Second Edition

The Counseling Experience

A Theoretical and Practical Approach

Michael E. Cavanagh
Justin E. Levitov

Loyola University, New Orleans

WAVELAND

PRESS, INC.

Long Grove, Illinois

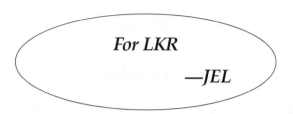

For LKR

—JEL

For information about this book, contact:
Waveland Press, Inc.
4180 IL Route 83, Suite 101
Long Grove, IL 60047-9580
(847) 634-0081
info@waveland.com
www.waveland.com

CONTENTS

PREFACE

Revising a successful text on counseling is a complicated task. Since much has changed in the field of counseling since the first edition was published in 1982, decisions about what to keep and what to revise were never easy. I sought to preserve that which continues to be useful and to update and incorporate that which years of research and clinical experience have added to the mental health profession. Thus, this edition covers the same three dimensions in counseling found in the first: basic human dynamics that are particularly relevant to counseling; a theoretical underpinning that accommodates many, if not most, specific theories of counseling; and the practical approaches that flow from the application of theory to the problems and issues that compose human experience. Additionally, advances in diagnosis and treatment, psychopharmacology, and treatment delivery systems that have evolved over the past twenty years are covered. The second edition also contains revised philosophical perspectives that underlie counseling initiatives in the twenty-first century, as well as updated clinical examples.

As a profession ages, its priorities often change, and the past twenty years have seen many alterations to counseling priorities. The present edition reflects these changes with a revision to the way the chapters are sequenced. The topic of ethics, for example, is now covered in chapter 3 instead of chapter 14 in order to reflect the increasingly important role now played by a formalized corpus of mental health ethics.

The translation of theory into practice offered in this edition is tailored to the needs of students completing undergraduate and graduate counseling programs. It is written to help such students face the challenges, problems, successes, and failures that arise whenever human beings try to be helpful within the counseling relationship.

While written principally for students, counselors may also find that this edition can be useful for clients who are actively engaged in counseling. Progress in counseling is often unnecessarily impeded because clients do not know what to expect, what the counseling process will require them to give, or how they can cooperate most effectively.

The fact that the original focus of the text was retained along with much of what was offered in the first edition exists as a tribute to Michael Cavanagh's insights and his understanding of the counseling process. I am pleased to have been given the opportunity to write this edition. I am grateful to Michael Cowan, Kevin Fall, Bruce Thompson, and Robert Watson for their suggestions, help, and encouragement. Whewellene Fischer's attention to detail and enthusiasm carried the manuscript through many important, yet time-consuming, revisions. Laurie Prossnitz's wise and incisive editorial direction, patience, and understanding proved invaluable. Thanks to my family—Kathi, Talya, and Jana—for their encouragement and for granting me the time to complete this book. Finally, I am deeply indebted to the many clients with whom I have worked over the past twenty years. The best and most complete understanding that I have of the counseling process comes through my contact with clients, people who by their decision to enter counseling demonstrate the courage to face their challenges, experience their pain, and search out the pools of strength and understanding that make change possible. I am thankful for the privilege granted to me by so many interesting and remarkable people.

Justin E. Levitov

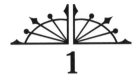

1

THE NATURE OF COUNSELING

Human experience is a labyrinth. Categories developed by social scientists, philosophers, and others map only a fraction of the terrain. Each explanation produces only a partial view, and while the accumulation of explanations may offer the promise of a greater and more comprehensive understanding of human behavior, mutually exclusive views outnumber more encompassing ones. This is not to say that such competing explanations are less useful, only that human behavior is so diverse that many perspectives are needed. Life's complexities and challenges often bring people to an early appreciation of the breadth of human experience. Based on their personal and professional experiences, counselors alternately embrace and ignore various explanations as they respond to the perceived needs of their clients. Differing views persist, but rivalry fades when we accept that human experience is constructed in such a way that we only deal with or understand select parts of ourselves and others at any particular point in time—the whole is never fully realized or experienced.

Like a visitor entering a city for the first time, we are largely reliant upon the experience of others to find our way through this labyrinth. Guides suggest what to pay attention to, what should be seen and how best to get there; they recommend things to do along the way, as well as places to stay and places to avoid. However, the perspectives, experiences, and priorities of the guides color their view of the city and shape their recommendations to travelers. While we could try to explore the city without help and forgo the assistance of those more experienced, it would be an overwhelming, if not impossible, task.

1

Applying the metaphor of the city to human experience suggests how we often learn about those elements of ourselves that we cannot directly discern. We rely upon the experienced observations of other people. Family, friends, teachers, and counselors offer information from vantage points unavailable to us. Counseling is one example of an important relationship within the labyrinth that offers perspectives and views that could not be developed alone. Skilled counselors aid clients by helping them realize aspects of themselves that they cannot directly observe or may not fully understand. Relationships of all kinds make it possible to more fully understand the labyrinth of our personal experience and communal human experience. While this chapter introduces the reader to the counseling process, it begins with a discussion not of the process but of a client. We make this choice because it mirrors the way we believe counselors should approach counseling—with emphasis on and priority afforded to the person in counseling. We open with an anecdote describing how one client entered the process.

INTO COUNSELING

*Paul, a prospective client, called to obtain an appointment. He enthusiastically proposed several potential meeting times and ended his conversation by stating, "I **really** want to get **into** counseling." The counselor scheduled the intake evaluation appointment, hung up, and began to ponder his new client's closing comment. What, he wondered, did it actually mean for this client to "get into counseling"? It was clear from the initial telephone conversation that Paul knew little about the process he was about to enter. But that did little to deter him. He wanted to get **into** counseling even though he needed experience with and information about the process before it could be used to achieve his goals or to reduce his difficulties. It was also clear from the brief telephone conversation that Paul's pain, coupled with the possibilities for change that he presumed to be within his reach, both scared and motivated him.*

Paul asked many questions during each of the three intake sessions. How long would it take? Would he have to review painful experiences? Would the process influence other parts of his life where difficulties did not exist? Do people ever fail to reach their goals in counseling? Could things get worse instead of better? Why did he need help when others did not? Would the counselor guide him? Would the counselor make decisions for him? How would he know if he had selected the "right counselor"?

Paul's questions reveal concerns similar to those experienced by many clients. Responses to each of these questions will be found in the chapters that follow, but Paul's "into counseling" comment deserves immediate attention because it offers a client-based conceptualization of the counseling process. When people enter counseling they enter a location, a private arena—a place to think, sample new ideas, explore thoughts and feelings, interact with others, confront challenges, develop solutions, and experiment with change. To construct such a place, counselors mold the clinical process into a form that reflects clients' needs and honors their experiences. Counselors do not prepare the site alone; as clients enter the counseling process, they help construct it. In Paul's case, he contributed to preparing the site with questions that brought his concerns to the surface and revealed how he might define his relationship with the counselor. Other clients will establish different priorities, and these differences will be reflected in the structure of the counseling relationship they create.

The idea of counseling as a cocreated space, different for each client, suggests features about the counseling process to counselors and clients. A working relationship, for example, based on empathy, understanding, knowledge, and sensitivity is fundamental. Counselor-client cooperation fuels not only the creation of the therapeutic relationship but also the process of change. Counselors also interact with other counselors in a cocreated space. For example, consultation and supervision, time-honored relationships among and between counseling professionals, take place within the labyrinth to enhance understanding and reflection.

While the relationships within the labyrinth that have been discussed involve direct human contact, other less direct experiences also are possible. Reading is one such example. Clients are often encouraged to read books (bibliotherapy) about their particular problems or difficulties, and counselor training relies heavily on texts. With this last fact in mind, we hope you will consider your encounter with this book as a relationship within the labyrinth. We encourage you to construct from your reading a place that challenges and supports you, one that expands your understanding of the human experience and your ability to help people. Finally, we hope that your sensitivity will help you understand the clients described in the case vignettes. They are people who have undertaken the challenging and painful task of admitting their problems, confronting difficult thoughts and feelings, and asking for help.

The remainder of this chapter identifies the strengths and limitations of counseling theory, discusses similarities and differences between counseling and psychotherapy, illustrates the importance of social science research, and defines counseling by introducing the basic components of the process.

Counseling Theories

Counseling theories offer an assortment of organized perspectives that guide a counselor's understanding of clients and their struggles, and help the counselor determine the best course of action. Most counseling theories balance theoretical explanations and practical applications, but the foundation of counseling theory is philosophy. Philosophy provides the keystone on which a more thorough understanding of the human experience is built. According to Mahoney (1991), "All modern sciences are the unmistakable descendants of what was once a relatively undifferentiated love of study called philosophy" (p. 23). The philosophical bedrock of counseling theory can be better understood by exploring two collections of questions. The first is offered by Tolbert (1972, p. 90) and it suggests that counselors and clients, like philosophers, must reckon with three fundamental problems:

1. Ontology—what is real?
2. Epistemology—what is true?
3. Axiology—what is good?

Williamson's five basic questions, the second collection, focus more specifically on counseling issues (1965, p. 154–157):

1. What is the nature of human nature?
2. What is the nature of human development?
3. What is the nature of the "good life" and the "good"?
4. What is the nature of the determination of the "good life"? Who determines what is "good"?
5. What is the nature of the universe and what is a person's relationship to that universe?

These questions confront all who wish to work with others in any type of professional relationship in which *change* is a goal. These questions require personal responses and are fundamental to counseling theories. While a more in-depth discussion is beyond the scope of this book, the reader is referred to Mahoney's (1991) work on the scientific foundations of psychotherapy for a comprehensive review of the relationships among philosophy, science, and theory.

Counseling theory also is practical. In fact, good counseling theory should strike a balance such that practical and theoretical issues interact in a way that illuminates both. Boy and Pine (1983, pp. 249–250) offer the following useful functions of theory:

1. Theory helps us to find relatedness, or some degree of unity, among diverse observations and experiences, particularly as these occur in counseling.

2. Theory compels us to observe relationships that we had previously overlooked.

3. Theory provides operational guidelines that help us in making provisional evaluations of the directions and appropriateness of our development as counselors.

4. Theory focuses our attention on relevant data by telling us what to look for.

5. Theory provides us with guidelines for helping clients modify their behavior more effectively.

6. Theory helps us to construct new approaches to counseling and point to ways of evaluating old ones.

Counseling theory is essential because it organizes and guides the counseling process while simultaneously making possible the creation and evaluation of new theory. Boy and Pine identify an additional and equally important use of counseling theory when they write that "one of the behaviors that characterizes any professional is the sense of a personal responsibility and public accountability in applying a theory" (1983, p. 251). The existence and use of counseling theory help to differentiate professional counseling from other activities.

Human experience can be defined and categorized in many ways. One such approach identifies four basic areas of experience: affective, cognitive, physical, and spiritual. Accordingly, each counseling theory offers a particular set of assumptions about human behavior and human experience by emphasizing some components and downplaying others within one or more of the four categories above. For example, some theories may emphasize cognitive elements while downplaying affective components. Different theories may be seen as different paths through the labyrinth. A single all-encompassing route does not exist, and the pursuit of such a grand theory might even be problematic. According to Ginter, "The attempt to build a unified theory of counseling is premature; it cannot be achieved now without gross distortions of the various theoretical views" (1988, p. 6).

Regardless of one's theoretical orientation, changes in behavior are evidence that some form of learning has occurred. Since various counseling approaches emphasize different forms of learning, they can be differentiated accordingly. Beitman (1987) called attention to the importance of the learning dimension of the counseling process very early in his book. Most counseling theories can be categorized by one of the following approaches to learning: (1) linear learning, (2) modeling behavior, or (3) systems approach.

The linear approach is based on stimulus-response (S-R) theory; it includes both classical and operant conditioning, although operant conditioning is more widely applied. Its premise is that, with the aid of a carefully managed program of rewards and consequences, individuals can be influenced to make changes in their behavior. Behavioral approaches to counseling capitalize on this form of learning. A role-modeling approach produces changes as well and this form of learning may also be found in various counseling theories. Also called vicarious learning, this approach posits that new behavior can be learned through observation of others. For example, a person who is having difficulty making friends can learn social skills by watching other people interact successfully. A systems approach implies that behavior forms and resides within a system. Widening the lens in this way brings into view the interaction of social, environmental, and individual forces. A systems approach, in contrast to both modeling and linear approaches, offers counselors a set of principles that has been widely applied in defining problems and developing interventions. According to Blocher (1987):

> Systems approaches are particularly useful in counseling because counselors are interested in very complex patterns of interaction between people and the various interrelated aspects of their environment. Not only are counselors interested in understanding such transactions, but they are also actively engaged in helping people solve problems, achieve goals, and develop competence within complex environments. (p. 107)

A systems approach accommodates many levels of complexity concerning the forces that form and maintain behavior. This fact has several implications for counselors. For example, a systems approach suggests that human beings exist in a homeostatic or balanced state; specific behaviors cannot be defined or changed in isolation from the system. This does not imply that the level of functioning is necessarily good or bad, only that it is balanced. Clients who remain in what may seem dire situations do so not because they necessarily want to but because they are in a balanced, albeit undesirable, state.

According to the systems approach, effective counseling efforts target the system—not the specific behavior. If the system changes, the behavior also will change. Behavior remains in force because influences from different sources hold it in place as they maintain homeostasis. Thus a balanced state suggests that the forces are equal; change occurs only when those forces are interrupted. A new, more adaptive set of responses may result when the forces that hold the behaviors in place are disturbed. Therefore, counseling from a systems perspective seeks to disrupt a balanced but undesirable state in order to establish a new homeostasis.

Each approach to learning produces a different paradigm upon which to build an understanding of human behavior and the forces that produce change. Effective counselors should recognize the influence of all three and be able to identify the conditions that dictate where each is influencing behavior. Effective counseling is predicated on properly matching interventions to clients and types of client problems, and to do this, counselors may choose to apply different learning theories based on specific presenting problems.

A working knowledge of at least one counseling theory is essential. Just as experienced travelers realize that the route taken first may not ultimately be the best one, but was necessary because other routes could not be identified absent the first, so too the first journey through human experience is necessary to identify and evaluate other routes. Counselors who take various routes through the labyrinth accumulate a working knowledge of several counseling theories. This enlarges their understanding of the human experience and their ability to work with a more varied client population.

Eclecticism is a term that simply means to select what appears to be best from a variety of sources. Theoretical eclecticism is formed by combining various theoretical positions, while technical eclecticism describes the process of combining various techniques. In the first edition of this book a "healthy eclecticism" was encouraged. This edition departs somewhat from that position; it now follows Lazarus and Beutler's (1993) argument favoring technical eclecticism but opposing both unsystematic eclecticism and theoretical eclecticism (theoretical integrationism).

Lazarus and Beutler (1993) argue that *systematic technical eclecticism,* selecting and employing techniques that experience has shown to be effective, is the single justifiable way to use elements of various theories. Unsystematic eclecticism, "the haphazard mishmash of divergent bits and pieces" (p. 381), and theoretical integrationism, "a gallimaufry of methods and ideas that have no consistent rationale" (p. 383), are discouraged. Clearly defined criteria for utilizing various counseling techniques and defensible methods for evaluating them overcome the deficiencies noted in unsystematic eclecticism and theoretical integrationism.

All forms of eclecticism are especially problematic for novice or inexperienced counselors because a blending of theories, in addition to the caveats already noted, can inhibit the process of learning a specific school of counseling. The risk that elements of different theories would find their way into an eclectic fabric because of chance rather than careful review further compounds the problem.

The techniques described in this book are potentially useful in many different approaches to counseling. Which techniques to choose and when to apply them are important professional decisions that need to be made thoughtfully and methodically. Systematic technical eclecticism has important clinical advantages that are not found in theoretical eclecticism and poses fewer risks for the client.

Additional support for learning one or more approaches and a guide to making the selection may be found in Wallace's *Theories of Counseling and Psychotherapy: A Basic Issues Approach* (1986, pp. 8–16). Eleven basic issues organize the study of each counseling approach:

1. conscious and/or unconscious determinants
2. conditioned behaviors and/or freely chosen behaviors
3. biological and/or social determinants
4. uniqueness and/or commonality
5. early and/or continuous development
6. psychological and/or actual environment
7. explanation of learning

8. importance of role assigned to self-concept

9. importance of group membership

10. number of and weighting assigned to motivational concepts

11. importance of reward

This enumeration of issues helps differentiate all of the major theories. An awareness of the scope of a given theory will help guide beginning counselors as they choose theories that best fit their world view and personal assumptions. Assonance between counselors' belief systems and the basic tenets of a particular theory is essential—counselors cannot successfully apply a theory that they personally do not find credible. Adhering to a particular counseling theory causes us to think and act in certain ways. It influences what we attend to and what we ignore. It suggests how we relate to ourselves and our clients. Counselors therefore need to make careful and informed judgments about the theories they choose to apply.

Watts (1993) offers additional guidance to those interested in selecting a counseling theory. He maintains that theories are learned intellectually and experientially. This suggestion that counselors need to think about and experience theory reemphasizes that theoretical and practical issues are both academically and personally important. Watts's detailed exploration of counseling theory and of the selection process helps counselors examine and choose counseling theories that are consistent with their personal values and beliefs.

While guiding readers in the selection of a specific theory is beyond the scope of this work, it is assumed that readers are familiar with at least one counseling theory. A personal understanding of the basic philosophies that underlie counseling theory and the knowledge of one or more counseling theories help counselors organize and explain to clients anything that seems confusing or overwhelming. There are, of course, caveats. The counselor must fit his or her approach to the client and not vice versa. While counselors should know at least one theory well, they must be willing to employ other theories or at least be able to offer clients alternatives. Students and counselors who follow one theoretical approach exclusively risk two pitfalls.

First is the tendency to perceive the person and the person's problems in a manner that is unduly restricted by one's own theoretical orientation. A client would be seen differently, and sometimes *very* differently, by a Freudian, Adlerian, Skinnerian, humanist, or Gestalt counselor. The causes and dynamics of all personal problems do not necessarily fit any one theory. Second is the tendency to turn counseling into an academic seminar in which clients end up learning more about a particular theorist than they learn about themselves.

It is notable that many founders of the major schools of counseling emphasized the tentative nature of their therapeutic approaches. They discouraged the view that specific theories and strategies are valid under every circumstance or with all people. For example, Freud (1953) wrote, "There are many ways and means of practicing psychotherapy. All that lead to recovery are good" (p. 259). In other words, because behavioral, psychodynamic, existential, cognitive, rational-emotive, Gestalt, and other approaches each emphasizes a different element or elements of human experience, they are useful with different people and problems. Multiple perspectives exist because each represents an attempt to explain something that cannot be fully explained—human experience. Because they offer only partial explanations, counseling theories are simultaneously valuable and limited. If we adopt those that are consistent with our personal values and belief system and employ them with appropriate clients we can be effective. However, improperly selected and applied theory can have undesirable results. Therefore, our concluding caveat might be: rely too heavily on a theory and risk losing sight of the unique person; ignore theory altogether and risk becoming disoriented, and thus losing sight of the unique person.

Counseling and Psychotherapy

There is little agreement among counselors on whether and how counseling and psychotherapy differ. As Hahn (1953) writes:

> I know of few counselors or psychologists who are completely satisfied that clear distinctions [between counseling and psychotherapy] have been made. . . . Perhaps the most complete agreements are (1) that counseling and psychotherapy cannot be distinguished clearly, (2) that counselors practice what psychotherapists consider psychotherapy, (3) that psychotherapists practice what counselors consider to be counseling, and (4) that despite the above, they are different. (p. 232)

Many people view the terms as synonymous, while others persist in stressing differences. The number of subspecialties found within the counseling profession makes identifying differences between counseling and psychotherapy more complicated. Counseling offered in some subspecialties differs markedly from psychotherapy while counseling in other subspecialties is virtually identical to psychotherapy. For example, counseling offered by Certified Clinical Mental Health Counselors (CCMHC) would probably be indistinguishable from psychotherapy, while counseling services offered by school counselors or vocational and career counselors might differ appreciably. Each counseling subspecialty prepares counselors to provide specific types of services to clients with specific needs and problems. The difference between psychotherapy and counseling across subspecialties varies with training and the focus of practice.

While a bold and distinct line of demarcation probably cannot be discerned, the following are some differences between counseling and psychotherapy suggested in the literature:

1. Counseling emphasizes a wellness perspective and embraces prevention; psychotherapy deals primarily with those who are seriously troubled psychologically.

2. Counseling includes educative, supportive, conscious oriented, and short-term interventions; psychotherapy focuses more exclusively on reconstructive, unconscious oriented, and long-term interventions.

3. Counseling is more structured and directed toward limited, concrete goals; psychotherapy is purposely more ambiguous and has goals that change and evolve as the client progresses.

Although there may be legal reasons to make such distinctions, counseling and psychotherapy are viewed as synonymous for the purposes of this work. There is so much overlap between the two that attempts to separate them would only do violence to our understanding of both. Moreover, such a separation would preclude a presentation of elements equally relevant to both.

We use the term *counseling* in this work, but we maintain that the principles contained in this book can be validly applied across mental health professions, and to a wide range of clients.

Effectiveness and Counseling Research

Researchers who seek to explore counseling effectiveness face an assortment of challenges. For example, what constitutes effective treatment? How can effectiveness be reliably measured? To what extent have effectiveness criteria been met? These criteria, in particular, can vary widely across client populations, counselors, clients' families and their employers—all may offer widely different opinions (Burck & Peterson, 1975; Goldman, 1976; Osipow, Walsh, & Tosi, 1980). In attempting to define effectiveness, controlling for problem type and maintaining consistency of treatment are major concerns. Other issues also can make it difficult to empirically evaluate the effectiveness of counseling, both as a discipline and as it applies to a specific client. It is not surprising then that the research literature has historically offered a wide range of conclusions about the efficacy of counseling (see Bergin, 1971; Eysenck, 1966; and Strupp, 1971).

Effectiveness research has improved in recent years with the advent of better criteria, improved methods of measurement, and the emergence of counseling protocols for various theories. Recent findings offer much greater support for the overall effectiveness of counseling. Lambert and Cattani-Thompson's (1996, p. 606) careful and comprehensive review of the conclusions of effectiveness research indicates that counseling is effective when compared with placebo and nontreatment conditions and that effectiveness research findings have important implications to clinical practice. These authors offer eight specific conclusions and urge that these findings be used to guide clinical judgments:

1. The general effects of counseling are positive at treatment termination.

2. The effects of counseling can be achieved in relatively short periods of time (5 to 10 sessions).

3. A sizable minority of clients (20% to 30%) requires longer treatment and perhaps alternative interventions or more intensive multifaceted efforts, but with these efforts clients will improve to a significant degree.

4. The effects of treatment seem to be lasting for a majority of clients, with follow-up studies suggesting little decline one to two years after termination.

5. Client outcome is largely determined by client variables rather than by the counselor or counseling per se.

6. The best predictors (and possibly causes) of success outside of client variables are counselor-client relationship factors.

7. Some specific techniques seem to be especially helpful with particular symptoms and disorders.

8. A portion of clients gets worse during counseling.

Despite improvements in effectiveness research, counselors may still be confronted with contradictory conclusions regarding many aspects of treatment, including the duration of treatment, appropriate types of interventions, the matching of interventions with specific psychological problems, the identification of those unlikely to benefit from treatment, and so forth. Research offers some guidance, but counselors often tend to emphasize clinical activities and invest less time in effectiveness research. In fact, Loesch and Vacc (1996) identify research as an enigma within the helping professions. They conclude that although many clinicians are trained to both consume and conduct research, very few actually do either—a particularly distressing situation in a field that is both in its ascendancy and challenged by conflicting research findings and confounding variables. While these authors see the possibility of increased attention to effectiveness research, both agree that "change will occur if and only if counselors and therapists use research results more effectively and engage in research practices far more frequently than is currently the case" (p. vi). Their *Research in Counseling and Therapy* offers a comprehensive view of counseling research that includes problems as well as achievements, while also defining a direction for the future.

While effectiveness research is extremely important, it is not of sole importance. Advances in basic social science and counseling research are of great value to counselors because they affect many clinical issues. Modern social scientists are reexamining not only basic assumptions about human experience but assumptions about the social science enterprise itself. The field of social science is still undergoing a major paradigm shift, and research into human development offers an excellent example of the effects of this reexamination. For example, human growth and development were traditionally studied by delineating a progression of behavior patterns across time. These so-called stages of development imply the presence of possible organic mechanisms that both produce and result from development and change. The formation of a conscience or the ability to reason at particular levels are examples of the presence of certain cognitive structures. Defining these structures and delineating the boundaries of particular stages traditionally occupied a very prominent place in developmental research. Nevertheless, "one of the most important developments in development has been the conceptual shift from stages and structures to systems and processes" (Mahoney, 1991, p. 147). According to Mahoney, "the general shift of interest within and beyond stage theories and toward the more complex dynamics of process theories has been accompanied by a reappraisal of the relationship between structure and function, with contemporary opinion acknowledging that these dimensions are inseparable" (p. 154). Stage theories tend to explain problems and develop interventions by determining the client's current stage of development and identifying strategies that will help the client evolve to a higher stage. Process theories, on the other hand, tend to be less concerned with developmental stages and more focused on the interpersonal processes that are in place at any particular point in time. The shift in emphasis from stages and structures to systems and process produces a deeper and broader view of behavior; it ultimately challenges counselors and social scientists to unite stages and structures with systems and processes.

Human behavior can be studied from a variety of perspectives. Two approaches are particularly useful: an empirical approach and a phenomenological approach. The empirical approach suggests that the methods used in the natural sciences can be usefully applied in the social sciences. Empirical experiments are designed to discover cause-effect relationships, to create categories (developmental stages), and to carefully control for extraneous variables. Human beings are complex, however, and these empirical procedures may tend to limit what is studied. Levels of control are much more difficult to achieve in life than they are in the laboratory, and ethical concerns appropriately limit how experiments with human beings are conducted. Therefore, a *phenomenological* or *human science* approach that emphasizes the subjective view of the client may be more useful because the complexity of the human experience is studied more completely but less empirically.

Changes in the focus of social science research are related to the transition to a systems and process framework. The delineation of stages and structures may be the result of relying exclusively on empiricism and the fundamentals of natural science. A phenomenological approach, on the other hand, offers counselors and social scientists opportunities that are often excluded from a natural science perspective (Hanna & Shank, 1995; Herman, 1997). Human science employs phenomenological methods and therefore encourages a more subjective approach to understanding human experience, behavior, and consciousness (Herman, 1997). Herman concluded that "the counseling profession is moving toward a new definition of science, one that emphasizes the eclectic and subjective nature of the activity" (p. 280). He cautions that researchers will need to "be familiar with strengths and limitations of both natural and human science and . . . accept quality research in both modes as valid knowledge" (p. 281).

Since human beings are always seeking meaning, advances in the study of meaning are of particular significance to counseling efforts. Mahoney (1991) described four major "metatheories" that pertain to meaning in the cognitive sciences. The first three include physical associationism, representationalism, and contextualism (p. 88–89). Physical associationism suggests that "the meaning of anything amounts to its net momentary associations with prior sensory experience," representationalism includes "cognitive mediation in the phenomenon of meaning," and contextualism holds that meaning is "dependent upon the context." Each advance more completely honors the complexity of human experience. The fourth and most recent development regarding meaning comes from *hermeneutics*.

Originally a term applied by biblical scholars to the interpretation of texts, hermeneutics has more recently been applied to the interpretation of human experience. A thorough discussion of hermeneutics is beyond the scope of this work, but a brief note is in order regarding this current trend in science and philosophy. Individuals interpret their experience based upon a set of personally held assumptions with the result that interpretation of any kind is not possible without a knowledge of individual personal assumptions. These assumptions are not static, but are transformed as individuals act on their interpretations and as their actions are reacted to by others. Assumptions change as the interpretation continues. A cycle of assumptions, interpretations, actions, reactions, and new assumptions is posited by hermeneutical theory (for a more detailed explanation see Cowan, 1995, pp. 5–8). Counselors may attempt to influence clients at one or more of the stages within the cycle. This philosophical perspective is inextricably linked to counseling because it supports a phenomenological understanding of human beings and because it respects how individuals produce meaning in their own lives and reflects the truism that the meaning people develop is unique.

The evolution of the understanding of meaning establishes a series of important philosophical developments that have influenced social science research. Mahoney (1991) concluded that "whether viewed from the perspective of connectionism, constructivism, or hermeneutics . . . it is increasingly clear that scientists studying complex phenomena have been jointly acknowledging the range and role of 'individual differences' in human knowing processes" (p. 93).

In summary, counseling effectiveness and research have been discussed from social science and philosophical perspectives. Effective counseling relies upon contributions from research, philosophy, and clinical experience; a model of practice that focuses on all three would be most effective. A scientist-practitioner model is therefore suggested because it emphasizes the interrelatedness of science, theory, and philosophy. Surely advances will continue to challenge and inform counselors as they offer clinical services based on a scientist-practitioner model.

A Definition of Counseling

Lewis Wolberg's classic text, *The Techniques of Psychotherapy* (1977), offers 36 different definitions of psychotherapy or counseling, each one written by a different theorist. Two examples will be helpful as we begin the process of defining counseling. Definition 21, "an emotional exchange in an interpersonal relationship which accelerates the growth of one or both participants" (p. 10), reveals important elements of the counseling process, as does definition 23, "a cooperative enterprise for clarifying purposes and modifying attitudes in the direction of greater integrity of personality" (p. 10). A careful review of all 36 definitions yields four common themes: the relationship, the problem (or issue), the goals, and the treatment. These common themes can be used to form a general definition of counseling. Each of the four will be discussed briefly here and then expanded upon in subsequent chapters.

The Relationship

Most definitions examined include direct references to the relationship between counselor and client. In a few, the relationship was incidental to the counseling process, but for many others it *was* the process. Concern with the nature and quality of the relationship between counselor and client has a long and distinguished history dating to Freud and is particularly important in the conceptual formulations of Sullivan (1953) and Rogers (1951). Beitman (1987) wrote that "professional psychotherapy is a complex process that is a unique subdivision of that problematic class of human activity known as interpersonal relationships" (p. 14) and that "no matter what theory one holds, individual psychotherapy is primarily a relationship between two people that is subject to the distortions common to any dyadic relationship" (p. 21). Teyber (1997, p. 11) further amplifies the importance of the relationship when he offers three basic assumptions for the interpersonal-process approach, each of which highlights a different and important aspect of relationship: "(1) Problems are interpersonal in nature, (2) familial experience is the most important source of learning about ourselves and others, and (3) the therapist-client relationship can be used to resolve problems."

That human beings both develop and resolve psychological and emotional problems through relationships suggests that relationships are generally important and that in counseling, the therapeutic relationship is particularly important. Counselors aid clients whenever they help them relate more effectively to themselves and others. Stated slightly differently, learning to relate better with others is important because many basic psychological needs are met only through interpersonal relationships.

How important is the counseling relationship? While authors may vary on the importance of the relationship to the healing process, every talking therapy relies on the formation and maintenance of a relationship that endures across time and change. This would be as true for existential approaches as for behavioral approaches. Regardless of theoretical orientation, counseling is therefore defined by the presence of a counselor-client relationship; one that must necessarily include an adequate degree of trust, mutual understanding, confidence, acceptance, and cooperation. Many theorists as well as practicing counselors maintain that it is the relationship that heals.

The Problem or Issue

Moving from the relationship to the reason for the relationship brings counseling's second common element into view. Each of the counseling definitions described by Wolberg implicitly or explicitly offers some method or methods for identifying and defining problems or issues. As might be expected, agreement across definitions about what constitutes a problem or an issue is limited. Strict psychiatric diagnoses and behavioral definitions are found as well as more general problem formulations like "the need for accelerated growth of one or both participants [in the counseling process]" (Wolberg, 1977, p. 10). The authors surveyed tended to define client difficulties according to the counseling theories, developmental theories, personality theories, and/or theories about psychopathology they embraced. Any theory forms a lens that brings into focus specific elements of behavior that are considered problems or issues while blurring other elements. The process of identifying problems along with different methods for classifying these difficulties will be discussed in later chapters of this book.

Goals

As with defining client problems, the goals of counseling vary according to theoretical orientation. Some theorists stress insight and cognitive changes; others emphasize emotional or behavioral change; and still others, in an attempt to be as inclusive as possible, opt for a very broad focus by stressing broad levels of change like "human growth and development." This difference in the formulation of goals is attributable to differing theoretical orientations. For example, strict behaviorists define change in very specific, measurable, observable ways, while other theorists emphasize goals that are less easily measured; for example, "clarifying purposes and modifying attitudes in the direction of greater integrity of personality" (Wolberg, 1977, p. 10). While a few approaches focus directly on a learning process with a goal of fostering clients' efforts to replace maladaptive behaviors with adaptive ones, most approaches contain one or more of the following general expectations:

1. increased intrapersonal and interpersonal competencies

2. personality growth (not solely symptom removal)

3. aid to "normal" people who are experiencing an obstacle to their growth as well as to psychologically disturbed people

The goals of counseling predictably vary across clients and with time. Goals, though subject to many forces, are often molded in the course of developing the therapeutic process.

Treatment

Just as various clinicians magnify or reduce specific aspects of human experience when defining problems or issues, so they select and create interventions consistent with their focus. These different approaches to treatment are easily identified. A cursory review of Wolberg's definitions yields examples of behavioral, client-centered, analytic, cognitive, and medical interventions, though other less common approaches might also be found. Thus, counseling may additionally be defined by the presence of treatment wherein differences regarding treatment modality and the focus of intervention vary predictably along the lines of individual theoretical orientations.

Taken together, the relationship, a delineation of the problem or issue, the formulation of goals, and a treatment program suggest a basic definition of counseling: **a relationship or alliance between a trained helper and a person seeking help wherein problems and/or issues are identified, goals are defined, and treatment steps are taken to achieve desired outcomes.** This definition is general enough to encompass the wide variations in problems, treatments, goals, and outcomes that are produced as clinicians embrace different assumptions about the human experience and counseling approaches above, and as they encounter different clients. A broad definition is warranted because, as stated earlier, the vastness of human experience and behavior demands many different formulations regarding human beings, their problems, and the means to their goals; thus, a definition of counseling must be inclusive.

Summary

This work presents and discusses the principles that underlie counseling. Readers can take these principles, mix them with the dynamics of their own personality, and eventually tailor them to the needs of clients. As with any journey to a new place, the first efforts to negotiate the labyrinth of human experience are rarely without false starts. What may seem straightforward in a book can become very complex in an actual counseling session. But after the newcomer has been through a long period of study and experience, paths will be discerned that not only clarify the client's struggle but also suggest ways the client might be helped. With time, counselors will be able to go with the client on a journey that neither party would be able or willing to travel alone. At this point, perhaps more than any other, counselors fully grasp the nature of the counseling relationship and the journey. Counselors also will come to understand that there is no perfect or ideal route, since each has its own limitations and advantages. The search for better routes through the labyrinth of human experience eventually leads to an appreciation of the infinite challenge of counseling.

Reflection Questions

1. Relationships are fundamental to counseling. What personal attributes might some counselors possess that would inhibit their ability to relate to clients? What attributes might advance their ability to relate to clients?

2. Respond to the following statement: "Counseling doesn't seem to help. I have read that people on a waiting list at a mental health center did as well as, if not better than, the people who had received counseling."

3. Some theories emphasize a systems approach while others focus on the individual. Describe the circumstances under which each approach would make sense to you. What support do you have for your position?

4. Since counseling is sometimes considered more an art than a science, counselors, as artists, are freer to "do their own thing" than are physicians or physicists. What is your response to this statement?

5. What might you discover about yourself or the field of counseling that could lead you to reevaluate your plan to become a counselor?

2

STAGES OF COUNSELING

A delineation of the stages of counseling offers clinicians a map to locate where they are in the process and suggests what tasks need to be completed at particular points. Similar to the steps found in most developmental processes, stages of counseling are neither discrete nor universally defined. Researchers define and sequence the stages of counseling differently (for examples see Beitman, 1987; Brammer, 1979; Carkhuff & Anthony, 1979; Egan, 1998; Weiner, 1975). These variations probably result from theoretical and philosophical differences found in various approaches to counseling. Virtually all researchers are in agreement about the termination stage while being at variance about the number and names of the other stages. Beitman's model probably contains the fewest number of stages: engagement, pattern search, change, and termination. The sequence presented in this text contains six stages: (1) alliance, (2) information gathering, (3) evaluation and feedback, (4) counseling agreement, (5) behavior change, and (6) termination. This series of steps was selected because it is broad enough to be useful with a wide variety of counseling theories.

Figure 2-1 depicts the six-stage sequence and reveals two major choice points with regard to initiating and maintaining the counseling relationship. The first occurs when client and counselor initially meet. The client often makes an uninformed decision to get help, and the counselor makes an uninformed decision to see the person; that is, the counselor does not know whether the prospective client is a reasonable candidate for counseling. The second choice point occurs after the first three stages,

Uninformed decision			Informed decision		
Stage 1	*Stage 2*	*Stage 3*	*Stage 4*	*Stage 5*	*Stage 6*
Alliance	Information gathering	Evaluation and feedback	Counseling agreement	Behavior change	Termination

Figure 2-1. Counseling stages.

when the client and the counselor have gained sufficient knowledge about each other and about the issues the client confronts to make an informed decision about whether the counseling should continue or be abandoned in favor of an alternative.

The six stages can be telescoped so that they fit both short-term and long-term counseling, just as any journey may involve visiting a number of points of interest for either a brief or an extended period. Counseling intended to last only five or ten sessions would therefore move through each of the stages in an abbreviated manner. Long-term counseling, on the other hand, might require five or more sessions to complete the first three stages and 50 to 150 sessions for the remaining three. Nevertheless, it is doubtful that any kind of counseling could be effective without spending at least some time at each stage because all are essential to the process. If a counselor omitted the alliance stage, there would be no counselor-client relationship; if the information-gathering stage were ignored, the counselor would remain unaware of the client's critical issues; if the evaluation stage were omitted, the counselor and client would be unable to make an informed decision about therapy and treatment options; without a counseling agreement, there would be no course to follow; if no changes were attempted, there could be no counseling results; and if the termination stage were ignored, counseling gains could be at risk because the client could be left without a sense of closure.

For the sake of convenience, the stages are presented here separately. These divisions are, however, not bounded by clear lines of demarcation. In fact, clients and counselors are often unaware of transitions from one stage to another. Flowing movement between or among stages is desirable because the counseling process might be obstructed by holding clients at certain stages or by forcefully structuring sessions around particular stages. For example, a persistent focus on gaining information to the exclusion of change activities may frustrate and overwhelm clients. In these cases, it would be more appropriate to obtain a sufficient amount of information, evaluate it, establish a contract, and then proceed to institute a program of change. Success at the change stage can often encourage clients to pursue other issues, evaluate them, establish new contracts, and proceed to other changes. Each stage must be passed through successfully, sometimes more than once, if counseling is to be effective.

Counselors need to reiterate completed stages because new information often surfaces as counseling progresses. For example, clients may admit to deeper or more serious problems well into the counseling process. Developments such as these often call for both counselor and client to return to earlier stages of the counseling process. The practice of reiterating the stages of counseling is also necessary because counseling is a dynamic recursive process, not a simple linear progression through a series of discrete steps.

This stage approach offers additional training opportunities. New counselors seem to understand and manage the process better if they are urged to ask themselves several questions continually:

1. What stage of the counseling process are they in?
2. How appropriate is what they are doing to the realization of the goals of that stage?
3. Should the counselor and client shift to another stage to better accomplish the current goal or goals?

A good example of an occasion in which a novice counselor would be well advised to reiterate an earlier stage would be one in which the counselor tried to garner information about the client before having forged a solid alliance with the client. The client cannot share enough information on which to base a good evaluation if the alliance is weak. The simple suggestion to limit information gathering in favor of alliance building often solves the problem. Novices appreciate such clear and effective suggestions since they can be made to recognize the problem and thus to accept guidance on the problem immediately.

Before proceeding to a discussion of the individual stages of counseling we offer an example of how ignoring a stage can produce problems. We describe the case from the perspective of Janet, a client just beginning the process.

THE CASE OF JANET

As Dr. Smith asked one question after another, Janet dutifully answered. While she did not see a list of questions, she sensed that through the years Dr. Smith had come to memorize a sequence of queries that seemed, at least to her, disjointed and confusing. This was not the first time Janet had consulted someone. In fact, her previous counseling experience had been very helpful. But a call to Dr. Steele's office saddened her; the counselor she had worked so well with had moved to another state.

Dr. Smith's questions continued as Janet thought to herself how much better it would have been to have seen someone else. Her first choice was obviously no longer available, but she seriously doubted that she would come back to Dr. Smith. She wondered to herself if Dr. Smith would ever ask about the counseling sessions with Dr. Steele. And she really wanted to talk about how disappointed she was about Steele's leaving. More questions filled the remainder of the first session. Eventually, Dr. Smith mentioned that they were out of time but suggested they meet next week at the same time. Apparently Dr. Smith had a lot more questions for Janet and hoped to get through the rest of them next time they met. Janet left the session with only one question: "How can I cancel the next meeting without talking to Dr. Smith?" She was certain that her cancellation would be met with even more questions, so she finally decided to call at a time when she would be sure to get the answering service.

This unfortunate but not uncommon example brings up several valuable points. Forming an alliance is the precursor of all effective counseling endeavors. Janet remains in an alliance with Dr. Steele. Dr. Smith's questions offer little to Janet as she contends with her feelings about Dr. Steele's leaving and do not help establish a new alliance with Dr. Smith. Dr. Smith not only fails to build this important component of the process but also loses the opportunity to learn more about Janet's counseling with Dr. Steele. By exploring previous counseling experiences counselors obtain invaluable information about the client. What, for example, could be more important than knowing how a client previously reacted to the counseling process? Information like this serves as a guide for understanding the client in the very part of the labyrinth where counselor and client will meet. The sections that follow offer a better way to proceed through the stages of counseling than that revealed in Janet's example.

Stage 1: Alliance

The therapeutic alliance, another term for the counseling relationship, is the basic ingredient of virtually every form of talking therapy; it would be impossible to overstate its importance. Teyber (1997) maintains that "this relationship is the therapist's *most important* [italics added] means of effective client change; it determines the success or failure of therapy" (p. 16). For example, the quality of the relationship between counselor and client actually determines what and how much will be shared by the client. In other words, the alliance must be strong enough to allow the issue or problem to be disclosed. A firmly established therapeutic alliance encourages the client to raise more difficult issues and enables the client to work through more complicated problems.

Unfortunately, the stages of counseling are not sequenced in order of difficulty; the first stage is also the most difficult one. This fact motivates seasoned counselors, but it complicates the training of new counselors. The counselor's personal and professional goals make failures at the alliance-forming stage particularly difficult to come to terms with. While further clinical experience helps novices to improve, beginning with the most challenging part of the process is often discouraging.

At the initial phase of counseling, counselors face a considerable task. They must rapidly develop a working relationship with a person whom they have never met. The nature and extent of the client's difficulties can either enhance or impede the formation of the therapeutic alliance, depending on several factors. Clients in severe emotional pain may be highly motivated to pursue a therapeutic relationship. Their pain and anxiety, when greeted with the counselor's empathy, can rapidly draw counselor and client together. On the other hand, clients who have experienced multiple difficulties in relationships may have considerable trouble engaging; the therapeutic relationship may appear to them as little more than another potential source of difficulty. Since many emotional and psychological problems are both raised and resolved within interpersonal relationships, clients will likely view the counseling relationship with apprehension, realizing that it is potentially both beneficial and problematic.

The client's relationship history always influences the formation of the therapeutic alliance. Many people pursue counseling because symptom relief cannot be obtained by relating to friends, family, or associates. People also enter counseling because they have encountered many different types of relationship difficulties (e.g., failed love relationships, social isolation, etc.). Many individuals predictably avoid and resist relationships because of a history of social problems or because they struggle with problems that produce a certain amount of interpersonal isolation. In other words, what clients need most also may be what they fear or try to avoid most. This is a particularly interesting, common, and important therapeutic paradox. Fear of intimacy, rising levels of anxiety, emotional distress, and other difficulties militate against the formation of the therapeutic alliance. This combination of relationship difficulties challenges counselors to develop personal and professional characteristics that will allow them to manage the myriad forces that inhibit alliance formation. Effective counselors usually overcome these problems by being well-informed, embracing a set of therapeutic attitudes, applying clinical skills, and working within a professional-ethical framework.

Rogers' (1957) classic article identifies the following time-honored requisite attitudes on the counselor's part: congruence, unconditional positive regard, and empathy. Trust and confidence flow from the alliance when these attitudes are verbally and nonverbally conveyed to the client. The counseling relationship hinges on the counselor's ability to share feelings of congruence, warmth, unconditional positive regard, and empathy with the client within the context of the therapeutic alliance. Emotionally vacant, mechanistic applications of technique fail to produce the alliance. Even the counselor's internalized feelings of congruence, unconditional positive regard, and empathy may not produce the therapeutic alliance if they are not communicated to the client.

Kottler and Brown (1992) identify several practical dimensions of the therapeutic relationship, including commitment, trust, empathy, confidentiality, and benevolent power (pp. 74–76). Counselors prepare clients for the work ahead by establishing a relationship that includes each of these dimensions. Clients are also influenced by surface issues that might include the counselor's appearance, the office decor, academic credentials in evidence, and so forth (Beitman, 1987).

Transference and countertransference issues may surface very early in the therapeutic alliance. These concepts are therefore introduced while discussing the alliance stage. A cautious appraisal of both transference and countertransference should be made at the earliest point of counselor-client contact.

Transference reactions occur when a client displaces or projects feelings, attitudes, or impulses that were part of some previous relationships onto the counselor. For example, the counselor who represents an authority figure likely will be reacted to in the same way the person has reacted to authority figures in the past. If the client has a history of being defensive, hostile, or ingratiating toward authority figures then the client is likely to behave similarly with the counselor. The client may react to the counselor's personal qualities with positive or negative transference. The way the counselor looks, speaks, sits, thinks, or emotes may trigger a transference reaction. A person may say, "I hate it [you] when you get that god-almighty expression on your face [because you are my father when you do that]," or "I like coming here [I like you] because I feel comfortable and understood [the way my mother always made me feel]."

Sometimes the transference is direct ["I don't like you"]; at other times, it is indirect—that is, directed at the counselor's profession ["I always felt people went into psychology to solve their own problems"] or directed at the counselor's work space ["Why is this room always so cold?"].

Counselors should bear in mind, however, that not all of a client's reactions stem from transference. Clients also relate to counselors directly. For example, a client who becomes angry with a counselor is not necessarily manifesting negative transference. The client's anger may be appropriate to the actual situation; therefore, it would be inappropriate to treat it as transference. Doing so would demean the client and preclude a productive relationship. For example, a devoutly religious person may not agree with some of the values of a counselor who views devotion to religious beliefs with skepticism. To label such a client's value conflicts with the counselor as transference fails to acknowledge a real conflict—one that should not remain unresolved. All instances of cognitive dissonance between the counselor and the client need not be ascribed to transference.

Counselors need to be aware that all transference reactions have a quality of resistance. As long as people are spending time and energy loving or hating the counselor, they are not progressing toward the mutually agreed-upon goals. How much resistance the transference creates determines the extent to which the counselor should address it. In general, indirect expressions of mildly positive transference should receive the least attention, and direct manifestation of intensely negative transference should receive the most.

Another approach to transference reactions is to deal with them in a direct, flexible, interpersonal manner rather than in an analytical, reductive fashion. For example, a counselor may reply to a woman who challenges him on being sexist by saying, "I agree that a sexist counselor would not be helpful to you. However, why don't we refocus on our goals, and if you see any concrete data to substantiate your concern as we go along, we can deal with it at that time." This type of response respects the woman's concern yet does not allow it to distract her and the counselor from the main purpose of counseling.

Countertransference consists of reactions by the counselor to the behavior of the client. These reactions are very important at all stages of the counseling process but especially important at the alliance-building stage. According to Teyber (1997), "the therapist's relationship with the client is the most significant means of effecting change. At the same time, the most likely reason for therapy to terminate prematurely is that the client's interpersonal coping strategies have activated reciprocal conflicts in the therapist, who has not been able to recognize or resolve his or her own issues" (p. 289). Such negative countertransference is exemplified when a counselor feels angry or bored with a client who has done nothing to merit such a reaction. As with transference, not all pleasant or unpleasant feelings toward a client are necessarily countertransference. A counselor may have reason to like or to be upset with a person and these reactions should not be dismissed as countertransference, but should be dealt with realistically.

Countertransference offers both advantages and impediments to the counseling process and to counselors themselves. For example, countertransference is advantageous when it teaches counselors something about themselves. A client may have a habit of responding in a way that angers the counselor. The counselor can study this accurately detected countertransference reaction and improve his or her level of insight and self-awareness. But countertransference can also be a hindrance to counseling because strong, inappropriate feelings—positive or negative—dangerously interfere with the counselor's clinical judgment. Countertransference reactions can be difficult to detect and hard to resolve unless the novice has recourse to professional guidance. Regular consultation and supervision may help to identify such personal animadversions while offering direction and support as counselors work through their reactions and make decisions about the client's future treatment (such as referral to another counselor). A more complete discussion of transference and countertransference may be found in Singer (1965).

And so the alliance stage is arguably the most important and challenging of all that make up the counseling process. The strength and quality of the therapeutic alliance affects every aspect of counseling. An effective therapeutic alliance can form when trust, unconditional positive regard, warmth, and empathy are present; yet, while necessary, these factors alone are not sufficient. Counselors should also be sure that the therapeutic alliance is formed in accordance with appropriate professional boundaries, and counselors must exhibit adequate professional knowledge and expertise in an interactive relationship with clients who need to appreciate and understand both the counselor and the counseling process.

Potential clients may not be able to establish an alliance for a variety of reasons. Counselors should not prematurely advance to a later stage if an alliance is not possible. Moving ahead in hope that an alliance can be formed at a later stage is a problematic solution. The therapeutic alliance is an indispensable prerequisite for the remainder of the process. If the counselor is unable to form a therapeutic alliance, he or she should refer the client to another counselor or recommend alternatives to counseling.

Stage 2: Information Gathering

The quantity and quality of the information that counselors have about their clients will dictate the validity of their evaluations, the accuracy of their feedback, and the soundness of their recommendations. Therefore, it is helpful for counselors to recognize the various areas of information that must be tapped. The information index in Figure 2-2 represents the main sources of information for the counselor.

Continuum A-B represents the time dimension. Information about the client's past helps the counselor understand how the client got where he or she is. Information about the present indicates how well the client is functioning currently, and information about the future tells the counselor about the person the client wishes to become. As these pieces of information are brought together, they can give a reasonably good picture of who the client is and what the client needs or wants.

Continuum C-D concerns the obtaining of both intrapsychic and interpersonal information. Intrapsychic information includes clients' perceptions of reality; their inner conflicts and how conflicts are handled; the relationship between who they are and who they think they are, and how they want others to think about them; as well as the client's beliefs, values, and hopes. Interpersonal information consists of the dynamics involved in how the client relates with others and whether these relationships are satisfying or dissatisfying to the client or to the people with whom he or she relates.

Continuum E-F denotes what the client thinks and feels about self, others, and relevant events. It is important not only to know the content of the person's thoughts and feelings, but also to recognize how these thoughts and feelings relate and conflict. For example, when asked how

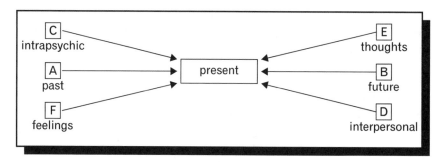

Figure 2-2. An information index.

she views her father, a woman responds, "I have nothing but the utmost respect for him." When she is asked how she *feels* about her father, she replies, "I resent him more than words can say."

The information index emphasizes caution in information gathering. Clients may lead counselors into talking about the past, discussing interpersonal relationships, or focusing on ideas to the exclusion of other equally important dimensions. Failing to obtain information from all the continua will produce a fragmented, inaccurate base upon which to found a clinical evaluation.

Questions

An intake interview based upon a series of questions is probably the most common way of obtaining information from clients. Various types of questions are used. Open-ended and closed-ended questions are the two major types, though most inquiries fall somewhere along the continuum between the two extremes. Murphy and Dillon (1998) describe counselor dialogue at the information-gathering stage with a more useful set of terms. According to these authors, questions and comments vary from "focal opening lines" to "nondirective opening lines." Focused questions are efficient and direct, but they also inhibit the flow of information beyond specific responses. The posing of specific questions illuminates some aspects of the client's life but leaves others in darkness. This problem can be reduced by adopting an alternative style of questioning. Though less efficient, more of the client's values and priorities surface with open, nondirective questions. For example, counselors can obtain very basic specific information and then simply ask their clients to share those aspects of themselves that they think would be important for the counselor to know. This approach encourages clients to produce the information in the form that is most meaningful to them, not in a form structured by the counselor. It also sets the stage for future sessions when the client will be more likely to take the lead in the process.

Questioning and interviewing are not one-way processes; counselors probably reveal more of themselves to their clients through their questions than their self-disclosures. Queries reveal the counselor's theoretical orientations, life experiences, and personal priorities. As you review the following semi-focused questions, consider not only the usefulness of the question in obtaining information from the client but also what asking the question suggests about the counselor.

1. "Why do you feel it would be a good idea to talk with me?" This question is meant to ascertain the person's motives for seeking counseling and his or her view of the problem. A person may reply, "I didn't think it would be a good idea—my mother did." A person may present the problem as feeling depressed, worried, insecure, confused, or scared. The counselor can then help the person describe the nature of his or her problem more specifically.

2. "How long have you felt this way?" The answer to this question gives the counselor some idea as to whether the problem is longstanding or of short duration. Counselors should be aware that people sometimes describe their problem as short-lived, but further probing indicates that it was present for a long time and only recently became activated.

3. "What do you think is causing these problems?" This question is meant to disclose how much insight the person has and how much responsibility he or she is taking for the problem. A person may answer, "I don't have the slightest idea," or "My boss is the cause of the problem," or "I've always been insecure, and this new job is hitting every insecurity I have."

4. "How have you been dealing with the problem up to this point?" The answer to this question will give the counselor some idea of the person's defenses, adaptive responses, and use of environmental supports. The person may answer, "I don't think it's a problem; my husband does," or "I've been distracting myself with work and probably eating and drinking too much," or "I have tried several alternatives that I thought a good deal about, and I've discussed it with my family, but I still need a little more help."

5. "What results do you expect from counseling?" The question is meant to elicit the person's expectations of counseling. One person may answer, "I don't have a clue about what to expect." Another person may respond, "I think you can tell me what I should do." A third person may reply, "I hope you will be able to help me see what I'm doing wrong so I can stop it."

6. "How much time and effort are you willing to invest in working on your problem?" Answers to this question will tell the counselor how accurately the person assesses the seriousness of the problem and how much personal motivation he or she has to solve it.

7. "Can you tell me some things about your past that you think may be helpful to my understanding of who you are today?" This question is

meant to get a psychological snapshot of the person. A detailed case history is rarely necessary as part of the information-gathering stage and may only serve to distract from current issues and affects.

8. "What are some of your strong points?" The answer to this question gives the counselor some idea of the person's strengths. It also gives the client an opportunity to bolster his or her self-esteem, which may have been diminished in talking about the problem.

An ear for what is missing is as vital as hearing what is said. People share as much of themselves by what they don't say as by what they do talk about. For example, clients who identify their strengths to the counselor without prompting suggest a set of conclusions that differs from that suggested by a client who focuses on difficulties and failures.

Interaction and Reaction

In addition to hearing the client talk about himself or herself, the counselor must have an opportunity to observe the client in action. Since there is often a discrepancy between what people say and what they do, the information provided by clients may be considered to some extent hearsay. That is, counselors need to examine the validity of the client's comments because unconfirmed hearsay information produces only a partially accurate picture of the client. Fortunately, counselors can become eyewitnesses to the client's dynamics through the counseling relationship as counselor and client interact. The counseling relationship itself offers a microcosmic view of the client's relationship style and produces important information about the client.

Though the term *interaction* has many definitions, in this case it means to challenge and to relate empathically to the client. By *challenging* we mean to probe the client in an interested, gentle, tentative fashion. Challenging differs from confronting, which is ordinarily inappropriate at this stage (see stage 5 for a definition and description of confronting). When a counselor challenges the person's perceptions, motives, insights, defenses, expectations, and values, the counselor invites the client to entertain the possibility that the client's way of perceiving reality and reacting to it may not be entirely accurate, or for that matter, helpful. For example, a counselor may ask, "Bill, you say your mom is pretty unreasonable. Is it possible that sometimes she is being reasonable but you don't want to see it that way?" The counselor creates some stress in order to see how the client reacts to it. Does the client handle the stress differently than the way he or she *claims* to handle stress? When challenged, does the client exhibit some behavior that he or she has successfully covered up in previous sessions? Does the client respond by attacking, withdrawing, or deftly avoiding the challenge? Does the client respond well, seeing the challenge as an opportunity to learn something about self or to clarify a situation? Counselors who are reluctant at this stage to challenge the client risk missing valuable information. Probing, even though it may be somewhat difficult for the client, is essential because important decisions about treatment options require sound and complete information.

Warmth is another component of interacting. Relating warmly means that the counselor naturally and genuinely communicates positive feelings toward the client. This affords the counselor a chance to see firsthand how the person responds to positive feelings. Are they accepted naturally or ignored? Do they produce suspicion or does the client seek them out and cling to them? Answers to these questions give the counselor information about how the person handles warmth: whether the person accepts it and grows from it or rejects it and deprives himself or herself of valuable psychological fuel.

A second way to elicit firsthand information is by *reacting*. To do this, the counselor must be finely attuned to his or her own reactions to the client and must be able to differentiate the sources of these reactions. A mastery of this level of discernment is very valuable to the client in all stages of the counseling process but is especially useful at the information-gathering stage. With experience, training, and supervision, counselors can make reasonable appraisals about the way they are actually reacting to the client. These appraisals become tentative hypotheses about the way others react when they interact with the client. For example, the client may produce reactions in the counselor that include such feelings as: threat, anger, sympathy, tenderness, affection, sexual attraction, frustration, confusion, distrust, repulsion, curiosity, and caution. This information can tell the counselor how the person tends to "make" other people feel, at least under certain circumstances. This material can give the counselor otherwise unobtainable information as to how the person "gets" others to treat him or her. The information gained from interaction and reaction affords counselors access to material that they could not obtain simply by asking questions and letting the client tell a consciously or unconsciously edited story.

The importance of the intake interview and the process of asking questions cannot be overstated. While supervising a number of his interns, an experienced counselor asked what were the three most important evaluation tools? Hands shot up and one intern after another offered a different way of gathering information. Psychological testing, *in vivo* observations, reviews of records, and other less common methods were discussed. The enthusiastic interns had many answers but none expected the supervisor's reply. He stated simply and clearly, "the intake interview, the intake interview, the intake interview"—not unlike the real estate broker's cry, "location, location, location." The point is that the intake interview is the counselor's most effective tool as he or she begins the process of counseling. Information gained through this interview will help the counselor make a number of critical decisions regarding the client's care.

With the importance of the client interview in mind, counselors may also rely on other sources of supplementary information including psychological and educational test results, records (work, school, etc.), and collateral interviews where appropriate (e.g., with family members). Blocher (1987) offers useful information about assessment methods beyond the interview, and Osipow, Walsh, and Tosi (1980) provide a summary and evaluation of various types of educational and psychological tests that can be used to gather information about clients.

.⚔︎.

Stage 3: Evaluation and Feedback

As information gathering draws to a close, the counselor and, to some extent, the client begin the process of evaluating the information, making decisions, and providing feedback. The evaluation weighs these factors: (1) symptoms, (2) causes of symptoms, (3) relief of symptoms, (4) readiness for counseling, and (5) client/counselor fit. Feedback consists of the counselor's sharing relevant information with the client. The purpose of feedback is to provide sufficient information to enable the client to make an informed decision with regard to beginning a course of counseling. How counselors share this information is particularly important. Both evaluation and feedback are covered in the following pages.

Symptoms

Symptoms are signs indicating that people are experiencing difficulty in one or more areas of their lives. Conceptually, there are two kinds of symptoms: those included in the formal diagnostic categories—for example, those presented in the *Diagnostic and Statistical Manual* of the American Psychiatric Association (*DSM-IV*)—and those generally not included in formal diagnostic classifications. Constellations of symptoms are used to form diagnostic categories such as depression, anxiety states, phobias, obsessions, compulsions, personality disorders (such as antisocial and passive-aggressive), and so forth. Clients may have heard of various *DSM-IV* diagnoses, but mostly they report specific symptoms like inordinate fear, anger, guilt, confusion, frustration, procrastination, feelings of inadequacy, over-sensitivity, fatigue, tension, jealousy, interpersonal conflicts, job inefficiency, and religious desolation. Clients often refer to their symptoms as their problem. For example, a client may tell a counselor, "My problem is that I'm *confused* and *tense* all the time."

It is important for counselors to assess the nature and severity of the symptoms. Some symptoms need immediate and direct intervention. For example, people who are deeply depressed, severely anxious, are currently addicted to alcohol or drugs, or who pose an imminent threat of harm to themselves or others need forms of treatment that produce more immediate symptomatic relief, and they may need to be carefully supervised (e.g., hospitalization). Their symptoms are life-threatening, and the intensity of the symptoms precludes the effective use of counseling. Attempting to counsel someone with severe symptoms may dangerously delay more appropriate interventions and should be avoided for both ethical and professional reasons.

On the other hand, less severe symptoms that do not interfere with counseling often produce sufficient amounts of distress that they actually motivate the client to pursue counseling and take better advantage of it. These symptoms can be monitored and used to gauge the progress of counseling. As the client improves, the symptoms should diminish and possibly change.

Causes of Symptoms

There are essentially two generic causes of symptoms: biological imbalances and other factors that significantly interfere with, or threaten to interfere with, a basic psychological need or needs. Biological imbalances are often treated with a combination of medicine, medical supervision, and counseling. Less severe problems may be treated with counseling, and slightly more severe problems may be treated with a combination of counseling and medical interventions. Symptoms best treated through counseling include those where basic needs like the need to experience a reasonable degree of security, love, esteem, accomplishment, stimulation, freedom, joy, or purpose are not met. When an important need is unmet, anxiety results and when anxiety persists, it either immediately or eventually produces symptoms. The intensity of the anxiety and the individual's coping skills interact to affect the development of symptoms.

Basic needs can be significantly interfered with in several ways:

1. Trauma: an objectively psychologically damaging event occurs. For example, clients might be damaged by the loss of a loved one, divorce, termination of a love relationship, serious financial setback, or loss of a job.

2. Family problems: the client is in an important relationship with someone who is behaving in ways that significantly interfere with the client's basic needs. For example, a client might remain in a marriage with a person prone to destructive behavior.

3. Interpersonal issues: the client behaves interpersonally in ways that discourage others from meeting his or her needs. For example, an individual senses the need to relate to others but acts abrasively and gets rejected.

4. Intrapsychic issues: the client has intrapersonal dynamics that ultimately interfere with need fulfillment. For example, a person feels inadequate and therefore does not allow others to get close enough to meet his or her needs; a person has unrealistically high self-expectations and pursues them to the exclusion of satisfying more basic needs.

These causes are rarely mutually exclusive. A man may behave abrasively with women (interpersonal maladaptive behavior) because he perceives himself as inadequate and fears rejection (intrapersonal maladaptive behavior). Hence, he rejects women before they can reject him. There also may be more than one cause underlying a symptom, and two or more causes may interact. The more skilled counselors become, the better they can see how causes and symptoms interrelate. Figure 2-3 shows the interaction between symptoms, anxiety, and the causes of anxiety. It is important that counselors identify and assess the cause(s) of the symptoms as accurately as possible since an effective resolution depends on an accurate diagnosis.

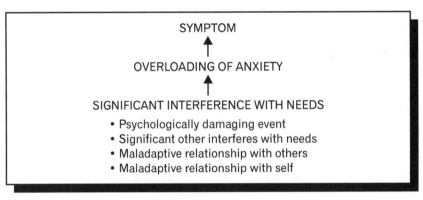

Figure 2-3. Interaction between symptoms, anxiety, and the causes of anxiety or stress.

Relief of Symptoms

The strategies to modify the behavior causing the symptoms depends upon the nature of the cause. If the cause is an objectively stressful event, then cognitive restructuring, ventilation, and reassurance may gradually allow the person to feel more secure, loved, or competent. This in turn reduces the stress, which diminishes the symptoms. If the cause is a significant other interfering with the person's need fulfillment, then the person can be helped to perceive and handle the situation more constructively or to withdraw from the relationship. If the person's maladaptive behavior in interpersonal situations is causing the symptoms, then the counselor can help the person develop better social competencies or a better sense of self, depending on the specific issue. If the cause is the person's intrapsychic conflicts, they can be identified and the person can be taught how to deal with them more creatively. The specific steps taken and the time required depend upon the nature of the behavior, its duration, and severity.

Readiness for Counseling

The decision to initiate a counseling relationship is difficult because counseling is appropriate for some people and not for others. The ideal situation occurs when the client is motivated to enter a counseling relationship and the counselor agrees with the efficacy of this course of action. Not everyone who needs and would benefit from counseling opts for it, and many people who desire counseling would not benefit. The following factors may help counselors assess the potential client's readiness and suitability for counseling. Each of these factors is on a continuum. A person at the positive end of the continuum on all these factors probably would not need counseling.

1. People who accept responsibility for their problems are likely to be better candidates than those who blame others. People who express some variation of "I need to learn how to handle things better" are likely to be better candidates than those who say, "If only my (husband, wife, boss, friends) treated me better, everything would be all right."

2. People who are motivated to "work" at feeling better are likely to be better candidates than those who want to feel better without changing their maladaptive behavior. Perls holds that "very few people go in therapy to be cured, but rather to improve their neurosis" (1969, p. 39). Although Perls may be overgeneralizing, his characterization merits consideration.

3. People with strong, intrinsic motivation to change are likely to be better candidates than those with weak intrinsic or primarily extrinsic motivation.

4. People who are psychologically minded are more likely to be good candidates than those who are not. Psychologically minded people are not only insightful but also are able and willing to appreciate the cause and effect dynamics of their behavior. For example, people who recognize that when they get angry at someone they deny it but later subtly punish that person are likely to be better candidates than those who absolutely deny their anger and therefore can make no connection between their anger and their passive-aggressive behavior.

5. People who have good interpersonal environmental supports tend to be better candidates than those who are interpersonally isolated. This is particularly true if the people who might support the client also tend to reward change and growth in others. Family and friends can strongly influence outcomes by either supporting or impeding progress.

6. People whose fears cause significant distress will likely be better candidates than those whose symptomatic (and problematic) behavior greatly reduces anxiety or provides pleasure through maladaptive means. Addiction to alcohol, drugs, or food; compulsive gambling; stealing; or sexually acting out all diminish the potential for counseling to be effective. Unfortunately, these problematic coping mechanisms reduce anxiety and therefore limit motivation to change.

7. The ability to communicate in ways that can be understood and to listen in ways that insure the assimilation of information improve the potential for counseling to be effective. Symptoms that significantly interfere with the ability to communicate seriously jeopardize effectiveness. For example, people with severe depression, agitation, withdrawal; those with cognitive disturbances such as hallucinations, delusions, disorientation, or memory impairment; and people with speech disorders such as mutism or echolalia may not be good candidates for counseling.

Great caution must be exercised in deciding who is a reasonable and who is a poor candidate for counseling (for further discussion about the selection of candidates for counseling, see Garfield, 1980, pp. 41–68). Persons who are not good candidates at present can be referred by the counselor to more appropriate types of intervention (detoxification, chemotherapy, weight control programs, hospitalization). Completing an alternative form of treatment may enable them to become reasonable candidates in the future.

It is sometimes appropriate for a counselor to accept a poor candidate into counseling. Clients such as these often experience great difficulty establishing relationships, building trust, and being able to express their thoughts and feelings. An extended period of relationship building is often necessary so that an effective therapeutic alliance can be formed. When working with clients who are poor candidates for counseling it is especially important that the counselor not offer the client any false hope regarding the effects of counseling.

Client–Counselor Fit

Not all counselors can help all people who seek their help. Counselors who expect to be able to work with anyone who comes to them entertain a potentially destructive assumption. Counseling relationships are similar to other important relationships: when serious, ongoing problems arise, it is often a consequence of two people trying to work together who probably never should have started together.

Counselors are human beings with weaknesses, biases, fears, angers, and values. They can learn to recognize areas where they are vulnerable and work to strengthen themselves; however, they also should recognize that some clients may be too disturbing to them. When this occurs, it is better to refer the client to someone else. For example, a counselor may have a difficult time relating to a very hostile, powerful, demanding client. Another counselor may experience inordinate stress relating with very passive, docile, clinging clients. Yet another counselor may have trouble accepting the client's presenting problem: child molesting, child beating, alcoholism, drug addiction, abortion, sexual promiscuity, rape. The more counselors know and understand about themselves, the more accurately they can assess which kinds of people and problems they can successfully counsel.

It is both a professional and ethical responsibility to screen people for counseling. Ordinarily, a counselor who agrees to counsel someone explicitly and implicitly communicates that the potential client has good reason to expect that counseling will be successful, that the counselor can work effectively with the person, and that the time, energy, hardship, and financial investment will be worthwhile. If one or more of these are untrue, such concerns should be carefully explored and discussed because serious professional and ethical issues may arise.

Counselors who agree to work with people who cannot be adequately helped through counseling tarnish the reputation of the profession. This leads to the conclusion that "counseling doesn't work" instead of "counseling doesn't work with certain people," who should have been referred to a more appropriate source of intervention. Counselors who intelligently screen potential clients perform a positive service to those seeking help and to the counseling profession.

Because of the complexity of human behavior, it is unlikely that an evaluation and recommendation for counseling can be made with absolute confidence and certainty. However, competent counselors can be reasonably confident about the hypotheses they develop in concert with a client regarding the potential effectiveness of counseling for that client. How these hypotheses are shared with clients is important. A careful, clear, meaningful discussion helps the client make sound and responsible decisions about whether to begin counseling. Frank discussions also help clients form reasonable expectations about the counseling process. This communication process is often called *feedback* and it is used at various stages of counseling. Feedback consists of the counselor's sharing relevant information with the potential client. The purpose of this information is to enable the person to make an informed decision with regard to beginning a counseling program. Four principles guide counselors as they provide meaningful feedback.

The first pertains to the characteristics of the information provided to the client. The information should be given as clearly, succinctly, concretely, and prudently as possible. Simple, jargon-free language aids clients' understanding of the process and invites them to take part in decision making. Short descriptions, clear analogies, sometimes even a simple diagram help clarify the important issues. Counselors also should instill a sense of concern (when it is appropriate) without creating a state of alarm; for example, saying "You've got some struggles or difficulties that need attention, but there is something you can do about each of them." Feedback, even with the most psychologically disturbed people, can be given in one session.

Second, the feedback should include both strengths and weaknesses. Usually it is better to begin with strengths and finish with weaknesses. When the order is reversed, the person may become so defensive or demoralized that he or she may tune out important parts of the discussion. The sequence is not set in stone; interspersing strengths and weaknesses also works well. The important point is always to include strengths in the feedback session, thus guarding against feedback sessions that are solely negative and problem-focused.

The third principle suggests that the client should be invited to ask questions both during and after the feedback. Questions should be answered in a straightforward, supportive manner. Sometimes clients ask a litany of questions in order to forestall the feedback process. When this is the case, the person can be invited to hold any questions until the end of the session.

The fourth and final principle pertains to the recommendations counselors make after communicating the feedback to the client. The counselor should explain that recommendations are not orders but rather are serious, well-thought-out suggestions. The following are some common recommendations:

1. Continue counseling on a weekly basis or more or less frequently as the seriousness of the problem dictates.

2. Continue individual counseling; or begin group, marital, or family counseling; or combine individual counseling with one of these other modalities.

3. Continue counseling, but with another counselor. This recommendation is made when the counselor feels someone else would be significantly more helpful, either because of a personality conflict or because the person's problem requires help outside of the counselor's area of expertise. When this recommendation is made, it should be done prudently and without communicating to the person that he or she is being rejected.

4. Recommend a more suitable type of intervention—for example, substance abuse counseling, a weight-control program, readings or a course in psychological health, a support group, or religious direction.

5. Recommend no further intervention because the person's difficulties are quite normal and are simply a part of the person's development and growth.

6. Recommend no further intervention because, as a result of the sessions up to this point, the person has gained sufficient insight and courage to handle the problems without further professional help.

7. Recommend no further intervention because, although the person has problems that merit counseling, he or she is not psychologically ready for counseling. The person may not be experiencing sufficient anxiety, or may be experiencing anxiety controlled by defenses that are currently impenetrable. In either case, the person's motivation and accessibility are insufficient for effective counseling. Counselors should exercise care not to convey that the situation is hopeless. The

difference between "not being ready" and "hopeless" should be explained, accompanied by an open invitation to return at some time in the future. On the other hand, these people should not be led to believe that they do not need counseling.

If the session(s) preceding the feedback progress the way they should, neither the feedback nor the recommendations will be a surprise. Counselors need not feel that the feedback should consist of dramatic insights and discoveries. Consciously and unconsciously, the counselor has been preparing the client for the feedback and recommendations as the evaluation progressed.

No matter what the recommendation, the client should not make a decision on the day of the feedback. The client should be encouraged to think about the feedback, assimilate it, and discuss it with others if so inclined. The counselor should be careful not to convey the attitude that the client would be foolish not to accept the recommendation or that the counselor does not care if the client follows the recommendation. A more helpful attitude is one that conveys, "I think the recommendation is a sound one, but what is more important is that this is *your* decision."

At this point, the client has a second decision-point as to whether to begin counseling. This time the choice is an informed one. The person understands much more about himself or herself, about the nature of counseling, and about the personality of the counselor. If the person chooses to continue counseling, he or she will be a much stronger candidate and counseling will continue with good momentum. If the person chooses not to continue counseling, this decision may save the person and the counselor a great deal of time, energy, and frustration.

≈⚖≈

Stage 4: Counseling Agreement

Although counseling has been taking place during the first three stages, both the counselor and the client possess much more information than they did when they began. Using this information as a frame of reference, the counselor and the client can come to an agreement on several important issues: (1) the practical aspects of counseling, (2) roles, (3) expectations, and (4) the goals of counseling. To formally appraise clients and potential clients of various aspects of the counseling process, many counselors use disclosure statements. Such statements include information about the counselor (training, experience, licenses, etc.), fees, length of meetings, and general expectations and responsibilities. The counseling agreement discussed in the following pages goes beyond what would be found in such a disclosure statement and focuses on counseling a particular client. This focus is based on the information gathered and the unique qualities of the developing alliance between counselor and client.

Practical Aspects

Practical aspects include how often the client and counselor will meet, the length of the sessions, the counselor's policy regarding canceled and missed appointments, and billing procedures. Even if there is no need to modify these based on the information gained from the first three stages, it is helpful to restate them in order to underline their importance. However, sometimes the counselor has learned information that warrants an adjustment to the practical arrangements to fit a particular client and situation. When this is the case, the counselor can explain the modifications and the reasons for them.

Roles

The second part of the agreement deals with role expectations. The specific roles depend on the counselor and the client. For example, the counselor may explain that his or her role will be the same as it was during the first three stages or that it will be more passive, reflective, varied, confrontative, direct, ambiguous, questioning, silent, active, or listening. It is helpful for the counselor to offer a brief explanation of why he or she feels that assuming a certain role will facilitate the client's progress.

It is important to remember that *assuming* a role is not the same as *playing* a role. When a man returns from work, he assumes the role of father, which is helpful and appropriate. It is hoped that he does not simply play the role in the sense of acting out a part. A counselor may legitimately assume a role in a counseling situation that would be inappropriate to assume in other circumstances, but the role should be a part of him or her, not simply an acting job.

The role of the client is also discussed. A counselor may feel it is helpful for the person to begin each session by discussing whatever concern or issue is uppermost at the moment. Or the counselor may suggest that the person's past requires more attention and should be the area of focus for a time. Another counselor may wish to concentrate on the present and on feelings, or a counselor may want to focus on what goes on inside the counseling room. One counselor may invite the person to relate personally as well as professionally, asking questions and getting to know the counselor, while another counselor may wish to remain more impersonal.

When both the counselor and client clearly understand and agree that their roles feel comfortable and will facilitate growth, they are in a better position to work as a synchronized team.

Expectations

Expectations can become more explicit than they were during the first three stages because each person has a better grasp of the counseling situation. The counselor shares his or her expectations regarding the responsibilities of the client. These might deal with honesty, making concerted efforts to reach the goals of counseling, placing a high priority on counseling, doing homework assignments, discussing counseling with others, and viewing counseling as a seven-day-a-week experience rather than a 50-minute-a-week visit.

The client can also share his or her expectations of the counselor. The person can tell the counselor what he or she would find helpful and unhelpful. Often in this early stage of counseling, however, people are not in a position to articulate clearly how the counselor can be of more help. Consequently, the counselor can encourage the person along these lines and invite him or her to keep the counselor apprised of growing and changing expectations as counseling progresses.

Goals

As a result of the first three stages, both the client and the counselor have a clearer picture of the problems and the possible solutions. Goal-setting is perhaps the most important part of this stage of counseling because it ties the process together. For this reason it requires an adequate amount of time and care. Properly formulated counseling goals share certain characteristics.

First, they are specific and measurable. For example, an agreed-upon goal might be that a person overcome his or her fear of getting a job. This goal is specific in that it zeros in on a clear target. It is measurable because the steps toward the goal can be readily charted, and it is relatively easy to determine how much progress has been made toward accomplishing the goal.

In contrast, a person may have as a goal to be more happy, less anxious or depressed, to become a better husband or mother, or to get to know oneself better. These goals are so general, abstract, and difficult to measure that they are unworkable. In this situation the counselor and client need to target in on what "more happy" actually means. Why exactly does the person feel tense? Why specifically does the person think he is not a good husband? The more precise and operational the goals, the better chance counseling has to achieve them.

Second, the goals of counseling should be realistic and should take into account the client's potential as well as all limitations in the client's environment. For example, two 38-year-old women wish to enter law school and each seeks counseling to help her make the psychological changes necessary to bring about this decision. For one of these women, this may be a realistic goal and for another it may not be. One woman is divorced, intelligent, and energetic. She worked as a court clerk and feels that she has the motivation and skills required of an attorney. She seeks counseling because she is not sure whether she wants to leave the security of her present job, whether she wants to make the sacrifices that both law school and a career as an attorney demand, and whether it will deprive her two adolescent children of the parenting they still need. She knows what she wants, but she is not sure that pursuing it would be a wise choice.

The second woman is married to a man who does not want her to go to law school. He wants her home with their four school-age children, and he would have to get another job to secure a loan to finance law school. The woman is of modest intelligence and has been depressed. The thought of going to law school has somewhat alleviated her depression. She has no knowledge of law but came upon the idea when she read about another woman whose life was changed when she became an attorney. She seeks counseling because she wants to learn how she can go to law school and keep her husband happy and children healthy. It is unlikely that the second woman's goal is one that can be attained in counseling, even though it is the same as that of the first woman.

Realistic goals are seldom of an all-or-nothing nature. For example, a man seeks counseling to help him relate more effectively at work. "More effectively" for this particular man may mean increasing his effectiveness by 20, 50, or 70%. It would be unrealistic to expect counseling to bring him to the point of functioning with complete effectiveness.

Third, the goals should be psychologically healthy. Some people's proposed goals are consonant with psychological growth. They want to become more assertive, autonomous, and confident; less angry, fearful, and confused. Other people, however, may seek counseling to maintain equilibrium through means that are not psychologically healthy. For example, a person may want to learn to survive in a work situation that is intractably damaging, to leave a family situation in ways that would be injurious to self and others, or to begin a project for which he or she is unprepared and that is doomed to fail. While it is the client's prerogative to choose his or her own goals, it is the counselor's responsibility not to become a collaborator in destructive behavior.

Fourth, goals are often hierarchical. Some clients have only one goal in counseling, such as the previously mentioned woman who wants to go to law school. Many people, however, have several goals. For example, a man may list the following goals: to be more comfortable sexually, to change jobs, to have a less conflictual relationship with his parents, to recapture religious fervor, to relate more comfortably with women on dates, and to lose 30 pounds.

While it may be helpful to establish a set of goal priorities, this task can be quite difficult and complicated. Goals are not isolated structures; they interact with one another in a complex system. For example, once the counselor knows this client better, it may become clear that the goals cannot be arranged in such an order that the client's goals will be immediately met. It may be that the inordinate pressure at work is causing ongoing damage, and until it is alleviated, the man is in no position to work on any of the other goals. Once that pressure is alleviated, the next step may be to refer the person to a medically supervised weight-control program through which he can lose weight and feel more presentable. While he is losing weight, the next step may be to explore the reasons for feeling sexually confused or uncomfortable about himself. When this issue is on its way to resolution, the next step may be to examine what makes dating an anxiety-producing experience and then to date. When the dating anxiety gets under control, the next step may be to understand and work on his conflict with his parents. When all these are reasonably under control, he may be at peace enough to be able to work on his religious doubts and conflicts.

Sometimes when the first two or three goals are attained, the rest take care of themselves. For example, in the case above, the man's conflicts with his parents and his religious doubts may be resolved as side effects of achieving the previous goals. One caveat must be noted: agreed-upon priorities must not be set in cement. When the counselor understands more about the client, it may become imperative to rearrange the priorities. In the scenario we've been discussing, the counselor may discover that until this man's religious conflicts are resolved, there will be no movement toward any of the other goals. A shift in priorities may be necessary when the client and the counselor work hard at attaining a subgoal but achieve no meaningful results. This could indicate that another goal or a hitherto unrecognized goal must be dealt with first.

Fifth, the goals belong to the client. Sometimes, especially when people bring general, abstract, or vague goals to counseling, the counselor gets trapped into making them more concrete and manageable for the client. For example, a man may say he is depressed but doesn't know why because he has a job, a wife, children, and a home—everything he could ever want. After several unsuccessful attempts to help the man articulate the cause of his distress, the counselor may decide why he is depressed: he is denying his disappointment with a marriage that has become drab; he resents the fact that his wife won't let him pursue work in another field; he feels guilty about having recently placed his father in a convalescent hospital; and he regrets not having as much time as he would like to spend with his children. Based on any of these conceptualizations, the counselor could craft specific goals: spice up the marriage, work on his relationship with his father, or learn time-management skills.

On the basis of these hypotheses, with which the client reluctantly and tentatively agrees ("You're the doctor—I expect you know more about these things that I do"), the decision is made to launch into trying to reach the counselor's goals. Of course, nothing good is likely to result from this counseling relationship because the goals are the counselor's and not those of the client. Even if the counselor is correct on all the hypotheses, the client has never claimed the goals for himself.

It is essential that the counseling goals be clearly owned by the client and that counseling not continue until this occurs. To spend a few sessions trying to clarify goals could be appropriate, but when the goal of counseling is to discuss the goals of counseling, this usually results in unproductive expeditions in which both the counselor and the client continually meet themselves exactly where they began.

Sixth, counseling goals should be evaluated frequently. Aiming at goals in counseling is similar to aiming at any kind of target. After attempting to hit the target a few times, it is sensible to have a look at how successful the efforts have been. Since goals are specific and measurable, it should not be too difficult to gauge progress toward them. When the counselor and the person agree that they are progressing in the right direction and on schedule, it provides a mutual sense of confidence and accomplishment that can add momentum to their quest. If, after a reasonable time, it becomes clear that the counselor and client have gradually strayed from the target or are progressing too slowly, they can consider questions like the following: Is there a prior condition that must be met? For example, the person may need more time to trust the counselor before becoming committed to the goal. Is there some deep ambivalence developing toward the goal as it gets closer to realization? Maybe a man is becoming less confident that divorce is the best thing for him at this point. In any case, it is much better to look at the target early and at short intervals to check your "aim" than to assume that counseling is squarely on target, only to discover later that it has been spiraling out of control.

Developing a counseling agreement may take from one to four sessions. If the counselor and client are still debating and negotiating an agreement after five sessions, it is likely that the client is not sufficiently motivated to use counseling, that there is a problem in the counselor-client relationship, or that the counselor is not sufficiently skilled to develop the agreement. A thorough discussion of the importance of counseling agreements can be found in Goldberg (1977, pp. 31–61).

Stage 5: Change(s) in Behavior

Exactly what occurs during this stage depends upon the nature of the client's problem and its causes. For example, cognitive restructuring, ventilation, and reassurance may be used to improve difficulties brought about by objectively stressful events. If maladaptive behavior patterns in interpersonal situations are producing symptoms, efforts may focus on helping the client develop better social competencies and a better sense of self. Intrapsychic conflicts require a slightly different approach. These patterns can be identified and the client may develop alternative strategies for managing them. The following are situations which counselors frequently confront while helping clients change their behavior.

Focusing on Responsibility

Clients frequently view counselors as psychological architects whose role is to provide a blueprint telling clients who they are, what their problem is, how they should solve it, and when they should take each step in the process. Even the most experienced counselor can be insidiously trapped into assuming this role. Unfortunately, when this occurs, the counselor is taking responsibility not only for the person's changes in behavior but for the person's life.

Counselors should resist manipulations and temptations to become managers for clients. If clients demand that someone take the reins of their life they may likely need more intensive treatment than traditional outpatient counseling can provide. The counselor's stance toward the client should always focus on the client's taking responsibility for the process. To do this counselors can encourage clients to control the session for themselves by:

- defining who they are (how they are feeling and thinking; what they want and what they do)
- identifying the problem(s) they wish to address
- defining how they wish to solve the problem(s)
- describing what strategies they intend to implement

Obviously, a person could respond, "If I could tell you all these things, I wouldn't be in counseling in the first place." While in one sense this retort is valid, in a deeper more important sense it is not. The assumptions underlying many counseling approaches maintain that the answers to these questions lie only within the individual. Therefore, the counselor's role is not to answer these questions, but to provide an environment and a relationship that improve insight and bolster the courage necessary for the client to answer the questions and to translate the answers into practice.

Inward Searching

Clients, like most people, often operate exclusively on an external level. Their approach to life is, "I've got a problem here, and I have to figure out a way to solve it." The focus is almost entirely on *the problem outside* of them and not on *the person inside*. As a result, they persistently experience the same types of problems.

For example, a 30-year-old woman comes to counseling because she is depressed that she cannot find a marriageable man. The more frantic and depressed she becomes, the more she sabotages her relationships with men. After several sessions of internal searching, she makes the following discoveries:

- She has a void within her that is comprised of feeling unimportant, unlovable, and purposeless, and she believes only a man can fill that void.

- She looks upon marriage as a psychological and social validation of herself. As long as she is unmarried, she and society look upon her as psychologically lame; as soon as she gets married, she will be seen as psychologically healthy. A good deal of the pressure she feels is not to get married but to feel good about herself.

- She thinks the best way to get a man is to be sexually active and has not realized that this is not going to get her a man who meets her qualifications. In other words, she is attracting exactly the kind of man she dislikes.

- She is very ambivalent about marriage. On one hand she wants to get married, but on the other she resents men because she needs them to make her happy. She fears her deep need for a man will enslave her just as her mother became enslaved to her father. She is fearful that if she does marry, she may find herself disillusioned, which would rule out her last hope for happiness on this earth. Her deep ambivalence is reflected in her behavior with men, causing her unnecessary conflicts.

As she works through these unconscious insights, she feels far less pressure to get married. She begins to fill her void intrapsychically with a clear appreciation for her worth and goodness, to which counseling introduces her. She fills the void with new friends, a more fulfilling job, and hobbies she always enjoyed until she began her "manhunt."

When she does date, she is more selective, acts in keeping with her deeper values, and relates more comfortably. Dates are no longer examinations that she can pass or fail, but evenings to enjoy in themselves. She still would *like* to marry, but she does not *have* to marry.

Fears often prevent clients from inward exploration. They are afraid of what they might discover. Therefore, skilled counselors actually help people work through the resistance and develop a sense of timing that guides them as they select the right moment to explore a given insight.

Utilizing Insights

Insights alone may bring about the psychological equilibrium necessary to reduce symptoms and create growth. In other words, the person's problem may remain, but the person has outgrown it. Therefore, the problem becomes less of a nuisance. But a second point of view argues that insight alone is not sufficient for change. Inward searching (insight) provides the blueprint but external behavioral changes are also necessary for personality growth. This view accepts that some human problems are unsolvable and suggests that counseling should address itself only to those that are subject to change. The benefits of introspection are thus combined with problem solving in a two-part process.

The woman in the previous example did not simply rest with her inner reflections and discoveries, but used them to chart concrete, observable changes in her daily life. She finished college, changed jobs, broadened her circle of friends and interests, changed her way of relating with men, returned to her religion, and used the psychological dividends of this change to fill her void and strengthen her being. As a result, she has not only solved the problem she brought to counseling but also has grown as a person.

Mirroring

Counselors act as mirrors where clients can metaphorically see themselves. Mirroring can occur directly or indirectly. Direct mirroring occurs when the counselor informs the client of the impression the counselor would form purely from the client's behavior. In mirroring, the counselor says, in effect, "This is the way you look to me now. If you agree that's who you are, what changes, if any, would you like to make? If you don't agree that's who you are, let's figure out why we have different perceptions." This is important because many clients are faced with distortions in the picture they have of themselves, and these distortions often lead such persons to behave in inappropriate and unhelpful ways. It is also important because very few, if any, people in the client's life would have the skills, concern, benevolence, and courage to reflect to the person how he or she appears. Clients benefit from the alternative views provided by someone who knows, respects, and has a professional relationship with them. With an additional and somewhat clearer picture, clients are in an improved position to make meaningful changes.

Equally important is indirect mirroring. This means the counselor reflects to the client how he or she is perceived in terms of the responses this perceived behavior elicits. The counselor might say, "I'm starting to feel confused (anxious, distracted, sympathetic, bored, frightened, etc.) as I listen to you talk about this issue." The message that the counselor conveys is, "When you act the way you are, this is the response you are likely to elicit from people. If you want that response, it's okay; but if you don't want it, let's see how and why you elicit it."

While counselors can never be emotionally neutral and totally objective about their reactions to the client, they can reasonably trust that their reactions to the client are likely to be similar to those that other people would have. This is priceless information for clients because they may be unaware of how their verbal and nonverbal communication affects others. People often wonder why others "always" manipulate, reject, seduce, misunderstand, or avoid them when all they do is behave in a manner they consider friendly and reasonable.

Both intrapsychic and interpersonal reflection must be done as nonthreateningly as possible. It is likely to be threatening to some extent because people generally become anxious when they hear something about themselves they didn't know, even when the feedback is positive. The only purpose of mirroring is to be helpful; it is never to put a person "in his place."

Confronting

A counselor may point out significant discrepancies in the person's behavior or lifestyle. This is different from mirroring, which simply reflects back to people who they appear to be. It also differs from challenging in that challenging is more gentle and invites clients to reexamine the accuracy of their perceptions; confrontation is more assertive and focuses on deeper motives and contradictory behavior.

Confrontation is one method of interpretation. Conflicting information or messages are brought to the client's conscious awareness: "You say you are this, but is it possible you are something different?" For example, a counselor might confront a client by stating, "Bill, you keep saying you want to save your marriage, but the way you've been acting makes me wonder if a part of you does not want to save it," or "Nancy, you tell me you want to use counseling, but you consistently forget what we talk about from one session to another and seldom work on anything between sessions."

Some cautions must be exercised regarding confrontation. The alliance between the client and the counselor must be strong enough to withstand the confrontation. In other words, clients may not like the confrontation, but if there is a strong therapeutic alliance they will appreciate that it is in their best interest. All of this presumes that there is a sound basis for elements of the discrepancy. Trust and professional respect diminish rapidly if counselors confront clients on patterns that are not part of a reality that the client can understand and accept.

Finally, counselors need to be sensitive to the nature of their motives. Is the confrontation actually a personal attack disguised as a helpful strategy, or does it stem from a counselor's sole interest in helping the client learn something important? If it is an attack, the tone will be, "Tim, who do you think you're kidding?" If it's a constructive response, the tone will be, "Tim, I'd like to share some perceptions with you and see what you think about them." For a thorough discussion of confrontation see Adler and Meyerson (1973).

Giving Support

Counselors offer reassurance and positive reinforcement and reduce people's anxiety by showing them the positive and hopeful aspects of a situation and by rewarding positive behavior with genuine and spontaneous encouragement and support. According to Frank (1961), "Efforts to heighten the patient's positive expectations may be as genuinely therapeutic as free association or habit training" (p. 385). Giving support can be a very effective aid to the counseling process, but it needs to be approached with caution. The reassurance must be justified by reality; hollow pep talks may backfire. Statements such as, "I'm sure things will turn out fine" or "I have faith that you'll do well" are usually ill advised. A more effective type of reassurance is, "Let's do our best, and, whatever happens, we'll work very hard together to handle it well." This communicates a more reality-based reassurance that focuses on the counseling relationship as a source of support and not on the success or failure of a particular event.

When using positive reinforcement, counselors should be careful about *what* they reinforce. A man may tell a counselor that he was *finally* able to assert himself at work. He proudly relates the incident to the counselor, who congratulates him for his willingness to take a risk and for successfully asserting himself. However, if the counselor had delved more deeply into the matter, he might have discovered that the "assertiveness" was a ploy to escape some rightful responsibility at work. In effect, the counselor rewarded the person for being manipulative and shirking responsibility. It is often difficult for counselors to delve into situations that the client proudly presents as evidence of progress. Counselors may feel pressure to allow clients to bask in their feelings of accomplishment because they do not want to appear distrustful or rude. However, careful and thoughtful examination of the client's report often helps to prevent reinforcing problematic behavior.

A second caution regarding positive reinforcement is that it can create a situation in which the client is changing to earn the praise of the counselor. This counseling relationship can never end because, as soon as talk of termination begins, the client regresses as he or she realizes that growth is meaningless without the praise of the counselor. Ideally, growth should be its own reward, and, as people progress in counseling, there should be less need for counselors to reward their efforts. However, in the first phases of counseling, when people's efforts are not yet sufficiently effective to produce rewarding results, it is often necessary for counselors to provide reinforcement.

Resisting Reverse Shaping

The counselor helps shape the behavior of the client through the judicious use of reward, expectation, insight, and confrontation. Reverse shaping occurs when the client does the same thing to the counselor. Because conscious and unconscious shaping is almost continually operative in all human beings, the shaping attempts of the client are probably as numerous as those of the counselor. Clients can subtly and not so subtly reward and punish counselors. Counselors who behave in ways that please clients may be rewarded with compliments or by clients demonstrating new evidence of growth. When a counselor displeases a client, the client is apt to regress or attack the counselor.

When clients' shaping efforts are obvious, they can be dealt with easily. But people who are "cooperative" and whose only wish is to get strong enough to handle their own problems can adroitly shape the counselor without the counselor being even slightly aware of it.

Some clients bring a script to counseling that has a bad ending. They hire the counselor as a facilitator who will help bring about the desired destructive ending in the most "officially approved" way possible. The ending of the story may be suicide, getting fired, getting rejected by loved ones, remaining in a destructive relationship, proving that one is hopeless, being hospitalized, or setting up the counselor to fail. Each progressive act is an escalated attempt to shape the counselor's behavior so that he or she will help the client bring about the destructive ending.

Counselors have tools to help them react constructively to reverse shaping. Every time the client creates a situation in which the counselor feels quite pleased or quite displeased, the counselor should consider possible motives: Why is this person telling me this (doing this)? How does he (or she) expect me to respond? Will my response be feeding into the person's strengths or weaknesses?

Counselors also can focus on the agreed-upon goals of counseling, despite the client's pressures to ignore them. This will eventually either spotlight the destructive ending of the script and allow the counselor to invite the client to change the ending or cause the client to terminate when he or she sees that the counselor is not willing to be shaped. If the latter happens, it is better to have it occur early than to have the counselor continue as a co-conspirator in the client's destructive behavior.

Interpreting

Interpretation introduces to clients previously unknown information about themselves. In other words, the counselor pulls back the blinds and permits the person to see behaviors that were relegated to the subconscious or unconscious layers of personality. The goal of interpretation is to increase self-knowledge. The more self-knowledge people have, the more able they are to change their behavior.

Clients repress or deny parts of themselves they do not wish to or cannot acknowledge. Therefore most interpretation centers on areas where clients have deceived themselves. However, these hidden elements (thoughts, feelings, defenses, motives, conflicts, or values) unconsciously influence clients' actions. People can vent these less-than-conscious behaviors without having to accept responsibility for them. For example, a man has unconscious negative feelings toward his family. He thinks he comes home quite late every night because he is too busy at work. His late arrival allows him to shorten the time spent in an unpleasant situation and to upset the people who are upsetting him without having to face exactly what he is doing and why. In the meantime, both he and his family are unhappy, and they feel there is nothing that can be done about it.

Interpretation ordinarily poses a threat to the client because the repressed material is not pleasant, otherwise it would not have been repressed in the first place. Also, the new information that stems from interpretation means the client will be challenged to let go of old behaviors and adjust current behaviors to the new information. For example, once the man who gets home late discovers what he is doing and why, he will feel more anxious and will tend to use the anxiety to change the situation in one direction or another. Therefore, it is not unusual for people to resist interpretation.

Because interpretation in counseling is a delicate and complicated operation, counselors should be familiar with the important issues involved. Counselors need to know *what* to interpret. For example, it is generally more helpful to interpret the client's defenses before interpreting the conflict itself. In this way the interpretation doesn't get intercepted and defused by the defenses. If a client describes a situation where he is dealt with unfairly by another, say a supervisor or a boss, the counselor might be tempted to interpret the specifics of the conflict. But it would be more effective to interpret the defenses that obstructed the client from seeing the conflict from various vantage points first, and then proceed to the interpretation of the conflict itself. Along the same lines, it is generally more helpful to interpret process (how and why the person is doing or not doing something in the counseling session) than content (what the person is saying). Basically, interpretation should be selective; only behaviors that are significantly affecting the client need to be considered.

When an interpretation is offered is as important as *what* is interpreted. Interpretations are more likely to be heard and acted on if the client is close to the level of awareness required to grasp the interpretation and is sufficiently relaxed and comfortable with the counselor, and when there is reasonable certainty that the interpretive hypothesis is correct. Finally, the effectiveness of the interpretation is linked to *how* the information is shared with the client. Counselors often introduce the client to interpretation gradually by beginning with less threatening interpretations. Also, interpretations should be phrased tentatively ("Could it be that . . . ?") and concisely since unnecessary words serve only to distract. Interpretation is probably more common in long-term counseling where deeper issues are explored than in crisis intervention and short-term counseling. A more complete discussion of interpretation may be found in Singer (1965).

Stage 6: Termination

Clients terminate the counseling relationship in a variety of ways. Ideally client and counselor work to a point where they share an opinion about termination. But counselors and clients prematurely terminate for a myriad of reasons. Counselors move, change professions, become ill, or sometimes elect not to continue counseling for ethical or professional reasons. Clients get transferred, develop symptoms that require referral to other professionals, become disgusted with the process, and so on. For these reasons, termination needs to be considered throughout the counseling process. Counselors can anticipate, but they can never know, when clients might elect to terminate counseling.

It is helpful to remember that termination is a *stage* of counseling and not simply the last few sessions. This stage could conceivably encompass as much as the last quarter of counseling. While it may seem logical for the counselor to begin preparing the client to leave counseling only during the termination phase, in actuality termination is an issue of concern from the outset of the counseling relationship. Each counseling session can be seen as microcosm of the total counseling effort. Each session contains alliance-building activities, information gathering, evaluation, goal setting, change, and termination. Sessions end, and clients learn very quickly how to deal with the breaks that occur between sessions. The fact that a week separates one session from the next is a clear and important message to the client that termination is possible and, moreover, the client has the resources and abilities to make productive use of the time between sessions.

Under ideal circumstances, at termination the counselor begins pulling back as a source of support, feedback, and guidance. The counselor's interest in the client persists, but it is demonstrated in a way that honors the client's increased independence from the counseling process. At this stage of the process the counselor offers more termination-oriented comments, such as pointing out the success the client is achieving. The counselor's overall message suggests to clients that they are doing more and more on their own and doing it well. This helps clients see that the distance already traveled in counseling is much longer than the distance that remains.

Counselors often notice that as counseling progresses to termination, the sessions become a place to check in. The client may say, "I've got a problem that came up last week. Let me tell you what I'm going to do about it, and if you've got any thoughts you can let me know." This level of autonomy is later elevated to another level: "Let me tell you how I solved a problem this week. I purposely didn't tell you about it because I wanted to handle it on my own. If you've got any thoughts when I'm through, I'd be glad to hear them."

Usually at about this time the topic of termination surfaces either from the client, the counselor, or both. While it is sometimes said that it is better for clients to initiate the subject of termination, this is not necessarily true. Sometimes the fact that the counselor brings it up first is viewed as a validation of the client's own thoughts and an affirmation of his or her progress. Also, some clients may assume that broaching the subject of termination is the rightful role of the counselor.

When initiating the topic, the counselor might say, "You seem to be doing so well that I'm wondering if you have given any thought to tapering off our sessions?" Of course, the counselor would ask this question only when the client has had good momentum for a reasonable period of time. The client may respond, "It's funny you ask that. We must be on the same wavelength because I've been thinking about it, too." Other responses might be, "I haven't given it much thought, but I suppose it is something we should start planning for" or "No, I haven't. Why? Do you think I'm ready to stop?" The counselor must deal with the dynamics underlying the responses. The last example likely indicates that the client and counselor are viewing things differently or the person is dependent on counseling and resistant to even the thought of terminating.

The client who initiates the topic of termination might say, "You know, I've been thinking that I may not need to come here as often because I'm handling things pretty well." The counselor may respond, "Why don't you tell me what you've been thinking about?" and react appropriately to the person's explanations.

After there is agreement that counseling has progressed to a point where terminating is an issue, the next step is usually to taper off the number of sessions. Generally, the longer the counseling relationship, the longer the tapering period. Usually the number of sessions is reduced from four each month to two. Sometimes that is sufficient but, with some clients, it is helpful to continue tapering to once each month and then to a "come in as the need arises" basis. Tapering is meant to avoid the shock of autonomy that can cause separation anxiety and regressive behavior, and must be tailored to each counseling relationship.

It is helpful to recall at this stage the nature of a *goal*; that is, it is something to aim at, but may not be totally achieved. Thus, counseling does not necessarily continue until the goals are ultimately and irrevocably attained. More often, counseling helps people to approximate their goals more closely and to live more effectively with the distance that remains between where they are and where they would like to be.

A related concept is that a person's growth toward goals does not terminate with the end of counseling. By the time clients terminate counseling, they should have built up a momentum that will continue to carry them in the direction of their goals. Clinical judgment regarding termination considers the relationship between how far a person has progressed and what additional benefits will accrue by continuing counseling. When people have a clear picture of their ultimate goals and good momentum in the right direction, they often are ready to finish the job on their own.

Finally, clients do not always terminate counseling with profuse feelings of gratitude toward the counselor. Although this can be discouraging or confusing to the counselor, it is understandable. When counseling has been a difficult experience for clients and has cost a great deal of time, energy, tension, hard work, and money, they may feel like amateur athletes after a grueling victory. They truly enjoy the victory but feel they contributed as much to it as the coach, and the coach is getting paid. Consequently, they may feel no special need to express appreciation. In some cases, clients still have not completely resolved the fact that they needed help or needed to depend on another person. Therefore, to thank the counselor would be admitting that they needed him or her. Obviously, it would be nice for people to resolve these feelings before the termination of counseling, but what is "nice" and what is "real" are sometimes two different things. Still other clients are people who have never been good at showing gratitude or saying goodbye; counseling may not have changed that. It doesn't mean these people did not benefit greatly from counseling, but simply that they cannot express their gratitude.

On the other hand, the fact that some people show apparent gratitude does not necessarily indicate they received a great deal from counseling. They may just be thankful that counseling is finished or that they got through it without having to face their deepest, most dreaded problem. The counselor can take satisfaction from having helped the client lead a better life, even though some clients' lives may never be more than marginally fulfilling. If a counselor wants greater satisfaction, he or she may have to, and probably should, find it outside of the counseling room.

Summary

It is important that counselors recognize the developmental dimension of the counseling relationship. When counselors possess a general theoretical and practical frame of reference, it lends both direction and order to what otherwise could be a chaotic and frustrating experience. An understanding of the stages of helping is beneficial to both counselors and clients. It is helpful to counselors because the stages act as directional markers that help counselors steer a steady course toward growth. It is helpful to clients because, once the sequence of stages is explained to them, they can feel a sense of security and purpose.

While this chapter introduces the stages of the counseling process, more specific information about engaging with clients, gathering information, evaluating information, structuring goals, effecting a change in behavior, and termination will be covered in the chapters that follow. This stage-by-stage overview should inspire readers to raise their own questions about the process of counseling and about what needs to be accomplished at each step of the journey.

Reflection Questions

1. What specific characteristics would you look for in a counselor at the beginning of the counseling relationship? Why is each of these characteristics important to you?

2. If you were limited to only *one* question in the information-gathering stage, what would you ask? Why would you ask it?

3. With regard to screening candidates for counseling, what one type of person and/or problem would you refer to another counselor? Why do you feel this way?

4. After a few sessions, your antagonism toward the person you are counseling reaches such a peak that it is obvious you can no longer be of help. When you recommend that this client see another counselor, the client retorts, "You just don't like me. That's why you want to get rid of me." What do you respond?

5. When you experience negative countertransference toward a client, how are you likely to show it? When you experience positive countertransference toward a person, how are you likely to show it?

6. What specifically would you like to hear from a client after the successful termination of a counseling relationship? What will it mean to you if you don't hear it?

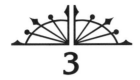

3

ETHICAL CONSIDERATIONS

If counseling theories can be said to map various routes through the labyrinth of human experience, then the code of professional ethics forms the rules of the road. Generally speaking, ethics may be defined as standards of professional conduct that seek to assure just, equitable, and effective treatment. In counseling, the observance of ethics means that the legal and human rights of the client are scrupulously protected by the counselor at the same time that just, equitable, and effective treatment are provided. Without this protection, people would understandably be reluctant to share crucial information with counselors.

That ethical considerations are broached in chapter 3 reflects the priority that this critical aspect of the counseling profession has attained. The chapter will include a discussion of several basic principles that underlie ethics as applied to mental health settings, along with an overview of the elements of a Counselor Disclosure Statement (CDS), a discussion of the ethics of professional responsibility, a discussion of sensitive issues and caveats regarding the counselor's influence, and finally, a summary that includes recommended readings in ethics.

To begin the examination of counseling ethics, we present the case of Susan. This case contains ethical concerns that range from the obvious to the subtle and from easily resolvable to very complicated.

THE CASE OF SUSAN

Only six months following her marriage to Ted, Susan began to develop many worrisome and debilitating symptoms. Though she had always been enthusiastic about her job, in recent months she was barely able to work more than three days a week. She had depleted all of her vacation and sick leave. When she remained at home she would stay in bed and stare at the walls for hours. She rarely ate unless Ted prepared something when he came home at night. Feelings of severe anxiety and hopelessness persisted day after day. Occasionally she slept through the night but mostly she tossed and turned until morning. Fears that she would need to miss another day of work only made her feel worse. Annual evaluations would soon be completed and Susan's supervisor had delicately expressed concerns about both the quality of her work and her attendance problem during Susan's annual review.

Susan's supervisor feared that without some form of intervention, Susan, a highly valued employee, might be in jeopardy of being demoted or even worse. At the end of the interview Susan's supervisor urged her to consider talking to someone in the Employee Assistance Program (EAP) office. She assured Susan that the talks would be completely confidential. Susan was swayed, but ultimately decided not to go to the EAP office. There had been too many rumors about the EAP counselor's leaking confidential information, and so the EAP option was out of the question; but she knew that she was getting worse and needed help. Susan still had the business card of a counselor a friend had seen several years ago. She reluctantly called the number.

The major reason she had selected Dr. Gray was that his office was on the opposite side of town. She did not want anyone to know that she was having trouble contending with her problems and was going to see a counselor. Though time consuming, traveling to an area of the city where no one knew her was the best way she could think of to protect her privacy.

Dr. Gray could see her the very next day, so she took the appointment—although with mixed feelings. She was somewhat relieved, but still worried whether Gray could guarantee the privacy she needed to quiet the shame she felt. The scary thoughts weren't going away: they were actually getting worse. Thoughts of killing herself and the fear that no one would even care if she succeeded made her feel so awful she could hardly bring herself to consider telling another person about them.

Dr. Gray was late for the appointment. Susan repeatedly fought the impulse to leave during the wait. Finally, after 30 minutes, Gray emerged from his office to greet her. He instantly observed that she was very anxious and upset. His hectic schedule allowed no time for brief breaks between clients to clear his mind and today was particularly bad. During yesterday's phone call, he sensed that Susan needed to see him immediately, but a full schedule caused him to squeeze her between two very demanding clients who always had trouble ending on time.

Gray's repeated apologies were greeted with tearful nods. Susan finally calmed enough to speak. Her greatest concern was for privacy, so she asked Dr. Gray how confidential the sessions would be. He could see that she was upset and assured her that everything she said would be held in strict confidence. "Everything?" she asked. "Absolutely everything," he calmly and warmly assured her. Clearly relieved, she began to fill him in on some de-tails. By the end of this abbreviated first session, she was asking Dr. Gray more questions than he was asking her. "How long will it take?" she asked over and over again. The same reassuring voice answered, "Not long—these problems are not too difficult, and they rarely require any other form of treatment or additional evaluation." She was again relieved. One of her ba-sic fears throughout this recent episode was that she would end up having to take medicine: after all, her father had had to take pills when he'd experi-enced similar problems several years ago. Susan did not like the idea that her father had also struggled with the same symptoms, so she was quite pleased that Dr. Gray avoided any questions about her family.

Dr. Gray calmly scheduled the next meeting and apologized once again for being late to the session. With regret in his voice he said, "We really could have used a little more time to talk today." Susan could feel his concern. Sure, he had been late for her session, but she understood that the next client was waiting and Dr. Gray needed to move on. This was probably a good thing, as far as Susan was concerned, since she was beginning to feel anx-ious again and feared having to tell him about the awful thoughts. Dr. Gray sensed her rising tension and quickly mentioned that he had worked with many people with problems similar to hers. He went on to calmly reassure her that she would be feeling fine in no time at all and then showed her out of the office. Gray patted her warmly on the back while promising he would be on time for the next session. Susan felt her anxiety diminish and began to look forward to next week's session. She had no reason to question the doc-tor's pronouncement that problems like hers never needed other forms of treatment, that they were not too difficult to treat, and that she would soon be fine. She even felt a little embarrassed for having worried that her symp-toms were as serious as her father's symptoms.

⚜️
Ethical Principles

Susan's first counseling experience might be summed up as "a trag-edy of good intentions." To explore how Dr. Gray ignored a number of ethical issues and to make recommendations about how Susan *should* have been treated requires a conscientious, thoughtful analysis of both the philosophical principles and the practical issues that underlie ethical counseling practice.

A philosophical basis always forms the bedrock that underlies codes of ethics, standards for professional behavior, and models for appropriate decision making. These basic philosophical principles can be very compli-cated because they address the entire field of ethics and not simply ethics as applied to counseling. While the study of ethics at this level can be very challenging, it will be found useful when the novice faces complicated clinical issues that cannot be adequately resolved through precedence and recognized methods of decision making.

The study of counseling ethics reflects the interrelationship of the values of the society and the values of the profession; standards are formed from the consensus discovered between the society and the empirical practices of the mental health professions. The existence of community standards for treatment and the principle of informed consent are both good examples of how professional and social values interact to shape the ethics of the counseling profession.

In keeping with the practical focus of this book, our study begins with some basic organizing principles that pertain more specifically to counseling or mental health issues than to a general, philosophical study of ethics. It is for this reason that we refer to Kitchener's (1984) five general, interrelated principles: *respect for autonomy, nonmaleficence, beneficence, justice,* and *fidelity.* These may be said to provide a fairly inclusive taxonomy of the important elements of mental health ethics. The sequential relationship of these should be noted, as each principle is built, at least in part, on that which precedes it—with the obvious exception of the first, as the respect for autonomy is the indispensable prerequisite of the counseling relationship. These principles will guide the discussion of specific ethical issues related to Susan's first counseling experience.

Respect for Autonomy

Respect for autonomy as a principle first decrees categorically that clients are individuals with specific personal freedoms and responsibilities. Acknowledging their ability to judge, make choices, and assume responsibility for themselves is the cornerstone of any effective counseling effort. The respect for autonomy basically challenges the counselor to cooperate with the client in a way that enables the client to properly balance personal freedom, responsibility, and regard for others. Clients need to understand the consequences of their actions and the reality that there are important limits to freedom: the concept of freedom must always be tempered by a sense of responsibility and a regard for others.

The respect for autonomy should begin with the initial contact and continue throughout the course of the counseling relationship. Counselors cannot assume that those who seek counseling do so with an adequate knowledge of the counseling process or any acquaintance with the alternatives (Hare-Mustin, Marceck, Kaplan & Liss-Levinson, 1979). Therefore the counselor is ethically bound to help both potential clients and current clients make informed choices regarding entering or continuing counseling. When counselors offer information about (1) the procedures, goals, and possible side effects of therapy, (2) the qualifications, policies, and practices of the therapist, or (3) the available sources of help other than therapy, they are supporting the client's autonomy. There are, of course, many other ways that counselors are able to nourish autonomy. The principle is so important and the opportunities for violating it so numerous that counselors would do well to examine all of their client interactions for acts that might diminish or restrict autonomy. For example, when Dr. Gray quickly decides that Susan needs counseling and that she will not require any other treatment or evaluation, he is ignoring her autonomy. Personal freedom and responsibility are basic goals in virtually all counseling theories, and they should be primary concerns in every counseling session.

The need to respect autonomy is categorical; all mental health professions incorporate it as a basic underlying ethical principle in their codes of ethics. According to Welfel (1998), "The connection between respect for autonomy and the codes of ethics is easy to see. The duties for counselors to obtain informed consent to counseling and to maintain confidentiality of disclosures made in session derive directly from this principle" (p. 33). The increasing use of the Counselor Disclosure Statement (CDS) may also be attributed to the necessity that counselors respect the client's autonomy from the very outset of the counseling relationship. Counselors prepare these written documents so prospective clients can learn important information about both the counselor (training, experience, etc.) and the counseling process. CDSs are discussed in detail in the next section of this chapter.

Nonmaleficence

Nonmaleficence essentially means to do no harm. This tenet derives from a portion of the Hippocratic oath (*primum nil nocere*) and it is considered "the most fundamental ethical principle for medical and human service professionals" (Welfel, 1998, p. 34). Counselors may honor this principle in a number of ways. A decision not to initiate a course of therapy, for example, may often be prompted by the realization that counseling might in and of itself aggravate the person's problem rather than ameliorate it. In other words, the process of counseling might prove a catalyst which could inadvertently *occasion* avoidable harm and thus the counselor would be well-advised not to initiate a counseling relationship in such circumstances.

Many counselors establish a two- or three-session evaluation period, thereby delaying the decision on whether to initiate a counseling relationship until certain important information about the client and the potential counselor-client alliance can be gleaned and sifted. Protocols such as these are in accordance with the tenet against doing harm.

Differentiating between issues that might usefully be discussed in counseling and those which might best be avoided until the client is ready is an example of how this ethical principle influences an informed clinical judgment. Apart from crisis management, clients generally need to have a certain amount of ego strength if they are to deal with more complicated, painful, and difficult issues. Clients and counselors also need to establish a therapeutic alliance that is durable enough to withstand the challenge of the issue(s) being confronted. For example, counselors would not want to deal with any intense emotional conflict that emanates from relationship difficulties if a sufficiently strong therapeutic alliance has not yet materialized. Monitoring the depth of the alliance and assessing the client's ability to handle difficult or painful issues are elements of the dictum that counselors first do no harm.

When counselors clearly define their areas of expertise and when they make appropriate decisions about whom to treat and whom to refer to other health professionals, they are adhering to the principle of nonmaleficence. This same principle also forms the basis of sanctions against *dual relationships*, which involve an improper deployment of the counselor's power in the counseling relationship.

The way Dr. Gray responds to Susan offers an object lesson in how honoring the principle of nonmaleficence can be complicated and challenging. This principle is particularly important in Susan's case because she is in such a frail state. Dr. Gray faces difficult choices about how to interact with her without causing harm to her. While she does not need to be overwhelmed with the seriousness of her symptoms, she does need honest information and feedback. Susan's case illustrates how counselors can be faithful to one principle at the cost of another. By applying the principle of doing no harm and protecting Susan from difficult information because of her frail condition, the counselor failed to respect her autonomy and, as will be seen, found himself in a situation in which his actions were at odds with the principle of beneficence. Because conflicts such as these frequently surface, counselors are encouraged to carefully explore alternatives and seek the advice of more experienced colleagues.

The vignette also illustrates how codes of professional conduct change over time in response to changing values and expectations. At an earlier point in the history of medicine, physicians commonly withheld information about a person's medical condition from him or her in an attempt to protect the patient (and often the patient's family) from the *harm* that such knowledge might inflict. While it is hard to imagine how withholding information about the seriousness of Susan's symptoms could be considered an acceptable course of action at present, such practices were common in eras that did not emphasize the duty to maximize the client's autonomy.

Beneficence

Beneficence entails the obligation to do good and to be of help. Clients opt to enter counseling because they expect to benefit from the experience; counseling professionals then offer to provide clients with interventions that will aid and benefit them. While there may be legal as well as ethical reasons that counselors avoid making empty promises about results (or about the projected duration of treatment), there is a consensual expectation that any counseling undertaken will tend to improve the client's condition, or at least prevent further decline. Counselors cannot proffer themselves as effective professionals without remembering that clients expect results. Professionals achieve and maintain their status when they bring about demonstrable progress.

Susan's experience offers a paradoxical example of the issue of beneficence. Dr. Gray apparently wants to do good and thinks the best way to achieve that goal is to minimize Susan's symptoms and offer reassurances—even if such reassurances lack substance. Acting beneficently toward Susan would produce increased discomfort in the short term, but in the long term the client would be provided a more realistic understanding of herself and the problems to be faced. She would then be in a better position to make decisions about her treatment and the steps that would need to be taken in order to improve her condition.

This is not at all unlike the conflict that many counselors face when they realize that a course of treatment has not shown signs of effecting the desired outcome and that the client needs to be referred. In both of these cases, acting beneficently is necessary but difficult. These examples also illustrate that ethical decisions become more complicated when ethical problems are not readily apparent (e.g., if one learns of the problem after the damage has been done), alternatives may be difficult to identify (e.g., if inexperience limits the number of alternatives a particular counselor is able to develop), or when the ethical course of action might be personally difficult to carry out (e.g., if counselors were to encounter conflict between what they personally feel they need to do or want to do and what is mandated by professional ethics).

Beneficence and nonmaleficence are complementary, and therefore closely related, ethical positions. Counselors must implement a therapeutic relationship that balances the need to do good and the proscription against doing harm. The tension produced by this opposition challenges counselors to make professional choices based on the client's needs and the counselor's competencies—a task that can be very complicated and difficult.

Justice

The principle of justice underlies the expectation that counselors will act fairly and equitably. Office policies and practices should insure that all clients have equal access to services and that appropriate accommodations for disabilities exist. A respect for and a proper handling of multicultural counseling concerns also fall under the heading of justice. Prejudice, discrimination, and bias are, of course, serious threats to the concept of justice, and counselors are therefore expected to identify potentially inequitable or unfair acts and practices so as to do no harm.

Justice and fairness issues surface in our vignette. Susan is not afforded equal access to her counselor. Even though Dr. Gray's intentions may have been good, his office procedures and schedule precluded Susan's having access to her counselor at a point in the counseling relationship when the need was greatest. Susan essentially left her first session with a sense (conscious or not) that the client seen before her and the one who followed her were treated more justly. Both had been afforded greater access to Dr. Gray.

Fidelity

Fidelity, the last of the ethical principles, "deals with faithfulness to promises made and to the truth" (Welfel, 1998, p. 37). The reader can easily see how fidelity relates to trust, an essential component of the counseling process, and to the other four principles listed. Clients tend to trust truthful and honest counselors, even if the truth is painful or difficult to deal with. Persons experiencing difficulties are best served when they sense that they and their counselor have an appreciation of the depth of the problem and, in spite of the difficulty, the counselor can be counted on to remain committed to finding the best way to help resolve the problem. Minimizing a client's problems erodes the trust between counselor and client, delays necessary alternative treatments, and may indicate that the counselor is inhibited by some countertransference that needs to be carefully analyzed.

The relationship of fidelity to respect for autonomy is particularly interesting and well-illustrated in the vignette. How will Susan make an appropriate autonomous decision about continuing a counseling relationship without accurate and honest information about her condition and treatment alternatives? Dr. Gray's reassurances may "help" for the moment, but he has not offered a complete picture of the depth or breadth of Susan's difficulties. Dr. Gray's empty reassurances (the promise of feeling better quickly) and limited treatment alternatives (counseling to the exclusion of further evaluation and other treatments such as pharmacotherapy) both mislead and misdirect her. Susan's symptoms indicate the need for a psychiatric evaluation and a medical physical examination. Dr. Gray's clinical assertions all but exclude these important treatment and diagnostic alternatives.

Disclosure Statements and Informed Consent

Codes of professional conduct, codes of ethics, and models of ethical decision making may all be thought of as translations of philosophical principles into practice. For example, the concept of informed consent, which relates mostly to the principle of respect for autonomy, implies that clients must understand the counseling process in order to actively and effectively participate in decision making about entering and remaining in counseling. Thus, counselors need to be acquainted with effective methods of conveying information about the counseling process to prospective clients. Additionally, counselors need to be able to suggest alternatives to prospective clients who are not interested in pursuing counseling or who would benefit more from other forms of treatment. Methods of informing clients about the counseling process and for exploring alternatives to counseling are covered in this section.

The requirement for informed consent has been treated as a consumer issue in some states, which have passed legislation requiring counselors to prepare a document that describes, in detail, critical aspects of the counseling process and specifically indicates the counselor's professional background, training, and areas of expertise. These Counseling Disclosure Statements (CDSs) are often provided to clients in advance of, or at, the first meeting. It is not too difficult to see that respect for autonomy and fidelity form the backbone of the CDS, but the concepts of nonmaleficence, beneficence, and justice also influence the content of these documents and dictate how they should be distributed. Clients eventually decide to begin counseling or to pursue alternatives due to many factors. Information given in the CDS, along with additional information gained from the counselor during the evaluation phase of the engagement stage, figure prominently in this decision.

Preparing a Counselor Disclosure Statement

A CDS is practical, effective, and not too difficult to prepare. Counselors licensed in the State of Louisiana, for example, are required to compose and distribute a highly detailed CDS to every client, and the Louisiana LPC Board of Examiners keeps copies of each counselor's CDS on file. The usefulness of this document is not limited to clients; the process of preparing the CDS is equally beneficial to counselors. It provides counselors with an opportunity to (1) explore many important elements of the counseling process; (2) clearly define their skills, abilities, and limitations; and (3) consider many practical aspects of the counseling process, including limits to confidentiality, billing, scheduling, client/counselor expectations, and so on. The Louisiana Counselor Licensure Law and the rules stemming from that law require that counselors complete a CDS that includes specific information about each of the following topics:

1. counselor identifying information
2. qualifications
3. description of the counseling relationship
4. areas of expertise
5. fee scales

6. an explanation of the types of services offered and clients served

7. code of conduct

8. privileged communication

9. emergency situations

10. client responsibilities

11. physical health considerations

12. potential counseling risks

13. confirming signatures of client and counselor (supervisor and counselor intern)

A discussion of each section of the CDS follows. You are encouraged to think about each section from the standpoint of both a counselor and a client, to consider what clients might be looking for in such a statement, and to think about how you might prepare a disclosure statement appropriate to the requirements of practice in your own state.

Identifying information. Basic identifying information is useful to the client because it identifies the counselor, designates where sessions are held, and determines how the client can contact the counselor. The counselor's name, mailing and office address, e-mail address, office phone, and fax number are usually included in this section. Though fax numbers and e-mail addresses are listed, clients should be cautioned about the lack of security associated with these forms of communication. Directions for getting to the office, when necessary, may also be included in this section.

Qualifications. This section describes the counselor's academic preparation, including colleges and universities attended and degrees awarded. The counselor's license number is also included along with the address and phone number of the licensing board. This allows clients to identify the counselor as licensed and to know under what board the licensure is administered. The address and phone number of the licensing board are listed so that clients and prospective clients can verify the information and contact the board if they have particular concerns.

Description of the counseling relationship. The counselor is to describe the counseling relationship and list the general goals of counseling in this section so that clients can become more knowledgeable about the process of counseling and aware of the potential outcomes. Counselors can further clarify the counseling relationship by identifying which theory or theories they subscribe to and by briefly, but clearly, describing the basic tenets of the theories and the techniques that will be used. The language used in this section should be appropriate for one's clientele and relatively jargon-free.

The boundaries of the professional counseling relationship also should be addressed. This helps clients identify the limits of the relationship early in the process. A written statement is an excellent way of accomplishing this goal. *Dual relationships* are said to exist "whenever counselors have other connections with a client in addition to the therapist-client relationship" (Welfel, 1998, p. 167). Sanctions against dual relationships can be found in the codes of ethics that govern each of the mental health professions.

Clients generally do not understand what dual relationships are, nor do they immediately see why they are conducive of ethical conflicts. While the serious harm caused by dual relationships in extreme cases—such as sexual relations between counselor and client—is common knowledge, clients may be confused by a counselor's refusing to accept gifts or declining a social invitation. While moving beyond professional boundaries may appear benign initially, the problems spawned by dual relationships surface abruptly, painfully, and dangerously. For this reason, it is a good idea to define dual relationships from the very outset of the process, to discuss how power differences between counselors and clients make these relationships potentially damaging, and to identify how such role confusions may effectively be avoided. While it is the counselor's responsibility to establish and maintain appropriate professional boundaries, clients need to understand why and how boundaries are demarcated.

Areas of expertise.   Because there are prerequisites that restrict by law the activities a counselor is allowed to perform and because there exist professional qualifications that, unfortunately, are less explicit, counselors attempt to provide a description of their areas of expertise in their CDS. These listings cover the areas of performance that the counselor's training and experience have prepared him or her to do most effectively. This disclosure is particularly important because many potential clients are naive about issues of expertise. They incorrectly assume that all mental health professionals possess hospital privileges and are equally qualified to prescribe medication; administer psychological tests; do individual, group, marital, and family counseling; help children, adolescents, young adults, the middle-aged, or elderly; and treat all psychological problems of any degree of severity. It is important to distinguish between legal and professional qualifications and convey this information to the client.

A license issued to a Licensed Professional Counselor (LPC) simply informs potential clients that the license-holder has met certain general standards and is not breaking the law by practicing counseling in that particular state. The license does not imply that the counselor is equally competent in all areas of counseling, any more than a medical license indicates a physician is equally qualified in all medical specialties. Therefore, individual counselors are responsible for accurately characterizing their areas of expertise. While these competencies may be thought of as narrow, such competencies tend to change over the course of time as counselors mature, gain experience, and obtain additional training. Counselors usually indicate the types of clients they are trained to help by listing specific diagnoses (e.g., depression, substance abuse, etc.), particular problems (e.g., academic problems, vocational or career issues, parenting, etc.), specific age groups (child, adolescent, adult), and therapeutic modalities (e.g., individual, couples, family, or group).

People who seek the aid of counselors have the right to know what the counselor's areas of specialization are and to request a referral if a given counselor does not seem to possess the requisite competencies. This is an important competency issue: counselors may be said to behave ethically when they limit themselves to working only with clients who have such problems as fall within their area of expertise, and counselors behave ethically when they refer certain potential clients to other professionals who are more experienced with certain types of problems.

An important and potentially serious ethical question arises when a counselor agrees to work with someone who has a problem that the counselor has seldom, if ever, treated—especially if there are other counselors in the community who are known to have experience with that type of problem. Counselors who wish to expand their areas of competence are encouraged to do so, but only under the supervision of a colleague who is appropriately skilled and experienced in the area of specialization.

In summary, mental health professionals are obligated to carefully and scrupulously delineate the scope of their professional preparation. In counseling, this calls for a careful review of one's areas of expertise, formal training, and experience. The licensure of the therapist guarantees the client of little more than that the therapist is licensed to practice counseling in that state, but the question of exactly whom a particular counselor is qualified to treat raises even larger and more serious professional and ethical questions that must be answered correctly.

Fee scales.   Prospective clients are entitled to information about the financial aspects and responsibilities of counseling. This will include fee scales, billing policies, methods for scheduling and canceling appointments, as well as the policy regarding missed appointments. The issue of insurance coverage is also important and should be covered at this stage as well. This is particularly serious because insurance claims usually require a psychiatric diagnosis and because this confidential information must be reported to the insurance company in order for the claim to be processed. It is not surprising that many clients opt to forgo filing insurance claims because of concerns about confidentiality—especially if coverage is limited to a very few sessions per year. Here again, the principle of informed consent directs counselors to explore all of the potential advantages and caveats associated with filing mental health insurance claims with the client's insurer.

The client should be informed as to the amount of the fees, when they are to be paid (after each session or monthly), and whether it is the counselor's practice to bill on a sliding scale under certain circumstances. Counselors who work in an agency should explain the agency's fee schedule and the likelihood of any fee increases in the foreseeable future.

It is important that counselors inform clients of the consequences of not making payments at the agreed-upon times. Counselors should also let clients know if they are planning to raise the fees during the period that the person is likely to be in counseling. The person should also be informed whether the counselor is legally permitted to accept third-party payments—for example, from insurance carriers, workers' compensation, or Medicare. These issues are important to the client, and they may surface as obstacles to therapeutic progress at a later point in the relationship. In cases in which the counselor's normal fee would be an undue hardship to the client, the counselor has an ethical responsibility, based on the principle of justice, to help such a person find appropriate help at a more affordable cost. Counselors also can comply with the principle of justice by offering sliding scale fees and pro bono services.

A related issue is giving the client an idea of the likely duration of counseling. Counselors should inform people as to the approximate amount of time they can expect to be in counseling. Many clients begin counseling thinking it will take only a few sessions or at most a few months. When this unspoken but expected termination date passes, the client may very likely conclude that the counselor is ineffective or that counseling itself does not work. If the client is paying a fee for counseling, any "extra" time can be the occasion of a valid hardship. It could be that a person might have willingly agreed to a six-month program but would not have agreed to a two- or three-year one. Some clients might suspect the counselor is unnecessarily prolonging the period of counseling for financial gain. While counselors cannot predict precisely how long counseling will take, they should at least be able to accurately distinguish between situations requiring short-term and long-term counseling efforts.

Counselors must also tell clients in advance if they are planning to be absent for any period of time, such as for sabbatical leave, a prolonged vacation, or medical leave, or if they will be moving from the area before the counseling process can be completed.

Explanation of the types of services offered and clients served. Potential clients vary greatly in their comprehension of the implications of the counseling process: some are experienced and knowledgeable, while others are quite naive. Counselors should be able to single out the theoretical orientation(s) that guide(s) their practice and concomitantly be able to characterize accurately the techniques they use in ways that people can understand. Prospective clients should know which modalities are likely to be used: group, individual, or family approaches, and why. Counselors should identify, in general, which types of clients they are trained and experienced to work with, and the CDS should specify the particular developmental stages (infants, children, adolescents, young adults, adults, and elderly) in which the counselor specializes. Material contained under "areas of expertise" may also merit inclusion in this section as well.

Code of conduct. Licensed mental health practitioners are professionals, and as such they adopt and adhere to a code of conduct. Counselors are further required by licensing laws in many states to follow a prescribed code of conduct or code of ethics. Prospective clients have an ethical right to know this fact, and the code itself should be available to them if they wish to review it. A CDS often includes a statement that indicates which code is followed and how a copy may be obtained. Brochures offering information about specific ethical issues (including dual relationships, limits of confidentiality, etc.) are very useful adjuncts to a copy of the disclosure statement and the code of conduct.

Privileged communication. The ethical issue of confidentiality and the legal concept of privileged communication should be completely described in this section of the CDS, along with exceptions/limitations and clear descriptions of special local or state regulations. Confidentiality can be a very complex ethical issue because it deals with the counselor's twofold responsibility: to the client and to society at large. Sometimes these allegiances pull the counselor in opposite directions, creating a great deal of tension.

According to Corey, Corey, and Callanan (1998), "Mental-health professionals have an ethical responsibility and a professional duty to safeguard clients from unauthorized disclosures of information given in the therapeutic relationship" (p. 155). In other words, counselors do not communicate, directly or indirectly, information that a client has shared within the context of a professional relationship unless the client has authorized the disclosure, the counselor has been compelled to do so by law, or the counselor has a clear duty to warn others or protect the client in potentially life-threatening situations (Corey et al., 1998).

The concepts of confidentiality and privileged communication are not synonymous. Privileged communication is the legal right existing by either statute or common law that protects the person from having confidences revealed publicly during legal proceedings. It means that certain professionals cannot be compelled to testify as to the content of any professional communication between themselves and the people they see in counseling. As can be seen, privileged communication is relevant only to legal proceedings. Historically, confidentiality was seen as a broader concept that imposed on the counselor the responsibility not to divulge information received in a professional capacity in court or in any other situation (Stott, 1981, pp. G1, G2). Recent Supreme Court rulings (e.g., *Jaffee v. Redmond*, 1996) have affirmed the importance of confidentiality to the process of psychotherapy. According to Justice John Paul Stevens, "Effective psychotherapy depends upon an atmosphere of confidence and trust in which the patient is willing to make frank and complete disclosure of facts, emotions, memories, and fears." Corey et al. (1998) view this decision as an indication of a potential trend that would improve privileged communication laws, making them stronger and able to be applied more broadly. Rulings and changes in codes of ethics regarding confidentiality reflect how privileged communication affects issues of confidentiality and how to some extent the professional concerns for confidentiality may affect laws governing privileged communication.

Confidentiality remains both a professional and a legal issue. When a case involving privileged communication enters the courts, the legal interpretations of confidentiality supersede the professional ones. In other words, counselors may adhere conscientiously to the code of ethics of their profession, but the court may rule that such a code is not fully compatible with the requirements of the law.

The rules governing privileged communication are not uniform throughout the United States or between federal and state jurisdictions. Different legal jurisdictions have different definitions of privileged communication; so a counselor in California may face an entirely different situation than a counselor in Iowa, even if the case were the same. For this reason, it is important that counselors learn the exact nature of the rules of confidentiality of their state.

Which professions are covered by the privilege also differs from one state to another. In some states, many helping professions are covered; in others, very few. In no states are paraprofessional counselors granted the right of privileged communication. It is important for counselors not to make the mistake of promising this privilege in jurisdictions that do not have it.

Exceptions to privileged communication. The basic professional and legal problem with the issue of confidentiality is that there is no such thing as *absolute* confidentiality. The ruling bodies of the helping professions and the courts agree that there are circumstances that militate against absolute confidentiality. The California Evidence Code lists thirteen exceptions to the basic privileged communication rule (Sections 911 to 1028). Some of them are worth mentioning because many other states have the same or similar exceptions and because clients need to be aware of these exceptions as they contemplate entering counseling.

Reasonable cause. Privileged communication does not hold in cases where the counselor has reasonable cause to believe that the client is in such a psychological state as to be dangerous to self or others and that disclosure of the communication is necessary to prevent such danger. The duty to warn potential victims of the risk that the client might cause injury to self or others "remains one of the developing areas of law and varies from state to state" (Bernstein and Hartsell, 1998, p. 153). While legal requirements differ across jurisdictions, the ethical requirement is fairly consistent: "Where the therapist feels the client presents a danger to self or others the therapist shall take 'reasonable steps' to prevent the antici-pated harm" (p. 153).

In practice, this is can be a particularly difficult exception, even though most people would agree it is philosophically sound. It is difficult because the concept of "reasonable cause" is so subjective. It is not uncom-mon for counselors to hear a person say, "I'm going to kill my husband when I get home!" or "Sometimes I'm almost overcome by an urge to kill myself." People can make such comments lightly or half-jokingly and commit the act an hour later. Others can make such statements in a very convincing way and yet not commit the act.

The duty to warn may also arise when clients with life-threatening transmittable diseases, (e.g., AIDS) engage in high-risk behaviors with people who are unaware of the client's illness and the attendant risks. The ACA *Code of Ethics and Standards of Practice* (Section B.1.d: Contagious Fatal Diseases) implies there is such a duty to warn:

> A counselor who receives information confirming that a client has a disease that is commonly known to be communicable and fatal is jus-tified in disclosing confidential information to an identifiable third party, who by his or her relationship with the client is at a high risk of contracting the disease. Prior to making a disclosure the counselor should ascertain that the client has not already informed the third party about his or her disease and that the client is not intending to inform the third party in the immediate future.

An ominous consequence of this exception is that counselors can be, and have been, successfully sued because, while they did not feel there was reasonable cause to inform the authorities or the victim-to-be, a court did. Counselors need to develop a protocol to guide them in deciding whether to warn and policies to govern the actions they will take to warn someone. The protocol and the policies must conform to ethical guide-lines and meet a "standard of care" consistent with other mental health practitioners working within the same legal jurisdiction. Consultation with other counselors, licensing board officials, and lawyers who have an expertise in mental health issues is extremely useful as counselors develop guidelines for dealing with situations where the duty to warn surfaces. By including this exception in the CDS, the client is made to understand that the counselor will take steps to prevent clients from injuring themselves or others.

Child victimization. Counselors are required to report child abuse and neglect by the Federal Child Abuse Prevention and Treatment Act (1987) as well as specific state laws. For this reason counselors are advised to become familiar with their state laws governing child abuse and ne-glect and to communicate this exception to confidentiality to their clients in writing. State laws usually dictate when and how the report must be filed and offer some guidance about what constitutes a reportable situation. The *suspicion* of abuse or neglect is all that is usually necessary. While counselors who fear legal reprisal from the alleged perpetrators may worry about reporting abuse without sufficient evidence, laws stipulate serious penalties for the "failure to report." Thus for clinical, legal, judicial, and ethical reasons it is better to err on the side of protecting the child. Protective Services and other agencies that deal with child abuse also offer assistance in determining the conditions that necessitate the filing of a report. This is a particularly important exception to confidentiality because a child's safety and well-being hang in the balance and because the perpetrator(s) may be among the child's family or friends. If the counselor does not bring such information to the attention of the authorities or the parents (assuming that they are not the perpetrators), the child will continue to be victimized. Once again consultation is essential; counselors should contact Child Protective Services personnel, other counselors, or lawyers with a specialty in mental health for additional information. Decisions should be carefully documented, noting not only the course of action taken, but whom the counselor consulted and why one course of action was selected over another.

Court appointees.   When a counselor is appointed by the court to examine a person and to prepare a report that will be sent to the court and to no one else, the person in the professional relationship with the counselor cannot claim the privilege. The purpose of this exception is that it would be absurd for a court to order a mental health examination, only to have the person being examined claim privileged communication. The *ethical* issue that this exception raises is whether a person should be forced to undergo a mental health examination. The *professional* question it raises is what kind of evaluation can be done on a person who has a deeply vested interest in appearing more healthy or more disturbed than he or she really is.

Criminal trials.   Privileged communication cannot be claimed when the purpose of a professional relationship is to examine the sanity or psychological competence of the person in a criminal trial. Again the purpose of the exception is self-evident, but it raises the same ethical and professional issues as the previous one.

Psychological injury and litigation.   There is no privileged communication in civil cases where the person in the professional relationship with a counselor introduces his or her psychological condition into a civil litigation. In other words, a person who is, or has been, in counseling cannot claim psychological injury due to an event but not allow the court to determine if the injury was present or partially present before the event, was caused or only partially caused by the event, or was a contributing factor in the degree of psychological damage caused by the event.

The reasonableness of this exception, as with many of these exceptions, can be validly debated on both sides. In one sense, this exception appears to be reasonable. In another sense it does not, because if the claimant had not sought professional help, he or she would probably be in a more advantageous position because there would be no professionally obtained and documented psychological information to divulge. In a sense, the claimant is being punished for having sought professional help.

Breach of duty. There is no privileged communication in a case where the counselor is accused of a breach of duty. This means that if a counselor is sued for malpractice by a client, the counselor cannot refuse to testify on the relevant issues by claiming privileged communication.

This exception and the one that precedes it demonstrate an important point—namely, that in all states privileged communication is granted to the *person receiving help;* it is *not* granted to the *counselor.* Although it is said that certain professionals are covered by the privilege, this only means that the people seeking help from such professionals can have them claim the privilege on their behalf. In other words, the privilege is not meant to protect the professional but only the person the professional has examined or treated in counseling. This is the reason that a person who sues a counselor for malpractice leaves the counselor unable to invoke the plea of confidentiality.

Furthermore, especially in civil cases, counselors may be asked by claimants with whom they have had or currently have a professional relationship to divulge information that the counselor feels will jeopardize the claimant's case or his or her overall psychological welfare. Although counselors may ethically choose not to reveal this information, legally they do not have that prerogative. The counselor who, under these circumstances, insists on silence can be fined and/or sentenced to jail for contempt of court.

Confidentiality in a counseling relationship is determined by ethical and professional concerns. Privileged communication, on the other hand, is a legal matter governed by laws. Counselors who claim the privilege for their clients should realize that state statutes, local statutes, and under some conditions, the presiding judge, will determine what will be covered under privileged communication. As has already been noted, conflict surfaces when the ethics of confidentiality suggest one course of action and the laws governing privileged communication mandate another.

There is a general rule that a person who is or has been in counseling cannot discuss some privileged communication in court but then decline to convey the remainder of the privileged information. Once the person voluntarily divulges *some* privileged communication, it opens the door to *all* relevant information.

In many states, when the client is judged to be psychologically incompetent or is under the age of 18, parents or legal guardians can waive the confidentiality privilege.

Depending on the specific jurisdiction, the fact alone that a person is in or has been in counseling may be considered privileged communication. For example, in California, the attorney general has given the opinion that such a relationship entails privileged communication (53 opinion of the Attorney General 151, 1970).

In many states, communications occurring in the presence of a third party are not deemed to be privileged communications. Although this rule does not apply to the counselor's professional associates, it may well apply to family and group counseling situations.

Finally, if a counselor is compelled to testify by the court, he or she cannot be prosecuted for violation of professional ethics or sued for malpractice. While this protection exists, being compelled to testify represents one more example of the potentially conflictual relationship between the legal concept of privileged communication and the ethical concept of confidentiality.

Confidentiality in specific work situations. In addition to the basic principles of confidentiality, there are related issues of which counselors should be aware in specific work situations. Counselors who are employed by certain agencies may be required by that agency, and perhaps by state law, to divulge information regarding the clients seen in counseling. Before taking a specific job, counselors should learn in detail the exceptions to the basic principles of confidentiality that will be required. Counselors who do not consider this factor may soon find themselves embroiled in professional, political, and legal struggles.

School districts may have policies that require counselors to divulge information regarding students in counseling. Such policies limit confidentiality with respect to behavior that would be grossly disruptive to the school, drug and alcohol abuse, venereal disease, and pregnancy. Some schools also have policies requiring counselors to obtain written consent from parents when behaviors in the sexual area are to be discussed.

In prison systems, the military, and industry, counselors may be required to pass on information garnered from evaluations and counseling that might involve a person's potential for violence or the ability to handle sensitive jobs. While such exceptions to confidentiality are inimical to the counseling process, there are some situations in which they are understandable. For example, a counselor working in a prison might learn of escape plans that include taking hostages, and the lives of many people would be in jeopardy.

In a military situation, a counselor might learn that a person has a problem which might pose a serious risk to self or others in the performance of duty. For example, a pilot may confide that severe anxiety attacks have almost led to a loss of control of an aircraft over populated areas on several occasions, but refuses to report this and has not requested a transfer to another type of assignment. In these and similar cases, the counselor must weigh the importance of confidentiality with the overall welfare of the client, as well as that of society at large.

If counselors choose to work in situations in which confidentiality may be compromised, they must do several things. They should always tell the client of the restrictions placed on confidentiality by carefully enumerating such limitations in the CDS and should reiterate that fact verbally during the initial session(s) with the client. Counselors must decide if they are going to adhere strictly to the policies of the agency, use their own judgment about confidentiality, or ignore the requirements completely. Counselors who lead employers to believe that they are abiding by such restrictions, when in fact they are not, may find they have created an ethical problem for both themselves and their profession. Finally, if counselors decide in good faith that they must divulge some information, it should be done in ways that preserve as much as possible the dignity and welfare of the client.

Records and reports. Another dimension of confidentiality deals with consultations, reports, and recording the counseling sessions. Recording the session can be done by note taking, tape recording, or audiovisual taping. If any of these procedures is to be used, the counselor should advise the client of this fact at the first meeting. If the procedures for recording sessions vary from client to client, then the exact procedure cannot be put into a written form applicable to all clients. If notes are taken, the counselor should explain how confidentiality will be preserved—for example, by using a code or pseudonym to protect the client's identity. If audio- or videotapes are employed, counselors can advise the client that these devices will be used only by the counselor. If the counselor wishes to share them with others for consultation or teaching purposes, permission must be obtained from the client and the client's identity should be disguised as much as possible. It is to be understood that counselors will *invite* the client to give permission but not attempt to persuade or pressure the client to do so.

With regard to sharing the records of sessions with other professionals, permission must be obtained from the client and the person's identity must be protected whenever possible. It is good practice to obtain permission *in writing* to play recordings or to bring the client's material into a professional consultation. What seemed to be a clearly understood and freely given consent a year ago may be something counselors wish they had documented as they later defend themselves in court.

Test results and clinical data communicated in report form also fall under the rubric of confidentiality. Before counselors send a report, they must receive written permission from the client. If at all possible, it is helpful to let the client read the report and *then* sign the release form to prevent a situation in which the client states, "But I didn't know he was going to divulge *that* information."

Clients must be able to gain access to their personal information and know how it is used. They not only have the right to see any reports, but must have a process whereby they can contest or call for a correction of information in the report. Counselors would do well to keep this in mind when deciding on the content and tone of records or reports.

Legally, and as a practical matter, a counselor does not have control over a report once it is sent to the recipient. For example, a counselor may send a report that is part of a job application to the head of personnel at a civil service agency. The head of personnel may then inadvertently leave it out on a desk, file it in a place where there is public access, or send a copy to a third party. A similar problem arises when counselors submit required confidential diagnostic information, claims, or reports in order for clients to obtain third-party payments—that is, when insurance companies, workers' compensation, or Medicare is paying for part of the counseling. For this reason, it is advisable to type in large print at the top of a report the following notice: "This report is confidential. The information therein is not to be communicated in any manner to anyone other than Alice R. Jones, to whom the report is sent." Although the legal standing of such a disclaimer is debatable, it demonstrates good faith on the part of the counselor and should be in his or her favor if a problem arises.

Because there are so many exceptions to privileged communication and confidentiality, counselors must identify these exceptions to the client in the CDS and in discussions as clearly and completely as possible. It is especially important to emphasize those exceptions that are relevant to a particular client's situation. Once prospective clients fully comprehend the nature of the exceptions to confidentiality, they may decline to enter counseling. While this may be an unfortunate decision if therapeutic progress is thereby sacrificed, it is the client's right and, in some situations, could be a prudent decision.

Emergency situations.   We apply the term *abandonment* to situations where counselors are not available to their clients when they should or need to be. Abandonment is a particularly serious violation of the counselor's ethical and professional responsibilities. For this reason, a set of instructions regarding emergencies should be available to clients from the very outset of the therapeutic relationship. Additionally, a policy regarding emergency contact that contains clearly defined criteria about when and how to contact the counselor is needed in order to let clients know when it is appropriate to call. This policy not only reduces the likelihood of nuisance calls but also insures that clients *will* call should problems develop. Clients should be provided an alternative list of emergency contacts that might include hospitals, crisis lines, and possibly colleagues who have agreed to help out in emergencies if the counselor cannot be reached for some reason.

Client responsibilities.   While the principle of the client's autonomy must inform the overall construction of the CDS, the section covering the client's responsibilities explicitly challenges the client to help shoulder the burden. If clients understand and accept that the responsibility for the success of therapy rests equally on their shoulders, they will participate more effectively in the counseling process. They may also make use of the information contained in this section to determine whether they are able and willing to involve themselves in the counseling process.

Most theoretical orientations expect clients to learn about the nature of the counseling process in order to assist in the formulation of goals and to cooperate in the assessment of their progress. Counselors who use certain theoretical orientations may also specify that completing homework assignments, maintaining a journal, and completing suggested readings are additional responsibilities of the client.

Responsibilities of a completely practical nature are often included in this section. For example the CDS might state that clients are expected to arrive on time, to meet regularly (weekly, biweekly, etc.), to obtain a physical examination, and so forth. Finally, clients are expected to inform the counselor of any other active counseling relationships. If the other counseling relationship predates the current one then permission is required from the first mental health professional before the new counseling relationship can proceed. This last requirement insures continuity in the treatment and cooperation among the network of mental health professionals engaged in helping the same client.

Physical health.   Both clients and counselors can easily assume that a particular group of difficulties or symptoms would best be treated through counseling when in fact other modalities might be more effective or appropriate. Symptoms can appear to have a psychological origin when they may in fact stem from nonpsychological sources. Impotence in men, for example, can be caused by certain blood pressure medicines, and various medical problems often produce symptoms that appear to be psychological. Incorrectly assuming a psychological source of difficulty or incorrectly suggesting counseling for a problem that could be treated more effectively in another way is unprofessional, unethical, and potentially disastrous. Medical treatments that might be needed could be seriously delayed if counseling were to be made the primary or exclusive form of treatment. While clients may actively refuse to consider that their symptoms might stem from some form of illness or disease, any pressure they may exert on the counselor to avoid medical or surgical alternatives to counseling does not relieve the counselor of the responsibility to insure that counseling be used only where it is appropriately indicated.

Requesting that clients obtain a medical physical examination reduces the probability of an erroneous diagnosis and invites the client to consider that symptoms can arise from various sources and that these symptoms can be effectively addressed in various ways. In addition, counselors should have clients list any medications they are taking and identify their physicians and any ongoing treatments they are receiving.

Potential counseling risks. People often enter counseling with a vision of its outcome that may include becoming symptom-free, significantly more effective, and happier than before counseling. However, counselors must often temper the client's vision with one that is more realistic and balanced. Clients need to be well-informed about both the potential benefits and the possible risks associated with counseling. For example, some clients are likely to feel worse before they begin to feel better. For some clients, a realistic counseling goal might go no farther than to reduce the level of symptom impairment. And with very troubled clients, meager gains, or in some cases maintaining the current status, could qualify as successful counseling.

People should also be advised of the possible consequences of personal changes brought about by counseling. Counselors cannot foresee the future, but experienced counselors can often evaluate a client and the environment in which the client lives and form some expectation of the possible effects a personal change may have on the client and on those around the client. When certain side effects seem possible or likely, counselors should share their impressions with the client at an appropriate time so that the client can better understand what he or she is doing and can freely choose to continue or discontinue counseling.

The following can be noted in the CDS as potential side effects that may result from successful counseling, given a specific person and environment:

1. Change in young clients can create significant tension in their parents. The parents may deflect this tension back onto the children, making matters worse.

2. Change in one spouse but not in the other can produce disequilibrium in a marriage and may even fracture it.

3. Change in a psychologically presexual client of any age can cause the surfacing of heterosexual or homosexual feelings that could be quite threatening.

4. Change in a client can lower the level of defenses, allowing previously repressed feelings of anger, fear, guilt, and depression to surface—sometimes with a vengeance.

5. Change can markedly alter a client's attitudes toward parents, marriage, spouse, children, divorce, careers, friends, or religion.

6. Change can drastically affect how significant others view the client. People who grow in independence may be viewed as ungrateful or selfish. Those who become more assertive may be seen as disrespectful and arrogant. People who become more honest may be seen as less lovable, less attractive, and less honest. Those who grow in warmth and tenderness may be seen as weak. Those who change their religious attitudes may be seen as heretics or

neurotic. Those who change their sexual behavior in one direction or another may suddenly be branded as "uptight" or "loose."

There are additional risks associated with specific types of counseling. Marriage counseling may cause partners to encounter greater difficulty in their relationship. Individual counseling can cause issues to surface that were not known or realized at the outset of the counseling. Family counseling could exacerbate problems between parents and children. Clients need to take into account all of these potential problems as they make decisions to begin treatment, terminate treatment, or move to a different treatment modality (to change from individual counseling, for example, to couples counseling).

Agreement in writing.   Disclosure statements usually end with a section set aside for the client's and counselor's signatures. Minors may sign the form along with their parents or guardians. Since counselor interns must work under supervision, the disclosure statement should include a place for the supervisor's signature. By signing, the client acknowledges that he or she has received, read, and discussed the disclosure statement and understands it.

Counselors are professionally and ethically compelled to honor their clients' autonomy and to obtain clients' informed consent. The CDS outline presented here offers one method for accomplishing both these necessary prerequisites. While counselors are not relieved from carefully discussing all these itemized topics with their clients, the need for written documents that confirm informed consent exists and will almost certainly increase (Bennet, Bryant, VanderBos, & Greenwood, 1990). The CDS outline may be a recent development, but counselors have used similar forms for many years. To obtain some historical perspective on the evolution of such documents, readers may wish to review Everstein et al. (1980, pp. 832–833) for additional examples of a client's rights statement, initial contract form, and informed consent form.

Alternatives to Counseling

Counselors have both professional and ethical responsibilities to inform people about alternatives to counseling. Before deciding whether to enter into a counseling relationship, the counselor and the prospective client must take into account many variables including the nature of the problem, the prospective client's psychological resources, the length of time counseling is likely to take, the strength of the person's motivation to remain in counseling, the realistic gains that counseling may impart, the amount of time and money the person can afford to expend, and whether other more appropriate methods of treatment might exist.

Prospective clients who are poor candidates for counseling or who need other kinds of help may be referred to such community programs as self-help programs; support groups for people with specific problems (for example, child abuse or battered wives); relaxation training; parents without partners; marriage encounter; peer counseling; courses in assertiveness, personal adjustment, sexuality, parent effectiveness, meditation, or group dynamics; and centers or clinics that help people with weight-control problems, substance abuse, pregnancy, religious problems, or stress. Also, some people will benefit from bibliotherapy (reading books that are relevant to the person's problem), pharmacotherapy (taking medications to relieve symptoms of anxiety or depression), biofeedback, or clinical hypnotherapy.

When and how alternatives to counseling are suggested and explained depends on each situation, but the counselor should exercise discretion. If the person is in an obviously anguished state, it may be more helpful to reduce some of the anguish over a period of one or more sessions than to deal immediately with the alternatives. It may be to the client's advantage to continue counseling while alternatives are considered.

The manner in which the counselor discusses the alternatives is also important. Alternatives should be described without personal bias. For example, a person might ask if hypnosis would help, and a counselor, who had negative feelings about hypnosis, could respond in a way that clearly reflected these negative feelings, even though hypnosis might prove to be of use in alleviating the person's symptoms.

Counselors should also make sure that a referral does not give the erroneous impression that they simply don't *want* to see certain clients. When counselors offer sound reasons why an alternative method may be more appropriate, they convey their commitment to being forthright and their desire to obtain the best and most appropriate help for the client.

Consider once again the case of Susan as we summarize this section. Susan will likely see Dr. Gray several more times. His promise of a quick and easy recovery will prove false and Susan's symptoms will likely worsen. Instilling false hope, limiting evaluation and treatment alternatives to short-term counseling, and failing to provide enough information for Susan to make an informed decision will have doomed the therapeutic relationship and precluded any potential benefits that might have resulted from counseling. This unfortunate situation underscores the fact that informed consent, respect for autonomy, nonmaleficence, beneficence, justice, and fidelity are not only essential principles of ethical practice but also factors that powerfully influence the course of the counseling relationship and the outcome of the counseling experience. The more surprises there are for the client, the more fraught with difficulties the process will be for both the client and the counselor. It is far better for a potential client to opt not to enter counseling on the basis of valid information than to terminate at a later date without having made any progress and harboring feelings of regret, disappointment, and acrimony toward both the counselor and counseling in general.

.⋊⅃⋉.
Professional Responsibility

Ethical practice ultimately hinges on how completely and consistently counselors manage their professional responsibilities. Counselors demonstrate professional responsibility by correctly knowing when to ask for help, by knowing what to do, and by doing what needs to be done regardless of how complicated or perplexing the issue. This task poses personal and professional challenges. While a code of ethics provides guidelines for treatment and professional conduct, it cannot specify what to do in every circumstance or with every client. These so-called *gray areas* can be particularly arduous for counselors. But gray areas are not the only source of problems. Issues that originate from within counselors themselves can be even more formidable—especially when the client's needs and the counselor's coalesce in ways that result in unethical or countertherapeutic conditions. Ultimately counselors have ethical responsibilities not only to their clients but also to themselves. This section serves to identify particular aspects of the counseling relationship to which counselors should pay special attention. Additional information about internal determinants that can adversely influence counselors will be found in the section entitled "The Counselor's Influence."

Responding Fully

Effective counselors respond fully to their clients. If counselors are to be sufficiently attentive and energetic with their clients, they must appropriately manage their personal and professional lives. They should not see clients when their attention, energies, and motivation are blunted by personal matters, social activities, overscheduling of appointments, and so on.

Experience teaches counselors to develop a schedule that accommodates both their own needs and the needs of their clients. Some counselors can see eight people each day and do an effective job while others, especially those with outside professional duties like teaching or consulting, may see significantly fewer clients per day. The determining factor is not just the number of clients a counselor can see but also the pace of the sessions. While counselors often schedule people "back to back"—that is, three or four people in a row—taking a brief break between sessions is advisable. Even a ten-minute break will allow the counselor to complete notes and prepare for the next client. The time of day is also a factor in scheduling since counselors are more attentive at certain times of day than at others.

Agency work can present problems in the area of scheduling because counselors do not usually have a great deal of control over when they see clients or how many clients they see. But scheduling problems can also arise in private practice, where a counselor's income depends directly upon the number of clients seen. When this is the case, counselors can rationalize seeing large numbers of clients at any hour of the day or night, whether or not they are physically and psychologically prepared to do effective work. A second source of income—such as teaching, research, or consultation—might reduce the temptation to see too many clients.

Counselors also need to be selective as to whom they choose to see in counseling. Counselors should only agree to work with people with whom they have some reasonable expectation of rapport and success. People with problems outside the counselor's area of expertise should be referred elsewhere. It is unethical for counselors to take on an "interesting case" if the counselor knows, or might reasonably be expected to know, that other means of help would more likely be successful. For example, a counselor may never have worked with a "pain patient" and may decide this could be a chance to learn something new, ignoring the fact that surgical intervention, biofeedback, hypnosis, or pharmacotherapy might be more effective sources of treatment.

Responsible client selection requires that counselors realize the kinds of people with whom they work best and which types they should avoid. With more training, maturity, and professional experience counselors usually become better able to help a more varied cross-section of personality types. However, counselors will find that they are poorly suited to deal with certain people, finding some personalities abrasive, distracting, or alienating in some other way. Responsible counselors willingly and routinely make referrals to other counselors not solely because they are too busy for a given case, but because they recognize their own professional and personal limitations.

Terminating Appropriately

Another area of professional ethics and responsibility is related to the question of how and when it is appropriate to terminate a counseling relationship. Since the autonomy of the client informs the goals of virtually all valid counseling approaches, counseling relationships are always considered to be of limited duration. Counselors should accord this aspect of the counseling process the same consideration given to the other stages. Even as counselors begin the process of establishing the relationship they should simultaneously be considering termination issues.

Termination problems arise in situations where the counselor (1) terminates prematurely, (2) extends the process beyond its usefulness to the client, or (3) fails to properly prepare the client for termination. Each termination error occurs for different reasons and produces different problems for the client.

Counselors act unethically when they prematurely terminate a counseling relationship for improper reasons. For example, a counselor may simply get bored, frustrated, or angry at the client and manufacture some "acceptable" reason to terminate. Feelings of boredom, frustration, or anger are not uncommon and are often an integral part of counseling. It is the counselor's responsibility to deal with them, both intrapersonally and interpersonally in some productive way, if possible. Clients rightly feel abandoned and confused if they are abruptly terminated. Their abandonment problems are further increased if the counselor's reasons for termination are perceived as being less than forthright.

Counselors act unethically when they maintain the client too long in counseling. An inappropriately prolonged term of counseling often can result when the counselor is improperly using the therapeutic relationship to meet personal needs. The counselor may find it pleasant, gratifying, or financially rewarding to see a client past the point where other, more responsible counselors would have successfully and appropriately terminated treatment. When this occurs it is a signal that the counseling relationship is corrupt and that the roles have reversed to the extent that the client is now taking care of the counselor. There are many reasons why this unfortunate situation occurs, but basically all point to a failure on the part of the counselor to properly define his or her role and to act accordingly.

Finally, counselors act unethically when they fail to properly prepare for the termination of the counseling relationship by systematically collaborating with their clients about this phase of the counseling process. Learning to properly manage the feelings and thoughts that are associated with such changes in interpersonal relationships is an important developmental task that counselors will have to discuss with their clients and, in this case, perhaps even model for them. This topic can be particularly challenging for counselors and their clients because the idea of termination often brings out separation and abandonment anxieties that are present in many people. Numerous clients predictably avoid the topic. Counselors can be equally affected. They are not immune to these same issues and may well skirt termination topics for the same reasons that clients do. For this reason, counselors are well advised to carefully explore and resolve their own personal issues regarding termination before they begin working with clients. If counselors and clients cannot properly and collaboratively prepare for termination, then the counseling relationship is simply one more counterproductive relationship.

Evaluating the Relationship

According to the codes of ethics, counselors are expected to establish and maintain a *therapeutic relationship* with clients. Therapeutic relationships honor clearly defined boundaries and employ interventions that are focused on the client's needs and goals and that are ethical, effective, and appropriate. It is unfortunate that counseling relationships formed with the expectation of being therapeutic may degenerate into damaging relationships. In extreme cases, the relationship may develop into an overdependent one that immediately or eventually becomes an obstacle to the goals of counseling and serves to diminish rather than aid the client. Or the relationship can become an angry, sadomasochistic one in which each partner treats the other in a destructive way. When a relationship takes on either of these characteristics, it is the counselor's responsibility promptly to terminate in an appropriate manner. The responsibility to terminate is not shared by the counselor *and* the client because the client may be getting so many needs met, albeit inappropriately, that he or she sees no reason to terminate the relationship. Overdependent or angry sadomasochistic relationships are often replicas of other counterproductive and destructive relationships in the client's life and possibly the counselor's own life. That relationships like this should occur at all is concern enough but that they should transpire in a "therapeutic" relationship is all the more tragic.

Counselors' Responsibility to Themselves

A final area of responsibility is that of counselors to themselves. Unfortunately, this is a dimension of ethics that is seldom discussed but nonetheless important. In order to be effective, professional and ethical counselors must take care of themselves both psychologically and physically. Since counseling is primarily a giving process, counselors have to "get" in other areas of their lives. It is necessary for counselors to have rewarding relationships and leisure pursuits outside of counseling. It is also important for counselors to keep in good physical condition because, while counseling is a sedentary job, it demands an energy and alertness that only physical conditioning can provide.

Counselors also have a responsibility to avoid being drawn into the role of manager, conservator, parent, or spouse to their clients. Counselors have a limited, well-bounded role in the client's life, and that role should be clearly defined from the outset and continually underscored throughout the course of the counseling relationship.

There are times when a client may expect, and even demand, that a counselor provide time, energy, and services that lie outside the limits of a reasonable counseling agreement. Counselors who accede to these expectations and demands may well be doing damage to themselves, to the other people in their lives, and to the client. It is as much an ethical issue for counselors to take care of their own overall health and psychological well-being as it is for them to safeguard the well-being of those they see in counseling.

⚶

The Counselor's Influence

It is important that counselors fully appreciate the fact that they hold a position of influence in the counseling relationship. This is true for several reasons. People who approach counselors for help often overestimate the counselor's knowledge, wisdom, and healing abilities. As a result, even the slightest nod of the head or casual remark can take on meanings of which the counselor is unaware. Counselors are usually more knowledgeable about mental health principles than clients are and, it is to be hoped, in better psychological health. Therefore, what counselors say and do may be more persuasive than the actions of other people in the client's life. Finally, people who are experiencing psychological pain are often suggestible and easily swayed by the influence of a person who presents himself or herself as a source of help. The client's fear of emotional abandonment (Sonne, 1994) may cause him or her to acquiesce to the counselor's perceived or imagined wishes in exchange for the maintenance of the counseling relationship.

Counselors can be influential in other ways that can cause problems. For example, "role slippage" (Smith & Fitzpatrick, 1995) develops from power differentials that are improperly managed by the counselor. Role slippage occurs when counselors unwittingly use their power in the therapeutic relationship to influence a client in a "dual relationship." An example of this type of problem may be seen in the case of a counselor whose client was a travel agent for a large international company. Over the course of their one-year counseling relationship, the client's employment was increasingly introduced into the counseling sessions. The counselor had taken a tour with this agency and had been so severely disappointed in the trip she decided to sue the agency for false advertising. As the lawsuit developed the client found herself answering the counselor's questions about the travel business during sessions that were supposed to be focused on the client's issues, not the counselor's legal worries. Eventually the counselor asked if the client would testify on her behalf during the upcoming trial. While the counselor's request was the most blatant attempt to improperly alter roles, it was not the most destructive. The trend that had been developing over the weeks leading up to the counselor's request was far more insidious and damaging. The client was confused and frustrated, wondering how it was possible to simultaneously feel used and ignored by her counselor.

Fortunately, the client found a new counselor with whom she developed a healthy, appropriate counseling relationship. Ironically, the issues that prompted her to seek counseling—her husband's critical illness, the prospect of his death, and attendant issues of grief and loss—also figured prominently in her decision to remain in an increasingly corrupt counseling relationship. This example illustrates that counselors *are* influential and that a client's fears and anxieties (e.g., loss or separation anxiety) may inordinately increase the counselor's level of influence. When a counselor's influence interferes with the proper goals of counseling, a red flag is raised from an ethical point of view. The following areas are particularly relevant to this subject.

The Counselor's Personal Needs

When a counselor's personal needs are introduced into the counseling process they may enhance, impede, or even reverse progress. The following are seven counselor needs that might well have adverse ethical implications should they attain prominence in the counseling relationship.

The need to control. When counselors exert inordinate control, they contaminate the decision-making processes of the client in ways that preclude autonomy. Little by little, the person becomes attached to the counselor's decision-making mechanisms and thus becomes a psychological robot. Even though such control is ostensibly benevolent, it undermines the person's attempts to define his or her own values and to make decisions accordingly. Counselors can rationalize their over-control by assuring themselves that their goals and the goals of the client are essentially the same and that the client only needs a little help to make some "good" decisions.

The need to be correct. When the need to be correct is too much in evidence, the counselor creates a dynamic in which he or she is always correct and the client is always wrong. Such a need will tend to manifest itself most clearly in situations in which the perceptions, interpretations, and values of the counselor and those of the client differ. When the counselor puts the client in the role of being wrong, this role reinforces the person's poor self-esteem and detracts from his or her self-confidence. It also subtly changes the therapeutic milieu from one in which a person can feel free to say anything and to explore attendant feelings into one in which a person must be careful in order to reduce the risk of being wrong. Counselors sometimes rationalize the need to be right by assuring themselves that their role is to present a version of reality to the client that is very likely to be more accurate than the client's own.

The need to rescue. The need to rescue is an exaggerated, destructive version of the need to help. Counselors with the need to rescue cast themselves in roles in which they pull clients off psychological cliffs. However, when clients become accustomed to being pulled off cliffs, they fail to learn the competencies necessary to rescue themselves, and they learn to expect someone else always to save them from facing the consequences of their behavior. While counselors may rationalize their rescue operations by assuring themselves that rescuing and helping are all but synonymous, this "rescuing" is counterproductive and unethical because it effectively undermines all efforts to honor beneficence or to promote autonomy.

The need to be important. Counselors who need to be important to their clients subtly or blatantly demand an allegiance in which they occupy a position of paramount importance. As a result, the client becomes a worshipful subject. This is one of the dynamics of the "guru" phenomenon in which people virtually hand over their lives—and sometimes the lives of their families—to the counselor. Counselors sometimes rationalize their need to be important by assuring themselves that they *should* be important in the person's life and by postulating that without this "transference" the counseling could not be successful.

The need to feel and receive affection. When counselors need to feel affection from their clients, they are at risk of compromising the integrity and effectiveness of the counseling process. There is a difference between a client's having some feelings of affection toward his or her counselor and a counselor's *needing* the client's affection. In the latter case, the focus is placed on the relationship between the counselor and the client rather than on the client's issues. And should the client sense such a need on the part of the counselor then he or she might, at least unconsciously, treat this as a means of neutralizing the counselor as a threat. Both these dynamics are inimical to effective and ethical counseling. While counselors may rationalize a need for affection by assuring themselves that a close relationship is the foundation of effective counseling, they are venturing onto a "slippery slope" that might prove most prejudicial to both counselor and client.

The need to create tension. Counselors cursed with a need to create tension continuously inject tension into counseling even when it is inappropriate and destructive. Unduly creating tension has several harmful effects: it creates a nervous distance between the counselor and the client; it is nothing more than an antidote to boredom; and, since the counselor is more adept at handling tension, such a counselor might be guilty of subordinating the counseling process to a personal need to "win" every confrontation. If treated like a sparring partner by the counselor, the client learns nothing more than how to take punishment and parry attacks. Some counselors rationalize this "need" by assuring themselves that good counselors should generate tension to enable personal growth, but vanity-driven efforts to create tension violate the principle of nonmaleficence.

The need to make money. There is a world of difference between providing a service for which one gets paid and providing a service primarily for the purpose of getting paid. When the latter need is operative, clients are treated as customers more than as human beings who need help. This need to make money is manifested in the counselor who schedules so many people that he or she is unable to be fully present for and attentive to each client, whose motivation is contingent on the amount of money the person is paying, and who charges higher fees than necessary. Such counselors rationalize this concern with money by assuring themselves that they have to make a living and that their fees are no higher than those of counselors who are far less effective.

It is important that counselors honestly appraise the nature and strength of their needs and become aware of whether such needs enhance or interfere with the counseling process. Basic personal needs that are healthy—for example, the need for affection—should be met primarily outside the counseling relationship. Needs that are basically unhealthy—such as the need to create tension—should be resolved in such a way that they do not affect the counseling relationship negatively. Hammer (1972, p. 21–32) offers a full discussion of counselor's needs and how they can affect the practice of counseling.

The Counselor's Personal, Moral, and Spiritual Values

Personal, cultural, moral, and spiritual values are integral elements of any person's life and they will necessarily be present in any counseling relationship. While an adherence to values of these types is usually congruent with sound counseling practice, there are important caveats. For example, problems will arise when counselors' personal values cause them to react to clients in ways that are countertherapeutic. Depending on a given counselor's value system, issues potentially productive of countertherapeutic reactions might include premarital sex, unmarried cohabitation, homosexuality, extramarital sex, abortion, divorce, spousal or child abuse, child molesting, incest, or a failure to live according to the tenets of (the counselor's) religion.

Problems may also arise when the client behaves in ways that the counselor considers immoral and this causes the counselor to view the client in a negative light. This negative view may range from condescension ("You don't seem to realize the wrongfulness of your behavior") to outright contempt ("You seem to be somewhat lacking in moral character").

While well-meaning counselors may try to override these involuntary feelings by reciting the canon of mental health precepts or by recalling some variation of the admonition to "hate the sin but love the sinner," such efforts are unlikely to succeed over a period of time. This is especially true if the client continues to participate in the behavior because he or she either does not view it as immoral or does not consider the behavior a therapeutic issue. The client's casual attitude toward the offensive behavior, conjoined with a possible inclination to chide the counselor about his or her differing values, might conceivably make it impossible for the counselor to maintain an accepting attitude. For this reason, the idea that counselors should not see people who possess values diametrically opposed to their own or who participate in behaviors that are morally repugnant to the counselor has some validity.

Does this mean that counselors should not have personal values or should put them on a shelf when they do counseling? Does it mean that counselors should *like* the behaviors of the people they see in counseling? The answer to both questions is, of course, no. Counselors possess personal values, and their values play an important part in the counseling relationship. The question is not whether counselors should bring their values into counseling but rather how best to do so. For example, a counselor working with a client who has a history of being physically abusive needs to make it clear that he or she finds such behavior unacceptable. At the same time the counselor must demonstrate that he or she values the client and believes they can work in a close, caring, and effective way.

How people behave (professionally and personally) is determined to a very great extent by personal, cultural, moral, and spiritual values. Value differences between counselors and clients are inevitable; methods for appropriately dealing with these differences must be found. Section 1.08 of the APA code states:

> Where differences of age, gender, race, ethnicity, national origin, religion, sexual orientation, disability, language or socioeconomic status significantly affect psychologists' work concerning particular individuals or groups, psychologists obtain the necessary training, experience, consultation, or supervision necessary to ensure the competence of their services, or they make appropriate referrals.

While the terms *cross-cultural* or *multicultural* counseling tend to connote situations in which the counselor and client do not share the same ethnic background, it is far more useful to define culture in the broadest possible terms. Thus counselors, responding to multicultural issues, would be expected to honor not only ethnic differences but a host of other potential differences including those that might arise from sexual orientation, religious or spiritual beliefs, types or forms of disabilities, and so forth. This broader definition proves its worth both clinically and ethically when one considers that "attention to multicultural issues is a natural outgrowth of discussion of respect for autonomy, fairness, and the obligation to do good for others" (Welfel, 1998, p. 245). Multicultural counseling efforts help counselors not only to identify differences but to develop appropriate methods for honoring these differences while providing useful and effective counseling services. While a sensitivity to cultural differences improves the quality of care, the absence of such a sensitivity can be devastating.

The challenge that cultural difference presents to counselors should evince an organized and effective response. Diller (1999) suggests that counselors need to become "culturally competent," and while there are many routes to fulfilling this obligation it would be best to concentrate on the steps that counselors personally need to take. According to Cross, Bazron, Dennis, and Isaacs (1989) counselors need to address five skill areas: (1) awareness and acceptance of differences, (2) self-awareness, (3) dynamics of difference, (4) knowledge of the client's culture, and (5) adaptation of skills. Once counselors accept that differences exist and that these differences affect both the counseling relationship and the counseling process, they are urged to examine their own beliefs, assumptions, values, and expectations. Such an examination often clarifies unexplored elements of the counselor's culture and highlights the areas where cultural blind spots or cultural conflicts may exist. To remain aware of how individuals miscommunicate, misjudge, and misinterpret one another is as important to remember as that cultural differences exist. By paying close attention to cultural differences, counselors add the "how" to the "why" and "what" associated with such difference. Ultimately counselors harmonize these differences by learning the client's culture (perhaps from the client) and by carefully tailoring their therapeutic approach. While this five-step process is specifically useful for counseling clients from a culture different than the counselor's own, it also has a more general application. *All* counseling is multicultural counseling, because cultural differences, broadly defined, always exist between the counselor and the client.

Counselors can improperly introduce their personal values into the counseling relationship by acting on their concerns rather than talking about them. When the counselor's personal values clash with the client's, the counselor may wish to redirect the client's thinking. For example, a counselor who believes that divorce is immoral may try to persuade the person to remain married, even though there is no therapeutic reason to do so. Or a counselor may believe that religion is simply a neurotic defense that must be discarded if counseling is to be considered successful.

Some counselors fail to see the difference between personal and counseling values: they view cultural, moral, religious, and counseling values as synonymous, even when they are not. For example, a counselor may be convinced that until a married person discontinues extramarital relations, he or she cannot expect relief from anxiety or that until a woman admits the wrongdoing of having an abortion and works through the unconscious guilt associated with it, she cannot expect to be free of insomnia. In these cases, the counselor's values have become improperly intertwined with his or her mental health principles, and the counselor may be attributing dynamics to the client that simply are not present. If introducing the client to phantom dynamics and then resolving them becomes a goal of counseling, damage will be done to both the client and the therapeutic process.

A third problem arises when the client seems open to accepting the counselor's personal, cultural, moral, or religious values. The counselor may feel he or she has been given an invitation to teach personal values to the person. The client may have had little moral education or simply may be suggestible and eager to achieve validation by assuming the counselor's values. At first this may seem like a beneficial development, but it may not be. Moral education can well be a valid part of counseling, but it should be moral education and not moral indoctrination. Moral education consists of objectively exploring with a person the rationale underlying various values and beliefs and the constructive and destructive consequences of certain behaviors. But it is the client who should freely and ultimately decide what values and beliefs are best suited for his or her overall growth. Whether the values the client chooses are consonant or dissonant with those of the counselor, the counselor's regard for the person should remain unalterably positive and caring. May (1967a) offers a rich discussion of religion, mental health, and counseling. Readers would do well to refer to this excellent work.

⚜

Summary

Professional ethics are rules of conduct that are meant primarily to protect the welfare and ensure the safety of clients and others. Ethics in counseling covers a wide range of issues, from more obvious ones such as confidentiality and privileged communication to more subtle ones such as establishing schedules that ensure proper client care. Adhering to a code of ethics does not ensure effective counseling, but violating ethics precludes effective counseling. It is the professional responsibility of all counselors to apprise themselves of the ethical issues in counseling and to communicate the most relevant of these to their clients. Only when people are confident their human rights will be scrupulously safeguarded can the foundation of a counseling relationship be built.

Remaining thoughtful, mindful, sensitive, and self-aware helps counselors not only to identify potential ethical problems but also to begin the process of working through ethical concerns in consultation with others. The practical matter of working ethically is best accomplished through contact with colleagues who are willing to participate in a frank exchange of intellectual views and a free expression of personal emotions involved in these important professional issues.

Adherence to a code of professional conduct is essential to effective counseling. Codes of conduct and values change over time and therefore warrant both serious and continuous study. Realistically speaking, a single chapter written by one or two authors can provide little more than a brief survey of a narrow range of ethical issues. Students are therefore urged to supplement the material in this chapter by reviewing the codes reprinted in Appendix A and Appendix B and by reading one or more books on ethics in counseling. Any number of books and articles on counseling ethics are now available. For example, Corey et al. *Issues and Ethics in the Helping Professions* (1998) offers an excellent review of the important ethical issues that confront counselors, while *Boundary Issues in Counseling: Multiple Roles and Responsibilities* (Herlihy and Corey, 1997) provides critical information, thought-provoking examples, and useful suggestions regarding therapeutic, professional, business, and personal relationships for counselors. The fifth edition of the ACA *Ethical Standards Casebook* (Herlihy and Corey, 1996) brings the ACA *Code of Ethics and Standards of Practice* (1995) to life with useful examples of each principle. *Psychotherapy: Standards, Research and Emerging Issues* (Welfel, 1998) not only explores the subject historically, philosophically, and clinically, but also compares and contrasts the ACA *Code of Ethics and Standards of Practice* (1995) with the APA *Ethical Principles of Psychologists and Code of Conduct* (1992) as well as with other codes. Finally, the reader can obtain important legal information covering a wide range of clinical issues from *The Portable Lawyer for Mental Health Professionals*, by Bernstein and Hartsell (1998).

Reflection Questions

1. Which specific criteria would you use to guide you in deciding whether to inform authorities that a client had voiced an intention to do harm to self or others?

2. You have obtained "a verbal agreement" from the parents of a teenage girl that whatever she tells you during counseling sessions will be confidential and that the parents will not be privy to it. Later, the parents become suspicious that their daughter is sexually involved with her boyfriend and demand that you confirm or deny the accuracy of this suspicion. When you refuse, they threaten civil proceedings, in which they will likely prevail. What do you do?

3. Your values are such that you oppose abortion. A young woman you have been seeing in counseling for six months becomes pregnant and wants you to help her decide whether to obtain an abortion. How could you handle this situation in such a way as to preserve the integrity of the counseling relationship?

4. After six months in counseling, a man says, "I read the other day that, legally, I have access to all the information you have that pertains to me. I just thought it would be interesting to see the progress notes you keep on me." How do you respond?

5. It is highly unlikely that there is any experienced counselor who, at one time or another, has not failed to comply adequately with one or more of the several ethical principles discussed in this chapter. Which ethical issue(s) do you feel that you as a counselor should be particularly careful about?

4

COUNSELING AS A
NEW EXPERIENCE

Counseling theorists would generally agree that if counseling is to be effective, it must be a new experience—a unique relationship in the client's life that provides opportunities to perceive self and life differently, to experience and express thoughts and feelings differently, and to behave in new ways. Such a view of counseling is consistent with Jourard and Landsman's (1980) optimistic conclusions about human potential and the ability to change: "Humans have incredible learning capacity, and when environments change, they have it in their power to learn new modes of conduct" (p. 402). Novel situations, especially those that challenge individuals to alter the way they perceive themselves and the world around them, can produce beneficial change. Such challenges bring up alternatives and uncover elements of oneself that would otherwise remain dormant. These newly discovered internal resources are especially useful when individuals attempt to pursue alternative ways of acting. Counseling is particularly useful, and often necessary, when the client's familiar relationships perpetuate a shared reality where rigid behaviors, feelings, attitudes, and ideas contribute to the client's difficulties.

Caveats, of course, exist—the challenges must not be so great that they overwhelm the person, yet they must be substantial and unprecedented enough to activate inner strengths and resources. The following vignette describes a young man who is trapped in patterns of behavior that limit his alternatives and access to his inner resources. He would likely benefit from a novel relationship that challenged him to explore alternatives and become more aware of his needs and wishes.

THE CASE OF STAN

In his second year of college Stan began to question his decision to major in engineering. For Stan, the seemingly harmless act of considering other college majors produced great fear and anxiety. He was quite young when he fully committed himself to the idea of becoming an engineer. His grandfather, someone whom he respected and admired, was a civil engineer, and when Stan was about six years old he spent the day "working" with his grandfather who was supervising the construction of a large bridge. While Stan was too young to know specifically what the study of engineering entailed, when he saw the scale model of the finished bridge and watched workers constructing the actual bridge, he felt that he wanted to be an engineer. That interest persisted, without interruption, until his second year of college.

Stan's father, on the other hand, cared little about the world of engineering and had long since rejected many of his own father's other interests. Their differences ran deep and persisted long enough to make it very difficult for them to talk much beyond exchanging simple greetings. This situation was exacerbated when Stan's father dropped out of college and took a job in an insurance company. While the insurance company wasn't necessarily exciting, it paid well. Stan's father liked the clients and his fellow workers and he progressed rapidly to a regional manager's position. He had established himself in the insurance business and had done this work exclusively for almost 25 years. Stan visited his dad at work from time to time, but these brief encounters with the insurance business made it very clear to him that he did not want to sell insurance or work in an office.

While Stan's father and grandfather did not relate well to each other, Stan got along well with each of them. He considered talking to his father about his academic and career concerns but quickly vetoed the idea. While he occasionally thought about talking to his grandfather about his difficulties he knew that it would be impossible for him to actually follow through. This was a very difficult and risky issue for him. He felt certain that neither his relationship with his dad nor his relationship with his grandfather could stand the strain if he honestly talked about his dilemma with either one of them. His grandfather would be crushed at the mere thought of him not pursuing civil engineering; his father would try to help but he would not know what to do and would quickly give up. Stan also worried that his decision to leave engineering might be interpreted as rejecting his grandfather in favor of his father. He feared that at some point his father might even gloat about his decision to leave engineering.

Stan sensed that he would not be able to force himself to finish something that he had lost interest in, but at this point he was too afraid to tell his family that his interest had waned. His problem was compounded by the fact that he had no idea what he really wanted to do. His fears became so strong and persistent that he would try to convince himself, each day, that this was just a stage. He hoped for an easy solution. He longed to return to the time when he seemed sure of what he wanted. He was beginning to realize that while he was not happy with engineering, he was equally unhappy not knowing what he wanted to study.

He spoke to a couple of his college friends, who were very sympathetic. They said that everyone attending college has the same problem and you deal with it by just taking a whole bunch of different courses until you happen onto one that you like. You then take one more course in the area and if you like that one, too, then that's what you change your major to. One of his friends, who used this system, was on his fourth major in two years. While Stan appreciated their willingness to help, he did not have much faith in this approach.

Stan finally decided that he would talk to his grandfather but he would not tell him about his struggles with majoring in engineering. No, he definitely did not want to disappoint his grandfather; his father had already done enough of that. He would just ask his grandfather questions about the work, much as he did when he was a child. In no time, the old enthusiasm would return and he would not need to bother investigating other college majors or struggle with making choices when he had already made a very good choice many years ago. He just knew his grandfather could get him back on the path.

This example illustrates that even in the face of deeply disturbing and increasingly painful consequences, people will paradoxically cling more intensely to established unproductive patterns. The anxiety does not motivate Stan to change; on the contrary it causes him to reject alternatives and to avoid trying even minor departures from what he has traditionally done. Jourard (1968, p. 73) throws light on the dynamics of Stan's behavior when he writes, "Our security and self-esteem are frequently grounded on a set of fixed beliefs, and whenever we encounter evidence which is dissonant with these, we may undergo an anxiety attack of such severity that those who are less healthy may seek to reduce their anxiety by denying or distorting the evidence which is in conflict with their beliefs."

While this example offers a useful lesson about how difficult it often is for people to change, it also identifies an important issue regarding the very foundation of the counseling relationship. The same resistance that keeps people from examining their decisions and assumptions may also interrupt the formation of the counseling relationship. Stan is having difficulty talking to family members about an important personal issue, and he is likely to encounter equal or greater difficulty discussing these same issues with a counselor. Since the probability of replicating old relationships that tend to maintain the status quo is quite high, Stan will very possibly attempt to re-create the relationship he has with his father or his grandfather as he interacts with a counselor. It is precisely this tendency to replicate relationships instead of creating a new and unique one that produces the first obstacle to the formation of the counseling relationship. Overcoming this tendency is essential because counseling can't be any more helpful than the client's previous relationships if these historical relationships are simply re-created.

Counselors who wish to establish and maintain effective therapeutic alliances need to pursue ongoing answers to two basic questions: How can I be a qualitatively different "significant other" to a particular client? How can I create an environment—a relationship—that is substantially different than any presently available to the client? While these questions do not appear complicated, answers to them must take into account that both counselor and client bring long and varied interpersonal histories to the therapeutic relationship. These histories deeply influence (positively and negatively) the formation of the therapeutic relationship. Successful therapeutic relationships result when counselors effectively understand and manage the clients' history as well as their own. Additional information about counselors' issues can be found in chapter 5.

This chapter's discussion of the maladaptive assumptions that clients cling to is meant to help clarify the twin tasks of realizing what forces hold sway over the client and how the counseling relationship must necessarily appear to the client as unprecedented and possibly puzzling. Recognizing and understanding these patterns will help counselors effectively negotiate the hazards along the route to a successful working alliance. When counselors recognize that people often perceive their problems as being caused by external forces, they will be better prepared to deal effectively with the clients' realistic and unrealistic expectations of counselors and the counseling process.

Client patterns should be kept in sight if they are to be explored and managed. For example, the counselor's efforts to exist as a qualitatively different "significant other" to the client may produce fear and anxiety and, as previously mentioned, prompt the client to attribute characteristics to the counselor that are found in relationships that the client has with others. This displacement or transference process allows the client to engage in familiar, accustomed patterns. Problems arise when transference reactions inhibit the formation of the therapeutic alliance, but these same reactions are helpful because vital information about the client and how the client relates to others is brought actively and immediately into the center of the counseling process. These interferences can simultaneously endanger the formation of the alliance and directly aid the counseling process. The counselor's ability to understand and use these forces dictates, to a great extent, how effectively the counselor and client align with one another and ultimately how effective the counseling effort may prove.

This chapter describes a number of inaccurate perceptions that can hinder clients. It concludes with a description of how counselors can assist clients by offering them a unique relationship. The magnitude of difference between the counselor's and the client's views may be quite large. The counselor must therefore play a key role in the early part of the engagement stage if the counseling relationship is to overcome the myriad forces that seek to shape it into an unproductive replica of an existing relationship in the client's life. The client's rights to informed consent and autonomy are of course to be scrupulously observed as the counselor properly, ethically, and cooperatively defines the boundaries and basic assumptions of the counseling relationship.

⚜ Externalizing Conflict

Unfortunately, people often assume that the cause of their problems lies outside of themselves. They struggle with what Adler referred to as the "if only" absurdity and enter counseling assuming that if it weren't for some external source of conflict in their lives they would be fine: "If only it weren't for my boss, my work would be a pleasure"; "If only it weren't for my mother, I could move away and have a great life"; "If only it weren't for my husband's drinking, we would have a very happy family"; "If only it weren't for my wife's social aspirations, I could relax and enjoy life."

Assumptions such as these immediately complicate the formation of the counseling relationship. If clients assume that the source of the conflict is external then they will labor under the misconception that the resolution will also be external. If the counselor does not agree that the source of the conflict is external, the client will recast the counselor as yet another external source of trouble. The list of external problem sources would then expand from a troublesome boss, a difficult spouse, and an insensitive parent to include an ineffective counselor. Counselors must emphasize from the outset that clients must focus on themselves. The counselor cannot do anything to change the client's boss, mother, husband, or wife. Rather, counselors should help clients discern whether there are changes they can make in their own behavior that would help alleviate their problems.

Many clients predictably refuse the invitation to explore their own behavior. Such clients are not inclined to change their behaviors unless the other offending party changes first. Other clients may respond with a certain amount of curiosity. Perhaps they have never before thought about how people can change and may suddenly become open to exploring alternatives; these people are often more willing to consider changing their behavior if it would prove helpful. Finally, some clients may respond by honestly evaluating their behavior and considering specific alternatives or at least admitting, "Well, I guess I could be more patient" or "I guess sometimes I exaggerate the conflicts and don't see his (her) good points." These people may be closest to the source of conflict, although they are still not quite on target.

Concluding that one's problems have an external source is not the only way that people fail to develop productive ways to make sense of their difficulties. For example, some people attribute the cause of their distress to their symptoms: "If it weren't for my insomnia (depression, anxiety attacks, fears, insecurities, drinking), life would be great." Symptoms are rarely the source of difficulty, and while it may be useful to treat symptoms it is also important to explore the underlying issues that give rise to them.

If clients can accept the fact that the answers to their questions lie within, then counseling can teach people that most psychological problems are internal and that environment is merely the arena within which the battles are waged. Many situational and interpersonal problems are externalized manifestations and reflections of internal conflicts. When clients externalize the solution to problems by expecting the counselor to fix blame somewhere, they are in effect exhibiting a lack of confidence in their own abilities, along with a loss of trust in themselves and a sense that they lack the necessary knowledge to identify their difficulties and deal with them.

The counselor in this case should probably side with the client at this point. This is not to say that external situations and relationships play no part in a person's problems. External factors do activate internal conflicts. People often misunderstand this dynamic, however, when they say, "My job must be the cause of my problem because I was fine until I got promoted." More likely, the stress of the promotion activated an internal dynamic that was latent until that point. For this reason, counselors can recognize that except for certain extreme circumstances, removing a person from an environment rarely leads to a solution to the problem. For example, if a client is experiencing difficulties at work, the solution is not necessarily to change jobs. If a client's marriage is causing the client distress, the logical solution is not necessarily a separation. These clients may experience great relief after a change of settings (which they inaccurately perceive as proof that they made the correct decision), but they are likely to carry their problem into the next setting.

The following internal factors—all of which can cause conflicts in the formation of the counseling relationship—tend to give the appearance that they originated in the environment whereas in fact they have only been reflected from the environment.

Negative Self-Appraisal

Negative self-appraisals are not maladaptive when they are accurate and realistic. They alert the person to issues that need to be looked at and dealt with. On the other hand, when people consciously or unconsciously harbor *unrealistic* negative feelings about themselves, they are vulnerable in their interactions with other people and their environment. Persistent, inaccurate, negative self-appraisals produce unrealistic, inaccurate, and dysfunctional beliefs that obstruct an accurate perception of self and interfere with interpersonal relationships. Examples of negative self-appraisal might include the following: "I am stupid," "I am unattractive," "I am unsophisticated," "I am immature," "I am lazy," "I am selfish," "I am uncaring," "I am cold," "I am needy," "I am weak," "I am immoral," "I am insecure," or "I am uninteresting." According to McGonicle (1988), harmful negativity can take three forms. People can be negative in a way that causes them to see all events as catastrophes; they can become bound by absolutes—psychological imperatives that take the form of "must" statements; or they can persistently recant or disavow their decisions by telling themselves that they did the wrong thing and "should have" done something else. Each of these patterns limits the person's alternatives and experiences while creating a profoundly negative self-perspective.

Clients troubled by a negative self-appraisal form and maintain relationships only with difficulty. Such a rigid negativity makes it very difficult for others to establish close personal ties. The "price of admission" for a relationship with someone who is unrealistically negative is often a willingness to share a similar negative perspective. Persons who are better adjusted tend to shy away from consistently negative individuals. Relationships become untenable because when the maladaptive perceptions are questioned by others, these individuals either fight or flee, inadvertently creating additional difficulties instead of solving problems. Because they sense only the reaction coming from the environment and not the patterns coming from within themselves, such clients continually blame the environment for their difficulties, thereby ensuring that the problems will continue unabated.

A telling example of this pattern may be seen in the client whose most distinctive feature was the ability to convert virtually anything that happened into a disaster. Difficulties and bad news were easily perceived as catastrophes. Making negative situations worse is far from uncommon, but this client exhibited an uncanny facility for framing even positive events as calamities. At one point the client dejectedly mentioned having recently received a promotion. The client exhibited during the session an animosity to this promotion. The client claimed not to be knowledgeable enough about the job, to lack management skills, and further stated that former coworkers would never respond to having him as a supervisor. This client was convinced that the promotion was a set-up by his superiors—an invitation to fail in an impossible situation. The client resisted the counselor's efforts to help him reconsider these inaccurate perceptions and eventually decided to reject the promotion. The client's bewildered supervisors offered to restore him to his previous position, but some self-destructive impulse prompted this client to reject all reconciliation and part company with the firm. This client returned to therapy only briefly before parting company with the therapist.

Counselors regularly encounter people who struggle with this pattern. Counselors should understand that some clients may pressure their counselors to view them in a negative light by behaving in ways that exhibit their negative attributes. Because a homeostatically balanced (if unproductive) state forms around the client's internal negative self-image, the client grows to expect others to affirm this pattern by perceiving the client negatively. Anything else might cause disequilibrium and distress. To be effective, counselors should scrupulously avoid the invitation to perceive the client negatively even though the client may exert excessive, unrealistic pressure in this direction. Egan's concept of *immediacy*—the process of exploring what is occurring, at a particular moment, in the counselor-client relationship—is particularly useful (1994). Resisting the client's single-minded negativity in favor of focusing on the client's internal struggles serves as a useful antidote to the counterproductive patterns caused by the patient's negative self-images.

Psychological Imperatives

Psychological imperatives, certain "musts" in a person's life that are perceived as compelling and absolute, produce varied difficulties. Such psychological imperatives can cause people to feel that if they do not accomplish a particular "must," they will be less worthwhile and life will be less livable. These psychological imperatives generally fall into one of three different categories: personal, interpersonal and social.

The following are some examples of common personal imperatives: "I must always be kind . . . attractive . . . strong . . . correct . . . loyal . . . unselfish . . . happy . . . carefree . . . successful . . . brave . . . loving . . . special."

Some examples of interpersonal imperatives are "I must be treated fairly . . . liked . . . loved . . . appreciated . . . rewarded . . . entertained . . . paid attention to . . . sought after . . . spoken well of . . . admired." "You must be perfect . . . docile . . . agreeable . . . kind . . . reliable . . . beautiful . . . interesting . . . industrious . . . religious."

Examples of social imperatives are "I must go to the right schools . . . have the right friends . . . enter a particular profession . . . be promoted . . . make a certain salary . . . have a certain position . . . get married . . . have a family."

These psychological imperatives make it very difficult for people to relate naturally and comfortably with others and with the world around them. They place undue pressure on themselves and expect people to treat them in ways that are unachievable, inappropriate, or unreasonable. People who struggle with this issue are unable to assume responsibility for their problems, but they are often able to assure themselves that if life met their "musts," everything would be fine.

Similarly, psychological imperatives distort the counseling relationship and inhibit the formation of the therapeutic alliance. Unreasonable client demands on the counselor can exist in many areas of the counseling relationship. Clients can dispute times for scheduled sessions, fees, frequency of visits, or approaches to treatment, but such complaints do not necessarily stop at practical issues. The arguments can even range to "social musts" where the counselor's perceived professional status within the community becomes an issue. The client feels that he or she must be treated by the "most well-known or highly respected" mental health professional in the community. The fact is that these so-called "musts" are actually incorrectly labeled. While clients may feel, at the extreme, that life is not possible without meeting these standards, clients often eventually learn to live comfortably and happily by placing these demands in proper perspective.

Conflicting Needs

The idea that one set of needs might conflict with another does not seem like a remarkable or surprising condition given the complexities of life. However, some people have incompatible needs that dramatically conflict with each other so as to produce difficulties. Significant conflict usually occurs because a more acceptable need is conscious, while the less acceptable one is subconscious or unconscious. The result is internal conflict if important elements of the disagreement are not consciously known to the client. For example, a man might have a strong need to be independent and an almost equally strong repressed need to be dependent. He protests that he does not want to remain at home with his parents, but they are putting so much pressure on him to remain that he feels he must. He blames his parents for manipulating him but at the same time responds to their "manipulations" with only a token struggle. He may enter counseling to get help in extracting himself from the clutches of his parents when in fact he is where he wants to be. The counselor who identifies only that the client wants to leave home would miss an equally important aspect of the client's conflicted state: namely that the client simultaneously and unconsciously hopes to remain in the safety of his parent's home. An alliance focused solely on the parent's "manipulations" would thus fail therapeutically. The counselor would need to be sensitive to hidden, conflicted feelings that could also jeopardize the formation and maintenance of the therapeutic relationship.

The potential for identifying surface conflict and missing subconscious or unconscious needs confronts counselors when they work with virtually any client. Perhaps the most elemental conflicting need is the one that every client enters with: the conscious desire to solve emotional difficulties without help and the emerging intense, though unconscious, need to seek professional assistance.

The following are some typical conflicting needs:

- independence versus dependence
- intimacy versus safety

- humility versus prestige
- sexuality versus chastity
- believing versus doubting
- belonging versus being free
- perseverance versus the need to get out of damaging situations
- altruism versus selfishness
- achieving versus relaxing

These conflicts produce inner tensions that are readily misunderstood as social or environmental problems. The result is that the client blames the environment or other people when, in fact, the stress exists as a function of the conflict within.

Thus, counseling can be a new and valuable experience for people who believe the sole cause of their problems stems from their environment or the people around them. The uniqueness of the counseling relationship gives clients an opportunity to learn that they may have created or perpetuated many of their conflicts. This understanding in turn helps clients lessen their inner conflict so the remainder of their lives can be significantly more satisfying and fulfilling. Perhaps the most basic insight that counseling seeks to impart is that the majority of struggles stem from unresolved internal conflicts rather than from external situations.

While the importance of factors internal to the client must always be considered, there may be times when the environment has become so intractably destructive that counseling efforts would be useless and a crisis management approach would be far more appropriate. Focusing on internal issues to the exclusion of serious external threats would be counterproductive and inappropriate. There are situations in which clients cannot safely and productively exist. Dowd (1976) cautions that "every counselor should constantly question what needs to be changed, the individual or the environment" (p. 142). In fact, "One of the implications of the new construct of mental health . . . is that modification of the environment is a legitimate counselor function. Individuals should not always be adjusted to their environment" (p. 142). Under these conditions counselors should be careful that the therapeutic process honors this fact and aids the client.

Misperceptions of Reality

Counseling offers the client an opportunity to perceive reality more effectively. It is important to realize that each of us makes sense of our world in ways that are consistent with how we see ourselves and how we are treated by others. Perception of reality is subjective, individualized, and deeply influenced, for better or worse, by many variables. For example, some people who enter counseling may be hiding from or manipulating reality in order to diminish their anxieties and meet their needs. While they think they are perceiving reality clearly and dealing with it well, their problems provide evidence that contradicts this belief. In fact, their decision to enter counseling may itself be a sign that their usual methods of dealing with reality are not working—anxiety that used to be controlled is now building. The problem of adhering to unproductive views of reality is further compounded by the fact that significant others in the person's life may continue to encourage less productive perceptions. In the example given at the beginning of this chapter, Stan's view of reality is no longer effectively managing his anxiety, and his efforts to change are further hampered by what he suspects his father and his grandfather would do if they knew of his uncertainty about a career.

From the very origin of the counseling relationship, counselors present alternative perspectives that regularly conflict with the way clients perceive their reality. For this reason clients often view the counseling process at first as alien and suspect. Counselors walk a fine line at the beginning of the counseling relation because they must challenge the client's perceptions or conclusions while simultaneously seeking to understand them. Counselors only achieve this goal when they realize that it is possible to understand the client's perceptions without necessarily agreeing with them. At the engagement stage it is particularly important for clients to feel that the way they make sense of the world around them is something that can be shared with and understood by someone else, even if the other person does not necessarily agree or see things the same way.

Avoidance, blaming, and overgeneralizing are three common ways that people unproductively deal with reality. Each affects the formation of the counseling relationship differently.

Avoiding the Present

When counselors ask clients to consider that the source of their difficulty resides within themselves they are encouraging clients to focus on themselves in the present. Such an introspective focus is at variance with the way many clients function within their day-to-day lives. For example, people become skilled at avoiding the present. Much of their time is spent reliving the past or planning the future. They revel in or mourn their pasts and fear or look forward to their futures. The process of resisting the present can be seen as a vicious circle. The more inept people are at dealing with the present, the more their past haunts them (because they didn't handle it well when it was their present) and the more they fear the future (because they have no present upon which to build.)

Commonly, when people enter counseling they talk mostly about yesterday and tomorrow. They may pointedly avoid the present—specifically as it exists between them and their counselors. Avoiding the here-

and-now obscures reality and stands in the way of sensing who they are, who others really are, and what the situation really is. This results because an accurate perception of reality demands focused attention on the present instead of dividing attention between the past and the future. To focus in this way, clients must become more open to experiencing the present on a variety of levels: to see it, to listen to it, to examine it with their minds, and to feel it with their hearts.

The significant others in clients' lives are often unable to help them deal with the present because of their own inability to do so. The majority of the communication between clients and their significant others dwells on the past and the future with a tacit agreement not to bring up the present. While friends and relatives may ask the person "why" questions ("Why did you do that?"), counselors ask "what" and "how" questions as they attempt to bring the client into the present. For example, counselors might ask, "What feelings and thoughts are you aware of right now?" "What is going on between us right now?" "How are you avoiding diffi-cult thoughts and feelings that are hard to talk about with other people?"

As clients become better able to experience the present and deal with it effectively—that is, when they fully enter into the counseling rela-tionship—unproductive anxiety attached to past and future events often diminishes and is replaced by a more constructive anxiety focused in the present. This form of anxiety is more desirable because it is more likely to motivate the individual to take the risks that are necessary to explore and act on alternatives. Further discussion of the importance of dealing with the present can be found in Perls (1969).

Overgeneralizing

When clients overgeneralize they establish unrealistic assumptions about themselves and others by focusing on a particular trait and over-generalizing it or exaggerating it to such a degree that other personal qualities become obscure. For example, people who overgeneralize may view themselves as consistently kind when they are also sometimes un-kind, or as generally intelligent when in fact they are competent in some areas and limited in others. They may see themselves as always altruistic when they are oftentimes selfish, or as wholly forthright and cooperative when at times they are closed and manipulative.

People may also exaggerate negative traits. They might perceive themselves as uncaring when they sometimes care deeply, as insensitive when they can be quite vulnerable, or as cold when they possess genuine warmth as well. Overgeneralizing is not limited to self-perceptions. Indi-viduals who overgeneralize may perceive others (parents, spouse, friends) by similarly exaggerating certain traits at the expense of others. They may incorrectly perceive some people as ideal when in fact they are just average human beings with varied strengths and weaknesses. They may see others as well-meaning when at times they are not or as trustworthy when they are sometimes untrustworthy.

The client's overgeneralization will extend to the counselor. Clients are quite likely to exaggerate certain traits that they observe or hope to find in the counselor to the exclusion of others. Helping clients toward a more realistic perception of the counselor is extremely beneficial. Clients are more likely to perceive themselves more completely and accurately when they are encouraged to explore their exaggerated perceptions of the counselor's personal qualities. This method of bending reality is quite common, so counselors can expect to be perceived either excessively positive or negative by many of their clients, especially during the engagement stage. Initially the client knows almost nothing about the counselor. The client's tendency to fill in the missing information at this point is quite high. Understanding how the client attributes traits to the counselor and what those traits are can be therapeutically useful. These findings can be used to guide the engagement process, to understand the client more deeply, and to tailor the counseling process.

Blaming

People commonly blame themselves or they blame others for the stress in their lives. It is an indirect, subtle way of avoiding reality that can persist through time because the pattern offers some rewards. When people blame themselves for a problem, they need not confront the other people involved; when they blame others, they do not have to deal with their own role in the problem. Both of these avoidance techniques leave much to be desired: when two or more people encounter a problem, it is likely that each of them has contributed to the situation in some active or passive way. The active form is often less difficult to become aware of than the passive form of "contributory negligence" and related issues of "victimization."

Many people who enter counseling tend to be either self-blamers or other-blamers. When people assign blame, they are often unaware that they have a further option: to view the stressful situation realistically and address their role in the creation and maintenance of the problem. In other words, if they can accept responsibility for contributing to the problem without blaming themselves, then they can help others see their responsibility without insisting that they accept blame. An adaptive person's attitude is "If I do this differently and you do that differently, it may solve our problem" instead of "I'm sorry; I won't do that again" or "Until you can see that this situation is your fault, we can't resolve this problem." Clients laboring under the delusion that every problematic situation is someone's fault should become aware that they are playing roles induced by indoctrination. This topic will be discussed further in the next section.

An approach that emphasizes shared responsibility without blaming and fault-finding is particularly important to any therapeutic effort. The counselor and client need to establish a cooperative working relationship where blaming and fault-finding are replaced by a more collegial mutual understanding. This is just as applicable to the counselor as to the client. Counselors should always guard against blaming and fault-finding because everyone is equally susceptible to these roles. Consider, for example, a worst case scenario where the counselor is a person who tends to find fault and the client is someone who embraces self-blame. The potential for a deeply troubled and counterproductive relationship is markedly elevated and the outcome potentially disastrous.

Obstructions to Insight

While theorists may disagree about the necessity of insight for the process of change, most would agree that coming to a clear and accurate sense of self is a worthwhile benefit of effective counseling. Difficulty with developing accurate insights is far from uncommon because many people pursue counseling with limited information about themselves and about how they relate to other people—including their new counselors. While it is impossible to know ourselves fully, it is possible to increase our range of awareness. This is an important goal of counseling. Knowing how clients encounter difficulties with insight helps counselors tailor counseling strategies to individual clients. Some clients may have a fairly complete view of themselves, but they may be unwilling to share these insights with others; that is, their uneasiness with what they know about themselves may cause them to deploy counterfeit images. Other clients may assume they know themselves quite completely, when in fact they have limited or unrealistic insights about themselves. Still other clients are admittedly confused about who they are.

The following sections will cover certain obstructions to developing and sharing insights that are commonly encountered in interactions with certain types of clients.

Counterfeit Images

There are people who enter counseling knowing reasonably well who they are. Their difficulties stem not so much from a lack of insight as from an inability to act on these insights. This condition is often brought about by fear. The amount of fear is related to the magnitude of the discrepancy between the client's perceived self and ideal self. Clients in the throes of a conflict produced by a reluctance to act on insights may create an image or public self to present to others. They may even present different images to different people, tailoring themselves to others and moving further away from a sense of who they really are. The creation of public selves compounds the problem because over time clients may begin to believe that their images, and not their real selves, are what people are attracted to. Conversely, they may fear that if their real selves emerge, the significant people in their lives will find them less attractive, or even repulsive.

Counselors can help clients examine the difference between what they know or think to be true about themselves and the images they may project, as well as examine the discrepancies that often exist among their various images. Exploring these differences is particularly important because of the psychological cost associated with trying to maintain and balance incompatible roles. If clients can be guided to cast off counterproductive roles, an overall economy will be achieved and clients may become able to allow more of their true selves to emerge. It's also possible that clients will consciously choose to continue with their images.

The same forces that cause people to present contrived images rather than their true selves also affect the counselor-client relationship. The counselor faces the same difficulty that others might when attempting to interact with the client—the client insists on presenting an image rather than engaging in the more difficult task of surfacing pertinent material. In the initial stages of the counseling process counselors must often engage equally well with many facets of the client's being, including images—public selves—as well as more inner elements of self.

Clients can be expected to resist the counselor's efforts to engage them if their counselors discount the images and press them to reveal difficult parts of themselves too quickly. It might be noted parenthetically that images or "masks" can be and often are used beneficially. The maladaptive images described in this section are troublesome because of their being rigidly held and because their presence keeps the client that much further from accurate self-perception.

Psychological Filters

Some people who enter counseling *think* they know who they are, but they are actually held from self-knowledge because important elements of themselves have become buried beneath layers of psychological filters. A deeper understanding or knowledge of their individual identity becomes obscured by these filters. *Indoctrination* and *the acquisition of roles* are two common psychological filters.

Indoctrination, which comes generally from society and specifically from parents and teachers, is based on repeated injunctions that focus on various aspects of self: "This is who you are; this is who you will be; and this is what life is about." Injunctions are endlessly repeated until the child and adolescent internalizes them and the injunctions become part of the person's life. Indoctrination is different from education. Education is based on the attitude "Let's find out who you are so that you can decide who you want to become; you will learn about life as it evolves."

Consider the example of a man who has been indoctrinated with the following injunction: "You *are* special, agreeable, asexual, religious, and athletic; you *will be* successful, industrious, cautious, obedient to the church, a leader, and a family man; and *life is* good, as long as you don't *enjoy* it." As this person develops, he recognizes that he can neither possess all these qualities nor possess any one of them to the degree to which he has been commissioned. He then starts pretending to others that he possesses these qualities. After pretending for a certain period of time, he begins to fool himself as well. By the time he is 25 years old, the indoctrination is complete; that is, he thinks he *is* what he pretends to be. He is like a person who has never looked in a mirror and who therefore must rely totally on others' descriptions of his appearance. Unfortunately, it is difficult, if not impossible, for him to develop any further without having a personal sense of self—one that can be set alongside the perceptions that others have of him.

Another common psychological filter arises from the *acquisition of roles*. All people have been assigned roles by society. Some people remain true to themselves despite such assignments, but others may give up their integrity and assume such a role as their identity. For example, instead of being a person who is a physician, a man or woman may *become* a physician and equate the personal identity with the role. The role dictates that one must always be correct, gentle, and available to one's patients.

The following are some of the problems thus encountered as a result of assuming the societally defined role of physician. If one must always be correct, one cannot admit mistakes to oneself, one's colleagues, or one's patients. This will cause both interpersonal difficulties and a tendency to continue making the same mistakes. If one must be gentle, it is necessary to repress and deny feelings of an ungentle nature. The concomitant frustration, confusion, and anger constitute a drain on the person's time and energy. If one must always be available to one's patients, one will deprive oneself and one's family of the important time they all need for personal growth and recreation.

When people become overidentified with their roles they become rigid and unable to explore alternatives freely. They are limited by the roles, not by themselves. Clients who struggle with this issue present interesting challenges during the engagement phase. They often describe the unhappiness they experience in their role but they do so as someone relating from the role rather than from a sense of self. Such persons are more likely to confide how difficult it is to live up to expectations that are associated with various roles they have adopted than to discuss how painful it is to suppress elements of themselves in the process of maintaining their involvement in a particular role. At engagement, counselors need to look beyond the injunctions and beyond the roles to envision the client's fuller potential, but an awareness of the client's psychological filters will help the counselor to better navigate these issues.

Confusion

Some people enter counseling confused as to who they are. While indoctrination and roles produce identity characterized by rigidity, confusion produces a self too fluid to be stable. These people may be confused because so many self-images are present to the mind that they are unsure or afraid to know which ones reflect their true identity. Confusion helps them keep aspects of themselves at a distance from each other. As long as they are confused and successfully confuse others, they stave off the anxiety that would arise if they allowed these aspects of themselves to emerge and confront each other.

During an intake interview, a woman may spend the majority of a counseling session listing all the things in her marriage she is unhappy about and how she envies the single women she knows. At the end of the session she might then state, "Oh, I'm so confused, I don't know what is happening." While the woman may report being confused, the counselor may come to the opposite conclusion. The counselor may realize the client is not confused in the usual sense, but rather is unable to admit how she feels and therefore hides behind confusion rather than admit to herself or the counselor the realities of her deeply troubled marriage. Honoring her confusion while developing an understanding of the pain and conflict that resides within her are both equally important at the engagement stage of the counseling process. The amount of confusion helps the counselor to estimate the depth of the pain and it offers a useful place to establish the focus of a therapeutic relationship. The client would not likely be ready to discuss the future of her marriage but she could, without much difficulty, begin the process of exploring her confusion.

The counselor should also be prepared to expect some confusion regarding the nature of the counseling relationship whenever difficult or painful issues are addressed. This type of confusion places special demands on the counselor. The client's confusion may easily draw the counselor into the position of the person who is expected to resolve the confusion—the one with the answers. This would be an unfortunate course to be made to take, because giving advice and reducing the confusion would likely breed the same form of dependence that contributes substantively to the client's current difficulties. The confusion is a symptom, but it is not the problem.

The therapeutic goal of helping clients understand themselves better and the therapeutic practices serving this goal distinguish counseling as both a new and a unique relationship. While people may have been told over and over again how to live up to their images better, they have seldom been invited to reexamine them. When people possess a clearer sense of self, they are more aware of their specific needs, values, attitudes, motives, strengths, and weaknesses. This knowledge helps them to make appropriate choices and pursue life with a greater potential for growth and happiness. While self-awareness, in itself, is not sufficient for growth, it is a necessary prerequisite.

✠

Misconceptions

People who pursue counseling often harbor misconceptions about themselves or their behavior. While these misconceptions contribute significantly to the client's difficulties they are surprisingly resistant to change. This is probably due to the fact that they are so frequently reinforced and because common misconceptions are shared by large segments of society.

There are several common misconceptions that clients often express from the very beginning of the counseling process. Counselors need to be aware of and able to develop useful methods for identifying and exploring each of them.

Insoluble Problems

People may enter counseling with the assumption that their problems are insoluble. There are several possible reasons for such a misconception. For example, they may have honestly looked for solutions but lacked the competencies either to recognize solutions or to carry them out. They may fear finding a solution because such a solution would require them to make the corresponding changes in their lives. Then again, they may have opted to accept others' assessment of their situation because it appears accurate or because it is easier to agree than to disagree with others.

For example, a woman may come to counseling complaining that her husband is abusive but that she cannot leave him. She says her parents and friends would disown her, she has four children who need a father, and she has only a high school education and no marketable skills. These basic assumptions are based upon a reality that she embraces, and they collectively establish that her problem is insoluble. From her perspective, she is in an impossible situation, and all her friends agree that this is true. She approaches the counselor with a paradoxical attitude: "There's nothing that can be done about my problem, but I'm here for you to do something about it."

The counselor would probably disagree with her since, in fact, there are several steps that the client could take to solve the problem if her underlying assumptions were different. For example, (1) she might try to get her husband to join her in counseling, (2) she might get counseling for herself, (3) she might go to appropriate social service agencies, where she could be directed to jobs, job training, child-care services, and other resources, or (4) she could get group counseling or join a woman's group in order to obtain support and encouragement. Although she may methodically and reflexively thwart the counselor's attempts to help her see that her problem is not intractable, the above options are all within her grasp.

Her relationship with the counselor is predicated on her expectation that the problem is a permanent fixture in her life. But the counselor's relationship with the client is predicated on hope—the existence of options where none seemed possible. This engagement, perhaps more than any of the others discussed in this chapter, demonstrates how much counselor and client can differ perceptually at the outset of the counseling relationship and how important it is for the counselor to carefully negotiate the boundary.

Unbreakable Promises

Many people believe that they must abide by their promises, regardless of the damage they or others may encounter because of them. Society tends to support this concept of fidelity, especially when promises involve important areas such as work commitments, friendships, and marriage.

As a general principle, it is better to keep promises than to break them. But it is counterproductive if a promise goes counter to the reason for which it was made. A commitment should not be made to the promise itself, but rather to principles that the promise presupposes (e.g., justice, growth, or support). For example, a marriage promise is made to aid the partners in their pursuit of mutual growth and understanding through a sense of love, respect, and justice. If love turns to hate, if justice is replaced by injustice, if the situation becomes irreversible despite honest efforts, then the marriage promise has outlived its purpose. Remaining in the relationship simply to keep a promise may signify that the person lacks sufficient understanding of the purpose of promises or has a vested interest in remaining in a destructive situation.

Although promises are often useful and important, they also can give rise to inappropriate behavior. Problems may develop (1) when a person views a promise as an end in itself rather than as a means to an end, (2) when the person, at the time of the promise, did not have sufficient self-knowledge or sufficient awareness of the situation to make a truly informed decision, and (3) when a promise is used to bind a person in an objectively damaging situation. The key word is "objective." The counselor's role is to provide an objectivity that the client cannot achieve alone. The counselor mediates between the client and the client's environment.

Society tends to reward keeping promises. Even when people are seriously damaged by remaining in commitments, they are likely to be viewed by a large segment of society as loyal and persevering; people who leave destructive situations are often viewed as weak and selfish. Consequently, people who are in a destructive commitment are caught in a double bind. If they keep their promise, they will continue to be damaged. If they break it, they risk being viewed with scorn.

Counseling may be the first opportunity for a person to evaluate the reasonableness of keeping a promise that is causing significant damage. If the client can place his or her promises in a proper perspective and clearly view the psychological and emotional damage that is being perpe-trated, then perhaps the client may find the courage to move away from a promise-keeping frame of mind toward a more just and growth-produc-ing alternative.

Victimistic Behavior

While there are people who are, in fact, victims in the truest sense of the word, many people inaccurately or incompletely characterize them-selves as being the victim of some destructive situation or person. Under closer scrutiny it may become clear that their own behavior, conscious and unconscious, is contributing to their being victimized. Such persons are, in a manner of speaking, *consenting victims*.

When consenting victims complain to others about their plight, they are likely to receive an amount of sympathy that tends to reinforce their perception of themselves as helpless victims. For example, a woman may complain to a friend that her husband comes home drunk almost every night and ruins the evening for the entire family. Her friend commiserates with her and offers suggestions, all of which are dismissed as unworkable. But it could very well be that the woman has a vested interest in her hus-band's coming home drunk for at least a couple of reasons: (1) deep down she may not want to feel too close to her husband because she finds him repulsive or (2) she may have a strong need to feel important to her chil-dren. As long as her husband comes home drunk, she is spared from hav-ing to interact with him in any meaningful way and also takes on a position of foremost importance to her children. She protects them from his drunken behavior and assumes the roles and responsibilities of both parents, thus making her children entirely reliant on her.

In a real sense, she would rather have her husband arrive home drunk than sober; consequently, she makes no serious attempts to confront him with his destructive behavior. She views herself as the long-suffering wife who must make the best of a difficult situation. This is the concept she conveys to others and for which society rewards her through sympathy.

Being a consenting victim can be a situation-specific trait; for exam-ple, the woman whose husband comes home drunk may be a consenting victim only in her marriage. Or it can be a general trait in that she is a con-senting victim in many or all of her relationships.

Unwilling victims, in contrast to willing victims, cannot foresee the damage they will suffer. They learn from the situation and take steps to see that it does not reoccur. Consenting victims tend to remain in situa-tions of continuing damage or tend to exchange one damaging situation for another. Following a destructive experience, unwilling victims might conclude, "I learned one thing: I'll never get myself into a situation like that again," while consenting victims would be more likely to lament, "Why do these things always happen to me?"

Established patterns of self-defeating or self-handicapping behavior are commonly found in consenting victims. The issue of victimistic behavior has important therapeutic implications. According to some researchers

> the incorporated self-handicapper strives to define his or her problems as resulting from the handicapping condition and to define that condition as a relatively peripheral aspect of himself or herself. For the contract to remain in effect, the individual must "suffer" and, occasionally, demonstrate the handicap's continuing effect. This typically entails some loss of freedom and, perhaps, the assumption of dependent status. . . . To the extent that self-handicapping becomes an exercise in self-defeatism, it rightfully becomes a focus for therapeutic interventions aimed at enabling the individuals to reconnect with his or her capacity for growth. (Higgins, Snyder & Berglas, 1990, p. 189, 205)

Victims may well create situations where a victim-perpetrator relationship is duplicated in the counseling relationship. Such clients perceive themselves as victims of the counseling process. For this reason, such clients are especially difficult because they are able to convert much of what the counselor does in counseling into affirmations of their victim status. Carefully planned, well-bounded therapeutic interventions can help consenting victims ultimately realize what they are doing, why they are doing it, and how they can make some basic changes within themselves so that being a victim ceases to be a viable option.

Inaccuracies

People perceive and interpret their experience in a way that is consistent with the assumptions they hold. When they communicate their view of reality to others, it is commonly accepted as factual. For example, Mary complains to her mother about her husband: "Bill has become so irritable with me lately, and I can't understand why." Her mother is likely to spend a good deal of time trying to help her understand Bill's problem. By doing so, she directly reinforces her daughter's notion that her perception of Bill's behavior is accurate. But it may not be. Her perception or interpretation may be inaccurate. There are several possibilities that could explain Bill and Mary's behavior.

First, Bill might not be irritable. Perhaps Mary is making unreasonable demands on him, and he is healthily declining to meet them. Mary would rather view his behavior as "irritable" than her demands as excessive.

Second, Bill might be irritable, not just with his wife, but with everyone. But perhaps Mary ignores his irritability toward others or rationalizes that it is justified. She then focuses on his irritability toward her and makes a personal issue of it. She asks, "What's wrong with me? What's wrong with him? What's wrong with our relationship?" instead of seeing the broader problem. Her attempts to answer these questions then lead to frustration, which only complicates the situation.

Third, Bill may be irritable for reasons that Mary is well aware of. Suppose she has been pressuring him lately to move to the suburbs, a move that will create significant financial and geographical burdens on the family. But Mary fails to see that Bill's irritability increases with the pressure she exerts. Since she does not wish to view herself as the cause of his problem, she cannot see any cause and effect relationship between her behavior and Bill's irritability.

Fourth, Bill may have always been irritable; it is nothing new. Bill has been irritable all his life, but Mary views it more clearly now. This may be because she is growing in psychological strength and is less inclined to deny the presence of his irritability, or it may be that at the present time she needs to scapegoat him as a means of explaining some problems she has begun to experience.

Unfortunately, the few people Mary can confide in may automatically assume that her perceptions and interpretations are accurate and inadvertently reinforce them. By the time she enters counseling, she will be convinced that her views are accurate. The more Mary's peers have reinforced her inaccurate views, the further she will be from an accurate assessment of her situation.

Self-Deception

People often are convinced that they know exactly what they are doing. They may be unaware of how they unconsciously deceive themselves or unaware that such deception is even possible. When people fail to understand this dynamic they view problems as having fallen into their lives as the result of bad fortune rather than as being the result of improper decisions. The following are some common examples of people who are deceiving themselves.

A man explains that he never remains with a job very long because he has yet to find one that really challenges him. He is aware that he is looking for challenge. He is unaware that he quits because he doubts his ability to do well once the honeymoon period on a job is over.

A woman complains that she has had a medley of unhappy love affairs and laments her bad fortune in finding the right person. She knows that she wants to be loved, but remains unaware of how difficult it is for her to become emotionally involved. While she beckons with one hand for people to come closer to her, she pushes them away with the other.

In these examples, the people appear convinced that they know exactly what they want and what they are doing. It may be only after they enter counseling that they can discover they are creating their own obstacles and frustrations because their needs and feelings are moving them in opposite directions at the same time. When people become aware of this, they are in a better position to make conscious, reasonable choices that will further their growth and sense of satisfaction in life.

Counseling may be the first opportunity for some people to consider the existence and the invalidity of their misconceptions and to replace them with more accurate views. When this occurs, people are freer to make decisions that further their needs and interests and are ultimately more advantageous to them.

Beginning a New and Unique Relationship

Thus far this chapter has focused on the types of general assumptions, distortions, and patterns that may keep clients from achieving an accurate view of themselves and of the source of their problems. All people have these blind spots, but all people do not enter counseling. Those who enter counseling sense that some part of the complete picture is missing. Counseling has the potential to fill in these missing parts by offering clients a new kind of relationship, one that is different from those obtainable from associates, friends, and family. Some people in a client's life may be concerned about him or her, but in a more passing, pragmatic way. Others may be genuinely concerned, but lack necessary levels of psychological health to be helpful. Still others might have a genuine concern and may be psychologically healthy, but may lack the knowledge of human behavior and/or the therapeutic skills to be of any real help to the person. Counselors offer clients a professional therapeutic relationship that is simply not achievable through contact with friends and family members. The following section discusses several of the basic attributes of the counseling relationship that contribute to making it unique and therefore more effective in rectifying or ameliorating the inaccurate perceptions discussed thus far in this chapter.

These factors cannot be considered in a vacuum. The counseling relationship is effective only when counselors bring to the relationship a sound knowledge of human behavior, conjoined with empathy, skill, sensitivity to the client's needs, appropriate levels of self-awareness, and a willingness to form a therapeutic relationship with someone they do not know. Perhaps Beitman (1987) best characterizes the challenge associated with forming an effective therapeutic alliance when he describes the goal of the engagement stage as being able "to emerge from the anonymity of the first few seconds into a pair of individuals willing to define and alter the maladaptive patterns of the person designated patient" (p. 43). The counselor then bears the greater responsibility during the earliest stages of the process because the client must be brought to face the facts. The discussion thus far has centered on factors in the client that perpetuate blind spots which may work against the formation of a client-counselor alliance. The following factors can be utilized by a skilled counselor in order to overcome such obstacles.

Interpersonal Honesty

People need and respond best to benevolent honesty, but they are often unable to obtain this reaction from others. Clients have probably received feedback in the past that was honest but too harsh to accept or feedback that was benevolent but not sufficiently honest to be helpful.

The combination of honesty and kindness can be very powerful and extremely useful. Effective therapists introduce their clients to the kindness in the world. Moreover, honesty and kindness on the part of the therapist can give rise to honesty and courage on the part of the client. The ability to convey this honesty with a benevolence that reflects a basic acceptance of the individual and the wish to be helpful further increases the beneficial effects. The counselor need not personally like the client in order to communicate warmth and compassion. An impersonal honesty conjoined with an abstract compassion should suffice. Warmth, carefully chosen words, and an invitation to the client to accept or reject the validity of honestly offered reflections will help form the alliance and make deeper and more honest discussion possible.

Benevolent honesty is obviously and critically different from the "I'm hurting you for your own good" style of honesty that many people are used to receiving. The difference is to be found not in *what* is said but rather in the *way* it is said. If an adolescent's parents tell him that he won't amount to anything if he does not do well in school, they are offering the same message that the counselor presents to the client: that success in school is important in life. However, the counselor's message expresses concern for the client's personal and academic and vocational well-being and conveys an empathic understanding of how difficult it is for people to discipline themselves to complete tasks that may not be particularly interesting.

Understanding

Genuine understanding helps people feel less isolated, accept aid from others, and learn to accept more of themselves. People who make the effort to understand others are rare because the act of understanding has substantial risks associated with it. For example, people may not want to understand others because they would have to respond differently than they might prefer. In this case, understanding is commonly replaced by advice giving, lectures, a scolding, pep talks, impatience, moralizing, or rejection. The failure to understand others can take active forms such as these or passive forms such as ignoring the reality of the person's situation.

Many clients may find an accurate perception on the therapist's part quite unsettling because it invites them to listen to themselves as well as to the counselor. They are accustomed to ignoring or defending themselves from advice givers, lecturers, critics, and so on. When the counselor begins to relate to the client without providing these usual responses, clients may be unsure about how to take advantage of the opportunity. While they may begin to recount their problems either girded for battle or silenced by fear, understanding responses cause them to gradually relax and collaboratively explore important issues and problems.

Intrapersonal Honesty

Counseling offers clients the opportunity to be honest with themselves. People often need to face their innermost thoughts, feelings, and experiences. While anxiety may have caused the person to repress these thoughts and feelings, their adverse effects often persist. When people become more honest with themselves, they often feel an increased sense of relief and personal integrity. This form of honesty improves the person's ability to develop useful insights, to deal more effectively with reality, and to recognize internal conflicts.

Intrapersonal honesty develops through contact with others. Jourard (1968) noted that the ability to share information with significant others benefitted people not only because they told someone else about their struggles but also because they were simultaneously communicating with themselves. The ability to share aspects of ourselves with others helps us become more honest with ourselves. Interpersonal and intrapersonal honesty are highly interrelated, and improvements in one benefit the other. People need to appropriately share the positive and negative thoughts and feelings that have remained unexpressed. As people develop inner strength through intrapersonal honesty, honesty in general becomes a part of their daily repertoire of responses. What clients are able to share with their counselors improves what they will be able to share with others as well as with themselves.

Risk Taking

Counseling offers a setting in which people can take risks, but where the potential for damaging consequences is greatly reduced. In counseling, people can overshoot or undershoot their responses, and the only price they pay is the honest reaction of the counselor couched in terms of the counselor's continuing positive regard. When clients eventually realize and trust the freedom that they have to experiment and take risks, growth becomes greatly accelerated. They learn that they can practice honest responses in counseling and increase their confidence to try their new behaviors outside of counseling.

Counselors can help clients take risks by realistically exploring potential outcomes and by encouraging the client to break down the risk-taking behavior into accomplishable steps. The counselor also can help the client identify emotional supports within his or her environment.

New Responses

Clients have probably received the same advice, admonitions, and emotional responses over and over again. The following sample responses likely have been heard scores of times and now have little or no effect:

- You need to get your mind off yourself. Maybe you should do some volunteer work with people who have some *real* problems.

- You're too sensitive and take things too personally. You should learn to laugh more at life and not take yourself so seriously.

- I know you are grieving about your loved one's death. But he is suffering no longer. I'm sure he is happier than we are, and you will see him soon.

- You should get your priorities straightened out because you're starting to lose touch with what's really important in life.

While each of these directives may be absolutely true they are not generally helpful because (1) they do not touch the underlying causes of the person's problematic behavior; (2) the messages lack empathy, warmth, strength, and hope, all of which are necessary to motivate people to change their behavior; and (3) when people repeatedly hear the same directives, they eventually tune them out. New responses ultimately emerge from the counseling relationship not because they are mandated but because empathic understanding, honesty, and support create an environment where they can take form and be acted upon.

While most new responses are valuable, some are significantly more important than others. The following discussion of psychological freedoms is one such example. When clients develop psychological freedom they are simultaneously opening the door to a greater array of responses and possibilities.

✥

Increasing Psychological Freedoms

Ultimately counseling offers people opportunities to explore and possibly increase their psychological freedoms. While the concept of psychological freedom stems from an existential perspective, it is useful in many different theoretical approaches. Many people who enter counseling lack psychological freedom. Some probably did not possess a great deal of freedom to begin with, while others may have had freedom at one time, but levels of freedom decreased as their problems increased.

Counseling can help people discover the specific freedoms that they lack and work to increase them. The counseling process first does so by reinforcing the assumption that individuals can control the amount of psychological freedom they have. This is an important insight because of the common tendency to view oppression as imposed by others. People who enter counseling often lack one or more of the following four basic psychological freedoms to one degree or another.

Freedom to Acknowledge Imperfection

To be human is to be imperfect. Each of us is composed of a wide range of qualities and characteristics. Our judgments about these qualities or characteristics classify them in categories that might include strengths, gifts, weaknesses, faults, and mistakes. A well-rounded and complete understanding of self is predicated on the ability to accept that which is deemed positive as well as negative. Pacht (1984) maintained that the pursuit of perfection is associated with a number of different psychological problems. People need to be able to admit that they were wrong, made a mistake, didn't know the answer, are responsible, or are sorry. Doing so offers many advantages:

1. If people do not have to hide their imperfections they have fewer barriers to intimacy and greater access to the other people in their lives.

2. They do not have to be on guard; less vigilance provides more energy for enjoying life and for creative pursuits.

3. People who acknowledge their imperfections experience empathy with greater ease and in more mutually fulfilling ways.

Ultimately the path to growth and change involves grappling with imperfection. As people grow in their acceptance of all of their qualities, they are freer to acknowledge themselves and to pursue life.

Freedom to Assume Responsibility for One's Behavior

Assuming responsibility is a basic prerequisite for understanding and enacting change. People must assume sufficient responsibility for their behavior and accept the consequences of their acts before they can improve the conditions that trouble them. Counseling can demonstrate to these people that they are responsible for all their behavior and help them recognize that the advantages of assuming responsibility far outweigh the superficial disadvantages. By assuming responsibility, clients stop blaming others and move away from symptoms of passiveness such as perennially waiting for something good to happen, waiting to be rescued, or experiencing a pervasive sense of helplessnes.

Freedom to Disappoint Others

Our lives are filled with our own expectations and the expectations that others have of us. When harmony exists between our expectations of ourselves and those of others, people tend to feel balanced and accepted. When discrepancies arise in these expectations, internal and interpersonal conflict arises. Stan, the college student introduced in the beginning of this chapter, offers a clear example of how difficult it is to make choices that run contrary to the expectations of others, and how difficult it is *not* to make these choices. He feels damned if he moves in one direction and damned if he moves in the other. His example also illustrates how important it is for people to be able to grant this freedom to themselves.

People who enter counseling often have problems that were caused by their inability to disappoint someone. Usually they find it easier to disappoint casual acquaintances than to disappoint loved ones. Counseling can help these individuals recognize this conflict, it can give them an opportunity to reassess what they want to do, and it can help them explore the consequences of their behavior. Ultimately, if what is expected of them runs contrary to their needs, counseling can help them develop the courage and strength to make appropriate choices, even if their decisions are disappointing to important people in their lives.

Freedom to Allow Contrary Feelings to Exist Simultaneously

Ambivalence of affect, or having "mixed feelings" about an issue, is a normal aspect of human existence that can either produce change or paralyze a person. For example, a man who "worships" his children is incapable of being a good father. Because he cannot entertain critical thoughts and feelings toward his children, he is unable to challenge, discipline, or present difficult reality to them or to allow them to fail. If he had a more realistic attitude that embraced both negative and positive aspects, he could become a more effective father.

When contrary feelings are allowed to coexist, tension surfaces. If the amount of tension is greater than can be tolerated by the person, repression of one of the contrary feelings will result. Since the repression is unconscious, the person recognizes only that the tension has been replaced by a lessening of emotional stress. Thus, many people who enter counseling say they either love their spouses or hate them, are proud of their friends or jealous, have faith in God or do not believe in God, or define themselves as either brave or frightened. The truth is that feelings are almost never unequivocal. The conscious anxiety people rid themselves of by repressing one of the contrary feelings only returns to haunt them in some other way. For example, a woman who "adores" her husband cannot understand why she is sexually uninterested, or the man who firmly believes in God cannot understand why he is terrified of death. If both these people could get in touch with their ambivalent and equivocal feelings, this would be an important step toward solving the problem.

When people learn to feel free to experience contrary feelings they can become conscious of the tension and anxiety associated with ambivalence. Feeling tension is useful as a motivational force to promote growth. Allowing contradictory feelings to coexist benefits clients in at least one additional way. Clients gain a more global, less rigid, understanding of themselves—one that allows them to realize that their feelings about people and themselves are dynamic; that is, they change over time. Accepting and accommodating this affective ebb and flow helps people better adapt to life's challenges.

Each of these four freedoms was discussed individually but they should not be seen as discrete or unrelated. They interact with each other. Effective counseling helps clients achieve a significant level of freedom in all four of these areas. The combined effect produces the most impressive and the most lasting results. Finally, it would be useful to reconsider Stan's difficulties in light of each of the freedoms. If he were to gain these freedoms, his confusion about a career would lessen. His ability to deal with the important people in his life would increase and he would be freer to talk to them about a much wider range of topics. He would have a more realistic view of himself and the choices that exist for him in the world. And he would experience far less stress and discomfort. His symptoms of anxiety, confusion, tension, and worry could all be interpreted as indicators that sufficient psychological freedom is not present in his life.

Summary

There are many sound reasons for interacting with clients in a way that does not replicate existing relationships in their lives. To achieve this goal of creating an environment that helps people to explore alternatives and to behave in new, more adaptive ways, counselors may find it helpful to ask themselves questions such as the following:

- If someone said to me what I am saying to this person, would I find it helpful or would I whisper to myself, "What else is new?"
- How many times has this person heard what I am saying to her and felt what I am conveying?
- Am I reacting much as anyone else would to this person, or am I responding like an effective counselor?

For people whose behavior is in the normal range, counseling can offer a new environment that removes the roadblocks to improved functioning. Counseling also can help people whose problems stem from psychological disturbances to unlearn maladaptive ways of thinking, feeling, and responding and to replace them with adaptive ones.

❧

Reflection Questions

1. The text states that most psychological problems emanate from within, and the environment is merely the arena in which battles are waged. How can this position be reconciled with that of many family counselors, who hold that problems in family members are caused not so much by inner dynamics as by the interaction of family members?

2. Both counselors and clients can be affected by psychological imperatives. Do you possess any imperatives that could adversely impact your work as a counselor?

3. The text suggests that in almost all human problems there is "contributing negligence," whereby the people involved are both perpetrators and victims. How could this concept be applied to a problem that arose between a counselor and client during the engagement stage of the counseling relationship?

4. Banal comments like "You're too sensitive" or "Don't be so serious" are common but usually unhelpful messages to people. They surface in conversation with others when painful or difficult topics are discussed, offered with the hope that they might actually be helpful. What banal comments would you be likely to make to someone who is struggling with a problem? Discuss why this comment would not be helpful by putting yourself in the recipient's place.

5. Regarding psychological freedom, how free are you to admit the mistakes you make as a counselor to yourself and to the client? How free are you to disappoint clients by not living up to their expectations?

5

THE PERSON OF THE COUNSELOR

When counselors and counselor educators discuss the factors that contribute to counseling effectiveness, a common argument surfaces. Proponents of the school of thought that emphasizes the counseling *relationship* as the healing force maintain that the counselor's ability to establish and sustain a close professional relationship is what really counts. They stress the importance of the counselor's personal qualities and downplay educational, theoretical, and clinical technique issues. For example, Perez (1979) states:

> What these research findings show is that experience, theoretical orientation, and technique utilized are not the critical determinants for effectiveness as a therapist. The implication is strong in these studies that it is the counselor's personal qualities, not his [sic] education and training, which are a more promising criteria [sic] for evaluation of his effectiveness. (p. 80)

While no one would argue for an exclusively educational, academic, and theoretical emphasis that ignored the counselor's personal qualities, a more moderate position that suggests that the counselor's personal qualities and theoretical, clinical, and academic preparation are equally important seems to make the most sense. As Corey (1977) writes, "My main point is that I think it is misleading to dupe student counselors into the idea that counseling is a science that is separate and distinct from the behavior and personality of the counselor" (p. 197). We subscribe to this position and suggest that personal qualities and theoretical/clinical issues are actually tightly interconnected. When counselors choose particular counseling theories they are acting in response to personal qualities, and when they offer counseling they are interpreting the counseling theory which they have adopted through their experience. In essence, a discussion that sets personal qualities against academic or theoretical issues is promoting a false dichotomy. Effective counseling cannot take place where one or the other is minimized, because the extent to which they influence one another is profound.

Lauver and Harvey (1997) suggest that counseling competence grows from the integration of three elements: the person, counseling knowledge, and counseling skills. They also offer a list of personal traits, including attitudes, beliefs, needs, abilities, and expectations, that counselors necessarily confront as they become counselors. In other words, the counselor's personality, the counselor's knowledge of behavior dynamics, and the counselor's therapeutic skills collectively influence the counseling relationship. This suggests two important points.

First, a helpful personality cannot compensate for inadequate knowledge of behavior and/or poor therapeutic skills. Human behavior is very complex, and while there is still a great deal to be learned, certain patterns have been documented and the therapist should be aware of them. Helpful personal qualities, knowledge of behavior, and counseling skills cannot be substituted for one another.

Second, counselors need to simultaneously enhance personal qualities and improve their knowledge of behavior and counseling skills. Some educational settings, if they are properly designed (e.g., those that emphasize both theoretical and experiential components), can improve personal qualities, academic knowledge, and clinical skills at the same time. These settings also can help counselors properly integrate these areas. There are situations where training may focus exclusively on theoretical or clinical issues, whereas therapy, group work, or consultation situations might focus exclusively on personal characteristics. Ultimately, what counselors learn about themselves needs to be integrated into their practical approach to counseling alongside what they learn about the theory and practice of counseling.

Advanced education and training are more likely to influence growth quantitatively than qualitatively if they are presented in a style that ignores the need for experiential activities within the educational process. For example, a series of lectures and readings can help counselors learn a good deal about the phenomenon of resistance in counseling, but academic knowledge cannot give people the patience or other personal strengths necessary to handle resistance. Firsthand, experiential activities are needed to supplement purely academic efforts and to enhance growth.

While clinical/theoretical issues will be covered in later chapters, this chapter discusses 12 personal qualities of an effective counselor. These qualities are not to be considered ideals, but necessary requirements for a basic level of effective functioning as a counselor. As counselors grow in these areas they can expect to reap personal benefits in their own lives as well as to become more helpful to their clients. While this chapter discusses only 12 qualities needed in counselors, counseling researchers have identified many additional personal characteristics that are relevant to effective counseling (see Brammer, 1979, pp. 27–43; Pietrofesa, Hoffman, Splete, & Pinto, 1978, pp. 117–205).

☆

Counselor Qualities

The discussion of each quality provides concrete descriptions of how the quality is manifested, cites specific reasons why the quality is important in counseling, and discusses potential obstacles that can interfere with the fullest development or expression of the quality.

Self-Knowledge

The self-knowledge required of counselors involves knowing themselves well enough to have a clear sense of what they are doing, why they are doing it, and to discern which problems are theirs and which belong to the client. Counselors with a sufficient degree of self-knowledge share certain traits.

1. They are well aware of their needs. As counselors, they recognize that they must be especially aware of their need to achieve, to feel important, to feel needed, to be superior, or to be in control. While none of these needs is inherently damaging, the more they mingle and compete with the professional imperative to be of benefit to the client, the less effective counselors will be.

2. Such counselors are well aware of their feelings. Feelings of hurt, fear, anger, guilt, or love will be part of every counselor's experience. None of these feelings is problematic in itself and can, in fact, contribute much to the counseling relationship. Problems arise, however, when counselors are not exactly aware of which feeling is operating at the moment. For example, counselors may be aware of their anger toward the client but may be unaware that the anger stems from a feeling of hurt. Similarly, problems arise when counselors are unaware of how their feelings cause them to react in decisions regarding counseling. For example, a counselor may be aware of sexual feelings toward the client but may see no connection between that feeling and deciding that this client should attend counseling more frequently. Problems also can arise when counselors become uncomfortable with the client's range of expressed emotions. The counselor should not obstruct a client's ability to express his or her full range of feelings.

3. Counselors with self-knowledge are aware of what makes them anxious in counseling and what defenses they are inclined to use to re-

duce the anxiety. Questions regarding or attacks on their knowledge, so-phistication, maturity, reasonableness, sexuality, strength, good inten-tions, and so forth, may well cause anxiety. Self-knowing counselors are aware of the defenses they would be inclined to use to ward off the anxi-ety: becoming passive and dormant in the hope that the client will feel ashamed and stop the assault; imperceptibly changing the subject; be-coming suddenly nondirective and reflective; making the client feel threatened; or using examples or analogies to deflect the perceived attack.

4. They recognize their strengths and weaknesses. A counselor whose strengths include a genuine affection for people can bring this af-fection into play when a session is filled with confusion and despair, thus providing the client a source of support. Counselors whose range of skills includes a natural affection will know when to make use of it. Effective counselors know their limitations as well. For example, counselors who know that they tend to blame others when things are not going well can use this knowledge to slow down their reflexive impulse to blame long enough to allow other options to present themselves. These counselors re-alize that because they are always growing, they will always have to ad-dress their own weaknesses. Conscientious counselors thus reassess their strengths and weaknesses on an ongoing basis.

Self-knowledge on the part of counselors is important for several reasons. First, counselors who have an accurate perception of themselves will be more likely to form accurate perceptions of the people who come to them. Blind spots in self-perception can cause blind spots in the coun-selor's whole perceptual field. For example, if some counselors do not re-alize that they enjoy discussing marital difficulties more than any other topic, they may unconsciously steer clients toward such discussions. This can lead to an unproductive cycle wherein the counselor concludes that if clients need to speak so much about their marital difficulties, then marital conflict must be the basis of their problems. A counselor possessed of self-awareness would not make such a mistake.

Second, the skills counselors employ to know themselves are the same ones used to know others. Consequently, the more self-knowledge counse-lors have, the better their chance to know others. For example, counselors who can see through their own attempts at self-deception are in a better po-sition to see through the ruses of the people they see in counseling.

Third, counselors who have acquired the skills necessary for self-knowledge are in a good position to teach them to others. For example, counselors who have developed the ability to see beneath their conscious motivations can teach these skills to the client.

Finally, self-knowledge permits counselors to feel and communicate genuine compassion to the client. When counselors are aware of and feel their weaknesses and strengths, they are in a much better position to re-late to the client empathically; they are in touch with how it is to feel ashamed, stupid, frightened, hypocritical, weak, jealous, irrational, or guilty. When counselors come to know and accept negative as well as positive attributes of themselves, they censor less and less of themselves and their clients.

One of the main obstacles to continuing self-knowledge is that counselors use the same defenses as everyone else to protect themselves from a painful awareness of their shortcomings—both personal and professional. They tend to congratulate themselves when things are going well in counseling and to blame any lack of progress on the resistance or poor motivation of the client. Either of these tendencies should raise a red flag. Counselors need to understand how deeply their personal needs are tied to others and how they use blaming to shield themselves from acknowledging any personal weaknesses.

Wholeheartedness

Wholehearted counselors add enthusiasm and adventurousness to the quality of self-knowledge and, therefore, devote themselves to improving their skills and understanding in every possible way. They thus share certain characteristics.

1. They continually increase their knowledge of behavior and counseling by reading relevant professional periodicals and books, attending conferences, and discussing their cases with colleagues. To these stores of public knowledge they add a private wisdom that stems from their personal experiences in life and counseling.

2. Such counselors seek new life experiences that will help them hone existing competencies and develop new skills. They do this by accepting risks, responsibilities, and challenges that cause them a certain amount of anxiety. They then use this anxiety to access previously untapped potential.

3. In order to increase their competence, wholehearted counselors try new ideas and approaches in counseling. The pursuit of greater expertise involves exploring and implementing new competencies. New theories and approaches are considered and old ones reconsidered with a new and deeper understanding. They are always looking for one more way to be more helpful to the next person they see in counseling.

4. Wholehearted counselors evaluate their effectiveness by scrutinizing each session with an eye to how it could have been more productive and by inviting ongoing, final, and follow-up evaluations from clients.

Wholeheartedness is important in a counselor because people enter counseling in order to bring *life* back into their lives. Halfheartedness on the part of the counselor will not help the client discover his or her maximum human potential. Clients are wholeheartedly concerned about improving their lives. They just don't know how to accomplish this goal.

One of the main differences between a friendship and a counseling relationship is that friendships may be casual, but counseling relationships are intense. Wholeheartedness is often precluded in conventional, hierarchical relations. Conventionality seldom allows a genuine wholeheartedness to manifest itself. Good counselors try to be models of wholeheartedness.

Such wholeheartedness also generates confidence in the client. Confidence is what gives the person the momentum to take risks in counseling that are necessary for personal growth. Clients make intuitive judgments about their counselor's competencies. For example, a person may tell a friend, "My counselor seems to be brilliant, but he is difficult to relate with" or "My counselor is a very caring person, but she doesn't seem to know what to do with me." It takes only a few sessions for a client to develop abiding confidence in a counselor or a nagging doubt that clouds each session.

A wholehearted dedication on the part of the counselor is also important for the efficient use of time in counseling. The more dedicated the counselor, the more likely he or she is to formulate specific goals and concrete methods. The counselor and client will share an ongoing sense of direction that enables them to evaluate progress and make appropriate changes to ensure continuing growth. The less wholehearted the counselor, the more time is spent on "fishing expeditions," unproductive discussions, and hit-or-miss stratagems.

Wholeheartedness may sometimes be countered by certain obstacles; chief among these is complacency. Any counselor who thinks that he or she should just stay put and not venture further is in danger of succumbing to stagnation. A stagnant counselor can only model stagnation to the client. Such a counselor is less able to stay abreast of the continuously changing conditions which every counselor must face.

Good Psychological Health

It is not reasonable to require that counselors be endowed with perfect psychological health, but they should be possessed of sound psychological health. The counselor should possess the qualities the client would like to develop. Psychologically healthy counselors share four traits.

1. They get their needs for security, love, nurturance, power, sex, and affirmation met outside of the counseling relationship. As a result, the need to be helpful in the altruistic sense can remain foremost in the counseling relationship.

2. Sane, healthy counselors keep their past and current personal problems out of counseling. They do not approach each session weighted with the unfinished business of their lives, such as unresolved childhood fantasies of heroism, romance, and sex; or conflicts regarding members of the same sex, opposite sex, or authority figures; or biases against certain socially disapproved behaviors, values, or personality types. They also do not allow their current personal problems to interfere with their work.

Counselors can learn to focus on a client with the same intensity and free-dom from distraction that a biologist enjoys while peering through his or her microscope. Counselors cannot afford to have many days in which their personal concerns impair their concentration or create the attitude: "You think you've got problems!"

3. Psychologically healthy counselors are aware of personal biases and weak spots, and this awareness helps them recognize situations that might activate these problem areas. They can separate what *they* would like for the client from what the *client* would like and avoid projecting their needs onto the client.

4. They are not only surviving in life but living it to the fullest. Their lives outside of counseling are stimulating and enjoyable. They read, write, travel, play, and enjoy the company of diverse friends and the pri-vacy of being alone. Because they maintain a balance in their lives, psy-chologically healthy counselors possess a strength they can share with others. They do not find counseling burdensome because they bring to it a buoyancy created by the richness of their personal lives.

Good psychological health is important in a counselor because per-sonal psychological health gives underlying support to the counselor's understanding of behavior and skills. Neither understanding nor knowl-edge is possible without sound psychological health. If not grounded in health, they can become forces that lead to confusion and damage.

Counselors are models of behavior whether or not they choose to be. Every counseling session has the potential to become a period of in-tense tutoring in adaptive behavior. When counselors lack psychological health, their frame of reference will be defective, causing the client even more anxiety. When this occurs, the counselor has become part of the problem rather than part of the solution.

The better a counselor's psychological health, the more helpful the counseling relationship is likely to be. Counselors in poor psychological health can become contaminated by their own needs, idiosyncratic per-ceptions, and distorted values, creating conflict, confusion, and iatrogenic (doctor-induced) symptoms.

One of the main obstacles to functioning in a psychologically healthy way is that counselors may allow the fears and dissatisfactions of their personal lives to create a pseudocommunity consisting wholly of counseling and clients. In this restricted community they may feel a sense of security, importance, and satisfaction. A vicious cycle begins: the more their needs are met in this pseudocommunity, the less they feel their need for family, friends, and avocations. And the less they fulfill their needs in other ways, the more they psychologically feed off the people they are supposed to be helping.

When counselors lack adequate psychological health to help a client, one of two things will usually occur. Either the client will possess enough psychological strength to sense the problem and therefore terminate counseling, or the client and the counselor will enter into a relationship based on neurotic collusion in which the problems of one feed on the problems of the other. This allows both parties to maintain their problems while sharing the illusion that progress is being made.

Trustworthiness

The quality of trustworthiness means that the counselor's behavior is "dependable, predictable, and consistent" (Lauver & Harvey, 1997, p. 57). Clients often evaluate the counselor to determine levels of trust by assessing nonverbal as well as verbal behavior. Counselors who inspire trust share any number of characteristics. Four are singled out here.

1. Counselors who inspire trust are reliable and consistent. They arrive on time for appointments and finish on time. They keep their promises and live by their agreements. They do not disappoint clients. While they have their good days and bad days, they do not appear to the client as temperamental or moody. They are not happy one time and depressed another; they do not exert maximum energy at one session and coast through the next; they are not wildly confrontational at one visit and placidly agreeable at the next. They do not make haphazard shifts in orientation or procedure from one stage of counseling to another. Their clients know what to expect from them before the session begins and are not forced to make adjustments to deal with unpredictable behavior.

2. They verbally and nonverbally assure the person that client confidentiality will be honored appropriately. They reassure their clients by letting them know that no client is ever spoken of to anyone without some compelling cause. Good counselors don't speak to their clients of other clients. They assure the client that all phone conversations, correspondence, and reports dealing with that client will be openly discussed and shared in a future session, and they make good on this promise. The parameters enjoined by professionalism are made as clear as possible to the client.

3. Counselors inspire trust when they listen nonjudgmentally and accept revelations with understanding and kindness. Such counselors never make a person regret having made a revelation. The counselor who is momentarily confused by a client disclosure makes sure that the client understands that the confusion is not disapproval. The counselor may bring up the revelation later, but only in such a way that the person does not feel haunted by it.

4. Trustworthy counselors are predictable, responsible, and professional. They are able to respond to the client totally so he or she feels confident that the counselor will miss little, if anything, of importance. They convey an awareness of who the client is by remembering pertinent information; this is effected by keeping records. They respond by answering

phone calls, by respecting appointments or suggestions, and by filling out any forms before the deadline. Furthermore, such counselors respond by seeking consultations when necessary, making intelligent referrals, and terminating counseling at the appropriate time.

Trustworthiness in a counselor is indispensable for numerous reasons. For one thing, a primary goal of counseling is to encourage people to reveal their innermost selves. If this goal is to be realized, the client must be made to feel that the counselor will understand and accept revelations without shock or disapproval. If the person does not feel this sense of trust, revelations will be superficial or nonexistent, thus frustrating the purpose of most counseling.

Clients need to trust the counselor's motivations and character. They need to believe that the counselor's main motive is to help them and that no motives on the counselor's part will override this. They should not be distracted by wondering whether they are being used as an experimental subject, surrogate need gratifier, or possibly just as a source of revenue.

Finally, when clients experience the counselor's acceptance and professionalism it helps them develop a deeper sense of trust in themselves. As they better understand their needs, feelings, strengths, and so forth, they can accept them more fully. When this point is reached, clients no longer fear, but can recognize and control, their behavior. Once people can trust themselves, they are capable of trusting others and mutual trust is the first step in establishing meaningful and satisfying relationships.

One of the main obstacles to counselor trustworthiness is a possible distraction with other matters. Such distractions can cause counselors to be careless: they may forget relevant material, lose track of time, or be unable to concentrate because they are preoccupied. Counselors who are busy people with hectic schedules and many commitments must be especially careful that these pressures do not interfere with their trustworthiness.

Honesty

Counselors exhibit honesty when they are transparent, authentic, and genuine. When counselors are authentic and genuine their clients are free to pursue the same traits (Boy and Pine, 1982). Authentic behavior is effected through honest interaction. Counselors who strive to be honest in their interaction with clients share the following four traits.

1. They are congruent; that is, their real self (who they are) is identical to their public self (who they allow others to think they are). They realize that honesty with clients means much more than simply refraining from lying to them. Because their behavior is informed by congruence, it reflects the attitude: "Who you see is who I am."

2. They realize their honesty may create anxiety in the person toward whom it is directed, and they are prepared to deal with this. They

do their best not to arouse gratuitous anxiety but realize that the client may be unaccustomed to uncompromising honesty. They also realize that the client may attempt to reduce the anxiety by denying the validity of the message, by attacking or withdrawing from the counselor, or by becoming emotionally upset. However, honest counselors do not allow predictable manifestations of anxiety to deter them from conveying information that ultimately could be helpful. They are able to place the client's anxiety in a proper perspective.

3. Counselors attuned to honesty have a clear and reasonable understanding of what honesty means. They realize they cannot share everything they think and feel during a counseling session. They know they must be selective as to what they express and yet not lose sight of sincerity. They operate according to four principles: (1) any significant emotional reaction involving the client will be surfaced within the same session that it occurs, thus allowing the reaction to remain fresh rather than become intellectualized, forgotten, or submerged so as to haunt or sabotage future sessions; (2) counselors may be distracted to a significant degree by something outside of the session, and when this is the case, this distraction will be explained to clients so they will not think they caused the counselor's confusion; (3) effective counselors reply to personal questions either by answering them outright or directly declining to answer them and then dealing with the implication for counseling; and (4) the counselor's honest need to ask a question must sometimes be denied immediate gratification lest it prove an unnecessary intrusion into the flow of counseling at that point. In other words, honest counselors give the client the same degree of honesty they would appreciate receiving.

4. When it is necessary to express a negative reaction to a client's behavior, they do so in an appropriate way. The following case history may illustrate this point.

A client who persistently alienated people by interrupting them behaved in essentially the same way with the counselor. After a couple of sessions it became clear to the counselor that the client needed to learn how off-putting this was. The counselor then said that she had something important to talk about but had reservations about being able to do so. When the client asked what the reservations might be, the counselor responded by stating that what she had to say might be hard for the client to hear and the client might try to interrupt the counselor as the information was shared. The client then became very quiet and alert. The counselor then went on to say that once she finished what she had to say, there would be time to discuss the client's reaction to the communication and time for looking at the issue. The client remained uncharacteristically silent during this disclosure as well. The counselor went on to say, "When you interrupt me when I am sharing something with you I feel frustrated and sometimes want to not finish what I wanted to say to you." She ended the disclosure by noting that in this particular situation the client had listened to her without interruption and that she felt very differently at the present moment as a result. The client asked the counselor if this could be a reason why people sometimes walked away from her when she was talking to them. The counselor suggested that while she never felt like walking away, it would not surprise her if others did. The dialogue continued productively from that point on. Timing, carefully worded responses, and honesty converge to help clients become aware of the effects of their behavior.

An honesty of this sort is important in counseling for several reasons. First, the transparency mentioned above allows the counselor and the client to get as close to each other as needed. Counselors who protect or hide parts of themselves from the client create a buffer zone that hinders intimacy. Psychological intimacy is important in counseling because it enables both the counselor and the person to relate directly and openly.

Honesty also permits the counselor to give constructive feedback to the client. Most people receive very little accurate personal feedback from others: much feedback is dishonest and distorted because it is tinted by the overly positive or negative attitudes of the person giving it. Counselors' interactions with their clients are informed by an honesty born of study, training, and commitment.

Also, honesty in a counselor is a genuine invitation for the person to be honest in return. It is one thing for counselors to verbally invite a client to be honest; it is another for counselors to initiate a client into honesty by being honest about themselves and their relationship with the client. A well-known and highly regarded counselor admitted openly to his client that he was baffled by the client's persistent symptoms. The client thereupon volunteered that he had stopped taking the prescribed anti-depressant medication without telling anyone. He eventually shared the source of his resistance and agreeably returned to the medication regimen. The counselor's honest report of his confusion inspired the client's (very pertinent) revelations.

The counselor may serve as a model of how to be honest in constructive ways. Clients may lack experience and encounter difficulty when they attempt to be honest. Counselors can model the ways in which one can be truly honest without unduly hurting other people. When clients witness the constructive expression of honesty and experience its beneficial effects, they will be more likely to be honest with themselves and the people in their lives.

If one main obstacle to absolute honesty in counseling were to be singled out, it would be the need to be liked and/or to remain as stress-free as possible. In cases where frankness would produce a predictably hostile resistance, counselors not dedicated to the principle of honesty might shy away from a confrontation regardless of the needs of their clients.

Strength

It is important that counselors have the courage to do what their deepest selves say is the helpful and just thing to do in counseling. The strength they need to accomplish this task stands at the midpoint between intimidation and weakness. Its paradoxical nature is difficult to master, and thus strength is often developed through experience. Strong counselors share the following traits.

1. They set reasonable and appropriate limits. Proper limits in counseling are important because they help define the nature of the counseling relationship, encourage the best use of time and energy, and clarify both parties' responsibilities. Counselors must set limits with regard to the length and number of sessions, accessibility to the client between sessions, the extent to which a counselor is willing to intervene in the person's life outside of counseling, and the professional charges and payment arrangements. Counselors set clear and reasonable limits and adhere to them despite pressure to make exceptions.

2. Strong counselors are able to say things that might be difficult for the client to hear and make decisions that might be difficult for the client to accept. There are times when a counselor must say things that will evoke hurt and anger in the person, no matter how kindly they are said. At other times, counselors must make decisions that will upset the person—for example, to increase or decrease the number of sessions, to refuse to intercede for the person outside of counseling, or to discontinue a counseling relationship. Although such steps may be difficult, effective counselors act according to their best judgment because their need to be helpful is stronger than their need to be liked.

3. Counselors who are strong are flexible. Their strength allows them to approach the counseling process and the client with an openness that invites new ideas, procedures, and challenges. They are willing to listen to and seriously consider the ideas and suggestions of the client. They are able to try new approaches to facilitate the counseling process and to redefine the limits of counseling in the face of new developments. They can tailor their philosophy of counseling to keep up with their professional and personal growth and to react appropriately to changes in the client.

4. They are able to remain separate from the client's situation. Their self-identity is clear enough to allow them to become involved in the client and the counseling process while remaining distinct enough to be of help. They empathize, but do not overidentify with the client. When the counselor overidentifies with the client, there is no longer a counselor in the room, but rather two people lost in the same subjectivity. Effective counselors are involved in the process of counseling, but not immersed in it. Their separateness allows them to resist being swept along by whatever turmoil of emotions is operative at the time. Strength in a counselor is important

because it allows the client to feel safe. The person can thus see the counselor as one who is able to remain steadfast in the face of all circumstances.

Counselors must have strength in order to withstand psychological assaults and manipulations on the part of the client. The "weaknesses" that a person brings into counseling can be very formidable. At times the client may try to verbally, physically, or emotionally overpower the counselor. At other times, the client may try to seduce the counselor with pseudocooperation, compliments, or effusions of gratitude. Counselors must be able to withstand all types of manipulation; they must be willing to accept manipulative attempts as an important part of the client's personality; and they must be able to use what they know about why people behave in these ways to help the client make desirable changes.

Strength also removes the counselor as a source of distraction to the client. When counselors are emotionally or psychologically weak, their clients may find themselves worrying as much or more about the counselor as they do about themselves. This may occur when a counselor lacks the strength to keep himself or herself separate from the client, to refrain from injecting personal needs into the relationship, or to allow the person to leave counseling, all of which are violations of professional codes of practice and ethics.

Finally, strength is important because it can induce strength in others. People often enter counseling because they lack the strength to be assertive, or to resist the manipulations of others, or to enter into intimate relationships without losing their selfhood. The counselor's strengths may in such cases be gradually shared with and modeled to the client, who can then grow in self-protection, self-sufficiency, and self-sharing.

One of the main obstacles to a counselor's being strong is the need to be an agreeable person—one who does not create anxiety in another. Effective counselors possess a "kind strength." Kindness without strength nurtures weakness; strength without kindness breeds resentment. A judicious combination of the two is conducive to and necessary for the client's growth.

Warmth

Warmth involves being kind, caring, and compassionate. Warmth is communicated largely through nonverbal means—through tone of voice, expression of eyes, posture, and gestures. Counselors who are able to convey warmth have certain traits in common.

1. They receive adequate warmth in their personal lives and are therefore able to share warmth with others. Counselors who are treated warmly by others in their personal lives learn to value kindness, caring, and compassion. When counselors behave in a distant or businesslike way toward their clients, it often means that they lack adequate warmth in their own lives.

2. They distinguish between warmth and effusiveness. Warmth is appropriate, and thus eases defenses and nurtures potential. Effusiveness is inappropriate, heightens defenses, and suffocates potential. The warm counselor is caring and freeing; the effusive counselor is needy, gushy, and smothering.

3. Counselors who convey warmth are nonthreatening. They allow people to feel comfortable and reasonably relaxed in their presence. Their message is, "I will do nothing to make you feel less a person." They do not send messages that declare, "To be accepted by me, you will have to be intelligent . . . interesting . . . docile . . . tough . . . reasonable . . . mature . . . moral." They accept people where they are and work from that point.

4. They are attuned to their own humanity. Their calm acceptance of themselves, weaknesses as well as strengths, makes them comfortable to others. Their caring, kindness, and compassion are not academic tools with which to prod and seduce people into growth. These qualities have become a natural part of their being and have evolved from dealing with their own insecurities, frailties, mistakes, and shortcomings. Their attitude is, "Let's see how we two imperfect people can collaborate to get you where you want to be."

Warmth is important in counseling because it lowers defenses. People bring into counseling the same defenses that caused them problems before they entered counseling. In fact, they may intensify their defenses upon entering counseling in order to manage the new and unfamiliar stress that counseling can produce. While verbal support is usually not sufficient to lower the client's defenses enough for the counseling process to be helpful, the counselor's perceived warmth is one quality that enables people to reduce their defenses and thus relate to themselves and to the counselor in a realistic fashion.

Warmth encourages sharing on an emotional level. There is an important difference between imparting personal data to the counselor and sharing the emotion-laden deeper parts of oneself. The professional skill of the counselor may well elicit information from clients; but a true warmth invites clients to share their being. It is important that such an expression of feeling receive a warm reception. Warmth is essential to the therapeutic relationship if new behaviors are to result. Once actualized, these new patterns are not confined to the counseling environment, but rather can become part of the client's daily life.

When people receive warmth, it eventually allows them to behave warmly toward themselves. This is important because many clients have either lost or never possessed the ability to be kind, caring, and compassionate with themselves and others. As they gain or regain this ability, better relationships outside counseling become an option.

An intellectualized approach to life can post an obstacle to expressing and receiving warmth. Intellectualized counselors specialize in figuring people out rather than exploring feelings. These counselors sometimes misunderstand the meaning of the concept of "professional distance" and use it to keep an emotional distance between themselves and the client.

Active Responsiveness

In addition to warmth, strength, honesty, trustworthiness, psychological health, and self-knowledge, counselors should have an active responsiveness. Counselors must be *dynamically involved* in the process of counseling. Active responsiveness involves striking a balance between being hyperactive to the point of distraction and being passive to the point of somnolence. Counselors who are actively responsive share the following traits.

1. They relate *with* people and not merely *to* them. They exchange ideas, feelings, and confusion and don't simply reflect them. They realize that they can be actively responsive either verbally or nonverbally and that their responsivity should be a help and not a hindrance to the process. They perceive themselves as bearing an equal responsibility with the client.

2. They challenge clients to become more aware of their feelings, be more honest and assertive, take more risks, become more committed, admit their mistakes, be more careful in their interpretations, and to try new approaches to problems. They challenge clients by developing a vision of a more fulfilling life and instilling a sense of what's possible.

3. Actively responsive counselors react to their clients in ways that elicit meaningful responses. They are willing to evoke responses that range from tentative, intellectualized ones to forceful, emotionally charged confrontations. In either case, the counselor invites people to be who they are so that they can become who they want to be.

4. They are willing to share an equal responsibility with their clients. Actively responsive counselors are responsible *to* their clients; that is, they actively try to help them achieve their counseling goals. This is in contrast to being responsible *for* their client in the sense of bearing their entire weight. It also is in contrast to accepting too little responsibility for the progress of counseling.

Active responsiveness on the part of the counselor is important because it communicates personal caring. When a counselor is obviously alert, asks thoughtful questions, gives insightful feedback, reacts emotionally, and shares responsibility for the helping process, the client feels the counselor's genuine enthusiasm, caring, and liking. People may feel that an inordinately passive counselor is professionally, but not personally, concerned. Inordinate passivity can make the client feel shortchanged—especially when the person is putting a great deal of time, energy, and sacrifice into counseling. One common complaint heard about counselors is, "He just sat there and listened, nodded a few times, repeated what I said,

and told me when my time was up." While this could be a distortion related to resistance, the complaint seems to be so common that one is led to
believe there must be some truth in it.

Active responsivity also stimulates and encourages the person to react spontaneously to the counselor. This gives the counselor eyewitness
information as to how the person relates with others. A little "mixing it
up" with the client will often elicit fresh information that the counselor
would have no other way of attaining.

When counselors are actively responsive to clients, they engage in
situational teaching. By their responsiveness, they are saying, "Watch me
relate with you. Watch how I assert myself without demeaning you.
Watch how I express my feelings, articulate my confusion, and admit my
mistakes." By observing the counselor in action, clients receive guidelines
and permissions that will help them relate more effectively both within
and outside of counseling.

Finally, clients need new ideas. Most people are in counseling because they have tried to solve their own problems with little or no success.
Although solutions lie within the client, others' ideas and reactions help
clients unearth their own answers. While clients often need to understand
how to make better decisions, how to delve into themselves to discover
answers to their questions, how to learn from mistakes, how to evaluate
the effectiveness of their behavior, and how to predict the consequences
of their decisions, they are not helped by advice or being told what to do.
When counselors advise and direct they short-circuit the development of
important internal processes that are needed if clients are to be able to understand themselves and act in response to themselves.

One of the main obstacles to active responsivity is the counselor's
fear of getting involved, which means getting close, being vulnerable,
making mistakes, and assuming an appropriate responsibility for the
progress of counseling. A misguided notion of what professionalism
means can lead counselors to remain distant, aloof, and passive, when
such passive nonresponsiveness serves to shield the counselor from re-
buffs rather than to further the counseling process.

Patience

An active responsiveness is fully compatible with patience. Though
actively involved, patient counselors allow situations to develop naturally,
without prematurely injecting personal ideas, feelings, or values. The following traits are found in counselors who are patient.

1. They tolerate ambiguity. Because human behavior is so complex,
there is a good deal of ambiguity in counseling relationships. It is not uncommon for effective counselors to experience momentary confusion and
say to a client, "I am confused, can you help me understand what is happening now?" The counselor uses this question as an invitation to the cli-

ent to trudge through the ambiguity, searching for some clarity and meaning. Impatient counselors perceive ambiguity as a threat and an obstacle rather than as a challenge and an opportunity. They may lack the ability to explore ambiguous feelings and may grasp at straws in an effort to assign meaning to the ambiguity.

2. Counselors who are patient can stand back and allow clients to follow their own path, even when the path looks more assuring to the client than it does to the counselor. Effective counselors may feel they know a shortcut, but they also understand how important it is for the client to make a personal decision after discussing it with the counselor, follow through on the decision, and learn from the consequences. A client who uses the counselor's shortcuts quickly gets to where the counselor wants to be, but this only increases the distance from where the client wants to be. The point is not so much *where* the person goes, as *how* he or she gets there.

3. Counselors possessed of patience are not afraid to "waste" time in the interest of growth. They realize that the client needs rest periods, digressions, and some coasting. The client is actively engaged in a stressful activity. The impatient counselor is like a football coach who sits resting on the sidelines for the first half of the game, then exhorts his players to give 120% in the second half. Because the coach is not playing the game himself, he may lose sight of the fact that a person needs a breathing spell from time to time.

4. Patient counselors refrain from expressing insights and questions that would interrupt the flow of a session and instead bring them up later. Impatient counselors brim over with insights, questions, and hypotheses about what would help the person use time better and get down to business. While "tightening up" a session is sometimes necessary, patient counselors realize that messages implying "You're not doing this well—here, let me help you" are more inclined to impede than to accelerate progress.

Patience is important because it allows the client to develop and progress at a natural pace. Counselors cannot force or accelerate psychological growth any more than a tree can be made to grow faster by continually watering it and stretching its limbs. Forcing an issue may introduce fears or resentment that impede rather than expedite the progress of counseling.

Patience in a counselor connotes more interest in the person than in the results. This may sound like a fine distinction, but it's one that clients feel instinctively. As a person in group counseling told the counselor, "I think you are more interested in the finish line than in those of us who are running the race." Impatience in a counselor implies more interest in a successful termination than in a struggling client.

In an atmosphere free of inordinate pressure to perform and produce, people are able to freely plumb their depths and sort out their needs, dreams, feelings, abilities, and values. They can then use them to chart a life course along lines drawn by what they can become rather than what they are supposed to be. Any restlessness on the part of the counselor deflects clients from an inward focus on themselves to an outward focus on the counselor; clients may easily be overwhelmed by a counselor's flood of ideas, interpretations, and solutions. Impatient counselors are like tour guides who rush people along. They end up being seen by their clients as nuisances.

One of the greatest obstacles to patience in a counselor is a need to be successful. Those counselors possessed of such a need focus not on the client, but on themselves; the client is simply a means to an end. The message to the client is, "I don't care who you are. What can you do for my ego?" Accelerating the counseling process so that the counselor—not the client—will benefit constitutes a gross violation of the ethical and professional standards that govern counseling. Such a drive to be successful, however, is not always one-sided. Clients can also place inordinate pressure on counselors to produce rapid results. Remaining patient when the client wants to move more quickly than is possible can be burdensome for even highly experienced counselors. Experience, training, and the opportunity to consult with other therapists can help counselors develop and maintain patience.

Sensitivity

It is not enough that the counselor possess self-knowledge, psychological health, trustworthiness, honesty, strength, warmth, active responsiveness, and patience. An effective counselor needs a certain sensitivity as well. Sensitivity means counselors are aware of the subtle dynamics and vulnerabilities present both in the client and in themselves. Counselors who are sensitive share certain traits.

1. Sensitive counselors are conscious of their own reactions in counseling, reading them as reflexively, skillfully, and attentively as they read those of the client. Because of this inner sensitivity, they know immediately if they are becoming frightened, incited, bored, distracted, sexually aroused, or just confused.

2. Sensitive counselors know when *not* to intrude. They recognize the early warning signs of defensiveness. This is in contrast to counselors who fear to probe because they lack confidence in their investigatory capabilities or those who probe according to their own agenda regardless of the needs of the client.

3. Sensitive counselors ask questions and convey information likely to be seen as threatening by the client in ways that take the person's specific vulnerabilities into account. They recognize the difference between being brutally frank and realistically helpful. They use language that avoids unnecessary pain without diluting the honesty of the message.

4. Sensitive counselors are naturally aware of their own vulnerabilities. They realize that they, like all human beings, have soft spots. They

know exactly where these spots are located and recognize how they tend to protect them. This enables them to understand and accept the nature of their vulnerabilities and to thus tread lightly with others.

Sensitivity in a counselor is important because it communicates safety. When clients feel the counselor's sensitivity, they are free to spend less energy protecting themselves and more time in discovering who they are and who they wish to become. Clients take comfort in knowing that the counselor can sense their reactions well enough to ensure that the counseling will be done carefully and in a way that prevents unnecessary pain.

Sensitivity also connotes sensibleness. Clients who perceive the counselor's sensitivity are confident that he or she will not ask them to do things beyond their capability. Moreover, these clients are confident that the counselor's plans are individually tailored to them.

Many people who enter counseling are unaware of their real problems. While they present symptoms as problems, their problems are often buried beneath layers of defenses and pseudoproblems. The sensitive counselor is empathetic, able to understand the deeper parts of the client's being and better able to help the client bring these deeper issues to the surface. Without this level of sensitivity, counseling remains superficial and symptom-oriented. Lasting effects are often not possible, though some short-term relief often results.

As clients become aware of their counselors' sensitivity, they become more sensitive to themselves. They learn to ask themselves the right questions and to recognize the telltale signs of denying and distorting their deeper issues. As clients develop these abilities, they become more sensitive to others, more accurate in their perceptions of others, and ultimately more accepting of people.

The chief impediment to sensitivity is self-consciousness. It should be avoided at all costs. Counselors who focus on their own needs for success, who continually plan their next move, and who habitually protect themselves against threat cannot be attuned to the subtle emotional nuances emanating from the client. Fear also poses an obstacle to sensitivity. Counselors might fear undisclosed aspects of themselves which they may be unable to see in themselves but which they can observe and react to in particular clients. Counselors, for a variety of reasons, may have such strong reactions to clients who struggle with particular problems that they are unable to develop sufficient empathy or sensitivity to be helpful. Counselors have no choice but to refer such clients to counselors who can be sensitive and empathic.

Freeing

We have seen that counselors not possessed of sensitivity, warmth, and so on are unlikely to be effective, but the greatest challenge of all to a counselor is to be freeing. Freeing counselors are able to exercise a significant influence in the client's life while honoring the client's need to create meaning through freely made choices. Freeing counselors will share certain traits.

1. They place a high value on freedom in their own lives. They make their own decisions and act according to their own expectations and values. They recognize that all freedom is relative and are willing to make compromises and sacrifices based on free choice instead of compliance. Because they experience the positive and sometimes exhilarating results of freedom in their own lives, they are ardent advocates of freedom in counseling.

2. They recognize the difference between manipulation and education in counseling. Manipulation means the counselor pushes a person into making decisions more desired by the counselor than by the client. It may look like a personal decision because the person dutifully makes it, but the only decision the person made was to please the counselor. So this person, who appears to be "making better decisions," is actually getting worse.

A manipulating counselor confuses *acting* better with *getting* better. Education means the counselor helps people clearly realize the options at their disposal and the possible consequences of all of them. The counselor then stands back and lets the person make the choice.

3. Freeing counselors understand the difference between superficial and true freedom and help clients appreciate this important difference. Superficial freedom means people can act any way they choose. True freedom means two things: first, that a person has the same capacity to choose to act or to choose not to act—that is, the choice is not controlled by overdriven needs, compulsions, or unbridled emotions—and second, that the results of the choice will not unnecessarily injure anyone. The freedom a counselor gives is not a license to behave selfishly or heedlessly—it is an invitation for people to assume complete responsibility for their behavior, enjoying the rewards and accepting the consequences.

4. They exercise and value true freedom in the context of the counseling relationship. They understand that in a counseling relationship, as in any other, freedom is restricted by the nature of the relationship. The nature of counseling is to help the person become more psychologically healthy. Both the counselor and the client are free to behave in ways that directly or indirectly achieve this result. To the degree that one or the other behaves in ways that significantly violate this goal, the other is free to terminate the relationship. This understanding of freedom allows both the counselor and the client maximum latitude in working toward the goals they have agreed upon, but it still protects each from being used by the other in a destructive manner.

Until clients are entirely free to be themselves, counselors don't know whom they are working with in counseling. The less free a person feels, the more it is the public, specious self, rather than the real, authentic self, that relates with the counselor. Consequently, many of the clues that the counselor picks up from the client and acts upon are false ones. Only when the person can speak any thought, express any feeling, ask any question, or consider any decision does the counselor truly know the client.

Freedom brings clients closer to who they really are. Many clients (as well as those not in counseling) live according to someone else's plan, often without realizing it. Typically, parents' plans are adhered to until they are traded in or added to by spouses' or friends'. Being freed allows people to see, perhaps for the first time, the marked discrepancies between who they are and what their conditioning says they should be. As they relinquish the needs, dreams, and values imposed from others in favor of their own, they can begin to shape a more fulfilling life.

Freedom reduces the need to rebel. People who do not feel free from others often rebel to establish independence. A young woman may refuse to attend college for no other reason than that her parents are pressuring her to do so. A young man may marry a woman primarily because his mother is doing all she can to prevent the marriage. Unfortunately, some people sequester themselves in order to establish a little freedom and control over their lives. They unnecessarily become martyrs for their freedom. When clients can develop a true sense of freedom, they become eligible to make choices that are good for them, regardless of the approval or disapproval of the significant people in their lives.

The more freedom people are allowed in counseling, the more freedom they can allow themselves. Most of the unnecessary restraints that people bring into counseling are self-imposed. They use other people as an excuse for not acting freely or they inappropriately assign blame elsewhere. Once they can develop the confidence to make free choices, they can allow others to act more freely.

One of the obstacles to being a freeing counselor is the skewed logic: "I know what's best for this client; this client wants to know what is best for him; therefore, it is my responsibility to prod him along the paths that I feel he needs to take." This obstacle may be overcome by bearing in mind that acting responsibly is profoundly difficult for anyone. When counselors are unable to manage their own freedom, when their choices are constrained, the client's freedom is at risk in the counseling relationship.

Holistic Awareness

It is appropriate that the last requisite quality here listed should be that of holistic awareness because it assumes and subsumes all the others. A holistic approach to counseling results when the counselor is aware of the whole person and does not approach him or her with tunnel vision. This does not mean that a counselor is an expert in all areas; it simply indicates an awareness on the counselor's part of the fact that people are multidimensional and that each dimension may affect others. Counselors who respond holistically share three traits.

1. They are acutely aware of the dimensions of personality and their complex interplay. They do not artificially restrict a person's problem to the one, two, or three dimensions with which they feel the most comfortable. Nor do they assume that a dimension is conflict-free until it has been adequately evaluated.

2. Counselors with a holistic view seek appropriate consultation and make intelligent referrals. They do not cling. While it would be unrealistic to refer a person to a specialist for every specific presenting issue, counselors should not diagnose and treat dimensions for which they are not qualified. For example, a counselor should not rule out the possibility that a depressed client might need medication or that a client's spiritual concerns and religious conflicts may need to be additionally addressed by pastoral counselors or clergy.

3. Holistic counselors are familiar with and open to many theories of behavior. While they may have more confidence in a particular theory, they recognize that there is no one theory or combination of theories that adequately explains all behavior. They attempt to fit their skills and theories to the client rather than putting the client into some slot consistent with their skills and theories.

A holistic approach in counseling is necessary because people have many dimensions. To focus exclusively on any one dimension could only seriously limit the effectiveness of counseling. The following dimensions of personality interrelate but are separate enough to consider individually: physical, emotional, social, sexual, and spiritual. The importance of understanding the nature and dynamics of these five dimensions may be seen in the following example.

A college student seeks help because he is underachieving. After discussing the problem for a while, the counselor discovers that the student has poor study habits. However, the counselor correctly suspects other issues underlie the client's poor study habits; in other words, the counselor realizes that the problem may be a symptom. Additional sessions reveal that the poor study habits stem from the student's depression. In trying to understand the depression, the counselor discovers that the student is harboring a great deal of repressed anger toward his father and has discontinued taking his thyroid pills since returning to school. This student's symptom—poor study habits—encompassed the intellectual, emotional, spiritual, and physical dimensions. Attending to the client from a holistic perspective prompted the counselor to consider varied sources of the client's difficulties and inspired a treatment plan that included medical treatment, counseling, and academic counseling that included study skills and time-management training. Each service was important to the client's overall success.

A holistic approach is also important because it is not uncommon for a problem in one dimension to get referred to a different one. A person's emotional conflict (anger) may manifest itself in the physical dimension (ulcerative colitis); a physical problem (diagnosed or undiagnosed diabetes) may manifest itself in the sexual area (impotence); or an emotional conflict (guilt) may manifest itself in the intellectual area (inability to concentrate). It is important to deal with the primary problem and not to waste time on the referred dimension.

By being holistically aware, the counselor can reduce the effects of an insoluble problem in one area by expanding growth in a different dimension. For example, a young woman's fiance has died, and she brings her inconsolable grief into counseling. After a few supportive sessions, however, the counselor becomes aware that the woman is actually mourning more for herself than for her fiance. She had been a shy, withdrawn person with a good deal of self-doubt. Her fiance protected her, made her feel worthwhile, and gave her a purpose in life. His death symbolized the snatching away of her hope for a happy and meaningful life. While counseling cannot bring back the woman's fiance, holistic counseling can help her resurrect herself. Through counseling she can not only regain her feelings of self-worth and purpose but regain a private ownership of them so that their existence no longer depends upon the presence of another person.

Obstacles to a holistic approach may come into play when counselors do not allow themselves to admit that they are unqualified, for whatever reason, to assist with certain dimensions of a client. Insecurity or a lack of humility may blind counselors to important aspects of their clients—aspects that should be addressed by other professionals if the client is going to be cared for properly.

The 12 qualities of self-knowledge were selected because their combined presence makes it possible for counselors to personally address major theoretical, clinical, and ethical issues when they provide services to their clients. Each was discussed individually because it is easier to present them in this fashion, but such a mode of presentation is potentially deceptive—these qualities exist within the same person and cannot be separated from each other. The 12 qualities actually form a gestalt, an entity that is much larger than the simple sum of the parts. With this fact in mind, we maintain that counseling effectiveness results when counselors are academically prepared, clinically competent, and able to combine the 12 enumerated qualities in ways that honor themselves, their clients, and their profession. Counseling is a complicated task. On the one hand counselors are challenged to know themselves well enough to be of service to someone else. On the other hand they are challenged by the differences they encounter in their clients. In other words, each counseling relationship is substantively different and requires the counselor to respond by calling the appropriate area of competence into play.

One way to understand more about the personal qualities that are found in effective counselors is to discuss the difficulties that arise when one or more of these areas need further development. The conclusion of this chapter discusses a few of the problems that new counselors may face as they begin the task of learning to help others.

⚜️

Beginning Counselors' Concerns

The complexities of counseling are probably felt by no one more strongly than by novice counselors. Most are rapidly overwhelmed by the need to understand and apply theory, the need for effective clinical skills, and the escalating need to know themselves well enough to be of help to their clients. They may encounter difficulty in any or all of these areas. For example, they may find they lack sufficient insight about themselves to be helpful to others or they may become uncomfortable with intense expressions of feeling. Novices also may find that they are unable to apply their theoretical training to particular clients or that their unpolished clinical skills cause them to be less effective than they want to be.

A discussion of the struggles that novice counselors face and how these struggles relate to the previously discussed 12 personal qualities is in order at this point because it alerts novices to potential problems and it suggests appropriate targets for change. New counselors can often remedy difficulties by strengthening the personal qualities that are related to the problem. The following discussion will involve seven common concerns, presented in the form of questions that beginning counselors may ask themselves or their teachers and supervisors. The answers that we offer were selected because they fit the overall philosophy informing this presentation. As you read through this section try to think how you would resolve each of these questions by selecting one or more of the foregoing 12 personal qualities to focus on.

Psychological Health

Do I have to be the very picture of psychological health before I can effectively help people? The answer to this question is no. It is a reasonable assumption that, all other factors remaining the same, the better a counselor's psychological health, the more effective he or she will be. While counselors seek to progress toward their ideals, the majority remain ordinary people who have a special interest in helping others. Their interest does not make them immune to the types of problems that the population in general experiences. Sometimes counselors are impatient, defensive, or arrogant. At other times they are irritable, distracted, depressed, or unreasonable. They can misperceive situations, introduce their prejudices into counseling, and like some clients less than others and treat them accordingly.

While counselors should work to modify these behaviors, they can also use them as a learning experience for the client. As clients see the counselor handle his or her imperfections and as they learn to deal with the counselor's humanity, real growth can take place.

However, a counselor whose lack of psychological health precludes self-knowledge, self-esteem, or an ability to relate smoothly and honestly with people is unlikely to be generally effective.

Harming Clients

Can I do irreparable harm to someone in a counseling session? The answer to this question is probably not. Fortunately, psyches are generally more resilient than bodies in the face of stress. One mistake in surgery could cause a patient to die, but a mistake in counseling is unlikely to result in a comparable catastrophe. This is not to say that clients cannot be seriously damaged in counseling, but such damage could only result from ongoing mistakes over a period of time.

It is unlikely that a counselor could "say the wrong thing" in a session or misinterpret a communication in such a way that would result in dire consequences. The stronger the counseling relationship, the more mistakes can be accommodated. On the rare occasion when a person decompensates into an acute psychotic episode or commits suicide, questions often arise: Did the counselor say or do the wrong thing? When such episodes occur, it is likely that they would have happened no matter what the counselor did or even whether or not the person was in counseling.

Counselor Responsibility

How much responsibility do I have for the people I see in counseling? It is helpful for beginning counselors to keep a number of points in mind when considering this question. First, the counselor did not cause the client's problem(s). Moreover, the problems were present for weeks, months, and most likely years before the counselor came into this person's life. Therefore, the counselor cannot reasonably assume responsibility for the basic causes of the person's problems. On the other hand, counselors are responsible for providing effective, competent care to their clients. They need to properly assess a client's difficulties and formulate a reasonable plan of treatment. Ethics codes delineate many counselor responsibilities. Being familiar with these codes and understanding that professionals are expected to provide services that meet the standards of practice of their profession help counselors define their scope of responsibility.

Assuming that a counselor has properly assessed a particular client, the counselor would not ordinarily be responsible for that client's behavior outside of counseling. However, if a client who was improperly assessed leaves the session and gets drunk, harms another person, or takes an overdose of sleeping pills, issues of legal and personal responsibility might surface as a result.

On the other hand, assuming responsibility about things that are clearly beyond the counselor's sphere of professional responsibility is grandiose, naive, and self-punitive. It is grandiose because it assumes that the counselor has the power to change a behavior that the client is unable or unwilling to change. It is naive because it reflects a lack of understanding of behavioral dynamics, especially of how people can use even the most salutary situations as instruments of self-destruction. It is self-punitive because the counselor berates himself or herself for something beyond his or her control.

Counselors are not responsible *for* the people they see in counseling, but they are responsible *to* the people seen in counseling. This means counselors do all that is reasonable and appropriate to help the person during the counseling relationship. This is the only valid contract with regard to responsibility. The counselor agrees to provide care, knowledge, skills, energy, honesty, strength, and hope. To promise and assume any more responsibility beyond this is unreasonable and, in all likelihood, countertherapeutic.

Caring and Accepting

To what extent can I or should I really care about and unconditionally accept the people I see in counseling? Caring and unconditional acceptance are terms used so much in the counseling literature that they may cause beginning counselors to simulate these sentiments artificially or to become discouraged because they cannot do so. But caring only evolves from coming to know the client. The more a person knows and likes another, the more he or she will care about the other. Conversely, the less a person knows another, the less genuine the feelings. Therefore, it is unrealistic to expect a counselor to care deeply and genuinely about a person during the first sessions of counseling. All counselors have a theoretical concern for people, but a personal and deep regard can grow only gradually as the counselor increases his or her knowledge and liking of the person.

Some beginning counselors wonder whether it is possible to care *too much*. A cursory examination suggests it *is* possible to care too much about a client. Caring too much in this sense is less likely to be grounded in a genuine, healthy caring than to stem from a counselor's overdriven need to be a rescuer or a success.

It is not unusual for a counselor to care somewhat more about a client than the client does. The hope is that the counselor's care will gradually become contagious and that clients will begin to care about themselves. However, when the counselor cares *significantly* more than the person, the counselor assumes responsibility not only for what happens in the counseling session but for the overall outcome of counseling. This type of counseling relationship is likely to end unsatisfactorily.

The concept of unconditional acceptance is a complex one. Does it mean that *whatever* the person does, the counselor's acceptance will remain unwavering? Does it mean the client can abuse the counselor by missing appointments, not paying bills, or using him or her in ways that are destructive? An unquestioning acceptance of this sort could only be countertherapeutic since it injures both the counselor and the client. It seems more reasonable and honest to set some limits on acceptance. These limits can be broader than those offered by society in general and perhaps by the client's friends and relatives, but they must be tailored to the goals of counseling. As long as the client's behavior is broadly consonant with the agreed-upon goals of counseling, the counselor is able to proceed. However, if the client's behavior continues to be dissonant with the agreed-upon goals of counseling, the counselor must reevaluate whether the client is someone who can be helped by the counseling relationship. If not, the counselor would be ill-advised to continue. The importance of this cannot be overstated. Proceeding with a counterproductive counseling relationship imparts tacit approval of countertherapeutic, even dangerous, behavior. The abuse of the counseling process in this way is probably one of the most serious abuses because the client rationalizes that because he or she is in counseling, steps are being taken to correct the difficulties, but the behavior still persists. Under these conditions the counseling relationship inappropriately shelters the client from responsibility and the pursuit of more adaptive behavior.

The basic values of counseling that take priority over caring and acceptance are beneficence (the promotion of good), nonmaleficence (the avoidance of harm), justice (fairness), and veracity (truthfulness). When the counseling relationship becomes unjust to either or both of the parties, it has outlived its purpose. Ethical principles underscore this point; for example, the *Code of Ethics and Standards of Practice* of the American Counseling Association states, "If counselors determine an inability to be of professional assistance to clients, they avoid entering or immediately terminate a counseling relationship. Counselors are knowledgeable about referral resources and suggest appropriate alternatives. If clients decline the suggested referral, counselors should discontinue the relationship" (ACA, 1995).

Lack of Experience

Won't clients know that I am just a beginning counselor, and won't that create some difficulties? While this concern is understandable, it usually rests more on the counselor than on the client. Of course, some clients challenge beginning counselors about their youth or lack of experience, but clients usually tend to assume that if the counselor has been placed by authorities in a position of trust, the counselor must be capable of handling the situation.

The occasional client who does challenge the counselor with regard to his or her experience can be assured in a matter-of-fact way that the counselor meets the professional requirements of the agency. Usually this straightforward approach will suffice. People who continue to make the counselor's age or experience an issue may be using it as a decoy from their real concerns, and their reaction can be handled as with any other form of transference and resistance. If the person pushes the point, and especially if it appears to have some validity, most agencies have a policy to guide the beginning counselor in this situation.

A counselor's concerns about lack of experience or ability to provide services to someone who is older also need to be carefully addressed. Confidence grows with experience; it is important for new counselors to understand that it takes time to become self-assured and to mature professionally. Such concerns are quite valid. They can serve to motivate new counselors to explore how differences in life experiences between counselors and clients affect the ability to be helpful. New counselors can thus identify the types of experiences they need to become more effective counselors.

New counselors tend to see differences between themselves and their clients as reasons why they may not be able to help or understand their clients, but in time counselors learn to look forward to these differences because they very often become the focus of the therapeutic relationship. Novice counselors might become intimidated if a client suggests they will not be able to understand a problem because they are too young. With experience, however, the same counselor will be able to reduce the amount of self-doubt that such a disclosure produces and pursue the wealth of information communicated by the client's statement. Such a client's comment is full of meaning, and it illuminates some of the client's assumptions: age differences are important, differences between people make useful discourse difficult, and it is difficult for people to understand each other unless they share certain commonalities. Critical comments about the counselor's level of experience or age may aid the progress of therapy if the counselor is not immobilized by feelings of insecurity and uncertainty. Counselors are formed by their experiences. Their earliest experience is that of an inexperienced person providing counseling services to people quite different from themselves. Everyone starts the same way.

Failure

What if I fail with a person I'm seeing in counseling and the client terminates? There are several general ways counselors can be unsuccessful. First, the counselor can make a large mistake or a sufficient number of small mistakes that cause the person to terminate counseling prematurely. Or the counselor might be competent and the client cooperating fully, but a "good fit" is still lacking—that is, the two people seem to be operating on different wavelengths. In a third case, the counselor may be working effectively, but the client wishes to sabotage counseling for some reason. Counselors who tend to be self-blaming will blame themselves for all three types of failure. Counselors who tend to blame others will blame the client for all three types of failure. The realistic counselor will attempt to judge accurately the cause for the discontinuance of counseling and react appropriately.

If the first cause seems likely, the counselor can learn from his or her mistake and avoid making it again. All counselors make an occasional mistake and even the best counselors have made significant mistakes but learned from them. If the counselor accurately judges that the premature termination is attributable to the second cause, he or she need not view it as a failure but simply as a "poor match"—something that can occur in any relationship. With the third cause, the counselor should view the situation as one that likely was unavoidable and that comes with the territory of counseling.

All professional people fail at times; failure is a price both counselors and clients may have to pay for taking risks and being human. As Corey (1977, p. 243) states, "We can't realistically expect to succeed with every client. Even experienced therapists at times become glum and begin to doubt their value when they are forced to admit that there are clients whom they are not able to touch, much less reach in a significant way."

Counselors need a number of competencies in order to be successful. Novice counselors face a steep learning curve as they begin the process of gaining experience and developing professionally. Counseling is a demanding task; counselors need to be psychologically healthy enough to be helpful to others while still caring for themselves. While new counselors need to be sensitive to the fact that they can be harmful to their clients, they need to be realistic about the limited potential for harm. New counselors are also challenged by the need to properly balance professional responsibilities, caring, and accepting. Finally, novice counselors must deal with the reality that they are inexperienced, but the manner in which they deal with this lack of experience probably outweighs any judgment a client may make. Counselors develop in all of these areas as they study theoretical, clinical, and ethical issues in counseling and as they receive proper consultation and support from supervisors, consultants, and peers. The progress from novice to professional counselor is an exciting and personally enriching journey.

Pitfalls

What are some pitfalls of which I can be aware as a beginning counselor? There are several potential pitfalls in counseling of which *all* counselors should be aware, although beginning counselors may be particularly susceptible to six of them.

Trying to do too much too soon.   Beginning counselors are often impatient to put their years of learning and practice to work. Impatience almost always leads to difficulties. For example, counselors' personal and professional insecurities may cause them to counterproductively push for early successes in order to buttress their confidence.

The counseling relationship and process, like most relationships and processes, cannot be rushed. Counselors who attempt to accelerate the process tend to be overly active and place undue pressure on their clients to make positive changes in their behavior. Clients, under this type of pressure, will firmly resist the process or will superficially comply with the counselor's expectations and then suddenly terminate by either disappearing or by becoming "cured." Problems that arise from placing undue pressure on the client can be observed in the case of a client who entered counseling because his wife had given him an ultimatum: either obtain counseling for his drinking problem or she was going to leave with the kids. The counselor immediately and exclusively defined the client's problem as alcoholism, sided with the client's wife, and began demanding that the client stop drinking. The client returned the following week ready to terminate. He announced that the problem was over and offered, as evidence, the fact that he had consumed no alcohol for seven days and that he felt great. The client refused to return and left the session 15 minutes early.

The same client was seen several months later by a different counselor. The client returned to counseling under a court order following his arrest for assault and battery. His new counselor suggested that the client attend three weekly evaluation meetings and that once they completed these sessions, they would decide together if there was a need for further counseling. These three meetings revealed that the client had been abusing other drugs, had a history of abusive behavior toward every member of his family, and had been abused by members of his family of origin when he was 11 years old. The client began a course of therapy and also agreed to obtain both a psychological and psychiatric evaluation. The results of each were used to develop a treatment plan that included group counseling, individual counseling, and medication. The client terminated abruptly after roughly three months but eventually returned after a six-month hiatus.

Teaching instead of relating.   New counselors have in common the fact that they have recently finished a college and graduate academic curriculum of from six to ten years. As students they were taught through lectures, discussions, and various experiential activities. A natural consequence of this experience is to reduce anxiety in counseling by teaching the client instead of counseling the client. The counselor may present a seminar on anger at one counseling session, a discussion on communication at the next, and a workshop on relationships at the third. This reduces the counselor's anxiety because it allows the counselor to think he or she is *doing* something, and it reduces the client's anxiety because it is less demanding to be a student than to be an actively participating client or patient.

Unfortunately, the more lecturing that occurs, the less counseling will take place. Beginning counselors can use their academic knowledge to help them understand the client and make the most appropriate responses. But simply passing on one's class notes to the client will impede the counseling process and relationship.

Being overly accommodating.   It is helpful for counselors to be reasonably accommodating as far as scheduling appointments, allowing the client to select the issues to be discussed at a particular session, and being accessible by phone. Sometimes, however, beginning counselors feel inadequate and seek to compensate for this by bending over backwards for the client, even though it will be detrimental in the long run.

Inexperienced counselors may set limits that are too broad or too changeable. They thus allow clients to control the session with extraneous content or by putting the counselor in the "hot seat." They allow fees to slide without payment. They schedule special sessions, take phone calls between sessions, and reschedule people even when it is inconvenient to do so. It is as if these counselors were saying, "I know I'm not a very good counselor yet, but I'll make it up to you in other ways." The problem is that the compensating behavior is countertherapeutic. It weakens boundaries in a way that may confuse the client. Structure, predictability, and clearly defined expectations are necessary in any working relationship— they are essential to a counseling relationship. When problems develop in a therapeutic relationship they can often be traced to weak or nonexistent boundaries, and such boundary problems may have been present from the first counselor-client encounter.

Attributing counseling problems to inexperience.   Certainly some problems arise in counseling because the counselor is a novice. However, many problems with which the beginning counselor must deal would arise with any counselor. The following are some typical examples.

A client prematurely terminates after only a few sessions and the counselor blames it on the fact that he mishandled the situation because of his inexperience. However, studies indicate that 37% to 45% of people who seek counseling in urban mental health centers prematurely terminate after the first or second interview (Garfield, 1980, p. 4). It is unlikely that all these people were seen by beginning counselors.

A client may tell a beginning counselor, "Well, it looks like neither one of us knows what to do right now." The counselor interprets this as a reference to her youth or inexperience, whereas the client would have made the same statement to any counselor at that point.

A client is very resistant to change and continually treads water or backslides in counseling. The beginning counselor is convinced that if he only had a few more years' experience, he could help the client through the impasse. In fact, the client may be objectively very difficult to work with and would present the same challenge to the most experienced counselor.

It is understandable and perhaps appropriate that beginning counselors feel somewhat insecure as they begin their career. However, it is important that they separate the problems they may create due to their inexperience from problems and behaviors that would be present no matter how skilled and experienced they were. Failure to do so may cause novice counselors to misperceive situations in ways that cause them to feel inadequate.

Assuming a "counseling personality."   Possibly because there is so much written about what a counselor should be, beginning counselors have a tendency to change dramatically when they walk into the counseling room. The young man who was smiling and laughing minutes before may now enter the counseling room with a ponderous or empathetic look plastered on his face. The young woman who was actively involved in a discussion at the water cooler may become passive and reflective as she settles into the counseling session. The young man is afraid to smile in counseling because he learned that counseling is not a social but a professional relationship. The young woman is passive and reflective because she learned that counselors should not intrude their personalities into the counseling situation. The result is that these counselors become caricatures of some so-called "effective counselor."

Counselors who overidentify with the role of counselor lose contact with the best counseling resource they have: themselves. Instead of asking themselves what they can do at this point in counseling, they ask what Jung would do at this point or what their supervisor would do or what the textbook said should be done. It is important that beginning counselors distinguish between *becoming* an effective counselor and *acting* like an effective counselor. The qualities of an effective counselor are not meant to be worn in counseling as a surgeon wears scrubs into the operating room. They are meant to be assimilated into the counselor's unique personality and to become a part of it, just as a coat of paint becomes a part of a building.

Ruminating after difficult sessions.   There is a difference between evaluating a session in order to learn from it and ruminating about it for hours afterward in a way that creates more self-torment than learning. Sometimes beginning counselors spend time second-guessing themselves after a difficult session. They ask themselves or fellow students or counselors, "Should I have said what I did, or would it have been better not to say it?" "If it was good to say it, should I have said it when I did or later in the session?" "Should I have agreed to see him twice next week, or did I get hooked into something I shouldn't have?"

Such questions can go on endlessly because the dynamics of difficult sessions remain unresolved. Counselors who spend a lot of time in post mortems should realize that whatever mistakes were made in the session, they will not be redeemed by brooding over them. Since they will likely discuss the session with a supervisor, they can limit their own postsession evaluations to 15 minutes, focusing on the one or two major areas of concern. They can scrutinize these areas and make a tentative plan for dealing with them in the next session.

While each of these pitfalls was discussed in the context of novice counselors, they can also adversely affect experienced counselors. New counselors are more susceptible in general, while experienced counselors become more susceptible when they work with particular client types. In other words, virtually any counselor could encounter these problems when confronted with the "right client." Basically, these problems are best explored and managed through the processes of supervision and consultation.

The novice counselor is subject to supervision. A case supervisor is responsible for the counselor's work, and regular meetings and observations provide the novice with support, information, and direction. Consultation serves the same purpose in the case of licensed counselors. While the consultant is not responsible for the licensed counselor's cases, the consultant provides support, information, and direction. Supervision and consultation can be provided in individual as well as group settings. There are advantages and disadvantages to each arrangement. The counselor's objectivity, judgment, and the ability to develop alternatives improve through contact with other professionals. Counselors of any ability benefit from and should obtain either supervision or consultation throughout their professional lives.

⚜ Summary

Each quality discussed in this chapter is a necessary trait of an effective counselor. As with vital signs in medicine, it is not good enough that *most* of the qualities are present. The absence or undevelopment of even one of the qualities could significantly interfere with the progress of counseling and could even cause counseling to be counterproductive. As Weiner (1975, p. 22) says, counseling "is not a benign procedure. Ample evidence indicates that it can be harmful as well as helpful to patients and that the major factors influencing good and bad outcomes reside in the therapist and how he [sic] conducts treatment."

It is also important to understand that these qualities do not operate in a vacuum. The personality of the client can influence the actualization of these qualities in a counselor. A very gentle, kind person may elicit great sensitivity on the part of a counselor while a boisterous, intimidating person may diminish the counselor's ability to be sensitive. This is not to say that the counselor's effectiveness varies with the client, but rather that it would be unrealistic for a counselor to expect to function at maximum potential with every client.

As has already been noted, for practical reasons the qualities are listed separately. In practice, however, they interrelate, and one quality either helps or hinders the others, depending upon its strength or weakness. Beginning counselors will find themselves applying these qualities in counseling "by the numbers"—that is, they will be aware of the extent to which each quality was present in a particular session and strive to optimize its operation in the next session. This is an important and necessary part of counseling, as long as it does not become distracting or compulsive. After some years of experience, however, counselors find that these personal qualities fuse with their knowledge of behavior and counseling skills to form a single growth-producing force. As Bugental (1978) writes:

> Just as an accomplished pianist (or any artist) is one who has thoroughly mastered the fundamentals of the craft in order to be free to be truly creative in expression, so the master therapist has incorporated the mechanics of the processes to the point that they are invisible. The pianist no longer "plays the piano" but only draws music forth from the instrument which has become integral to the artist. The therapist no longer "does therapy" but relates so authentically with the client because the skills are integrated completely into the professional's way of being. (p. 44)

Reflection Questions

1. In terms of self-knowledge, what are two of your greater strengths that would help you as a counselor? What are two of your greater weaknesses that could interfere with your effectiveness as a counselor?

2. Of the 12 qualities of an effective counselor discussed in this chapter, which two do you feel you most possess and which two do you feel you need to work on the most?

3. The text states that the client's significant emotional reactions should be discussed within the session in which it occurs. What is your reaction to this concept? Could you imagine a situation that would represent an exception to this principle?

4. The text states that honesty is necessary for a counselor to be effective. What are some situations that could arise in counseling in which you would find it very difficult to be honest?

5. Of the seven concerns typical of beginning counselors, which one do you feel reflects your greatest concern? Do you have a concern that was not mentioned in the text?

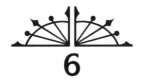

6

COMMUNICATION IN COUNSELING

Counseling relationships form and are maintained through a unique communication process. Counselors employ a specialized form of interaction that is distinctly different from the patterns that are found in friendships or work relationships. Counseling communication bridges the psychological space between the client and the counselor for a very specific purpose, over a limited period of time, structured on clearly defined boundaries, in pursuit of an efficient path to helping the client.

The model presented in the chapter is a hybrid, selected because it is practical and, for the most part, uncomplicated while still including the basic elements of therapeutic communication. For purposes of presentation we have divided the chapter into two parts: client communication and counselor communication. The information in this chapter comes mostly from the related disciplines of psychology and counseling (for additional information see Beier, 1966; Ivey, 1994; Murphy & Dillon, 1998; Ruesch, 1973). The philosophy, sociology, and anthropology literature also contain an abundance of information on general patterns of communication (nontherapeutic); this research, though not covered in the following presentation, is also quite useful for counselors.

Client Communication

Clients communicate with counselors at a number of levels about different sorts of topics. One way of structuring an analysis of these levels is to categorize them into one of three dimensions and then to further distinguish how closely the communication actually reflects the client's innermost self. This structure contains three dimensions—personal, contextual, and relational—and three levels that range from comments that reflect what the client feels is expected of him or her (Level III) to comments that reveal the client's innermost "true self" (Level I). Analyzing communication in this way helps the counselor answer the question, "What is the *real* message that the client is trying to convey to me?" It also reminds the counselor that communication needs to be approached from all three directions because the goal is helping clients communicate accurate messages at each level and to advance from Level III comments to Level I comments. Each of the dimensions and the levels within each are discussed in the following sections.

Personal Dimension

The personal dimension consists of messages that clients send the counselor regarding themselves. These messages are formed at three different levels and they can be either true or false at any level.

Level III messages.   Level III messages say, "This is who I want you to *think* I am." For example, a person may communicate with his behavior, "I want you to think that I am a very cooperative person." If the message is accurate (that is, the person is truly cooperative), no problem will arise. But if the message is false, the less perceptive counselor may be lulled into a sense of complacency while the client actually resists the process of counseling. The less psychological strength or ego strength people possess, the more likely they are to send false Level III messages, not only in counseling but in the other parts of their lives. Because false Level III messages are not backed by actual behavior, conflicts arise both for the client and for those who believe the false message.

Counselors can ask themselves during a session, "This person obviously wants to be viewed as cooperative (or intelligent, stupid, benevolent, strong, weak, etc.). Does the client want me to believe this because it is true or because believing it helps the client avoid a painful or difficult reality?"

Level III messages, like all messages, can be sent consciously or unconsciously, and obviously or subtly. When the false message is communicated unconsciously and subtly, it takes a very vigilant counselor to see through it. When counselors learn that they have been misled by clients, it is often because they believed false Level III messages. If counselors are regularly exposed to false Level III messages they should evaluate the level of engagement between the counselor and the client to determine whether the therapeutic relationship is durable enough for the client to be more honest and to discuss issues at a deeper level. It would not be wise to criticize the client for false statements, because the client's need to falsify information may say more about the quality of the therapeutic alliance than it reveals about the client.

Level II messages. The Level II personal message is, "This is who I *think* I am." It reflects the image that clients have of themselves, whether or not it is accurate. If it is accurate, no problems will arise. If it is inaccurate, problems can occur both inside and outside of counseling. Examples of Level II messages are "I have superior intelligence," "I am a kind person," "I am boring," or "I am neurotic."

Clients often have inaccurate self-images that consciously and unconsciously cause them to further some destructive need. For example, a person may think he is intelligent not because he *is* but because he *needs* to think he is. As long as he thinks he is intelligent, he can blame his problems on the ignorance of others. By the same principle, as long as a person views herself as helpless, she need not move in any direction with her life.

Counselors should consistently question the validity of Level II messages. The client who communicates "I think I am kind" may need to feel kind because he is actually hostile. If the counselor believed the false message, the client's hostility might be overlooked by the counselor or labeled as something different, since kind people obviously do not behave in hostile ways.

Level I messages. The Level I message is, "This is who I am." It reflects the true nature of the person at that time. In other words, if a person is fearful, he or she communicates "I'm scared." The person with modest intelligence communicates "I had better lower my aspirations." The person who is angry communicates "I'm furious. Maybe I'm not supposed to be, but I am."

While counselors do not need to help clients operating at this level become more accurate in their comments, they do need to help and support the client as the client reacts to and deals with revelations at this level.

Consonant and dissonant messages. In psychologically healthy people, all three message levels are consonant. They can be diagrammed as follows:

Level III   A   I want you to think that I am frightened.

Level II   A   I think I am frightened.

Level I   A   I am frightened.

The letter A signifies that all three messages match.

People with less psychological health are inclined to send dissonant messages. The following diagrams reflect some of the combinations that can occur. The letters signify the difference in messages.

Level III   B   I want you to think that I am reasonably happy.

Level II   B   I think I'm reasonably happy.

Level I   A   I'm depressed.

Level III B   I want you to think that I'm not angry with you.

Level II A   I think I am angry at you.

Level I A   I am angry at you.

Level III C   I want you to think I have no sexual concerns.

Level II B   I think I'm sexually confused.

Level I A   I experience strong homosexual feelings.

No matter how much or how little psychological health people have, they are likely to communicate in a consonant way when dealing with innocuous issues. However, the less psychological strength a person has and the more threatening the issue, the greater the likelihood of dissonant messages.

The implications for counseling are obvious. Counselors can usefully classify or rank client comments on one of three levels: other's expectations, idealized self-perceptions, and accurate self-perceptions. As counselors gain experience and improve their skills, they become better able to determine the accuracy of the client's Level II and Level III messages. The counselor's ability to correctly classify the client's comments and to determine the accuracy of Level II and Level III messages have strong therapeutic implications. Most clients offer dissonant messages when they discuss the more serious and therapeutically important issues in their life; therefore, correcting the dissonance in the client's messages helps the client obtain a more accurate sense of self. More simply stated, one of the goals of counseling is to improve the client's understanding of self in reference to particular problems in his or her life by reducing the number of dissonant messages that are associated with those problems.

Contextual Dimension

Contextual messages deal with the content of the message. There are three levels of contextual messages.

Level III messages. Level III contextual messages communicate, "This is what I know you probably want me to discuss." While clients usually enter counseling with some idea of what the counselor will want them to talk about, over time they learn what topics the counselor does in fact favor. The counselor's favored themes generally reflect the counselor's theoretical, clinical, professional, and personal biases. For example, while one counselor might tend to value a discussion of the client's cognitive assumptions and the way the client thinks about important issues, another counselor might pursue a discussion of the client's emotional reactions to events and exclude cognitive issues completely. Different counselors may focus on emotions, childhood issues, dreams, cognitive assumptions, communication patterns, and so forth. Unfortunately, clients may consciously and unconsciously pursue topics they think the counselor prefers, rationalizing that counselors "must know what they're doing," when other topics would be far more useful for them to explore.

Level II messages. Level II contextual messages follow the theme, "This is what I *want* to talk about." Though these topics range from benign to very painful they are often presented as familiar and safe; clients have rehearsed them so completely that they no longer communicate their innermost thoughts and feelings. Clients offer these topics more as scripts to be read than as deeply emotional, personal experiences to be shared. The psychological area that the script covers may need attention. Counselors can help the client discard the script and communicate about the area in a more spontaneous, less defensive way; or, if the area the script covers is of little current importance, the counselor can help the client shift attention to more productive, often more threatening, themes.

Level I messages. Level I contextual messages communicate, "This is what I *need* to talk about." These topics deal with the deepest layers of hurt, fear, anger, guilt, confusion, and despair and eventually must be dealt with if clients are to effect any significant change in their behavior.

Effective counselors accept that the early stages of counseling are often replete with Level III and Level II contextual messages. Counseling is likely to begin with Level III communications because the client is better prepared for social than for therapeutic communication. This fact raises a question about the usefulness of the client's earliest contextual messages (we will refer to these early messages as the client's "story"). The story must be carefully explored, even though it may suggest something very different from what is really troubling the client, because the client's story contains clues of all types. Some clues expose deeper, more important issues, while others reveal the client's defense mechanisms. Thus, some stories are eventually forgotten as clients move deeper into the counseling process because the stories were actually distractions from the more important issues, but other stories produce themes that persist throughout the course of treatment. Either way, counselors need to carefully explore the story: it is the earliest contextual message offered by the client, and it might be the most important one.

As counseling progresses, clients often alternate between Level III and Level II contextual communication. Sessions are filled with dialogue, but the important Level I topics are clearly missing. This is a particularly challenging stage for the counselor because it can erroneously signify that easy communication and good rapport have been established when in fact, clients are continuing to defend against engaging difficult issues by (1) offering topics that they want, instead of need, to talk about or (2) discussing issues they have determined to be of interest to the counselor.

Most people have a collection of comfortable topics that they want to talk about. These themes are usually easy for the counselor to identify because they often portray clients in a way that is consistent (not necessarily positive or negative) with the way the clients see themselves. For the most part, counselors have little difficulty shifting the focus to more productive topics. On the other hand, counselors are less sensitive to identifying topics that the client has surmised to be important to the counselor. This is because counselors are pleased, rather than disturbed, when the client seems to embrace ideas or assumptions that are consistent with the counselor's. Counselors erroneously interpret the congruence of focus as a positive sign that the client is evolving in the counseling relationship. The client is not developing; the client is simply adapting to the counselor. Too much questioning on the part of the counselor is often to blame for this condition.

Ironically, highly specific questions often reveal more information about the counselor than they elicit about the client. For example, a counselor who frequently and exclusively questioned a client about family dynamics was surprised to notice that this client never shared critical information about other important areas of his life. The client was someone who desperately looked to others for support and direction and quickly deduced the counselor's assumptions about life and behavior from the questions she asked him, and so essentially gave the counselor what he believed she wanted to hear. Ironically, the counselor felt very pleased with the quality of interaction. She felt they were both on the "same page" and never sensed any difficulty with the way they were relating to each other. After all, the client held identical assumptions to hers, without their ever having talked about the counselor's exclusive research and clinical interest in family dynamics. This example offers the following lesson: if the client seems to enjoy the level of communication and experiences little or no anxiety, it is likely that the topic is probably not one of the areas or themes that the client *needs* to address. On the other hand, if the counselor changes the focus to an area that seems important but has been conspicuously absent from the sessions and the client reacts emotionally to the change, Level I communication may have been broached.

Level I communication becomes more common during the latter stages of counseling. The client's smooth, easy voice is often replaced with one that is tight, hesitant, and filled with emotion, because the material being discussed is significantly more meaningful and thus more threatening.

Relational Dimension

The relational dimension deals with the messages that clients send regarding their views of the counselor. Three levels of sincerity will be discerned.

Level III messages. These are probably the most confusing to understand. Basically these messages occur when clients second-guess how their counselors would like to be perceived by them. Stated more succinctly, but somewhat less clearly, a Level III relational message is, "This is who I want you to think that I think you are." One example of this type of message is, "I want you to think that I think you are a very competent counselor and that I am very lucky to be seeing you." The supporting dynamics of this statement could be to curry the counselor's favor so he or she will treat the client kindly and gently and not cause any significant degree of anxiety.

Another example is, "I want you to think that I think you are an arrogant, uncaring person who helps people because it makes you feel superior and affords you a nice income." The underlying dynamic here could be to keep the counselor at a distance so the counselor cannot get close enough to the client to broach vulnerable areas.

Conscious and unconscious Level III relational messages often dominate the early stages of counseling. This is not surprising because social interaction contains many Level III-like messages; it is only to be expected that this would carry into counseling. Effective counselors recognize the importance of not being deceived by these messages, but they also understand how to make good use of the information contained in them. The client is both reacting to the counselor and projecting onto the counselor. Early attempts to correctly distinguish the client's honest reactions to the counselor from the client's projections onto the counselor contribute to the client's improved sense of self and simultaneously enhance the therapeutic alliance.

One clue to Level III responses is that the sentiment the client expresses toward the counselor has little, if any, basis in reality. For example, a woman may tell her counselor after only four sessions, "I can't tell you how much better I am feeling about myself already because of your help." Or a man may say after a few sessions, "I'd like to bring up some religious conflicts I'm having, but I can tell you're not a person who puts much stock in religion." As the client develops more psychological strength and trust, he or she will gradually gravitate to Level II and eventually Level I relational messages. The transition to Level II responses may be heralded by the client's realization that much of what he or she concluded about the counselor was more a function of what the client needed the counselor to be than of how the client assumed the counselor wanted to be perceived.

Level II messages.   A Level II relational message is based on who the client *wants* or *needs* the counselor to be. The client tends to exaggerate the counselor's abilities and skills in either a positive or negative direction. For example, the client might ask, "I am certain that you know what I need to do, so why won't you tell me?" This question, and others like it, tell volumes about the client's expectations of people and, indirectly, their expectations of themselves. Additionally, because Level II relational messages are filled with transference information, skillful counselors can use information obtained at this level of communication to unearth many of the client's important issues.

Level I messages.   Level I relational messages reveal how the client actually perceives the counselor. In other words the client is telling the counselor, "This is who I *really* think you are." These messages are comprised of the true thoughts and emotions that the client has regarding the counselor. The ideas and feelings may be positive, negative, or ambivalent, but they are genuine and are offered to the counselor as possible aids in the growth process. Counseling sessions that contain many Level I relational messages suggest that appropriate levels of trust between the counselor and the client have developed and that the counseling relationship is robust enough to effectively manage the range of emotions that are associated with deeply honest disclosures and insights.

While the move from Level III to Level I personal, contextual, and relational communication may seem like the primary goal of counseling, the truth is that exploring messages at all three levels is what is most important. Abundant, useful information about the client and the way the client relates to others can be gleaned from all three categories at all three levels. Focusing on one level to the exclusion of others may cause the counselor to rush the client and to ignore important information in the push to Level I communication. Both of these outcomes limit the overall effectiveness of any counseling effort.

Problematic Communication

Both senses of the world problematic are intended here. The communication patterns discussed in this section provide the counselor with spurious information, but this very disingenuousness on the part of the client will reveal how the client's behavior habitually creates problems.

Controlling Messages

Clients often send messages meant to modify the counseling environment or relationship. The more vulnerable clients become, the less they can allow others the freedom to respond as they desire. Vulnerable people tend to constrain others so that they can respond only in certain prescribed ways. Evoking the responses they want allows these people to interact with others, while feeling safe from threat and damage. When counselors recognize controlling verbal and nonverbal messages, they can help clients explore their need to control the session. When counselors fail to appreciate the client's controlling responses, the counseling relationship becomes no different from any other unhelpful relationship that the client has experienced.

The emotional climate.   Clients can control the counseling situation in several ways. One way is to create an emotional climate that is comfortable for them. For example, the client may pursue a positive climate of friendliness and kindness in order to prevent the counselor from intruding into vulnerable or painful areas. The warmth of the climate can blunt the counselor's effectiveness if the counselor consciously or unconsciously adopts the goal of keeping the relationship friendly. Once this friendly climate becomes established, it successfully restrains the counselor from acting in therapeutic ways (nonfriendly, often anxiety-producing).

The client also can create a negative emotional climate—one that is filled with skepticism and antagonism. This negative climate keeps the counselor distant and may grow so intense that the only reasonable option is to terminate counseling and refer the client to someone else.

Finally, clients may send unclear, self-canceling, double messages that serve to confuse the counselor. This confusion may successfully confound the counselor to the point that he or she is only marginally effective.

As long as counselors feel restrained from making certain responses and constrained to make others, or if they experience inordinate confusion, it is likely they are being manipulated in a manner meant to distract them from their goal of helping the client.

The counselor's responses. A second way clients control the counseling process is by evoking specific responses from the counselor that may, unfortunately, be used by the client to maintain his or her current level of maladjustment. The evoked responses can blind the counselor to important issues, or the counselor's evoked responses can be used by the client to reinforce the client's faulty assumptions. For example, a client may cause the counselor to miss important issues by inviting the counselor to discuss work-related problems exclusively, thereby making it difficult to explore other potentially more important areas. Clients may also elicit responses that reinforce their own faulty assumptions by evoking angry or rejecting responses from the counselor. In this case, the counselor's angry reactions affirm the client's assumptions that no one likes her. The client may have a vested interest in maintaining this assumption because it allows her to continue to withdraw from others or to behave in a hostile manner toward others.

Lack of awareness. Clients are often unaware of how they control their interpersonal environment through communication because the process has become automatic and subconscious. Clients commonly and incorrectly think they are not communicating anything significant or that they are not communicating at all when careful examination reveals something much different. Skillful counselors can often identify messages that the client is unaware of, but more importantly, messages that actually suggest just the opposite of what the client believes is being shared. Because clients are unaware of what is being communicated, they may think they are inviting one type of feedback when they are really inviting a different type. Being unaware presents many communication conflicts. For example, clients tend to feel misunderstood, falsely accused, and surprised by other people's reactions. Clients frequently encounter similar difficulties when they attempt to communicate internally. They become confused and surprised at their own formulations. It will be found that communication problems and the related lack of self-awareness that accompany them may well become very productive areas for counselors to explore with their clients.

Skilled manipulation. People quickly learn that various verbal and nonverbal messages tend to produce particular responses in others. For example, if a client tells a counselor, "I'm so fortunate to have you as my counselor," the probability of a positive response is great. If a person tells a counselor, "If you were more interested in helping me than seeing as many patients as you can, I would be doing a lot better," a negative response will all but certainly result.

The more vulnerable clients are, the more likely it is that they will find a way to elicit constricted, highly predictable responses from the counselor. Such persons will have developed an ability to manipulate others so they can continue to deny some parts of themselves and exaggerate others; doing otherwise would produce more anxiety and disorientation than they believe themselves capable of managing. Clients do not manipulate counselors because they want to but because they feel that they must do so if they are to survive.

With regard to this principle, it is helpful for counselors to be mindful of the following points.

1. Clients often attempt, through the messages they send, to sculpt the counselor into a familiar likeness. They try to evoke responses that form the counselor into an old friend or an old enemy. They do this so they will be able to predict the counselor's responses and deflect the counselor from areas in which they are vulnerable.

2. Counselors should be aware of their vulnerabilities because it is these vulnerabilities that can be tapped into by the client's manipulative communications. For example, if a counselor needs to be esteemed, the client may send the message, "I know some people who don't like you." If the counselor falls for this, the rest of the session will be spent discussing the counselor and the message rather than the client, the client's problems, and the client's avoidance behavior.

3. When the counselor successfully avoids responding in the anticipated way to manipulative communications, tension increases in the counseling relationship. The counselor's refusing to be manipulated challenges the client to relate to an unpredictable, unconstrained counselor; clients often react with consternation and anger if they have occasion to conclude that the counselor is not "playing fair." When this occurs, it is important for counselors to handle the situation gently but firmly, clearly explaining what is happening.

4. Counselors must detect provocative communications if they are going to react to them successfully. Since the client has lifelong experience

in bringing about obfuscation by manipulative means, counselors are especially vulnerable to reacting to such baited messages, especially in the initial stages of counseling. Counselors who discover that they have taken the bait can disengage themselves from the evoking messages and help clients discover what vulnerabilities are being protected. If counseling becomes conflict-ridden or stagnant, it often means the counselor has been successfully manipulated to the point where the counseling process is either being seriously disrupted or is frozen in a state of confusion or inactivity. Such occurrences often signal a need to consult with a supervisor or colleague who has the benefit of an outside view.

5. Counselors can determine whether or not their responses are being evoked by the messages of the client. One way is for the counselor to have a reasonably firm grasp on the proximate and long-range goals of counseling. When counselors have a clear view of where they want to go, they will be more sensitive to attempts to lure them in other directions. When counselors lack this grasp, they are more open to unproductive excursions chartered by the fears and vulnerabilities of the client.

A second method counselors can use to determine whether their responses are free or elicited by the client is to ask themselves some questions:

- Do I feel completely comfortable with the way I am responding right now, or is my response stronger, weaker, or vaguer than I really feel?

- Am I responding in a way a "nice person" should or in the way a courageous, helpful person would?

- How does the client react when I respond in an unanticipated way? For example, how does the client react when the message invites me closer and I remain in place, when he pushes me away and I move closer, or when she attacks me and I step aside?

If the client reacts with anxiety and anger, it could be that the counselor didn't react in the way the client planned. On the other hand, if the client easily assimilates the counselor's move, it could be that no evocative message was sent.

Third, counselors can examine their ongoing attitude and approach toward clients. If counselors feel they must consistently react to one client delicately, another harshly, one sympathetically, and another good naturedly, it may be that their responses are being elicited by their clients. Counselors who are genuinely free (who have not succumbed to their clients' manipulations) react to the reality that is present in each session. In other words, the reality may call for empathy one day and confrontation the next. Counselors who have one continuing approach to a client may well be playing by some subliminal ground rule laid down by the client in the very first session. This would be the same ground rule the client lays down for everyone because it protects him or her from reality. However, such an attitude may also underlie the majority of the client's problems.

6. It is helpful for counselors to know what cognitions and emotions are likely to be evoked in them. Obviously, no one can declare that a particular cognition or emotion is automatically an evoked one, but some seem more likely to be evoked than others.

With regard to cognitions, clients sometimes imply to the counselor that they need extra support, attention, gentleness, toughness, guidance, protection, consolation, or warmth. Commonly elicited emotions are anger (in order to reinforce some negative self-image the person holds), eroticism (to distract the counselor from dealing with the real issues), confusion (to create a smokescreen that brings counseling to a standstill), guilt (so the counselor is less demanding), fear (so the counselor is kept at a safe distance or must work harder and show more concern), and helplessness (so the counselor is discouraged from making further efforts).

Counselors who typically experience any of these cognitions and emotions while with a particular client may need to carefully examine the source of both.

Communicating through Symptoms

Psychological symptoms also can be interpreted as coded messages. People often code messages because they lack the ego or psychological strength to absorb the anxiety that would be released by dealing with the actual uncoded message. A client who is in a marriage filled with pain and fear might code her experiences and report that she is tired and lethargic much of the time. The symptom is shared far more easily than the deeper and more painful messages that would reveal the problems in her marriage.

Types of messages. Typically, there are as many as four message combinations. In the first combination, the client sends a coded message to himself about himself. For example, a man may develop a phobia that prohibits him from going to work. The true message he is sending himself is, "You are beginning to have sexual feelings toward a woman at work, and this is a betrayal of your marriage." Since this man would define infidelity as the worst thing that he could do, he cannot send such an unmitigated message to himself. Consequently, he codes the message into abnormal symptoms: "You're afraid to leave home, but you don't have the slightest idea why." This coded message has facilitative value because it accomplishes two things: it rescues him from the anxiety-producing situation at work, and it does so while protecting him from the true message, which would also produce anxiety. His phobia causes less distress than if he had gone to work and been faced with the specific possibility of infidelity.

In the second type of message, the client sends a coded message to herself about a significant other. For example, a woman's true message to herself is, "I deeply resent my husband because he is more interested in everybody and everything than he is in me." She cannot tolerate owning this message because it would mean facing her own feelings of inadequacy, reappraising her idealized image of her husband, and confronting him with the real message, which she is loath to do. To avoid the severe anxiety that would be created by such realizations, she develops symptoms and sends herself the coded message, "I feel very depressed, and there is absolutely no reason because I have a good life and a lovely family." She cannot understand why she is depressed because she doesn't want to. By encoding her real communication, she trades a specific anxiety for an anonymous depression.

In the third message combination, the client sends a coded message to a significant person other than the counselor. For example, adolescents often resent their parents, but lack the psychological skills and strengths to communicate their resentment directly and effectively. Consequently, they may telegraph the resentment through the medium of delinquent behavior: "You make me feel inadequate as a son, so I'm going to make you feel inadequate as parents." His delinquent behavior allows him to deliver his message with great force without having to assume responsibility for it, and the coded message makes it even more difficult for his parents to recognize the problem. Eventually his coded behavior (delinquency) is answered with a coded response on their part. They blame his behavior on the influence of his "no-good friends." His resentment is never discussed, and their anxieties about how to properly raise their child are never dealt with. They all fail to recognize the real dynamics because the messages were coded.

In the fourth message combination, the client sends encoded messages to the counselor. A woman may tell her counselor: "I'm so depressed I don't think anyone can help me." The counselor must decipher the possible true message hidden in this woman's depression and reflected in her statement. There might be several possible true messages that are being masked by the woman's symptoms:

- Assure me that there is hope because I'm bordering on despair and that panics me.
- I don't intend to help myself; so you and my husband better start giving me what I want if you want me to get better.
- I want you to tell me I will get better so that I can prove you wrong, since proving people wrong is my only source of satisfaction these days.

Implications for the counselor. It is important for counselors to correctly understand their clients' verbal and nonverbal messages in order to discover the larger issues that underlie their symptoms. Much of counseling is spent deciphering messages coded in the form of symptoms. Until the real message is brought to the surface, only superficial progress can be made; there exists no reason for the disturbance to stop because neither the counselor nor the client really knows why the latter is in counseling until the key messages inherent in the symptoms become known.

Up to this point, the client thought he or she was in counseling because of discomfort caused by symptoms. But it is now clear that the discomfort was only a side effect of some deeper, more powerful inner message. Only at this point can clients make an authentic decision for or against counseling, because only at this point do clients actually know—for the first time—why they are there.

Discovering the message hidden beneath the client's symptoms does not in itself ensure progress. The client must first decide whether to accept or reject ownership of the decoded messages. If the messages are owned, the client can then, and only then, decide whether he or she wants to strengthen the areas of weakness reflected in the communication or whether he or she would rather terminate counseling and look for some other solution to the problem.

Nonverbal Communication

It has been suggested that more than half of what people communicate to others is shared nonverbally (Birdwhistell, 1970). People may also tend to place more credence on nonverbal cues than on what is said. "How clients (and clinicians) say things is as important as what they say" (Murphy & Dillon, 1998, p. 65). Therefore, counselors should be keenly aware of the presence of nonverbal communication and able to appropriately interpret these messages and use nonverbal communication therapeutically. The following are some basic concepts regarding nonverbal communication in counseling.

Relationship to Verbal Communication

Nonverbal communication is an important factor in counseling because it qualifies the verbal communication. According to Knapp (1978, pp. 9–12), nonverbal behavior can alter verbal interpersonal communication by: (1) confirming/repeating, (2) denying/confusing, (3) strengthening/emphasizing, or (4) controlling/regulating verbal messages. The messages that a person's body sends may be congruent with what is being said verbally or give a completely different message. The following examples show how nonverbal messages can influence responses.

Congruent nonverbal communication means that the person's nonverbal behavior substantiates the verbal communication. For example, a client may state, "I'm really glad to be here today," and the person's face and body language indicate this is true. She is genuinely smiling, her eyes reflect the happy expression on her face, and her body is relaxed.

Amplified nonverbal messages communicate even louder and stronger than the verbal message. For example, a man may tell a counselor in a rather casual, matter-of-fact tone of voice, "I'm not feeling so hot this week, Doc." His benign tone and colloquial phrasing give the impression that he is no more than slightly disconcerted. But his face reveals agony. His eyes are dark and foreboding; his mouth is wincing and dry; he holds his head down and stares at the floor; his hands are strangling each other; and his legs are crossed at the ankles in a very awkward, taut manner. The counselor translates "not feeling so hot" as "I'm very anxious and depressed, and I'm scared!" The counselor will try to help the client put this nonverbal message into words in order to get more in touch with exactly how he feels, why he feels it, and what he can do to get some relief.

Diluted nonverbal messages subtract from the verbal message. A woman in counseling says, "Yes, I think I'm making pretty good progress" but the tone of her voice is much more tentative than the verbal message. Her eyes are saying "I think this is what you want to hear; so here it is." Her face has a frozen smile, her hands are fiddling with her purse, and her back is at a 30-degree angle from the back of the chair. The counselor translates her nonverbal behavior as saying, "I think I'm making a *little* progress, but this counseling has not been much help so far."

Nonverbal behavior can be used to *deny* verbal messages. For example, a man says to a counselor, "I think this is going to be the last time I come in, because we don't seem to be getting anywhere." But the tone of his voice is not convincing. His voice has a pleading quality that indicates, "What I really need is for you to care enough about me to give me some reasons to stay." His eyes say, "Please don't believe what I'm saying," and he lingers in much the same way as a child might when he announces to his parents that he is going to run away from home in five minutes.

Nonverbal communication also can convey a message completely *disconnected* from the verbal one. A woman may say to her counselor, "I'm so worried about my mother moving in with us that I can't think straight. I know she will be hard to live with and . . ." The counselor, watching and listening intently, sees and hears two separate topics. The verbal topic is the woman's mother. The nonverbal topic is the counselor. In barely perceptible ways, this woman is communicating anger toward the counselor. She is glaring at him in a way that does not fit the topic. Her voice has an angry edge, her mouth is tight, and her words are clipped. She interjects little asides such as, "I can see you're amused by all this." So while the woman is discussing her mother, she is throwing darts at the counselor, and her affect is much more congruent with dart throwing than with concern about her mother. The counselor can now help the woman separate the two distinct topics, which are not intertwined at all, and one of which the client is probably unaware she is communicating toward the counselor. Helping the woman see her anger is the counselor's first priority.

Counselors must "listen" to two sets of messages: what is said (the verbal content) and how messages are expressed (vocalizations).

Categories of Nonverbal Behavior

There are many ways that nonverbal behavior can be categorized. For example, Lauver and Harvey (1997) describe four categories: eye contact, space (physical distance between two people), body position, and body movements. Murphy and Dillon (1998) identified four similar categories including appearance, body posture, facial expressions, and clinician nonverbal communication. Their last category is particularly useful because it helps remind counselors that they, like clients, communicate nonverbally. Four general categories of nonverbal communication should be singled out: anatomy, movement, sounds, and dress.

Certain *parts of the body* communicate. The eyes can send messages that one is happy, sad, alert, dull, distracted, frightened, angry, loving, confused, relaxed, guilty, seductive, mischievous, playful, or ashamed. The mouth can communicate that the person is happy, sad, cocky, angry, cynical, frustrated, disbelieving, perplexed, mocking, bored, tense, or relaxed. The contours of the hands, legs, and feet give general messages of being relaxed or tense. One's overall posture communicates relaxation, withdrawal, defensiveness, aggression, anxiety, or uninvolvement.

Movement denotes how people move their anatomy. Eyes can stare into space, flit frantically around the room, avoid contact with the counselor's eyes, or glare. Arms, hands, or fingers can remain at ease, gesticulate wildly, cling tightly to each other or the arms of the chair, fiddle with objects (such as purses, pencils, and note pads), point menacingly, gesture in seductive or loving ways, or protect like a shield. Legs or feet can shift frequently, kick menacingly, tap nervously, twist tensely, or rest peacefully.

Sounds are nonwords that come from a person and often elaborate on word or content communication: sighs, groans, whines, laughs, snorts, wheezes, gasps, coughs, sniffles, belches. Included in sounds are tones of voice, which can be high, low, harsh, unsure, tight, happy, sad, frightened, sarcastic, angry, surprised, powerful, or weak.

Dress often communicates what people feel about themselves and what kind of interaction they would like with others. Clothes can be used to camouflage the body, enhance appearance, declare independence, reflect casualness, get attention, invite ridicule, appear interesting, or communicate despair or apathy. Included in dress are personal hygiene, hair, makeup, jewelry, and perfume.

All the elements listed under anatomy, movement, sound, and dress communicate something about the client. Clients may or may not be aware of what they are communicating, but counselors need to be particularly vigilant in order to observe nonverbal cues. In fact, effective counselors perceive so much nonverbal communication in each session that they must consistently decide which messages to comment upon, which to file away for later use, and which to let pass.

Translating Nonverbal Communication

It is not possible to assign universal meaning to any particular verbal or nonverbal behavior. Specific communication patterns do not have the same meaning for all people, nor do they mean the same thing for a particular person at all times. The interpretation of meaning is not static because communication is a dynamic process. For example, a man who folds his arms across his chest may at one time find it the most relaxing way to sit. At another time he may be protecting himself from what his counselor is saying, covering his stomach (which he recently noticed was getting larger), trying to muffle the sounds his stomach is making, or attempting to avoid hitting or hugging the counselor.

A woman who fiddles with her appointment book during a session may be nervous and wholly unaware of what she is doing. At another time she may be trying to convey how busy (heavily scheduled) she is to the counselor. At still another time, she may have brought the book into the meeting for a very practical reason; perhaps she just wants to find a good time to schedule the next counseling session.

Hasty and assertive translations of nonverbal behavior into "obvious" messages can cause problems in counseling. Verbal and nonverbal messages are kaleidoscopic; that is, they often take on different shapes, colors, and configurations, depending upon the situation. The skilled counselor may say, "I've noticed that your words are saying one thing but your face seems to be saying something different." The counselor then invites the client to clarify the situation. A less skilled counselor may say, "Your mouth is saying some very nice things to me, but your eyes indicate that you're angry. What are you angry about?" This counselor's interpretation is hasty and precludes further clarification. All the client can do is admit the counselor is correct or be seen as resistant, lacking in trust, or deficient in insight.

Counselors can communicate nonverbally in all the same ways as do clients. It is important for counselors to realize that people in general are fairly astute at picking up nonverbal messages, since psychological survival—especially during the early years of life—depends largely on how accurately one perceives nonverbal communication.

Some counselors tend to think they have more control over their nonverbal behavior than do their clients. A counselor may be listening to a client and say to himself, "Who does this guy think he's kidding?" The counselor is completely oblivious to the barely perceptible sneer at the corner of his mouth and the look that says, "I hope you don't think I'm so stupid that I'm buying what you're saying." Instead of verbally communicating these thoughts and feelings, the counselor says, "Good. Well, I think I'm getting a clear picture of your relationship with your wife. Let's meet next week at the same time." The client leaves the session aware of the deception. On a deeper level, the client may register a sense of distrust that may not even be conscious, a distrust that may significantly interfere with future sessions, much to the confusion and consternation of both client and counselor.

The best protection against this type of situation is for the counselor to communicate inner thoughts and feelings verbally, even if they are apt to increase the tension level between the counselor and the client. For example, the aforementioned counselor could have said, "You say you had an affair to help you become a feeling person again so that you could bring that warmth into your marriage. Is it possible that, in addition to that reason, there were other motives less easy to think or talk about?" Here the counselor's reservations are put to a potentially helpful purpose.

Generally, if the counselor is thinking or feeling something about the client, he or she is probably communicating it nonverbally. The counselor must decide whether the message will also be communicated verbally. Verbal confirmations of nonverbal messages may be helpful if they reduce confusion and provide information useful to the client. People regularly receive nonverbal messages but they less often have the opportunity to actually verify them, and they rarely have a chance to discuss these feelings and thoughts with others.

Silence as Communication

Silence in counseling is important communication in and of itself. Perhaps one of the most challenging skills that counselors develop is the management of silence within the counseling relationship. While most people appreciate the opportunity to be silent and to quietly reflect, in counseling, silence can be threatening and confusing. We offer three different types of silence (creative, neutral, and conflictual) so that counselors can properly distinguish one from another and react to each type appropriately.

Creative Silence

A creative silence is one during which the client is reflecting on what has just been said or felt. A woman may have just said, "I've never thought about it in this way, but I think I've always resented my son because my husband enjoyed being with him more than he enjoyed being with me." The woman then stops and stares at a spot in space. She is obviously contemplating what this insight means. Various thoughts are passing through her mind, and she is experiencing a wide range of emotions. She may remain silent for a minute or five minutes, relating solely with herself. This is a creative silence because something new is happening that may evoke pleasant or unpleasant feelings, or a mixture of the two.

One key indicator of creative silence is the "staring at a spot in space." This often signifies intense rumination. During this time, the counselor should remain quiet—that is, do nothing but watch and wait. The counselor's silence invites the client to take all the time that is needed to sort through his or her thoughts and feelings. Moments like this are very productive for the client because they can learn much more about themselves. Also, the fact that the counselor and client manage the silence effectively suggests the existence of a strong therapeutic alliance.

It would be obtrusive for a counselor to interrupt this silence with inquiries such as, "What are you thinking about?" This is a sure way of causing the person to lose a train of thought. Nor is it helpful for the counselor to interrupt with statements such as, "It seems that you are on to something." People can be allowed to come out of these silences on their own. Sometimes a person is not ready to share the thoughts and feelings that arose during the silence. The client may need time to assimilate the insights and become more comfortable with them before communicating them to the counselor. In this case, the counselor can be sensitive to the client's hesitation or reluctance and suggest that the situation be discussed at the next session. While it is true that some of the spontaneity of the insight may be lost in sharing it later, it is a smaller price to pay than for manipulating the client to share things against his or her will or before it would be appropriate or safe to do so.

Neutral Silence

Neutral silences usually flow from not knowing what to say. Initial counseling sessions sometimes have neutral silences when the client is at a loss as to what to say next. People don't know what they want to say. They don't know what is important and what is not, what the counselor wants or doesn't want to hear. Unlike creative silence, where the eyes may fix on a particular spot, during neutral silence the client's eyes may nervously flit from one place to another and intermittently stop to look imploringly at the counselor as if to ask, "What am I supposed to do now?"

The longer the counselor allows this silence to continue, the more tension will build up inside the client, further short-circuiting his or her ability to focus on a particular area of importance. The counselor can wait until it is clear that the silence is not a creative one, then step in by saying, "Can you tell me what you're feeling right now?" Counselors who wait out such silences with the expectation that the person should be allowed to find his or her own way out of the silence may be expecting too much in the early stages of counseling. Once the client has gotten used to the counselor, a longer period of waiting could be more appropriate, as long as it is benevolent and patient.

Conflictual Silence

Conflictual silences may be caused by fear, anger, or guilt. People may be frightened to talk either because they were hurt the last time they did or because the matter that should be discussed is threatening. They may be angry at the counselor and thus using the silence as a passive-aggressive way of communicating the anger without taking much of a risk.

Generally, when people are frightened their nonverbal behavior says, "I really don't want to be here." When they are angry at the counselor their behavior says, "I'm not going to help you out one bit." The guilty person avoids the counselor's eyes and squirms.

When it is at least somewhat clear that the silence is caused by fear, gentle questions and reassurances can reduce the fears. Often, once the client can see that the counselor is attuned to the fear, this is enough to free the client to begin speaking. Advising people that it may be good to talk about their fear, but that the choice is theirs, assures them of freedom and control in the situation. If the fear is causing strong reluctance to talk, it may be better to drop that particular topic and go on to less threatening ones so that the client doesn't become immersed in tension and frustration.

When the silence is motivated by anger, it may evoke anger in the counselor, who then nonverbally communicates "I'm not going to talk until you do." In this situation, the passive-aggressive behaviors of both parties can produce a serious therapeutic impasse. It is therefore better for the counselor to confront the issue as soon as the presence of anger becomes obvious. The counselor might say, "You seem to be communicating something to me by your silence. Can you tell me what you're feeling more directly?" This may immediately generate an open and honest dialogue. Even if it doesn't, it's a healthy response on the part of the counselor, which lays some groundwork for a better exchange later in the session.

When faced with conflictual silence, a counselor can communicate with his or her attitude, "We have a problem here, and this is my way of trying to solve it as quickly and easily as possible." If the person refuses to cooperate, the counselor can patiently wait until the person is ready. Time is not being wasted because every minute of silence signifies the intensity of the emotion and the extent of the person's inability to handle it well. This information will be helpful later when dealing with the significance of the situation.

Silences in counseling need not be feared or avoided, but may be viewed as very helpful instruments. While silences are viewed socially as undesirable, they should be viewed therapeutically as opportunities for growth.

Counselor Communication

We have covered several general ways that clients communicate with counselors. Obstructive as well as helpful patterns were discussed. The previous section also included general suggestions about how to remedy clients' verbal and nonverbal communication difficulties. This section will focus on specific communication skills that counselors need in order to productively interact with clients.

While counselor communication has been analyzed by various authors, the elements of counselor communication are remarkably similar across the literature. When differences are found they almost always occur because certain authors emphasize particular skills over others. One example of the similarities can be illustrated by comparing two different works: Cormier and Cormier (1991) and Egan (1994) divide counselor communication into two major headings: listening responses (e.g., clarification, paraphrase, reflection, and summarization) and action responses (e.g., probe, confrontation, interpretation, and information giving). Counselors employ eight different communication responses in this analysis. Egan discusses four basic communication skills (attending, listening, empathy, and probing) and several challenging skills (e.g., advanced empathy and confrontation). The similarities between the two models are obvious; the differences between them minor.

Doyle (1998) singles out many of these same skills but organizes them around what he describes as counselor roles and sub-roles. Viewing elements of counselor communication in this way guards against an oversimplified view of the process. Before introducing the various responses that counselors use when counseling clients, Doyle describes the personal traits and abilities counselors need in order to work effectively. While he covers the major types of responses (e.g., reflections, paraphrasing), he equally emphasizes the importance of assuming the role of one who genuinely listens and attends to another. Counseling effectiveness demands good technique and genuineness—neither will suffice without the other. Communication skills (sub-roles) are placed into one of three main categories: (1) primary role, (2) intermediate role, and (3) advanced role. Each major role corresponds to a different stage of therapy.

The primary role is used to establish the counseling relationship, so it contains listening skills sub-roles. The intermediate role includes sub-roles that can be used to share information with the client, to question or probe the client for information, to manage the client's questions, to deal with silence, and to establish the counseling relationship. Intermediate role responses are used to further define the counseling relationship, to identify problems, and to recognize how silence can be used effectively. The advanced role contains sub-roles that counselors employ to help the client develop alternatives, to encourage the client to act, to assess progress, and to integrate changes. Skills and roles are presented together in order to emphasize the previously noted relationship between the skill of the counselor and the person of the counselor.

We have selected a single model around which to structure the final section of this chapter. Brammer and MacDonald's (1999, p. 70) seven skill clusters were chosen because they contain a wide assortment of counselor responses. In fact, the array is so inclusive that counseling offered according to any particular theory could be accomplished by using some or all of the following:

1. listening skills
2. leading skills
3. reflecting skills
4. challenging skills
5. interpreting skills
6. informing skills
7. summarizing skills

Effective counselors, regardless of the particular theory to which they subscribe, need to be able to master each of these seven areas. While some counseling theories may emphasize one skill over another, all are important. In general, these skills are used to gather information, define problems, convey empathy, motivate the client to pursue deeper insights or feelings, develop alternatives, interpret experiences, share emotions, and take action. As we discuss each skill area we will include various counselor responses, some taken from Brammer and MacDonald (1999), others from Cormier and Cormier (1991), Egan (1994), and Doyle (1998). It would be useful to also consult these references directly since the following does not describe any one of them completely.

Listening Skills

Listening skills are covered more extensively than the other skill clusters in Brammer and MacDonald because the ability to listen is probably the counselor's single most important skill. Without this, counselors would be unable to collect the information that is needed to determine the client's strengths, weaknesses, and problems, and it would impossible to form and maintain the therapeutic alliance or measure the effectiveness of the counselor's efforts with the client. It is not surprising that counselors probably spend the majority of the time in counseling sessions listening to their clients. Ironically, human beings usually find it very difficult to listen effectively. Careful training, persistence, and a willingness to explore the personal issues that may obstruct the counselor's ability to listen are all prerequisites. The rewards gained by good listening skills more than justify the efforts invested in learning to listen effectively. When counselors carefully and consistently attend to clients, the latter not only respond to the attention paid to them (the result of the counselor placing them in the center of the therapeutic relationship) but also begin to listen to themselves more effectively. In other words, the listening skills that counselors use to communicate convey the counselor's positive regard for the client, while at the same time offering a useful model for effective listening that the client can adopt. The combined benefit improves the client's personal awareness and the client's ability to be aware of others.

Fast-paced, distraction-laden lives and limited free-time make it very difficult for people to find themselves in a setting where someone can fully listen to them. For many people, a counseling session may be the first time that anyone has listened to them deeply enough and long enough to be of help. The following are some considerations that help differentiate the type of listening that is found in counseling sessions from daily communication with others.

Listening and hearing. It is important to distinguish between hearing and listening. A counselor could hear everything a person says in a session and not listen to a single word. *Hearing* is the physiological reception of sound. A person hears the rain, the laughter of children, the sound of a train. *Listening* is the physiological reception of sound plus its psychological interpretation. Hearing is a relatively simple process; listening can be very complex. People seldom create barriers to hearing, but they often construct barriers to listening.

The following is an example of the difference between hearing and listening. A woman begins a counseling session with the statement, "Boy, I'm glad to be here." The counselor responds, "Well, that's good. What shall we talk about today?" The woman begins to relate an incident that she says she wants to share with the counselor. The counselor's response indicates that while he may have heard what the woman has said, he has not listened. If he had, he would have asked himself the following questions:

- Is she trying to convince herself that she is glad to be here? Why wasn't she just glad to be here? Why did she go to the trouble of announcing it?

- If she is glad to be *here,* where is she glad that she is not—with her husband, her children, her work, herself?

- Did she say this as a response to my statement during our last session that she seemed to be losing interest in counseling?

- Is she finally settling into counseling and loosening up her resistance?

- Is she softening me up for something she wants some feedback on later in the session?

- Or is she simply genuinely glad to be here?

This client's simple, declarative statement was chosen to illustrate the kinds of questions that a listening counselor entertains. Of course, most statements in counseling are grammatically and psychologically more complex. Moreover, since most messages a client sends to a counselor in the initial stages of counseling tend to have several layers of meaning, it is important for counselors to realize that one simple statement may encompass many different meanings.

Obviously, counselors cannot ruminate over every statement the client makes without missing at least every other sentence in the session. However, as counselors become more experienced, they become selective, listening more fully to one statement than another, but always listening. For example, if the woman in the preceding example starts each session with this comment, it probably does not mean very much. If, however, she seldom or never begins a session in this way, the counselor may well entertain all the possibilities mentioned. The counselor can then select which questions to follow up with, either by immediately responding to the woman or by using the questions to make more sense out of the ensuing portions of the session.

Functions.   Listening serves several purposes in counseling. Clients need not only to be heard, but to be truly listened to. It is probable that people who pursue counseling have talked about their problems with many others, but have had few actually listen to them. Friends and family members are often unable to listen because they are themselves involved in the client's difficulties, and when they can listen, they often prefer to listen to something pleasant rather than to problems. It is therefore likely that by the time people seek counseling, they have either been unsuccessful in finding others who can and are willing to listen to them or the people who they found are no longer willing or able to do so. The functionality of being heard—otherwise absent in the client's life—is thus introduced.

Listening is also important because people need to listen to themselves talk out loud. Thoughts and feelings become solidified and more real when spoken aloud. People can then get a handle on their thoughts and feelings and choose to do something constructive with them or to reject them as invalid and search for more valid ones. As people speak aloud and know they are not only heard but listened to, they become introduced to themselves. It is not unusual in counseling for a person to say, "I never knew I felt that way, but now that I say it, I guess I do." When counselors listen, they invite people to become who they are.

Finally, listening to a client is important because it can teach clients how to listen. One of the problems that may bring people into counseling is an inability to listen very well to themselves or others. In the first stages of counseling, people typically talk a good deal but listen very little. Counselors who model listening behavior thus enable their clients to identify an area of weakness and take steps to remedy it. Listening can be taught both indirectly through modeling and directly by tutoring people in how to develop alternative interpretations for messages and then how to evaluate them. When clients learn to do this effectively, they will be spared many avoidable problems in their lives.

Barriers.   Counselors benefit greatly from carefully studying the common barriers to effective listening. Egan (1998, pp. 75–79) has identified eight obstacles that affect virtually every counselor. These include the following:

1. Inadequate listening: the counselor is distracted by his or her own thoughts and reactions.
2. Evaluative listening: the counselor judges what the client is saying instead of attending to it.
3. Filtered listening: the counselor screens what the client is saying through the counselor's own cultural, political, professional, or personal filters.
4. The use of labels as filters: the counselor sees the client not as a person but as a diagnostic label (e.g., "the depression").
5. Fact-centered rather than person-centered listening: the counselor questions the client in an attempt to obtain as many facts as possible without ever developing the themes and patterns that make the facts therapeutically useful.
6. Defensive rehearsal: the counselor engages in an oblivious internal dialogue (rehearses what to say) while the client is speaking.
7. [Overly] sympathetic listening: the counselor becomes so emotionally connected with the client's pain that he or she becomes unable to help the client.
8. Interrupting: the counselor's responses block or halt the client's.

Counselors remain vulnerable to putting up these barriers throughout the course of their professional lives. While inexperienced counselors are more prone to listening problems, counselors, regardless of their level of expertise, can become distracted by personal problems and react to particular clients in ways that blunt the ability to listen. Several of the more common obstructions to listening are discussed in greater detail in the following paragraphs.

People often are unable or unwilling to listen to others. These two conditions are responsible for what is arguably the largest barrier to effective communication. While people can't help hearing a message, they can choose whether or not to listen to it. Both the counselor and client may realize that if they truly listen to a message or become aware of its different levels and possible meanings, it could be anxiety producing. For example, if a client hears the counselor say, "I will be going away for a month in July, but I will have a colleague cover my calls," the client may respond, "Oh, that's good that you'll get a chance to get away." This woman hears the message but doesn't want to listen to it because that would mean having to get in touch with its real, personal impact:

- Does the counselor really care about me if he so easily leaves me for a month?
- What if I really need him? Will I be able to get in touch with him?
- I resent his palming me off on some colleague whose name I don't even know and furthermore don't want to know.

- Will I be able to function for four full weeks without my counselor?
- I really feel hatred for him right now for being so cavalier about our relationship.
- Have I become *this* dependent on him?

On some level of awareness, this woman probably realizes that if she truly listens to the message, she will have to deal with the accompanying anxiety. She would be forced to decide whether to keep it to herself or share her thoughts and feelings with the counselor, neither of which she wants to do. She removes herself from this dilemma by not really listening to the counselor. When the counselor repeats at the end of the session that this will be their last session for four weeks, such a client may well act shocked and surprised, as if she were completely unaware of the counselor's vacation plans.

Too much inner noise (internal dialogues) makes it difficult for the counselor to attend to the client. For example, counselors may *hear* the client but *listen* to *themselves*. They may be thinking about the research papers they are in the midst of writing, what they will say to their spouses that evening, or where they will have lunch and with whom. Hearing the client but listening to oneself will naturally occur off and on throughout a counseling session. But if it becomes a common occurrence, the counselor must examine the reason for this and do something to solve the problem.

Counselors who find themselves thinking back or ahead often miss the client's messages. A counselor who reviews the facts may well ignore the evolving theme—the therapeutically significant message. For example, a counselor may think back to what a person has just said: "Did the client say he waited for his boss for 25 or was it 30 minutes?" The client's comments are thus ignored while the counselor tries to recall an essentially insignificant fact. Or the counselor may be thinking ahead: "What additional questions will I need to ask the client so that I can fill in the missing pieces?" Again the counselor loses valuable listening time. The average person speaks over 200 words in one minute, and this doesn't count the amount of nonverbal communication, which may be even more meaningful. Losing "only" a couple of minutes in a session can be a costly experience. To prevent lost listening time, counselors should stop the communication instead of thinking back. They can say, "Could we stop a minute? I'm still back on what you just said and need to understand it better before we go on." In terms of thinking ahead, the counselor should listen to each word and, when the person is finished, say, "You've said some important things. Let me take a minute to clarify them in my own mind so then I can share some of my reactions with you." In both cases, the counselor is freed to listen more completely.

Clarifications are questions that the counselor asks the client in order to better understand the client's comments, to get the client to discuss more, and to verify the accuracy of what was stated. For example, if a client said, "I am here because my wife asked me to; the idea of talking to a counselor makes me feel very nervous," a counselor could use a clarification response and ask the client, "Are you saying that you really don't want to be here?" This question would be used to clarify the client's intent regarding counseling. The counselor could also paraphrase the client's comment. This causes clients to pay more attention to what they are saying. In this case the counselor might say, "Based on what you said it seems to me that you are here because your wife told you to come here." The paraphrase, in this case, encourages the client to focus on his wife's involvement in his decision about counseling. At this point the client has explored cognitive but not affective concerns.

Leading Skills

The skills which come under this heading serve to invite the client to actively participate in the counseling process, to guide or focus the client when necessary, and to explore particular topics more deeply. Probes in the form of open or closed questions are commonly used. Open questions encourage the client to explain or explore (e.g., "How did that happen to you?"), while closed questions call for a specific answer (e.g., "Did you arrive on time?").

Returning to the example of the man who entered counseling at his wife's request, a counselor might ask a closed question like, "Do you have any reason to be here?" This question could be answered with a simple yes or no response. Either answer prompts a follow-up open question. If the client said no, the counselor could ask, "How will you be able to do something that you do not want to do?" If the client answered yes, the counselor could respond by asking, "What are your concerns and how do you think counseling could help?" Counselors are able to learn a great deal about their clients by effectively navigating between open and closed questions. Of course, too much questioning is clearly undesirable; but carefully selected and applied leading skills offer direction while stimulating clients to talk more about themselves, their strengths, their struggles, and their hopes.

Reflecting Skills

Reflecting skills help clients in a couple of ways. Clients learn more about their own feelings and thoughts and they gain a sense that the counselor understands them emotionally and cognitively (reflections can convey counselor empathy).

Basically the reflection of feeling is used to help the client link feelings to their comments. The counselor restates what the client has said but emphasizes the affective elements of the content. In our example, the counselor might state, "You feel anxious when you think about talking to a counselor about yourself." This helps the client sense his feelings and test whether this is actually how he feels. This reflection is also useful because, if it is accurate, it would lead the counselor to examine whether the client's fears regarding counseling are inhibiting his involvement in the process more than his resentment toward his wife for pressuring him to go. Clarifying the major source of his resistance is critical. It will determine, to a very large extent, whether this counseling effort will be successful.

Reflections need to be offered tentatively since not all will be correct. By carefully noting how the client responds, counselors can often assess the accuracy of their reflections. For this reason, reflections should be offered once the counselor has a good sense of how the client reacts to feedback and at a stage in counseling where the counselor has some confidence that the client could and would correct the counselor's incorrect reflections.

Challenging Skills

Brammer and MacDonald (1999) identify four helping skills in this category:

1. *Recognizing* feelings in oneself as a helper.
2. *Describing* feelings in oneself and sharing them with the helpee.
3. *Feeding back* reactions in the form of opinions about his or her behavior.
4. *Self-reflection* as a form of self-challenging.

These skills are quite useful and for the most part self-explanatory. Returning once again to our example, it would be very important for the counselor to examine the feelings about working with someone who does not want to be there or who is there at someone else's request. The counselor would need to make these feelings known by describing them to the client and offering some opinions about the situation. Ultimately, the client would be invited to challenge himself by personally reflecting on the situation.

The counselor might indicate a reluctance to work with someone who does not want to be involved. Or, the counselor might admit to the client that many people are reluctant to start but the fact that the client came at all is cause for optimism. The important point is that the responses are accurate and consistent with the counselor's reaction to the client. Different clients produce different reactions and clients are entitled to hear the particular reaction that they produce in the counselor. These challenging efforts are ultimately aimed at encouraging clients to self-reflect—to challenge themselves.

When counselors challenge clients they run the risk of increasing the client's level of resistance as much as improving the client's level of insight. Therefore, challenging skills must be used carefully and judiciously.

We have not discussed *confrontation,* a skill that easily meets the criteria for a challenging skill. The term is loaded with meaning, and therefore is commonly misunderstood by clients as well as counselors. People generally think it means to get face to face with the client and dispute differences. But this would be an incorrect interpretation. It actually means to raise the client's awareness about discrepancies in the client's behavior. In our example the counselor might confront the client by simply stating, "You do not want to be here, yet you are here and you are talking to me." Discrepancies exist in all forms of behavior. Helping clients identify and respond to discrepancies improves their level of understanding and encourages them to consider alternatives.

Counselors take some risks when they employ challenging skills, but taking properly calculated risks can produce remarkable results. Challenging risks are reduced if the working alliance is strong and the levels of trust are high. Clients will explore more difficult areas and will constructively respond to challenges if they feel the counselor is knowledgeable, genuinely caring, and is willing to remain with them as they work through the feelings/reactions that were released by the challenging response. A client summed it up best when she said, "A lot of people have said the same things to me at different times in my life. You were the only one who was willing to hang around after you said them and help me sort it all out." The client's comment emphasizes that counselors need to assess their level of commitment to working with the client as they make judgments about what challenges and confrontations to offer.

Interpreting Skills

Interpreting skills allow counselors to offer their ideas about why the client reacts or behaves in certain ways. The goal is to introduce new and different information to clients so they can improve in insight and gain a better understanding of self. Counselors interpret behavior according to their theoretical orientation and personal assumptions. Therefore, interpretations should always be offered to the client as matters for consideration rather than as indisputable statements of fact.

The counselor working with the client in our example might interpret the client's introductory statements in a variety of ways. For example, the counselor might say, "I wonder if you are actually here because you are looking for someone who will listen to you rather than someone who will tell you what to do. You might even be interested in making some decisions for yourself and just need a place where you can explore the possibilities." The interpretation comes from an existential theoretical perspective and invites the client to consider more internal reasons for his decision to follow his wife's advice.

According to Egan (1982), interpretations also help the counselor to convey "accurate advanced empathy." This level of empathic understanding occurs when interpretations are offered that bring the client to a clearer or more poignant realization of internal issues that were only partially realized or understood. If the client in the example comes to a realization that the counselor not only understands that he wants to take more control over his life but may even have ways to help the client take this control, it becomes easy to see how strong the client's reaction would be to the counselor's empathic understanding of him.

Of course not all counseling theories would support the use of interpretation as an appropriate counselor response. Proponents of psychodynamic approaches would rely heavily upon interpretations, while Gestalt therapists would likely resist the use of any interpretation. Fritz Perls, the founder of Gestalt therapy, was adamantly opposed to interpretation. Gestalt counselors would expect clients to be solely responsible for interpreting their behavior.

Informing Skills

While advice-giving has historically been shunned by counselors, clients often have a clear and pressing need for information. Counselors need to be prepared to answer questions about community resources, treatment alternatives, symptoms, and so forth. Offering information to clients in a way that does not make decisions for them but rather outlines alternatives is an essential element in effective counseling. It makes little sense for a client to wander aimlessly when specific useful information can be provided. For example, while completing a post-doctoral internship at a local university medical center, a counseling intern encountered a woman who was interested in seeking employment after having remained at home to raise her children for over twenty years. The intern asked his supervisor if it would be a good idea to tell the client about a local program that specialized in helping women return to the workforce. The supervisor urged the intern *not* to tell the client about the program because it would breed dependence and infantilize the client. The client never received the information about the program and left therapy a couple of weeks later, complaining that it wasn't helping. This story exemplifies the fact that sometimes clients need information to solve problems or improve their situations. This client would have been helped by a program designed to deal with precisely the issues she was confronting. The supervisor's theoretical orientation and assumptions blocked the intern from being able to freely offer this information to the client.

With respect to the example of the client whose wife pressed him to enter counseling, we could offer several useful pieces of information. For example, it might help the client to know that people do better in counseling if they find personal reasons for being there. The offer of couples counseling as an alternative to individual counseling might also be in order since the client's wife is so strongly linked to his participation in counseling.

Summarizing Skills

Summarization helps the client recognize common themes and understand how seemingly disparate comments may be cognitively and affectively linked messages that together form important personal themes. Counselors summarize by linking collections of paraphrases or reflections. With regard to our example the counselor might state, "This must be very difficult for you; what your wife is encouraging you to do is something that makes you feel very anxious; it is something you said you do not want to do. This is a situation where difficult feelings confront you if you move in either direction." The counselor might also ask the client if there have been other times in his life where this theme surfaced, either at work, in his childhood, or possibly in school. An affirmative response is likely. It the client does affirm the pattern, the counselor can expect to see nonverbal and verbal messages that are often associated with a "eureka" experience. Clients may seem surprised that the counselor was able to see something so important and pervasive when they could not see it themselves. While the client might conclude that the counselor possesses some uncommon insight or remarkable ability, the truth is that the counselor used essentially one tool—active listening. At this point it is also wise to remind the client that these insights, patterns, and themes were revealed directly from the counselor's interaction with the client. The client told the counselor all that was needed to develop the themes.

While the example that we used to illustrate each of the seven skill areas is oversimplified, it does show how one or two brief client comments can be productively explored. The responses serve to clarify what the client is saying, allow the counselor to express empathy to the client, explore the counselor's reactions to the client, offer the client useful information, identify important themes in the client's life, and in some way motivate the client to change. The client in the example is very likely to sense that the counselor understands his struggle and his emotional reactions because the combination of listening responses affirms the counselor's interest, warmth, empathic understanding, and positive regard for the client. While the client came because someone else requested that he do so, there is some hope that he may choose to remain for his own reasons.

⋇⋇⋇

Summary

Communication is the heart of the counseling relationship. As long as lines of therapeutic communication are open, ideas and feelings can flow freely between the counselor and the client. The challenge associated with this form of communication arises from the fact that both pleasant and unpleasant ideas and feelings must be shared and discussed in the process. Counselors must remain open to various messages, some of which may be very difficult to hear, and others challenging to understand. Open lines of therapeutic communication also contribute to the formation of a therapeutic alliance that is based on trust, empathy, and a willingness to explore difficult and painful topics as well as issues that are less emotionally charged. Counselors realize they must continuously work to maintain effective lines of communication, yet they understand that the counseling process is time-limited and markedly different from the other relationships in a person's life.

Reflection Questions

1. This chapter states that some commonly evoked emotions are anger, eroticism, confusion, guilt, fear, and helplessness. Every counselor has at least one area of vulnerability. Which of these six reactions would you be most vulnerable to? Why?

2. What is your strongest asset as a communicator, and what quality do you need to improve in order to be an effective counseling communicator?

3. Regarding listening to messages, a person says to you after three sessions, "I'm really lucky I got you for a counselor. You seem to really care about me and understand where I'm coming from." Describe at least four dynamics that could be supporting the client's comment.

4. The most common barrier to listening is that people simply don't want to listen. What kind of content in a counseling session would you find difficult to listen to?

5. Some counselors purposely sit in certain ways, talk in measured tones, and look chronically empathetic. They do this in an effort to communicate care, warmth, and acceptance. They don't know it, but what are they *really* communicating?

7

COMMON CLIENT ISSUES

Ultimately, the client's psychological issues are *subjectively* defined through the counselor's eyes. While clients participate, to a greater or lesser extent, with the counselor in the process of determining what is troublesome to them, the counselor's judgment is usually the larger force in the process. But caveats exist because evaluating the clinical significance of various client issues is an imperfect process. One major reason for this is that whenever human beings attend to stimuli they simultaneously ignore others. In other words, the same selective attention that makes it possible to focus on particularly important client behaviors brings with it the inevitability that other equally important aspects of the client will be ignored. The counselor's assumptions—conclusions drawn from personal experiences and interpretations of both theoretical and clinical training—determine which aspects of the client will be attended to and which will be ignored. These assumptions also influence the meaning that the counselor will assign to the client's behavior. In summary, when counselors determine the client's issues they are biased by their assumptions in at least two ways: (1) they selectively attend, and (2) they interpret meaning.

While any theoretical approach to counseling establishes how issues are defined, the range of approaches can be divided into two major groups. We shall label one group *biased to psychopathology* and the other *biased to wellness* and immediately pose an important practical question. Would it be better for counselors to attend more to the problems, issues, and symptoms associated with specific mental disorders, or to attend more to the issues that are common to all clients—their psychological strengths as well as their weaknesses? While a strong ethical and professional argument exists for attending to both psychopathology and wellness—counselors must correctly determine if counseling is an appropriate treatment alternative—it is helpful to explore how each model influences the counselor's assumptions and behavior.

Traditionally, mental health services have relied upon the medical model, emphasizing attention to the client's psychological problems and symptoms and the need for diagnosis. This model maintains that one can study pathology, classify symptoms, establish a diagnosis, and ultimately treat the problem successfully. The implication is that for each diagnosis there is an appropriate and effective treatment alternative. While this holds for certain disorders, there are many that cannot be unerringly diagnosed, and still others that have no useful treatment alternative even if accurately diagnosed. In other words, the model works well when curable conditions are correctly diagnosed and treated. On the other hand there is a cost associated with a model that emphasizes pathology.

Barnard (1994, p. 135), in the introduction to his work on resilience, asks this question: "As our clients often underestimate their own resources and potential, do helpers fall victim to the same phenomena?" He finds "that helpers are often overattentive to client deficits and pathology to the detriment of acknowledging family and other client strengths and resources brought into the therapeutic arena. Much of our professional training results in an overreliance upon pathological lenses which is to the disadvantage of both client and helper." Thus while counselors must correctly identify clients who may need psychiatric or medical treatment in addition to or instead of counseling, being overly focused on psychopathology can be detrimental. A wellness perspective offers a suitable alternative.

Where the study of symptoms with a view to diagnosis is important in the bias to psychopathology, the study of psychological strength is what is most salient in the bias to wellness. While the existence of psychological strength is not too difficult to prove—it is the force that explains why some people are able to deal very effectively with trauma and crisis on their own while others cannot—determining the components of psychological strength is more complicated. There are probably as many ways to define psychological strength as there are theories of personality and counseling. For example, ego strength, a term taken from the analytic literature, and more recently, resilience, are both used to describe essentially the same concept, though each one is offered from a different theoretical orientation. The *Source Encyclopedia of World Problems and Human Potential* defines ego strength from a psychoanalytic point of view.

> Individuals differ considerably in the forms and effectiveness of the functioning of their egos and this gives rise to the concept of ego strength. An individual of strong ego tends to have the following characteristics: objectivity in apprehension of the external world; objectivity in self-knowledge or insight; organization of activity over longer time

spans; maintenance of schedules and plans; ability to conceive and act on a self-selected course of action; ability to choose between alternatives; direction of drives into socially useful channels; and resistance to immediate environmental and social pressures. The related concept of ego stability refers to the normal as opposed to the neurotic, and to an emphasis on real situations as opposed to imagination and wishful thinking. The ego-weak individual is less capable of productive activity because . . . energy is drained into the protection of warped and unrealistic self-concepts due to a distorted perception of reality and self.

This description of ego strength emphasizes the value of self-knowledge, behaving responsibly, self-direction, being objective, and making effective choices. While most of these concepts are also found in a more general description of psychological strength, the ability to establish and maintain close personal relationships is noticeably and predictably absent. Analytic theory would tend to minimize the importance of interpersonal relationships so a definition of ego strength would be less likely to contain this element of human behavior. On the other hand, intimacy and the importance of interpersonal relationships are stressed in most other descriptions of psychological strength.

In general, levels of psychological strength profoundly influence the quality of one's life; deficiencies often cause people to experience greater than necessary amounts of dissatisfaction and distress in their lives and, in many cases, to seek counseling. Since psychological strength profoundly affects how people respond to challenging or traumatic events, clients are often aware of the need for greater strength in order to resolve the important issues in their lives.

Thus effective counseling is predicated on the counselor's ability to identify and capitalize on the client's strengths. When counselors assess the client's overall level of functioning, when they assess the client's ability to deal with complicated or painful issues, and when they develop treatment plans, they rely upon an ability to estimate how strong the client is psychologically. Because psychological strength explains human growth and development, counselors must understand this concept and the elements that comprise it. The remainder of this chapter offers one model of psychological strength.

We have introduced common client issues by focusing on the related concepts of psychological strength, ego strength, and resilience because doing so emphasizes the importance of a bias to wellness. A bias to psychopathology will be addressed in chapter 8 where various psychiatric diagnoses and more detailed information about psychopathology are covered.

The theoretical model described in this chapter is meant to be broad enough to comfortably accommodate many, if not most, theoretical positions. In other words, while counselors of various theoretical orientations help clients increase their psychological strengths in different ways, their goals are, for the most part, similar to those presented here.

This model of psychological strength is composed of several interrelated elements: *need fulfillment, intrapersonal competencies,* and *interpersonal competencies.* These elements interact with each other; that is, a change for the better or worse in one is likely to cause a similar change in the other. For example, a person who lacks self-direction (an intrapersonal competency) may tend to lack assertiveness (an interpersonal competency), which may reduce the chances of ever experiencing a satisfactory degree of freedom (a psychological need). By the same principle, the more freedom a client gains, the greater the capacity for self-direction and, consequently, for a reasonable self-assertiveness. Each element is important for the functioning of other elements, and each element is important in itself. The following discussion will focus upon each in turn.

Human beings are subject to a variety of physical and psychological needs. Fulfilling these needs is essential because the more healthy needs people meet, the more psychological strength they come to possess. And the more psychological strength people have, the more they handle stress constructively and behave in ways that ultimately bring them realistic amounts of satisfaction and happiness. Conversely, the less psychological strength people possess, the more ineffectual they are in the face of stress and the more dissatisfaction and distress they experience.

Intrapersonal competencies are methods that people use to become more internally conversant. These abilities make it possible for people to relate to the environment in ways that are need-fulfilling because they promote a greater awareness of thoughts, feelings, and needs. On the other hand, decreased intrapersonal effectiveness makes it very difficult for people to know their thoughts, feelings, and needs, and thus they do not relate satisfactorily to their environment and ultimately experience greater levels of distress.

Interpersonal competencies consist of the methods that people learn to use in order to interact with others. Interpersonal competencies afford people the opportunity to understand others and in turn themselves in a social context. These competencies are necessary because the more effectively people relate with others, the more they can learn about themselves and the more likely they are to get their appropriate interpersonal needs met. When people relate ineffectively with others, they are likely to experience isolation, frustration, despair, and loneliness.

Intrapersonal and interpersonal competencies are not ordered hierarchically—they interact on the same plane. Thus the counselor would not necessarily help a client increase a sense of self-direction (intrapersonal competency) in the counseling session and then encourage him or her to be assertive (interpersonal competency) inside or outside of counseling. As opportunities for self-direction arise, they are capitalized upon, and as opportunities for assertion arise, they are met. As one dimension of the psyche feeds the other, the person grows in strength. Figure 7-1 illustrates each of the dimensions in relation to the other.

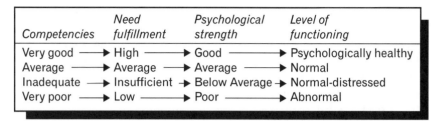

Figure 7-1. Relationship between the dimensions of psychological strength.

The figure illustrates the following concepts:

1. As people increase their intrapersonal and interpersonal competencies, their need fulfillment increases. Increased psychological strength, a major determinant of one's level of psychological functioning, is directly related to increased need fulfillment.

2. People who seek counseling can be roughly categorized, with respect to distress levels, into one of two groups. Clients who experience high-normal levels of distress form one group. These clients experience distress levels within the outer limits of the normal range and experience symptoms including discouragement, irritability, confusion, indecision, frustration, hurt, resentment, guilt, jealousy, interpersonal conflicts, employment difficulties, procrastination, and the inability to concentrate. The second group experiences abnormally high levels of distress. People who are functioning on the abnormal level experience more serious and impairing symptoms such as those seen in the transient stress disorders, personality disorders, psychoneuroses, addictions, somatoform disorders, and psychoses.

3. The general goal of counseling is to help high-normal distressed and abnormally distressed clients to reduce distress levels, fulfill unmet needs, improve intra- and interpersonal communication, and thereby increase psychological strength and ultimately improve their overall level of functioning. How much clients can be helped to improve depends upon the seriousness and duration of their symptoms, as well as their potential to develop intrapersonal and interpersonal competencies and their ability to fulfill basic needs.

Need Fulfillment

It is extremely important that people have the psychological strength, ego strength, and resilience needed to fulfill their psychological needs. The more psychological needs people fulfill, the better able they are to overcome challenges and the stronger they become psychologically. The relationship between need fulfillment and psychological strength is similar to the relationship between nutrition and physical strength. Proper nutrition ensures that a person can do physical exercise well enough and safely enough to increase physical strength. As physical strength builds, the capacity for greater amounts of exercise increases. Similarly, as need fulfillment increases, the capacity to deal effectively with greater challenges increases and psychological strength increases.

People who are able to fulfill their needs are usually psychologically strong enough to adapt to life's challenges; they enjoy good psychological health. Those who get their needs met adequately enjoy normal psychological functioning—that is, they are relatively free from distress even if they are not psychologically robust. People who get their needs met to an inadequate degree usually experience symptoms of distress, within either the normal or the abnormal range. Thus the motivation to seek counseling is often related to the difficulties that people experience as a result of being unable to adequately fulfill important, basic needs.

Glasser (1965) stresses the importance of psychological needs when he raises these questions:

> What is it that [counselors] attempt to treat? What is wrong with the man in a mental hospital who claims he is Jesus, with the boy in and out of reform schools who has stolen thirty-eight cars, the woman who has continual crippling migraine headaches, the child who refuses to learn in school and disrupts the class with temper outbursts, the man who must lose a promotion because he is afraid to fly?
>
> Do these widely different behaviors indicate different [psychological] problems requiring a variety of explanations, or are they manifestations of one underlying difficulty? We believe that, regardless of how [one] expresses [one's] problem, everyone who needs [counseling] suffers from one basic inadequacy: [being] unable to fulfill essential needs. The severity of the symptom reflects the degree to which the individual is unable to fulfill [such] needs. (p. 8)

While Maslow's hierarchy (see Maslow, 1968) provides one widely used model of human needs, others have developed equally useful classifications. For example, Capuzzi and Gross (1995, p. 394), referring to Glasser's control theory, find that "human beings are born with five needs: belonging; power (competence, achievement, recognition, self-esteem, and so on); fun or enjoyment; freedom or independence (autonomy); and survival." While each of the needs Glasser identified will be addressed (directly or indirectly), the model presented here uses labels that are somewhat different, though the differences are minor. The eight needs that will be covered in the next few pages were selected for two important reasons: (1) they are common to all people, and (2) people seem to experience the most difficulty meeting them. Clients differ markedly as to how successfully they meet these needs, so estimating need levels in each area for every client is important. Counselors can also use this information to develop appropriate treatment plans.

Giving and Receiving Affection

The need to give and receive affection is presented first because of its importance. Human beings are social creatures with intimacy needs, and they must be able to express and receive affection throughout the course of their lives if they are to function effectively. Most people are probably more familiar with the need to receive affection than with the need to give it. Receiving affection allows a person to feel warm, accepted, and lovable. When people are treated affectionately they are better able to acknowledge their affection for others because the effects are reinforcing to them and the behavior is modeled for them. Although being treated with affection produces obviously desirable reactions, some people have great difficulty receiving affection. They may give it but not allow others to give it to them, because when people give affection, they often have more control of the situation (the relationship) and thus feel less vulnerable than when they open themselves up to receive affection.

Giving affection is an important need because when people give affection, they can appreciate the effect it has on others and can ultimately feel more loving toward themselves. On the other hand, when people fail to express their love, they experience symptoms similar to those of people who withhold anger. People who do not share much affection often tend to feel frustrated, useless, and emotionally arid. People resist offering affection to others for the following reasons: (1) they have no affection to give, (2) they feel that demonstrations of affection would be rebuffed, or (3) the significant people in their lives are not capable of receiving affection. Fear of rejection and anxiety about not having any affection to share with others make it very difficult for people to develop intimate relationships.

Counselors can help clients discover the primary impediment to getting one or both of these needs met. If the primary problem is within the client, the counselor can help him or her discover the assumptions and feelings that are interfering with the ability to adequately fulfill these basic needs. If the basic problem lies in the inability or unwillingness of significant others to meet these affectional needs, the counselor can help the client identify and act on appropriate alternatives. However, both of these courses of action are based on oversimplifications. The truth is that counseling in the area of affectional needs can be especially anxiety producing for clients because it may bring to light the possibility that they do not feel lovable or that a relationship with a significant other is not founded on love but on some other need or emotion, and both of these are painful realizations. People usually psychologically defend themselves from this type of emotional pain. Clients who live in isolation from significant others do so because the alternative—the prospect of giving and receiving affection—is far more distressing than the pain of emotional isolation.

Counseling offers clients a setting where they can carefully explore their affectional needs. As the client learns to accept the counselor's positive feelings as genuine and learns to share positive feelings toward the counselor, the person's affectional needs can be explored. The client can then become more confident and motivated to meet his or her affectional needs outside the counseling relationship. For a discussion of the importance and dynamics of affection, see Fromme (1972).

Being Free

People need to have a reasonable amount of free choice in their lives. Free choice implies that individuals make decisions on the basis of who they are and not because of who they are supposed to be or what other people want them to do. A reasonable degree of freedom at work, in the family, and with friends is all but essential. While most people accept that certain responsibilities, once freely chosen, reduce freedom to a certain extent, they are still able to maintain sufficient overall freedom in their lives to remain psychologically healthy. This concept emphasizes the link between freedom and responsibility. Human beings cannot function effectively if one is divorced from the other. Responsibility without freedom is life without choice, meaning, and purpose; freedom without responsibility is egocentric, reckless, and destructive. However, the appropriate amount and type of freedom that people need is determined, to a large extent, by cultural patterns. Appropriate acts of free choice in a Western middle-class family could be considered inappropriate, selfish behavior in a traditional Asian family. Counselors should continuously seek to understand the concept of freedom within the cultural framework that defines it.

People who lack sufficient freedom tend to be robots at work, servants at home, and taken advantage of by their so-called friends. The less freedom they enjoy, the more automatic, mirthless, and resentful they become. They have discovered that certain benefits accrue from being a servant—namely, they do not have to assume responsibility for their lives or try to exact their freedom from others. People may lack freedom because they have erroneously assumed that a willingness to sacrifice personal freedom is a sign of love. Such people may equate love with the sacrifice of freedom. They remain unaware that love and freedom are not mutually exclusive but mutually inclusive and are in direct proportion to each other. People may also lack freedom because they remain in relationships with people who make demands that interfere with their freedom. A parent, spouse, or friend may effectively imprison one through subtle manipulation or pressure, making one effectively lose touch with oneself.

Counseling can help clients understand the relationship between their lack of freedom and their unhappiness. Clients may ideally be brought to recognize what causes their lack of freedom and understand how, in some cases, this serves to protect them from greater anxieties. Ultimately, counselors help clients not only to discern the freedoms they do have, but also to act. Freedom is latent even in the most imprisoning situations and relationships.

Often when clients pursue freedom, their behavior creates anxiety in others. For example, a man who is in an unfree relationship with his mother will find that she will suffer disequilibrium as he becomes more free. Counselors often have a dual role of helping the client deal with personal anxieties about becoming free and helping the client cope with the anxiety of the other person in the relationship. At first freedom can be very anxiety producing, but after the initial anxieties diminish, clients usually experience a sense of exhilaration that they may have never previously felt (and that is surprising to them).

Freedom is an essential part of the counseling relationship. It is also an important ethical concern. Ironically, counselors who unduly pressure clients to seek freedom in their lives, defeat their purpose. People evolve to freedom; they are not driven or ordered there. Counselors should be careful not to lose sight of the importance of the client's free choice. They must consistently honor the client's right to choose, even when a particular choice is contrary to one the counselor might prefer.

Play

Play increases people's strength while affording need fulfillment. According to Shaffi and Shaffi, "Play enhances the child's mastery over the environment and [the child's] own impulses and increases [the child's] adaptive behavior. Play is the mother of discovery, creativity, and invention" (1982, p. 42). While children and adults are acutely aware of the child's need for play, many adults think that play is *only* for children as if the need for play were inversely related to maturity. This assumption is incorrect—mastery of the environment and the joys that discovery, creativity, and invention bring are as important to adults as they are to children. Indeed, play can potentially improve the psychological health and well-being of adults as much as of children. Despite this fact, play is an often undervalued and poorly understood psychological need. Adult play was considered so important by one local psychotherapist that he established a basic requirement that anyone whom he treated had to have a hobby and had to be actively engaged in it throughout the course of therapy. While clients were reportedly surprised by the demand, most came to appreciate the value of play. People who look forward to involving themselves in a pleasurable event or activity have a buoyancy that helps them ride above the drudgery and hurts that are part of daily life.

What constitutes play varies from one person to another. Play can be hiking, skiing, swimming, playing tennis, or bicycle riding. Play can be writing, reading, painting, sculpting, or playing or listening to music. Play can consist of relaxing with friends, experiencing the joy of an intimate relationship, playing with a child, or helping people who are less fortunate. Unfortunately, for many adult clients, play is mostly a memory. Their fears, angers, hurts, and guilts have expunged play from their lives, leaving them in situations devoid of joy in which they are unable to grow. This mirthless, uphill journey leaves them seriously questioning whether it is worth the trouble.

For many people, play may never have been part of their lives. They are unaware that they are missing anything. Others may sense that play is missing, but lack the competencies to bring it back into their lives. To compensate for this, they may attempt to substitute compulsive behaviors for play by working excessively, overeating, or engaging in substance abuse, promiscuity, or gambling. Because compulsive behaviors do not fulfill basic psychological needs, these individuals may find themselves compulsively seeking pleasure that does not improve their level of psychological strength but rather creates a secondary set of problems.

Clients who lack adequate amounts of play, leisure, or joy need to recognize the importance of these activities and understand why they have been living without them. Counseling not only can help clients discover the particular creative and inventive experiences that would bring joy into their lives but also can help them develop the competencies to make such events happen.

Receiving Stimulation

People need a healthy amount of variety and change in their lives. They need to experience invigorating relationships and new challenges in order to remain fully alive. While they are tied to necessary routines, they also consciously allot time for new experiences in their friendships, at work, and in leisure pursuits.

People who lack adequate stimulation become immersed in unvarying routines of work, socializing, and recreation that are dulling and suffocating. Those who continually experience the same things tend to remain the same people; that is, they fail to grow. They have no new things to think or feel, to challenge them to grow, or to talk about with others. They feel bored and boring. These people could range from the housewife who is locked into the same routine of housework and mothering to the successful businesswoman who is locked into a rut of paperwork and meetings. Many people who seek counseling do not realize that their apathy, low morale, and general discontent may stem from a lifestyle that, whatever merits it has, is unbearably repetitive. Unfortunately, boredom can be a sanctuary for some people because, while they do not enjoy being bored, it is less anxiety producing than undertaking new behaviors that might revive their lives.

Counselors can introduce clients to the importance of stimulation and help them relate at least some of their apathy and discontent to their suffocating lifestyle. Some clients simply need to enliven themselves in small ways; others need to make radical changes, such as going back to work or school or getting out of a stifling relationship. In either case, clients will need the insights, competencies, and courage necessary to make the changes in order to become psychologically refreshed.

Counselors should also bear in mind that counseling should be a stimulating experience. Counselors who are so nondirective that they continually rehash the same subject matter do little to whet the person's appetite for stimulation. While it is not the counselor's role to entertain, effective counselors relate in ways that are varied and challenging enough that the person feels stimulated and alive.

Feeling a Sense of Accomplishment

Clients must observe and appreciate the positive results of their efforts. Success strengthens clients and motivates them to pursue greater accomplishments. In fact, effective therapy from a behavioral perspective may be seen as a series of successes built upon other successes. The tasks that clients attempt can range from parenting to a project at work to playing golf. The task must be matched to the client's interests and abilities because when people succeed at tasks that matter to them, they attend to the results of their labors and they achieve a sense of satisfaction that strengthens them.

Some people rarely experience a sense of accomplishment. They may try very few things; so their sense of accomplishment is meager. Or they may try too many things, which results in each success being canceled out by an equal number of failures. Some people attempt a reasonable number of tasks but lack the competencies to perform them satisfactorily or find themselves in situations that do not allow success. Still other people do not accomplish things because it would make them feel responsible for accomplishing even more, which they are either unable or unwilling to do.

Many people who seek counseling say, "Things just aren't going well. I seem to make a mess of everything. I'm beginning to feel there's no use in trying any more." Sometimes the feeling that they are gradually accomplishing something in counseling rekindles the possibility that they can accomplish things in other areas.

People seek counseling because they do not feel effective at home, at work, with their friends, or in all three areas. Counselors can help these clients pinpoint their specific areas of incompetence and begin to develop the competencies necessary to become more effective.

Clients should be able to meet some of their needs for accomplishment in counseling. Counselors can begin with a series of less difficult tasks, noting and reinforcing the successful completion of the steps. As the tasks become more difficult and the person's confidence increases, the person is able to carry a sense of accomplishment into tasks of graduated difficulty outside of counseling.

Having Hope

Clients need to feel a sense of the possible—that it is possible to be freed of their depression, that they will be able to mend their marriage, or that they can make things better at work. According to Jerome Frank, "Humans are time-binding creatures, so assumptions about the future have a powerful effect on one's present state . . . hopelessness can retard recovery or even hasten death . . ." (1973, p. 136). In other words, when clients experience hope, they are motivated to continue their efforts to make things better. Even when the light at the end of the tunnel is dim, it can have a drawing power that generates movement in its direction.

However, when hope is lost or is so dim that it loses its power to motivate, people stop trying and experience despair. Losing hope can be a gradual and insidious process that has no clear beginning and no obvious end. People can imperceptibly slide into despair about themselves, their relationships, or their work. They surrender and are imprisoned by despair without ever consciously realizing what happened.

Some people have never experienced much hope because they were essentially taught that they were hopeless. Others do not experience hope because they have tried so many things in so many different ways, all to no avail. And still others do not want to experience hope because they realize that if they do, they will have to move in directions that are frightening. They purposely suppress their hopes and expectations out of fear.

Counselors help clients realize that there is always hope. When people come to counseling in a state of near hopelessness, it is often because (1) they are viewing a situation as hopeless when in fact it is not, or (2) the *situation* they are in is hopeless, but *they* are not. People view situations as hopeless when in fact they are not either because of an inability to see the various ways the situation can be salvaged or because they need to see the situation as hopeless in order to escape responsibility for changing it. Some situations, of course, *are* hopeless. For example, a woman's husband may be a hopeless alcoholic in the sense that he does not wish to stop drinking or abusing her. But *she* is not hopeless. She has the freedom to choose to remain in the destructive marriage or to leave it and make a better life for herself.

Counselors are in a unique position to offer people realistic hope because they probably have experienced clients with similar or worse problems and helped them grow and move on. By demonstrating the hopeful possibilities *within* counseling, the counselor can strive to engender in the client a hopeful attitude outside of counseling.

Having Solitude

Solitude, being alone and quiet with oneself, is a basic way that people keep track of who they are. People who meet their need for solitude make sure that their needs and values do not become buried under the mountain of daily activities that seem important but are essentially irrelevant to their growth and happiness. People who make time for solitude enjoy a sense of peace, purposefulness, and strength. Unfortunately, most people do not recognize their need for solitude. They have become so distracted by everyday events that they view solitude as unnecessary, as wasting time, or as a luxury they cannot afford.

People who do not recognize their need for solitude or who recognize it but are too busy to meet it gradually become strangers to themselves. They lose touch with who they are and serve other masters, meeting the needs and upholding the values of other people or of institutions, rather than their own. Although they may be successful at work or devoted parents, they are strangers to their own needs, feelings, and values and thus behave in ways that are contrary to their best interests. People may avoid solitude because they are frightened to become reintroduced to themselves, since it may result in a radical revision of the lifestyle in which they have invested so much.

Counselors can help clients understand the importance of being quiet and alone. At first clients often do not realize how solitude will help them with their financial worries or their problems with their children. Once they begin to understand, they are likely to protest that they lack the time. Gradually, the counselor can help these clients work through their resistance, especially if the counselor provides time in counseling for quiet reflection. Counselors can invite such clients to take five or ten minutes out of a session to remain quiet and focus on what is really going on within them. Frequently, they are surprised to discover that the more they sense their deepest thoughts and feelings, the clearer their sense of self becomes and the more relaxed they feel.

Having an Existential Purpose in Life

Viktor Frankl, in *Man's Search for Meaning: An Introduction to Logotherapy* (1992), illustrates the profound value of establishing meaning and purpose within one's life. He reveals how concentration camp prisoners, forced to the bare edge of physical survival, could still successfully pursue the existential elements of freedom, choice, meaning, and purpose. People who are aware of their need for an existential purpose in life look for and often produce a deeper sense of meaning for themselves. Instead of wanting to get something from life, they want to give something to life. They seek to contribute, by doing something directly or indirectly to make life a little easier, freer, or happier for others.

Unfortunately, many people remain unaware of their need for an existential purpose in life. A fast-paced, technologically advanced society

offers little time and few external rewards to individuals who are searching for meaning within their lives. People can easily quiet the search for
meaning with the pursuit of material possessions. Success becomes more
linked to possessions, a prestigious high-paying job obtained at a young
age, or some other easily measured indicator of achievement. People who
are unaware of this existential need skim along on the surface of life, taking what each day brings, but have no theme that ties their days into a
meaningful whole.

Some people get so many material needs met that they never give the
existential emptiness within them a chance to surface. Others, however,
may gradually realize that what they are doing each day may have an importance of its own but does not make sense on any deep or lasting level.
These people may experience a sense of existential frustration, although
they may suffer its symptoms without recognizing its cause. They may offer a general complaint: "There's something missing in my life, and every
time I think I've found it, it evaporates, leaving me with a worse feeling."

Counselors can provide many clients with their first opportunity to
learn that life can be more than endless cycles of working to pay bills and
seeking excitement to diminish boredom. Of all the psychological needs
mentioned, this one requires the most psychological strength; it is primarily altruistic, the most abstract of the group, and it requires people to integrate deep thoughts and feelings.

When a client approaches counseling feeling that "something is
missing," and the client is not experiencing depression or some other disorder, then he or she is likely sensing an existential dilemma. Counselors
can help these clients discover how to create purpose and meaning for
themselves through offering something to others. When people recognize
what they have to offer and want to give, it may entail only minor revisions in their lifestyle, or it may require them to make major changes. In
either case, counseling offers a setting where they can explore freedom,
choice, meaning, and purpose. For a more complete discussion of the
place of purpose in life in psychological maturity, see Frankl (1992).

With regard to need fulfillment, counseling has five goals:

1. Introduce clients to their specific needs, since frequently people
   who enter counseling are experiencing psychological weaknesses
   but have no idea of the cause.

2. Help people acquire the courage and competencies to meet these
   needs. It is also important for these people to move away from
   significant others who refuse or are incapable of meeting these
   needs and to move toward those who are interested in a mutually
   fulfilling relationship.

3. Help clients realize that it is *their* responsibility to get their needs
   met and not the responsibility of others. It is up to *them* to get freedom in their lives, to create a stimulating lifestyle, to give life mean-

ing, to ignite a sense of hope in themselves, to relate with people who are both willing and able to enter into a mutually fulfilling relationship, and to refrain from relating with people who are not.

4. Help meet some of the client's needs, not to the extent that the client becomes dependent on the counselor, but in a way that encourages the person to meet additional needs with people outside of counseling.

5. Help clients recognize that they sometimes block their own need fulfillment. They may act counterproductively because they fear getting close to people; are angry at people, which prevents them from accepting concern or love; or experience unresolved guilt, which prevents them from enjoying life.

Intrapersonal Competencies

People get their needs met according to how well they relate with themselves and others. Intrapersonal competencies are learned abilities that help people relate well with themselves. One function of intrapersonal competencies is to increase the quantity and quality of the person's need fulfillment.

People relate with others in much the same way that they interact with themselves. When people relate with themselves comfortably, they tend to relate comfortably with others. Conflictual interaction with others often signifies analogous internal communication difficulties.

People who seek counseling often lack intrapersonal competencies. Consequently, the friction from their internal conflicts spills over into interpersonal relationships, causing tension. However, as was mentioned previously, clients often perceive their problem as stemming from something they are *doing* or something someone else is *doing*, and not from something they are *being* (i.e., someone who panics, is impatient, is in despair, etc.).

Intrapersonal relationships are actually based on three competencies: self-knowledge, self-direction, and self-esteem. (For a discussion of the place of the self in a healthy personality, see Combs & Snygg, 1959; Jourard & Landsman, 1980.) While there is some overlap in these areas, they are separate competencies. Self-knowledge says, "I know who I am"; self-direction says, "I make my own decisions"; and self-esteem says, "I am a worthwhile person."

Self-Knowledge

Self-knowledge is an ideal of mental health, but it is uncommon to have full self-knowledge. Clients often lack adequate self-knowledge because they do not understand their strengths, weaknesses, needs, feelings, and motives. The following are some examples of people who might be said to possess inadequate self-knowledge:

A man may hide his *strengths* from himself because this allows him to get his deep dependency needs met by having to rely on others. He prefers to be ineffectual and dependent rather than strong and autonomous. He comes to counseling complaining that he cannot seem to "take hold of life" when in fact his problem is that he cannot take hold of himself because he does not wish to know himself and act accordingly.

A woman may hide her *weaknesses* from herself while exaggerating her strengths. This permits her to feel strong, but the price she pays is a chronic sense of frustration that stems from entering situations in which she cannot be effective. She blames her failures and frustrations on the stupidity of others. She would rather think she is stronger than she is and fail than to admit her weaknesses and succeed at a more realistic level.

A man may hide *needs* from himself. He denies his need for prestige and exaggerates his need to help people less fortunate than he. He gets a job helping poor people but finds himself continually and increasingly frustrated with it. He blames his supervisor and takes a similar job, which activates the same frustrations. He would rather be frustrated and think he has a strong commitment to the poor than admit he needs a job that pays a decent salary and gives him some prestige and happiness.

A woman hides *feelings* from herself. She hides anger toward her husband and wonders why she has become sexually less responsive to him. She would rather be sexually unfulfilled for no apparent reason than to admit her anger to herself, handle it constructively, and become sexually satisfied.

A man may hide *motives* from himself. A counselor, under the guise of being confrontive, actually uses counseling to vent his hostility on people who cannot hit back. He would rather have a dwindling practice, which he blames on the economy or on people's unwillingness to change, than admit his hostility, learn to handle it more appropriately, and have a psychologically and financially rewarding practice.

People who possess inadequate or poor self-knowledge have learned to hide the more threatening parts of themselves in order to reduce anxiety levels. They were taught that they should have certain qualities, and any thoughts and feelings contrary to these qualities will have produced unmanageable levels of anxiety. They thus respond by employing defense mechanisms to hide dissonant qualities and reduce anxiety. In contrast, people with good psychological strength have learned to take anxiety in stride.

Inadequate self-knowledge is associated with several common client problems. Self-alienation is one such problem. People who lack adequate self-knowledge behave, in effect, like two or more individuals living within the same body; one is familiar, while the other is a complete stranger. When the familiar part of the person moves in one direction, the alienated part or parts stay anchored in place or actually move in an opposite direction. These psychological tugs-of-war cause friction, which may manifest itself in symptoms and/or interpersonal difficulties that the client usually blames on external situations.

A second problem results from the fact that alienated parts of the self significantly influence behavior. These aspects of personality do not disappear, but they manifest themselves in disguised ways, much to the confusion of the person and those around him or her. For example, a father may love his son but also have some deep but unrecognized feelings of resentment toward him. These feelings may appear in his relationship with his son in one of two ways. He may overcompensate for the resentment by being "too loving" toward his son and then spoil him and, in the process, fail to properly parent him. Or the father may wish to address the problem but is perplexed by the fact that every time he makes a conscious attempt to get closer to his son, he only succeeds in pushing him away. The result of both dynamics is that he injures his son and their relationship, all the while protesting that he has done everything possible to have a good relationship with him.

A third problem is that a lack of self-knowledge leads to poor decision making. Obviously a personal decision can be only as good as the data on which it was based. People with inadequate self-knowledge make decisions on the basis of faulty or incomplete data; hence, their decisions are rarely in their best interests. A young man decides to follow a very difficult course of study in college. Despite his modest intelligence and a history of academic problems in high school, he "knows" he is smart enough to handle it well. After wasting great amounts of time and enduring many frustrations, he quits school, blaming the academic game-playing of the professors.

Those who lack self-knowledge may find that their unrecognized parts taint their perceptions. For example, a man hides his deep feelings of inadequacy. His boss tells him, "Tom, I'd like you to help me with this new account—aw, no, skip it—I'll let Fred handle it." In reality, the boss said this because she wants Tom to work on a more important account. Tom, however, perceives that she thinks he is unable to handle the account successfully. Tom's hidden sense of inadequacy has led to a misperception of the boss's comment. As a result, Tom lapses into one of his frequent episodes of depression, which further increases his unrecognized sense of inadequacy.

A fifth problem is that these people ironically avoid situations that could introduce them to their unrecognized parts. For example, a woman thinks she is well adjusted emotionally and sexually. On a less than conscious level, she is frightened of intimacy and doubts her sexuality. Every time she begins to get close to a man, she discovers some flaw in him that she cannot tolerate and uses this as a reason to break off the relationship. She laments that there seem to be no decent, eligible men around anymore.

Sixth, people with insufficient self-knowledge may manipulate others and be manipulated according to their unrecognized parts. For example, a student's unrecognized area is that he doubts his intelligence. He manipulates his girlfriend into writing his term papers for him because he is "too busy" or "too lazy." As long as he can avoid putting his intellect to the test, he does not have to face his perceived inadequacy. This student's girlfriend may have an unrecognized feeling that she is not very attractive or interesting. Hence, she allows herself to be manipulated by her boyfriend because she feels she has to give him *some* reason to continue to see her. The collusion that takes place in the relationship is seen in the contract. The boy says, "If you allow me to think I'm intelligent by writing good papers that I pretend I could have written if I had the time, I'll allow you to feel attractive and interesting by continuing to see you." Such collusion is common and ultimately useful. Studying the contract between two people illuminates hidden behavior patterns in each.

A seventh possible problem is that people with poor self-knowledge project unrecognized qualities onto others in an effort to deny the presence of these qualities in themselves. For example, a woman may have an unrecognized need to be successful at any price. She perceives her colleagues as backstabbers and criticizes them for their ruthlessness. By doing this, she successfully distances herself from the possibility that she possesses similar qualities. As a result, however, she is continually suspicious of others at work, which causes unhappiness in her and her coworkers.

Since it is likely that many clients will be found to lack adequate self-knowledge, it is helpful for counselors to recognize how this lack can manifest itself in the counseling situation. Such clients rarely focus on the true cause of their difficulties—themselves. They tend toward convincingly blaming other people and situations. Counselors must realize that the first place to look for the cause of difficulty is the accuracy of the person's self-knowledge. If the person seems to lack self-knowledge, counseling can focus on this point. If it turns out that the person's self-knowledge is adequate, this frees the counselor to look to other areas of the self and then to the interpersonal area.

Unrecognized parts of a person are at the core of resistance in counseling. While the recognized part wishes to progress in counseling, the unrecognized parts remain stationary or move in opposite directions. Areas of resistance provide the counselor with clues as to where the source of inexplicable difficulties lies.

Another indication of the presence of unrecognized areas is the tendency of people to taint their perception of the counselor and project their unrecognized parts onto the counselor. In a sense, the counselor becomes a blank screen onto which the client projects such unrecognized areas. For example, when clients read behaviors into the counselor that are not present or accuse the counselor of behaviors he or she is not participating in, these misperceived behaviors must have come from *some place*, and usually their source is within the unrecognized areas of the client.

Clients may seek counseling for help in making an important decision—for example, whether to marry, continue their education, begin a particular career, or get a divorce. Unfortunately these clients often define their problem too narrowly. The problem may not be that they can't "make up their mind" but that they don't "know their mind." Counselors who fail to realize this and help clients through a particular decision may be actually hindering their clients from gaining a deeper knowledge of themselves and blocking access to information on which to base important decisions.

Finally, counselors should be aware that people with inadequate self-knowledge tend to unconsciously deflect the counselor's attention from such unrecognized areas. For example, they do not introduce for discussion areas that may lead the counselor into an unrecognized area. Or, they attempt to manipulate the counselor away from these areas by discussing decoy issues or by focusing on the counselor. Such clients may seek to enter into a contract of collusion that reads, "I won't introduce you to your unrecognized areas if you don't do it to me." Finally, they can "protest too much" as a way of covering up unrecognized areas and thus, because they are so convinced, persuade the counselor that he or she is wasting time probing a particular area.

Self-Direction

When individuals are self-directed they simultaneously direct their lives and assume full responsibility for the consequences of their behavior. The more people direct their own behavior, the more they live according to their nature and the better they develop a repertoire of behaviors that will be consistent with self-direction. Three important such behaviors are self-confidence, self-reliance, and self-control. People who seek counseling often lack adequate self-direction and may manifest this deficiency in one or more of the following behaviors.

Self-confidence. Self-confidence is an integral part of self-direction because people must be capable of trusting themselves before they can actually direct their lives. People who seek counseling have often learned to distrust their abilities, perceptions, motives, and judgments. They learned self-distrust either because they were taught by their parents and others that they were wrong a good deal of the time or because they were overprotected to the extent that they had few opportunities to test themselves and strengthen their self-confidence.

People who lack self-confidence may experience one or more of the following problems. They may distrust themselves globally or just in some crucial area—for example, their ability to enter into intimate relationships. They may have good reason to doubt their abilities because they never have developed them to a workable degree, or they may possess good abilities but lack the confidence to test them. In either case, they may suffer frustration because they know what they want but lack a confidence in the ability to achieve the goal.

Second, they may experience difficulties making choices. Because they distrust themselves, they either decline or put off making decisions. In either case, important needs are not getting met. Frustration and anxiety increase both in themselves and in others who are affected by their decisions.

Third, they may react poorly to failure. A failure is not simply a failure to them but a validation of their lack of abilities and judgment. Instead of saying to themselves, "I didn't do that well," they say, "See how stupid I am."

A fourth result is a reluctance to take risks. Because they distrust their abilities, perceptions, motives, and judgments, they fail to take the ordinary risks necessary to grow psychologically.

Fifth, people who lack self-confidence may behave in ways that make them psychologically invisible. Their meek and passive demeanor can make it easy for them to be passed over professionally and socially.

A very serious problem may arise when such people attempt to undermine the self-confidence of others. It can be threatening for people with little self-confidence to relate professionally and socially with those who are self-confident. They may counterproductively seek to reduce the threat by attempting to undermine other people's self-confidence. This can be done by targeting their colleagues' weak points and hitting them with such accuracy and frequency that their colleagues are hurt and forced to defend themselves. While this tactic may seem to offer a certain amount of protection, it predictably tends to alienate people and reduce interpersonal need fulfillment.

In counseling, individuals who lack self-confidence need a fair amount of support before they feel ready to take risks either within or outside of counseling. Such clients are likely to test the counseling process and the counselor a good deal before they risk any significant exposure. They may attempt to use the counselor as a manager by contending, "You know more about these things than I do; you tell me what to do." It may take a while for such clients to understand the dynamics of counseling and to accurately perceive the counselor's role.

Such clients may view routine counseling setbacks as proof of their inadequacy. Counselors should help clients understand that for every two steps forward in the counseling process, there is often one step back.

Clients who lack self-confidence may extend their lack of self-trust to the counselor or the counseling process. They often begin counseling by declaring that they do not believe in it but are there only to please a friend or loved one. Counselors can help these people articulate clearly the exact nature of their distrust and fears and help them associate such feelings with their own lack of self-confidence.

Another tactic used by clients who lack self-confidence is to attempt to undermine the counselor's confidence. Clients may astutely sense the counselor's weak points and play on them to distract the counselor from the client and from the goals of counseling. When counselors feel off balance or defensive with a client, this form of undermining may be occurring.

Counselors should determine whether the client's lack of self-confidence is appropriate. The counselor cannot blithely assume that a client's competencies, perceptions, and judgments are fine and all that the client need do is recognize the fact. The client may actually lack certain competencies, and such deficiencies may thus warrant a certain lack of self-confidence. When this is the case, the counselor's task will be to help the client strengthen these areas, thereby increasing the client's self-confidence legitimately.

If the counselor ascertains that the person is not weak in abilities, perceptions, or judgments but merely lacking in confidence, at least two explanations are possible. The client may feel inadequate as a result of unrealistically high self-expectations. In this case, successful efforts to reduce the client's unrealistic expectations may well increase self-confidence. The other possible explanation is that the client may be consciously or unconsciously using poor self-confidence as an excuse for not living life fully. This could be passive-aggressive behavior aimed at disappointing loved ones, or it could be caused by unresolved guilt that will not allow the person to enjoy life. Whatever the cause, the counselor can help the client understand and overcome it.

Counselors should realize that pep talks do not increase a client's level of self-confidence. Clients no doubt have heard such pep talks from friends and family. In place of pep talks, an effective counselor creates an atmosphere in which clients can freely and clearly articulate the specific areas in which they lack confidence. Then the clients can explore the reasons for their lack of self-confidence and develop methods for solving the problem.

People with low self-confidence can learn to develop healthier, more adaptive perspectives on their mistakes and failures. When counselors help clients understand that even the most effective and psychologically healthy people make mistakes daily, they are more likely to develop a freedom to err (or tolerance for personal error) that will permit them to take reasonable risks. Mistakes and failures can increase self-confidence when one learns something important from them and comes to understand how to apply what was learned to future situations.

Self-reliance. Self-reliance, like self-confidence, contributes to self-direction in the presence of self-knowledge because of its basis in good internal communication. An absence of self-reliance often derives from an inadequate appreciation of one's strength and connectedness. Need fulfillment may be adversely impacted as a result.

People may have failed to learn adequate self-reliance because they remained dependent upon others for needs that they could fulfill themselves. Dependency obstructs development of the competencies necessary to create situations in which need-fulfillment can occur.

When people lack self-reliance, they may experience one or more of the following problems. They may experience a low-grade but ongoing sense of resentment toward themselves for being incapable of meeting their own needs. This self-resentment may show in feelings of self-deprecation, or it may be projected into a resentment of others. They may also resent others because they must rely on these people for psychological support. Their deep need and deep resentment of others often cause them metaphorically to "bite the hand that feeds them": that is, they tend to drive away the very people they need.

Second, they find it difficult to attend fully to tasks because they are always on the lookout for sources of psychological nourishment. Other things in life, such as school and work, are perceived as boring since their real focus is on receiving attention, support, and affection.

Third, they experience interpersonal problems. It is difficult for these people to truly love because their love is conditional. It is based on the principle, "I'll nourish you as long as you nourish me." Checks and balances in the relationship are carefully monitored, and temporary shortages or stoppages of support are met with anxiety and frantic renegotiations.

Because these people often depend on a relationship for survival, they are reluctant to be completely honest in the relationship. They would rather prostitute themselves psychologically than place the relationship in jeopardy. This forced distortion of the true self further weakens the person and makes him or her even less self-reliant; so leaving the relationship, even when it is abusive, becomes very difficult. When such symbiotic relationships do terminate, clients are likely to feel acutely depressed and helpless, believing themselves incapable of taking care of themselves. When relationships terminate, these individuals are likely to latch onto another person; they sense that they need another in order to survive.

Because people who lack self-reliance tend to lean on others, counselors should be especially vigilant about allowing this to happen in the therapeutic relationship. A counselor may inadvertently step into such a role and incorrectly assume that therapy is progressing well because of how easily the client has settled into a "good relationship" with the counselor. However, if the counselor becomes a primary source of nourishment, the client is prevented from becoming self-reliant and from seeking his or her own psychological fulfillment.

A counselor might encourage a client involved in a relationship that fulfills the client's dependency needs to become self-reliant. As the client attempts to become an equal partner in the relationship, however, disequilibrium might be the result. The partner who was playing off the dependency need of the client might lose his or her balance. At this point the client may need to choose a priority: becoming strong or keeping the partner. Sometimes these relationships can be transformed, but more often they cannot— especially if the partner is not growing at the same rate as the client. In such a case, the client may need to end the relationship and experience the symptoms of withdrawal from an unhealthy emotional attachment. While counselors can help clients through such periods, they must resist the client's predictable need to replace the previous unhealthy relationship with one that is equally unhealthy. The client's attainment of self-sufficiency is an overarching goal throughout the process. Anything that might retard this accomplishment should be avoided. Counselors should also remember that a lack of self-reliance severely limits psychological strength and that psychological strength is what clients need to overcome the forces that pull them into dependent relationships. In many cases, the client should be coached in incremental steps in developing psychological or ego strength before being encouraged to withdraw from a dependent relationship. There are many ways that counselors can help clients develop increased self-reliance.

People who lack self-reliance can be encouraged to branch out emotionally. Instead of relying on a few sources of emotional support, it is important for people to develop new friends, relationships, and interests. In other words, the more resources one has, the less reliant one will be on one or two sources of survival and happiness. When clients learn to branch out, their overall welfare cannot be significantly damaged by the loss of any one relationship or job.

Counselors should remember that some clients who lack self-sufficiency overcompensate for it by assuming an "I don't need anybody" attitude. Deep down these clients have strong dependency needs that are hidden behind a facade of independence. These individuals may have an approach-avoidance relationship with the counselor. They may be tempted to become dependent on the counselor, but they will have equally strong needs to remain independent. Because either getting closer to the counselor or moving away would create anxiety, clients may feign indifference. The counselor should use every means available to help the client grow in self-reliance.

Self-control.   Self-control is a necessary part of self-direction because it helps people channel their energies and allows them to guide their own lives. Healthy self-control is based on good internal communication. The wishes or impulses present to the mind are considered in conjunction with possible consequences and the need to manifest higher values within the persons's subjectively perceived range of possible options.

People who lack adequate self-control have failed to master two important developmental tasks. They did not learn the ability to sacrifice short-range gratification for more important long-range goals, and they did not learn the importance of becoming their own masters rather than the servants of others or of alien parts of themselves.

People who lack adequate self-control tend to come up against problems. First, they manifest poor self-discipline. These people are more interested in gratifying their desires than in meeting their work or social responsibilities. They expend time and energy unproductively or only on projects that interest them, ignoring those that may be equally or more important. They lack a realistic motivation. Consequently, unless they are goaded by external pressures, they fail to attend to the unexciting but necessary tasks of daily life. Finally, undisciplined people seek immediate gratification. They have difficulty sacrificing the pleasure of the moment for more important long-range goals.

Second, they often lack the ability to be *self-governing*. People who have difficulty governing their lives are controlled by internal or external pressures that cause them to make decisions that seriously impair their need fulfillment and which they may later regret. For example, they may be controlled by an irrational conscience and conform to an inflexible moral code or set of stringent ideals that may cause them to make decisions contrary to their best interests. Sometimes their "shoulds" have so successfully taken over their conscience that they actually think *they* are making the decisions rather than an unrecognized imperative. They may also be unhealthily governed by authority, which can include parents, bosses, older people, or their church. They thus follow the dictates of authority rather than their own carefully considered attitudes and beliefs.

Additional problems arise when they are governed by what other people think. Before making any consequential decision, they worry how others might judge them. They may frequently lament, "I really know what I need to do, but it would kill my parents" or, "I know what I'd really like to do, but my friends would disown me or think I was crazy." This attitude confines them to a restricted roster of possibilities.

Finally, they may experience problems because of their raw needs and feelings. Their needs and feelings have probably not been sifted through a socialization process that allows them to work toward a harmony between themselves and others. If they want something, they think they have to have it now. If they feel something, the feeling is as likely to be expressed destructively as constructively. Hence, it is not they who govern their behavior; their behavior is governed by their whims and impulses. When needs based on greed or feelings of frustration and anger override one's socialization, behavior that is proximately or ultimately self-defeating may ensue.

The counselor should first help the client recognize that undisciplined behavior is self-defeating. Clients may then come to realize that while their behavior helps them skirt immediate anxieties, it deprives them of the orderliness and consistency necessary for true happiness and fulfillment.

Because clients with inadequate self-discipline often fail to perceive the immaturity and unreasonableness of their behavior, counselors may need to confront them with the weakness of their rationalizations, excuses, and self-justifications. Since the person's poor self-discipline is also likely to manifest itself in the counseling relationship, the counselor will have ample opportunity to mirror to the person a clear reflection of the causes, dynamics, and results of his or her undisciplined behavior.

People who lack self-discipline must be dishonest a good deal of the time in the hope of avoiding the consequences of their unorganized, disordered, or damaging behavior. As long as they can avoid facing the consequences of such maladaptive behavior, they have little motivation to change. Therefore, it is important that counselors encourage people to be honest with others about their lack of self-discipline and to accept that growth may entail some discomforts.

Counselors can help clients understand the causes of inadequate self-discipline. People can learn what fears may have made it difficult to concentrate on important tasks; what angers may have caused them to disappoint, use, or damage people; what hurts foster the attitude "I've got to take care of me because no one else will"; and what guilts are causing the self-defeating nature of their behavior.

While working on the underlying causes of the lack of self-discipline, counselors can help clients begin to take small, practical steps toward a self-motivated self-discipline. Clients can be encouraged to be on time for appointments, to decline making commitments they have little intention of fulfilling, to map out a few basic priorities and allot time for each, and to pick one or two projects they will satisfactorily complete.

People who are governed by their irrational consciences often seek counseling to help them meet their "shoulds" in a more effective manner. They tell the counselor that they should be a better spouse, parent, child, friend, or worker and seek help in misrepresenting their true personalities even better. Counselors can help these clients realize the folly and destructiveness of their "shoulds" and focus on what they need to do in order to grow into fuller human beings.

Clients who are governed by authority tend to automatically cast the counselor into the role of authority figure and demand that he or she assume the role. Were the counselor to decline to fulfill this role, the client would experience the anxiety attendant to being on a rudderless ship. Were the counselor to ask the client, "What do you want to do?" the client would react with astonishment and perhaps say that no one had ever asked that question.

People who are governed by what other people think will resist behavioral change because they feel that new behaviors might create conflict. Counselors can help demythologize the clients' feeling that others care so much what they do, and help them develop the strength necessary to act, even when the action will upset others.

Clients who are governed by their raw needs and feelings tend to flood the counselor with pressing issues ("You've got to write a note to my teacher saying that I'm too upset to take the exam"). They also tend to splatter the counselor with whatever feelings of fear, anger, guilt, or hurt are brimming over at the time. By reflecting to these individuals the manipulative and destructive quality of their behavior, the counselor can invite them to design more appropriate alternatives. Counselors also should assiduously avoid reinforcing these behaviors by not allowing clients to make use of such strategies in the counseling environment.

Self-Esteem

Self-esteem, like the other intrapersonal competencies, depends on good internal communication. People perceive themselves as being capable, benevolent, and worthwhile when they can relate the known facts about themselves to their true values and to an accurate assessment of outside forces affecting them. Failures of self-esteem thus involve a failure of self-communication at the deepest levels.

People may lack adequate self-esteem because they were taught that they were not competent or lovable, or because they were ignored or made to feel unimportant, inadequate, unattractive, or burdensome. As people grow through adolescence into adulthood, their feelings of unlovableness may cause them to behave in unpleasant ways, giving rise to further self-esteem problems.

People who lack self-esteem may exhibit one or more of the following behaviors. They may perceive themselves with disrespect and disaffection and treat themselves accordingly. Whether they realize it or not, such people do not like themselves and would not choose themselves as friends or life partners. They view themselves as stupid, evil, weak, boring, or unattractive, and relate with themselves as they would to a person who possessed such failings. Consequently, they ignore themselves; that is, they fail to take care of their own needs or attend to their basic values. As a result, they become weaker and more self-alienated, which only adds to their poor sense of esteem. They may also treat themselves poorly by making bad decisions, such as entering into or remaining in damaging relationships or jobs. They settle for less in life because they feel they do not deserve more, or they invite destruction because it seems to be an appropriate fate. They may recognize the self-limiting and self-defeating aspects of their behavior only to protest that they are unable to stop them. Or they may blame their unhappiness on other people or situations, such as work, society, religion, or fate.

Second, people who simply underrate themselves without despising themselves often attempt to get others to meet their esteem needs to compensate for their lack of self-esteem. They function on the principle, "Since I don't respect or like myself very much, I *doubly* need you to respect and like me." In other words, they seek from others what they cannot give themselves. Like everyone, they have a self-esteem void and an other-esteem void, both of which need filling. However, they attempt to fill *both* of these voids with the esteem of others, something which cannot be done. Not realizing this, they often compulsively seek others' esteem by an endless series of behaviors that drive them further from behavior that could fill their self-esteem void.

A third behavior typical of those who lack self-esteem is attempting to fill the void with artificial substitutes. Because the emptiness of the void causes boredom, loneliness, or pain, they attempt to fill it with food, drink, or drugs. Or they may attempt to fill it with prestige, which is different from esteem in that it invites people to see the person as successful, something quite different from seeing the person as good per se.

Fourth, they may overidentify with a role. When clients do not view themselves as worthwhile, they overidentify with a role that they perceive as making them worthwhile. A man does not play professional sports; he *is* a professional athlete. A woman does not practice medicine; she *is* a physician. A man does not do religious work; he *is* a priest. A woman is not married to John Smith; she *is the wife of Senator John Smith*. These people do not possess a privately owned sense of self-worth; so they must borrow it from a role. As long as such a role is available, they are unlikely to grow to any significant degree. And if the role discontinues, they are left with nothing.

Fifth, they cannot let others become psychologically intimate with them. Because they view themselves negatively, they cannot allow others to get close lest they come to share the same view. Consequently, they keep others at a distance through obvious or subtle tactics, or they place a pleasing facade between themselves and the people whom they invite to come closer. In either case, their deepest needs fail to be met. In the first case, other people are too far away to meet their needs, and in the second, it is the facade that receives the love and respect, not the person. These people are left with the assumption that if others really knew them they would not like them or care about them.

A sixth behavior is a capriciousness in the choice of friends and co-workers. People with low self-esteem tend to choose friends on the basis of how people will meet their esteem needs. People who continually show respect, admiration, and liking are accepted as dear friends and valued coworkers. People who relate more matter-of-factly, even though they are good and enjoyable people, are discarded as deficient or poor company. Consequently, such clients may end up having very few friends.

People with sound self-esteem have a reservoir to draw upon; so if they lose some self-esteem it causes only temporary disequilibrium. People with superficial self-esteem have no such reserves; hence, a sudden blow to their sense of worth can cause acute anxiety or depression. Failure to receive a promotion is seen as a catastrophe; rejection by a lover is seen as devastating. Such individuals tend to go to great and inappropriate lengths to win and keep jobs and friendships and relentlessly attempt to retrieve them if they are lost.

Another problem is their inability to forgive themselves. Just as one can forgive a loved one more easily than a person whom one dislikes, the person with low self-esteem ruminates and broods about transgressions. This occurs even when others have forgiven the person. These people use their guilt in a self-tormenting way that stubbornly withstands all attempts by others to help them return to the business of living. Sometimes these people permit the guilt to lie dormant until something nice happens to them. Then they stoke it up and allow it to spoil any pleasant experience.

Finally, people who dislike or hate themselves may get their esteem needs met in negative ways. Since they feel they can never be the best, they may set out to be the worst. They may well be able to get some people to respect or admire them for the strength, cunning, callousness, or courage they manifest in antisocial behavior. This can be seen in the 10-year-old class bully or the 30-year-old prison inmate who likes prison life because he enjoys significantly more respect in prison than he does "on the street."

While a lack of self-esteem may be hard for clients to detect within themselves it is often obvious to the counselor. The way the client walks, stands, dresses, or talks may all give evidence of a lack of self-esteem. But sometimes people who experience low esteem do not present an obvious picture; they may appear self-confident, buoyant, and energetic. Under these conditions it may take time and highly developed listening skills for a counselor to see through the facade.

When counselors remember that one of the ways people learn to feel unlovable is by being treated in unlovable ways, they realize how important it is for them to relate to the client in a positive, nonrejecting way. At times this can be a challenge because people who dislike themselves often dislike others (including the counselor) proportionately. Consequently, the client may become very unpleasant, and if the counselor is not perceptive enough to see through the behavior and understand its causes, the counseling effort will be severely compromised. The counselor who chooses to see only likable clients will not help those who need the most help.

Clients who lack self-esteem are likely to be ambivalent toward counseling. The part of their personality that wants to learn to behave in ways more in keeping with healthy values and realistic expectations wants to cooperate. However, the part that feels ugly or unlovable may unconsciously make them feel they do not deserve esteem or happiness and may work to sabotage counseling. Often it is necessary to invite and allow the client to get in touch with the perceived ugliness, share it with the counselor, and place it in a more realistic, understanding, and forgiving light. Sometimes this can be done simultaneously with learning new behaviors; at other times it must be done prior to attempting to encourage any overt behavior changes.

Such clients may attempt to induce the counselor to meet their esteem needs. They may grow in counseling for the sake of earning praise from the counselor rather than growing for the sake of growth and self-acceptance. Counselors should be aware that, while some rewarding can be a necessary and important part of counseling, offering excessive rewards may simply give the client other-esteem rather than help him or her develop self-esteem.

As alluded to previously, clients who lack self-esteem may also attempt to induce counselors to help them fill self-esteem voids with artificial substitutes such as other-esteem, prestige, material acquisitions, or love relationships. While any of these goals could be a valid pursuit, in itself, none is really the same as self-esteem. This is often a difficult insight to help people attain because most people are convinced that if only they could get a desirable person to love them, they would have all the love and esteem they need, and their problems would be solved.

Counselors should be aware that clients who lack self-esteem are not truly helped by being told they are better than they think they are. Psychological pep talks may create a temporary and superficial positive self-concept, but it is likely to deflate at the first setback. While people may possess an inherent worth by the fact of their existence, they must acquire a sense of self-esteem. Counselors can help clients pinpoint and change behaviors that detract from their sense of worth.

Clients lacking in self-esteem are likely to bring into counseling their reluctance to allow people to get close to them. It may take time and a good deal of testing before the client will allow the counselor to get close enough to share the client's negative view of himself or herself. The counselor will need to be patient, sensitive, empathic, and gentle to achieve this goal.

Interpersonal Competencies

Interpersonal competencies are learned abilities that allow people to relate with others in mutually fulfilling ways. Interpersonal competencies complement intrapersonal competencies in that both are necessary for psychological growth and need fulfillment. When people relate well with themselves and others, they will experience positive need fulfillment. Difficulties in one or both sets of competencies will interfere with need fulfillment and may cause psychological dysfunctions.

Interpersonal competencies act as bridges that link the individual with the external environment. The more bridges a person has and the stronger they are, the more needs will be met and the more psychological resources the person will have to share with others. People who seek counseling often lack one or more interpersonal competencies; hence, one of the goals of counseling is to help people unlearn unproductive ways of relating and learn new, more fulfilling communication skills. There are many interpersonal competencies. The following discussion presents some of the competencies that seem to present the most difficulty to people who seek counseling.

Sensitivity to Oneself and Others

When people communicate effectively with others, they must be attuned to themselves as well as to the people with whom they are relating. In other words, they need effective levels of intrapersonal communication so that as they talk and listen, they remain aware of their own thoughts and feelings and take into account this awareness in making appropriate responses to others. Predictably, many people who seek counseling are poorly attuned to themselves. For example, as they listen to someone, they may be responding intellectually to what the person is saying, but unable to sense their own emotional reactions. After they leave the encounter, they may begin to experience the feelings of fear, anger, hurt, guilt, or love that were present, but subconscious, during the conversation.

Being sensitive to others means that people perceive the deeper thoughts and feelings that lie behind another's words and actions. For example, a man tells his wife that he will not be able to go away with her for the weekend as he had promised because he has to prepare a project for work. His wife assures him that she understands and that it is all right. However, he does not see the hurt look on her face that disappears in a flash, or hear the false lightness in her voice. He will be confused by her inattentive and passive-aggressive behavior over the weekend because she assured him that she understood.

Being sensitive to others also means having a sense of empathy with them. People with empathy intuit others' thoughts, feelings, sensitivities, and vulnerabilities and use this information with great care and discretion. They recognize the right and the wrong time to say things. They also anticipate the needs of others; for example, they know without being told directly that a person needs to be given some affection or encouragement or to be left alone.

A lack of sensitivity to self and to others profoundly interferes with mutual need fulfillment. Sensitivity allows people to detect thoughts, needs, and feelings within themselves and others. How deeply people are able to relate to others is to some extent governed by how sensitive they are to themselves as well as to others.

In counseling, these clients often experience difficulty concentrating on their reactions or those of the counselor. For example, after delivering some emotion-laden statement to the client, the counselor may ask, "Well, what have you been feeling?" The client may react with a dumbfounded look and reply, "Oh, I was so busy listening to what you were saying that I wasn't thinking or feeling much of anything."

When appropriate, counselors can invite clients to explore the thoughts and feelings that lie beneath their words. Over time, clients can learn to ask themselves, "Are my words communicating what I am really thinking and feeling, or are they simply camouflaging my real reactions?"

Sensitivity can also be taught by direct example. For example, a counselor might say, "What I am wondering is whether I should let you continue with what you are saying or tell you that I feel frustrated because I am interested in how you feel, but I think you are using your words to hide your feelings." Here the counselor models how a person who is aware of what he or she feels and who is willing to disclose the information to another can deepen the level of communication and at the same time improve the relationship.

Counselors can also help clients learn how to become more sensitive to others within the limits of the counseling session. In individual counseling the counselor might invite the client to practice identifying the counselor's thoughts and feelings by asking the clients questions such as, "What do you think I'm really saying and feeling at this point?" In group settings the client might complete a similar exercise by trying to identify thoughts and feelings in another member of the group. Both approaches may be useful. Exercises like this can help reveal how and why the client remains insensitive while simultaneously disclosing many of the interpersonal problems that insensitivity produces. Couples counseling contains many examples that attest to the effectiveness of this approach. Spouses are often surprised at how incorrectly they read one another's thoughts and feelings and are saddened by the amount of marital conflict they experience that is directly attributable to one or the other acting on the basis of incorrect conclusions. When people lack sensitivity they are insensitive to both themselves and others. So when they do try to read others' thoughts and feelings they usually end up projecting hidden parts of themselves into others. While they assume they are perceiving some aspect of the other person they are actually perceiving unacknowledged feelings within themselves.

Assertiveness

Being assertive means that people have learned to get from life what is rightfully theirs and to communicate in ways that are constructively honest. Assertive people do not permit others to block their paths to legitimate need fulfillment.

On the other hand, nonassertive people must rely on the beneficence of others to get their needs met. Either they passively wait to be cared for or they indulge in behaviors meant to earn donations from others. Such people either try to exist by meeting a limited number of their needs and desires or they become dependent upon some person or persons who regularly provide for their wants. In the latter case, the price the person pays is often high. For example, the person may exchange significant amounts of personal freedom in order to remain in such a relationship. When nonassertive people experience psychological pains, they unfortunately often ask the wrong questions: "What's wrong with people that they don't meet my needs?" "What's wrong with me that people won't meet my needs?" In fact they should be asking, "What's wrong with me that I don't go out and create situations in which I can meet my needs myself?"

Nonassertive behavior may stem from a person's lack of self-esteem. For example, a person may ask, "Who am I to ask for what I need and say how I feel?" It could also originate from inadequate self-confidence in that the person feels others can take better care of him or her. Nonassertive people may have lacked assertive models; hence, they have never had an opportunity to learn assertive behavior, even though their self-esteem is adequate.

Counselors motivate clients by emphasizing the disadvantages and costs of being unassertive and by identifying opportunities both in and out of counseling where the client can begin a series of increasingly difficult assertive responses. Counselors can model assertive behavior in the counseling sessions and offer role-playing experiences that give the client a chance to practice assertive responses. Each intervention has merit, and most clients will need to use all of them.

The opposite extreme of nonassertiveness is aggression. Aggressive people not only take what is appropriately theirs but intrude in the lives of others in unjust and inappropriate ways. They interrupt people, intimidate them, manipulate them, make inappropriate demands, criticize in destructive ways, and take over situations. They often become loud, boisterous, and impervious to others' feelings. These patterns are difficult to change principally because aggressive behavior produces results while camouflaging fears or weaknesses. For example, aggressive people are often fearful of being ignored and overcompensate by making it impossible for people to ignore them. They may also be hostile people whose aggressive behavior is meant to vanquish others.

Although aggressive people often get short-term needs met by their behavior, they tend to alienate others, which prevents them from entering into intimate, long-term relationships that would satisfy deeper and more meaningful needs. While these people may be surviving on a daily basis, their needs for intimacy, esteem, and acceptance remain largely unmet.

In counseling, such people are likely to behave aggressively toward the counselor, challenging his or her policies and personal qualities and making inappropriate demands. In these situations counselors can act as a model of assertiveness, standing by their policies yet not meeting force with force. Counselors can also gradually invite these clients to recognize how their aggressive behavior, despite its short-term benefits, severely limits them. As these clients see the self-destructiveness of their behavior more clearly, they are in a better position to envision more constructive alternatives.

Being Comfortable with Oneself and Others

Being comfortable with oneself and others means being open—that is, "Who you see is who I am." Such people are interested in the issues and the people with whom they are communicating. They react spontaneously because they do not use censoring mechanisms to delay their reactions in order to erase parts of themselves they don't want others to see.

In other words, they become part of the interpersonal process instead of being spectators observing from a safe distance.

People who are uncomfortable with themselves become self-conscious to the point that they are a distraction to themselves. They reflexively sift their reactions, holding back those that may create anxiety and offering inauthentic responses to please others. They continually listen to an inner voice that asks, "How should I react now?" "What will make them accept me?" "What had I better not do or say?" They function on the principle, "Who you see is not who I am but who I want you to think I am."

The basic cause of self-discomfort is fear. People who are not comfortable with themselves fear that if others see them as they really are, they will be thought less of, rejected, or may lack some power or control in the situation. Hence, they view many interpersonal encounters as contests to be won or lost rather than as opportunities for cooperation and fulfillment. Their self-consciousness often causes them to act tense, stilted, and guarded, which makes other people uncomfortable. In this milieu of mutual discomfort, few if any needs will be met by either party.

Clients will bring their discomfort into the counseling situation and possibly create an environment in which the counselor "catches" the self-distrust. The counselor may begin to feel tense, distracted, or irritated. Counselors in this situation can insulate themselves by establishing clear boundaries that separate them from the client's insecurities and by helping the client limit such anxieties so that they do not overwhelm the counseling process. For example, a counselor may say, "Let's see if you can put into one sentence your major concern right now." Often when clients can isolate their greatest concern, they experience a certain peace, even if the concern itself is anxiety producing. This occurs because clients no longer need to expend effort trying to camouflage the concern from themselves or their counselors.

Allowing Others to be Free

People who have a sense of freedom will allow others to be themselves. Because they allow themselves to be free, they enable others to interact with them in a relaxed, mutually beneficial, and satisfying way.

People who have not come to value freedom insist on conditions others must meet before they will be accepted. Some common conditions such controlling people stipulate include the following:

- you must be intelligent and logical
- you must be serious and correct
- you must agree with me
- you must not hurt my feelings
- you must be who I want you to be

In other words, controlling people carry with them a kind of psychological pillory into which others must squeeze their psyches if they wish to relate. The problem with this is that secure people will not wish to subject themselves to these conditions, and insecure people may accept them but demand more than they will give. In the first case, the controlling person is left with few, if any, people to relate to; in the second case, the controlling person pays a high price for a basically damaging, maladaptive relationship. Neither case produces adequate mutual need fulfillment.

People who value freedom allow others to meet their needs as they see fit. Controlling people have difficulty doing this. Controlling people demand exclusive relationships where under threat of retribution, the other person must meet their needs and seek no personal satisfaction from other relationships. Such an unarticulated ultimatum will quickly be brought to bear should the other person attempt to get his or her needs met from other people or in other situations.

People who have failed to develop this competency are both frightened and needy. Their fear causes them to set up conditions for relationships that screen out secure people, whom they would perceive as threatening, and admit insecure people, who will meet their needs without posing a threat. Some people are controlling because that is the way others treated them and they have had no opportunity to learn any other way of relating with people.

Controlling people are very likely to bring their unspoken demands into counseling. They commonly refuse to relate with the counselor unless the following conditions are met:

- you let me control the counseling situation
- you share my religious and philosophical values
- you promise you will be able to help me
- you agree not to make me face realities I don't want to see
- you agree with my perception of my problem

These conditions are usually presented immediately, so the counselor must be ready to react quickly to them. Obviously, counselors cannot agree to any conditions that would lock them into an unprofessional role, and when the counselor communicates this fact, tension almost always arises. The counselor must also resist the client's conditions for another reason—because the counseling relationship will be ineffective if it does no more than mirror the other nonproductive relationships in the client's life. The counselor must calmly explain that the counseling relationship is based upon mutual freedom. During the agreement-building phase, which may last for one or a few sessions, the counselor gives the client important data upon which to make a decision about the counseling relationship. If the client understands what the counselor is saying, he or she will make a more informed decision as to whether to continue with counseling sessions. If the client chooses to continue, the counselor can gradually help the client recognize the fears and needs that are behind the client's conditions (demands) so that they can be dealt with and either reduced or else expressed in more constructive ways.

On the other hand, if the client insists that the conditions are nonnegotiable, he or she may decide to terminate the sessions. If this occurs, it may be interpreted as a sign that although the person may need counseling, he or she was not an appropriate candidate for counseling at that time. Since rigid controlling behavior signifies a lack of psychological strength, controlling clients who opt out of counseling may be understood to be people who correctly realize that the process would be too disorienting for them. In other words, they understand, at some level, that they lack the ego strength to commit themselves to counseling. If the counselor handles the situation in a firm yet understanding manner, the client is likely to re-enter counseling at a time when he or she is more able to benefit from it.

Realistic Expectations of Oneself and Others

People who have realistic expectations of themselves realize that they have imperfections. Consequently, they do not always pressure themselves to be correct, intelligent, benevolent, selfless, kind, mature, sensitive, firm, interesting, or attractive. Although they realize that each of these qualities may be a virtue, they also recognize that there will be times and situations in which they fail to exhibit such qualities—perhaps spectacularly.

People with unrealistically high expectations of themselves generally react to their shortcomings in various ways. For example, they may seriously think they should meet their unrealistically high expectations, which causes them to focus more on themselves than on the interpersonal event. They are so focused on trying to meet these expectations that they ignore the other person, using him or her as an audience for the performance. On the other hand, they may realize that they cannot meet their high expectations; and hence avoid all but the most necessary and superficial interpersonal situations in order to protect their pride. Unfortunately, people who have unrealistic expectations perceive others as audiences to perform for or to avoid, instead of as individuals to relate with.

People who have unrealistic expectations of themselves may have been taught that they have to be better than they are in order to earn praise and love. Others were taught that they had to be superior to everyone else; hence, they developed goals for themselves that in their mind would make them better than others. These perfectionistic individuals often think, "I can forgive others much easier than myself," as if to say, "I expect *others* to make mistakes, but I don't expect *me* to make mistakes."

In counseling, these people often present their self-ideals as their goals for counseling. They want counselors to help them reach their ideals rather than help them face and accept themselves as they are. This can produce tension when the nature of counseling is explained to them; they may view it as a place where they must learn to experience inferiority. As the counselor helps these clients understand the folly of their expectations, the fears and myths that created them, and their self-defeating nature, these clients can gradually learn to accept themselves and—as a result—others.

Some people have unrealistic expectations of others. They experience frequent frustration and conflict in interpersonal relationships, which significantly reduces the potential for mutual need fulfillment. The following are some typical unrealistic expectations of others:

- people must like me
- people must be reliable
- people must be fair
- people must not hurt me
- people must be there when I need them
- people must think of me first
- people must be totally honest with me
- people must not break promises
- people must not use me
- people must not talk about me behind my back

Of course, most people cannot meet even half of these expectations. Consequently, those who harbor these unrealistic expectations may either give up trying to relate with others in meaningful ways or else endure an endless series of hurts, frustrations, and fractured relationships.

People sometimes learn to have unrealistic expectations of others from having had unreal expectations foisted on them. They will naturally feel that if such expectations were made of them, it is logical they should make them of others. Or unreal expectations may have been created to cover weaknesses in themselves; for example, a woman may demand that people love her because she lacks the ability to love herself.

People with unrealistic expectations of others will probably bring such expectations into the counseling situation. These clients will expect the counselor to be someone he or she can never be and perhaps should not be. The unrealistic expectations will be obvious when friction develops in the relationship. Friction can stem from the client's feeling of being double-crossed: "You're supposed to be kind all the time, and you're not being kind" or "You're supposed to be right all the time, and you were wrong." Counselors should be careful not to fall into the trap of thinking they must meet their clients' unrealistic expectations. Counselors who do this tacitly agree that such expectations are reasonable. As counselors help these individuals discover the causes of their unreasonable expectations and the problems such expectations may create, their clients can begin the gradual process of reconsidering such expectations and replacing them with those more firmly grounded in reality.

Self-Protection in Interpersonal Situations

People who have learned this competency have confidence in their ability to handle whatever happens in a relationship without being personally affected. They have successfully learned the art of psychological self-defense, so they feel free to travel in any kind of interpersonal terrain. They will have learned to spot potential dangers in interpersonal relationships and head them off. If they do find themselves in a difficult situation, they will be able to extricate themselves.

People who lack this competency fear situations where they feel powerless to defend themselves. They may be frightened of any of the following interpersonal situations:

- being manipulated into being someone they do not wish to be or into doing something they do not want to do
- becoming trapped and imprisoned by the other person
- being deceived and ultimately rejected
- building hopes that will be dashed
- being used as a crutch, punching bag, crying towel, or sexual release
- experiencing feelings they cannot control—for example, feelings of dependency, sexuality, anger, or jealousy
- doing something that will seriously hurt the another person

These people feel that the probability is high that one or more of these situations could occur, causing psychological distress. As a result, they either do not allow themselves to become close enough to people for these events to occur or they relate with only a very few people who, while tried and true, continually offer the same bland responses.

Such individuals have never learned how to avoid interpersonal traps by anticipating them and taking appropriate action; for example, saying "I'm sorry, but I can't do that or be that; so let's try a different way of relating." And if no constructive way of relating could be found, they are unable to say, "I'm sorry; I have to leave this relationship now." They have not learned why feelings well up inside them as they get closer in a relationship or how to handle these feelings. As a result, they either avoid relationships or approach them tentatively with an apprehensiveness that tends to doom the relationship.

One reason people may have failed to learn this competency is that they have seen others who were trapped, enslaved, and damaged in relationships. They thus assume that such events are an ordinary part of interpersonal relationships and therefore make a decision to never allow to happen to them what they saw happen to a mother, father, sibling, or friend.

They also may need to avoid close relationships or endure conflictual ones as a way of keeping themselves in a state of unhappiness they feel they somehow deserve. Or they simply may not have had sufficient modeling in protecting themselves.

It is common for clients who have not learned self-protection to bring their sense of interpersonal powerlessness into the counseling relationship. In fact, these fears may become more pronounced in counseling because people who lack the ability to protect themselves may view counselors as powerful enough to take control of them and their lives. As a result, they relate to the counselor from a distance and continually survey the area for possible traps. It is essential that clients learn to be wary, when appropriate, and counselors must be prepared for an initial distrust on the part of the client. It is important that counselors not discount the client's fears because they have some validity in the overall world of interpersonal relating. The best way to increase clients' sense of security in interpersonal relationships is to assist them as they develop skills to be free from stifling interactions and to develop competencies that will provide the basis for need-fulfilling and growth-inducing relationships.

Summary

To approach common client issues from a wellness perspective, the counselor must first appreciate the degree to which psychological strength and the related areas of need fulfillment and interpersonal and intrapersonal competencies work together to support the client's well-being.

The counselor's first decision—largely a subjective one—is to estimate the client's strength in terms of the competencies required for successful need fulfillment, for successful relationships with others, and for a successful and realistic relationship with oneself. There is a reciprocal relationship between strength and these areas of competence. The failure to exercise strength in one area may contribute to problems in other areas so that one's overall strength is thereby diminished.

Eight important needs are involved: (1) the need to give and receive affection, (2) the need to be free, (3) the need to play, (4) the need for stimulation, (5) the need to feel a sense of accomplishment, (6) the need to have hope, (7) the need for solitude, and (8) the need to feel a purpose. Counselors can help clients recognize needs they might be unaware of, help clients find the strength to free themselves from situations that prevent them from having a fuller degree of strength, help clients understand that it is up to them to take full responsibility for their well-being, judiciously fulfill appropriate needs in order to help the client feel stronger, and help clients recognize behavior that keeps them from fulfilling their needs.

There is an important intrapersonal component involved in having strength. One's self-knowledge, self-direction, and self-esteem all play a part in successful relationships with others as well as contributing to the strength derived from successful need fulfillment.

Many people have unacknowledged and thus unknown qualities which they will either project onto others or experience in such a confused way that the resulting anxiety may distort their perceptions or interfere with rational decision making. The decision to enter counseling is often made for reasons not clear to the client. The counselor may then encounter unconscious projection or resistance of various sorts. The counselor should be aware that the areas the client avoids are probably more important than the areas the client is most willing to talk about.

Self-direction is an important intrapersonal competency, involving self-confidence, self-reliance, and self-control. Self-direction is impossible without self-confidence because people who do not trust themselves will fail to make important moves for fear of the consequences, and thus rely on other people to direct their lives. A distrust of self can cause a distrust of others, and the resulting resentment can lead to actions that may alienate others and thus perpetuate low self-confidence. The counselor should be aware that distrustful or resentful behavior often signals low self-confidence. Clients who exhibit resentment may also have low self-reliance. Without self-reliance, clients will depend on others and may believe that other people are responsible for gratifying their wishes. The counselor should be aware of any unreasonable demands. The counselor can help the client become more self-reliant through encouragement and by carefully adhering to boundaries that respect the client's ability to develop self-direction, self-control, and ultimately self-confidence.

Self-control is essential for effective self-direction, and like all intrapersonal competencies it depends on an internal awareness—in this case, that some impulses are not consistent with other areas of equal or greater importance. Counselors can suggest ways that clients may develop forms of freely chosen self-discipline and they can call attention to irrational imperatives imposed on the client from without.

Self-esteem involves a perception of oneself as worthwhile because of an internal consistency between behavior and values and not because of the opinions of others. People with self-esteem treat themselves with respect, whereas a lack of self-esteem may result in behavior harmful to oneself. Strong, mutually fulfilling relationships require a self-esteem that is not dependent on others and that will not be seriously affected by small reverses. The need for self-esteem is so vital to functioning that people may resort to substitutes, such as over-identifying with some social role. A sense of guilt may sometimes serve as a substitute, as may destructive behavior. Counselors often can gauge the degree of self-esteem by the client's willingness to open up to the counselor. Where self-esteem is low, the counselor should not offer pep-talks or try to provide some substitute for self-esteem, but rather make the client aware that self-esteem must come from within.

Among the most important interpersonal competencies are sensitivity to oneself and others, assertiveness, the ability to be comfortable with oneself and others, the ability to allow others to be free, realistic expectations of oneself and others, and the ability to protect oneself. Sensitivity to oneself and others must often go beyond words, and counselors can often model such sensitivity to clients or create situations that will teach sensitivity. Assertiveness involves a relation to others that is neither nonassertive nor aggressive, but appropriately straightforward. Being comfortable with oneself and others is important if there is to be openness in a person's relationships, and the counseling relationship may not be fully open if the client's fears of disclosure are not properly understood. The ability to allow others to be free is such a basic interpersonal competency that counselors must make clients aware of any tendency to be controlling and must firmly refuse to be controlled. People with realistic expectations of self and others tolerate shortcomings without undue disappointment or frustration. When clients have unrealistic expectations, especially unrealistic expectations of counseling, the counselor should help them examine and discover the causes of such expectations. Self-protectiveness allows people to feel comfortable in a variety of situations because they have the ability to disengage themselves from situations likely to be counterproductive or harmful to them. The ability to protect one's self makes it possible to engage in a greater number and wider range of potentially fulfilling activities.

Reflection Questions

1. What are the risks and benefits associated with defining the client's issues from a bias to psychopathology? From a bias to wellness?

2. Of the eight psychological needs discussed in this chapter, which two do you get met the most, and how does getting them met increase your effectiveness as a counselor? Which two do you get met the least, and how does failing to meet them decrease your effectiveness as a counselor?

3. What cautions should counselors be mindful of when meeting the need for hope in their clients?

4. A subtle yet destructive dynamic can occur in counseling when clients who lack self-esteem seek to earn the counselor's esteem rather than their own esteem. How could you tell whether a client is progressing for the sake of growth or for the sake of winning your esteem?

5. No one is perfectly assertive in all situations. What stressful event(s) could occur in counseling that would lead you to choose to respond aggressively? What event(s) could arise that would lead you to choose a nonassertive response?

8

MENTAL AND
EMOTIONAL DISORDERS

The previous chapter identified common issues that may bring people into counseling. While the number of generally healthy people who enter counseling because of one or more of these basic issues continues to increase, many individuals who are motivated to seek counseling suffer from diagnosable mental or emotional *disorders*. While counselors can usually help clients manage common issues through the exclusive use of counseling or psychotherapy (they respond well to "talking therapies"), other treatment options are often needed to help clients with more serious symptoms. In order to make appropriate decisions regarding treatment and referral, counselors must be able to properly diagnose the client's condition and must be aware of the treatment alternatives appropriate for various problems. This chapter describes several of the more prevalent types of mental and emotional disorders (general anxiety disorders, dysthymia, and personality disorders) by identifying basic diagnostic criteria for each one and by calling attention to appropriate treatment alternatives. Since the medical model forms the backbone of the diagnosis (and treatment) of mental and emotional disorders, introductory information about the medical model is offered first. It encompasses biological versus environmental determinants of behavior, use of medication, and physical illnesses that produce psychological symptoms.

An appreciation of the nature-nurture controversy involves understanding the basis of the medical model as applied to human behavior. We

begin with this topic because important, far-reaching changes have occurred on both sides of the controversy in the years since this book was
first published. At present, counselors need to be thoroughly familiar with
the biological, medical, and psychological factors known to influence behavior because the accumulating pool of knowledge better enables them
to make appropriate professional decisions regarding the care and treatment of their clients.

The nature-nurture controversy implies that there are two primary
sources or determinants of behavior and that the relative contribution of
each is, at any point in time, debatable. The medical model and the search
for biological determinants are associated with the nature side of the argument while environmental (e.g., social, cultural, spiritual, and familial) determinants form the nurture side. Beginning in the 1960s and continuing
into the early 1980s, the theoretical tendency was to attend to environmental more than biological issues, but in recent years the pendulum has
swung—in some cases dramatically—to the other side. Some of the discoveries that fueled this change have been so profound that many mental
health professionals, even those who were skeptical of the medical model as
it is applied to behavior, have come to appreciate the influence of biological/
chemical determinants of behavior and favor the judicious use of psychotropic medications as an effective adjunct to counseling or psychotherapy.

The evidence has been compelling: (1) advances in psychopharmacology including new, more effective, more easily tolerated (fewer and
milder side effects) medicines and unexpected uses for existing medicines;
(2) refined imaging techniques that make it possible to study neurological
changes that underlie behavior in increasingly minute detail; and (3) genet-
ics research that is helping to establish biological links to many medical, including psychiatric, problems. Rapid progress has been achieved as
discoveries in any single area dramatically influence the others. For example, improved imaging techniques aid pharmaceutical researchers in the
attempt to localize activity in the brain and test how various compounds
produce specific neurological changes. Advances such as these make it possible to develop medication that is more specific to a given condition: compounds that work exclusively on a particular site without affecting others.

It would be foolish and dangerous for counselors to ignore such important biomedical discoveries. On the other hand, it would be equally
unwise to overlook environmental sources of distress/support as well as
the advances in counseling theory that have occurred over the past 20
years. If there is one lesson that emerges from the accumulated evidence,
it is that effective treatment is predicated on the counselors' ability to simultaneously consider all of the forces that interact to produce complex
human behavior. By doing so, counselors can provide improved counseling services and are better prepared to make appropriate referral recommendations to their clients. Preston, O'Neal, and Talaga make the point
best when they write:

New discoveries in the neurosciences refined technical advances in psychotherapy, and a large number of outcome studies in both pharmacotherapy and psychotherapy have made it abundantly clear: People are complex. Mental health problems spring from many sources; and reductionist, unidimensional models are simply inadequate to explain the wide array of mental and emotional problems people experience. Likewise, no single approach works for all problems. Certain disorders clearly respond better to certain interventions, whereas others require alternative approaches. (1997, p. 4)

These same authors emphasize the need for an "integrative approach" to treatment. They suggest using assorted treatments and a team approach where professionals representing different disciplines cooperate in the care of the client. Examples might include: (1) a depressed client who is being treated collaboratively by a counselor who sees the client each week for cognitive behavioral counseling and a psychiatrist who prescribes and supervises the client's antidepressant medication, or (2) a child diagnosed with Attention Deficit Disorder (ADD) who receives weekly behavioral therapy from a counselor; whose parents attend bi-weekly ADD support groups; who is seen weekly by a learning specialist at school; and whose pediatrician prescribes and monitors the child's medication, in this case an antidepressant.

Whenever counselors collaborate with other mental health specialists they rely upon a shared understanding of (1) the medical model as it applies to mental health conditions, (2) recognition of the potential benefits of medication for conditions where effectiveness has been well-documented, and (3) familiarity with diagnostic criteria/terminology. Collaboration is simply not possible without a common language and shared perspectives.

The information contained in this chapter alone will not be sufficient for mental health practitioners—the field is much too broad and the advances too rapid. Counselors will always require ongoing training in order to remain current. While there are many fine works on the subject, there are two which offer counselors an excellent introduction. Each should be read carefully by anyone who plans to work with individuals who experience mental or emotional disorders. *The DSM-IV Training Guide* by Reid and Wise (1995) provides a sound introduction to the use of the *DSM-IV. The Handbook of Clinical Psychopharmacology for Therapists* by Preston, O'Neal, and Talaga (1997) combines up-to-date information on diagnosis, treatment, and medication. Their *Handbook* also includes useful guidelines for referring clients to psychologists, physicians (family or internal medicine), and psychiatrists for evaluation to determine if medication should be included in the treatment regimen. The work emphasizes the need for professional collaboration and contains many practical suggestions.

Any attempt to explore the influence of biological and environmental factors by positing a dichotomy (e.g., the nature-nurture controversy) reveals the fact that different professional camps hold competing views but distorts a very important reality: biological and environmental factors are inextricably linked. The greater, more useful, and eminently more difficult challenge is to understand how nature and nurture are linked and how they influence one another. In other words, it might be better to talk about a "nature-nurture accord" rather than controversy. The following discussion of causality will emphasize the need to grasp how environmental and biological forces interact.

Determining Origins of Symptoms

Causality

Sufficient cause. It is important to distinguish between sufficient causes and contributing causes. A *sufficient cause* is an event that, by itself, produces abnormal symptoms—that is, no other cause is necessary. For a situation or event to be a sufficient cause, all people who experience it must react with mental and emotional disorders. For example, organic damage can be a sufficient cause for mental and emotional disorders. Serious damage to the central or autonomic nervous system alone can account for mental and emotional disorders, even in previously psychologically healthy people.

However, there are no nonorganic sufficient causes in mental and emotional disorders; that is, there is no psychosocial event that produces mental and emotional disorders in all those who experience it. There are some internal and external situations that have the potential to precipitate mental and emotional disorders, but they do not absolutely and categorically do so. For example, the loss of a loved one may have a high precipitative potential, but many people adjust without developing a mental or emotional disorder.

Yet people commonly speak of causes being sufficient when, in fact, they are not. People say, "His wife's death caused him to have a breakdown." "He went into a bad depression because he got fired." "She went crazy because she heard her husband was unfaithful to her." For these to be sufficient causes for abnormal symptoms, everyone who experiences any of these situations would have to demonstrate mental and emotional disorders. Since few people experience abnormal symptoms as a result of any of these events, one must view them as contributing, but not sufficient causes.

This is not merely a theoretical distinction, because to mistake contributing causes for sufficient ones will render the treatment superficial and ineffective. For example, to provide only grief counseling to a parent who is *seriously* depressed over the death of a child is inappropriate. The client should be evaluated by a specialist to determine if medical problems are contributing to the client's difficulties and to determine if antidepressant medication is needed in addition to counseling. In the course of offering grief counseling, the counselor might also learn that the death of the child was a contributing cause, but the fact that the parent was and is unhappily married and had overinvested himself or herself in the child is another important contributing cause. Counseling here would necessarily entail marital counseling to make the marriage stronger. If that doesn't seem to progress well, a third contributing cause—such as the individual's deep need to suffer in order to atone for earlier guilt-producing behavior—should also be explored. The point is that all of these avenues are important because the client's reaction to the loss is a complex behavior and the counselor must explore all of the available routes to improvement if he or she is to be effective.

Contributing cause. A *contributing cause* is an event that significantly creates stress in a client but does not, in itself, account for psychological symptoms. Both external and internal situations can be contributing causes for abnormal symptoms. External situations are events that occur in a person's life that produce strong reactions (e.g., loss of a job, accident or injury, loss of a loved one, etc.). Examples of internal situations that can be contributing causes are the client's particular attitudinal or emotional dimensions (e.g., pent-up anger, feelings of inadequacy, impatience, emerging fears of intimacy, and insecurity).

Many abnormal symptoms stem from a combination of biological factors coupled with external and internal stresses. Examples might include: (1) a college-age man with a family history of depression and inordinately strong dependency needs combined with the loss of a girlfriend, or (2) a bright, hard-working woman who has a predisposition to elevated levels of anxiety, strong feelings of inadequacy, and who has just received a new promotion.

Logic

Basic principles of logic as they apply to mental and emotional disorders can help counselors as they explore the complexities of human behavior. One principle suggests that if two events are related to each other it does not mean one has caused the other. For example, a significant relationship between the existence of learning disabilities in children and learning disabilities in their parents can be established. Does that mean that the parents *caused* learning disabilities in their children? The answer is, of course, no. While parents who have learning difficulties of their own may have trouble helping their children to learn, it is doubtful that they caused the problem in the child. Most likely, the relationship between the child's learning difficulties and the parent's learning problems is spurious, and the child's problem is the result of a third factor that caused learning problems in both parent and child. A neurological problem that affected the father and was inherited by his child is a good example. The basic truth is that correlational evidence cannot be used to establish cause-effect relationships. Events can coexist because of chance or, as has been shown, they can coexist because of a third overarching factor that actually caused both of the events that appear to be causally related.

Temporal contiguity, the proximity of events in time, is another logical issue that influences how counselors and clients explain psychological symptoms and their causes. Specifically, the fact that one event immediately follows another does not mean that the first event caused the second. A young woman moves away from home and gets an apartment with a female roommate. From the day she moves out of her home, she experiences anxiety symptoms. The "obvious" interpretation is that she is experiencing a separation anxiety caused by the abrupt breaking off of an overdependent relationship with her parents. However, the real source of the anxiety attacks is her strong, negative reaction to her new roommate—she fears she selected the wrong person. To treat the separation anxiety as the cause of the symptoms will result in no symptomatic change.

Also, the fact that one event can lead to a second event does not necessarily mean that the first event is the only possible cause of the second. In human behavior, one event is rarely a necessary and sufficient cause for a second event. For example, a counselor can reason as follows: Those who repress anger suffer from depression; Mr. Smith suffers from depression; therefore, he must be treated for repressed anger. But in fact, Mr. Smith is not repressing anger. He is depressed because he is lonely, feels helpless, has an endocrine dysfunction, or has a combination of all three. To treat Mr. Smith for repressed anger will lead to much wasted time and frustration.

Although these considerations may be academic in nature, the failure to understand them in a counseling setting can waste time and energy at least and at most cause damage to the client. Counselors and clients are vulnerable to establishing inaccurate cause-effect relationships and proffering inaccurate assumptions about the nature of mental and emotional disorders. A classic example can be found in the following true story. During a meeting of psychiatry residents the chief of the service posed the following question: "Under what conditions can the physician establish that the patient's physical complaints are psychosomatic (caused by mental or emotional rather than medical problems)?" One resident responded immediately by stating that "complaints would be identified as psychosomatic whenever it was possible to establish a psychological dynamic that could explain their existence." The chief of the service responded to the resident with another question: "When would it *not* be possible to develop a psychological explanation for the existence of symptoms?" While the humorous presentation of the second question lightened the mood, the importance of the resident's erroneous and risky conclusion struck everyone. Mental health practitioners can *always* develop a psychological explanation for the client's symptoms, but the psychological explanation they develop is not always correct and more importantly is not always useful. It should also be noted that faulty logic does not end with counselors: clients commonly apply faulty logic to explain their symptoms to themselves as well as to others. As counselors explore the logical relationship between and among events and symptoms they also need to reckon with the client's assumptions.

Medical Aspects of Mental and Emotional Disorders

The mind-body connection has been, and remains, an area of widespread interest. For example, the influence of patients' psychological states on the outcomes of surgical procedures is as important a question as understanding the psychological effects produced by certain chemical compounds, medications, or diseases. While this important research area is beyond the scope of this book, readers may wish to read *Philosophy and the Brain* (Young, 1987) and *Organic Unit Theory: The Mind-Body Problem Revisited* (Goodman, 1991).

The body can affect the psyche in a number of ways. A basic working knowledge of this relationship will help counselors appropriately select people for counseling and make intelligent referrals when the possibility exists that nonpsychological factors may be causing or contributing to the symptoms associated with particular mental or emotional disorders.

The following points may be helpful for counselors to remember when dealing with clients who have been diagnosed with a mental or emotional disorder, or clients who exhibit psychological symptoms that may, or may not, be caused by a mental or emotional disorder.

Physical Examination

It is always a good idea to refer clients for a thorough physical examination as part of the counseling evaluation. Ideally, it would be helpful to work with a physician who is attuned to psychological as well as physical health issues and knowledgeable about psychotropic medications and the psychological effects of non-psychotropic medicines. Equipped with this understanding, the physician is in a better position to gear the examination to identify medical conditions that could be responsible for psychological symptoms or medications that could be producing psychological distress and identify the need for psychotropic medications. Unfortunately, health insurance programs often limit who insured parties can see, so counselors regularly confront the problem of helping the client identify an appropriate physician from a small list of approved providers. Counselors need to become familiar enough with the medical community to identify at least one or two physicians with whom they can consult from each of the major plans. When an acceptable alternative does not exist, clients often have to assume the expense of consulting with a physician who is outside the plan.

It is also important to understand that one examination at the beginning of counseling is not always sufficient. A counselor cannot realistically assume that the results of a medical checkup done 6 or 18 months earlier are still valid. This is particularly true in some disorders, such as anxiety and depression, because psychological stress can trigger biochemical reactions that may increase or otherwise change the client's symptoms. Also, a latent medical disorder present at the time of the first medical examination can become active during the intervening period, causing psychological problems that could have been prevented with proper advance medical treatment.

Medications and Mental and Emotional Disorders

Many mental and emotional disorders are treated with effective psychotropic medications alone or in combination with counseling or psychotherapy. There are seven major classes of medications including (1) antipsychotics, (2) anxiolytics (antianxiety drugs), (3) antidepressants, (4) hypnotics, (5) lithium, (6) obsessive-compulsive disorder management preparations, and (7) psychostimulants. For example, moderately to severely depressed clients should always be evaluated by a psychiatrist or other physician to determine if antidepressant medications should be used. Selective serotonin reuptake inhibitors (SSRIs) like Prozac, Paxil, or Zoloft, as well as other types of antidepressants, have been shown to be very effective either alone or in combination with counseling. For some conditions, a counselor's decision to rule out the use of medication constitutes unethical behavior and malpractice. Counselors have been successfully sued for failing to offer or recommend alternative treatments to clients who would benefit from them.

The large number of currently available psychotropic medications makes it difficult but no less important for counselors to be up-to-date on the conditions these medicines are being used to treat and their effectiveness. A further challenge exists because psychotropic medications, while they are developed to treat particular disorders, are often proven effective at treating disorders for which they were not originally intended. For example, certain SSRI antidepressants have been found useful in treating obsessive-compulsive disorders. A counselor could easily assume that a client, who entered counseling taking an SSRI antidepressant, was diagnosed with depression when in fact the medication was being used to treat another disorder. Because psychopharmacology is such a rapidly expanding field, many counselors appropriately rely upon professional relationships with psychiatrists, pharmacists, and regular training experiences.

It is also important for counselors to be aware of the relationship that exists between various medications and the symptoms of mental or emotional disorders. One situation that can arise in this regard occurs when a client who is taking a nonpsychotropic medication develops psychological symptoms. For example, while giving his history to the counselor, a man mentions that he is taking something to control his blood pressure. Since the "something" is unlikely to be a psychiatric medication, the counselor pays little attention to it. However, if the counselor had asked the man to bring the bottle of medication to the next visit, the counselor would have seen that the prescription was for Inderal. If the counselor had consulted the *Physician's Desk Reference*, he or she would have seen that the potential central nervous system adverse reactions associated with this medication include: "light-headedness; mental depression manifested by insomnia, lassitude, weakness, fatigue; reversible mental depression progressing to catatonia; visual disturbances; hallucinations, vivid dreams, an acute reversible syndrome characterized by disorientation for time and place, short-term memory loss, emotional lability, slightly clouded sensorium, and decreased performance on neuropsychometrics" (*Physician's Desk Reference*, 1999, p. 3308).

If this client's chief complaint is depression, it raises the following questions: Is the depression purely psychological in nature? Is it a side effect of the medication? Is it caused by the interaction between psychological and physical factors? Although such questions cannot always be easily answered, it is important that they be asked in order to prevent avoidable mistakes.

A second type of situation that can arise occurs when clients take prescribed psychotropic medications. For example, Valium, a commonly prescribed antianxiety compound, not only can reduce anxiety and tension but also has such potential adverse reactions as confusion, depression, headaches, and changes in libido. Paradoxical reactions are also possible with this medication; these include "acute hyperexcited states, anxiety, hallucinations, increased muscle spasticity, insomnia, rage, sleep disturbances, and stimulation" (*Physician's Desk Reference*, 1999, p. 2736). Although these side effects may be uncommon, a counselor cannot assume that the medication is devoid of psychological side effects. Therefore, it is also important for counselors to have a general knowledge of the indications (uses) and the adverse reactions associated with many general medications as well as psychotropic medications. The brain does not differentiate between psychotropic and nonpsychotropic medications; either class of compounds can produce psychological symptoms. Additionally, many people are prescribed and take both classes of medicine at the same time. This is particularly common with elderly clients because they often have multiple health problems and because they are commonly treated by several different specialists. Unfortunately, when medicines are combined the potential for physical and psychological adverse reactions increases. These so-called synergistic effects can be quite serious; they are developments that demand immediate attention. Counselors can reduce the potential for trouble by urging their clients to tell their doctors what they are taking, including any over-the-counter preparations, and what has been prescribed for them by other physicians. Many counselors routinely obtain a release of information to consult with the client's physician(s). This is especially helpful when troubling symptoms surface since most doctors value the counselor's observations and will use the information as they make decisions regarding the client's medication regimen.

While counselors benefit on many levels from professional relationships with psychiatrists, they also need to be able to collaborate effectively with primary care physicians and specialists. According to Beardsley, Gardocki, Larsen, and Hidalgo (1988) the majority of prescriptions written for most classes of psychotropic medications are written by nonpsychiatric medical doctors (e.g., internists, family medicine physicians, general practitioners, pediatricians, etc.). This fact suggests several important issues for counselors. First, many clients, for better or for worse, may be taking psychotropic medications that were prescribed by their primary care physicians, not by psychiatrists. On the positive side, clients who need medication and who are unwilling for any of a number of reasons to go to a psychiatrist can obtain a prescription for needed psychotropic medications from a primary care physician. However, counselors should be aware that sometimes physicians, who have limited experience treating clients for mental or emotional disorders, misdiagnose and in turn misprescribe psychotropic medication. This happens for many reasons: (1) the client may lack the ability to accurately describe his or her symptoms, (2) the physician may not be sufficiently skillful at obtaining the necessary information, or (3) the physician may lack experience prescribing psychotropic medications. A good example of this problem occurs when depressed people describe themselves as "nervous" or "tense" because they lack the vocabulary to be more precise. A primary care physician who fails to explore the client's experiences more deeply before making his or her own assessment of the client's subjective state may incorrectly prescribe tranquilizers to help relieve the "tension." Tranquilizers, in this case, can actually increase the client's existing depression, which may in turn cause the client to request increased dosages because the amount taken seems ineffective.

Counselors can be very helpful to physicians as they make decisions about which medications to prescribe and in what dosage by providing the physician with a comprehensive client history, a clear description of the client's symptoms, and well-founded diagnostic impressions. Clients ultimately benefit when counselors develop strong, professional relationships with nonpsychiatrist physicians who understand and are willing to collaborate with nonmedical mental health professionals in the treatment of their patients' psychological difficulties.

Clients sometimes enter counseling already taking one or more psychotropic medications (see Figure 8-1 for a general classification and Appendix C for a more complete listing of individual medications). These clients, in particular, should be evaluated by a physician to determine the efficacy of the medication regimen. Some medicines may be useful, while others may no longer be warranted, and still others may cloud the clinical picture in a way that would make it impossible to develop an accurate diagnosis of the client's clinical symptoms. While counselors may raise concerns to the client and his or her physician about the need to discontinue a particular medication because the counselor thinks it might be unnecessary or is confusing the clinical picture, he or she must be mindful that sudden discontinuance of medication can produce serious medical problems. Physicians need to carefully monitor clients whenever there are changes in their medications. Many medicines have to be tapered off over a lengthy period of time. For example, immediate withdrawal from central nervous system stimulants (e.g., Adderall or Dexedrine) "usually results in extreme fatigue, and mental depression; changes are also noted on the sleep EEG" (*Physician's Desk Reference*, 1999, p. 3004). Mild feelings of depression and listlessness may persist for weeks or even months after the last dose.

Serious withdrawal symptoms can also be seen in people who have become dependent upon barbiturates (Nembutal). "Abrupt cessation after prolonged use in the dependent person may result in withdrawal symptoms, including delirium, convulsions, and possibly death" (*Physician's Desk Reference*, 1999, p. 458). According to other researchers, common withdrawal symptoms associated with the cessation of barbiturates are anxiety, tremors, insomnia, vomiting, and rapid heart rate. Between the sixteenth hour and the fifth day after cessation, convulsions may occur, and an acute psychosis often develops (Coleman, Butcher, & Carson, 1980, pp. 346, 348). Both sources suggest the need for careful medical supervision because the cessation symptoms can be life-threatening.

For these reasons, it is important that counselors refer clients and potential clients who are taking medications to a physician for medical evaluation. If the physician and counselor agree that withdrawal from the medication should be initiated, both can work together to help the client taper off, both psychologically and physically, from the medication, thereby avoiding potentially serious health problems.

---

antipsychotics
anxiolytics (antianxiety drugs)
antidepressants
hypnotics
mood stabilizers (lithium)
anti-obsessional
psychostimulants

Figure 8-1. General classifications of psychotropic medication.

While counselors need not be experts in pharmacology, it is important to have at least a general understanding of the effects of medication on a person's psychological and physical functioning. This understanding insures that the counselor will have a more cautious attitude about medication in general. Such vigilance can help prevent avoidable errors and incorrect conclusions.

Organically Caused Psychological Symptoms

It is helpful for counselors to have some familiarity with psychological symptoms that can have nonpsychological causes. Endocrine dysfunctioning, for example, can produce symptoms that might cause people to presume that they were experiencing a psychological problem and pursue counseling. The following are some of the psychological symptoms of endocrine disorders that might be seen in counseling (Vinicor & Cooper, 1979).

Hyperparathyroidism.   In its milder form, it causes neurasthenic personality changes that are insidious: loss of initiative and interest, fatigue, depression, and memory disturbances. An unsuspecting counselor could diagnose such a client as having a dependent personality, a dysthymic disorder, or an adjustment disorder with depressed mood. In its more progressed form, this disease causes severe anxiety, paranoia, disorientation, and hallucinations, which could be mistaken for psychoses of a psychogenic nature.

Cushing's syndrome.   Over 50% of people who have this disease experience the following symptoms: weakness, emotional lability, anxiety, and depression. Psychoses may be seen in one-half to two-thirds of all people with this disorder. The development of psychological symptoms may clearly antedate the physical manifestations; so a medical examination at the beginning of counseling may not detect its presence.

Addison's disease.   Over 80% of people who have this disorder experience psychological symptoms. These include easy fatigability, apathy, and irritability. In its more severe form, Addison's disease causes marked depression, paranoia, delusions, and thought disorders.

Hypoglycemia.   Some typical psychological symptoms of this disease are headaches, confusion, poor judgment, hysterical behavior, and schizophrenic-like and manic-depressive-like symptoms. People with reactive hypoglycemia manifest such symptoms as sweating, tachycardia, palpitations, and tremulousness, which could well be misdiagnosed as symptoms of a psychogenic anxiety disorder.

Hyperthyroidism.   The common psychological symptoms of this disorder are memory impairment, increased anxiety, irritability, aggressiveness, restlessness, and hyperactivity.

Myxedema. In its milder form, myxedema causes the following symptoms: depression, psychomotor retardation, memory failures, difficulty in concentrating and abstracting, and deterioration of intelligence. In its more severe form, the disorder causes confusion, delusions of persecution, and hallucinations.

Neurological dysfunctioning, like endocrine dysfunctioning, can cause symptoms that are the same as those seen in psychogenic disorders. Some common neurological disorders that can cause psychological symptoms are cerebral infections, encephalitis, vascular accidents, brain tumors, cerebral traumas, and degenerative disorders (presenility, Huntington's chorea, Parkinson's, Pick's and Alzheimer's disease). The major symptoms that can occur as the result of neurological disorders are the following:

1. Disorientation in time, person, and place.

2. Memory impairment. (The client may have long-term memory loss but, more typically, has short-term memory loss and may confabulate to fill in the memory gaps. Memory impairment may be the most common symptom of brain disorders.)

3. Impairment of comprehension, calculation, knowledge, and learning.

4. Impairment of judgment. (The client cannot make appropriate decisions and may exercise poor judgment.)

5. Lability and shallowness of affect. (The client may shift quickly and inappropriately from apathy to hostility or from laughing to weeping.)

6. Emotional impairment. (The client emotionally overreacts with inappropriate laughing or crying, or a blunting of emotional responses occurs.)

7. Loss of impulse control. (The client is unable to inhibit inappropriate sexual and aggressive urges.) For further discussion of these symptoms, see Martin (1977, p. 581).

All these symptoms could also be those of a psychogenic disorder. Since no counselor is in a position to make these critical differential diagnoses alone, it is important to make appropriate referrals to other professionals, so that all dimensions can be covered adequately.

Since the symptoms of mental and emotional disorders can have varied sources and because each source may be treated differently, counselors serve their client's needs and interests best when they pursue a holistic understanding. By recognizing that the client's condition exists as a function of biological, medical, psychological, spiritual, emotional, and social concerns, treatment options can be tailored to the client's specific needs. This integrated approach challenges counselors to become knowledgeable about each of the aforementioned areas, to develop appropriate referrals, and to be able to work with an interdisciplinary team of mental health professionals.

⚖

Diagnosis

Diagnosis in counseling means that the counselor makes a clinical judgment as to the nature of the client's mental or emotional difficulties, develops hypotheses as to the cause, and formulates a counseling program that will have the best chance for success. Some counselors do not relate comfortably to the idea of diagnosis. Counselors who oppose diagnosing may view it as labeling people in ways that will be detrimental to them; they may feel that diagnosis is identified with the medical model, which they reject; or they may feel that diagnoses are useless and harmful because they are so unreliable. To simply label a client and mistake this for treatment is harmful. To enter specific diagnoses into permanent medical records may cause problems for the client. Whether or not the counselor chooses to "officially diagnose" the client in terms of records or insurance forms is a matter to be decided between the counselor and the client. Thus while many of the popular objections to diagnosis have a degree of validity, the need to develop a diagnosis or a diagnostic impression of the client persists for good reasons.

While diagnosis is a part of the medical model, it is also used in many other fields as a method of defining problems (specific conditions) for the purpose of correcting or ameliorating them. Diagnoses are most useful when the problem or condition can be reliably identified, correctly differentiated from other problems or conditions, and when the diagnosis has an effective treatment associated with it. For example, certain infections can be reliably diagnosed. That is, different pathologists would arrive at the same conclusion concerning the pathogenic microorganism responsible for the infection. The diagnostic process might also include a sensitivity test—a laboratory procedure that is used to narrow the scope of medications considered and to determine which medicines would be most effective in resolving the infection. With a reliable diagnosis and the results of a sensitivity test, the infected individual has a high likelihood of being successfully treated. In this example a reliable diagnosis leads to an effective treatment; the outcome supports the process.

The diagnosis of mental and emotional disorders is not as *clean.* Mental and emotional disorders are not as easily differentiated from one another, as various microorganisms are, so the potential for mental health professionals observing the same client to come to different diagnostic conclusions is higher. Recommendations for treatment also vary widely for many mental or emotional disorders. Therefore, once a diagnosis is made, the range of choices is not as readily narrowed down. Mental health professionals often find themselves in situations where there is disagreement concerning the diagnosis and debate about how the client should be treated. However, this situation should not be used as a reason to denigrate the need for diagnosis. Diagnostic impressions remain useful because they are hypotheses about the client's condition that can later be refined. Furthermore, these same diagnostic impressions suggest treatment alternatives that can be explored and evaluated. While it is true that clinicians often disagree about a particular client's diagnosis, this situation occurs in all fields where judgments of people or performance are made; it is not a sufficient reason to abandon the process of diagnosis.

Multiaxial Assessments

The intake evaluation requires a series of careful judgments about the seriousness of the client's symptoms, the need for referral to medical or other mental health specialists, and the exact nature of the treatment plan. A multiaxial or five-axis assessment helps in making these determinations because it organizes the evaluation process so that the client can be assessed more completely. Each of the following axes is associated with a different source of difficulty. A complete multiaxial assessment for a client would include information about each of the following:

Axis I   Clinical disorders
          Other conditions that may be a focus of clinical attention

Axis II   Personality disorders
          Mental retardation

Axis III General medical conditions

Axis IV   Psychosocial and environmental problems

Axis V   Global assessment of functioning (American Psychiatric Association, 1994, p. 25)

According to this diagnostic statistical manual, "A multiaxial system provides a convenient format for organizing and communicating clinical information, for capturing the complexity of clinical situations, and for describing the heterogeneity of individuals presenting with the same diagnosis. In addition, the multiaxial system promotes the application of the biopsychosocial model in clinical, educational, and research settings" (American Psychiatric Association, 1994, p. 25). While, as we have suggested, counselors may be reluctant to diagnose clients, the need to properly organize the client's symptoms and communicate information to other health professionals makes multiaxial assessments essential.

Assessing Mental or Emotional Disorders

The assessment itself is only as good as the information it is based upon. While a careful history is the cornerstone of the assessment, counselors should be careful not to simply take the word of the client. Clients significantly overestimate or underestimate the nature and the duration of their symptoms for conscious and unconscious reasons. They may also deny the existence of extremely important symptoms or behavior patterns—a situation that can seriously jeopardize the accuracy of the diagnosis and, in turn, the effectiveness of the treatment. For example, clients may not disclose that they are abusing drugs or alcohol yet their symptoms may be directly caused by one or both. In this situation the counselor is missing a significant piece of the client's clinical picture. Over time, counselors develop ethically appropriate methods for obtaining information from other members of the client's family in addition to questioning techniques that can work around the client's denial mechanisms.

An example of just such a question is used in assessing the client's alcohol consumption. Since most people who abuse alcohol tend to underestimate the amount they consume, asking how much someone drinks is usually ineffective. Instead of asking how much the client drinks each day, the counselor might ask how much alcohol the client would have to consume for him or her to feel drunk. The report of excessive amounts to become drunk usually indicates a greater likelihood of alcohol abuse. This question is not useful, however, when interviewing people who have consumed alcohol to excess over very long periods of time and are now in the advanced stages of alcoholism. While their dependence on alcohol persists, their level of consumption actually drops because of advancing alcohol-related organ disease.

The degree of seriousness of a mental or emotional disorder is not always obvious, but an assessment of the degree of seriousness is still important. While some clients present themselves in a highly agitated state and appear to be acutely disturbed, it may become clear that the client is actually only mildly or moderately disturbed—far from severely impaired. This is because clients may consciously or unconsciously exaggerate their symptoms to impress the counselor with the seriousness of the situation, a "cry for help"; or it may be because some people typically overreact to situations as part of their personality.

On the other hand, clients can appear to be very matter of fact and low-keyed about their symptoms. They may assure the counselor that if he or she presently lacks the time to see them, they can return at a later date and that it is not serious. It is important to remember, however, that many people who explode into a rampage of destructive behavior are described by others as appearing "perfectly normal" only moments prior. Counselors need to be perceptive, skillful with their questions, and able to actively listen in order to make reasonably accurate assessments of the severity of the client's symptoms.

Cultural factors deeply influence all people, and they must always be considered when making decisions about behavior patterns and symptoms. Not everything that looks like a mental or emotional disorder is one, nor is everything that looks like normal behavior necessarily to be ignored. A man may suddenly quit his job even though he has no immediate means to support his family. At first glance, this may appear to be an impulse control problem, a symptom common to several mental or emotional disorders. But under closer scrutiny, the counselor may discover that the man was placed in a situation in which he had to violate an important value or quit his job. His integrity was more important than what his friends would think or his immediate comfort. Another man might have kept the job, and his decision would have been viewed as adaptive. The problem in this case is that the person has kept his job but lost a significant amount of self-respect, which eventually manifests itself in depression. As these examples reveal, counselors must be careful as to what they label as normal behavior and what they diagnose as symptoms of mental or emotional disorders.

The process of correctly diagnosing mental or emotional disorders can be quite complicated and time consuming. Many counselors establish a three-session intake process where they meet with the client for an hour each week. During that time they develop a diagnosis and a recommendation for treatment, make referrals to other needed professionals, and decide whether to begin a course of counseling. The following example illustrates some of the practical issues involved in diagnosis and some of the questions that would have to be resolved before an agreement could be reached regarding a course of treatment.

A woman seeks the help of a counselor because she is depressed following the death of her child. Is her depression a reaction to the loss of her child (an adjustment disorder), or did the death exacerbate a depression that is secondary to her dependent personality (personality disorder)? Is the death of the child only one of several dynamics involved in her dysthymic disorder (a more serious affective disorder), or is her depression mostly caused by taking Diupres (a blood pressure medicine that can produce symptoms of depression [*Physician's Desk Reference*, 1999, p. 1783]), or by hypothyroidism, carcinoma of the pancreas, or a viral illness (organic affective syndrome)? These are not simply academic questions. It makes a critical difference that the diagnosis is correct; treating a client for an adjustment disorder when in reality the client has a personality disorder or is experiencing some organic dysfunction that is producing psychological symptoms can make a huge difference in the outcome (for a further discussion of this point, see Small, 1972).

࿇

Specific Mental and Emotional Disorders

The following presentation focuses on three different mental and emotional disorders: Generalized Anxiety Disorder (GAD), Dysthymic Disorder, and Dependent Personality Disorder. These specific disorders were selected because counselors frequently encounter clients who will be diagnosed with them. While clients who have more serious psychological problems occasionally seek out counselors, they are more often treated by other mental health professionals. For example, individuals who are diagnosed as having thought disorders, or individuals who need to be treated for major depression are more appropriately treated by psychiatrists, and cases of this nature may be infrequently encountered. These clients almost always need to be treated with medication; many may need to be hospitalized; and still others may have other medical problems that complicate the treatment for their particular mental or emotional disorder.

While counselors do not generally treat people who are diagnosed with extremely severe mental or emotional disorders, they do need to be aware of the symptoms of these conditions. Without this knowledge, counselors would be unable to correctly determine which clients need to be referred and who has the requisite skills and expertise. Counselors benefit greatly from knowing the symptoms and also from having the experience of interviewing individuals who have any of a number of severe disorders. While such experience is very useful it will not completely eliminate error in judging whether counseling is the appropriate treatment alternative. Some conditions, Bipolar Disorder for example, are very difficult to identify without an extended evaluation. A client at one point in a bipolar cycle could be mistaken for someone who is exhibiting the symptoms of a less serious disorder (Generalized Anxiety Disorder, Dysthymic Disorder, Personality Disorder).

The discussion of each of the following disorders includes diagnostic criteria, suggestions about the psychosocial causes of the problem, and suggestions for treatment. A more complete discussion of biological causes is beyond the scope and focus of this book, but nonetheless important. The importance of a holistic approach cannot be overemphasized. The psychosocial aspect is discussed because the counseling process addresses these elements more than it does the equally important biological determinants.

Generalized Anxiety Disorder

Generalized Anxiety Disorder (GAD) is one of 12 types of anxiety disorders that share one or two common features: "clinically significant anxiety and, for some, avoidance behavior" (Reid & Wise, 1995, p. 179). "The essential feature of Generalized Anxiety Disorder is excessive anxiety and worry (apprehensive expectation), occurring more days than not for a period of at least 6 months, about a number of events or activities (American Psychiatric Association, 1994, p. 432). Clients diagnosed with GAD persistently imagine, predict or anticipate anxiety-provoking events to the extent that they remain in a state of alert (Preston, O'Neal, & Talaga, 1997). These same authors note that GAD is not commonly treated with psychotropic medications unless the symptoms are severe or psychological treatments prove ineffective (for specific recommendations about when medication may be needed for various anxiety disorders, see Preston et al., 1997, p. 97).

In the early stages of this disorder, clients typically try to identify the anxiety as having some external source. For example, if exams are approaching, certain students may assure themselves that they are nervous about the exams, even though they have never been nervous in this way before. When the event that is supposed to be the precipitant passes, the anxiety may remain or even increase. In such a case, the exams would not really be the cause of the attendant anxiety.

Symptoms.   The following are some typical symptoms of a generalized anxiety disorder.

Muscle tension.   People may experience tremors of hands and feet, generalized agitation, fatigability, restlessness, trembling or muscle tension.

Autonomic hyperactivity.   These symptoms include increased perspiration, palpitations, clammy hands; upset stomach, difficulty swallowing, frequent urination, diarrhea; dizziness, light-headedness; shortness of breath, hyperventilation, exaggerated startle response; weakness in the knees, ringing in the ears, inability to relax or sleep; and muscular tension in neck, shoulders, and lower back.

Apprehensive expectation.   The client feels that he or she is going to go crazy, die, do something that will cause public embarrassment, be arrested, or be confined to a mental hospital. The client may also fear that similar events may happen to loved ones.

Cognitive disruption.   The client feels confused and unable to concentrate, tends to be obsessed with anxious thoughts; experiences difficulty remembering; has little fantasy life except for morbid ruminations; has difficulty making decisions; and reviews mistakes, real or imagined. When sleep is eventually possible, frightening dreams occur.

Some people who suffer from a Generalized Anxiety Disorder may also experience *panic attacks*. These are recurring periods of acute panic that can last from a few seconds to an hour or more. These attacks are of sudden onset, mount to high intensity, and then subside. During the attack, many of the symptoms of anxiety previously mentioned can occur, but in terrifying intensity. These attacks can occur from several times a day to once a month or once every few years. When people experience their first anxiety attack, they may call a physician or ambulance because they feel they are having a heart attack.

Anxiety in its milder and moderate forms is sometimes marked by analgesic behavior such as sleeping, drinking, or eating too much; working too hard; and taking tranquilizers. When people suddenly stop any of these behaviors, it is not unusual for them to experience increased levels of anxiety, which often causes them to revert to the analgesic behaviors.

People whose anxiety is of a more chronic than reactive nature often manifest the following behaviors: the inability to relax; rapid, loud, and rambling speech; inability to listen or comprehend directions; chronic irritability; low frustration tolerance; nervous laughter; inability to stop oneself from making foolish or hostile statements; and accident proneness.

Many people who experience anxiety-arousing conflicts feel trapped in their jobs and/or relationships. They lack the psychosocial competencies either to handle the unpleasant situation constructively or to extricate themselves from it successfully.

Causal factors. Although there are many theoretical explanations of anxiety disorders, the following is a summary of the psychosocial explanations, based upon analytic, cognitive, existential, and cognitive behavioral perspectives.

Overly stringent conscience. Sometimes anxious people repress normal feelings (e.g., aggression or anger) because they have been taught that merely entertaining such feelings, much less acting upon them, is psychologically and/or morally wrong. They quickly find themselves in a bind—the more they repress these feelings, the more anxiety builds; the more the feelings approach consciousness, the more anxiety increases. Finally, the anxiety breaks through consciousness, but its sources remain repressed or enter consciousness in disguised forms.

Anxiety-arousing conflicts. These conflicts include the classic ones, especially approach-avoidance and avoidance-avoidance conflicts. A woman may have a strong desire to quit her job and pursue a better one, but her anxiety emanating from unwarranted fears of not finding another job prevents her from acting. A man may be miserable being married but experience an equal amount of anxiety when he considers getting a divorce.

Unrealistic expectations. Some anxious people are laboring under unrealistic expectations placed on them by themselves or others. These expectations put great pressure on such people, which they dutifully accept. As the pressure mounts and the impossibility of meeting their expectations becomes more clear, anxiety symptoms surface.

Self-alienation. Some people have lived according to the roles that others have assigned them for so long that they have become alienated from themselves. Anxiety is both a symptom of the alienation and a motivational force to change (become less alienated). Unfortunately, anxiety levels often increase as individuals begin the process of becoming more aware of themselves. The increase in anxiety often obstructs the client's efforts at reducing levels of self-alienation.

Reactivation of prior stress. People may find themselves in situations that rekindle long repressed ideas and feelings. For example, a man who had been physically abused by his father some 30 years earlier arranges a reunion with his father so that he can introduce his own son to him. Because his parents divorced shortly after the abuse was discovered, the man had no contact with his father until he recently located him to arrange the meeting. As the date of the reunion approached the man began to experience severe worries (anxiety) about his son, particularly his son's safety. He became so anxious about the child's well-being that he canceled the meeting with his father. Because he had repressed his early recollections of the abuse, along with the anger and fear that accompanied them, he saw no connection between his symptoms and his father's visit. Many different, seemingly unrelated stimuli can evoke anxious reactions. For example, a movie, television program, or play; a book or a piece of music may contain subliminal cues that activate the anxiety related to a prior experience without pulling the actual event into consciousness.

Counseling implications. The following are some considerations that counselors may find helpful in working with people who are experiencing a Generalized Anxiety Disorder. Counselors can remember that anxiety is contagious. Sometimes even experienced counselors get caught up in the anxiety of the client and make decisions that are premature and that they later regret. While anxiety disorders are obviously to be taken seriously, it may be helpful to know that, despite how acutely disturbed these people often appear, only 5% or less decompensate into psychosis (Coleman et al., 1980, p. 249). Counselors will be more helpful if they can maintain some distance between the client's anxiety and themselves.

The counselor should explain what is happening to the client in a clear, nonthreatening manner. Of all psychological disturbances, a Generalized Anxiety Disorder is one of the most frightening and mystifying to people. Clients are often saturated with anxiety without the slightest notion as to its cause. Consequently, they have anxiety about their anxiety, the combination of which potentiates the anxiety.

A counselor who understands the nature and dynamics of this disorder can offer at least tentative explanations and give assurances that none of the anticipated catastrophes is likely to occur. Clients are aided and supported by the fact that the counselor understands what is happening, has seen people with this disorder many times before, and can offer realistic hope based on past experiences.

Counselors who understand some of the more common causal factors can explore each one and render assistance in specific areas. For example, people with overly stringent consciences can be helped to understand the adaptive nature of feelings such as anger and fear and the damage caused by suppressing them inappropriately. People experiencing anxiety-arousing conflicts can be helped to bring them into greater awareness and to understand how to deal with them more directly and constructively.

Anxious clients' fantasies and dreams often give clues as to the sources of their anxiety. For example, a man may go to sleep each night fantasizing that he received the report of his mother's death, or a woman may have a recurring dream that she was fired from her job. The content of fantasies and dreams may provide a portal through which the causes of a client's anxiety may be discovered.

It is more helpful if counselors don't feel that they must discover the exact cause of the anxiety symptoms. If counselors place this imperative on themselves, their anxiety, coupled with that of the client, could become explosive. It would be helpful to identify the specific cause or causes, but people can be greatly helped without such knowledge.

Sometimes the originating material is so deeply repressed that it will never be uncovered. The counselor still can help the client change cognitions about the anxiety, learn psychosocial competencies that will increase self-esteem, and show the client constructive outlets for the anxiety. Many people with Anxiety Disorders have successfully terminated counseling without ever discovering the specific cause of their anxiety.

As has been noted, certain individuals with GAD benefit from various antianxiety medications. Support groups are also useful, as are various books on the subject. *The Anxiety Disease* by D. Sheehan (1983) and *Anxiety and Its Treatment* by Greist, Jefferson, and Marks (1986) are both valuable adjuncts to counseling.

Dysthymic Disorder

Mood disorders are a basic diagnostic group distinguished by "the development of an abnormal mood characterized by depression, mania, or both symptoms in alternating fashion" (Fauman, 1994, p.167). A number of criteria are used to differentiate each of the disorders in this group. Judgments about which disorder the client is experiencing are based on whether the client experiences depression, mania, or both and the intensity, duration, and level of impairment. While counselors need to be familiar with all of the disorders within this group (see Fauman, 1994, pp. 165–207), the specific mood disorder that counselors most commonly encounter and treat in their clients is *Dysthymic Disorder*.

The basic feature in this disturbance "is a chronically depressed mood that occurs for most of the day more days than not for at least two years" (American Psychiatric Association, 1994, p. 345). Children may exhibit irritability as well as depressed mood and the duration of symptoms is one year rather than the two years for adults. While depressed the individual would experience at least two of the following symptoms:

1. poor appetite or overeating
2. insomnia or hypersomnia (excessive sleeping)

3. low energy or fatigue
4. low self-esteem
5. poor concentration or difficulty making decisions
6. feelings of hopelessness (Fauman, 1994, p. 180)

Additional criteria help insure that the individual is not exhibiting symptoms that would be more appropriately diagnosed as something other than Dysthymic Disorder. These elimination criteria seek to prevent individuals from being diagnosed with Dysthymic Disorder who are actually experiencing a major depressive episode, who are in the depressed phase of a bipolar or cyclothymic disorder, and whose depressed mood is the result of substance abuse, medication, or a medical condition.

Dysthymia "has an early and insidious onset (i.e., in childhood, adolescence, or early adult life) as well as a chronic course" (American Psychiatric Association, 1994, p. 347). Women are more than twice as likely to develop Dysthymic Disorder than men, though it affects both sexes equally among children. Dysthymia can coexist with several other disorders including, for example, personality disorders.

The symptoms of Dysthymic Disorder are significantly milder and different than those associated with Major Depressive Episodes. Knowing the more serious symptoms of depression aids counselors in a couple of ways. First, the existence of a Major Depressive Disorder within the two years (one year for children) that symptoms are studied to establish a diagnosis of Dysthymic Disorder precludes the client from being diagnosed with Dysthymic Disorder. Second, a portion of people who are correctly diagnosed with Dysthymic Disorder will develop the symptoms of a Major Depressive Disorder. These people must be identified quickly because the treatment regimen for Dysthymia differs from the regimen for a Major Depressive Disorder. The following are some of the more general symptoms associated with depression (specific information can be found in American Psychiatric Association, 1994, p. 327).

Emotional manifestations: dejected mood (feeling miserable, hopeless, blue, sad, lonely, unhappy, discouraged, ashamed, worried, useless, guilty); negative feelings toward the self (feeling stupid, sinful, worthless, ugly, perverted, selfish, crazy, weak, unlovable); reduction in gratification (things that were once pleasurable are now boring or even aggravating; these can include eating, sex, work, hobbies, and relationships).

Motivational manifestations: paralysis of will ("I can't go to work tomorrow"; "I can't get dressed today"; "I can't even talk to you"); avoidance wishes ("Leave me alone"; "I need to get away by myself"; "I just want to daydream"); suicidal wishes and tendencies ("I would be better off dead"; "I hope I don't wake up in the morning"; "I can see only one way out of this").

Physical manifestations: loss of appetite and weight loss; sleep disturbance (trouble going to sleep, waking in the middle of the night, waking too early, sleeping excessively); loss of libido; psychomotor retardation (slowed speech, decelerated movement).

Cognitive manifestations: low self-evaluation ("I'm no good"; "I'm incompetent"; "I'm evil"); negative expectations ("I'll never feel better"; "I'll never be able to return to work"; "Life is over for me"); self-blame ("It's all my fault"; "I deserve what is happening to me"; "I've caused my son's divorce"); impaired thinking (loss of concentration, memory loss, morbid ideation).

Causal factors. There are several theories about the causes of depression that deal with hereditary, biochemical, and psychosocial factors. Each of these causes must be carefully explored for any depressed client because based upon the cause, certain treatments have been shown to be more effective than others. For example, clients with a family history of depression where family members have been successfully treated with specific antidepressant medication need to be carefully assessed to determine if they would also benefit from antidepressants. Since talking therapies focus on the psychosocial dimension, we offer some of the more widely held psychosocial explanations of depression, realizing that this is only one of several, no less important areas.

The experience of a significant loss. Some common losses that can precipitate depression are the loss of or separation from a loved one. The common denominator in these losses is that they cause a client to feel less esteemed, important, and loved. These losses may be real, symbolic, or imaginary, but they can have the same damaging effect.

Malignant interpretation of the loss. Losses in themselves are not sufficient causes for depression; otherwise everyone who experienced a loss would become clinically depressed. An important variable in loss is how the client perceives its meaning. For example, one woman may have a mastectomy and continue to live her life as before. Another woman, interpreting the operation as causing her to be "no longer a woman," may react with depression. A man who loses his wife through death may view the event as the end of his life, while another man, though grief-stricken, recuperates and continues to live life well.

Restricted sources of need fulfillment. The more people put "all their eggs in one basket," the more problems arise when the basket falls. A man who devotes his entire life to rearing his children may experience depression when the children leave home. A woman who lived for her career may become depressed when she retires. If these people had several sources of satisfaction, the loss of one or even two would not be as devastating.

Completion of a goal. Ironically, some people experience depressive symptoms after they achieve a desired outcome. This partially explains "promotion depression," in which the client feels depressed after winning a promotion, and "vacation depression," in which the client looks forward to a holiday, but experiences depression and irritability when it arrives. When people set goals for themselves they may find that the acquisition of the goal becomes their entire purpose in life. Everything in life revolves around the goal, and the pursuit of the goal is the client's main source of gratification. Once the client has reached the goal—examples might include winning an election or completing a book or play—there is nothing left but a large vacuum. People may discover that they are able to pursue a goal but unable to enjoy their accomplishments.

Learned helplessness. This is the fatalistic belief that one cannot control important events in one's life. For example, a woman may lament, "My husband left me and I am incapable of living life on my own." These people have learned early in life that they are victims of circumstances, life can be cruel, and they might as well accept the fact that there's nothing they can do to change things. When life is good to them, they are happy; when life is cruel to them, they become and remain depressed.

Strong anger that is not adequately or constructively expressed. Sometimes it is less the loss itself that causes depression and more the anger at the loss. Some people tend to be self-blamers—"How could I have been so stupid?" "How could I have been so selfish?" Others blame those around them but cannot communicate the anger and thus strangle on it. In either case, excessive amounts of internalized anger chokes these people to such a degree that they can't move in any helpful direction.

Excessive number of life responsibilities. Some very conscientious and/ or compulsive people assume an almost overwhelming number of family- and work-related responsibilities. After a while, two things become clear to them: they are emotionally and physically exhausted and there are several important responsibilities remaining unmet. This combination fills them with a sense of frustration and hopelessness that numbs them physically and psychologically. This withdrawal acts as a defense against the pain of trying to accomplish things that cannot be accomplished.

Atonement of guilt. People who feel that they are worthless or have committed serious sins may use depression as a form of self-punishment. They feel they don't deserve to be happy because of who they are or what they have done. Consequently, they stop living fully as a way to deprive themselves of happiness they feel they do not deserve.

Predisposing personality. Some people who become depressed have personality traits that make them susceptible to various precipitating events. Without the precipitating event, no depression would ensue but the combination of predisposing personality traits and the precipitating event produces the depression. There are identifiable cognitive sets that are associated with a predisposing personality. The first is a tendency to overinterpret events in a negative direction; normal setbacks and failures are perceived as traumatic. The second is low self-esteem. Such clients tend to view themselves as inadequate and worthless, and normal frustrations and failures seem to them to prove the negative self-concept is valid. Third, the clients view themselves as helpless and hopeless. When confronted with obstacles, they surrender. The combination of these negative cognitive sets causes a client to be inordinately vulnerable to stress, loss, and failure. (For a more complete discussion of cognitive counseling for depression, see Beck, 1976, p. 263, or Raimy, 1975, p. 100.)

Counseling implications. In light of the previously mentioned symptoms, counselors can aid dysthymic or mildly depressed clients the following ways.

Providing understanding and appropriate empathy. This is especially important because depressed people are often shunned by others, including loved ones.

Becoming familiar with the general causes of depression. This familiarity will enable counselors to help people strengthen the weaknesses that underlie their depression. For example, although counselors cannot reinstate a loss, they can help people reinterpret it in more realistic ways. This will provide a stronger psychological foundation that will better absorb future stress.

Being aware of the pitfalls associated with counseling depressed people. One trap, for example, is to "catch" the client's depression, a countertransference condition where the counselor is swayed by the client's sense of hopelessness. This trap is easy to get caught in because the counselor's suggestions and plans are often met with several "good" reasons as to why each is unworkable. A second trap, or countertransference reaction, occurs when the counselor becomes angry and frustrated with the depressed client. This reaction adds to the depression because the client already feels angry and frustrated, and the counselor's feelings are interpreted as substantiating the client's own feelings of despair. A third trap is to inadvertently reward the depression. If counselors listen for hours on end to the feelings of depression without constructive, reality-oriented interpretations or goals, their patience, understanding, and empathy may be reinforcing the very symptoms they should be helping to resolve. The client may soon learn that it's more gratifying to have a sympathetic ear than to actively change the depressive behavior.

Interpreting depression as an unproductive way of expressing fear and anger. In some cases, depressed people can't move because they are too frightened. Until the underlying fears are discovered and worked through, the depression will not lift. Depression can also be a very effective passive-aggressive behavior; that is, a message to significant others, "You've ruined my life; now I'm going to ruin yours." Until the anger can be conceptualized and effectively dealt with, the client has a vested interest in holding onto the depression.

Focusing on the overall goals. Counselors need to remain aware that the main goal of helping depressed people is not only to help them become free of symptoms, but to help them strengthen the preexisting weaknesses that made them more vulnerable to depression.

Counselors must select carefully among the five noted recommendations. Treatment has to be tailored to individual clients. A client may benefit from some of the foregoing interpretations and recommendations and not from others.

Individuals diagnosed with Dysthymic Disorder have an increased risk of major depressive episodes; counselors should carefully monitor the client's progress throughout the course of counseling. Many, if not all clients, should be evaluated by a physician to determine if medication should be used as an adjunct to counseling. Research suggests that roughly 50% of dysthymic clients can be helped with antidepressant medications (Preston et al., 1997). Excellent self-help texts for clients are also available. *Feeling Good: The New Mood Therapy* by David Burns (1999) and *The Depression Workbook* (1992) by Mary Ellen Copeland are both good choices for clients with depressive mood disorders.

Personality Disorders

There are 10 different Personality Disorders and all share in common "an enduring pattern of inner experience and behavior that deviates markedly from the expectations of the individual's culture, is pervasive and inflexible, has an onset in adolescence or early adulthood, is stable over time, and leads to distress or impairment" (American Psychiatric Association, 1994, p. 629). Each personality disorder can be further categorized into one of three different clusters. Odd or eccentric behaviors link the disorders found in Cluster A; they include: Paranoid Personality Disorder, Schizoid Personality Disorder, and Schizotypal Personality Disorder. Cluster B includes Antisocial Personality Disorder, Borderline Personality Disorder, Histrionic Personality Disorder, and Narcissistic Personality Disorder, all of which share dramatic or erratic patterns of behavior. Finally, anxiety and fearfulness characterize Cluster C disorders: Avoidant Personality Disorder, Dependent Personality Disorder, and Obsessive-Compulsive Personality Disorder.

Symptoms. While the *DSM-IV* describes six General Diagnostic Criteria for Personality Disorders (American Psychiatric Association, 1994), people with Personality Disorders exhibit many of the following characteristics:

Maladaptive habits. These are long-standing and uninterrupted maladaptive habits of behavior that can be traced to early childhood or at least adolescence. They may stem from flaws in the personality structure caused by failure to learn one or more important psychosocial competencies—for example, how to relate comfortably with people (schizoid personality), how to develop a sound value system (antisocial personality), or how to be self-reliant (dependent personality).

Resistance to change.   The maladaptive behavior pattern is deeply ingrained and resistant to change.

Minimal distress.   Minimum subjective distress is experienced more as a dull, continuing ache than as acute pain.

Problem to others.   These disorders frequently cause more distress for others (spouses, parents, friends, coworkers) than for the client who has the disorder. This is because the symptoms are ego syntonic to the client. For example, people suffering from Dysthymic Disorder will complain about the symptoms. They will express a discomfort with how the disorder is impacting them; that the symptoms are not a part of their normal functioning (ego-dystonic). People with Personality Disorders do not complain about the symptoms of the disorder, but about the manner in which others are interacting and impacting *them.* Their patterns of interaction are viewed by them as "normal" (ego-syntonic), while the response to their behavior is seen as the problem. Therefore the client's distress comes through others who interact with him or her.

Lack of insight.   People view themselves as normal and lack insight into the basic flaws in their personalities.

Inflexibility.   The maladaptive behavior is inflexible and repetitive. The client employs the same defective behavior in all situations, failing to learn that what has not worked well in the past is unlikely to work well in the present.

Symptom dominance.   People organize their lives around their symptoms. For example, schizoid people tend to choose associates and jobs that will allow them to remain essentially withdrawn emotionally.

Symptom variability.   The symptoms may increase or decrease throughout life, depending on the nature and strength of stress at any particular time.

Secondary symptoms.   The client may develop secondary symptoms as a result of the primary pathology. For example, a compulsive personality may develop ulcers or headaches; a schizoid personality may experience depression due to minimal need fulfillment.

Weak motivation.   The motivation for counseling is usually tenuous. These people are often referred by relatives, friends, or employers because their behavior has been socially disruptive. When they are self-referred, their goal is usually to rid themselves of a secondary symptom—such as headaches, depression, insomnia, loneliness, boredom, or frustration. However, they are seldom interested in changing the maladaptive behavior that is causing the secondary symptoms.

Causal factors.   The psychosocial causality underlying personality disorders is that critically important psychosocial competencies were inadequately learned. The nature of the inadequately learned competency or competencies differs for each of the 10 personality disorders; causality can best be discussed in terms of each specific disorder.

Counseling implications.   It is likely that a significant number of clients have personality disorders. Secondary symptoms frequently mask underlying personality disorders, which could give the false impression that counselors seldom see people with personality disorders. It is not atypical of dependent personalities, for example, to experience marked depression as a result of a fractured relationship. These individuals may seek counseling and offer depression as their chief complaint. Since the client reports feeling "fine, in fact, very good" prior to the breakup of the relationship, the counselor may automatically assume the client is experiencing a posttraumatic stress reaction or an affective disorder precipitated by the loss of an important relationship.

People with personality disorders have a "string of beads" dynamic. The beads represent episodes where their maladaptive behavior gets them into trouble, and the string represents the basic personality flaw that causes and supports their symptoms. Counselors who do not take a careful history may devote their attention to the newest "bead" and ignore the string, which will continue to support symptoms long after the current therapeutic encounter.

People with personality disorders are often particularly challenging to work with in counseling. This is ordinarily true because their problem is deeply ingrained, it causes them relatively little subjective anxiety, and they lack insight into their personality flaw or flaws. Of the 10 types of personality disorders, the only one discussed in this chapter is the Dependent Personality Disorder. The chronic help-seeking and overreliance on caregivers, such as counselors, makes Dependent Personality Disorder a common clinical presentation in counseling.

Dependent personality.   According to the *DSM-IV* (American Psychiatric Association, 1994, p. 668), Dependent Personality Disorder is "a pervasive and excessive need to be taken care of that leads to submissive and clinging behavior and fears of separation, beginning by early adulthood and present in a variety of contexts, as indicated by five (or more) of the following:

1. has difficulty making everyday decisions without an excessive amount of advice and reassurance from others,

2. needs others to assume responsibility for most major areas of his or her life,

3. has difficulty expressing disagreement with others because of fear of loss of support or approval (note: does not include realistic fears of retribution),

4. has difficulty initiating projects or doing things on his or her own (because of a lack of self-confidence in judgment or abilities rather than a lack of motivation or energy),

5. goes to excessive lengths to obtain nurturance and support from others, to the point of volunteering to do things that are unpleasant,

6. feels uncomfortable or helpless when alone because of exaggerated fears of being unable to care for himself or herself,

7. urgently seeks another relationship as a source of care and support when a close relationship ends,

8. is unrealistically preoccupied with fears of being left to take care of himself or herself."

The basic feature of this disorder is seen in people who passively allow others to assume responsibility for major areas of their lives because of a lack of self-confidence and an inability to be self-reliant. They subordinate their needs to those of others, on whom they depend in order to avoid accepting responsibility for their behavior.

As with most personality disorders, the precise causal factors are based on speculation and inference. The following are some hypothesized causes of a dependent personality disorder.

Parental attachment and overprotection. Parents greatly overmet these people's needs when they were children to the extent that they learned others can meet their needs more successfully than they can. Moreover, because these people were discouraged from becoming self-sufficient, they lack the psychosocial competencies for being instrumental in their own need fulfillment.

Weak self-identity. As a natural consequence of the first cause, these people are so reliant on others' definitions of who they are that they never develop a sound sense of themselves. Consequently, they must rely on others not only for need fulfillment but also for a sense of identity. When relationships develop problems, such people experience severe anxiety because the situation threatens not only their need fulfillment but also their entire sense of self.

Rewarded dependent behavior. In order to be accepted and loved, these people behave in very pleasing, docile, and loving ways. As a result, they are often viewed as helpful, polite, caring, loving, and self-sacrificing. These behaviors are often rewarded by others; that is, the behaviors bring about the intended result. Moreover, dependent people are rewarded because when they hand their lives over to others, they are relieved of the critical responsibility of making their own decisions.

As with all people with personality disorders, clients with dependent personalities present special challenges to counselors in the formation of the counseling relationship. Such clients may appear to be model patients because they often seek counseling on their own and will do anything to help the counselor help them. Unfortunately, these clients may look forward to counseling because they view the counselor not only as benevolent but also an expert caretaker. While they appear to be motivated to become involved in the counseling process, their deeper motivation may be to get the counselor to take care of them.

By adulthood, most people with dependent personalities have learned that they cannot hand over their lives to people in an obvious way, because that frightens people away from them. So with assurances such as, "I know I have to do most of the work myself" and "I don't want you to manage my life; I just want some feedback from you," the dependent client begins to develop another dependency relationship.

Consequently, counselors need to be careful not to allow these people to assign them the role of caretaker. While counselors need not be harsh in this regard, they can remain steadfast in their role as a counselor and not assume the role of mother, father, husband, or wife. For a more thorough discussion of the specific steps counselors can take to avoid being drawn into a dependency relationship, see Leeman and Mulvey (1973). The following are some relevant considerations.

Sometimes establishing a short-term counseling relationship with the client, right from the outset, can be helpful. The limit on the number of sessions may motivate the client to gain all he or she can from counseling, while reducing the potential for becoming dependent upon the counselor and the counseling process.

Counselors can make it clear verbally and behaviorally that they will not make decisions for the client and they will not offer advice. Instead, the counselor offers the client a setting in which he or she can freely discuss plans for action and obtain meaningful feedback. This strategy offers what likely was absent in the client's child-parent relationship. As children develop, their relationship with their parents also needs to change. Parents assume control of infants because the infant's survival depends upon the parents' ability to meet the baby's needs. But as children develop, the relationship needs to evolve from a directive one to a consultative one. Counselors can model this more adaptive type of relationship with their clients.

Counselors can focus on the client's dynamics and outside relationships rather than focusing too heavily on the counseling relationship. One way of focusing on the client's dynamics is to assess the client's cognitions, especially those that deal with self-esteem, self-reliance, and the catastrophic expectation that drives the client to seek caretakers. Counselors can directly focus on changing behavior to increase independence rather than on learning how to develop newer and better dependency relationships. For example, counselors may ask, "What could you do differently that would increase your ability to make decisions?"

Clients who have Dependent Personality Disorder present both interesting and difficult challenges to counselors. The potential is quite high for counselors to be counterproductively drawn into the center of the client's dependency issues, by making decisions for the client, taking responsibility for the client's behavior, and inadvertently limiting the client's opportunities for developing a greater sense of self. To work effectively with such clients, counselors must be able to immediately establish clearly defined boundaries, manage the client's conscious and unconscious attempts to interact with the counselor in counterproductive ways, and protect the integrity of the therapeutic alliance. To accomplish this task counselors benefit greatly from experience working with clients who have personality disorders and from consultation with and supervision by other experienced counselors.

General Considerations

The effects of a mental or emotional disorder can significantly disrupt people's lives and the lives of those around them. The level of disruption can be explored along several dimensions—we offer two that are particularly useful to counselors as they develop treatment plans. First, depending on the severity of the mental or emotional disorder, the client's overall *level of functioning* may be variously affected, ranging from minimal to profound levels of impairment. The client's level of functioning is a critical concern when determining if the client is a suitable candidate for counseling. People with very severe symptoms may be adversely affected by or may not benefit from counseling until the severity of their symptoms can be reduced by medications and, in certain circumstances, hospitalization. For example, a client who is experiencing the symptoms of a major depression, including suicidal ideation, would be an inappropriate candidate for weekly outpatient insight-oriented counseling.

If counseling is appropriate, the client's assessed level of functioning will be used when decisions are made about session frequency and in setting therapeutic goals. For example, the counselor may decide to meet weekly with a client whose symptoms are mild and more frequently with a client who has moderate symptoms. Similarly, the goals of a client with a more debilitating mental or emotional disorder will likely be more modest than those of a client with mild or moderate disorder.

The second dimension is the *duration of the mental or emotional disorder* (chronicity). All other variables remaining the same, the longer a client has been symptomatic, the more time it will take for the client's condition is improve. Chronicity helps counselors make judgments about whether clients can expect to be involved in short-term or long-term therapy. Unfortunately, many clients enter counseling incorrectly assuming that desired changes will come about in only a few sessions, even though they understand that their symptoms have been present for years. Because such clients often fail to even ask about the duration of counseling, counselors need to take steps to insure they understand that long-term treatment may be indicated and necessary.

Using Counseling

It is not true that the more distress people have, the more motivated they will be to use counseling well. More important than the amount of distress is the ratio of the degree of psychological strength the client possesses to the amount of distress he or she experiences. Some people who have a fair degree of psychological strength and whose level of distress is mild are often willing to work as long and hard as necessary to change their behavior. Other people who have only modest or little psychological strength yet have moderate or severe distress, may feel they are better off with their symptoms than without them; they will quickly abandon counseling. It is probably fortunate that they do so because attempts to deal with particularly difficult personal issues without an appropriate amount of ego-strength can be significantly more destructive than helpful. These clients should be encouraged to explore methods for improving their ego-strength and receive supportive therapy before attempting to deal with overwhelming personal issues. Pharmacotherapy and support groups are also potentially useful alternatives to counseling.

Symptom Remission

When symptoms abate in counseling, it does not always mean that counseling has accomplished its goal. Symptoms can remit for reasons other than the fact that the client has become stronger psychologically. Sometimes symptoms disappear when they have served their purpose by getting the client to seek counseling, by getting the attention of family members, or when pressure is temporarily relieved by talking with a counselor. Although the symptoms are no longer present, the client's behavior may continue to be maladaptive. Clients such as these have a fairly high threshold. They directly recognize their discomfort only when it reaches severe levels. Subsequently, relatively minor reductions in distress drop the symptoms below the threshold and the client is no longer motivated to continue, despite the fact there is a pressing need for help. It is important for counselors to understand this and be able to discuss it clearly with the client. These clients make themselves known to counselors by calling in a crisis, coming in for one or two sessions, and deciding there is no further need for counseling only to return several weeks later in crisis. Their defenses make it almost impossible for them to sense levels of distress that would alarm and motivate most people to take steps to resolve the source of difficulty.

Counseling and crisis intervention are two different processes, and people who only come to counseling in crisis never obtain the benefit of counseling. This fact can be difficult to explain to clients but it is very important to do so.

⚹

Summary

Even though some counselors may limit their practice to clients who do not have mental or emotional disorders, they still need an extensive working knowledge of the medical model; professional relationships with physicians, psychologists, and psychiatrists; familiarity with multiaxial diagnosis; and a willingness to cooperate in a multidisciplinary approach. This knowledge affords counselors the ability to properly determine who they are capable of treating, who must be referred, and to whom referred clients should be sent. It also allows counselors to collaborate with other mental health professionals as they offer their portion of an integrated approach to helping clients who have mental or emotional disorders.

Human behavior is complex: it is formed through the interaction of many forces including biological, psychosocial, environmental, spiritual, cultural, and so forth. While clinicians have historically tended to favor one source over another, it is no longer useful to do so. Counselors more accurately understand their clients and help them more when they consider all of the sources. By doing so they are better able to develop integrated treatment plans that include careful medical assessments to rule out physical sources of psychological symptoms, screenings to determine if clients will benefit from pharmacotherapy, and carefully conducted evaluations to determine if counseling is appropriate for the client. The integrated approach offers clients advantages that do not exist when mental health professionals work in isolation.

⚹

Reflection Questions

1. What aspect of counseling clients who have mental or emotional disorders is the most anxiety-producing for you? Why?

2. What is your attitude toward formal multiaxial diagnosis? If you think diagnosis is helpful, what about the real possibility that a diagnosis in some form will return to haunt the client later in life? If

you think it is unhelpful, what will you do when the agency for which you work or the insurance company who will pay for the counseling requires a diagnosis?

3. What are some cautions counselors should keep in mind when working with clients who are diagnosed with Dependent Personality Disorder?

4. What is your attitude about hospitalization and medications for people with psychological problems? What symptoms would cause you to recommend hospitalization to a client? What type of symptoms would a client have to be experiencing before you referred the client to a physician for a medication evaluation?

5. A client tells you, "I'm more depressed now than before I started counseling." How will you respond to this?

9

MANAGING REALITY

Each of us establishes and maintains our own view of reality. We accomplish this by selectively attending and interpreting events (infusing meaning into what we observe). Selective attention is vital because the sheer volume of stimuli striking us at any point in time would immediately overwhelm us. Interpretations are necessary because we must make sense of what we observe in the context of our own lives. In other words, we must filter and shape reality so that we will not be overwhelmed by it, so that we can establish and act on priorities within it, and make sense of our experiences. However, shaping reality has both advantages and disadvantages: (1) assumptions we hold about ourselves and the world around us can decrease our objectivity as well as increase it, and (2) assumptions can protect us from painful experiences yet they can simultaneously distort, even obscure, important parts of our psychological selves.

How we selectively attend to and interpret reality defines who we are. Our uniqueness is conveyed in the idiosyncratic ways that we perceive and interpret reality because perceptions and interpretations are influenced by assumptions, experiences, needs, levels of psychological strength, and levels of self-awareness. Our perceptions and interpretations are a mixed blessing; they can seriously limit as well as increase our ability to comprehend internal and external realities. The more we know ourselves—that is, become increasingly aware of our deepest needs, feelings, and motives— the more we can make decisions and act in ways that honor our true feelings, needs, and desires. On the other hand, the more that parts of self are hidden, unexplored, or obscured, the more confused and lost we become.

Hidden, unexplored, and obscure parts of self exist for good reasons. The hidden territory is usually comprised of needs, feelings, and motives that, if recognized, would create significant amounts of anxiety. While one main goal of counseling is to reduce the area of uncharted self so the client can obtain a more accurate and potentially more helpful view of self, efforts toward this end must be balanced against the client's fears and anxieties. If clients become too heavily stressed, an unconscious system will begin to distort their view of reality to restore a balance between their anxiety levels and the amount of psychological strength they possess. Such an emotional trauma would inhibit rather than accelerate progress in counseling.

Anyone's ability to continue to function becomes seriously threatened when anxiety levels exceed that which can be effectively managed. The unconscious processes that protect people from threatening parts of reality are traditionally called *ego defense mechanisms*. While defense mechanisms have been commonly perceived as pathological at the extreme and inhibiting at a minimum, this view is inaccurate and limiting. Vaillant offers a more clinically useful perspective when he writes, "Ego mechanisms of defense imply a restorative process and by no means connote the abnormal. Rather, defenses have much in common with the behavior of an opossum vigorously and alertly playing dead or with a grouse seeming to nurse a 'hurt' wing in order to protect her babies. Such smooth functioning actions are a sign of health" (1977, p. 9). While such mechanisms are always employed for the same reason—to restore psychological homeostasis—different sources of anxiety and different amounts of anxiety call for different types of defenses. People deploy various defense mechanisms (Vaillant, 1977, p. 10):

1. to keep affects within bearable limits during sudden life crises (e.g., following a death)

2. to restore emotional balance by postponing or channeling sudden increases in biological drives (e.g., at puberty)

3. to obtain a time-out to master changes in self-image (e.g., following major surgery or unexpected promotion)

4. to handle unresolvable conflicts with people, living or dead, whom one cannot bear to leave

5. to survive major conflicts with conscience (e.g., killing in wartime, putting a parent in a nursing home)

How much protection is needed varies from person to person and across time. However, defense mechanisms, of one type or another, can be found in all people, not solely in individuals in psychological distress. The presence of defense mechanisms should not be interpreted as a sign of pathology.

Defense mechanisms should not be studied in isolation from the psychological system within which they operate. That system includes anxiety sources (both internal and external), psychological strength (resilience formed from experiences, insight awareness, etc.) and defense mechanisms. The role of defense mechanisms, within the system, is to regulate how much anxiety a particular person is exposed to by distorting reality. Defenses can be ranked on a continuum that varies from extreme levels of reality distortion to very mild levels of distortion. Defenses that severely distort reality are considered *primitive* while defenses that honor reality are termed *adaptive*. An array of defenses is necessary because individuals need varying degrees of protection, depending upon the amount of anxiety that is being produced and the individual's levels of psychological strength. For example, a person with low levels of psychological strength who is not confronting a particularly anxiety-provoking situation will not require much from defense mechanisms to maintain a psychologically balanced state. On the other hand, if the same person encounters an emotionally distressing situation that overcomes his or her level of psychological strength, he or she will need to rely more on defense mechanisms to maintain a balance.

This introduction to defense mechanisms reveals several practical conclusions about how counselors should understand these regulatory mechanisms. First, the defense mechanism should not be confused with the client's psychological issue or problem. When we observe defense mechanisms in a client we are observing the regulating portion of a homeostatic process activated to help the client adapt—we are not observing the underlying issue(s) that produced the excessive anxiety. The relationship of fever to infection offers a useful analogy. Just as the human body wards off infection by an increase in temperature, excessive amounts of anxiety are lessened through defense mechanisms. The existence of fever and the existence of defense mechanisms mean essentially the same thing: there is an insult (infection or emotional trauma) to the system and mechanisms are being activated to control it.

Second, defense mechanisms are necessary for all people, no matter what their level of psychological health. Psychologically robust individuals need the protection these defense mechanisms afford as much as others do. The only difference is that robust individuals rely on more adaptive mechanisms than those less robust in order to manage anxiety. Anyone, no matter the level of psychological strength, can be overwhelmed by traumatic events. It is at these times that defense mechanisms perform one of their most important roles.

Third, defense mechanisms use energy, sometimes extreme amounts, leaving individuals lacking energy for other important activities. Under ideal circumstances, people would not expend any more energy on defense mechanisms than is absolutely necessary to control the anxiety.

Fourth, defense mechanisms distort reality, sometimes profoundly. Again, under ideal circumstances people would not want defense mechanisms deployed that distort reality more than is absolutely necessary. This is because reality distortions inhibit psychological growth by making it more difficult to identify deeper thoughts, feelings, and motives.

Finally, it should be mentioned that defense mechanisms, like fevers, can become problems themselves, especially when they exist for lengthy periods at intense levels. Long periods of particularly high fevers can produce serious health problems, even death. Similarly, defenses that severely distort reality and are applied over long periods produce profound negative effects. Once again, the mechanism is not causing the problem, but rather is trying to balance it; but defenses can be overtaxed and overwhelmed. The level of distress a person experiences can be greater than that which can be balanced through defense mechanisms because of insufficient psychological strength, overwhelming anxiety sources, or both. Such individuals need other forms of treatment including medication or hospitalization before counseling can be of use to them. Counseling, in these circumstances, could dangerously tax an already overburdened system.

Taken together, these points offer a practical understanding of defense mechanisms, and they suggest how defenses come into play in the counseling process. For example, because defense mechanisms serve a very important regulatory function, their elimination should never be a goal of counseling. Instead, counselors should focus on helping clients reach a point where primitive mechanisms can be replaced by adaptive mechanisms (those that require less energy and cause less reality distortion). This strategy insures the client will be protected from excessive amounts of anxiety and yet still helps the client improve levels of psychological strength by carefully exploring deeper and more threatening parts of the self that would be inaccessible if more primitive defenses were in place.

Coping Mechanisms Instead of Defense Mechanisms

The phrases *coping or adaptive mechanisms* and *coping or adaptive tactics* will be used in place of *defense mechanisms* throughout the remainder of this chapter. This terminology is consonant with the paradigm shift illustrated in the introduction to this chapter: that is, the recognition that such mechanisms and tactics play an essential role in maintaining psychological equilibrium. The term *defense* has negative connotations and implies that defenses need to be reduced, avoided, or eliminated. For example, it is common to hear counselors talk about helping to rid the client of defenses—a goal that is inconsistent with the notion of a homeostatic system where coping mechanisms are vitally important. Similarly, a psychologically healthy person might be defined as one who is free of defenses—a conclusion that is also inconsistent with the model presented in the introduction. It is more helpful for counselors to see their clients not as defending themselves, but as adapting or coping within the restrictions of their psychological system.

An Underrated Dynamic

Adaptive or coping mechanisms are a vital but underrated dynamic in human behavior. It is all too easy to remain unaware of how these mechanisms reshape reality—it is difficult to value a dynamic that resides beneath conscious awareness. People are often unable to recognize, for example, that they *need* somebody more than they love him or her; or that someone is not as fond of them as they think; or that they hurt people, and not always for their own good; or that they are freer in a particular situation than they pretend to be, or less free than they would like to think; or that they are less competent in some areas than they think; or that their altruism is sometimes a camouflage for self-serving behavior. Clients may tend to judge themselves harshly for "fooling themselves" once they adopt more mature coping mechanisms that allow larger amounts of reality to filter in.

Early Learning

People adopt coping mechanisms very early in life. For example, three-year-olds might typically use the primitive mechanism of denial ("I didn't spill my milk"—even though there is milk all over the table and no one else has been in the room); or of projection ("You made me spill my milk"—even though there was no one within 15 feet).

As people develop emotionally and intellectually, they may discard primitive mechanisms for more adaptive ones. For example, a college student may no longer use denial ("I didn't cheat on the exam") but may have evolved to rationalization ("Sure I cheated. I'm not going to let some neurotic professor's unfair exam keep me from getting into law school, where I can learn to help thousands of poor people"). By using rationalization, the student has turned cheating not only into acceptable behavior but into virtuous behavior. Such rationalization, of course, continues to distort reality.

"Preferred" family coping mechanisms, a particular adaptive mechanism that most or all the family members use, are common. For example, projection as a family defense can be seen in the following family counseling dialogue:

> *Husband to counselor*: My wife's problems are beginning to interfere with my whole life. I'm even starting to get in trouble at work.
>
> *Wife to husband*: If you'd take a stronger stand with the kids and not let them run the house, it would reduce my problems by 90 percent.
>
> *Teenage daughter to parents*: I don't think things were that bad until we started this stupid counseling. Now the doctor has us all upset.

This interchange reveals a shared method for managing anxiety that interferes with problem-solving; the projections presented by the family members reduce anxiety by obscuring each member's contribution to the problem and, in turn, by obscuring lines of responsibility. This coping mechanism works—but only at a cost.

Individual clients as well as families can be helped to replace less-adaptive coping mechanisms with more adaptive ones. This process helps them recognize realities that were previously obscure. Ideally, a client can be helped to reach a point where acknowledging and dealing with certain realities through the use of adaptive coping mechanisms produce less anxiety than results from denial. The more a person or a family has used primitive coping mechanisms, and the larger the repertoire of primitive coping mechanisms employed, the longer it will take to evolve to more adaptive coping mechanisms.

Anxiety-Producing Situations

People with good psychological strength can allow a great deal of threatening material into awareness without feeling inordinately anxious; they do not have to rely upon primitive coping strategies. On the other hand, people who lack psychological strength frequently employ very primitive coping mechanisms to block or avoid a reality perceived as threatening. For example, a young man views himself as a good student but receives a final grade of "C" in a course. The dissonance between the idea he has of himself and the reality of receiving a "C" causes anxiety. To reduce the anxiety, the young man uses the defense of projection ("The professor is incompetent; that's why I got a 'C' ") or rationalization ("My roommate had serious psychological problems that affected me all semester"). By employing such defenses, the young man can continue to perceive himself as a good student when, in fact, he is simply an average one.

It would seem that people tend to hide the negative parts of themselves and acknowledge only the positive ones. However, this is not always the case. Coping mechanisms found in some people paradoxically hide the positive traits and emphasize the negative ones. For instance, take the case of a young woman who perceives herself as unattractive and uninteresting. Although she does not especially like feeling this way, such feelings protect her from social involvement. In other words, behaviors associated with her negative self-concept protect her from the risk of being hurt or rejected by eliminating the possibility of becoming emotionally involved. When a young man asks her on a date, this creates cognitive dissonance between her negative self-concept and the positive reality. To reduce the anxiety resulting from such cognitive dissonance, she assures herself that he must have been dared by his fraternity brothers or has some other nefarious motives.

This young woman has an unconscious reason for tilting a positive reality into a negative one: she can remain withdrawn. The reality that she is more attractive and interesting than she thinks produces anxiety because it opens up the possibility of intimate relationships and the risks that such relationships bring. The emotional cost of her isolation and the pain associated with perceiving herself as unattractive and uninteresting are less threatening than the pain she expects will come from a close relationship in which she may be hurt or rejected.

It is important for counselors to realize that for people with negative self-concepts, positive reality can be as threatening as negative reality is for people with positive self-concepts. This situation is often difficult for counselors to reconcile; one would not expect that individuals would feel safer by embracing negative self-perspectives. Counselors should not impulsively contradict their clients' negative self-concepts by assuming such clients would willingly embrace a more positive self-concept. The client's difficulties might appear simple to resolve: all the client need do is realize how much he or she is esteemed by others. Counselors can easily find themselves in a tug-of-war with these clients, insisting the client has some very positive points while the client insists otherwise. If this occurs, the counselor is likely to become frustrated and eventually communicate the sentiment, "How could you be so blind as not to see how attractive you are!" With this, the client wins the tug-of-war. The counselor's angry response confirms that the client's negative self-perceptions are accurate because they are shared in this case by the counselor. Counselors should be aware of paradoxical behavior patterns of this nature. Helping clients appreciate the value of their negative self-concept and the coping mechanisms that support it is far more effective. Over time these clients can be helped to develop the psychosocial competencies they need to deal effectively with the threatening reality.

Problems with Coping Mechanisms

One problem with coping mechanisms, especially more primitive coping mechanisms, is that disavowed parts of the personality do not simply cease to exist; while they cannot be seen, their effects persist. The uncharted psychological territory affects a person's behavior in a very real way. An adolescent boy may deny that he is angry with his father, but the anger still affects their relationship.

A second problem is that functioning with hidden parts of one's personality is analogous to navigating with an inaccurate map. The map tells people where all the smooth roads are, but it fails to apprise them of the dead-end roads and cliffs. The navigator will thus travel a confused and perhaps dangerous course, often repeating the same mistakes and arriving at the wrong places.

A third problem with coping mechanisms is that they divert energy that could be used for psychological growth. The more coping mechanisms people need to employ, the more energy they must allocate. People who must rely on multiple primitive coping mechanisms are often fatigued, apathetic, and susceptible to illness because of their depleted energy and resistance.

Counseling Implications

Responding to coping mechanisms. While, as has been shown, coping mechanisms can inhibit psychological growth, at other times these mechanisms can be extremely helpful. For example, in crises they buffer a pain that would, in its raw form, cause great anguish. In these cases, coping mechanisms allow a client to retreat, recoup, and eventually return to the painful reality and deal with it more effectively. However, when people lack psychological strength their need for more primitive coping mechanisms increases, even though maintaining such an array of coping mechanisms can be cumbersome, energy depleting, and weakening. In this situation, the counselor can help the client adopt more adaptive coping mechanisms while simultaneously helping improve the client's level of psychological strength. To accomplish this, counselors help the client understand their need for more primitive coping mechanisms, explain their usefulness up to this point, and invite the client to assess whether these primitive tactics are still necessary, or whether some less intense mechanism might serve the same purpose. The goal is to help the client ease away from one set of coping mechanisms as another, more efficient, set takes its place.

For example, a client may start out by saying, "My wife's drinking is causing our family to disintegrate." The counselor might respond, "I'm sure her drinking is creating some real problems at home. Could it be that if you could learn how to handle her drinking more effectively, things could get a little better?" If the husband can abandon the mechanism of projection, he might reply, "I see what you mean. Maybe I'm contributing to the tension because I don't *want* to deal with the problem well. In fact, I wonder if I don't use her drinking sometimes as an excuse to misbehave."

If the husband is not able to evolve to a more adaptive mechanism, he will reply, "Well, we had a happy family before she began to drink. If she would stop drinking, we could be the same happy family again." The counselor may want to press further: "I understand what you're saying. It's only that sometimes how we handle a problem can make things easier or harder, and I'm wondering if it's possible that you could handle the problem a little better." The client might then reply, "Well, it could be I'm not handling it very well. I'm sure open to suggestions." Or the client may respond by saying, "Hey, I *told* you; it's *her* problem. I don't need anyone putting another trip on me—I get enough 'trips' right now, thanks." This is a door-closing response. For the counselor to pursue the point any further would only fortify the mechanism, thereby increasing the length of time it would take to replace it with a more adaptive mechanism.

Appreciating a client's coping mechanisms differs greatly from more aggressive and potentially damaging approaches metaphorically described as *shoving* the client's coping mechanisms or *ripping away* the client's coping mechanisms. When counselors appreciate the client's adapting mechanisms, they may gently test to see how much support these give to the client. Shoving or ripping at the coping mechanisms results in the client's falling off balance or pushing back equally hard to maintain a balance. The following is an example of defense shoving.

A man may tell the counselor, "I love my wife so much; I don't know why I hurt her this way." A counselor may shove this man's coping mechanisms by stating, "Well, I think you *need* to feel that you love your wife so much. Nevertheless, it sounds to me like you may have strongly mixed feelings toward her, and that's what's causing the behavior you're concerned about."

The counselor's interpretation may be correct, but because he or she shoved an interpretation at the client instead of reaching for an insight, the client's coping system may have inadvertently been reinforced. This kind of "too much too soon" response is a major cause of people stopping counseling as the ultimate protection against a shoving counselor.

Counselors who are inclined to rip away coping mechanisms generally exhibit one of the following characteristics. They may have difficulty creating a nurturing atmosphere. They may be impatient and want to "cut through the garbage and get the job done." This may be a good axiom in business or politics, but it is ordinarily a damaging one in counseling. They may be hostile and attack the client under the guise of being helpful ("I'm hurting you for your own good"). The following is an example of a counselor ripping away the client's coping mechanisms.

A man may tell a counselor, "I didn't go for any job interviews again this week. I had a bad cold during the first part of the week, and my car broke down after that." The counselor may inappropriately reply, "Nonsense. You didn't go for job interviews because you are petrified of getting a job. You are scared that you'll fail the interview or that you'll get the job and bug everybody so much like you always do that you'll have to 'resign' your third job this year."

Although this type of counselor reaction might, in very rare cases, be helpful to a particular client at a particular point in counseling, for the most part it would not be a therapeutic response. The counselor's insights are delivered in a way that is harmful to the client and counterproductive to the process. This is particularly unfortunate because the only time that ripping away coping mechanisms "works" is when the client's protective mechanisms are about to fall away anyway. The question then arises: Why set up a state of antagonism when support, empathy, and understanding would work just as well? The adversary system may work well in a court of law, but it is rarely, if ever, useful in counseling.

Counselors can also take no action regarding the client's coping mechanisms—they remain and function undisturbed. Since one main goal of counseling is to gain a deeper understanding of self, it would be atypical for the counselor to ignore the client's coping mechanisms. But there are several situations when a counselor may not wish to disturb coping mechanisms.

The first situation occurs when the counselor and the client make an agreement to avoid extended discussion of emotionally charged topics. The counselor implicitly communicates, "If you will admit that you really want a divorce, I'll not challenge the assertion that you still love your husband very much and that you've done everything possible to keep the marriage together." Although "cutting deals" in counseling may not be the best way to help people grow, it may be necessary at times. In this example, it could be that progress in counseling has come to a standstill because the woman cannot admit to herself that she really wants to divorce her husband. If the obstacle can be removed by the woman's admitting she wants a divorce, this will open the door to examining the whole situation more clearly and helpfully. The counselor may later confront the woman with her role and responsibility in the deteriorating marriage.

The second situation in which a counselor may not want to stress a client's coping system is in a crisis situation. For example, a man may come to a counselor in a state of panic. He tells the counselor that his wife just left him and took the children with no warning. He is acutely agitated and torn between killing himself and killing her. He relates a litany of wrongs that his wife has perpetrated on him and the children and clearly sees himself as the victim and his wife as the villain. The client's need for effective coping mechanisms is at its highest. Interfering with those processes would not be appropriate because they are helping the client deal with a very difficult and emotionally intense situation.

Allowing the coping mechanism to remain does not mean that a counselor agrees with or reinforces the distortions that the mechanisms produce, since this would be dishonest and cause significant problems later in the relationship. Counselors can listen to the client and respond sympathetically, but to agree with the reality distortion can be ultimately quite harmful. In the previous example, the counselor could respond, "You feel very angry, frightened, and confused. If your wife did all the things you say, I certainly can understand it." The client may be so agitated that he may not even hear this response but may feel the support. Or the client may respond, "Well, she *did* do them—there's no doubt about that," to which the counselor nods in understanding. Or the client may respond, "Hey, don't you *believe* me that she did all those things?" The counselor may answer, "It's very hard for me to know, because I wasn't there. But I think we have a problem here that needs solving, no matter who or what caused it."

To agree with the client's distortions—that is, for the counselor to respond, "Your wife sounds like a very disturbed person"—would be burning bridges that may be useful later in counseling. For example, getting the husband to accept his responsibility in the situation will be harder. He will undoubtedly tell his wife what the counselor said, thus creating a great obstacle to her joining them in counseling. Deep down, the man himself may lose confidence in a counselor who was induced to choose sides so easily.

Clients' use of coping mechanisms. Many potential clients seek counseling because their overworked coping mechanisms are no longer protecting them. For example, the system may have been successful in helping the person evade difficult parts of reality, but the price (energy loss and reality distortions) for such evasion has been so high that the person decides to enter counseling. Second, the overworked coping system may have worn thin, and previously hidden thoughts, motives, and feelings begin seeping or flooding into awareness. This can occur if the coping mechanisms are becoming less effective or if new sources of distress have overtaxed them. Under these conditions, entering counseling in a very anxious state is common for people traumatized by the realization that whatever had been protecting them is no longer working.

It is important for counselors to realize that people bring into counseling the same coping mechanisms that were present before counseling began. They will cope with the counseling relationship by using the same mechanisms used in the other relationships in their lives. However, astute counselors are in a unique position to help clients safely explore their coping strategies within the context of the counseling relationship.

Skilled counselors understand that clients may depict a reality that sounds far better than it actually is; they know how to glean the difference between what the client reports and what the client may be experiencing at deeper levels; and they can help the client appreciate the difference. The following is an example of how the client's coping mechanisms can obscure the counselor's understanding of the client. In this and other examples throughout this chapter, keep in mind that clients can make similar statements and *not* be distorting reality. However, in the following examples, assume that the client's statements and the counselor's interpretations are based on a reality that has been filtered through the client's primitive coping mechanisms.

The client may come into counseling and tell the counselor, "I didn't feel like coming today, but I knew it would be good for me. I'm trying not to give in to my scared self—so here I am." The counselor may be deceived by this coping mechanism and reply, "Well, that's a good sign! It sounds as if your healthy self is beginning to gain some control."

But if the hidden part of the client could have spoken, it might have said, "I don't think I'm getting anywhere in counseling. But if I didn't come today, it would have made me face that realization more squarely, and then I would have to do something about it. I would have to either end counseling or talk about my feelings of discouragement. I'm not ready to do either; so it's easier for me to keep the appointment and pretend that things are progressing nicely."

Counselors' use of coping mechanisms. Of course, counselors also employ coping mechanisms, both in their personal lives and in counseling. A counselor's knowledge of behavior does not preclude the need for protecting himself or herself from overly difficult or excessively painful experiences. In fact, a knowledge of behavior can be used to help the counselor evolve from a less adaptive system of coping mechanisms to a more adaptive one and to be able to teach this to their clients.

Unfortunately, a knowledge of behavior can be *abused* to justify actions that would otherwise have been unjustifiable. For example, a person may have been rather timid about expressing anger before studying counseling. However, now that he or she understands that "a counselor must be confrontive" to help clients face themselves, the person feels justified in insulting and lambasting clients. The counselor's countertransference issues in the form of pent-up frustrations and anger have, through the magic of rationalization, become a "therapeutic tool."

The following example shows how a counselor's coping mechanisms may cause him to mislead himself and, consequently, mislead the client. A counselor tells a client, "I think I've been getting lenient with you and letting you drag your feet in counseling. I'm going to have to get a little tough with you, but it's for your own good." The client responds, "Well, maybe that's what I need. I usually function better if someone gives me a kick once in a while to keep me honest." Although neither the counselor nor the client may be aware of it, the hidden part of the counselor might be saying, "This guy's passivity reminds me so much of my father's, which I hated. I can't do anything about my father now, but I can 'beat up' this guy under the guise of 'toughening him up,' and that will make me feel better."

While this example illustrates that counselors are susceptible to reality distortions, it also shows just how destructive these distortions can be in a counseling relationship. Counselors must recognize that their coping mechanisms can produce misperceptions of themselves and their clients and that they are always vulnerable to these distortions. Personal counseling, consultation, supervision and at times recording sessions with the client's permission are probably the only ways that such countertransference issues can be detected, explored, and remedied. Counselors, no matter what their level of experience, should consult with supervisors and colleagues throughout their professional lives.

The common factor in each of these examples is that both the counselors and the clients heard what they were able to hear and were closed to hearing alternatives. Counseling progresses only when both the counselor and the client can approach each other with an openness that allows them to hear and understand one another's experience of themselves and the world around them. Counselors who cannot achieve this with a client should not work with that client.

Counselor and client negotiations. The client's coping mechanisms can negotiate with those of the counselor and vice versa without either being aware that it is happening. This unconscious dynamic is as powerful as it is subtle. The concealed agreement between the counselor and the client evolves from the basic theme, "I won't unearth your most hidden parts if you don't unearth mine." The covertness of this agreement cannot be overstressed. The following is an example of coping mechanism negotiations between a client and a counselor.

A woman in counseling has two deeply hidden parts: one is that she would like to leave her husband and find a more affectionate, healthy mate; the second is that she has deep religious doubts hidden beneath religious fervor. The counselor also has two deeply hidden parts: he doubts his skills as a counselor, and he feels guilty for charging a large fee.

The specific agreement (if it could be known) between the coping systems of the counselor and the client may read as follows. Client to counselor: "If you don't make me look at my desire to leave my husband or my serious religious doubts, I won't make you face your inadequacy as a counselor or your guilt for charging more than most other counselors." The "No Trespassing" areas are clearly posted. These two people could meet for a hundred or three hundred hours and discuss every conceivable topic and problem without either one trespassing. In so doing, both could feel that progress has been made, pointing to what, in reality, are only superficial changes in behavior. Both terminate counseling feeling that it was a successful endeavor. And according to their hidden parts, it *was* successful. Both paid their respects to mental health without having to face themselves or make any significant changes. The good feeling that accompanies the termination of counseling stems from the relief that the hidden parts were not unveiled.

The negotiated agreement between the counselor's and client's coping systems may be enforced through comments made to each other during counseling sessions. The counselor may approach one of the client's deeply hidden and highly sensitive parts by stating: "You say you love your husband, but do you ever feel, deep down, it would be nice to relate with someone different for a change?" or "You tell me frequently how thankful you are for a strong religious faith, but sometimes I wonder if, deep down, you have some doubts that aren't easy to look at?"

The client's response pressures the counselor to return to the agreement. To the latter question, she replies, "Where in the world did you ever get such an idea? The one thing I have to cling to is my faith, and you're trying to take that away from me! I thought you were supposed to be *helping* me, not *destroying* me. I'd be better off talking to a priest. At least *he* would appreciate my values and have the skills to help me live them out. And he'd be an awful lot cheaper, too."

The message is clear: "You'd better back off or you'll get hurt." The counselor receives the message and responds, "I didn't mean to upset you. The question just passed through my mind. If you feel comfortable with your religious beliefs, I guess that's all that's important." The counselor realizes he has touched upon an area protected by primitive coping mechanisms, but comforts himself with the idea that the client is not ready to deal with the situation; so he tags it for a later time. After the counselor backs off and the woman feels safe, she apologizes for her outburst and assures him that she is fortunate to be seeing him. The counselor tells her there is no need to apologize, that it was a healthy exchange, and both move onto less threatening and less important topics.

Some people are able to detect the deepest fears in others. While most skilled counselors possess this ability, many clients also have it. The more hidden or unaccepted fears counselors have, the more vulnerable they are to being directed by the client. In the previous example, if the counselor felt reasonably confident in his skills and felt justified in charging his fee, he might have responded to the woman's outburst in one of the following ways:

- Could you tell me more about why you are upset with me?
- Could we talk more about the idea that your faith is all you have to cling to?
- You seem to feel that sometimes I don't know what I'm doing or that I say some very foolish things.
- Let's talk about my fee for a few minutes since that seems to be concerning you.

The counselor displays both self-confidence and a genuine concern for the client by gently remaining steadfast and helping the woman carefully explore one or more emotionally charged issues. The counselor may or may not advance too far, this time, but either way the therapeutic relationship is enhanced because the client experiences the counselor as strong and empathic. The strengthened therapeutic alliance leads to the realization that eventually the counselor and client can successfully confront deeper fears, together.

Common Coping Mechanisms

Authors differ on the number of coping (defense) mechanisms that are available to human beings, how best to categorize them, and what part they play in counseling. For example, Anna Freud's *The Ego and the Mechanisms of Defense* (1966) defines the major mechanisms and offers many insights about the influence of these mechanisms and their analytic significance. George Vaillant takes a different view in his classic text, *Adaptation to Life* (1977), based on a longitudinal study that describes 18 different mechanisms, classifies each into one of four levels, and illustrates each mechanism's effect by offering detailed, often moving accounts of the subjects' lives. Though this work has been justifiably criticized for its exclusive sample (successful men), the findings are both useful and illuminating. While a discussion that compares the perspectives of different authors would be beneficial, in the interest of brevity only one particular model has been selected because it is useful in many different approaches to counseling.

Several classification schemes have been used to categorize coping mechanisms. For example, one way of classifying these mechanisms identifies them according to whether they are fight, flight, or compromise responses to a threat. In this scheme, projection, reaction formation, and denial are "fight" mechanisms. Intellectualization is an example of a "flight" mechanism, while compensation and sublimation are both "compromise" mechanisms. While it is interesting to see how each mechanism focuses on a different reaction to threats, the clinical value is limited. In contrast, Vaillant's (1977) four levels of mechanisms define levels of psychological functioning, and offer the most practical value from a counseling standpoint. They include:

I   "Psychotic" Mechanisms

II   Immature Mechanisms

III "Neurotic" Defenses

IV   Mature Mechanisms

Since Level I contains the most primitive mechanisms and Level IV the most adaptive, the hierarchy can be used to determine how adaptive the client's coping mechanisms are. This hierarchy also can be used to decide if, over time, a client is deploying more or less adaptive mechanisms; it can be used as a rough gauge of psychological growth. The following discussion of specific coping mechanisms is organized according this hierarchy. Space does not permit a discussion of all of the mechanisms that Vaillant identified for each level, but the mechanisms selected were chosen because counselors commonly encounter them, both in their clients and in themselves, and because they are easily distinguished from each other.

Level I—"Psychotic" Mechanisms

Denial.   Denial is the inability to acknowledge threatening aspects of reality. It is a primitive mechanism that severely distorts reality and obstructs access to deeper elements of self. The following is an example of denial in a client that illustrates why it is called a psychotic mechanism when it occurs in adults.

Client: You always see me so late in the afternoon, you must be pretty tired by the time you have to listen to me.

Counselor: Does it seem to you that I'm tired when we meet?

Client: I don't know what you are talking about. Why are you asking me if I think you are tired?

Counselor: You feel that maybe my concentration may be running a little thin by this time?

Client: No. I still don't know what you are talking about. Why are you asking me about your concentration?

Counselor: Could it be that you feel I'm not as interested or energetic when we meet?

Client: I still don't know what you are talking about. Why are you so worried about your energy levels, I thought we were here to talk about me?

Depending on the situation, the counselor can continue dealing with the denial. For example, he may say, "Well, why don't we spend just a few more minutes on this because I'm picking up some concern from you that may be legitimate. If you had a choice, would you choose an earlier time?" On the other hand, the counselor may drop the issue, either because it is relatively unimportant compared to the issues he knows will be dealt with in the session or because he feels that pursuing the matter at this time will be fruitless.

Counselors may also discover situations where denial protects them from anxiety. For example, a client may say, "Why does counseling cost so much? You must admit that you guys charge outrageous fees. What if I didn't have the money? Would you see me anyway?" Anger surges within the counselor, who responds with a tight voice, reddened face, and forced smile: "You are concerned about the cost of counseling?" The client responds, "Are you *angry* that I asked that?" The counselor responds too quickly, "Of course not! It's a very reasonable question. Don't worry. If I were angry, I would tell you." The problem is that the client *does* know it, and the counselor *doesn't*. The counselor is teaching the client, firsthand, how denial avoids unpleasant reality.

Level II—Immature Mechanisms

Projection. The defense mechanism of projection performs two functions. First, anxiety is reduced when the individual's unacceptable impulses, thoughts, and desires are attributed to others. Second, it reduces anxiety that would come from taking personal responsibility because the blame for a person's shortcomings, mistakes, and misdeeds is transferred onto others.

A married woman tells her counselor that she is seriously considering termination because she "knows" that the counselor thinks she should leave her husband, and she feels she never wants to do that. In fact, the counselor is not leaning in one direction or the other. The woman is projecting onto the counselor her unconscious desire to leave her husband. In projecting these feelings onto the counselor, she can terminate counseling rather than acknowledge and accept her desire to leave her husband.

Projection is a coping mechanism that is equally available to counselors. For example, counselors can easily blame the client for any lack of progress. Counselors can assure themselves that if only the client were more motivated, less passive, more mature, or less resistant, counseling would progress nicely. But the first question the counselor should ask is, whether he or she could be doing something differently to help untrack the client.

Counselors also use projection when they attribute their own motives or feelings to the client. For example, a counselor may tell a client, "I've noticed in the past few sessions that you seem to be placing an emotional distance between us." In fact, it is the counselor who is withdrawing emotionally because she is beginning to feel personally attracted to the client and fears it.

Level III—"Neurotic" Defenses

Intellectualization. Intellectualization interferes with or cuts off such normal emotional responses as anger, hurt, fear, or guilt from the event that caused them. It does this through thinking, rather than feeling. The following example shows the client's intellectualization of a painful event: "I was deeply upset when my fiancee broke up with me last week, but now I'm seeing the situation much more clearly. She was raised in a 'dysfunctional family,' used to getting her own way with men and having them fall all over her. She was attracted to me when I was still in the dependency stage of our love. At that point her wish was my command. Of course, the more I babied her, the more she worshiped me. However, being in graduate school really accelerated my maturity. I'm no longer a starry-eyed adolescent. I want a mature woman who wants a husband to relate with and not a daddy to play with. She obviously couldn't handle this change in me; so she is off trying to find someone else to order around. I can't tell you how lucky I feel that this happened *before* we were married."

This young man unconsciously employed his intellect to sever his feelings from awareness. He is deeply hurt that his fiancee broke off with him. He feels confused, inadequate, lost, and vengeful. His counselor will have to help him reconstruct the relationship and identify the feelings as they actually existed. This will enable the young man to identify his feelings so he can deal with them more constructively.

Counselors also can intellectualize in the counseling relationship. A client states, "I'm really depressed today, and I don't know why. But this is the first time I've ever felt that it would be nice to have a fatal disease and die." The intellectualizing counselor responds, "Well, by now you should know why you're depressed. Remember we talked before about how repressed anger causes depression. You are furious at your husband, but felt if you told him he would go out and get drunk again. You allow him to manipulate you covertly with his drinking problem. As long as you do that, you will be depressed."

In reality, the counselor may be alarmed at the woman's increasing depression. However, instead of recognizing these fears and sharing personal concern, the counselor lectures her and effectively squelches his feelings rather than using them to help the woman.

Rationalization.   Rationalization allows a person to present logical and socially approved reasons to justify behavior and to soften disappointments or failures. The following is an example of how clients may rationalize.

A woman may say to her counselor, "I canceled our appointment last week because my mother was sick, and I didn't feel I should leave her alone. And then I was having trouble with my car and felt if it broke down, that would really create problems for me. And I had to study for a final exam that I had to take that night."

The counselor is aware that none of these excuses sounds particularly valid, and the sheer number of them indicates maybe there is more to the canceled appointment than the woman is admitting to the counselor and possibly to herself.

The counselor may respond, "It seems that last Tuesday was a very tough day. Nevertheless, I wonder if there was something about coming to counseling last week that didn't feel just right to you, even if none of the other things had happened." If the real reason for the canceled appointment is barely out of consciousness, this response could invite it into awareness. If the real reason is further from awareness, more work will be necessary.

Counselors may also use rationalization in counseling. For instance, a counselor receives a note from a client stating that he is terminating because he thinks he is getting worse instead of better. To soften the disappointment and the possibility that she made some mistake with this client, the counselor assures herself that the man's motivation for counseling was poor and that it is better that he terminate now instead of wasting more time. This allows the counselor to avoid considering the situation any further. If the counselor had looked at reality squarely, she might have understood the reason for the note and contacted the man. They possibly could have met another time to discuss the situation and attempt to resolve the problem. Whatever the man's final decision, the counselor would have learned something and felt better about the situation.

Repression.   Repression means that a thought or feeling is intercepted before it reaches awareness. A client may assure the counselor, "I'm not upset that you canceled our appointment last week. You need a day off just like anyone else." This statement alone could be an indicator of repression, or it could be accurate. The nonverbal communication that accompanies the statement often gives telltale signs that repression is operative. If the client says it a little too jovially, defensively, or casually, it could show that some resentment is being repressed.

Depending on the circumstances, a counselor may wish to deal with the discrepancy between the statement and the accompanying nonverbal communication or just tag it and come back to it later. If the counselor deals with it immediately, he or she may start with a general approach and narrow it to a particular one. For example, the counselor may state, "A lot of clients feel upset when their counselor cancels an appointment. Is there a part of you that feels a *little* upset?" The client may answer, "Well, I hadn't thought about it, but now that you mention it, I was a little irked." With gentle encouragement, the client may acknowledge some anger and be able to talk about it.

On the other hand, the client may respond, "No. As I said, I can understand why you'd need a day off. If anything, I felt relieved that I didn't have to come in." Again, depending on the circumstances, the counselor may drop it there or continue, "The reason I asked is that you seemed to be trying to convince me that you had no upset feelings; so I was wondering if you felt that maybe you shouldn't have those feelings."

The client may respond, "Well, you've done so much for me, I guess I feel that I don't have the right to feel angry with you, just because you miss one session." This statement presents a clear possibility that, with a little permission from the counselor, the client can probably release some feelings. Or the client may reply, "As I told you *twice*, I wasn't angry. It sounds as if you would like me to have been angry, but I assure you I wasn't!"

This statement is a door-closing one; so, the counselor probably would be better off dropping the topic but remaining alert to unconscious leakage that would suggest that the client was upset. For example, the client may go on to state, "You'd think with a two-week interval, I'd be brimming over with things to talk about, but I really have nothing to say. Why don't you talk today for a change?" On the other hand, there may be no observable leakage, which suggests the client is either too frightened to loosen the repression or is not repressing any feelings.

Obviously, counselors cannot stop clients at every turn and search them for coping mechanisms; however, counselors can realize that repression can be damaging for people even by repressing just a little thought here and a little feeling there. The repressed issues begin to accumulate, making it ever more difficult for the client to reach important realities. If a counselor can teach a client in "here-and-now" circumstances to bring up repressed issues and deal with them, there can be much transfer of learning to situations outside of counseling. So when the woman goes home and her husband says, "I'm sorry I'm home late for dinner; I hope you're not upset," she may now say, "Well, I am upset, and here are the reasons."

Counselors may also discover their own use of repression as a coping mechanism to screen out threatening ideas, feelings, and motives. For example, a counselor may fear a particular client. Instead of admitting these fears and dealing with them constructively, he represses them. This causes him to avoid topics where the client's feelings, especially anger, might surface, to take an unnecessarily accommodating approach to keep the client at a distance, or to create a situation that leads him to suggest he cannot continue to see the client. So while conscious feelings of fear may have caused the counselor some anxiety, which he could have dealt with constructively, his repressed feelings sabotage the counseling relationship.

Reaction formation.   Reaction formation enables an individual to flee from disturbing feelings or desires by assuming their opposite. The following example shows how this defense can be used by a client. A woman says to her counselor, "Remember last week when I said I don't think counseling has helped me one bit; in fact, I thought it made me worse? Well, I gave that a lot of thought during the week and came to realize that for me even to have said that to you was proof of the tremendous amount of progress I've made. My only concern now is to adequately show my appreciation to you."

This woman may have scared herself with her honesty and anticipated being rejected by the counselor, just as her parents had rejected her when she was "too honest." She quickly recouped and did an about-face, guaranteeing that she not only would not be rejected but would be accepted more than ever.

The counselor can help this woman by responding, "I think you said some very important things last week, and I'm afraid we're going to lose them if we just move to the next topic. I'm sure you had good reasons for what you said, and it would be helpful for us to go back and take a further look at them." This type of response will help the woman recognize how she typically switches from her real feelings to their opposite to avoid assuming responsibility for them.

Counselors also can succumb to reaction formation. They can be overprotective to hide their deeper feelings of apathy. They can be optimistic to cover their feelings of discouragement. They can be overly accommodating to camouflage their feelings of dislike. They can be overly strong to mask their feelings of weakness. They can be overly active to compensate for their feelings of boredom. The problem is that these deeper feelings will subtly emerge and contaminate their counseling efforts.

Level IV—Mature Mechanisms

Suppression.   This is an excellent example of a mature mechanism, one that is highly adaptive. The mechanism does not distort reality, instead it manages anxiety by allowing the individual to put off dealing with the conflict to a more appropriate time. The individual is consciously or subconsciously aware of the source of the anxiety. The conflict is not denied, projected, or displaced, it is clearly attended to and will be addressed later at more appropriate time and place.

For example, a client who has been spending an inordinate amount of time tutoring her older child tells her counselor that her younger son will now also need tutoring. She received a note informing her of this fact shortly before meeting the counselor for her weekly appointment. She begins to describe how sad she feels and how worried she is that she will not have enough time to help both children. She stops talking, begins to tear up, and then explains that she will need to create a schedule starting that very evening so that she can help both kids. Finally she says, "I have a lot of feelings about all this; I am angry, sad, worried, and frustrated. I know I really need to talk about them with someone but this is not the time. Can we talk about some ways to problem-solve and return to the feelings next week?" The counselor quickly agrees, realizing that the need to take care of the tutoring issue was taking precedence over the issue of the client's emotional conflict. With the scheduling problems out of the way, and a tutor from a local university hired to help both children, the client returns the following week ready and able to explore her feelings. She decides to discuss the sadness she feels for both children and the pride she sensed in herself for not behaving the way her own father did when she needed his help as a school-aged child. He had become angry when she asked for help with schoolwork, and she vowed to herself that she would not do the same to her own children.

Effective counselors often can model this coping mechanism and thus help clients evolve to more mature and adaptive mechanisms. Suppression can be taught to clients. Counselors will sometimes suggest that the client work on a particular issue during a session and then suppress it until the next session. The metaphor of a long-term project that is worked on for an hour each week and then put on a shelf until the next week is very useful to clients.

There are other mature mechanisms. Humor will be covered in the next section as a coping tactic. Altruism, anticipation, and sublimation are equally adaptive coping mechanisms that share the "ability to integrate reality, interpersonal relationships, and private feelings" (Vaillant, 1977, p. 385). They are mechanisms that foster growth and development while continuing to provide protection from conflict, precisely because they are efficient, do not distort reality, and improve relationships.

Coping or Adaptive Tactics

Although coping mechanisms and coping tactics share a common goal, they are different behaviors. Coping mechanisms serve a more intrapsychic purpose; that is, they protect people from their threatening parts. Coping tactics protect by preventing others from discovering the threatening parts of the person. People employ adaptive or coping tactics to protect themselves by keeping people at a safe distance and deferring responsibility for their behavior. In other words, coping mechanisms are oriented more toward *intra*personal protection, and coping tactics are oriented more toward *inter*personal protection.

One is likely to see the following coping tactics in counseling. As with coping mechanisms, people employing these behaviors may be completely unaware of their protective function or only partially aware of the shielding service that the behavior provides. The following discussion focuses exclusively on the client because, although counselors can also use coping tactics, the ones discussed here are more likely to be used by the client.

Pedestaling

The client places the counselor on a pedestal when the client's attitude toward the counselor is, "I admire, trust, and respect you greatly. Just tell me what to do, and I'll do it." In the client's view, he or she is simply realistically acknowledging the wisdom, benevolence, and expertise of the counselor. However, on a deeper level, pedestaling has several coping functions.

First, placing the counselor above the client makes it difficult for the counselor to confront the client directly. The dynamic is similar to that between an adoring son and his father. How can the father present anxiety-producing reality to his son who so looks up to him? When the father does, the son's reaction says, "And I thought you really loved me." In the counseling relationship, the pedestaling client attempts to negotiate a similar arrangement with the counselor: "I'll admire and appreciate you as long as you don't do anything to increase my anxiety."

Second, the client who is in an inferior position to the counselor defines his or her role as following through on the counselor's suggestions. The counselor who attempts to get the client to look for causes and solutions to issues is met with the retort, "I don't know the answers to these questions. That's why I came to you—*you're* the expert; *you're* supposed to tell *me* what to do."

Finally, since this client has come to counseling to get answers to problems, the client is not interested in being "analyzed." This means the counselor is not invited to question the client's motivations or feelings or to offer insights, interpretations, or any opinions that would create anxiety.

In a short time, the counselor discovers the limitations of trying to operate from a pedestal. Unwary counselors can be caught in this dynamic by allowing themselves to be disarmed by respect and docility. While they remain on their pedestal and offer suggestions, inevitably they are faced with the reality that the client has not grown in any substantive way.

Counselors who are going to be helpful must remove themselves as early as possible from the pedestal. This needs to begin in the first session by carefully reorienting the client to the proper role of the counselor. There may be a period during which the client will make repeated efforts to hoist the counselor back on the pedestal, but the counselor can strenuously resist these efforts while pointing out the reasons for the resistance.

Humor

Humor is considered a very adaptive, mature, and productive coping tactic (see Vaillant, 1977). Humor softens the intensity of difficult realities while still allowing the individual to gain a sense of the reality rather than denying or repressing it. Although humor can be healthy and have salutary effects, it can also be employed as a shield. Deciding when the client is using humor adaptively and when the client is using humor to shield parts of self can be complicated. Understanding how humor is commonly used for protection offers some insight into how counselors can assess what service humor is performing. We discuss three ways that it can be used as a coping tactic.

First, it can be used to derail an important dynamic in counseling. For example, just as the counselor and client evolve to the brink of an important insight, the client makes a humorous remark, thereby derailing the dynamic. The counselor now has the choice of dealing with the shielding nature of the humor, for which she will be viewed as "too serious," or she can participate in the humor, rationalizing that the client is not ready for the insight.

Second, humor can be used to express anger at the counselor. This usually takes the form of a "just kidding" joke. The client laughingly says to the counselor, "Gee, you look more depressed than I do. Is there anything I can do for you? Ha, ha, I'm just kidding." By couching the anger in humor, the client does not have to take responsibility for the angry feelings and, at the same time, the counselor cannot respond in anger because the client claimed to be "just kidding." The counselor has the choice of letting the comment go, facing the client with the dual nature (humor and anger) of the comment, or laughing at the comment to prove that he or she is a "good sport."

Third, humor can be used to conceal a client's deep anxieties. The amount of humor and laughter some people exhibit during a session is directly correlated with the amount of anxiety they are feeling. They relate painful memories and events with laughter and a wide grin. They tell the counselor "and then my father hit my mother" as if it were the punch line of a joke. The artificial humor these people inject into situations protects them in an often unhelpful way from their painful feelings. These people work on the principle, "If I don't laugh, I will cry." Counselors can smile along with these people or gently confront them with the discrepancy between what they are saying and feeling and the humorous facade.

Agreeableness

Some clients are very agreeable; that is, they agree with everything the counselor says and does, no matter how negative or unsubstantiated it is. They seem continually to nod their head in agreement, even before the counselor has said anything with which to agree or disagree. Agreeableness has several protective functions.

First, it precludes any tension or conflict arising between the client and the counselor. This client has low stress tolerance and manages to escape the ordinary stresses of life by being agreeable. However, stress is an important catalyst for growth, and to the degree that clients avoid everyday stress, they will remain stagnant or regress.

Second, agreeableness can camouflage important parts of the client's personality. As long as the client agrees with the counselor, he or she need not make any personal declaration or revelation. The counselor's attempts to relate with the client are deflected by statements such as, "I see," "I'd really like to help you, but I just don't know the answer," and "I hate to admit it, but I think you're right." The agreeable client's attitude toward the counselor is, "You tell me who I am, and I'll agree with you" instead of "Let me tell you who I am, and I'll agree with you when I think you're right and disagree when I think you're wrong."

Third, agreeableness relieves the client from taking responsibility for decisions. If these clients agree with and cooperate with the counselor, they do not have to make their own decisions and experience the anxiety that comes with making choices.

One indication that a client's agreeableness has become a coping tactic is when the agreement with the counselor does not manifest itself outside the counseling relationship. For example, a man heartily agrees that he should confront his boss with how he feels and may spend a whole session preparing for the confrontation. At the next session, the man does not mention the confrontation because he forgot it as soon as he left the counselor's office. In other words, agreeable people feel that agreeing to something is as good as doing it, especially when it reduces their anxiety within the counseling session.

Counselors can initially develop incorrect assumptions about clients who employ this tactic because they seem open, cooperative, and motivated. The shielding function of the client's agreeableness becomes obvious when the counselor recognizes the inconsistency: pervasive agreeableness that it is not matched by action.

Cuteness

Adults can be cute in many ways, all of which are vestiges of childhood behaviors that worked, and still work, to rescue them from facing the inappropriateness of their behavior. Cute behaviors are mostly nonverbal and involve the eyes, the mouth, the tilt of the head, and gestures.

These nonverbal behaviors communicate messages such as:

- Oh, there goes silly me again.
- Gosh, do you really think I did that on *purpose?*
- I know it wasn't nice of me to do that, but it *was* funny.
- Oh, darn it—I tried *so* hard but messed things up.
- Oh, you're not going to be upset with me, are you?
- I know that sometimes I'm mischievous, but I don't mean to hurt anybody.
- Let's stop being so serious; let's play for a while.

Cute behavior performs the following shielding functions. First, when these people perceive themselves as being cute, it hides the real destructiveness of their behavior. Instead of facing the damage they are doing to themselves and others, they tend to view their behavior in a semi-humorous way. Since they do not quite take themselves seriously, their anxiety seldom reaches a point where it will motivate them to change their behavior.

Second, their cute behavior is meant to seduce the counselor into enjoying and protecting them, just as one does a child. They can offer a powerful invitation that reads, "Come on, let's be cute together." The counselor is invited to play and flirt with the client. The purpose of this dynamic is to get counselors to abandon their role and allow these people to continue with their irresponsible behavior.

Third, cute behavior often places the counselor in a no-win situation. If the counselor accepts the invitation to indulge the cuteness, counseling will not be effective and, in fact, will not occur. If the counselor declines the invitation and attempts to point out the protective function of the behavior, the client is likely to pout and accuse the counselor of being a "stuffed shirt" or of not liking the client.

Confusion

Of course, there are times when clients are genuinely confused; however, confusion may also exist as a coping tactic. By understanding some of the protective functions confusion can perform, counselors may be able to assess whether the client is confused or needs to be confused to protect himself or herself. Clients act confused for several reasons.

First, confusion can act as a smokescreen to protect the client from facing unpleasant reality. For example, a man reports obvious indications that his employer no longer is pleased with his work and would like to terminate him. However, instead of being in touch with his hurt, fear, guilt, and resentment, he reports only that he is "terribly confused by what's going on." His confusion acts as a buffer between himself and threatening feelings.

Second, if a client is confused, he or she can delay taking any action. In the previous example, since the man cannot figure out what is going on, he does not have to move in the direction of confronting the reality of his employment problem. While the confusion protects the client from the anxiety that realizing his plight would produce, it also robs him of valuable time and energy that could be better invested in evaluating what he needs to do to resolve his employment problem.

The client's confusion can be contagious and cause the counselor to become confused also. Consequently, both people stumble through the fog being equally ineffectual and removed from the more important issues. Moreover, prolonged confusion in counseling causes frustration in both the client and the counselor. The more confused they become, the more frustrated they become. They blame each other for the miasma in which both are caught. As they struggle with their frustrations and subtly or overtly blame each other, they become two stages removed from touching the issues that are causing the client's difficulties.

Acting Stupid

Acting stupid is different from being ignorant. Acting stupid means that, on a deeper level, people know what they are doing and what consequences are likely to flow from their behavior. Being ignorant means that people genuinely cannot grasp the meaning and possible consequences of their behavior. One example of acting stupid is seen in a married man who spends an increasing amount of time with his unmarried secretary after work. Over a time, they date frequently, and although she assures him that she is not interested in marriage, she dates no one else. They become intensely involved both emotionally and sexually, and the woman begins to pressure the man to leave his wife and marry her or she will break off the relationship. This situation fills the man with anxiety and consternation, and this distress brings him to counseling. He assures the counselor that he had no intention of getting into "this mess" and now wants the counselor to help him get out of it. Although an objective observer could have predicted this complicated outcome, the client is utterly surprised and at a loss as to how the whole situation occurred.

This example illustrates the several protective functions that result from this coping tactic. First, it protects the client from anxiety-producing reality. The man did not want to face either his deteriorating marriage or the fact that he was actively and volitionally creating a romantic relationship with his secretary, the result of which could only be a source of great stress no matter how it turned out.

Second, it allows people to avoid assuming responsibility for their behavior. When the situation caves in on top of them, these people can appear astonished and wonder what went wrong. The man mentioned in the example defines himself as a victim both of the woman and of circumstance. His question to the counselor is, "How could this have happened to me?"

Third, acting stupid and its destructive results can focus on a bogus problem. The client defines his problem as one of naiveté and stupidity. He asks the counselor to help him become less naive and more intelligent; in other words, he wants to define the problem in intellectual terms. In fact, however, he is not naive or stupid, but wants things that he is unable to admit to himself or for which he is unwilling to accept responsibility.

Helplessness

Some people present themselves in counseling as helpless. They do this in various ways: They cannot figure out what their problem is; they do not know what is causing the problem; or they do not know what to do to solve the problem.

Helplessness is a coping tactic when it induces the counselor to take over for the client. Clients such as these define the counselor's role as telling them what their problem is, what caused it, and how to solve it. By doing this, these clients remove themselves as a creator or contributor to the problem and pass the responsibility for solving it to the counselor.

In addition, when clients remain helpless, they cannot move because no one, including the counselor, can successfully make them move in the direction of growth. So while such clients protest that they want to solve their problems, they also ensure that things will remain the same.

Clients who persistently employ helplessness as a coping tactic can cause the counselor ultimately to agree with them. The counselor may try budging the client in one direction or another, but to almost no avail. After repeated attempts and increasing frustration, the counselor may give up and agree that the client is helpless. This further reinforces the client's position, which is, ironically, what he or she really wanted from counseling.

Being Upset

Some clients are genuinely upset and have a right to be. Others, however, use being upset as a coping tactic. Being upset can function as a shield in two ways. It can provide sufficient distraction so that the client does not recognize what is causing the upset or what obvious steps must be taken to solve the problem. For example, a woman may be so upset that her child is using drugs that all she can do is be upset. She does not have to consider her contributions to the problem; she does not have to think about what she must do now to help her child and her family resolve the problem. Being upset is easier and safer for her than to face reality and handle it as well as possible.

Second, when clients use being upset as a coping tactic, they must be treated so delicately that the counselor is like a surgeon who must try to operate on a patient without making an incision. Clients such as these may be asking for help but may actually be telling the counselor to leave them alone. Attempts by the counselor to encourage these clients to confront the people and situations that are obstacles to their growth are met with some version of, "Handle me carefully or I'll just fall apart (or blow up)." Counselors cannot be effective if they feel they must treat the client as if he or she were a Ming vase or a keg of dynamite.

Religiosity

Religiosity is different from healthy religious belief and spirituality. Religiosity is a client-held perspective on religion that interferes with his or her ability to make spiritually and psychologically healthy decisions. These people may do things that are psychologically destructive because they feel their religion tells them to do so, or they may refrain from making decisions that would be healthy because they feel their religion forbids it. They perceive religion more like a prison rather than a guiding, freeing, and loving influence. Their position in counseling is that they are suffering but can do nothing about it since to go against their religious beliefs would substantially increase their suffering. Religiosity has several shielding functions that protect people from further anxiety.

Such clients may suggest that they are waiting for God to send them an answer. They participate in counseling in a perfunctory way because they feel that the only real solution will come from God. The less they trust and use counseling, the more they regress and the more they call upon God for help, which further removes them from counseling. They have trouble allowing counseling to help them because it is difficult for them to integrate the guidance and comfort they gain from their spiritual beliefs with their counseling experiences. What may seem like deep faith in God, in this case, is actually religiosity, a coping tactic that has surfaced to manage the anxiety that is being produced by a difficult issue in the client's life. Under these conditions it is impossible for the client to be supported and comforted by his or her faith and spiritual beliefs. In direct terms, the client is waiting for God to intervene; the client will obtain relief without having to face the painful reality.

Religiosity can be a shield when it allows a client to suppress "sinful" feelings such as anger, lust, jealousy, resentment, doubt, and distrust. These individuals often feel that getting in touch with such feelings would make them feel worse. In fact, if they were not religious people, they would likely create another reason for not getting in touch with these feelings because they are so threatened by them.

Religiosity can also be used as a shield against allowing the counselor to get close. By asking counselors to respect their beliefs, such people keep the counselor at a safe distance. The counselor who attempts to loosen the bonds of the client's unhealthy beliefs is met with some variation of the response, "If you were as religious as I, you would understand and affirm my position."

Finally, these people often approach counseling looking for a counselor who shares the same religious beliefs. While it is valuable for clients to work with counselors who honor, understand, and accept their spiritual beliefs, clients such as these are often looking for someone who will affirm *all* that they do and say. This is, of course, an unworkable premise. Change produces anxiety; religiosity is a coping tactic that the client may deploy to obtain affirmations for *not* changing, thereby avoiding the anxiety connected with altering one's beliefs and behaviors.

Sanford illustrates how psychological and spiritual issues can merge when he writes, "A person with a strong ego is able to cope with, adapt to, or overcome life situations. A person with a weak ego, on the other hand, is not able to cope with life and as a substitute erects defenses or relies on various neurotic devices. Out of this comes the egocentricity so dangerous to a relationship with God" (1987, p. 22). The same author opposes "psychologizing" spiritual and religious issues. Ultimately, human beings can benefit differently and collectively from their spiritual and psychological experiences. Forces like religiosity that prevent integration inhibit growth on both planes.

Decoying

Decoying is a coping tactic where the client presents superficial problems to the counselor to protect deeper ones. With these people, counselors must work their way through a medley of decoy problems until they finally reach deeper and more important issues.

For example, a college student's presenting problem is that he is unmotivated academically and socially. As this problem evaporates under examination, the next problem that enters the picture is that he has a conflict with his father. The time and energy spent on this problem do not change his low motivation. The next problems that appear concern his girlfriend, his roommate, his studies, his weight, his poor self-concept, and finally, with great anguish, he reveals the death of a sibling years prior. It is with the resolution of the last problem that he becomes motivated and reports taking a more active interest in studies and social activities. Counseling soon ends because the man's presenting distress has been resolved. It could be that the counselor successfully worked through the decoy targets to the real one. It could also be, however, that the client's feelings of sadness and loss associated with the death of his younger brother were a decoy problem and that he "got better" because the counselor was getting dangerously close to the real problem.

Perhaps the real problem is that the young man believes that to be worthwhile he must be a great success professionally, marry a beautiful woman, and have a large family. Deep down, however, he does not want to be a great success. He would much prefer to have a nonprofessional job that would afford him a modest income and allow him a good deal of stress-free time to enjoy life. He also is very ambivalent about marriage and would prefer to remain single for a long time, if not forever.

He is faced with the choice of being "successful" and unhappy, or of living according to his deeper needs and values and feeling like a third-class citizen. As graduation approaches, his anxiety increases because he will have to choose his path in life. Therefore, the poorer he does in school, the longer he can put off graduation, and the need to make a choice.

This example illustrates the following functions of decoying: (1) it allows the man to think he is working to solve his problem while allowing him to shield it from himself and the counselor; (2) it allows the counselor to think that the positive changes in the man's behavior reflect a solution to the problem. This leads the counselor to agree with the man's assessment that he is ready to stop counseling; and (3) it allows the man to return to his symptoms shortly after he leaves counseling, so he can continue to forestall graduation.

Summary

Human beings rely on coping mechanisms and coping tactics to maintain balance. Clients exhibit, in the counseling relationship, the very same mechanisms they have employed throughout their lives. Therefore, much time in counseling will be spent exploring how people are shielded from anxiety and developing more adaptive ways to protect themselves from anxiety-producing realities. When primitive coping mechanisms and coping tactics are employed, the route to helping the client becomes more complicated and it takes longer.

Counselors ultimately guide their clients through an exploration of their coping mechanisms in an effort to improve awareness, insight, and psychological strength. Since clients are, for the most part, unaware of coping mechanisms and tactics, counselors need a practical understanding of them and the clinical skills necessary to help clients learn more adaptive mechanisms. This can be a very complicated task. While coping mechanisms are sometimes obvious, more often they are almost imperceptible. With increased experience, counselors become better able to detect the more subtle types of coping mechanisms and tactics.

Counselors can help the client recognize the protective nature of the behavior in ways that do not reinforce continued reliance upon them. This can be a particularly challenging task because coping mechanisms and tactics are well integrated into the individual's personality.

Counselors should also realize that they will be affected simultaneously by their own coping mechanisms and tactics. When counselors realize that this is happening they can begin quietly and calmly to sort through the distortions and clarify boundaries that were blurred by coping mechanisms. Such a process is extremely helpful to clients because it offers a safe environment for them to explore how more primitive coping mechanisms interfere with their relationships and it models how to apply more adaptive mechanisms in the counseling relationship. Over time clients learn to apply the same strategies to the personal relationships in their lives. Abrupt accusations, thinly veiled as "insights," are useless; they only serve to produce more resistance and they lessen the chance that the client will adopt more adaptive coping strategies. When counselors are sufficiently relaxed, they can express some variation of, "I'm beginning to see something happening here, and I think it would be helpful for us to discuss it."

Finally, it is important that counselors learn to become increasingly familiar with their own coping mechanisms and coping tactics. They can accomplish this through experience with clients, supervision/consultation, and by participating in individual or group counseling. As counselors learn more about their own coping mechanisms and coping tactics they can begin to sense when they are shielding themselves. Over time they become able to say to themselves, "Be careful, you're beginning to slide away from the real issue here by denying that it is important or by needing to be agreeable more than wanting to be helpful."

Reflection Questions

1. Of the seven coping mechanisms discussed in this chapter, which one do you think would be the most difficult for you to detect? Why?

2. Of the seven coping mechanisms, which would you prefer to use to shield yourself from excessive levels of anxiety? Under what specific circumstances are you likely to use it?

3. Of the ten coping tactics, which one would it take longest for you to identify in a client? Why?

4. Of the ten coping tactics, which one would you be most likely to use and under what circumstances?

5. A subtle trend may be developing in counseling in which counselors assume that people *really do* know exactly what they are doing, though they pretend they do not. Why do you think this trend is occurring? What problems do you see with it?

10

COGNITION AND AFFECT

Counseling theories offer hypotheses about the forces that produce behavior, provide definitions of what would be considered healthy as well as unhealthy patterns, and identify methods for improving or changing behavior patterns, ideas, beliefs, and so forth by concentrating on either the cognitive, affective, physical, or spiritual components. For example, analytic approaches stress the importance of intrapsychic issues and early developmental experiences; existential counseling theory emphasizes the importance of self-awareness and the need for individuals to establish meaning and purpose in their lives; and cognitive theories place a premium on the way in which thoughts influence behavior.

While all of the foregoing approaches are useful, they also are limited because they each focus on one route through the labyrinth of human experience. This is in no way meant to be a criticism of counseling theory. It would be impossible to travel all the routes, so we *must* choose one or another of them if we wish to take the journey. However, we should be mindful that whenever we emphasize one of the forces that produces behavior, others that may be equally important are downplayed, and in some cases ignored. For example, rational-emotive-behavior therapy (REBT) and cognitive-behavioral approaches reject the influence of underlying intrapsychic conflict as causes of behavior (Kalodner, 1995) and stress that the way one thinks about events influences how one feels and acts. While it is true that REBT or cognitive-behavioral approaches can be very beneficial to many clients, other clients may obtain better results through alternative counseling approaches that might emphasize the spiritual or affective aspects of human experiences.

Cognition and affect are discussed separately in this chapter. However, within people no such distinction exists. As you review this information keep in mind that feeling, thinking, physical experiences, and spiritual experiences can never exist apart from one another. There are no clear lines of demarcation; these forces constantly influence one another.

☙

Part 1: Cognition (Thoughts)

Rational-emotive-behavior therapy and cognitive-behavioral approaches to counseling emphasize the relationship between thoughts, feelings, and behavior. These approaches are based on the notion that behavior results from how a person perceives, interprets, thinks, remembers, imagines, decides, and reasons. (For discussions of the role of cognition in counseling, see Beck, 1976; Ellis, 1973, 1989; Vaimy, 1975.) Differences in perception offer one explanation of why two people who experience the same event may react quite dissimilarly.

For example, two men experience the death of their wives. One man perceives the loss as the end of his world. He feels that, without his wife, life has no meaning and he is unable to function. This perception causes him to feel devastated. As a result, he becomes clinically depressed and is eventually hospitalized after he threatens to take his own life in an attempt to "join" his deceased wife. The other man perceives the death of his wife as a great loss, but he does not equate his wife or his marriage with life itself. He feels great sadness and pain, but he is not devastated. After a reasonable period of grieving, he lives a productive and fulfilling life.

While cognitive approaches to counseling are relatively new, the belief that thoughts significantly affect behavior is as old as recorded history. Epictetus, in the first century, wrote "Men [sic] are disturbed not by things but by the view they take of them." George Kelly states: "Events do not tell us what to do, nor do they carry their meanings engraved on their backs for us to discover. For better or worse, we ourselves create the only meanings they will ever convey during our lifetime" (1970, p. 3). Cognitive assumptions (hypotheses, beliefs, constructs) are created by people to help them control and make sense out of their lives. In 1924, the philosopher Hans Vaihinger wrote, "It must be remembered that the object of the world of ideas as a whole is not the portrayal of reality—this would be an utterly impossible task—but rather to provide us with an instrument for finding our way about more easily in the world" (p. 15).

.⚕.
Faulty Assumptions

We are often guided, comforted, supported, and motivated by our assumptions, but we can also be misled, confused, and inhibited by them. In other words, assumptions may or may not be accurate; that is, they may fit reality or distort it. Faulty assumptions, irrational beliefs, and erroneous beliefs (all three will be used interchangeably) are potentially damaging to the individual and therefore a common focus in counseling.

Development

According to REBT and cognitive-behavioral theorists, faulty assumptions are learned (the question of whether biological predispositions to assumptions exist remains to be answered). Since learning is a complex process, faulty assumptions can be acquired through varied paths.

Incorrectly interpreted direct experiences are probably the most common and easily understood route to the formation of faulty assumptions. For example, a girl's first date turns out poorly. Rather than viewing the boy as insensitive, scared, or inept, she generalizes that *men* are insensitive and cruel. Faulty assumptions also can occur through vicarious learning experiences. A boy observes how his father is manipulated and harshly treated by his mother and generalizes that women are cruel.

Faulty assumptions can also come about as a result of direct instruction. A boy is told repeatedly by his father and his uncle that "it is wrong for boys to cry." He needs no further proof; the two most important male figures in his life have instructed him not to cry.

Symbolic logic can be applied in a way that also leads to the formation of faulty assumptions. For example, when a girl sees anger destroy her parents' marriage, she incorrectly concludes that anger is bad and must be avoided at all costs. Unfortunately, she fails to distinguish between destructive and constructive forms of anger. Because her major premise is false, her conclusions are erroneous.

Misconstrued cause and effect relationships commonly produce faulty assumptions. A child may conclude that he caused the arguments between his parents that eventually led to their divorce when in fact their differences, though he was deeply affected by them, had nothing to do with him.

These five methods of learning may be referred to as *natural learning*. However, another form of learning, one that is motivated by the need to reduce anxiety, also produces assumptions. A high school student lacks the psychosocial competencies to relate well with his peers. He must either accept this fact or "learn" that his problems are not his fault. He withdraws from his classmates, and the classmates leave him alone. The fact becomes contorted into a faulty assumption: "My classmates don't like me. I know this because they ignore me." He decides that it is not his problem because he has never done a thing to harm his classmates. This young man has successfully created a belief system to help balance his disturbed dynamics. In other words, he has taught himself that he is "OK" and his classmates are "not OK," thus reducing his anxiety about his real or perceived inadequacies.

Errors in thinking. Faulty assumptions form when people draw erroneous conclusions from their experiences. There are many ways to misinterpret; the following are some of the more typical errors people make.

Overgeneralizations. You can't trust anyone. Women are manipulative. Men are exploitive. No one at work likes me.

All-or-nothing concepts. Either I get accepted in graduate school or my life is over. Either you love me unconditionally or you don't really love me. Either you will help me or there is no more hope.

Absolute statements. I must obey my parents. I should keep promises. I must be nice. I should be right.

Semantic inaccuracies. I failed versus I made a mistake. This is the end versus this is a setback. I must get the promotion versus it would be better if I got the promotion. I can't do it versus I won't do it. I know so versus I think so. I hate him versus I dislike him. I love him versus I really like him. I feel devastated versus I feel bad. She is hostile toward me versus she is angry at me. I am panicked versus I am frightened.

Time discernment. What was valid in the past is not necessarily valid in the present. What is valid in the present will not necessarily be valid in the future. For example, a person may state, "Counseling doesn't work for me because I tried it a few years ago with no results." Or another person may say, "They're not thinking of giving me a promotion now; so I don't think I'll ever get one."

Characteristics

Temporal dimensions. While faulty assumptions are constructed about events in the person's past, present, or future, they affect present behavior. For example, a person may have a faulty assumption related to the past: "My parents didn't love me." She avoids getting close to people because she reasons that if her parents didn't love her, who else could find her lovable? Another person may have a faulty assumption related to the present: "I don't have any marketable skills." He seeks jobs significantly below his capabilities and outside his areas of interest. Each of these faulty assumptions can create significant amounts of anxiety and unhappiness in the lives of those who hold onto them.

Faulty assumptions, regardless of when they were formed, influence behavior only when they are held in the present. In other words, many people experience difficulties because they continue harboring faulty assumptions. For example, when a client says, "I know my parents wished they'd never had me," it puts him or her in a helpless position. What can he or she possibly do about this now? But if a counselor examines the issue more closely, an update of this faulty assumption will likely surface: "If people don't like me, I must be worthless." This assumption, unlike the one that gave rise to it, can be explored, tested. Whether or not the person's parents wanted him or her, for all practical purposes, becomes irrelevant.

Patterns of faulty assumptions. People who enter counseling may have one very influential faulty assumption that significantly hinders them, a series of minor faulty assumptions that, taken together, cause severe limitations, or both.

Faulty assumptions often can be placed into a hierarchy of clusters. For example, a student may believe she must be a great success if she is to be a worthwhile person. From this general faulty assumption evolve the following specific faulty assumptions in descending order of influence:

1. The best way to be a great success is to be a lawyer.

2. The best way to get into law school is to get accepted at a particular university.

3. The best way to get into a particular university is to spend every free second studying.

4. The best way to avoid temptations not to study is not to have friends, dates, or get involved in activities that will waste time.

It is not surprising that by October of her senior year of high school, this student begins experiencing severe anxiety attacks. She has ignored all of her psychosocial needs since elementary school and will soon take college entrance examinations. She knows, without question, that the rest of her life will be determined by her performance on these exams. Since it is too late for a counselor to work with faulty assumptions 3 and 4, counseling would begin by focusing on faulty assumption 2, at least to effect some short-term relief. However, to help this young woman avoid needless anxiety, the counselor will want to explore the highest faulty assumption, the one that is responsible for the cascade that followed it. If someone had done this during her freshman year, high school would have been a growing and joyful experience.

When friends, relatives, and associates fail to understand the erroneous beliefs that goad others into inappropriate and self-defeating behaviors, they cannot be helpful. For example, the young woman's mother kept telling her not to worry, and her father told her not to study so hard. Her high school counselor said he was confident she would do well, and if she didn't, it wouldn't be the end of the world. But the young woman is asking herself, "How can *I not* worry—my entire happiness hinges on this test. How can *I not* work so hard—that's like telling a man whose house is on fire to take his time getting water! And my counselor says, it's not the end of the world if I don't get into the right school. It's not the end of the world for *him!*" Each person focused on the symptoms instead of on the faulty assumptions that spawned them.

Underlying deficiency. Faulty assumptions can always be traced back to an actual or perceived deficiency within the individual. For this reason, faulty assumptions are not only important indicators of a client's difficulties but also indicators of what the client lacks to be reasonably well adjusted. The following faulty assumptions include what the individuals espousing them might have as a deficiency within themselves.

1. *Faulty assumption*: "I can't talk in front of a group of people."
   Translation: "I'm a phony and can fool people individually, but a whole group will see through me and see my shallowness."

2. *Faulty assumption*: "I must get accepted into college or I'll die."
   Translation: "I feel stupid, but if I get into college, I won't feel stupid anymore."

3. *Faulty assumption*: "It's better to lie than to tell people something that might hurt them."
   Translation: "I am very vulnerable. If I hurt other people, they will likely hurt me back, and I'll be annihilated."

The list also reveals that the translation of one faulty assumption is frequently another faulty assumption; for example: "If people hurt me, I will be annihilated." It is important to demythologize this belief, but it is even more important to identify its source.

Resistance to Change

Faulty assumptions are resistant to change. A client will rarely surrender a faulty assumption that has been embraced for many years by the mere application of logic, argumentation, and instruction. When faulty assumptions are essential to the person's functioning, people may not only cling to them, but they may fight to preserve them. Whenever counselors confront clients' faulty assumptions, they take risks, regardless of clients' apparent willingness to examine their assumptions. An understanding of some of the resistance forces involved helps to explain why change is so difficult.

Many faulty assumptions are kept private, hidden even from the client. This is one of the reasons it requires time and patience for counselors to identify specific assumptions and to help the client become aware of them.

A second reason is that some of the more crucial faulty assumptions have been present since childhood. They are deeply integrated into the client's character—their psychological equilibrium depends upon their presence. For example, a man may be in a destructive marital relationship but believes divorce is out of the question because it would be completely unacceptable to his family and friends and devastating to his wife and children. Being unhappily married is at the core of his life. If he were suddenly to correct this faulty assumption, it would cause dramatic shifts in his life and his self-concept. He might be free to think about changing his occupation, or moving to another state. He would have to face his issues or develop another faulty assumption to protect him because the bad marriage would no longer fill that role. He would tarnish his image with his family and friends, which he assumes would lead them to reject him. When all is considered, he would have to learn how to live alone, take care of himself, and risk finding out if others would feel about him the way he imagines they would if he were to get divorced. Thus, it is perhaps easier for this man to retain the faulty assumption that he must remain married.

A third reason for the difficulty in changing faulty assumptions is that people invest time and energy collecting evidence to prove the faulty assumption correct. They are not likely to surrender it easily. To do so would mean he or she would be faced with the realization that years of psychological conflict were unnecessary and may have been completely avoidable. Unfortunately, some people become more invested in being "right" than in being peaceful or happy.

Maintenance

Faulty assumptions persist and resist change because they are regularly "proven" correct. People can reinforce their own faulty assumptions in various ways. For example, a woman erroneously believes that she is superior to other people. She "proves" this assumption to be "true" every day through the following methods:

1. *Selective inattention.* When people surpass her in ability, she does not notice it or ascribes it to something else.

2. *Selective attention.* When she occasionally does do something superior, she focuses on it for a long time so that it seems as if she is consistently doing superior things.

3. *Fictitious rewards.* She is appointed office manager because no one else wants the job but assumes it is because she is special.

4. *Solicited feedback.* She asks people for "honest feedback" in a way that manipulates them into reinforcing the faulty assumption.

5. *Intermittent reinforcement.* Just as her faulty assumption begins to falter for lack of evidence, someone tells her she is superior, which revives the faulty assumption.

6. *Cognitive dissonance.* When information that contradicts her faulty assumption is presented—for example, she doesn't receive a pro-

motion—she reduces her anxiety by assuring herself that the company is saving her for something better.

Along with all the classic coping mechanisms and tactics, these errors in thinking shield this woman from having any reason to question the faulty assumption.

People who acquire erroneous beliefs that reflect a *negative* attitude toward themselves may employ an additional method to "prove" their faulty assumptions: self-fulfilling prophecy. For example, a boy whose faulty assumption is that he is uninteresting anticipates that his first date will be a disaster. The tension the faulty assumption creates makes him nervous and almost mute on the date. In a very real way, he has prophesied what would happen on the date and made it come true.

Unfortunately, when people have faulty assumptions of another, especially someone they work with or relate closely to, they can pressure the other to fit their erroneous beliefs, thereby proving the assumption. Sometimes in a marriage a husband will have the faulty assumption, "My wife wishes she had not married me." Because he feels rejected or resentful, he begins to act negatively in the relationship. When his wife finally loses her temper and says something, the response easily evoked is, "See, now it's finally coming out."

A person can also help maintain a faulty assumption by finding and entering into relationships with other people who share the same or similar faulty assumptions. The result is that each reinforces the other's erroneous conclusions. A man and woman who both believe that "you can't trust anybody" may successfully exclude most other people from their lives; so the only trustworthy people left are each other. They may fall in love and get married. Each brings home horror stories that reinforce their faulty assumptions. After a while, they become so emotionally isolated, even from each other, that one or both develop psychological symptoms and cannot figure out why. The mutual faulty assumption may be so subtle and ingrained in the relationship that a counselor may have great difficulty discovering it.

Significant others can inadvertently, indirectly, and with the best intentions, reinforce another's erroneous beliefs. A teenager retains the faulty assumption that she must go to the senior prom with a particular boy or the year will end with depression and despair. Rather than pointing out the faultiness of the girl's assumption, the mother gladly helps the girl plan the best way to fulfill her wish.

People can also directly reinforce another's faulty assumption. For example, a mother has the faulty assumption that her worth depends upon how much she can do for her children. When she does all that they ask, they love her and tell her what a great mother she is. When she tries to discipline them or asks them to help with chores around the house, they become angry and distant. The reinforcing quality of the noted social behaviors help to maintain these erroneous beliefs.

Examples

Most faulty assumptions can be categorized into one of four categories: those regarding oneself ("I'm uninteresting"), others ("My wife doesn't respect me"), life ("Life is cruel"), and spiritual ("God doesn't like me"). Since faulty assumptions regarding oneself are often at the core of those in the other three areas (although the other areas are also important), the following ten examples represent some of the more typical erroneous beliefs people bring into counseling.

I must be loved by everyone I love. People who hold this assumption do not want to be loved by everybody—just the people they are attracted to, respect deeply, or love. This could be a parent's assumption regarding his or her older children or older children regarding their parents. It could be people dating each other or people married to each other. When the love is not reciprocated or not returned in the specific ways these people desire, they are "crushed," "devastated," or "heartbroken" and behave accordingly. In fact, of course, they are none of these. They are hurt, perhaps deeply hurt, but this is a long way from devastation. Ellis (1984) refers to this irrational belief as "awfulizing." It is accomplished by exaggerating an incident into a catastrophe. Catastrophic expectations immobilize people. They may fear that if they make the wrong move, they will die. What they fail to realize is that being immobilized is a form of dying in itself.

Like many faulty assumptions, this one presents a no-win situation. If such a person "gets" the other person to show love, it has been accomplished through psychological prostitution, thus losing self-esteem. If the person is unsuccessful and is rejected, the other person has been lost, which causes the "devastation." In either case, the damage is done.

People learn this faulty assumption from their parents and society. Such erroneous beliefs often serve to insulate them from knowing their deeper needs and desires and from taking responsibility for themselves. As long as they are distracted by whether or not others love them, they are rescued from getting to know themselves and taking personal responsibility for their lives and their happiness. If they are happy, it is because someone loves them; if they are sad, it's because they are not loved. Their well-being is contingent on others. Counselors can help these people understand the damage they are doing to themselves by attaching their psychological well-being exclusively to others.

People must treat me fairly. Some people work on the assumption, "I treat people fairly; so others should treat me fairly." This assumption is usually a double myth. Although the person believes she treats others fairly, a close examination of her behavior generally reveals that she is capable of treating others unfairly, as is anyone else. In the second part of the assumption, she fails to discriminate between what people should do and what they actually do. People should treat each other fairly, but in reality they sometimes or often do not.

Deep down, such clients realize they can't always be treated fairly because people are imperfect. But they pretend that they don't know this and can respond to injustice by saying, "Well, if this is the way things are, I quit." This dynamic is similar to that used by a child when he sees his team is headed for certain defeat. He takes his ball and goes home, thus rescuing himself from defeat while enjoying a sense of righteousness.

People with this faulty assumption may have learned it through interaction with others and therefore need to be reeducated. More often, however, this faulty assumption was learned in order to hide the fear of failure. Such people delude themselves into thinking they are willing to take the risks necessary to attain success and happiness. On a deeper level, however, they are frightened to take the required risks. Therefore, they use real or perceived injustices as excuses for withdrawing from difficult situations. Counselors can help these individuals see the dynamic supporting the faulty assumption and help them change it.

Happiness is THE goal in life.   People who harbor this faulty assumption generally acquire one or more of three cascading faulty assumptions: (1) that happiness resides outside themselves (hence, they are always looking for it); (2) that once they find happiness, it will be theirs forever; and (3) that there is only one path to happiness.

Because this faulty assumption is constructed on one or more of these three myths, these individuals will experience far less happiness than they would had they possessed a valid assumption regarding happiness.

If the person directly learned this assumption from significant others, counselors can help by demythologizing its foundations. Happiness does not lie outside of oneself, it is a by-product of facing reality and handling it well. And there are as many paths to happiness as there are paths in reality. People who harbor a faulty assumption regarding happiness usually have one main happiness target: They must be a physician, attorney, or engineer. They must get married. They must have children. They must be financially and socially comfortable. They must be more successful than their friends. They must live in a certain area.

Sometimes this faulty assumption is not learned naturally but is learned to balance the person's dynamics. These people are, on a deeper level, fearful of success and happiness. They realize that if they narrowly target happiness, they will never hit it. Ironically, such a belief creates a certain equilibrium for them. They are deluding themselves into thinking they can handle success and happiness but never have to put themselves to the test. Counselors can help these individuals understand the service that this faulty assumption provides and offer to teach them a better option.

I'm at the mercy of my environment.   This irrational idea causes individuals to see people and situations as unchangeable. This view avoids stress and the risks that would be entailed in changing the situation. A wife sees her husband's reluctance to relate on a "meaningful level" as intransigent. As long as she does, she doesn't have to confront him seriously, which may evoke responses she does not want to hear.

People may also perceive events as causing automatic, prescribed reactions. A woman may react to her husband's death with the belief that life is also over for her. She believes this because this is how she was taught to react, or because a coping mechanism employed to protect her from the pain of her loss blocks the option of living out the rest of her life in a full, loving, and satisfying fashion. When people have directly learned this assumption, counselors can help reeducate them. When the learning has been motivated by the person's fears, counselors can help these people learn the protective role that faulty assumptions play in their lives and help them understand how they can develop the psychosocial competencies to master their environments.

Other people know better than I what's good for me. Those who believe this fail to discriminate between being an expert on things and being an expert on a particular person. Lawyers are experts on the law; physicians, on medicine; counselors, on mental health; and members of the clergy, on religion. But none of these experts is an expert on any particular person, except, of course, himself or herself.

People with this erroneous belief would not walk into a store and tell the salesperson, "Pick out a suit that you think I will look good in and I'll take it." Yet, they go to experts for advice (even next-door neighbors can be experts), and implement the suggestions into the most important and often the most personal areas of their lives.

These people have learned from their parents and society that everyone else has better ideas, or they have created this belief system to shed responsibility for their own lives. If another's suggestion works well, such people delight in this and learn to consult the same person in the future. If the advice doesn't work, they blame the giver and learn not to return to the same person for future help. Regardless of the outcome, such people continue to shed responsibility for their behavior and learn nothing more about themselves and the people or situations that were creating issues.

When working with clients who believe that others know better, counselors must be especially careful not to be seduced into becoming just one more advice giver. Doing so would only further perpetuate this destructive dynamic. Counselors may find it difficult not to take on the role of advice-giver, partly because such clients can be skillfully manipulative. For example, individuals with this faulty assumption often preface their remarks to the counselor with, "I know you don't give advice and I don't want your advice, but. . . ." They then immediately proceed to ask for advice.

I must get what I want.   Some people operate on the assumption, "If I want it, it is critically important to my well-being that I get it; if I don't get it, I will be devastated." These people have been conditioned, or have conditioned themselves, to believe they have voids that only specific people and things can fill.

For example, a woman who is a professor wants a promotion. If she does not get it, she either disintegrates or girds herself for a battle to the death. A young man wants a specific woman to love him. If she doesn't, he seriously contemplates killing himself.

It is interesting that as people approach middle life, they have forgotten most of the things they did not get and "could not live without." People with this faulty assumption confuse wanting something, which means desiring it, and needing it, which implies it is necessary for survival and well-being.

People learn this assumption naturally or construct it to further their ends. They discover that when they communicate that they *must have* something, the chances of getting it significantly increase. For example, a man in college learns that when he tells a professor he *must* get at least a "B" in a course or he won't graduate, or get into graduate school, or maintain his scholarship, he is likely to get a "B." If he doesn't get the grade, he can focus his energy and wrath on the professor instead of on himself. This is an example of a faulty assumption that creates, at least on a superficial level, a "no-lose" situation.

Counselors can help such individuals recognize the difference between *needing* something and *wanting* something. They can help them understand that while it would be nice to get what they want, it is not a disaster if they do not. Counselors can also point out that to the degree people *must* have something outside themselves—a promotion, for example—they lack something within themselves—a sense of personal worth, for example. Since inner gaps cannot be adequately filled by external factors, the counselor can help these individuals develop the inner resources that will diminish the overbearing strength of their needs for psychological and material acquisitions.

I am controlled by my past.   Some people believe their lives could be significantly better if they had a different history. They frequently assure themselves and others that "if it weren't for the fact that

> my father was an alcoholic, I could relate to men better."
>
> my mother was divorced three times, I wouldn't be fearful of marriage."
>
> I was put back in the fourth grade, I would have more confidence in my intelligence."

People who believe they are controlled by their past fail to understand that their problem is not the past, but their *attitude* toward the past. Some people have had objectively terrible pasts and nevertheless become self-actualized; others with objectively good backgrounds have become psychologically disturbed. Counselors can help such clients understand that one's past is never a sufficient cause for happiness or sadness. Many people harbor the faulty assumption that they are controlled by the past as an integral part of their dynamics. As long as they use their past as an excuse to live ineffectively, they can avoid current responsibility for their maladaptive behavior. Their attitude is that they have been dealt a "bad hand" in life and are simply playing it out and trying to cut their losses. Counselors can help these individuals recognize the destructiveness of their assumptions and invite them to develop new competencies to handle the present.

I have to be special. Although they would deny it, most people with this faulty assumption feel that being "special" means being superior to others. Such people will often strive to be special at any cost to themselves or family. If they cannot be special in a positive direction, they will be special in a negative one. As one person said, "Either I'm going to be the best person in the world or the worst. In either case, I'll be different from everyone else."

Many people learn this faulty assumption because it has strong environmental supports. Others cultivate this belief system to compensate for feeling very "unspecial." If they succeed in feeling special, they do not have to address their feelings of deep inadequacy. If they are unsuccessful, they can give up ("If nobody is going to appreciate my specialness, to hell with them"). They assume the life position of the unwelcome hero, retire from life, and live off the meager psychological pension that their faulty assumption provides for them.

Counselors can reeducate people with this assumption to understand that the opposite of "special" is not being "mediocre" or "ordinary," but simply *being*. Being means giving and getting the most out of each moment without being distracted by society's grading system.

There is a "worst thing" that can happen to me. Since such "worst things" usually include being wrong, failing at something, appearing foolish, being rejected, being deeply hurt, or being alone, people who harbor this faulty assumption live their lives giving wide berth to even the slightest possibility of any of these events occurring. This is analogous to a boat captain steering a course miles distant from beautiful islands because of the possibility of becoming grounded on one. For example, people may avoid rejection by not allowing themselves to get emotionally close to anyone or by making others so reliant on them that they cannot possibly be rejected.

Individuals with this faulty assumption trade happiness for safety. They are seldom happy, because the closer they get to a good relationship or situation, the more their worst-thing anxiety increases. They avoid worst things by not allowing their possibility. This prevents catastrophe on the one hand and the realization that they lack, or feel they lack, the psychosocial competencies to get what they want on the other. They remain frozen at a point of safety between discovering their inadequacies and experiencing catastrophe.

Counselors can help these people learn that no external event can ever be a worst thing. Not only have people survived, but many have grown through all the "worst things." Worst things can only develop internally when people believe that a person or situation can devastate them.

It's too late for me to change.   Superficially, the feeling that this faulty assumption generates is despair. People who harbor this faulty assumption feel they have grown too old to make any substantial changes in their lives. "Too old" may be any age from 20 to 70. On a deeper level, however, these people often feel a sense of relief. They are like the soldier who surrenders and feels resentment and despair. However, on a deeper and more honest level, he is relieved. He realizes he can live out the duration of the war within the safe confines of a prison camp.

As with all faulty assumptions, one of the largest problems is that a person can make the assumption true by firmly believing that it is so. People who think that it is too late to change react with amusement, then disbelief, and finally resentment.

There is sufficient evidence to indicate that middle-aged and older people can make substantial changes in their lives, but these data are seldom persuasive to these people. The rejoinder is often, "Well, that's nice for them, but they aren't me."

This faulty assumption can be naturally learned from society. Most often, however, it is a self-taught assumption carefully constructed to permit the person to surrender to people, circumstances, and life in general.

Counselors can help these individuals understand that they have a choice between either surrendering or remobilizing psychosocial forces. It is possible for them to make valuable changes in the way they think and, in turn, the way they act and feel.

✦

Considerations for Counselors

Counseling from a cognitive perspective often takes the form of teaching or instructing the client and disputing irrational beliefs through a variety of methods. While Ellis (1979) and Wallace (1986) maintain that effective counseling requires much more than a warm, empathic relationship, they do agree that good rapport and acceptance are necessary ingredients. The following points may be used to guide counselors whenever they encounter the client's irrational beliefs (faulty assumptions) and when they choose to confront them.

Patience

It may take time for clients to identify the faulty assumptions that underlie their symptoms, though the behavior that results from adhering to them is very obvious. As clients develop trust in the counselor and in the process (this is especially true for cognitive approaches), they will become better able to identify, test, and correct faulty assumptions. Because teaching plays such an important role in the counseling process, clients also need time to develop confidence in what the counselor knows and what the counselor recommends to the client.

Unhelpful Reactions

Counselors can inadvertently *reinforce* rather than correct faulty assumptions. A man matter-of-factly tells the counselor that his wife has made it clear she is going to leave him. She left a note and has gone to live with her mother. This launches the client and counselor into a long discussion on how to react to the situation, a discussion punctuated with signs of genuine warmth and empathy from the counselor. The problem is that the man's wife has *not* made it perfectly clear that she plans to leave him. The man's wishful thinking or catastrophic expectation was produced by an angry exchange with his wife that ended with her visiting her mother for the weekend to cool off.

Counselors can also inadvertently *induce* faulty assumptions. A counselor may view the client's request to taper off in counseling as a sign of resistance. The suggestible person accepts the counselor's faulty assumption, and a half-dozen sessions are spent attempting to uncover the source of the assumed resistance. In fact, the person was making good progress and had made a reasonable request.

Counselors can inadvertently *reward* false assumptions by encouraging expression of the accompanying emotions. Sometimes the catharsis that accompanies the affective results of a faulty assumption actually reinforces it. A student who believes that she is going to fail an important examination would benefit most from a careful assessment of her assumptions regarding her academic abilities and a plan to use what time she has left to prepare. A counselor who encourages her to openly express her fears and anxieties about failing is rewarding the faulty assumption instead of disputing it. In a real sense, the counselor who allows deep catharsis under these circumstances is saying, "I agree with you. You have good reason to be upset." When in fact, the person either does not have good reason to be upset or interferes with solving the problem by being upset.

Countertherapeutic Faulty Assumptions

Faulty assumptions about the counseling process and the counselor jeopardize the overall effectiveness of counseling. These irrational beliefs need to be explored as the counseling relationship forms. Describing the phases of the therapeutic process to the client allows them to respond, revealing both their accurate and faulty assumptions about it. The phases include (Livneh & Wright, 1995, pp. 340–341):

1. establishing rapport with the client
2. identifying the problem(s)
3. setting goals
4. explaining rational-emotive therapy to the client
5. showing the client the irrationality of her beliefs
6. showing the client that he is maintaining the disturbance by continuing to think illogically
7. disputing and attacking these irrational beliefs
8. teaching the client how to think logically and empirically
9. discussing the more general irrational beliefs held by society

By discussing each phase and by teaching the client about the process (item 4), the counselor invites discussion about the client's rational and irrational beliefs concerning why they think they are there and what they expect to happen to them. From this beginning, clients gradually bring more difficult issues into the counseling process.

Validity

Counselors can realize that not *all* assumptions are faulty. Counselors who tend to define their main role as detectives hired to find faulty assumptions see them everywhere. A man may have the assumption, "I'm not very intelligent" and may have mapped out his life to accommodate it. His assumption may be valid and tampering with it and his life plans may be a destructive pursuit. It is important that a counselor have sufficient evidence that an assumption is false before assuming that it is. Otherwise, the *counselor's* faulty assumption leads to an attempt to change the client's valid one.

Shared Faulty Assumptions

Counselors and clients can share the same faulty assumption. This is the cognitive theorists' version of a countertransference issue. For example, the counselor and the client may have had negative experiences with marriage. When the counselor hears the client say, "I'll never try marriage again—what a neurotic institution it is!" the counselor "empathizes completely." The counselor misses the point that institutions are only as healthy as the people that comprise them. Counselors must be particularly scrupulous about testing their own beliefs to avoid perpetuating erroneous beliefs by sharing them with their clients.

Hiding Assumptions

The best way to protect a faulty assumption from the scrutiny of a counselor is never to mention it. This is for the most part an ineffective strategy because the pernicious effects of the faulty assumption are easily observed in the client's behavior. Counselors should be alert to this possibility, consider separately each clue conveyed by the client, and identify how each clue connects to the originating faulty assumption. Clients often seem surprised and somewhat in awe of the counselor's ability to identify the faulty assumptions that underlie behaviors. While it may look to them like a remarkable feat, it is not. All that was needed to establish the presence of one or more faulty assumptions was detected in what the client says and does.

Dispelling Assumptions

Counselors cannot reason, argue, or talk a client out of faulty assumptions. They must present evidence that disputes the client's assumption, not once, but over and over again until it becomes irrefutable. Counselors themselves can be a source of evidence when they don't live up to the faulty assumptions of the client; for example, when they are not shocked by "shocking" revelations and when they do not reject the person when he or she becomes angry with them.

Insight is not considered a goal in cognitive approaches—behavioral change is. This is because people often obtain insights but fail to achieve any change in behavior. Counselors who emphasize a cognitive approach not only dispute faulty assumptions but they also identify alternative ways of behaving for the client. Clients are expected to actively change their behavior through "homework," role play, modeling, and other proactive strategies.

Entangling the Counselor

Counselors risk unwittingly becoming an integral part of the client's irrational belief system in at least a couple of ways. The counselor can become a target for the client's faulty assumptions. A client may harbor the assumption, "People don't like me unless they can use me to get something they want." It is clear that the counselor likes the person; so the obvious question is "What does the counselor think I can do for him?" The counselor will sense a wariness in the relationship but may not realize its source.

Second, clients can project their faulty assumptions onto the counselor. Since people often assume that their beliefs are shared by many other people, clients are likely to assume that the counselor feels about them the same way they do. A man may retain the faulty assumption, "I'm not very smart" and be convinced that the counselor shares it. The man's reaction is either relief brought on by the idea that the counselor won't challenge his assumption, or anger—"It's all right for me to think I'm stupid, but I don't want my own counselor to think I'm stupid."

Both of these examples illustrate the importance of carefully exploring the client's assumptions for those that directly affect the counseling relationship. These are often the easiest for the counselor to dispute and the safety of the counseling setting makes it more likely to achieve desired changes in behavior.

Proving Faulty Assumptions

Clients can manipulate counselors into "proving" that a faulty assumption is valid. One week a client tells the counselor, "I'm not as intelligent as you think. You expect too much of me." Instead of examining the irrational beliefs that underlie the client's faulty assumptions, the counselor replies that the client is certainly as intelligent as the counselor thinks. At the next session, the woman announces she is quitting counseling because she's "much better." In essence the counselor responds, "How can you be so stupid as to think that? We haven't begun yet." The counselor has just proven to the woman that her faulty assumption was correct.

One of the main problems with faulty assumptions is that a person can make them "come true." For example, a person may believe that if his or her spouse leaves the relationship, it will be the end of the world. The spouse does leave and the person does make it the end of the world (by committing suicide) or the end of the spouse's world (by committing homicide). Counselors must be careful not to inadvertently dare a person to make a faulty assumption come true. The counselor's role is to teach the client to think rationally, to realize that no event inevitably causes psychological disaster, and that the client does have constructive alternatives for responding to even the most traumatic situations.

New Realities

Changing from a faulty to a valid assumption does not necessarily and automatically bring with it the psychosocial competencies to deal with the new reality. Challenging faulty assumptions is only one aspect of the process of behavioral change that is expected from counselors who use cognitive methods. Counselors are equally obligated to develop alternatives, to support the client's efforts, and to take a very active role in counseling. Our assumptions guide and direct our behavior. They are like a ship's compass—they identify the direction that the ship is moving and make it possible to go from one location to another. If the compass is disturbed we become uncertain about direction and can quickly become lost or disoriented. The same is true when assumptions are disturbed. Counselors therefore must prepare their clients in advance for the disorientation that always occurs whenever clients correct their assumptions or beliefs.

This section addressed practical issues regarding cognitive approaches to counseling. A deeper theoretical understanding of the influence of thoughts on behavior can be obtained from studying one or more of the excellent texts that exist on the subject and from books that illustrate how these approaches can be used to treat specific disorders (for examples see Beck, 1976; Ellis 1973, 1989; Vaimy, 1975). Clients also benefit from reading one or more books that emphasize practical applications of cognitive-behavioral counseling theory. *Feeling Good: The New Mood Therapy* (Burns, 1999) is an excellent example of how a cognitive-behavioral approach can be presented in a way that is helpful to a wide range of people who confront the symptoms of depression.

⚖

Part 2: Affect (Feelings)

Whether emotional reactions stem from an accurate or inaccurate interpretation of reality, they must be understood and dealt with adaptively if personality growth is to occur in counseling. The interaction between cognitions, emotions, and actions reflects a system of reciprocal causality. Albert Ellis came to the following conclusion:

> Just as cognitions importantly contribute to emotions and actions, emotions also significantly contribute to or "cause" cognitions and actions, and actions contribute to or "cause" cognitions and emotions. When people change one of these three modalities of behaving they concomitantly tend to change the other two. (1979, p. 194)

The word *emotion* is a derivative of the Latin word *emovere*, which means to move out. The purpose of any emotion is to move a person toward safety and need-fulfillment and away from harm and need-deprivation. All of the basic emotions are necessary for survival because each has a specific contribution to make to the stability of a person's overall functioning. For example, people need love, but they also need hurt, which teaches which situations are damaging; fear, which anticipates threat and warns of impending danger; anger, which removes obstacles to need fulfillment; and guilt, which helps one avoid hurting oneself or others.

The following discussion tends to oversimplify a very complex human phenomenon that has not surprisingly proved itself to be exceedingly difficult to study. As Strongman writes, "Specific human emotions are extraordinarily complex; the names used to describe them cover a multitude of behaviors and experiences. This complexity makes them virtually impossible to study with precision and agreement between researchers" (1974, p. 148). However, emotions play an important role in counseling and need to be discussed, even though the discussion must necessarily be oversimplified. For a more thorough discussion of the theoretical aspects of emotions, see Arnold (1960, 1970); Candland, Fell, Keen, Leshner, Tarpy, and Plutchik (1977); Izard (1977); Plutchik (1962).

Although there are many definitions of emotion, the one given by Arnold is a clear and useful one; she defines emotion as "the felt tendency toward anything intuitively appraised as good (beneficial), or away from anything intuitively appraised as bad (harmful). This attraction or aversion is accompanied by a pattern of physiological changes organized toward approach or withdrawal. The patterns differ for different emotions" (1960, p. 182). Feelings can also "convey knowledge about a person's relationships with the world. For example, fear indicates that the person is facing a relatively powerful or uncontrollable threat. Happiness typically indicates one's harmonious relations with others, and anger often reflects a feeling of injustice" (Mayer & Salovey, 1997, p. 9). When emotions function properly—that is, according to their purposes—they energize and give direction. For example, if a man is angry at his boss, his anger may move him (energize him) toward his boss (point him in a direction) in order to resolve the problem. However, there are points along the continuum from the experience of an emotion to the process of acting on it, where the process can break down, as these examples indicate.

1. A person can *repress* the emotion so it neither energizes nor gives direction. Example: a man may repress his anger at his wife. In this case, the anger grows and eventually spills over into symptomatic behavior, such as depression or passive-aggressive behavior toward his wife.

2. A person may lack adequate control over an emotion. Example: a man who is angry at his wife may physically assault her.

3. A person may be energized by the emotion but have no direction. Example: a man may feel intense anger, but can find no place or person to focus it on.

4. A person may be energized by the emotion, but displace it. Example: a man who is angry at his boss may improperly direct his anger onto his children, his wife, or himself.

Clients commonly encounter one or more of these four situations.

The related processes of understanding and managing emotions begin with the ability to label them correctly. Unfortunately, both counselors and clients often use generic words to describe emotions. For example, clients may use nonspecific terms like anxious, nervous, tense, and stressful to describe their feelings. They may also report their judgment of the feeling rather than the feeling itself. For example, a client may reply that he or she feels "good" or "bad" rather than joy, anger, fear, and so forth. Since correctly specifying emotions is important because it makes the cause of the emotion and the appropriate direction for the emotion more discernible, vague terms have little practical therapeutic value and actually interfere with the counseling process. Therefore, counselors aid their clients whenever they help them correctly identify the specific emotions, or combination of emotions.

Specifying emotions can be accomplished through a straightforward four-step process. The client must first discover what specific emotion is causing the generic feelings. For example, a counselor can help a woman discover that she may be anxious because she is frightened, or tense because she is angry, or that a stressful situation may really be a hurtful situation. Then the counselor can help her arrive at directionality—that is, "*Who* are you angry at?" or "*Who* is hurting you?" Next, the counselor can help the woman discover the reason for the specific emotion: "*What* is causing you to feel guilty?" or "*What* is causing you to be fearful?" The final step entails asking, "*How* have you typically handled this emotion in the past and with what results?" and "*What* can you do to resolve this feeling constructively?"

While human beings experience and can identify many different emotions in the initial phases of the counseling process, it is sometimes helpful to limit discussion to the five basic emotions of love, anger, sorrow, joy, and fear. According to Warga (1974), the range of human emotion is produced from these five basic emotions. Four of the five basic emotions form two continua: the love-anger continuum is one; the sorrow-joy continuum is the other. A range of feelings corresponding to different points along each of these continua exists. For example, the sorrow-joy continuum might be composed of the following levels: "sorrow - grief - despondency - happiness - ecstasy - joy" (Warga, 1974, p. 191).

Feelings are also differentiated with respect to their focus. For example, a person might be angry at someone else but when the anger is focused on himself or herself the anger is called "frustration." An examination of how different terms are used to describe the same underlying feeling when it is directed at various people also gives us an opportunity to illustrate how counselors can help clients by limiting discussion to the five basic emotions. By being told that frustration is not one of the five basic feelings, the client is forced to identify the underlying feeling—anger in this case—and to specify the direction in which the anger is directed—in this case at the client himself or herself. Thus frustration is properly identified as self-anger and both the counselor and the client can make this the focus of the therapeutic intervention.

The fifth basic feeling is fear. The discussion of this feeling has been saved for last because of its peculiar effect on the other four basic feelings. According to Warga (1974), the presence of fear makes it difficult, if not impossible, to experience any of the other four basic emotions. This explains why it is so difficult for clients to identify other feelings when they are truly afraid and why it is so important to help the client resolve as many fears as possible before moving to other concerns.

Fear, anger, hurt, and guilt are probably the emotions that are most identified by clients as troublesome and as reasons for pursuing counseling. Jealousy, shame, shyness, depression, grief, loneliness, and discouragement can often be traced to some combination of hurt, fear, anger, and guilt. Fear, anger, hurt, and guilt are also commonly categorized as "negative emotions" or "bad feelings" even though such judgments are often therapeutically counterproductive. It is more valuable to identify this cluster of feelings as those that announce the need for change, something that many people find difficult to think about, and even harder to do. By contrast, if a person can feel some amount of joy, then it is often possible to link the joyfulness to particular people or events and continue to experience the enjoyment associated with these same people and events.

At the extremes, emotions can be used to motivate us to grow and make valuable changes in our lives or they can cause us to become paralyzed and repressed. This fact underscores how important it is for counselors to understand the role emotions play and to be able to help clients productively harness the power emotions produce. The more counselors understand the dynamics underlying each of these emotions, both in the client and in themselves, the more they can help people understand and use emotions in a growth-producing way.

Fear

Fear stems from anticipation of a specific physical or psychological threat. Since psychological threat comprises the vast majority of the fears of clients, this dimension of fear will be discussed in detail. Fear is a word few people entering counseling use because people, especially adults, aren't supposed to have fears. Consequently, people entering counseling use words that reflect fear but are distant enough to be more acceptable, such as tense, worried, anxious, upset, confused, indecisive, insecure, miserable, nervous, restless, and bored. When a counselor can help the client translate these inadequate synonyms into the word *fear*, the causes of such fears and the paths to resolution become clearer.

Since fear usually evokes a fight or flight response, anger is a common disguise for underlying fears. When people respond to a threat with a fight response, they reflexively feel anger and mistake the anger for the actual feeling of fear. It is helpful for counselors to realize that most angry people are really frightened and most angry responses aimed at counselors are actually fear responses. Recognizing this, counselors can cut through the decoy of anger and help clients learn more about their fears.

Because the psyche has a wide flank to protect, human beings are exposed to many threats and, consequently, experience many fears. The following four fears are common ones that people bring to counseling. Each has a protective quality that can help people avoid harm. However, when fears are too numerous or intense, they either paralyze people into inactivity or energize them to attack needlessly.

Fear of Intimacy

People with an inordinate fear of intimacy react to this fear in several ways. They may construct a psychological moat, creating a safe distance between themselves and others. The moat may be obvious, so that others perceive the person as "emotionally distant," or it may be covered by a false bridge of extroversion and friendliness.

Others with this fear manufacture pseudoconflicts to avoid intimacy. As they grow closer to other people, they consciously or unconsciously pick a fight or concoct a problem that creates distance and brings welcome relief. Such fights are common—especially in the early phases of the counseling process. Still others develop a counterphobic reaction. These people *push* for intimacy in a relationship in a way that is "too much, too soon." This approach invariably scares off the very people with whom the individual wishes to become intimate.

When counselors help clients resolve fears associated with intimacy there are several strategies that should be employed. The first is that counselors can expect clients to handle the fear of intimacy in the counseling relationship in the same ways they do outside of counseling. If the counselor recognizes this and points it out in helpful ways, it can provide an important, on-the-spot learning experience.

Second, counselors can help clients develop the psychological competencies needed to approach intimacy with confidence. For many people "intimate" is simply a synonym for "trapped" or "foolishly vulnerable." Counselors can help such clients learn to approach intimacy with prudence and assertiveness, which allows them in turn to enjoy its beauty while significantly diminishing the risks.

Third, counselors can help clients manage the intimacy issues that arise within the counseling relationship. Whenever people share deeper parts of themselves with others they feel emotionally closer to them. Because the counseling relationship is one-sided with respect to the sharing of intimate information, client self-disclosure produces a type of "artificial" intimacy between the client and the counselor. The term artificial is used here to underscore the fact that this intimacy is contrived; it occurs because clients, in the course of counseling, are expected to and do share intimate parts of themselves with the counselor. Though such disclosures often make clients feel emotionally close to their counselors, this artifact of the client's sharing deeper parts of the self in a counseling relationship should never be confused with the intimacy that develops between two people as a result of their *mutual* sharing and mutual vulnerability. Effective counselors understand this process, establish appropriate professional boundaries so that an effective therapeutic alliance is retained, and help the client manage feelings and reactions appropriately. If counselors fail to help clients deal effectively with this form of intimacy, they can substantially reinforce the client's original fears of intimacy in other settings. If they fail to maintain the appropriate boundaries they can create havoc for the client and cause serious psychological and emotional damage in the process.

Fear of Rejection

People with an inordinate fear of rejection can react to it by emotionally, if not socially, withdrawing from situations in which rejection is possible. These people feign a lack of interest in whether they are accepted by others in order to soften the blow should rejection occur. Typically, they may relate most easily with those who are not likely to reject them—for example, with other psychologically needy people, with children, with animals, or with such things as work, hobbies, or cars.

They may react by being anonymous. Such people do not allow themselves to be known beyond the outer, most superficial layer of their personalities. This is a protection against being known, which to them means possible or likely rejection. Additionally, people who fear rejection may try to preclude the possibility of being rejected. This is attempted in one or all of three ways. First, they may attempt to buy guarantees of non-rejection by being nice, ingratiating, and overly helpful. Second, they may become weak and helpless—patterns that often evoke a sympathetic response from others. Third, they may anticipate rejection and be the first to reject in order to save themselves some anguish.

There are several counseling implications regarding the fear of rejection. The first is that most, if not all, people who fear rejection tend to discount, harshly judge, and reject themselves. They fear that others will see the parts they themselves see as objectionable, thereby evoking further rejection. Counselors can help such clients to become more self-accepting and thereby lessen their inordinate fear of rejection.

Second, many people who fear rejection place a high priority on being accepted by others. Counselors can help such clients explore and reevaluate their priorities. These clients can be encouraged to place more value on knowing themselves and being honest with themselves, and less value on striving to gain the acceptance of others. This approach places the focus on the client and who he or she wants to become.

Third, it is helpful for counselors to realize that some people who inordinately fear rejection *want* to be rejected. For them, being rejected is painful, but less so than being accepted and becoming symbiotically dependent. As one person said, "I'd rather feel rejected and free than accepted and trapped." Obviously, being accepted is not really synonymous with being trapped, but it is to people with strong dependency needs.

Finally, both the counselor and the client will have a fear of rejection. The client's fear will often create marked ambivalence toward the counselor and the counseling relationship. On the one hand, the client wants to open up; but, he or she has probably been rejected in the past for opening up far less with more trusted people. Counselors have both personal and professional needs to be accepted by the client. However, counselors cannot allow their personal needs for acceptance to interfere with their professional needs and responsibilities.

Fear of Failure

People often respond to the fear of failure by refusing to take risks. These individuals operate on the principle, "If you don't try something, you can't fail." Or they may belittle success. This strategy entails diminishing everything so that nothing has much importance. Getting into college or graduate school is "not important." A particular boyfriend or girlfriend is "no big thing." Examinations and interviews are "stupid." Such people often overprepare for projects and social engagements in an effort to prevent failure. The time and effort spent on overpreparation simply increases anxiety, but does not guarantee that failure will be prevented.

There are several counseling implications for the fear of failure. First, people who fear failure will perceive counseling as an endeavor in which they will succeed or fail; subsequently, they will react to the fear of failing in counseling as they would to other similar situations. The counselor should be aware of the presence and meaning of these behaviors and reflect them back to help such clients see the destructiveness of their responses.

Second, most people with an inordinate fear of failure underestimate their strengths and overemphasize their weaknesses. Counselors can help such people develop a realistic picture of strengths and weaknesses and help them begin making decisions that lay stress on the former and downplay the latter.

A third implication is that most people with an inordinate fear of failure operate on an all-or-nothing principle: they want *big* success or *no* success. People suffering from a fear of failure convince themselves that they are not in a position to be immensely successful; so they don't have to try anything. Counselors can help such clients recognize the self-protective nature of this habit and learn that the road to success is paved with dozens of small, sometimes imperceptible triumphs.

Fourth, the fear of failure can affect the counselor and in turn the pace of counseling. The counselor, responding to a fear of failure, may move too quickly at times, in an effort to bring success closer, or hesitate at times, in an attempt to avoid failure. When the counselor's fear of failure becomes tied to the client's progress, objectivity and, in turn, effectiveness are reduced.

Anger

Many people have been taught that anger is a negative emotion. As a result, people often deny being angry or use less-threatening synonyms, such as upset, frustrated, disappointed, confused, annoyed, or hurt to semantically distance themselves from the anger. Because anger can be expressed in such potentially destructive ways, counselors often need to help clients identify and express their anger in ways that lead to positive action.

Causes and Purposes

Anger often results when obstacles block the fulfillment of an individual's perceived needs. The intensity of the anger is contingent on the strength of the perceived need. A man who wants the weekend off will be angry when he is told he must work on Saturday. But he will be less angry than if he were denied a promotion that he feels he deserves. Since needs are subjective, people vary greatly in what they consider their needs to be. For example, a highly controlling person may identify as critical certain needs that others would consider insignificant.

When another person creates the obstacle to need fulfillment, the anger is often directed toward the other person; that is, it is *other-anger*. Anger also can be focused at oneself. In other words, people can interfere with their own need fulfillment. For example, a woman in college *needs* to get a "B" in a course, works hard at the outset, but inadequately prepares for the mid-term examination, thus earning a "C." Whether or not she admits it, she is angry at herself. This is one example of *self-anger*.

The general purpose of both other-anger and self-anger is to energize one to bring about eventual need fulfillment in the frustrated area, though the target of each form of anger is different. The purpose of other-anger is to energize behavior that will either remove the obstacle to need fulfillment or remove the person from a situation where an important need is consistently unmet. In the example of other-anger, the employee denied the promotion can use his anger to appeal the decision and, if the appeal is unsuccessful, can use the energy to decide whether to remain in this particular work situation. The purpose of self-anger is to energize the individual to change behavior that is interfering with his or her need fulfillment. In the example of self-anger, the student can channel the anger into understanding why she slacked off and how she can increase her efforts so she can raise her final grade.

When anger is not channeled appropriately, various problems arise. First, people who are responsible for frustrating their own needs usually blame others. The self-anger that could have motivated them to change their behavior gets displaced or projected onto others. Such people will continue to block their own need fulfillment and those who were scapegoated will retaliate directly or indirectly for the unjust anger they received.

Second, people whose needs are being interfered with by another person or persons feel anger but turn it back toward themselves (self-anger). Here again, the anger is misdirected so it cannot be used to motivate appropriate changes. Misdirected self-anger also reduces the individual's self-worth, self-esteem, self-confidence, and his or her ability to correctly identify and fulfill needs. Self-anger spawns greater amounts of self-anger.

Third, other-anger may be channeled in the appropriate direction (outwardly), but may be expressed destructively. For example, a wife may be angry at her husband but may express it in disguised, veiled ways or in displaced ways, such as becoming angry with the children instead of with her husband. These destructive expressions will only create more conflict, and the cause of the need frustration will remain.

Fourth, self-anger may also be channeled in the appropriate direction (inwardly), but may be expressed destructively. Instead of using self-anger to change some maladaptive behavior, people simply use the anger to scourge themselves, just as a parent may yell at a child with no thought of helping the child learn from the offense.

Counselors can help clients correctly differentiate self-anger from other-anger at the appropriate target and express it constructively.

Manifestations of Self-Anger

There are several common destructive manifestations of improperly managed self-anger. However, a note of caution can be kept in mind. It is impossible to attribute a specific dynamic to a particular behavior. For example, to say that crying is a manifestation of sadness is naive. Crying could also indicate fear, anger, hurt, guilt, joy, gratitude, or an allergy. The following behaviors are commonly associated with people who turn anger against themselves in destructive ways.

Depression. People who experience depression can unconsciously punish themselves by avoiding happiness in their lives. The key to relieving this type of depression is to identify and understand the self-hatred.

Addictions. Included in addictions are alcoholism, drug dependency, compulsive gambling, and compulsive work. The self-anger may not be seen in the actual behavior, but in the inevitable self-defeating effects.

Wrong people and places. This involves choosing as friends or associates people who are insecure or disturbed or choosing to live and work in situations that cause needless stress and unhappiness.

Reckless behavior. This behavior is seen in a person who takes needless and careless risks—psychological, physical, or financial.

Martyrdom. Martyrdom implies unnecessary suffering under the guise of love, charity, fate, or religious fervor.

Degrading behavior. This comprises any behavior that makes a person feel ashamed. It could include allowing oneself to be abused emotionally, physically, or sexually, or initiating behavior that is self-degrading, such as stealing, sexual misconduct, cheating, lying, or causing oneself public embarrassment.

Counseling Implications of Self-Anger

Counselors should be conversant with the manifestations and dynamics of self-anger. It is fruitless for counselors to confront the behavior directly—for example, to tell a client he should choose better people with whom to associate, that she is becoming an alcoholic, that he should lose weight, or that she is being masochistic. It is likely the person already knows that the behavior is not helpful and is in counseling to learn how to change it. Efforts to help the client change the behavior must be accompanied by excursions into the possibility of self-anger as the underlying cause.

If the self-anger is appropriate—that is, the result of an action that is harmful to themselves—counselors can help these people channel the anger into changing the offending behavior. For example, if a student cheats in school, the self-anger may be used to discover and remedy the causes of the cheating.

The self-anger may be inappropriate. For example, a police officer may despise himself because he arrived at a crime scene moments after a fellow officer was wounded. He holds himself personally responsible, even though everyone agrees there was no way he could have gotten there any quicker and if he had, there was little he could have done to prevent the shooting. The self-anger and self-rejection that stem from needing to have been at the scene to protect the other officer cause him to behave in self-defeating ways—to lose interest in his work, to withdraw from other officers, and to pick fights with his wife and children. Counselors can help people develop more realistic expectations and a self-accepting attitude.

The self-anger also may be inappropriate if it is being mischanneled toward the self when it should be directed toward others. For example, a young woman may actually be angry at her mother, who has manipulated her to remain at home. Instead of feeling the anger toward her mother and directing it toward a solution, she bends the anger inward because it is safer to feel depressed than to be angry with her mother. Counselors can help these people recognize the true target of their anger and utilize the anger to encourage growth-producing changes.

Counselors can also be aware that people who indulge in these behaviors are very likely to bring them into the counseling relationship. Sometimes these behaviors can be very subtle. For example, clients may too easily accept a counselor's interpretation that reflects negatively on them. The counselor states, "I think you're using your depression as a weapon against your husband." The client replies, "I never looked at it that way, but I think you're right. How awful of me!" The counselor congratulates himself both on the accuracy of the insight and the obviously palatable way he communicated it. In fact, however, the client is simply accepting another hammer with which to hit herself over the head as part of her self-anger.

Counselors should also look for traces of self-anger in themselves. Under the guise of being honest, liberating, tough, or cautious, counselors may be setting up a failure experience for themselves and the client.

Manifestations of Other-Anger

The following are some common examples of destructive other-anger—that is, anger channeled toward others, whether or not it should be. The same caution should be exercised here as when examples of self-anger were discussed. Other-anger is a frequent dynamic underlying these behaviors, but it may not be the *only* dynamic and, in some cases, may not be present at all.

Moralism.   This term denotes perverting morality to demean other people. The theme of moralism is either, "You are a bad (weak, sinful, selfish) person and you'd better face up to it and mend your ways" or a more "compassionate" version: "It's not your fault that you are not as good (strong, moral, religious) as you should be. Let me help you become like me."

Hostile talk.   This includes ridiculing, acerbic comments, odious comparisons, sarcasm, tantrums, complaining, destructive criticism, gossiping, and being hostile under the guise of honesty.

Shutting down.   A person may shut off emotions in the presence of the person toward whom anger is directed. The person is saying, "I'll share my mind with you but I won't share my heart with you. This is your punishment for making me angry."

Purposeful ineptness.   A person may behave ineptly because the results will punish the people toward whom anger is directed. Examples of purposeful ineptness are motivated forgetting ("Oh, I forgot to pick up your dress at the cleaners for the party tonight") and nonthinking behavior ("Oh, I didn't mean to embarrass you in front of your boyfriend").

Victimizing.   The angry person may cause others to be wrong or to fail by placing expectations on them they can't possibly meet, by making people dependent, then using or rejecting them; by competing with people with the primary motive of *beating* them rather than simply winning; and by placing people in a double bind, "damned if you do, damned if you don't" situation, leaving them with the appropriate feeling "I can't win."

Ambushing.   The person will find some reason, sooner or later, to attack or reject someone. It may be done obviously ("You'd better not cross me, or you're going to be sorry") or by a much more subtle attitude that says with a smile "I'm going to give you enough rope until you hang yourself."

Passivity.   An angry person may refuse to budge in a direction that would be helpful to the person toward whom the anger is directed. A wife wants to buy a new house, which the couple can afford, but her husband has to "think some more about it." A husband wants to take his wife out for an evening, but she is always "too tired."

Counseling Implications of Other-Anger

Manifestations of other-anger may be directed at the particular person or people toward whom the person feels angry, or they could be part of a generalized, diffuse anger that includes all people as targets. The common element is that the person does not connect the behavior with anger and, in fact, may vehemently deny the possibility ("After all my parents have given me, how could I be angry?"). The challenge for the counselor is to help clients see at least the possibility of a connection between the behavior and anger, without arguing the point.

As with self-anger, it is important for such people to recognize when other-anger is appropriate and inappropriate. Making this distinction helps people deal with anger constructively. Similarly, counselors can be aware that people who indulge in other-anger behaviors outside of counseling will bring these same behaviors into the counseling relationship.

Counselors can also exhibit the destructive behaviors associated with other-anger. Counselors can be moralistic ("You're being kind of neurotic about this"), engage in hostile talk ("I wish I were taping this session so you could hear how phony you sound"), shut down ("Why is it so necessary that you see me emote?"), be purposefully inept ("I'm sorry I'm late again—I went overtime with my last patient"), or ambush ("I didn't say anything, but I knew if you kept missing our appointments you'd eventually fall off the wagon"). There are several thoughts about anger a counselor can keep in mind. It is true that a counselor cannot call "time out" at every turn to examine whether a piece of behavior is motivated by self-anger or other-anger; by necessity, some behavior must be allowed to pass. But when one of the previously mentioned behaviors occurs enough to suggest a pattern, or if it occurs only once but in a very dramatic way, the counselor can focus on it and examine it with the client.

Everyone indulges at times in destructive self-anger or destructive other-anger. Usually, the overall psychological health of the person and/or the relationship can absorb these mistakes. Problems arise, however, when people experience so much anger that it significantly interferes with their own need fulfillment or that of those closest to them.

Hurt

Hurt is the feeling of pain people experience when they are psychologically injured. This emotion is grossly underestimated in the field of mental health. While anger receives more attention, hurt may cause at least as many conflicts and, in fact, is at the heart of many problems with anger.

Causes

A person can be injured psychologically and suffer pain in a couple of ways. People can experience pain through the normal course of everyday interaction. A person feels injured because someone says, does, or fails to do something. For example, a man may feel hurt because his supervisor got all of the accolades for a very successful, long-term project that the man completed himself. Life is full of hurtful inequities that can affect anyone simply as a function of participating in the activities that make up our lives. Hurt can also come about as a result of naiveté. A person who harbors an unrealistic expectation may feel hurt when it is not met. For example, a woman in college tells her new roommate several potentially embarrassing secrets about herself. She becomes terribly hurt when she learns that her roommate shared this information with five other students at supper that evening. This type of hurt is more preventable than other forms.

Aside from experiencing pain through the normal course of daily life, there are various dynamics that share in common the fact that some people seem to invite being hurt. An example would be the case of someone who invites being hurt in order to use the hurt to feel justified in behaving in some destructive way. For instance, a man desires to have extramarital sex but his conscience and self-concept won't permit him to experience it. So, on less than a conscious level, he sets up a situation whereby his wife will hurt him. When this occurs, he assures himself that he now has a justifiable reason to seek extramarital sex ("If that's all she thinks of me, I'll find someone who really cares").

People may create situations in which they will be hurt in order to atone for unconscious guilt. A man may have treated his deceased father poorly and never dealt with the resultant guilt. Consequently, he unconsciously allows himself to be hurt as a way of assuaging his guilt feelings.

Some people may unconsciously allow themselves to be hurt in order to manipulate others. For example, a woman allows her husband to abuse her psychologically, then uses the guilt he feels for what he has done to manipulate him.

People can be hurt by standing in the path of other people's growth. For example, overprotective parents exhort their adult son to remain at home rather than pursue a career opportunity in another city. Despite their pleadings, he decides to move out on his own. Consequently, they feel terribly hurt.

People commonly invite being hurt by misinterpreting another's behavior. A woman may be told by her roommate that she plans to move out soon. She interprets this as meaning her roommate no longer likes her. In fact, the roommate likes her a great deal but can no longer afford the rent and is too embarrassed to tell her roommate her true reason for moving.

An awareness of the causes of hurt leads to several practical implications for counseling. First, the counselor's initial response to a client's feelings of hurt can be to help the client experience the feelings as completely as possible. The more the client can feel, and share, the more healing can take place. Deeper, more persistent sources of pain require more time. Clients often need to build strength as they deal with the pain. Thus, helping clients to limit the amount of pain they experience is as important as encouraging clients to experience the pain they feel.

Second, a counselor can help clients perceive hurt more realistically. Living life fully makes people vulnerable to everyday sources of emotional injury. Also, the closer people become in a relationship, the greater the chances of getting hurt. Clients can be helped to understand that these types of hurt are badges of growth, so they will no longer need to ask, "What's *wrong* with me that I get hurt like this?" A counselor can also help clients realize that some hurts can be brushed off. When a hurt stuns and knocks people down, they can learn to perceive it in a way that allows them to recuperate and return to the business and joy of living. Even very deep psychological injuries can be overcome; people do not have to feel that they will be destroyed by them.

Counselors often help clients realize that they may have been hurt in retaliation for a hurt they perpetrated themselves. For example, a woman embarrasses her boss in front of several customers. Later in the day, she is very hurt when her boss criticizes her in front of her coworkers. With the counselor's help, she comes to see the relationship between the two events.

Clients and counselors need to realize that they can experience hurt in counseling; open and honest relationships, including the counseling relationship, inevitably provide the occasion for one person or another to feel hurt. Honesty as well as misperceptions, misunderstandings, mistakes, conflicting needs, motives, and values are all potential sources of hurt. While the best way for a client and a counselor to avoiding hurting each other is to relate superficially, it is also the way that limits personal growth. Being hurt and learning how to react well to it is a necessary part of human growth and development. Learning to deal with hurt within the confines of the counseling relationship helps clients learn adaptive ways of responding to their feelings that can be exported to comparable situations in their daily lives.

Constructive Reactions

When people react to hurt in a growth-producing way, they admit the hurt and handle it constructively. Handling hurt well—that is, in a way conducive to healing and growth—entails four steps. The first is to admit the hurt. The second is to examine what the hurt means. When people are hurt, they can ask some important questions: Am I being too sensitive? Did I have an unrealistic expectation? What does the hurt mean in the context of our relationship? Did I misperceive the hurt? Did I deserve to get hurt? Is there a vulnerability within me that needs strengthening?

The third step, when it is appropriate, is to check out the possible meaning of the hurt with the person causing it. This dialogue may help heal the hurt so that the relationship can continue, perhaps stronger than ever. Or the dialogue will deepen the hurt, thus focusing the nature of the problem more clearly. When dialogue is not possible, people remain stuck with the hurt but can realize they have control over how much they allow it to interfere with their lives. The final step is to learn a lesson from the hurt that will help prevent a similar situation in the future.

A counselor can teach these steps directly and by modeling them. Counselors can lead clients through these steps and explain the reason for them and their importance. If a client is not used to reacting to hurt well, this process may have to be repeated. The deeper the hurt, the more difficult it will be to help the client focus on the process. Counselors need not be distracted by the amount of hurt; the procedures remain the same for small hurts as for larger ones. Counselors can also model these steps by the way they react to being hurt by the client. Clients often make hurtful comments that counselors need to be able to confront effectively.

Destructive Reactions

While people may not choose to react to hurt in destructive ways, they often do. The following illustrate some of the more maladaptive ways individuals react to hurt.

Denying the hurt. People deny feeling hurt because they view it as an admission of weakness. They state, "Don't be silly. I'm stronger than to be hurt by something like that." Others deny hurt because they view its admission as a criticism of the person who hurt them. They ask, "How can I be hurt when she did it out of love?" Still others deny hurt because they don't want to give the offender the satisfaction of knowing that he "got to them." A fourth way to deny hurt is to intellectualize: "I'm so used to being hurt that I'm beyond the point of hurting." Counselors can help these individuals understand that when hurt is denied, it increases.

Hurting back. Some people react to hurt by hurting back. They may do so reflexively, without thinking, or they may save the hurt and use it at a more opportune moment. Sometimes people hurt back by hurting someone other than the offender. A man may have been hurt by his wife but hurts the children as a way of getting back at her.

Counselors can help people realize that when they hurt another in retaliation, the hurt in the relationship becomes compounded. Moreover, retaliatory hurt often causes guilt, which adds to the stress of the situation. The original hurt becomes only one-third of the overall dynamics.

Disguising hurt. Some people disguise their hurt by covering it over with another emotion that is easier to admit and communicate. A person may claim, "I'm not hurt; I'm just angry" (or disappointed or depressed). The problem with disguising hurt is that it produces the same difficulty that develops when people try to hide any feeling. Sooner or later the hurt will overcome the coping mechanism and permeate the person.

Counselors can help people recognize that hurt is often a significant part of their fear, anger, and depression and that the sooner they can get in touch with hurt, the sooner the secondary emotion will disappear.

Wallowing in hurt. People may admit hurt, savor it, and invite others to share their hurt feelings. The underlying dynamics of wallowing in hurt are that the person needs to suffer in order to atone for unresolved guilt, to get attention, and to manipulate others by causing them to feel sympathetic and guilty.

Counselors will find these people especially challenging because they have a vested interest in hanging onto their hurts. The counselor's efforts to help them will be met with significant resistance. However, it is incumbent on the counselor to demonstrate to this type of client how self-destructive the behavior is and to point out the secondary gains associated with expressing hurt in this way.

Anesthetizing hurt. Instead of dealing directly with hurt, some people care for their hurt with psychological analgesics: food, drink, sex, sleep, drugs, and work. Counselors can help these clients understand that the problem with psychological painkillers is that they compound the original problem. While they deaden the conscious hurt, the deeper hurt remains to cause symptomatic behavior. Moreover, these psychological analgesics often cause guilt, which significantly increases the original anxiety the hurt actually caused.

Hiding from future hurt. Having been hurt, these people, consciously or unconsciously, decide never to place themselves in a similarly vulnerable position. This is the "burned child" reaction to hurt; that is, the child who is burned on a stove may decide never to go near a stove again. This child was not taught how to remain around stoves without getting burned.

The counselor can demonstrate to these clients that they are paying an enormous price for safety. People then can be helped to reenter situations of risk, to prevent hurt, and to handle hurt constructively when it does occur.

Hurting oneself. Paradoxically, when some people are hurt, they respond by hurting themselves further. For example, a child may be scolded at supper and refuse to eat his dessert even though he wants it. An adolescent is hurt by her parents and reacts by not studying for a test, which she fails. A man is hurt by his wife and refuses to have sex that evening, even though he looked forward to it all day.

The dynamics of self-hurting behavior are twofold. The first dynamic is to make the offending party feel guilty. The message is, "Look what you've done to me. You've hurt me so much I don't even care about myself anymore." The second dynamic is to punish oneself for being vulnerable. This dynamic is generally seen in people who define themselves as "tough" and/or "perfect" and who feel ashamed that they have succumbed to hurt. They feel, "If I'm so stupid as to be hurt by this person, I *deserve* to suffer even more."

Counselors can help these individuals recognize that self-hurt is a very destructive dynamic that breeds resentment, weakens the person, and discourages others from getting close. Counselors should also realize that they are vulnerable to hurt. It is helpful for them to recognize the strategies they knowingly and unknowingly use to avoid hurt. While these stratagems may protect the counselor, they may also create undesirable buffers in the counseling relationship.

Guilt

Guilt is the feeling of discomfort that people experience when they think, feel, or act in ways they consider wrong, bad, or immoral. While guilt and shame are often confused for each other there are sound therapeutic reasons to differentiate one from the other. According to Nugent, "Guilt involves acknowledging a specific inappropriate or destructive behavior and making amends. The attitude leaves self esteem intact. Shame, on the other hand, is a feeling that one is fundamentally unworthy, bad, or inadequate" (1994, p. 213). Guilt plays an important role in psychological growth and happiness—shame does not. When guilt is appropriate, it helps people refrain from behavior that damages their sense of self-esteem and that places a distance between them and others. Guilt can motivate a person who has participated in guilt-producing behavior to rectify its damaging effects and to change future behavior. Appropriate guilt is a preserver and restorer of self-esteem.

Guilt is appropriate when people behave in ways that legitimately reduce their self-esteem. The word *legitimately* is an important qualifier for several reasons. People may have unrealistically positive expectations of themselves and may feel self-hatred when they fail to meet them. For example, a young man feels appropriate anger toward his parents because of the inordinate pressures they place on him. He inappropriately berates himself for having these feelings.

A person's sense of being lovable may depend on another person's evaluation. For example, a young woman who recently graduated from college wishes to move out of her parents' home, but when she broaches the subject, her parents send her some variation of the message, "How could you be so ungrateful as to leave us by ourselves?" The daughter finally manages to gain enough strength to move out, but she is flooded with guilt because her sense of self-esteem is largely interwoven with what her parents think of her.

A person's sense of self-esteem can be tied to unreasonable moral absolutes. When people are unable to behave according to these absolutes, their self-esteem is diminished. Some common moral absolutes are that anger is bad, sex is sinful, self-fulfillment is selfish, obedience is good, promises should be kept, and loyalty is a virtue. What makes these moral injunctions absolute is that they admit no exceptions. In reality, anger can be destructive, but it also can be constructive and, in fact, in certain situations it would be immoral *not* to express anger. The same kinds of qualifications can be applied to the other moral absolutes.

Counselors can help people recognize when they feel guilty and help them discern whether the guilt is appropriate or inappropriate. The results of this discernment will suggest the next step to take.

Types of Guilt

It is important for counselors to understand that there is not one monolithic dynamic called *guilt*. In reality, there are at least three common sources of guilt: psychological, social, and religious. This distinction is not merely theoretical because the specific kind of guilt will dictate the particular path to resolution.

Psychological guilt.   This occurs when people behave in a way that goes against their self-concept. Unlike social guilt, which is interpersonal, psychological guilt is intrapersonal—that is, it deals with individuals' relationships with themselves.

Social guilt.   This stems from being psychologically or materially unjust to another person. The social dimension of a value system tells a person there are certain ways to behave in order to help others, and there are certain ways not to behave because such behaviors damage others.

Religious guilt.   This occurs in the case of people who feel that their behavior violates their religious or spiritual beliefs.

It is important that counselors understand the difference between the three kinds of guilt because resolving one does not resolve any of the others. A man may confess his sins to a minister and be relieved. However, after the good feeling wears away, he begins to feel troubled again. He feels forgiven by God but does not feel forgiven by himself or by the people he has damaged. The self-punitive feelings that stem from this realization could cause him to misbehave again, thus repeating the cycle. In counseling, a person may resolve the psychological guilt that accompanied a particular behavior only to be left with the social and religious guilt unresolved.

Guilt can be either *conscious* or *unconscious*. If an individual lacks the psychological strength to deal with guilt, coping mechanisms will intercept it and repress it. This allows a person who may be permeated with guilt to state, "I've never done a thing that I've felt guilty about in my life."

When guilt is unconscious, it cannot be used as an instrument of growth because, for all practical purposes, it does not exist. Furthermore, unconscious guilt causes self-punitive behavior as a way of atoning for the guilt. While this self-punishment relieves some of the anxiety caused by guilt, it causes its own set of problems. First, because the self-punishing behavior is motivated by unconscious guilt, there is no control over it, so it can invade the important and precious areas of the person's life—for example, work performance and love relationships. Second, self-punishing behavior almost always damages loved ones, which adds even more guilt as fuel for the destructive process.

Third, because the person is not aware of what behavior caused, or is still causing, the unconscious guilt, it is likely to continue, causing a relentless cycle of self-punishing behavior. Finally, the more self-punishing behavior the person indulges in, the more he or she is filled with self-dislike or self-hate. This causes its own vicious circle.

Manifestations

It is difficult to distinguish clearly self-punishing behaviors from self-anger behaviors because there is often a good deal of overlap. However, some behaviors are likely to be motivated more by unconscious guilt than by self-anger.

The conviction that there is something wrong with oneself. Despite repeated reassurances to the contrary, people may believe there is something physically or emotionally wrong with them.

Indecisiveness. As long as people allow themselves to remain between the horns of a dilemma, two things are happening. First, they experience a good deal of tension, and second, they are unable to get needs met in the particular situation.

Experiencing disappointment. This is the "Is that all there is?" syndrome. These individuals are always looking forward to some happiness, only to be disappointed when they reach it.

Psychosomatic or hypochondriacal symptoms. Psychosomatic symptoms are real physical symptoms that are caused as much by psychological factors as by physical ones. Hypochondriacal symptoms are magnified physical complaints that are imagined or are real. When such symptoms are caused by unconscious guilt, pain is very frequently part of the symptomology. It is interesting to note that these symptoms often get worse just prior to some event that a person is looking forward to enjoying.

Overdriven needs.   An example of an overdriven need is the need to be perfect. The perfectionist sets unattainable goals for self and others. Consequently, the person is continually disappointed. Another is to assume inordinate obligations. This person manages to assume obligations of a type or variety that effectively prevent enjoyment of life. A third is to worry. Such people move from one crisis to another. The solution of each problem only opens the way for more.

Habitually embarking on doomed ventures.   This behavior occurs in friendships, marriages, business ventures, and political causes. It is the "signing up for failure" syndrome. Each failure is met with surprise, even though others saw the "handwriting on the wall" from the start.

Snatching defeat from the jaws of victory.   This type of individual does well until the very end and then manages to self-destruct. The student who has an "A" going into the final examination does not show up for the exam.

Religiosity.   The relevant characteristic is that religion is used as an excuse to suffer and to be unhappy. This is motivated not by a positive attitude toward God but by a negative, guilt-ridden attitude toward oneself.

Counselors can help people recognize the possibility that some of their self-created problems are prompted by an urge to be self-punishing. When the client can entertain this as a possibility, the counselor may be able to help the client trace the self-punishing behavior back to its possible causes. These guilts may be appropriate or inappropriate or of long or short duration. In any case, the guilts can be uncovered so that the client can resolve them constructively.

Atonement

Conscious guilt provides an opportunity for constructive resolution through the process of *atonement*, which means that the person uses the guilt constructively to become more at one with the self and with the people who were damaged by the misbehavior. Unlike the resolution of guilt through self-punishment, the main goal of atonement is not simply to reduce anxiety but to heal as many wounds as possible and to make changes in order to decrease the likelihood of the same behavior occurring again. Counselors can help clients learn a process of atonement.

Acknowledging the guilt feeling.   This entails the admission, "I feel guilty." The counselor can help the client become aware that guilt can be disguised by other emotions and help the client ferret out such emotions.

Discovering the true source and magnitude of the guilt. Guilt can be displaced from one behavior onto another. A woman who is actually guilty of not being as loving as she could be toward her children may displace this guilt. She may think that her guilt stems from not visiting her own mother more often. She finds it easier to feel guilty for not being a good daughter than to feel guilty for not being a good mother.

Guilt can also be inordinately intense. A student may cheat on an exam and feel great and prolonged guilt, totally out of proportion to the situation. This same student behaves abusively towards his girlfriend but denies this deeper and more profound source of guilt. The existence of the second source of guilt explains the disproportionate guilt reaction to cheating on the exam. The counselor can help this man separate the two guilts and atone for each separately.

Atoning for appropriate guilt. Once appropriate guilt is isolated, it must be atoned for or it will continue to cause unconscious self-punishing behavior, which is always destructive, not only to the guilty person but often to innocent bystanders. Atonement must be appropriate to the specific kind of guilt the person is experiencing.

Psychological guilt—that is, guilt that stems from violating one's self-concept—must be atoned for differently than *social guilt*. The counselor should first help clients discern whether or not their self-concept in this particular area is appropriate. If a client's self-concept is inappropriate and based on ideals rather than on reality or if the self-concept is inappropriately negative, the basic problem is the self-concept and not the guilt that flows from violating it. The counselor can help the client align the self-concept with reality, and this will diminish the amount of inappropriate guilt the person feels.

If the self-concept is appropriate, then the counselor can help the client discover why he or she behaved in a way that violated it. For example, if part of a client's self-concept is that he is honest, but he lies during a confrontation with his wife, the counselor can help the man understand why this occurred. What needs, motives, fears, and angers prompted him to lie rather than to tell the truth? If telling the truth would have caused significantly more problems, what is going on in the overall relationship that is manifesting itself in this no-win situation? The answer to these and similar questions will give the client information that, if acted upon, will decrease the potential for similar behavior in the future.

Social guilt (guilt that stems from damaging another, directly or indirectly) can involve attempts to undo the harm. The counselor can help the client understand that merely apologizing to another ordinarily does not constitute atonement. How atonement is accomplished depends upon the kind of damage. If a client's reputation is damaged, attempts can be made to undo the harm. If the client cheated another out of monies or goods, they can be returned.

Sometimes direct atonement may be impossible—for example, if the damaged person is deceased. Atonement in this situation can be indirect or symbolic. This may be done by taking a special interest in the welfare of one's own family or friends or by doing volunteer work. In other situations, it may not be possible to rectify the damage. In these cases, counselors can help people accept this reality and learn from it so they can avoid similar mistakes in the future.

Religious guilt (guilt for behaving in ways that place a distance between oneself and God) stems largely from one's view of God. People who view God as one who can be vengeful, hurt, disappointed, authoritarian, or jealous will experience guilt when they fail to achieve the level of perfection this view of God requires. This is an especially difficult situation. The counselor who attempts to help the client modify his or her negative image of God will be met with resistance and anger. The counselor who attempts to raise the client to a level of perfection that surpasses human nature is attempting the impossible. The counselor who is not religious may be unable to empathize with the client in this situation. The counselor who shares the client's negative view of God may simply compound the guilt.

Counselors can help clients understand that harsh views of God often are projections of one's views of parents and/or teachers. As people's psychological health and self-esteem increase, they will relate to a God who is psychologically healthy and loving. In fact, for religious people, progress in counseling can often be measured by how their image of God changes from a frightening, angry, and authoritarian figure to one that is comforting, loving, and freeing.

In an age that has often viewed guilt as a neurotic and unnecessarily bothersome emotion, it is important for counselors to recognize that appropriate guilt is a useful emotion because this form of guilt generates adaptive behavior. Counselors can help clients separate appropriate from inappropriate guilt so that they can grow in the self-worth that is produced by constructively handling guilt and thus be freed of the self-disparagement caused by inappropriate guilt. Counselors can assist people who have overly stringent consciences develop more realistic attitudes toward themselves and people with weaker consciences to more fully appreciate the hurt that their behavior causes themselves and others and to use this appropriate guilt to guide their behavior. Dealing with emotions is an important part of counseling. When emotions are appropriate in nature and strength, they energize the person to behave adaptively. When they are inappropriate, they further distort the person's perceptions and consequently contribute to the formation of maladaptive behavior.

Emotional Intelligence

To this point we have discussed specific emotions, how they are likely to adversely affect individuals and what counselors can do to help clients manage specific feelings more effectively. We have also discussed how thoughts influence feelings and behavior; but a more systematic and inclusive way of understanding emotions and their reciprocal influence on other personality characteristics is clearly missing. Part of this gap may be filled by an emerging construct called *emotional intelligence*. Emotional intelligence research offers a sound theoretical perspective along with hypotheses about the influence of emotions that can be translated into practical methods for improving emotional intelligence. According to Salovey and Mayer (1990, p. 189), emotional intelligence is "the ability to monitor one's own and others' feelings and emotions, to discriminate them, and to use the information to guide one's thinking and actions." These same researchers identified three primary domains of emotional intelligence: (1) accurate appraisal and expression of emotion, (2) adaptive regulation of emotion, and (3) utilization of emotion-based information.

We have already illustrated the importance of correctly identifying and expressing feelings; the ability to process emotional information hinges on the individual's success in this domain. Of course people differ greatly in their ability to identify their feelings so strategies that improve this ability are crucial.

While the dynamic was not previously identified as *the adaptive regulation of emotion*, methods for adaptively regulating emotions were covered in the discussion of coping mechanisms and coping tactics in chapter 9 and alluded to in this chapter in the sections dealing with faulty assumptions. Human beings use many different activities to manage their emotions; some are adaptive (e.g., changing the way they think about an event, deploying more adaptive coping mechanisms, or vigorous exercise) while other methods are maladaptive (e.g., gambling or substance abuse).

In the context of emotional intelligence, adaptive regulation of emotions is enlarged to include the adaptive regulation of emotions in others. While the idea of adaptively regulating other people's feelings is rarely discussed in counseling theory, it has a well-established place in the counseling process. To be more specific, counseling efforts are usually focused on helping individuals adaptively manage their *own* feelings, but counselors are able to discuss emotional issues with their clients because of their ability to help *others* adaptively manage feelings. The question of how much clients benefit from being able to adaptively regulate other people's feelings after having the process modeled to them has not been answered empirically, but anecdotal evidence abounds. When clients report that they were able to sit quietly with their children and calmly discuss issues that previously produced intense emotions and angry arguments, they are describing their ability to adaptively manage feelings in others, as it was modeled for them by the counselor.

The utilization of emotion-based knowledge is a domain that has implications for career counseling as well as mental health counseling. Moods can positively and negatively influence various types of problem solving and they affect how persistently people pursue tasks (see Salovey & Mayer, 1994, p. 315). Counselors can aid clients by helping them to rely on emotional information and emotions as they solve problems and make life decisions. Problem-solving and decision-making are not exclusively cognitive processes. Emotional information and emotions are equally influential and necessary for effective functioning.

By 1997, Mayer and Salovey had modified and expanded their earlier definitions of the construct to this formulation:

> Emotional intelligence involves the ability to perceive accurately, appraise, and express emotion; the ability to access and/or generate feelings when they facilitate thought; the ability to understand emotion and emotional knowledge; and the ability to regulate emotions to promote emotional and intellectual growth. (1997, p. 10)

Their exhaustive study of emotion has identified a systematic route to emotional and intellectual growth via a model that honors the reciprocal relationships that exist among several personality traits, including social intelligence, individual intelligence, and emotions. The model offers many opportunities for counselors as well as teachers to help others improve their level of functioning by addressing the various domains that make up the construct of emotional intelligence.

It remains to be seen how counselors will use the wealth of information that is coming from research into emotional intelligence, though one way that counselors may be able to apply findings in clinical settings is through systematic skills training. For example, Saarni (1997, pp. 47–58) has identified eight different skills associated with emotional competence. While her work pertains to children, these skills are equally valuable for adults. They include the following eight skills:

1. Awareness of one's emotional state, including the possibility that one is experiencing multiple emotions, and at even more mature levels, awareness that one might also not be consciously aware of one's feelings due to unconscious dynamics or selective inattention.

2. Ability to discern others' emotions, based on situational and expressive cues that have some degree of cultural consensus.

3. Ability to use the vocabulary of emotion and expression terms commonly available in one's (sub)culture and at more mature levels to acquire cultural scripts that link emotion with social roles.

4. Capacity for empathic and sympathetic involvement in others' emotional experiences.

5. Ability to realize that an inner emotional state need not correspond to outer expression, both in oneself and in others, and at more mature levels the ability to understand that one's emotional-expressive behavior may impact on another and to take this into account in one's self-presentation strategies.

6. Capacity for adaptive coping with aversive or distressing emotions by using self-regulatory strategies that ameliorate the intensity or temporal duration of such emotional states (e.g., "stress hardiness").

7. Awareness that the structure of relationships is in part defined by the quality of emotional communication within the relationship.

8. Capacity for emotional self-efficacy: The individual views her or himself as feeling, overall, the way he or she wants to feel.

While this list of skills or competencies can be used to help individuals pursue emotional competence and self-regulation, they are not all that is needed. Emotional competence and self-regulation are valuable skills but they cannot be expected to overcome adverse social and economic forces. Saarni writes, "I seriously doubt that any 'instructional program' in the skills of emotional competence will have an effect on children at risk if there is no concurrent pragmatic effort to ameliorate the desperate circumstances of their daily life" (1997, p. 59). Her words of caution are equally applicable to counselors. While counselors may focus on the client's internal processes (cognitive, emotional, physical, and spiritual), they cannot ignore the crucial need to eliminate serious external sources of distress.

Summary

While counselors who espouse various approaches to counseling may disagree about how influential irrational beliefs and faulty assumptions are, none would argue that they are irrelevant. An understanding of how faulty assumptions form, how they influence behavior, and what can be done to change them are important to most counseling efforts and essential to others (e.g., REBT, or cognitive-behavioral therapy). The role of the counselor is also affected by adherence to an approach that focuses on the client's cognitive processes; the counselor's role becomes that of teacher. Clients are instructed on how to identify their difficulties, establish goals, challenge assumptions, develop behavioral alternatives, practice new behaviors, and transfer what they have learned into their daily lives. Many clients benefit from counseling approaches that target their irrational beliefs and faulty assumptions. All counselors, regardless of their theoretical orientation, must determine what place cognitive issues have in the counseling approach they offer to clients.

Counselors also help clients manage their emotions by taking steps to ensure that clients correctly identify not only what they feel, but the target or direction of their feelings. The tendency to misinterpret and misdirect feelings is so high that counselors often devote much time in counseling to this task. Emotional expression is both culturally and individually determined, so counselors need to understand the influence of emotions on the individual as well as the ways emotions are affected by social and cultural forces. Emotions, when correctly managed, can serve as guides and motivational forces that improve the quality of one's life.

The concept of emotional intelligence offers counselors a unique model that illustrates the reciprocal relationship between emotions and other personality traits. Models for skills training and strategies for productively harnessing emotional information are available. Continued research in this area will doubtlessly influence clinical practice in the future.

To be effective, counselors must be able to address, to a greater or lesser extent, the client's cognitive, affective, physical and spiritual concerns. While adherence to a particular theoretical approach may tend to bias counselors in one direction or another, that bias should not preclude attending to all four areas. Saarni's realistic prediction that emotional competence skills training cannot and should not be expected to overcome the effects of living in desperate circumstances underscores the fact that counseling should never be used to direct people to adapt deplorable conditions. Some clients may reveal thoughts and express feelings that may mislead counselors into helping clients change behavior, when it is their living conditions that really need to be changed. In cases such as these, the client's thoughts and feelings are correctly reflecting the depth of despair that comes from living in dire straits. Thus, while counselors often selectively focus on particular elements or characteristics of a client's personality, they must also attend to the whole person (external as well as internal determinants of behavior).

Reflection Questions

1. Many people enter counseling with the faulty assumption, "Other people know better than I what's good for me." How can even experienced counselors be led into reinforcing this assumption, and what steps could be taken to prevent this from happening?

2. Which two of the faulty assumptions covered in the chapter are you most likely to adopt during times of stress? How will adopting these erroneous beliefs affect your work as a counselor? How would you deal with them?

3. Most people have a fear of failure. How could your fear of failure affect the way you conduct counseling?

4. It would seem that if counselors have deep insight into themselves, they might feel a certain guilt about their role as counselors for at least a few reasons. What could some of these reasons be? How might a counselor handle the guilt in constructive ways?

5. How can skills training for emotional competence be applied to adults?

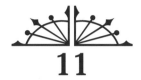

11

RESISTANCE IN COUNSELING

Even when clients know what life changes they need to make and are motivated to make such changes, fears and anxieties combine to produce a form of ambivalence that often leaves them mired in failed attempts to improve. Ironically, the internal forces that produce psychological and emotional difficulties in a person's life, the very same forces that motivate people to seek alternatives, also obstruct the change process. Wachtel (1982) illustrates this important perspective on resistance when he writes:

> It is in the very nature of psychological problems that the patient is hampered from doing what must be done to make things better. The very problems the patient comes to therapy to try to solve make it difficult for him [sic] to cooperate in their solution. This dilemma is the heart of the concept of resistance. The concept refers not to any willful malevolence or opposition on the patient's part but instead to the difficulties inherent in attempting to encounter and master feelings and experiences that have previously seemed so overwhelming they must be avoided and denied at all costs. (p. xix)

The counseling process can and often does increase the client's resistance because it can surface feelings and bring overwhelming experiences into the client's awareness. Therefore, the need to properly manage resistance throughout the course of counseling is essential—resistance, to a greater or lesser extent, is present at all times and in all counseling relationships.

Resistance is a force that has both benefits and liabilities. It helps by offering protection from potentially destructive, overwhelming feelings, insights, and experiences. It hinders because it can block efforts to explore more difficult emotions/insights or make necessary changes. Successful counselors must appreciate the value of resistance in situations where it is warranted and be prepared to help the client overcome its grip in situations where it blocks efforts to improve. Because resistance in counseling is so common, counselors as well as clients need to understand the complex forces that produce it and the obvious, as well as often subtle, signs that confirm its presence.

Resistance as it is applied to psychotherapy and human behavior has its origins in the psychoanalytic literature. It is a concept very closely related to defense mechanisms (see chapter 9 for a more complete discussion of psychological defenses and Weiner 1975, pp. 160–201 for more information about resistance). The assumptions that counselors hold about resistance influence the way they perceive their clients and the routes they select to help them. Both classical and modern definitions of resistance can be found. Classical definitions are rooted in psychoanalytic perspectives. For example, according to Greenson, "Resistance defends the neurosis, the old, the familiar, and the infantile from exposure and change" (1967, p. 77). And while Bischoff and Tracey's operational definition, "any client behavior that exhibits a reluctance, on the part of the client, to participate in the tasks of therapy as set forward by the therapist" (1995, p. 488), is a bit more general it still offers a serviceable example of a classical, psychoanalytically oriented description of the term. These classical definitions reflect several important assumptions: (1) the client is reluctant to do something that he or she *should* be doing; (2) the tasks of therapy as set forward by the counselor are useful and beneficial to the client; and (3) the client will improve if the resistance is eliminated. Unfortunately these inherent classical assumptions can be individually and collectively inaccurate. For example, some tasks outlined by the counselor may be inappropriate for certain clients; the clients know it and correctly choose not to comply. For some clients, reluctance to follow through on certain tasks may have much more to do with cultural patterns and norms than psychological resistance (Brammer & MacDonald, 1999). Asian clients, for example, may be following a well-defined cultural norm when they refuse to discuss personal or family matters with an "outsider" even if the outsider is a mental health professional.

Finally, many clients are not consciously acting in opposition to the counselor—they are acting and behaving within their capabilities and skills. While it might be perversely comforting for counselors to delude themselves into believing that the only thing that stands between the client's recovery and his or her current plight is overcoming the client's decision to combat the counselor's efforts, it simply is not true. This overly simplistic view of resistance can only distort reality in a way that limits the potential benefits of counseling.

Kottler (1986) offers a concise description of resistance from a more modern perspective when he writes, "Resistance, in all its manifestations, is hardly the nuisance and obstruction to treatment that Freud once believed. Whether clients are overly compliant or dramatically hostile, we now understand that they are doing the very best they know how to keep themselves together" (p. 72). Bischoff and Tracey (1995) also provided a more modern and circumspect definition of the term: "resistance encompasses aspects of client experiencing above and beyond 'noncompliance' and in essence may at times represent an enactment of healthy mechanisms (e.g., a boundary that differentiates self from other)" (p. 488).

Each definition of resistance directs counselors to view their clients in a different light. The classical view identifies resistance as client interference in the therapeutic process while the modern view emphasizes that clients are doing the best they can given their circumstances and, moreover, when clients refuse to comply with the counselor's requests they may often be acting in healthy and appropriate ways.

Ultimately resistance must be understood within the framework of the client's life experiences, relationships with other people in the client's life, and within the framework of the counseling relationship. At the most basic level within the counseling relationship, "client behaviors must be understood in a context that includes the previous therapist behavior (e.g., the sequential unfolding of events)" (Bischoff & Tracey, 1995, p. 493). While resistance has rarely been studied as an interactive process, the need to do so has been well documented. We will seek to consider the interaction between counselor and client throughout the remainder of this chapter as we discuss the concept of resistance from a more modern (less analytic) perspective.

Common Resistance Themes

Regardless of which theoretical orientation a counselor subscribes to, resistance forces will surface in the course of the counseling relationship and they will have to be worked through. Mahalik (1994) offers the following expanded list (enlarged to accommodate a variety of different counseling theories) of resistance categories that are likely to be encountered in counseling:

1. opposing expression of painful affect
2. opposing recollection of material
3. opposing the therapist
4. opposing change
5. opposing insight

While some theoretical orientations tend to emphasize one or more of the preceding areas of resistance over others, all are important. We will discuss each under the premise that individuals exhibit such opposition in an attempt to maintain an internal homeostasis, or a balanced state. However, this homeostasis should not be confused with a psychologically healthy state since, as we will show, human beings can just as readily establish a balance through the use of maladaptive behaviors as they can with adaptive ones. Thus, seemingly maladaptive behaviors are often tightly embraced by the individual because they are necessary to the maintenance of the balance, even though they are often deeply problematic. In simple terms, human beings resist that which is painful, confusing, disorienting, and threatening because moving away from any balanced state, even maladaptive balanced states, produces one or more of these unpleasant, unwanted reactions.

Beitman (1987) referred to the area that must be traversed between the status quo and change as the "Great Abyss." The metaphor of a large bottomless pit helps counselors understand why clients are hurt, confused, disoriented, and threatened by change and more importantly, why they would be willing to embrace a balanced but maladaptive set of circumstances rather than run the risk of making changes. Clients must traverse the abyss if they are to change, because it is impossible to simultaneously clutch old patterns of behavior and begin new ones. There must be a point of confusion and disorientation during the period when old patterns are relinquished and new ones are enacted. It is this period that people resist most intensely. This fact makes it easier to see that counselors can expect client resistance in each of the noted five areas because they are precisely the points where people are most vulnerable—changes or profound insights in these areas directly threaten the client's internal psychological balance.

For our purposes, there are essentially three major reasons why clients may be reluctant to cooperate with their counselors. These reasons are: (1) great amounts of emotional pain often accompany change or personal growth, (2) seemingly maladaptive behavior may be performing a "valuable" service for the client, and (3) motives that are actually countertherapeutic may bring people to counseling. The following discussion of each of these reasons also illustrates how one or more of the five resistance categories listed earlier combine to form various resistance themes.

The Pain of Growth

The pain of growth in counseling is analogous to what a person in physiotherapy experiences when muscles are being stretched and exercised in new ways. There is almost always a price to pay for becoming stronger. During the initial phase of counseling, it gradually becomes clear to the client that a good deal of hard, continuous work lies ahead. The client learns that there is no magic and few, if any, shortcuts. It is at this point that clients often ask only half-kiddingly, "Can't you just hypnotize me and get this all over with quickly and painlessly?"

Behavioral change, of any kind, usually involves stopping old behaviors and beginning new ones. Both activities create tension and anxiety. When this occurs, the client may want to slow down, stop for a while, or quit. At this point it is particularly important for the counselor and the client to cooperate in determining whether such requests are examples of resistance that need to be overcome or appropriate alternatives that warrant serious consideration. Choosing to stop or slow down may be more beneficial for clients whose ego-strength will not be able to carry them through the change process or support them sufficiently as they confront difficult emotions and insights. Counseling is not appropriate for everyone who seeks it. A careful evaluation of client resistance can and should be used to help counselors determine which clients are suitable for counseling.

Starting new behaviors. The counseling process typically challenges clients to begin new behaviors and helps them adjust to the change. For example, clients may find that it has become particularly important to *be more honest* with a significant person or persons in their life, even though they realize that such honesty is likely to create anxiety in both themselves and the other person(s). Therefore, resistance is an expected reaction to the fears and anxieties most people encounter when their behavior may cause significant others to alter the way they perceive them. Under these conditions some clients, in an attempt to avoid even the opportunity for being honest with significant others, may resort to bargaining with the counselor: "If I'm honest with my mother when I go home this weekend, can I wait awhile before I'm honest with my father?" Such pleas clearly reflect the pain involved in sharing deep thoughts, feelings, and questions with loved ones.

Clients may also realize through counseling that they need to *become more self-reliant* even though they may paradoxically fear such self-reliance and independence. Being overreliant on others not only for advice but also for acceptance is a common theme for many people who enter counseling. Being confused and uncertain about what to do are common symptoms of overreliance on others. For example, a client might state, "I'm so confused. My mother says that I should go to college; my father says I should work or go in the service first; and my fiancee says we should get married and move to Virginia." When the counselor responds, "What do you want to do?" the look on the client's face makes it obvious that no one had ever asked him what *he* wanted to do, and he had never asked the same question of himself. The client may then direct the counselor to tell him what to do and even leave counseling abruptly when the counselor turns the question back to the client. The process of taking responsibility for ourselves and our decisions can be very painful and disorienting.

Individuals in counseling may have to *admit self-deception,* a form of self-protection that often occurs when people encounter difficulty accepting particular feelings and motives. Individuals may deceive themselves into thinking that they feel one way when they actually feel another. For example, a man may enter counseling certain that he loves his work and gradually realize that he resents the fact that he chose not to pursue a different and potentially more attractive profession. A woman may feel that she deeply loves her husband and eventually discover through counseling that she is very ambivalent toward him. These discoveries are particularly painful and difficult because: (1) they produce amounts of cognitive dissonance; (2) the client will feel an intensified need to act on the new insight; and (3) intense feelings of discomfort often surface (e.g., guilt, anger, and frustration).

Clients also may also discover self-deception with respect to their motives. A man may enter counseling saying he wishes to become a mathematics teacher in order to help high school students. He soon discovers that while he likes mathematics, his decision to become a teacher has more to do with his parents' expectations than his personal wishes. At this point he is confronted with a difficult decision: does he continue to deny his motives in favor of his parents' expectations or does he begin the process of exploring alternatives?

Clients may also discover that they have to *reexamine basic beliefs, assumptions, and values.* Many enter counseling unaware that the resolution of their frustrations and conflicts will require the reevaluation of a basic belief, assumption, or value. Since these basic elements are critical to the way in which people understand themselves and the way they make sense of the world around them, they are difficult to change and difficult to acknowledge because they are so completely integrated. People may tend to accept them as universal truths rather than ideas that are open to debate and change. For example, a man may have always uncritically accepted the idea that once he married he would never get divorced. After five years in a strife-ridden marriage, this basic assumption is being severely tested. Or, following the death of her mother, a woman who had grown up with a particular set of religious beliefs begins to scrutinize and challenge aspects of her faith that had never been questioned previously. She worries how she will continue to function with such profound questions rocking what she had previously experienced as an unshakable foundation.

While it may be important, from a developmental perspective, to test basic beliefs, assumptions, and values, changing such basic elements of the way people make sense of the world around them can be very threatening and complicated. Such changes are usually quite disorienting and they are understandably resisted, often strenuously.

Stopping old behaviors. Clients may have to *stop a favored behavior.* Some common favored behaviors, though clearly counterproductive, are abusing alcohol/drugs, having an affair, pitying oneself, impressing people, manipulating others, and withdrawing from people. While each of these can meet needs and reduce tension, it may become clear in counseling that such behaviors are self-destructive and, until they stop, little progress can be made. Many of these behaviors are addictive and stopping them, even those that are not addictive, often causes painful psychological and, at times, physical withdrawal symptoms.

Clients may also have to *give up positive as well as negative pretenses.* The process of self-deception allows people to act as if they possess something they actually lack. They may pretend to be effective workers when, in fact, they are mediocre. They pretend that they are liked by many people when, in fact, their admirers are few. They pretend they know more than they do; that they are happier than they are; that they are braver, more caring, and more interested in changing than they are. People may also cling to "negative" pretenses; that is, they pretend to be weaker than they are; less happy, competent, attractive, or intelligent; more fragile, depressed, scared, or hopeless than they really are. Just as people may resist being honest with others, they may also resist being honest with themselves. The counselor's task is to help clients work through their predictable anxiety and resistance so that they can obtain a more realistic view of themselves.

Clients may have to *terminate an important relationship or job.* When it becomes obvious that a relationship or job constitutes an unhealthy environment, the client must seriously consider terminating it. Ending relationships or changing relationships can be excruciatingly painful, so painful that some people would prefer to terminate the counseling relationship rather than the unhealthy personal relationship. In modern societies, one's identity is tightly linked to a career—leaving or quitting a job or profession can be traumatic. When people have studied and worked for years to become a member of a profession and discover that it was never the right profession for them or that they have outgrown it, such a change can be intensely disorienting and anxiety provoking.

They may have to *learn to take personal responsibility and stop making excuses.* It is a rare person (in or out of counseling) who readily accepts responsibility for personal difficulties and failures. Clients frequently displace the responsibility for their shortcomings. A woman, when asked why she had an affair, responds "My husband was more interested in his work than in me." An adolescent boy explains his poor performance in school as due to his father's drinking problem, and the father blames his drinking problem on the son's rebellious behavior.

Most counseling theorists would agree that the process of change demands that clients take responsibility for their behavior (Beitman, 1987). Clients may cling tenaciously to their excuses for problematic behavior because once the excuse is dropped, the responsibility for the behavior falls to them. And in accepting responsibility, he or she must do something active to rectify the situation.

Psychologically strong people would find the eight behavioral changes described here as anxiety producing and painful; clients with weakened ego or lack of psychological strength will find these changes all the more difficult. Unfortunately, when counselors fail to appreciate how difficult such changes can be for people, they can become frustrated. While clients may need to be encouraged, direct advice to "just go do it" is rarely followed and is more indicative of an empathic failure on the part of the counselor than any viable therapeutic intervention. In other words, if counselors are too directive they will increase levels of client resistance (Bischoff & Tracey, 1995).

The Functions of Maladaptive Behavior

Clients may resist changing behavior because they have a vested interest in maintaining the status quo. All behavior is need-based, and the more frequently a person participates in a behavior, the greater the need that is being met. Therefore, when people enter counseling with maladaptive patterns, there is always a compelling need and reason for it.

People will cling to maladaptive behaviors until there is good reason to believe that the substitute behavior will be equally satisfying or anxiety reducing, or until the maladaptive patterns lose their ability to reduce anxiety. A person may opt to work excessively because he or she feels uncomfortable at home with family. Problems may build in the family beyond that which can be managed by simply working longer hours. Once the work proves ineffective as a means for controlling the levels of anxiety emanating from the client's relationships in the family, the client must seek some other method to achieve a balanced state. It is at times like this that counseling can have its most profound effect because the client is motivated to relinquish a maladaptive pattern that is not working and anxious to find something that will. In other words, the emotional pain is sufficiently high to motivate the client to find something that works better than the current maladaptive methods.

Maladaptive behavior can provide several psychological services for the client. While these services are not psychologically healthy, they do play an important role in the client's dynamics. Throughout the following discussion, alcoholism will be used as one example of a maladaptive behavior that provides various services for the client.

Fulfilling psychological needs. Maladaptive behavior can fulfill a person's psychological needs, albeit in a destructive way. For example, the alcoholic may find that when he is intoxicated, he receives significantly more attention than when he is sober. The attention may be positive (for instance, his family may protect and nurture him), or it may be negative (for example, his family may scold and ridicule him). In either case, he learns that when he is intoxicated, others automatically pay attention to him. When he is sober, he is often ignored. This reflects how maladaptive behavior meets important psychological needs when a person lacks the competencies to get these needs met in constructive ways.

Providing distraction. Maladaptive behavior can provide a distraction from the basic, more painful to address, problems. While the alcoholic defines his problem as alcoholism, alcoholism is actually a symptom of deeper and more complicated issues. In other words, the alcoholic's drinking is an effect, not a cause. He may drink to excess because he feels painfully inadequate, is terrified of life, is filled with rage, has failed miserably, is permeated with guilt over long-repressed behavior, or because of a combination of some or all of these issues. It is "simpler, easier, and safer" for him to tie all these issues into one package and call it "alcoholism." He will likely resist giving up the package for fear of discovering his problems are worse than he had thought.

When counselors invite clients to relinquish their maladaptive behavior, they must offer something in its place. The process of helping clients replace destructive patterns with constructive ones is often a long and arduous journey, made possible by the fact that the counselor and client cooperate with one another to achieve the same goal. They overcome or work through the resistance forces and simultaneously move toward improving the client's life.

Countertherapeutic Motives

The third reason that clients are ambivalent about changing is because they may enter counseling with such strong fears about change that they unwittingly adopt motives that oppose change. The following are examples of various countertherapeutic motives.

To get permission not to change. Some clients are actually seeking assurance from the counselor that they are fine just the way they are. Although they confidently tell the counselor of their willingness to do anything to make their lives less conflictual, their behavior in counseling suggests otherwise. Under the pretense of searching for behaviors that need to be changed, they are unable to look very earnestly. In fact, they may unknowingly steer the counselor away from discovering maladaptive behavior patterns. Such clients might voice some variation of the sentiment, "Gee, this is disappointing. We turned that last topic upside down and every which way, and we found nothing to work on." When the counselor does discover a problematic area, it is often difficult or impossible for the client to see, or the client denies that the behavior is problematic. The counselor's suggestions for change are politely and subtly ignored, resisted, or declined. The client's hidden motive is that sooner or later the counselor will have to admit, "Well, I've evaluated you thoroughly, and I have to give you a clean bill of health." Thus the actual goal of counseling for these clients is to obtain support for maintaining the status quo.

To validate a decision. Some people have, whether or not they are aware of it, already made a decision to leave a marriage, change jobs, get married, have an abortion, quit school, or begin or end a relationship before they contact a counselor. They are merely bringing the decision to an expert for a stamp of approval. These clients are often unaware that they are trying to validate a decision. On the surface, they seem to be wrestling with the decision and appear open to whatever the counselor has to say. But on a deeper level, they are selectively accepting only what the counselor says in support of their decision, sifting out what does not agree. The counselor's attempts to give equal consideration to the other side of the issue are often met with well-disguised resistance. The client may respond, "That's a good point. I hadn't thought of that. I'll have to give it some serious consideration." But the client returns to the next session proclaiming, "I was so busy this week, I didn't have time to think about it"; "I thought about it and even discussed it with some of my friends, but we all agreed it was nothing to worry about"; or "Let's see. What *was* it we were talking about last week?"

To prove that someone else is to blame.   The "someone else" may be a child, parent, spouse, friend, or boss. Counseling sessions are viewed metaphorically as court appearances in which the judge (the counselor) will be swayed by a preponderance of the evidence to rule in favor of the client. For example, parents may enter counseling with their 17-year-old son for the stated purpose of "improving our communication." But the real purpose is for the parents and the counselor to gang up on the boy and agree that he is the source of the family's problems. The counselor's attempts to improve communication are successful only when the communication provides evidence against the boy. When the communication focuses on other important areas or hints that the parents may share the responsibility for the family's difficulties, the parents are no longer interested in improving communication. At this point, the parents are likely to protest to the counselor, "See, now *even you* are starting to think the way he does!"

To vent hostility on another.   These clients view counseling as an armory where they can obtain ammunition to defeat their foes. A person may enter counseling with the implied message to family and/or friends, "Look what you've finally done to me." This message is subtle, hidden beneath protestations: "I know I'm the cause of so much conflict at home" or "My family and friends have been saints to put up with me for so long. I decided to give them a break and get some help." Gradually, however, the real motive for entering counseling surfaces. The client returns home from counseling sessions and says, "I thought it was all my fault. But now I'm learning you are part of the problem, too." After a while, the messages become less benign: "Dr. Smith says you are trying to mold me into someone I'm not." Then, "Dr. Smith wonders how I've maintained my sanity as well as I have living in this situation." Finally, "Dr. Smith says that you need counseling as much as I do, and if you don't get it, I'll have to move away." Whatever the counselor says or does is translated by the client into ammunition against others. The client unwittingly drafts the counselor as a forceful ally against family, friends, and associates. Efforts to focus the client on this dynamic or undertake other issues are met with strong resistance.

To manipulate others.   Such clients may enter counseling unconsciously motivated not so much to improve but rather to qualify as "psychologically infirmed." They reason that if they can make "the clinic" an important part of their lives, people will start treating them better. Once they can present themselves as disabled, people will take better care of them, protect them from stress, relieve them of responsibility, and understand and forgive their misbehaviors. These clients appear to be fragile so that no one wants to be responsible for pushing them "over the brink." When the counselor refuses to pamper such clients, they react with massive resistance. If the counselor gets enticed into treating the client as fragile, there will be no conflict but there will also be little in the way of personal growth and change.

To prove they are beyond help.   This category is closely related to the previous one. It is a form of manipulation where the focus is on getting others to give up on them. Clients may want to prove they are beyond help for a couple of reasons. One is that they have several people tugging at them to become someone they do not want to, or cannot, become. They figure if a doctor makes the pronouncement that they are beyond being helped, then everyone else will leave them alone. The second reason is that if someone diagnoses them as "hopeless," they will not have to persist in trying to make changes. These people usually paint only the gloomiest picture of themselves and their environment. They make it clear that if the counselor has any sense at all, the consensus will be that there is nothing to be done. Attempts to help the client are scorned as a waste of time and met with bemused resistance. Every time the counselor spots a vital sign, the client quickly explains that it was merely an illusion.

To defeat the counselor.   Transference forces can sometimes cause clients to symbolize the counselor as a hated parent, spouse, friend, boss, or society in general. These individuals have identified with their internal aggressor; that is, they have become proponents of their pathology because they find it easier to join it than to fight it. The client's hidden and countertherapeutic motive is to defeat the counselor. Attempts will be made to outsmart, outfight, and outseduce the counselor. Obviously, the counselor's attempts to promote the client's growth will be used against him or her. Although these people are difficult to work with, many of them can be helped. The parable of the child who picks a fight with a much larger child is a good metaphor. When the bigger child holds his ground without fighting back, the smaller child begrudgingly respects the other child at first and later learns to like and admire him. The same dynamic is possible in counseling.

To satisfy others.   Unfortunately some people are manipulated into counseling against their will. A parent, spouse, friend, boss, or judge presents counseling as part of an ultimatum: "Either get help or I'll leave you" (or "you'll be fired" or "you'll go to jail"). This individual chooses counseling as the lesser evil. Obviously, this is not an ideal situation therapeutically, but it is not inherently unworkable. If the client's attitude is, "Well, this can't hurt; so I might as well see what happens," it may be only a short distance to helping the client see the benefits of counseling. If the client's attitude is, "Well, I'm here; but you can't make me relate with you," the distance from this point to cooperation is significantly greater but not necessarily infinite. The counselor may need to take one of several positions: (1) I do not see clients who do not come in on their own, (2) I will play along for a while until one of us gets tired, or (3) As long as you're here, maybe we can agree on something worth working on. The first and last positions are better than the second one principally because the second position casts the counselor as more of a baby-sitter than a helper.

The unhelpful motive that brings a person into counseling need not be irreversible. Counselors can help clients gradually realize what their deepest motive is and help them to understand the negative consequences that flow from it. The counselor then can help the client replace the unhelpful motive with a more constructive one. Occasionally, a client loses all interest in counseling once the negative motive surfaces. When this occurs, it is probably better in most cases to agree to discontinue counseling. The client can be assured, however, that the door is always open in the event that his or her motivation changes.

Methods of Resistance

When people offer resistance in counseling, there are often perceptible signs. While it is possible to misinterpret resistance in clients, the following indicators are among the more common ways that resistance surfaces in counseling. These indicators are a type of defense tactic that tends to reduce the amount of time and the number of opportunities that the counselor and the client have to focus on the client's issues and to achieve the agreed-upon goals of counseling (other defense tactics can be found in chapter 9).

Attitude toward Appointments

Being late for appointments is a fairly common and reliable (especially when a pattern of behavior emerges) sign of resistance. By being late, the client loses precious minutes of an already limited amount of time. By the time the client catches his or her breath, explains the reasons for being late, apologizes, and listens to the counselor's reaction to the tardiness, another 10 or 15 minutes of counseling have elapsed. Elapsed time is not necessarily wasted time, as long as the counselor can help the client understand the meaning of being late for appointments. If being late be-comes an event that causes the counselor and client to discuss resistance and helps the client come closer to discovering the particular reasons for the resistance, the time would be well spent.

Other possible signs of resistance are failing and canceling appoint-ments. A failed appointment means that the client, without any forewarn-ing, missed a scheduled time to meet. Failed appointments need to be carefully processed since they are often seen as a significant expression of resistance. Fear and anger often form the dynamics underlying failed ap-pointments and both feelings should be addressed. Failed appointments may also signal difficulties in the therapeutic relationship. Since failed ap-pointments can be interpreted as a sign that the alliance is not strong enough to manage the levels of anxiety that are surfacing, counselors are urged to seriously consider the need to return to an earlier stage of the counseling process in order to strengthen the alliance.

People have full lives so an occasional canceled appointment is to be expected. On the other hand, a pattern of missed sessions (i.e., canceling every fourth or sixth session) raises the suspicion that resistance is surfac-ing and therefore the pattern needs to be addressed. A counselor can of-ten obtain a clue as to the cause of the resistance by closely examining what was discussed in the session or sessions that preceded the failed or canceled appointment.

Missed sessions are not the only clues to resistance regarding ap-pointments. Requests to increase or decrease the frequency of meetings can also indicate the presence of important resistance issues. For example, when a client suggests that the frequency of sessions taper off in the initial or middle phases of counseling, resistance should be considered as a rea-son for the request. It might mean that the client is beginning to explore some particularly difficult area or is feeling overburdened by the counse-lor's expectations. Since requests for fewer meetings may also be driven by practical matters (e.g., financial resources), counselors are well advised to carefully explore the underlying reasons for any and all changes re-garding appointments.

Evading Questions

One common form of resistance can be found in the client's reluc-tance to answer questions. While clients rarely refuse outright to answer the counselor's appropriate requests for information, it is common for them to avoid the question by answering one that was not asked or to pose another question in response to the counselor's question. The pro-cess can be so automatic and unconscious that the client does not realize it has occurred.

For example, a counselor might ask, "How are you and your hus-band dealing with your decision to enter the substance abuse treatment program?" The woman replies, "Well, my husband's been away on business so much it seems that I never see him. That's something I've meant to talk about. I've found myself wondering if he needs to be away that much or if he's looking for excuses to get away." She continues tearfully, "I even have to admit that I wonder what he does when he is away." The counselor, ignoring the original question, responds to the client's query and replies: "How do you mean, you wonder what he is doing?"

If this sequence continues, the session will end, and the counselor will have (1) not received an answer to the original question, and (2) forgotten that the question was ever asked. Tracking a client's unanswered questions by reviewing tapes of counseling sessions can be very helpful in managing this form of resistance. This method makes it possible for counselors to determine not only how often clients fail to respond but which personal issues they avoid by not responding.

Refocusing Attention on the Counselor Instead of the Client

If attention (positive as well as negative) is focused on the counselor, it limits the amount of attention that can be placed on the client. For example, a client may spend an inordinate amount of time praising the counselor. Such attention places the counselor in an uncomfortable position because when this happens the client's issues are not being properly addressed, but if the counselor interrupts and refocuses on the client, the counselor will appear unappreciative and rejecting. Nevertheless, the counselor must gently remind the client about the importance of concentrating on the client and his or her concerns.

Attention can be focused on the counselor in a negative way. As soon as the counselor approaches a delicate area, the client may say, "Why are you smirking?" The unwary counselor may spend the next ten minutes denying or defending the meaning of his or her facial expression and ignoring the client's issues in the process. Client criticisms of the counselor are always important issues to address, but it is equally important to be able to properly determine when they need to be the focus of the work and when they are distractions from other more important issues. Other examples of critical client comments, where counselors need to make a wise determination between what needs to be addressed and what needs to be treated as a distraction, might include:

- Why do you always ask about my relationship with my parents?
- You seem half-awake today. Didn't you get enough sleep last night?
- It really bugs me when you just sit there with a deadpan look and your hands folded neatly on your lap.

The unwary counselor can be successfully detoured away from the client's deeper and more important concerns without fully realizing what actually happened.

Entertaining the Counselor

There are some people who intentionally or unintentionally seek to entertain the counselor. In the process, they avoid attending to their own issues. For example, some may use humor, while others may intrigue the counselor with glibly offered psychological insights and behavioral dynamics. Still other clients may dramatically play the part of each person they mention, thereby converting weekly sessions into miniplays. Counselors easily get caught up in the entertainment and look forward to weekly sessions with the client much as one anticipates seeing a good play. This may be a difficult resistance to deal with because it is very likely that the client has used entertaining to avoid deeper issues throughout his or her life. The counselor must be able to demonstrate an interest in and a concern for aspects of the client beyond those that are simply entertaining.

False Claims of Improvement

Some clients defend themselves by claiming improvements when they have not been achieved. They may bring new insights to counseling, easily establish rapport, or tell the counselor that he or she is the first person to whom they have ever really opened up. They may make it clear that the counselor is teaching them a great deal about themselves and human nature, or place the counselor on an intermittent reinforcement schedule by assuring, "This was the best week I've ever had" or "This was a great session" or "My roommate has seen so much progress in me, *she* wants to see you in counseling." But they are not truly advancing.

These statements are not necessarily indications of false claims, but if they are not matched by real and observable changes in behavior, they probably are. Counselors must focus on behaviors and not get distracted by the client's claims. A counselor might ask, "Oh, what specifically has your roommate seen in you that makes her feel you are progressing well?" If the answer is, "I don't know. I didn't ask her" or "I think she sees I'm happier," the counselor may be appropriately wary that the client is making false claims.

Forgetting

Forgetting is seen in statements such as, "I never can remember what we talked about in a previous session"; "I was going to tell you about a conversation I had with my parents this week, but I've just blocked on the main point I wanted to tell you"; and "You're right. I was going to start filling out job applications this week, and I forgot all about it until you just mentioned it."

Anyone can forget, but forgetting in counseling takes on a particular meaning because the matters discussed in counseling usually rank quite high in importance in the client's life. Consequently, to forget matters that are central to a person's growth often indicates resistance. When forgotten material is eventually remembered, counselors gain useful information about the client's resistance and what issues the resistance protects.

Conditions for Counseling

Trust and understanding are important components of the counseling relationship. All clients should expect to be understood and be able to trust their counselors. However, sometimes clients imply that they will "open up" only if the counselor meets certain "special" requirements, which are usually impossible and often inappropriate to meet. A client may suggest that he or she will discuss a particular matter if the counselor will use the information in a particular way or relate to him or her in a specific manner. For example, a client might agree to discuss a substance abuse problem if the counselor promises not to use the information to suggest taking a certain step—such as entering a substance abuse treatment center.

Conditions such as these are inconsistent with successful treatment outcomes. Counselors risk a great deal when they enter into agreements with their clients that define how they will conduct themselves whenever such conduct is inconsistent with ethical and professional clinical practice. A counselor should explore the client's underlying reasons for requiring special conditions.

Controlling Content

No matter how much the counselor intervenes, the client retains a great deal of control over *what* is discussed in the session. Sometimes clients present counselors with a map that deftly excludes one or two very important territories. The counselor may realize after several months that the client has never mentioned a child who died, a first husband or wife, a grown child, or the subjects of work, adolescent experiences, friends, or religion. Yet each session had been filled with what appeared to be relevant and pressing issues. While the counselor may accidentally stumble into one or more of these undisclosed areas before it is time to terminate, a better strategy is for the counselor to be as vigilant about what the client fails to discuss as what the client shares. Experience helps counselors inquire about important hidden patterns that the client would never bring up or is not aware of consciously. When a counselor discovers these patterns and shares them with the client, it enriches the counseling process because it changes the way the client sees himself or herself and the way he or she is perceived by the counselor.

The client also controls what will be discussed in any specific session. The client may state at the beginning of a session, "I know we agreed to talk about my problems with my mother today, but I just had a fight with my roommates and that's all I can think about." The counselor who is not sensitive to the client's resistance may respond, "Well then, maybe we should talk about that and leave your mother until next week," never exploring the change from one topic to the other with the client.

The client also controls *how* he or she will communicate material to the counselor. A client can inadvertently minimize important material. For example, a client may offhandedly say, "Oh, by the way, I didn't get the job at the telephone company, but the computer company asked me back for a second interview, and I'm kind of excited about that." The counselor responds, "Oh, that's a good sign. What kind of work would you be doing if you got the job?" instead of asking, "Do you know why you didn't get the job at the phone company?" If the counselor had asked that, the client may have replied, "I was afraid you'd ask. In the interview they asked me if I would take orders just as well from a man or woman, and I told them that I thought that question, in itself, was sexist. Afterwards, I realized I blew it."

The client may downplay or overemphasize material as a way of controlling the distance between the counselor and the client's vulnerabilities. In other words, the counselor is at the mercy of the client's ability and willingness to communicate relevant material. This fact underscores the importance of a good therapeutic alliance—one built on respect, trust, and empathic understanding. Appropriately high levels of trust can carry the client through his or her fears and permit the sharing of very emotionally intense information.

Making Excursions into the Past

Some people spend great amounts of counseling time describing their past experiences. Story telling is another name for this form of resistance. Even though the past is painful to the client, it is often less frightening than facing the present. One fairly accurate sign that describing the past may be an escape from the present is the client's inability to focus on the present for more than a few minutes. Before the counselor realizes it, the client has used some present situation to catapult the discussion back into the past. When the counselor attempts to hold the client in the present, he or she is likely to be accused of not being interested in the client but only in results.

Limiting the Counselor's Influence

This is seen when the client creates situations in which the counselor is "damned if you do and damned if you don't." A client may tell a counselor, "I wish you would give me more feedback." When the counselor does, the client responds, "If that's the kind of feedback you are going to give me, you can keep it."

Another client may say, "I want to talk about my father today, since I've had some really strong feelings about him this week." As the session nears the end, the client says, "Is it time to go already? Why did you let me ramble on so long about my father? I had several other things I wanted to discuss today!"

The counselor who is limited in this way cannot move far in the direction of effectively helping the client. For example, the wary counselor who has gotten burned by previous "damned if you do damned if you don't" traps may try to prevent a similar outcome by stating: "Before you start talking about your father today, maybe you should decide how much of the session you want to spend on him so that we don't get caught short on time like we did last week." The client angrily responds, "Look, this is very important to me! I can't time myself like you time a roast in the oven!"

The client blocks either route the counselor takes. To help this client, the counselor will have to continually point out the motives and consequences of this dynamic until the client begins to understand the reasons for it and hopefully chooses to replace it with some more productive way of interacting. While it is difficult to interact with a client who exhibits this form of resistance, it helps to remember that the client has good reasons for resorting to such an intense approach, and the client's fears are surfacing amidst a counseling relationship in which they have a better chance of being dealt with appropriately than in any of the client's other relationships.

Counselors need to exercise great caution when considering how people resist in counseling. The frustrations inherent in working with people whose issues also block their ability to improve makes it all too easy to overemphasize and misunderstand resistance and to view clients as rivals. Struggles can quickly develop between the "growth motives" of the counselor and the "resistant motives" of the client. Counselors must conscientiously avoid becoming suspicious detectives, ferreting out pockets of resistance and, upon finding one, accusing the client as if he or she were purposely recalcitrant. Thus it is particularly important for counselors to understand that it is not always a sign of resistance when a client declines to accept or refuses to carry out a specific suggestion. Clients can resist growth, but they can also resist what they may correctly identify as damaging.

Dealing with Resistance

Since a significant portion of a counselor's time is spent on resistance, counselors need to be able not only to recognize it but to deal with it effectively. Ramey (1998, p. 20) offers a useful approach when he writes, "Instead of ignoring or overpowering resistance, as is done with the traditional disease model of treatment, it is better to focus on the resistance so the client is able to discover the strength and function of resistance. Merely labeling the behavior as resistant and expecting that the client will no longer resist or deny is not effective, nor does it acknowledge the potential and the creative side of the resistance." The following points can be kept in mind by counselors when they attempt to deal more effectively with resistance.

Relaxed Vigilance

At the extremes, some counselors seem to find resistance everywhere; others never see it at all. An attitude of relaxed vigilance with regard to resistance is probably the most helpful and effective one. Counselors can easily disturb the counseling process by being too "picky." For example, it is quite natural for some clients to begin a session by remarking on the weather or asking the counselor how he or she is. The brief amount of time spent in what might be called "warm up" is quite adaptive. Labeling it and treating it as resistance would, in most cases, disturb the flow of the counseling process. On the other hand, if small talk continues for five or ten minutes into each session, resistance might well be an issue.

Along the same lines are friendly questions asking counselors if they are going away for their vacation, what courses they teach, or if they restrict their practice to certain types of individuals. Counselors sometimes create resistance by reacting to each casual statement as if it were resistance.

On the other hand, some counselors are not vigilant and rarely, if ever, identify patterns of resistance. They view the client's avoidance behavior as normal or "within his or her rights as a patient." It could be that these counselors view resistance as a negative commentary on themselves; hence, they do not wish to see it. It could also be that they lack the strength or skills to deal with resistance. If they do not see it, they do not have to handle it.

Correct Labeling

Before behavior is labeled and reacted to as resistance, it is important that the counselor be correct. Some behaviors that appear to be resistance are simply part of the ebb and flow found in relationships and in the counseling relationship. For example, people can sometimes arrive late or forget what they were going to talk about without it necessarily qualifying as resistance. Other behaviors that appear to be resistance may be very appropriate reactions to some mistreatment by the counselor. For example, counselors who want to discuss a particular "pet topic" because *they* need to, regardless of whether the client has more pressing issues with which to contend, are likely to meet with a healthy refusal that cannot and should not be called resistance.

It is particularly helpful for counselors to accumulate sufficient data regarding the client's resistance over a period of several sessions. By doing so counselors can identify a pattern that can be shared with the client. Concrete information about the pattern helps the client recognize and discuss resistance themes and increases the likelihood that the client will see that pattern as a form of resistance. Carefully worded and well-documented observations can become "eureka experiences" when shared with clients; important insights that are presented as clearly defined patterns are more easily changed.

Differentiating between Types

While resistance can be categorized in various ways, we offer three basic categories: content, characterological, and relational. These three types are quite similar to those described by Blatt and Erlich (1982): episodic (content), fundamental resistance to change (characterological), and transference (relational). It helps to identify which type of resistance the client exhibits because, as you will see, each type is managed differently. It is also important to recognize that "all three types of resistance always occur in an interpersonal field within the therapeutic dyad" (p. 75).

Content resistance means the client resists discussing specific areas that are particularly threatening. Some common thoughts and feelings that are resisted are those involving hurt, anger, sex, jealousy, distrust, loneliness, dishonesty, and hypocrisy. Communication may progress smoothly until an especially threatening area emerges. This resistance is not too difficult to manage. In most cases strengthening the therapeutic alliance is all that is needed to create a setting where the client can share more about particularly difficult issues.

Characterological resistance refers to a type seen in people who have a basically defensive personality. They typically avoid ideas, feelings, insights, and situations that pose a threat. These individuals often have a preferred mode of defense; that is, they typically use intellectualization, withdrawal, attack, or some other specific avoidance behavior. Their character defenses are found in the counseling relationship just as in any other relationship. Managing characterological resistance is more complicated than content resistance because the client's character defenses make it much more difficult to strengthen the therapeutic alliance. Persistence and patience are needed to help the client trust enough to adopt a less defensive style. Seemingly minor misunderstandings can produce rapid regressions to highly defensive states.

Relational resistance may exist between the client and the counselor. It manifests itself in the client psychologically withdrawing from or attacking the counselor. The reason for this resistance is often found in feelings of hurt, fear, or anger toward the counselor. People may feel hurt because the counselor does not seem to genuinely care about them; or people may fear that they are becoming too dependent on the counselor; or they may feel angry at the counselor for not giving in to their wishes. Another type of relational resistance is *transference*, in which the client displaces positive or negative feelings from a significant other in his or her life onto the counselor. Transference reactions can have both positive and negative effects. According to Gelso and Carter (1994, p. 298), "Transference itself may generally be viewed as a resistance, since its aim is to obscure awareness of what seems too painful to be known consciously" (see Gill, 1982, for a detailed examination of this phenomenon). They add, however, that resistance "in the form of positive transference can actually serve as an aid to the alliance." Transference reactions can produce increased amounts of resistance yet they can also make it possible for the counselor and client to work more effectively together.

Relational resistance is more complicated than content resistance but probably less complicated than characterological resistance. The advantage that relational resistance has over characterological resistance is that the relationship, in this case the therapeutic relationship, is the focus of the resistance. Clients who experience relational resistance are much more likely to explore this form of resistance in the form of transference or by direct discussions with their counselors.

While it is important for counselors to correctly identify which type of resistance the client is exhibiting, overlaps are commonplace (e.g., content resistance is prevalent in clients who also experience characterological resistance). Mistaking one form for another can also produce problems because counselors may try to manage resistance with an inappropriate strategy. For example, a counselor might incorrectly conclude that a client is reluctant to talk about his checkered employment history because of content resistance, but the truth is that the client's angry style of dealing with others is the major reason that he has lost so many jobs. That style is actually a form of characterological resistance that also produces patterns that might easily be mistaken for relational resistance.

Sharing

When the counselor feels confident that he or she has properly identified patterns of resistance that are interfering with the client's goals for change, it is important to begin the process of working through this resistance with the client. The counselor can share the behaviors upon which the belief is based and invite the client to discover what they mean. For example, a counselor might say, "I've noticed that you've been late for our sessions four out of the past six times. Do you have any idea as to what this could mean?"

If the resistance is close to awareness, the client might reply, "It probably means that I look forward to these sessions with the same degree of enthusiasm as going to the dentist." This rather forthright reply opens the door to exploring the nature of the resistance. People whose resistance is marked and deep will respond as they would to any threatening reality, "I wasn't late the last four times. I was late twice, and you were late once!" Another person might respond, "No, I don't have any idea what it means. But you obviously do; so why don't *you* tell me?" In these examples, the client is reluctant to examine the resistance. This presents one of the more challenging situations in counseling. If the counselor backs off, the outward signs of resistance will decrease but the effect of the resistance will persist. If the counselor pursues the issue too intensely, a great deal of tension may arise and resistance levels will increase. While each situation is different, as a general rule, it is most helpful to pursue the issue of the client's resistance by being forceful enough to motivate the client but not so forceful that the resistance increases and obstructs the client.

One approach could be, "Well, I see an important issue here, and I think it would be good to see if we can agree on the accuracy of my observations first. Then we'll see if we can understand what you think and feel about it." This attitude will be less threatening and more inviting than saying, "How can you say you don't see a problem when you've missed four out of the last six sessions! You say you want me to help you but, at the same time, you are tying my hands behind my back."

It can also be helpful for a counselor to ask clients to assess their progress over the last few sessions. Clients are often able to admit that something has happened to inhibit progress. Counselors can also compare what has been going on, or not going on, in recent sessions with the agreed-upon counseling goals. Discrepancies often become points of enlightenment.

Sometimes, when resistance is excessive and seemingly intransigent, a counselor must deal with it more directly. The counselor may offer the client the options of working with the counselor in understanding and hopefully reducing the resistance, focusing on some related but less threatening issue, or even possibly taking a break from counseling until the client is ready to deal with the issues.

A Positive Sign

No matter how clients react, it is very important for counselors to understand that resistance to growth and change is part of the human condition. In some cases resistance is an indicator that counseling is moving forward; in others it signals that the counselor does not have a strong enough alliance to pursue a particular issue with the client; in still others it may mean that the client has correctly decided to resist that which is not in his or her best interest. Effective counselors must continuously explore all three possibilities as they provide counseling services to their clients.

How and Why Counselors Resist

Typically, when resistance in counseling is discussed, the focus is on the client. However, counselors also exhibit resistance, and when counselors are resistant they are no more aware of it than clients are of their resistance. Ironically, the most persuasive evidence that counselors can resist is the fact that counselors often resent discussing that the possibility even exists; that is, they resist the concept of resistance in themselves. The following are some of the more common sources of counselor resistance.

Need Gratification

The counselor who is getting some basic needs met from the client will resist any interference with getting those needs met.

Personal relationship. The counselor finds the client attractive in one way or another and wants to foster a personal relationship as well as a professional one. The client may find this flattering and conspire with the counselor to draw out counseling as long as possible. Both discover a new problem each time counseling is about to terminate. The goal of counseling in this situation is not the client's improvement, but the continuance of the relationship between the counselor and the client.

Punishment. Improperly managed, intense countertransference reactions may cause a counselor to negatively symbolize the client in a specific way (that is, view the person as resembling a disliked parent, sibling, ex-spouse, or friend). Or the counselor may negatively symbolize the client in a general or stereotypic way (that is, view the person as a typical male, female, or member of a particular ethnic group). Although the majority of the counselor's motives are to help the client, unfortunately the counselor's unresolved feelings for someone in his or her past find their way into the counseling relationship and the client becomes a target for these feelings. Tragically, the counselor, under the ruse of being "honest," "strong," and "helpful," roughly pushes the client's nose in reality, destructively criticizes the client, and even encourages the client to take unreasonable risks that result in failure.

Control. Sometimes a counselor's need to control is stronger than the need to be helpful. The counselor has a set idea as to what the client needs to improve, and will not deviate from that. The counselor may think the client's growth hinges on getting a divorce, quitting a job, moving out of the parental home, or facing a past experience more fully. The counselor's tunnel vision interferes significantly with exploring other areas of the client's life that are equally, if not more, important. These counselors shrink the client to fit their narrow definition of what is helpful and unhelpful.

Lecturing. Sometimes counselors are on a philosophical bandwagon. They have found a particular theory or activity helpful and want to share its salutary benefits with their clients. The theory could be that of Freud, Adler, Frankl, Skinner, Rogers, or others. The activity could be meditating, jogging, praying, or dieting. Although any and all of these theories and activities could be therapeutic, their level of helpfulness depends on each individual. Adler's specific thoughts may greatly benefit one client, but they may be of little or no help for another.

Counselors should realize that counseling is different from lecturing and proselytizing. If people want to understand a particular theory or practice, they should attend workshops and read books on it. This will be infinitely less expensive than counseling and probably more informative. Theoretical and clinical discussions interfere with the client's development; at the end of counseling the client has gained a working knowledge of a theory and/or technique but may not have grown much as a person. Unfortunately, the client does not realize this because he or she confuses intellectual enlightenment in a theoretical sense with personal growth and development.

Dislike for the Client

Sometimes counselors may actually dislike the person they see in counseling, just as a client may dislike the counselor but continue in counseling. A disliked client may be seen because the counselor needs the income, because the client was assigned to the counselor by the clinic in which he or she works, or because the client has challenged the counselor in some way so that if the counselor terminates, the client wins some undeclared contest. Although the counselor tries hard to be professional, dislike for the client shows, and this significantly interferes with the growth process.

Signs of Counselor Resistance

The signs of resistance in the counselor are much the same as those seen in the client. The counselor may do any of the following:

1. cancels appointments or comes late (counselors always have "good reasons" for being late; clients seldom do)
2. talks *at* the client instead of listening *to* and talking *with* the client
3. daydreams and dozes off
4. talks about himself or herself instead of about the client
5. forgets pertinent information about the client
6. sets up impossible requirements
7. suddenly discovers that the client has "a special problem" and tries to refer the client to another counselor who specializes in the problem
8. refuses to consider as important the areas that the client perceives as important
9. acts either sarcastic or "buddy-buddy" with the client
10. introduces areas of discussion that are of interest to him or her but are not necessarily helpful to the client

While counselor resistance is important it is not something that can or should be resolved in the counseling relationship. Counselors are obliged to take the necessary steps to discover their resistance patterns and to adequately manage their resistance in their counseling relationships with clients. Consultation and supervision are the most common methods for accomplishing this, and individual or group counseling may be additionally necessary. When counselors work through their own resistance they are less likely to exhibit destructive resistance patterns with their own clients. Moreover, they are in a much better position to help clients experiencing difficulties that are similar to those that the counselor has worked through. A classic example helps illustrate the point. A counselor who had never experienced the death of an immediate family member made it a common practice to avoid talking to clients about such losses. She would happily refer the client to someone skilled in helping people deal with the loss of a loved one. Another counselor, like the first in the sense that he had never lost anyone in his immediate family, tended to minimize the feelings of clients who were dealing with loss issues. Audiotapes of this counselor's sessions revealed that his resistance was blocking clients from deeply exploring appropriate hurt and pain. The counselor eventually pursued individual therapy and quickly learned of deep-seated fears attached to the thought of losing his own parents. Working through these fears and understanding how they caused him to react in counseling sessions with his own clients freed him from resistance patterns that were unhealthy.

Summary

The classical view of resistance as an obstructive force that must be overcome in counseling has been correctly and adaptively replaced by a more accurate and workable perspective: clients are doing the best that they can given their experiences, strengths, weaknesses, and resources. They do not consciously block progress; they react in the best way they know. The counselor's task is to create a therapeutic alliance that is strong enough to help the client overcome predictable fears that are associated with change and overwhelming insights.

There are common patterns to resistance that can be found in all counseling relationships. For example, clients exhibit resistance around scheduling/meeting appointments, dealing with complicated or difficult issues, managing their relationship with the counselor, and pursuing change. When counselors explain to clients that these issues commonly surface in counseling and that there are varied ways of working through them, they build the client's trust and respect because they reveal their knowledge of the process and their willingness to persist. When clients understand that the counselor is in it, so to speak, for the long haul, resistance forces become more easily identified and much more manageable.

It is valuable to define counseling at least in part as the study of resistance. Appreciating the client's resistance and helping him or her manage these forces in ways that liberate and allow productive change and growth are activities more consistent with a modern perspective on resistance. Resistance both protects clients from that which might overwhelm them and interferes with their progress; it is one major reason that they have come to counseling. Brammer and MacDonald (1999, p. 57) have identified seven reasons why clients may offer resistance in the counseling relationship:

1. It is not easy to receive help.
2. It is difficult to commit oneself to change.
3. It is difficult to submit to the influence of a helper; help is a threat to esteem, integrity, and independence.
4. It is not easy to trust strangers and to be open with them.
5. It is not easy to see one's problem clearly at first.
6. Sometimes problems seem too large, too overwhelming, or too unique to share them easily.
7. Some cultural traditions deprecate giving and receiving help outside the family.

Each of these seven themes will be found in varying amounts in every client. Counselors will help clients manage resistance more effectively if they can keep these themes in mind, thus conveying to the client that they have a deep and personal understanding of how difficult it is to be a client. Such counselors will be more skillful at constructing a therapeutic relationship that will help the client overcome the conscious and unconscious forces that once protected them but now inhibit them in their efforts to improve.

Resistance is also found in counselors. These forces are particularly problematic because of their adverse effect on the client. Counselor resistance must be managed outside of the counseling relationship, either in supervision or consultation sessions. While supervision and consultation can help manage many counselor-based resistances, counselors may also need to pursue counseling for themselves.

Reflection Questions

1. A client misses key appointments and, when he does show up, accuses you of lacking sufficient interest in him. What is going on here? What is your gut response to his accusation? How *should* you respond? How *will* you respond?

2. Forgetting is a common and subtle form of resistance. How might you differentiate between forgetting (a benign lapse of memory) and forgetting as a form of resistance? How might you respond to clients who begin to establish a pattern of forgetting to complete important therapeutic tasks?

3. Name three behaviors that the counselor might display in the course of a counseling session that the client *should* resist.

4. Of the five motives for resistance in counselors, to which one might you be most susceptible?

5. Counseling is probably the only profession in which a great number of people who seek its services are often quite ambivalent about obtaining them. Why is this so and what challenges does it present to you as a counselor?

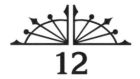

12

ISSUES THAT COUNSELORS FACE

U p to this point, much of our attention has been focused on the issues that clients face. We have offered some general explanations of why people who seek counseling experience emotional and psychological difficulties, what counselors can do to be of help, and how counseling can be accomplished in an effective, professional, and ethical manner. Regardless of which approach to counseling one employs, the effectiveness of the effort relies heavily upon one fundamental element of the counseling process: the counselor-client relationship. Counseling requires a commitment (often long-term) to and involvement with an individual who is likely to be experiencing a range of difficult and unpleasant feelings, conflicting thoughts, dire or painful circumstances, disturbing interpersonal relationships, or who has experienced various forms of trauma. Obviously, the formation and maintenance of such a deep clinical association with another person brings with it a number of challenges and hazards. The personal hazards and challenges that counselors face as they interact with clients form the focus of this chapter, and appropriate means to deal with these are suggested.

A counseling relationship is a microcosm of the human experience; examples of both the positive and the negative aspects of human nature will be found in this relationship. While the client's issues are basic concerns, the counselor's issues (personal and professional) are also important to the extent that the success of counseling is contingent upon how effectively the counselor manages the influences of both sets of issues. For better or worse, the counselor's issues deeply influence the counseling process. It goes without saying that effective counselors need to carefully maintain their physical and psychological health, but they also need to be continuously aware of the ways in which their life experiences, personal issues (resolved as well as unresolved), and level of professional training influence their efforts to help others. The counseling relationship is where counselor and client meet to explore the client's problems and issues, to identify strengths and weaknesses, to establish goals, and to pursue beneficial change on various levels (e.g., behavioral, emotional, or attitudinal). The counselor's personal and professional issues also play an important role in the way the counseling relationship is formed and maintained.

Though the counseling relationship appears as a single structure, according to several authors (Greenson, 1967; Gelso & Carter, 1994) it is formed from three related yet distinguishable components: "a working alliance, a transference configuration, and a 'real relationship' " (Gelso & Carter, 1994, p. 296). The successful counseling relationship can therefore be identified as a process that relies upon the counselor's ability to properly manage the working alliance, to elucidate the client's transference issues (and the counselor's countertransference issues), and to establish a well-bounded, psychologically healthy "real relationship." Conversely, problems in the counseling relationship may occur when the counselor's issues produce disturbances in one or more of the three components of the counseling relationship. We have therefore opted to categorize each of the issues that counselors face into one of three groups based on whether the particular issue is predominantly associated with transference/countertransference, the therapeutic alliance, or the "real relationship." Transference/countertransference issues are presented first because these issues deeply influence patterns that may be found in the remaining two categories, although it should be kept in mind that issues from any of the three categories can to some extent affect the others.

When countertherapeutic patterns arise in the counseling relationship, counselors often fail to identify the internal issues that form the source of their reactions while they usually sense the symptoms or reactions that the countertherapeutic patterns produce. For example, frustration (hostility), chronic boredom, or suffering (emotional pain) signal the existence of counselor issues related to the transference/countertransference component of the counseling relationship. Difficulties in the therapeutic alliance can surface as errors in clinical judgment, manipulative interactions, and termination problems (inappropriately hurrying or delaying termination), while poor management of the counseling relationship diminishes the real relationship. Clients play an important role in the formation and maintenance of countertherapeutic patterns, but the ultimate responsibility for identifying and correcting these difficulties rests with the counselor. We will discuss each of these three configurations and some of the patterns that can result within them. Categorizing these patterns in this way makes it easier to identify them and thus to resolve them.

ᐅᐅᐅ

The Transference/Countertransference Configuration

The transference configuration includes the client's transference as well as the counselor's countertransference (Gelso & Carter, 1994). In earlier chapters, transference and defense mechanisms (coping strategies) on the part of clients were examined, but countertransference—the counselor's transference to the client—has not been discussed as completely. It has been noted that the way clients react in the course of counseling is linked to the way that counselors interact with them. Resistance on the part of the client, for example, needs to be understood in the context of the interaction between counselor and client. Since clients are deeply sensitive to the counselor's mode of interaction it is especially important to consider the potential effect that countertransference can have on the counseling process. Additionally, countertransference issues can cloud the counselor's judgment and produce unhealthy distortions in the counseling relationship.

According to Hayes and associates (Hayes et al., 1998, p. 468), "The clinician's use of the self as a therapeutic instrument can be influenced greatly by countertransference. On the one hand, countertransference may cause therapists to act defensively in accordance with their own needs, perceive clients in distorted fashion, and exhibit poor clinical judgment. On the other hand, the insight that may be gleaned from countertransference can deepen therapists' awareness of relationship dynamics and provide valuable information about the course of treatment (Gelso & Carter, 1994; Gorkin, 1987; Singer & Luborsky, 1977; Tauber, 1954)."

Countertransference, like transference, is to be found in all therapeutic relationships; its presence is intrinsically neither good nor bad. Rather, it is the extent to which the counselor can identify countertransference forces and manage them that determines whether they improve or block the therapeutic effect of counseling. A basic principle identifies when helpful versus problematic uses of countertransference exist: when countertransference reactions are "acted out" between the counselor and the client, growth is blocked; when countertransference reactions are "worked out" between counselor and client, the latter's potential for growth is enhanced. One proviso must yet be kept in mind: the counselor should be aware of the countertransference reactions if he or she is to be able to work things through rather than act things out. If the counselor discovers countertransference, appropriate clarification is in order.

An example will help to clarify this principle and illustrate how countertransference can be productively used in the counseling process. A young man began weekly counseling sessions with a counselor who was about the age of his father. The client described his father as a demanding and highly critical person who often pressed his will on others and who was especially directive with members of his immediate family. Because father and son had struggled through so many conflicts, neither held much hope for any improvement in their relationship.

By a twist of fate, the counselor had a son who was about the same age as the client. Similarly to the client, the counselor's son was confused about a career path and was reluctant to take any steps toward securing employment in spite of having graduated from college more than eight months before. The counselor, because he had lost confidence in his son's ability to find a suitable job on his own, spent a great deal of time making recommendations and outlining various scenarios for his son to follow. And he did exactly the same thing to his client, unaware that his behavior in the two cases was identical. The counselor had unwittingly become very directive. In clinical terms the counselor was "acting out" his countertransference instead of working it out with his client. Though the client was not aware of what was happening, his comments to both the counselor and to a close friend offered important clues. The client told his friend that the counseling sessions felt a lot like the unproductive talks he had been having with his father, and he told the counselor that he wanted to quit because he needed the time to look for work. He refined this decision by saying that if stopping counseling was not an option, he was certain that they would have to reduce the frequency of the sessions from weekly to monthly meetings.

The example illustrates how easily and unconsciously destructive countertransference patterns can emerge. By acting out the countertransference, the counselor misses an opportunity to work through a collection of issues that are adversely affecting both himself and his client. If the sessions were to continue to follow the same course, the counselor and the client could only replicate the troubled relationships in each of their lives without thereby improving.

It would have been far better for the counselor to recognize the heightened potential for countertransference because of the counselor's and client's complementary real-life roles. Had the counselor attained a clearer awareness he might have been able to work through rather than act out the countertransference. He might have revealed to the client his own uncharacteristic urges to suggest courses of action to the client and that he was aware of an amount of frustration within himself when he sensed the client's uncertainty and confusion concerning career goals. The client might then have responded that this was exactly the way his father acts when talking to him, and he might even add that he wonders if there is some behavior pattern of his that contributes to his dad's reactions. The client might also mention that this pattern of interaction is not limited to his father, but that his friends often become annoyed at his indecision and that many of them either make fun of him or just tell him frankly what they think he should do.

By working through countertransference issues, this client would have gained useful information about how another person, in this case the counselor, saw him; furthermore, it could have motivated him to explore issues within himself that might contribute to this troublesome behavior pattern. The counselor's countertransference reactions would then have been harnessed in a way that helped rather than hindered the client's progress.

While the example was presented to illustrate countertransference issues, it also illustrates how difficulties in the configurations that form the counseling relationship deeply influence progress in other areas and, in turn, the overall effectiveness of the counseling process. For example, a counselor who possessed the clinical skills and theoretical sophistication to form an effective therapeutic alliance might still encounter many complications in the overall counseling effort if countertransference reactions were poorly managed.

Frustration and Hostility

The previous example illustrates what may happen when a counselor's frustration is acted out instead of worked out. Frustration and hostility are important concerns in counseling because counselors are often exposed to the client's frustration and hostility and because counselors may themselves experience such feelings toward their clients. While counselors generally think of themselves as well-meaning people who want to help others and who expect to be appreciated, they may find that their efforts evince hostility from their clients. And while the client's frustration and hostility toward them may confuse and frustrate counselors, their own frustration and hostility toward their clients will tend to scare and surprise them. Counselors frequently need help managing these feelings in both cases.

Sources. The client's as well as the counselor's hostility may flow from several sources. Most often, such hostility is a reaction to deep-seated fears. This explains why the more some people feel threatened, the more they attack. Unfortunately, people are usually unable to realize that fear is the cause of their anger and so remain uncertain or unaware of what frightened them. The anger causes them to focus outward rather than inward, protecting the area of vulnerability from both others and themselves but also forming a barrier to exploring the source of their fears. This coping mechanism keeps them from their fears but it also keeps them angry.

The more frightened clients are, the more they will view both the counselor and the counseling process as threatening. Clients may fear that (1) they will become too dependent on the counselor, (2) the counselor will reject them, or (3) the counselor will introduce them to disturbing parts of themselves. For one or another of these reasons, clients may use their anger to keep both their fears and their counselors at a safe distance.

Not unlike the client's frustration and hostility, the counselor's frustration and hostility toward the client are also fear-based. Counselors may fear (1) that their interaction with clients could cause them to be become aware of disturbing parts of themselves, (2) that clients might harm or injure themselves or others, or (3) that their clients will reject them. While it is helpful for counselors to understand that most hostility directed at them is generated by fear (and that they can try to help the client concentrate on the fears that are causing the hostility), dealing with their own fears is quite another matter. *Consultation, supervision,* and *personal counseling* offer counselors three different and useful forums for managing hostility toward clients as well as other forms of countertransference. The last section of this chapter discusses each of these alternatives.

Hostility stems in part from *frustrated needs*. When people are unable to meet basic psychological needs, their ability to stand up to stress drops dramatically. Such individuals become oversensitive to stimuli. As one woman said, "What was once simply a leaky faucet now sounds like a crashing waterfall. What once sounded like two children playing quietly together, now sounds like a yard full of screeching kindergartners." Such clients will respond to the counselor's well-intended comments or questions with some variation of, "How dare you think that about me!" The client's hypersensitivity will result in an overreaction in counseling as well as in other life situations.

Counselors themselves enter the counseling relationship with various expectations and needs. Problems may quickly arise should the counselor's needs become enmeshed with the client's behavior. Inappropriate frustration on the part of the counselor can pollute a counseling relationship should the counselor's attempts to help the client fail and the counselor's misdirected needs to feel successful, effective, or appreciated through the client not be met.

Hostility is often directed at a counselor who comes to embody some *external* or *internal conflict* of the client's. The counselor may then stand for or symbolize a feared or disliked parent, spouse, ex-spouse, or authority figure. The counselor may also pose a threat by espousing the cause of freedom to an overcontrolled person or by presenting an image of effectiveness to a client who feels a sense of failure. These transference reactions also may appear in the form of countertransference reactions and thus affect the counselor. Clients may come to symbolize a feared or disliked parent, ex-spouse, or other important person in the counselor's history.

Hostility can result from the *intense pressure* clients may feel from other people and from within themselves. A troubled client may be likened to a balloon that is extended to its fullest. The slightest pressure may cause the balloon to burst. Should the counselor create the slightest bit of pressure, the client is likely to explode at the counselor. A cascading shower of negative feelings can be difficult and disconcerting for the average counselor. Counselors are by no means immune to the same pressures: under certain conditions they may also displace similar pent-up feelings onto their clients. However, such a displacement of feelings on the part of the counselor is clearly inappropriate and counterproductive. Counselors need to come to grips with such feelings and be prepared to manage them outside of the counseling relationship.

Hostility and frustration are not always the result of transference. Some hostility directed toward the counselor may be quite appropriate because the counselor may be (1) relating with the client in an unjust manner, (2) putting forth a lukewarm effort to help the client, (3) continually focusing on the client's negative behavior, or (4) continually suspecting the client's motives. While an explanation focusing on transference may be convenient, it may not be accurate. Properly distinguishing between client reactions that show transference and those that are accurate responses to the counselor's behavior is essential to effective practice. Making such distinctions requires a level of emotional and professional integrity and the aid of consultants and colleagues or supervisors.

Dealing with hostility and frustration. In most effective counseling relationships, counselors commonly encounter periodic expressions of hostility from clients. As this is to be expected, it may be a cause for concern when such hostility does not surface. The problem is often related to the counselor's inability to confront the client. For example, countertransference issues that block the counselor's ability to confront clients may cause counselors to skillfully and assiduously avoid challenging clients in ways that could evoke hostility. They unconsciously enter into a pact that neither one will confront the other, often a symptom of what has been referred to as *benign countertransference*. Clients who see such counselors often view counseling as a "pleasant experience" and their counselors as "awfully kind" but they also sense that very little gets accomplished. At the other extreme are counselors who seem to always find themselves in the midst of battles with their clients. The *hostile countertransference* found in these counselors causes them to produce counseling sessions that sound more like family feuds than therapeutic encounters. Such counselors reflexively react to the client's hostility with their own hostility, never addressing the causes.

When counselors and clients learn what causes their hostility and frustration, they are in a better position to use their feelings productively. Counselors should be prepared to be the targets of both just and unjust hostility. Counselors who consciously or unconsciously avoid situations that will result in being targeted are not able to help their clients work through the coping mechanisms that block their growth. In a sense, counselors are like sparring partners. They must absorb some punishment so that the client's strengths and weaknesses can be diagnosed, but they don't permit themselves to be damaged. If the counselor acts like a punching bag that merely absorbs punishment, the client may feel a great release of tension, but will learn nothing about himself or herself. Thus, unresolved countertransference issues can cause counselors to become hostile or benign influences in the client's life instead of productive influences.

In summary, counselors experience varying amounts of frustration and hostility toward clients for the same reasons that clients feel hostile toward them. Clients may pose some threat to the counselor's self-concept, or the counselor may be experiencing levels of personal frustration that flow over into the counseling relationship. The client may symbolize a disliked person or highlight a latent weakness in the counselor. Properly working through feelings of frustration and hostility within the counseling relationship offers clients a valuable opportunity for psychological growth; acting out hostility and frustration produces destructive consequences. Counselors who find themselves in disputes with their clients will need to quickly assess their contribution to the problem and take immediate steps to rectify it.

Boredom

Boredom, while markedly dissimilar from feelings of hostility and frustration, is another common reaction that counselors may encounter. While people may become tired or lose interest for many different reasons, they commonly cite an uninteresting topic or person as the source of their boredom. Are there uninteresting topics or clients in counseling? The short answer is yes, and there are valid reasons for counselors to become bored: (1) clients often struggle with serious psychological problems that limit their levels of uniqueness, individuality, and vibrancy, and (2) people who share a common psychological diagnosis may tend to sound similar to one another in counseling, even though in their well state, they are very different. However, in order to form a therapeutic relationship the counselor must relate to the client's unique qualities, not just the symptoms of the disorder. When patterns of boredom develop in counselors, potentially serious problems often develop.

Beginning counselors seldom experience boredom principally because of the novelty of their experiences. Each day they encounter a client with a different problem, try out newly acquired skills, and assume new responsibilities. But like any other behavior that is repeated, counseling can become routine. After a counselor sees 25 or 50 depressed people, he or she may begin to look for patterns associated with the disorder and begin to ignore other equally important qualities that are unique to the client. Thus while experience improves skills and expands knowledge it can also interfere with the formation of a productive counseling relationship.

Problems created by boredom. Boredom distances the counselor from the client, and it does not escape detection. Clients easily sense the separation—even the most disturbed people can tell when the counselor is bored and distracted. The distance that boredom creates deprives the client of a sense of security, acceptance, and empathic understanding—essential elements to all forms of counseling. Counselor boredom itself is not the only problem. The counselor's inappropriate reactions to boredom create additional difficulties. For example, when some counselors become bored they daydream and substitute fantasy for the rigor of counseling. While bored counselors may delude themselves into thinking they can listen to a client with one ear and attend to their own thoughts with the other, they cannot. Clients are not fooled by well-timed nods, grunts, smiles, and frowns offered by the counselor in order to create the impression of full attention. Most clients are aware of the attempted ruse and resent it, even though they may not raise the issue directly. Counselors may also attempt to deal with their boredom by inappropriately provoking the client emotionally in an improper attempt to artificially add intensity to the session. This unprofessional practice disturbs the counseling relationship, distracts the client from focusing on more important issues, and obscures the problems that are developing in the counselor-client relationship.

Whether the counselor inappropriately daydreams or tries to get the client to react emotionally, he or she ignores important pieces of information about the client. The client may feel that what he or she has to say is important, but that the counselor is not astute enough to recognize it; or the client may conclude that the information is not important, since the counselor did not react. Ultimately, the counselor's boredom leads him or her to react inappropriately to the client. The problem compounds itself, and as the counselor becomes *more* indifferent and detached, so does the client—the "counseling process" grinds painfully to a halt.

Solutions.   When counselors find themselves bored, they must first assess their contribution to the emotion. If the counselor is tired or distracted by outside concerns, the counselor will need to take appropriate corrective action. In addition to rectifying the situation, the counselor will also need to explain to the client: "I'm sorry. I'm distracted today. Could you repeat the last of what you said so that I can catch up with you?" When a problem arises in counseling, it is very important for the client to know what contribution both the counselor and client make to the problem and what responsibilities each has in resolving the difficulty.

If a counselor feels that he or she is doing everything reasonable to be attentive but the client's presentation is lifeless or wearisome, then the counselor may need to communicate this reaction to the client. The counselor may state, "The way you are talking and the things you are talking about make it difficult for me to concentrate on what you're saying. I do not want to lose contact with you; so maybe we'd better talk about what's going on." The client may respond positively by saying something like, "You know, I *knew* you were getting bored. In fact, I'm boring *myself*. I'm glad you stopped me."

On the other hand, the client may respond in an obviously offended way and say, "Well, I'm sorry. I didn't mean to *bore* you. I didn't realize that I was here to entertain you." The counselor can simply respond, "I know what I said was difficult to hear. It was difficult for me to say, because I knew you might feel hurt. But I do feel that it's important for both of us to remain alert, and any time I'm losing my alertness, I have to tell you so that we can see what the problem is. I'm sure there will be times when I am talking and you drift off, and I hope that you will also be willing to tell me."

It is important that the counselor not only confront the issue of boredom but also help the client understand its meaning and dynamics—first in the context of the counseling relationship and then later in terms of other relationships in the client's life. Boredom may be linked to (1) clients who are so repressed that little or no emotion surfaces in the sessions, (2) clients whose fears produce heightened levels of resistance that block sharing any meaningful material that could evoke a negative reaction from the counselor, (3) clients who live such passive lives that they have few if any fresh experiences to talk about, (4) clients who may use boredom as a form of resistance designed to protect by neutralizing many of the counselor's abilities, or (5) clients who may unconsciously use boredom as a way to frustrate the counselor.

Counselors can make changes in the way they schedule counseling sessions to counteract boredom. They may reschedule clients to a time when the counselor and the client are more alert. They may see the clients for two half-sessions a week instead of one whole session. They may have the clients keep a journal and go over parts of it at each session. And sometimes it is helpful to take a more active, confrontational approach to cut through the client's lethargy. Group counseling can also be used as an adjunct to individual counseling as a means of sparking some affect within the client.

Counselors can also bore clients. They can bore clients with a bland, sedentary manner that causes the client to feel that he or she is talking to an inanimate object or to someone devoid of feeling and thought. Counselors also bore clients when they overtalk, speaking at length about some dynamic that has come up in counseling, about their favorite theories, or about their personal lives. Self-disclosure has only a limited use in most counseling approaches, and countertransference issues are more likely behind the counselor's impulse to talk excessively than any clinically defensible rationale. Unfortunately, many clients suffer in silence while the counselor relates stories that are essentially useless and boring.

Counselors who keep their reactions succinct and clear and their questions short and to the point will not be boring. They are less likely to see their clients react with glazed, drowsy eyes; finger or toe tapping; or bland, uninterested facial expressions. When these indications appear, counselors can address themselves to the signs and ascertain their meaning, but they must also be willing to accept partial responsibility for the boredom present in the counseling relationship.

Suffering and Emotional Pain

The client's suffering and emotional pain appear in counseling in two ways: (1) clients pursue counseling because they are experiencing emotional pain and suffering; and (2) the client's emotional pain and suffering surface as a direct result of counseling. A person beginning grief counseling following the loss of a loved one is a common example of the former. A couple who learn in the course of marital counseling that one member of the couple no longer wishes to remain in the marriage provides a good example of the second possible case. Regardless of how emotional pain and suffering become part of the counseling process, the fact is that counselors are regularly exposed to the intense pain of their clients and often play an important role in helping the client work through these very difficult emotions.

Suffering in the counselor. In order for counselors to be effective they must be empathic and when they are empathic they are affected by their own pain and suffering as well as that of their clients. Counselors realize that in the course of counseling there will be times when they will need to confront clients knowing full well that many confrontations are designed to invite the client to explore painful or difficult situations. While they may realize that such pain is necessary if the client is to grow, the necessity of this course does not reduce the client's pain. The decision to pursue such a course should never be easy or its necessity taken for granted.

Counselors may also experience anguish when the client is psychologically hurt due to damage caused by other people. While the client may cry out for help, the counselor realizes that the pain will lessen only as the client's natural healing process begins to function. Counselors help their clients most by being present with them as they endure pain or grieve the losses. The impulse to remove the pain from the client may be more a function of the counselor's uneasiness with such intense feelings than of the client's problems with them.

Inadvertently causing pain in the client may also give rise to suffering in the counselor. By some action or inaction, the counselor may be responsible for emotionally hurting the client and causing iatrogenic pain. This suffering is perhaps the most severe that counselors must endure because they realize they are the cause of a pain that may have little or no therapeutic value. To spend several precious counseling sessions helping a client deal with suffering caused by the counselor can be both painful and humiliating.

Generally, it is useful for counselors to share their feelings, pain, and suffering with the client so long as guilt-producing or sympathy-provoking statements that focus attention on the counselor are avoided. The counselor must share such feelings in a way that reflects both genuine empathy and supportive strength to the client.

Suffering in the client.   The desire to reduce suffering is a primary reason that many people choose to become counselors. Ironically, a common side effect of a counselor's work is that he or she *causes* suffering because suffering is an inherent part of personal growth. Counselors must reconcile their desire to soothe hurt with the realization that most effective counseling necessarily entails suffering.

Counselors are instrumental causes (although not primary causes) of suffering for a number of reasons. They must introduce people to painful insights. Because of a counselor's probing, a mother discovers that she is jealous of her daughter, whom she loves dearly; a father discovers that his busy schedule has caused his son or daughter to feel unloved by him; a son gradually realizes that he has been exploited by a parent; or a married client is led to the realization that his or her spouse has serious problems. Insights such as these can be excruciatingly painful.

Counselors can cause suffering when they must prod a client to grow, despite the client's strong needs to stagnate or regress. Clients may plead with counselors to leave them alone or allow them to regress. But an effective counselor can kindly but firmly encourage such clients to move in the direction of growth, to accept their protests as desires to avoid the suffering, and to cooperate with them as they explore the pain that may well motivate them to change.

Counselors who are unable to encourage or to allow people to suffer do damage. Some counselors may believe they are helping clients by shielding them from painful feelings but in most cases they are indirectly signaling that the client is too weak to deal with these important feelings. Counselors send the same inappropriate message when they try to become more supportive than the client needs them to be. While there are situations when clients need to be shielded, it is important to be able to distinguish between those that are driven by counselor countertransference issues and those that are based on sound clinical judgment. There are cases where the counselor's reluctance to deal with emotional pain may inhibit the client more than the client's own resistance.

Counselors may also inappropriately cope with the client's suffering by becoming hardened and matter-of-fact about it. They are actually detached from their clients and clearly unempathic. They may even become counterphobic—that is, cause some unnecessary suffering in clients as proof to themselves that they are not afraid to see people suffer.

Still other counselors become cynical about or angry at people who are suffering. Their distorted view of suffering sees it as a manipulative ploy to force the counselor into doing something he or she does not wish to do, into feeling sorry for the client, or into feeling guilty for being instrumental in the suffering.

Effective counselors recognize that change is always accompanied by varying amounts of emotional pain and suffering. Counselors learn to help clients explore these important but difficult feelings and they realize that they must be affected by their own as well as the client's feelings if the process is to be productive. For a further discussion of the role of suffering in counseling, see May (1967a, pp. 157–162).

⚘

The Working Alliance

The working alliance is the formal therapeutic relationship. The strength of the working alliance is based on the extent to which counselor and client "agree on the goals of their work, agree on the tasks that are useful to attain the goals, and experience an emotional bond with each other" (Gelso & Carter, 1994, p. 297). To develop a working alliance counselors need a sound technical understanding of the counseling process, experience in translating theoretical knowledge into clinical practice, a serviceable method for understanding the client and his or her symptoms, and the ability to tailor a treatment plan to the client that honors his or her psychological strengths and weaknesses. The therapeutic alliance relies heavily, but not exclusively, upon the counselor's knowledge of theoretical, technical, and clinical skills. Problems that develop in the working alliance include manipulating clients, poor clinical decisions, and poorly managed or inappropriate termination. Each will be discussed in detail.

Manipulation

Manipulation occurs when a counselor employs veiled tactics to induce the client to meet the counselor's needs. The result is always detrimental. For example, a counselor induces a client to remain in counseling under the rationalization that the client needs to develop more competencies when, in fact, the counselor has actually manipulated the client so that the counselor could get his or her personal needs met in the relationship.

It is important to distinguish between manipulating and confronting. In confronting, a reasonable amount of pressure is placed on a client in a forthright manner by bringing conflicted views, values, behaviors, feelings, and so forth into the client's awareness. For example, a counselor may place some pressure on an unemployed client to schedule job interviews by stating, "It seems that two patterns surface when we talk: Each week you clearly illustrate to me how important it is for you to obtain a job, and yet you share that you have not had time to complete the job application forms." This situation is different from manipulation in two important ways. First, the pressure is created within the client by surfacing the contradictory elements of the client's behavior. Second, the purpose is to help the client resolve the internal conflict. In manipulation the counselor's need takes precedence and the conflict is therefore between the counselor and the client—not within the client. Thus in manipulation, the resolution of the conflict emphasizes the counselor's needs at the expense of the client's.

Manipulation is a process that can be identified in many forms of interpersonal relationships. People resort to this tactic for many reasons. Clients often seek to manipulate counselors, and counselors may inappropriately tend toward manipulating their clients. Client manipulation of counselors will be covered first.

Manipulation of the counselor. Clients may seek to manipulate counselors for one or more of the following reasons.

To meet needs. When clients feel intense pressure to meet one or more particular needs they may unconsciously set up the counselor as the one to satisfy this need. While it is legitimate for a client to get needs met that are appropriate to a well-bounded counseling relationship, it is unhealthy for a client to manipulate counselors to meet such needs and to manipulate counselors into meeting inappropriate needs. The boundaries of the therapeutic relationship become blurred, dangerous ethical violations become more likely, and the client is blocked from the pursuit of healthy and appropriate relationships. For example, clients needing to feel secure may manipulate the counselor into taking care of and protecting them. They can do this by inducing the counselor to make decisions for them; to represent and intercede for them in conflicts with parents, spouses, teachers, or bosses; to spend inordinate amounts of time with them (prolonged or extra sessions, phone calls, letters); and to give assurances and make promises that are unrealistic and inappropriate, such as, "No matter what you do, I would never reject you."

A counselor who has strong needs to protect, nurture, guide, and be depended upon will be particularly susceptible to such a client's manipulation. Under the rationalization that the client needs a "psychological bodyguard," the counselor inappropriately assumes the crippling role of benevolent protector.

People with unmet needs for love may attempt to manipulate the counselor into loving them or at least having "special" feelings for them. These attempts may include being sexually seductive, ingratiating ("You're the best counselor I ever had"), overcooperative in a superficial way, or "dressing up for the counselor"—that is, discovering which qualities the counselor finds attractive and assuming these qualities to please him or her. Counselors who are not receiving sufficient love in their own lives will be especially susceptible to these manipulations and may adopt a "my favorite patient" attitude toward the client. This can weaken the counselor and taint his or her perceptions. Such a counselor is unable to entertain the possibility that the client is unconsciously manipulating the counselor to their mutual detriment.

Sometimes clients have destructive needs—for example, the need to be rejected. If they can get the counselor to reject them, they can prove that they are worthless, unlovable, and beyond hope. This "proof" then serves as a license to indulge in more self-destructive behavior.

These individuals behave in abrasive ways toward the counselor. Typical provoking behaviors are coming late for, canceling, or failing appointments; making inordinate demands on the counselor for time, adjustments in fee, and goodwill; asking hostile questions of the counselor; annoying the counselor by putting feet up on the desk or leaving in the middle of a session for an "important appointment"; or divulging what goes on in counseling to friends and relatives in a derogatory way. These behaviors can eventually result in the counselor's terminating the relationship.

To neutralize a threat. Counselors, by definition, are a source of threat to clients. The reason is that one of their main roles is to confront people with aspects of reality they have a vested interest in avoiding. Such confrontations are anxiety producing and sometimes painful. Some common and subtle ways the client attempts to neutralize this are seen in the following ploys, although they are seldom articulated as boldly.

1. *Bribing*: "I'll work hard on this area (problems at work) if you don't confront me with a more threatening area (problems in marriage)."

2. *Blackmailing*: "If you don't confront me with my school fears, I won't confront you with your phoniness."

3. *Distracting*: "Let's talk about my boss today. You'll find that more interesting than talking about whether I've moved out of my parents' house yet."

4. *Seducing*: "I think if you could hold me really tight and I could feel your warmth and strength, it would do more for me (and you) than if we talk about my boring parents."

5. *Assaulting*: "Let's talk about whether you ever feel guilty just sitting there listening to people and making a fortune instead of about why I get drunk three times a week."

Most counselors have an area that is particularly susceptible to manipulation. Clients could manipulate the counselor by making statements that tap into these vulnerable areas.

I thought you'd be more *understanding* than that.

I thought counselors weren't supposed to be *judgmental*.

I know you're a *compassionate* person; so I'm not afraid to tell you that. . . .

I know you're a *reasonable* person and wouldn't make unreasonable demands on me.

You're the only person I can *trust* not to hurt me.

You're somebody I could fall in *love* with, but I know it would be inappropriate.

I know you *care* about me as a patient, but I don't think you care about me personally.

How can you say that! I thought you were more *sophisticated* than that.

I thought you had a *sense of humor,* but I guess you don't.

You told me you wanted to be *helpful* to me, and now that I could use your help, you don't want to give it.

It is helpful for counselors to know what their vulnerable areas are so they can diminish their susceptibility to manipulation.

Important points.   There are several important points to consider regarding clients who tend to manipulate counselors. First, most of the time when people manipulate counselors they are unaware of what they are doing. Their manipulative behavior is being guided by unconscious needs, feelings, and motives. When confronted with their manipulative behavior, people commonly react with genuine hurt, confusion, anger, and denial.

Second, it is counterproductive for the counselor to take a defensive attitude ("You can't manipulate me") toward people for two reasons. One is that people *can* manipulate counselors, especially people who have used manipulation as a survival technique for 20 or 30 years. The second is that such an attitude will invite a challenge and/or put people on the defensive for no good reason.

Third, it is unhelpful to assume a cynical attitude toward people who manipulate counselors. Since *all* people manipulate counselors, cynicism would be an integral part of every counseling relationship. The helpful counselor can learn to manage and confront manipulation without resorting to cynicism.

Manipulation by the counselor.   Counselors, as we have already illustrated, can harm clients through manipulation. The following are some examples of how this can occur.

A counselor wishes to terminate a woman because he has become bored or irritated by her. Instead of dealing with and communicating these feelings, he either leads the woman to believe that she is progressing significantly better than she is or tells her that she is not ready for the next phase and should take a vacation from counseling.

A counselor wishes to get into a personal relationship with the client to meet his or her own needs for affection and warmth. Rationalizing that the client *needs* to show warmth and affection, the counselor offers himself or herself as someone with whom the client can practice.

A counselor feels that religion is contrary to psychological health. Without relating this belief to the client, she gradually weans him away from his religious beliefs, which have, until now, assumed a place of importance and support in his life.

A counselor needs to feel successful so she encourages a client to apply to graduate school or accept a promotion under the pretext that this would be a good opportunity for growth. In fact, the counselor is using the client to meet her own needs to feel successful and is less interested in whether such a move would be beneficial for the client.

The common denominators in these examples are that the counselor is not being honest with the client, is motivated primarily by personal needs, and is encouraging behavior that either is or could be detrimental to the client.

Counselors should remember that the most effective ways to help clients change bear no resemblance at all to manipulation. This axiom is as valid when applied to clients as to counselors. The point is that the more counselors realize that they are capable of harming a client through manipulation, the more they can take steps to prevent this.

Errors in Clinical Judgment

All counselors make mistakes. The subject matter that counselors work with—namely, human behavior—is infinitely complex and subtle. It does not lend itself to precise measurement; highly reliable and valid diagnostic procedures; or standardized, universally accepted treatment protocols. Therefore, it is imperative that counselors realize they will make mistakes and be ready to admit and learn from them. This awareness helps counselors realize that the potential for errors makes it important for them to be open to consultation and supervision experiences where they can be frank and honest and where they can develop methods to correct mistakes and errors.

Being weak.   Just as clients are better able to manage their emotional difficulties if they have sufficient levels of ego strength, counselors are better able to manage the rigors of the counseling relationship if they are strong enough to confront both themselves and their clients. Just as many problems with children can be traced to weak parents, many problems in counseling can be traced to weak counselors. Weak counselors allow themselves to be pressured by the client. They do not function according to their initial judgment, but accede to the client's opinions and wishes.

While it is important to realize that there are weak counselors it is also important to realize that counselors may be strong with some clients and weak with others. Basically strong counselors trust their judgments, are willing to expose their clinical decisions to other trusted and respected professionals, and stick to their decisions so long as they prove to be helpful.

The following is an example of how counselor weaknesses can create myriad problems. A counselor determines that marital group counseling is the appropriate choice for a woman who has come to him for evaluation and treatment. When she refuses his recommendation, he agrees to see her in individual counseling. He then suggests that her husband join them immediately for conjoint sessions. She refuses this recommendation by insisting that she needs time in individual counseling to "get used to it" before her husband joins them. After some discussion, she convinces the counselor that this "makes sense." Two months pass and the counselor and client form a fairly strong alliance in the eight weekly sessions. The counselor decides that couples counseling would be a problem at this point because he has formed a counseling relationship with the woman and not with her husband. The counselor urges the client to obtain couples counseling from another counselor—one whom neither of them has worked with before. The client refuses this suggestion and counters by stating that since the counselor already knows a lot about their problems through her work with him, then he should see them both. Eventually, the husband is invited to counseling, but he insists that he can come only on Saturdays, the counselor's day off. The counselor feels that as long as the husband is motivated to enter counseling, he might as well see them on Saturday mornings. He wants the couple to discuss their sexual relationship, which appears to be the heart of their problem, at least according to everything he learned in his eight sessions with the wife. The husband refuses to discuss their sex life in front of "a stranger" and insists "there's nothing to discuss anyway."

The counselor convinces himself that the man needs more time; so he allows the couple to discuss superficial issues for a dozen sessions. Meanwhile, the couple has not made a payment for four months. The counselor does not want to broach this subject, because the husband's motivation for counseling is precarious and he may use the counselor's "money grabbing" as an excuse to pull out of counseling.

Between sessions, the counselor gets a call from the woman, who says she is extremely upset and is going to swallow a bottle of tranquilizers. Although the counselor would ordinarily call the police, he does not do so, because the woman's husband is a police officer and the couple would be embarrassed. Consequently, he goes to the couple's house and remains for two hours until the husband arrives.

Only the wife appears at the next session. Her husband hit her for "pulling the suicide routine." He announced he did not want any part of the "counseling scene" because it was ruining what little marriage they had. She tells the counselor that after he punched her, they talked more than they had in years and agreed that they could make the marriage work without counseling. She assures the counselor that they will pay off the bill someday, but she would appreciate it if he could be patient. The counselor assures her there is no rush.

If the couple's dynamics had been slightly different, she might have committed suicide, or her husband might have killed her, or the couple could have sued the counselor for anything they concocted. Had the counselor been strong enough to trust his judgment and set limits accordingly, the damage would have been prevented, either because the couple would not have cooperated and quit or because the counselor's strength would have served as the adhesive the couple needed to grow.

Not admitting errors. Problems increase in counseling when counselors ignore or fail to admit their mistakes. The truth is that even experienced counselors make errors, sometimes serious ones. It is not the presence or absence of mistakes that separates effective from poor counselors; it is their willingness to admit their mistakes both to themselves and to the clients and their willingness to take steps to correct the errors.

There are several ways that counselors avoid admitting mistakes. Ironically, one way is never to take a risk. The counselor who only sits, nods, and makes reassuring sounds is unlikely to make an obvious mistake. Although these counselors do not view it as such, they are making one large mistake—the mistake of being afraid to take the risks with the client that are necessary for growth in counseling.

The second way to avoid admitting mistakes is to deny that the client's problems are worsening or the counselor's ability to help is being diminished. The client is getting more depressed, but this is misinterpreted as a "good sign." The counselor views his own daydreaming through a quarter of each session as "only human, considering the time of day."

Third, counselors can deflect the responsibility for any problems that arise onto the client. Counselors may incorrectly assure themselves that if only the client were more cooperative, intelligent, motivated, or courageous, counseling would be progressing nicely.

The fourth way to avoid admitting mistakes is to believe the seductive myth that one does not "make mistakes." Everything that happens in counseling is considered "grist for the mill." This erroneous belief is based on the concept that there are no right or wrong ways to proceed—only different levels of understanding and communication between the counselor and the client, levels that will naturally come to approach each other in time with care and warmth.

The fact is that counselors *can* make mistakes in counseling. They overinterpret or underinterpret situations; they react prematurely or too late; they are more directive or more nondirective than is helpful at the time; they get decoyed away from important issues; they interrupt too soon or not soon enough; they think they always know more about the client than the client does; they affirm and confront at the wrong times; they don't smile when they should, and they laugh when they shouldn't; they are tough when they should be gentle and gentle when they should be tough; they stand by the limits they set when they should be more flexible and are flexible when they should stand by the limits; and they daydream through important information.

Effective counselors will sit quietly for a few minutes after each session and examine it for any mistakes they might have made. They then try to discern why they made the mistakes—what need, fear, anger, insensitivity, or impatience momentarily took control. They take these concerns to consultation and supervision sessions where they are able to disclose honestly what has happened and listen closely to suggestions and interpretations. These counselors then plan how they will avoid the same mistake in the future while taking steps to rectify any effects that might have been produced.

Effective counselors also admit mistakes to the clients. They do this for four reasons: (1) the counselor accepts the critical role honesty plays in the counseling relationship and honors it by being honest, (2) the client should be helped to separate what mistakes belong to whom so that the appropriate person can take responsibility for rectifying them, (3) the counselor admits the mistake as a way of teaching the client the acceptability of mistakes and the importance of admitting them to others, and (4) the counselor knows that the client probably realizes the counselor made a mistake and is watching to see if the counselor is secure enough to admit it.

Termination Problems

Counseling relationships terminate in a variety of ways. Three ways are fairly common. First, counseling can terminate when the agreed-upon goals have been achieved to a reasonable degree and the client is ready to proceed without the support of weekly counseling sessions. A second situation arises when the client wishes to terminate prematurely—to stop counseling before the goals have been met and before the counselor deems it advisable. A third case for termination arises when the counselor decides to terminate further counseling sessions even though the client wishes to continue. These last two situations will be discussed below.

Premature termination. When a client wishes to terminate prematurely against the advice of the counselor, counselors become vulnerable to making one of two potential mistakes. First, they can immediately perceive this as a situation in which "fault" must be established. To persons of such mind-set, it must be either the client's fault or the counselor's. Counselors who readily accept the blame may inappropriately berate themselves at the expense of exploring the client's contribution. An equally probable scenario is that the counselor will blame the client and feel the need to make this known, thereby compounding any problems already in existence.

It would also be a mistake to be cavalier about the situation. An attitude such as, "Fine. I've got so many clients anyway, I can easily schedule somebody in your place," would be callous.

The counselor's first response should be to find out why the client is saying he or she wishes to discontinue. Often, such a statement on the part of the client is, in actuality, meant to communicate something else and is not meant to be translated literally. The following are some possible translations of what premature termination by the client can mean:

- an attempt to see if the counselor really cares about the client—to see how willingly the counselor acquiesces to the request
- a test to see how secure the counselor is and how well he or she handles obstacles
- an attempt to get the counselor to express some positive feelings toward the client, who feels only criticism from the counselor
- a chance to hurt or punish the counselor for perceived or real injustices perpetrated by the counselor
- a sign that the client is experiencing some very anxiety-producing feelings toward the counselor—fear, anger, or dependency
- an indication that the client can foresee some frightening subject arising in a future session and wishes to avoid it
- a manifestation of defense mechanisms shifting, causing the client to feel euphoric and optimistic, whereas he or she felt depressed and hopeless the week before
- a fear that the counselor is going to reject the client (so the client chooses to reject the counselor first)
- a sign that the client has found a "cure" elsewhere (for example, in love, religion, or a psychological "get rich quick" fad)
- an indication that the client has not been truthful with the counselor in some important area and realizes that he or she must either tell the truth or end counseling
- the client feels the counselor is too strong or too weak and wishes to change counselors
- the client feels the counselor does not truly understand what the client is trying to say
- the client feels the counselor is casting him or her in some inauthentic role
- the client feels the counselor is incompetent

These are typical issues that can be present, some or all of which can be explored in one way or another to establish the true reason for the client's stated wish to discontinue counseling. In the majority of cases, if this exploration can be done in a spirit of helpfulness and not seen as a threat or a dare, the client can be led to understand the underlying issue. Consequently, the client is in a better position to make a good decision about remaining in counseling.

But what if the client still opts to discontinue counseling? Every counselor can expect that some number of clients will choose to discontinue counseling before goals have been attained. There are often valid reasons for such premature terminations. For example, some counselors will not be as helpful to a particular client as another counselor might have been. Frankly acknowledging such a possibility is in the best interest of both counselor and client in such a case.

A second thing to bear in mind is that not all people are equally ready for counseling, and not all people's readiness remains the same throughout counseling. A client's fear may increase during counseling and then manifest itself in either resistance or apathy. Either state may exist for a long time; so nothing gets accomplished. Under such conditions it might be better for the client to discontinue counseling, at least for the short term.

Third, the counselor may be relating with the client in a potentially helpful way, but one which the client cannot handle. The client wants a "special" relationship and, not finding it, now chooses to look elsewhere. Not all clients who engage the services of an effective counselor complete the course of treatment. Similarly, a client's refusal to fill a prescription from a physician does not reflect on the physician's competence. Counselors can control only so many variables; the rest are controlled by the client and the people in the client's environment.

Whatever the final issue, the counselor's attitude and message to the client is important. A helpful attitude may be seen in the statement, "Well, I understand (or am trying to understand) why you feel the way you do. I think if you feel that strongly about it, you should take a rest from counseling. I hope you'll remember that the door is always open here for you. If you ever feel a need to talk, I would be happy to see you. I would like for you to do well, and I'll drop you a note to keep in touch." This attitude allows the client to avoid feeling guilty, either for making a mistake or for hurting the counselor's feelings. The client need not feel rejected because the counselor makes it clear that he or she cares about the client and offers a standing invitation to return. The client need not be angry because the counselor handles the termination without directing anger at the client. Finally, the client need not feel hopeless, since the counselor does not imply that without the counselor's help, he or she would be doomed.

Counselor-initiated termination. Sometimes a counselor will wish to terminate a counseling relationship even though the client does not. There are both good and poor reasons for such a desire. Some sound reasons might be the following:

1. Despite repeated efforts on the part of the counselor, the client has been "entrenched" for some time and shows little or no inclination to act in ways that will be helpful. A defensive position has been staked out and the client refuses to budge.

2. The client is using counseling in a destructive way; that is, he or she persistently relates to the counselor in an unhelpful way or uses counseling for motives other than growth.

3. Something has happened in the counseling relationship that has caused the counselor to have strong feelings of either attraction or

antipathy toward the client. Thus the counselor feels it would be in the best interest of both parties to terminate this counseling relationship.

4. The client is as ready to terminate as he or she will ever be, but is still dependent on the counselor. The client would like to see the counselor forever, but the counselor clearly sees that it is time for the client to move toward greater independence.

The counselor may also wish to terminate counseling for poor reasons. One such reason would be when a counselor becomes angry at the client. Because counselors are human, they may react angrily to clients, just as clients may react to them with anger. But if the counselor, in the midst of anger, terminates a counseling relationship for no better reason, this can be damaging to both parties.

Sometimes the client can get a counselor so angry that he or she feels like saying, "Look, if you're so unhappy with the way I do things, or if you're so indifferent to the benefits of counseling, maybe it would be better if we stopped right now." There has probably never been a counselor who *has not* felt this sentiment. But, as we have already noted, working it out and acting it out are two very different behaviors.

Counselors would do best to remember that by terminating the client, they might well be playing into his or her dynamics. The client may seek rejection from the counselor to avoid the stress of counseling, to prove how incompetent the counselor is, or to demonstrate his or her own helplessness.

If a counselor can articulate this anger in a clear and firm way, such a course should preclude the necessity of acting it out, unless the counselor just wants to get rid of the client and is merely trumping up an excuse. Clients who are rejected by angry counselors learn either how totally unacceptable they are or how totally insecure counselors are. In either case, some lasting damage is likely to result.

As previously mentioned, a counselor may terminate a client who continues to do damage to the counselor or to the relationship. Even then, however, the termination should be based on a recognition of this dynamic and not solely on the anger of the counselor.

A second poor reason for termination is when the counselor is bored with the client. Boredom, as noted earlier, undermines the counseling relationship and may or may not be a just reason for termination of counseling by the counselor. If the client is boring as a part of intransigent resistance, then termination might conceivably be a reasonable course. But if the client has a personality that is naturally bland and uninteresting, the counselor should reevaluate any inclination to terminate by bearing in mind the following considerations.

First, the client had the same personality when the counselor agreed to see him or her in the first place; so to terminate after this agreement was entered into might be said to be unjust. Second, one of the reasons this client is in counseling is probably due to having a boring personality. For a counselor to act toward this client the same way everyone else does is hardly the behavior of a helper. Rather than terminate the course of treatment, counselors can call upon their ingenuity to make the sessions more productive.

Regardless of the soundness of the reason, it is a very difficult situation for both the counselor and the client when the counselor chooses to terminate the sessions. There is no anxiety-free way to accomplish a termination. The counselor must possess the strength to say, "As I've discussed with you on several occasions, I'm concerned about our situation, and I honestly feel that it has come to the point where it is in our best interests to stop trying to work together." Abandonment issues are always a concern at this point in the process and counselors are encouraged to take steps to ensure that the client receives the names of appropriate referrals.

Depending on circumstances, the terminating experience may range from relatively matter-of-fact to highly turbulent. Both counselor and client are likely to feel a mixture of failure, frustration, and resentment. This is why it is important to give advance notice of any recommendation to terminate and to bring the subject of termination up early in the session so that feelings can be addressed in a timely manner. Termination of any kind requires adequate preparation and time. Terminations that are handled in a healthy, productive way do much to help clients accept that the counseling relationship, like all human relationships, has a beginning and an end. Ultimately, if clients can terminate comfortably, then the separation fears that have prevented them from forming other relationships in their lives will be lessened.

The Real Relationship

According to Gelso and Carter, "The real relationship is seen as having two defining features: genuineness and realistic perceptions. Genuineness is defined as the ability and willingness to be what one truly is in the relationship—to be authentic, open, and honest. Realistic perceptions refer to those perceptions that are uncontaminated by transference distortions and other defenses. In other words, therapy participants see each other in an accurate, realistic way" (1994, p. 297).

While this third, and final, component of the therapeutic relationship is the one that has been discussed the least it is critically important. Though different theoretical approaches attach more significance (e.g., client-centered) or less significance (e.g., psychoanalytic) to the real relationship, it not only exists in all counseling relationships, but it also affects and is affected by the other two components, that is, the working alliance and the transference-countertransference configuration (Gelso & Carter, 1994).

The importance of the real relationship component in counseling implies that counselors must be prepared to genuinely and realistically relate to their clients. While counselors may be more comfortable in adhering strictly to the roles that the duties and responsibilities associated with the therapeutic alliance require, how well counselors relate to their clients at a real level is of the utmost importance. Real relationships contain a level of intimacy that must be carefully understood in context. Counseling is an emotionally intimate experience, but the intimacy that forms in the confines of such a professional relationship should never be confused with the type of intimacy associated with friendships and love relationships. The intimacy in counseling relationships forms from the client's self-disclosures to the counselor: it is a "one way intimacy" (see Kottler, 1986, p. 48). The intimate exchange is formed from the client's disclosures and the counselor's empathic response to them. The closeness that the client feels to be generated by these disclosures is an intimacy which is to some extent contrived—the client's role is to impart important cognitive and emotional information to the counselor. It is therefore easy for clients to mistake or confuse the intimacy that this sharing with a counselor produces with the feelings that develop for friends or lovers. Counselors must therefore take special care to maintain adequate boundaries and help clients understand that the feelings of intimacy that result from counseling have little in common with intimacy produced in friendships where both partners hazard risk and disclose themselves to one another as a relationship of mutuality forms.

Novice counselors may easily succumb to an erroneous conviction that the client's feeling for them is something other than the intimacy associated with a well-bounded and carefully managed counseling relationship. Intimacy is a powerful force in the counseling process but it must be managed very carefully. It is as potentially harmful when abused as it is helpful when appropriately applied.

Distorted perceptions that prevent counselors from forming healthy, real relationships with their clients may cause them to substitute a destructive emotionally detached or attached relationship in place of a real relationship. An effective counseling relationship involves a balance between perceived attachment and acknowledged distance.

Destructive Relationships versus Real Relationships

There are at least two types of destructive relationships in counseling; those that are emotionally detached and those that are emotionally attached. Both of these will be discussed in terms of their characteristics and effects on counseling. Emotionally involved relationships, those that exist at the healthy midpoint between attached and detached, form the basis for real relationships and will be discussed last.

Emotionally detached relationships. Counselors who relate in an emotionally detached manner refrain from getting close enough to the client to be empathic. They do not reveal anything of themselves; personal information and opinions that would be appropriate to share are withheld, and they block necessary levels of emotional involvement. Such counselors adopt a role that is passive, reflective, and didactic.

Counselors are moved to relate in an emotionally detached manner because they were trained in this fashion (a leftover from the medical model of treatment), because they are frightened by their client's emotions, or because their personality does not lend itself to this level of emotional interaction. Counselors who are distant cannot truly get close enough to the client to be helpful. Since they cannot experience the client's thoughts, feelings, and perceptions sufficiently well, an unreal understanding of the client develops that is coupled with an empathic failure. This gives the client the accurate impression that he or she is misunderstood and emotionally isolated from the counselor.

When counselors are anonymous, they offer little of the personal data that is necessary to create a sense of trust and rapport. They expect clients to share their most intimate and vulnerable areas with a virtual stranger. Because of the counselor's anonymity, the client also cannot build a sense of identification with the counselor or with his or her mental health values.

When counselors are emotionally detached, their sole involvement is intellectual. Since human beings are composed of emotional, intellectual, physical, and spiritual elements, detached counselors attend to only one-fourth of the client's experience. Clients with this type of counselor often feel that they are treated as a symptom or a condition and not as a person. It is difficult for any client to relate openly with a counselor when he or she cannot sense the counselor's concern, understanding, and acceptance.

On the other hand, clients who need to relate to a counselor in an emotionally detached way use the counselor as a director, tutor, or mentor. They hold the counselor at a certain distance and thus prevent the development of understanding and empathy. Because these clients relate in formal, polite, and respectful ways, the counselor finds it difficult to see what lies behind this social facade. Clients who relate intellectually rather than emotionally deprive themselves and the counselor of the opportunity to experience and share important feelings. The counselor's attempts to deepen the counseling relationship are met with resistance clearly signifying that the client wants to keep the relationship on an intellectual plane.

Gradually, the effective counselor can help the client understand the important difference between the tutorial experience, which the client wants, and a therapeutic experience, which necessitates that the counselor and client interact on emotional and spiritual as well as intellectual levels. Progression from a role-to-role relationship to a person-to-person relationship can be swift with clients who have developed levels of trust, who are working in a well-bounded professional relationship, and who have been correctly oriented to counseling. For those who have an emotional investment in remaining in a detached relationship, the change must be far more gradual and modest. Trust levels are not sufficiently high to press for such dramatic change. As long as a counseling relationship remains on an emotionally detached level, however, the effects of counseling are likely to be superficial and transient.

Emotionally attached relationships. An equally undesirable relationship may form if either the counselor or client is emotionally attached. "Emotionally attached" means that the counselor or client inappropriately depends upon the other for fulfilling basic needs. Needs that are met in this type of relationship might include the need to feel secure, to receive and give love, or to feel admired and needed. Emotional attachment may arise because the counselor is unable or unwilling to establish and maintain appropriate boundaries and because the needs of one party are not being appropriately met outside of the counseling relationship.

Counselor to client. Counselors who, for a variety of reasons, have not learned to meet their needs through relationships in their daily lives run the risk of becoming emotionally attached to clients. Resultant problems may be characterized as parental (the counselor can relate as an overprotective parent), fraternal (the counselor can function as the client's best friend), or romantic (the counselor can function as a lover or spouse). Counselors need to remain alert to signs that indicate they are becoming emotionally attached. Such counterproductive and potentially dangerous attachments are a possibility when the counselor:

1. looks forward to seeing the client as a way of brightening up the day or week
2. finds the significant people in his or her life lacking when compared with the client
3. extends the time of the sessions, beginning early and/or ending late
4. fantasizes about the client between sessions
5. allows or encourages between-session contacts that are not permitted others (for example, phone calls, letters, or extra visits)
6. makes adjustments in fees that would not be made for others
7. finds the sessions are more recreation than work
8. is jealous of the other close relationships the client has and subtly downgrades or discourages them
9. worries about the client between sessions in ways and to degrees that he or she does not worry about others

The negative results that arise from a counselor becoming emotionally attached to a client stem from the fact that such a relationship corrupts and destroys the basic assumptions upon which counseling rests. For example, in a healthy counseling relationship the counselor brings a critical level of objectivity and clinical perspective to the counseling relationship. Counselors who are emotionally attached lose objectivity, and clinical judgment decays as they allow themselves to be drawn deeper into the client's perceptions.

Rather than help their clients make decisions that are to the clients' benefit, emotionally attached counselors angle clients into decisions that will best meet the counselor's needs (for example, to continue in counseling when the client could function sufficiently on his or her own). Instead of possessing a strength that clients depend upon and from which they can draw inspiration, attached counselors are inordinately vulnerable to manipulation and therefore are a weak foundation upon which to rely for support.

Counselors should be able to remain stable, despite the mood shifts and crises of the client. But the counselor who is emotionally attached rides the moods and suffers the anguish of the client, thus nullifying the ability to provide objective feedback. Whereas a competent counselor encourages clients to relate with others in maximally fulfilling ways, emotionally attached counselors inappropriately provide levels of satisfaction and fulfillment to the client that lower his or her motivation to relate with people outside of counseling. Even worse, the emotional attachment may also cause the counselor to jealously block the client from interacting with others. Effective counselors are strong proponents of reality; but attached counselors offer the client an unreal and wholly inappropriate relationship that can be deeply injurious.

When counselors become involved in emotionally attached counselor-client relationships they do no service to their clients and violate professional and ethical standards of treatment. Such clients often require long-term counseling to undo the adverse effects of attached relationships but they are predictably reluctant to do so. Their suspicions and fears of being used again are heightened by their previous experiences. Counselors need consultation and supervision opportunities to help them realize when emotional attachment is looming and what steps need to be taken to correct the problem immediately.

Client to counselor. A client can also become attached to a counselor without the counselor consciously encouraging or desiring it. While this is partially understandable because some clients feel that the counselor is the only one who accepts him or her, the counselor's reluctance to act on signals that such an attachment is beginning may passively encourage some enmeshment.

The following are some typical signs of this kind of attachment.

1. The client wants a special relationship with the counselor; that is, the client wants to be the counselor's "favorite client." These clients often ask, directly or indirectly, if and how much the counselor likes them and how they rank against the other clients the counselor sees.

2. The client wants between-session contacts (that is, phone calls, letters, or extra visits). Sometimes the client may make creative gifts for the counselor or bring presents, often of a personal nature.

3. The client's demeanor—verbal and nonverbal communication—reflects the signs of someone "falling in love." The client's eyes say "I love you," and the client lingers after the session in a way that says "I don't want to leave you."

4. The client feels hurt and rejected when confronted with some unpleasant reality by the counselor, such as the reality of the client's attachment to the counselor.

5. The client fantasizes about the counselor between sessions and sometimes makes the counselor an imaginary friend who is always there to protect and guide.

6. The client compares the counselor with the significant people in his or her life and judges the counselor to be superior to them: "If only I were married to you instead of Jim" or "If only you were my mother."

The following problems might result should the client become emotionally attached to the counselor. The client may (1) lose interest in working on relationships outside of counseling because he or she has everything needed in the person of the counselor; (2) be less than honest to avoid harming the relationship; (3) make it difficult for the counselor to set and enforce limits without feeling selfish or rejecting; (4) overperceive the counselor's care and understanding and underperceive the counselor's messages that he or she wants the client to become more self-sufficient; (5) "get well" for the counselor and remain so only as long as the counselor treats him or her nicely; as soon as the counselor proves upsetting or speaks of tapering off the sessions, the client "gets sick" again; (6) work halfheartedly at problems and concoct problems as counseling approaches termination in order to extend the relationship.

The effects that result from a client's emotional attachment to a counselor are detrimental to the counseling process and present a formidable challenge to the counselor. When the client becomes emotionally attached, the counselor must take steps to reduce and then hold the attachment within reasonable limits. This can be done by setting limits and scrupulously abiding by them, despite pressure from the client to make exceptions. Additionally the counselor will need to relate in a totally honest fashion, refusing to modify needs, perceptions, values, or strengths to accommodate the inappropriate needs or fantasies of the client. The counselor also can deal openly with the manifestations of the emotional attachment, pointing out its nature and its detrimental effects.

The counselor must continually walk a thin line between being consumed by and rejecting the client. In the last analysis, however, it may be better for the client to terminate counseling or be terminated than to continue making failed attempts to form an appropriate counseling relationship and thereby reinforcing weaknesses and producing serious damage in the process. Referrals for group counseling, social skills training or, in some cases, another counselor, exist as useful treatment alternatives for clients who develop such unhealthy attachments to counselors.

Real relationships. The real relationship is a healthy relationship that forms between a counselor and a client where the level of emotional connection lies equidistant between the detrimental extremes of an emotionally detached and an emotionally attached relationship. Real relationships form over time when roles and responsibilities are clearly defined and when the process is sufficiently well-bounded. Real relationships also form because the emotional intimacy generated in the counseling relationship is understood as a part of the counseling process and correctly differentiated from the forms of intimacy found in friendships and love relationships. This understanding fosters deeply empathic exchanges and a vibrant counseling relationship. Ultimately what is learned in the counseling relationship can be generalized to personal relationships.

The real relationship in counseling is built on a recognition that the counselor and the client are separate and distinct people. They are also partners in a counseling enterprise that emphasizes rights, responsibilities, freedoms, and independence. So while levels of emotional intimacy exist in the counseling process, this intimacy is managed in a way that honors shared goals for client independence. The intimacy in the counseling relationship is ultimately used to help the client become stronger. While counselors must be sufficiently involved emotionally to produce levels of empathy and to prevent the negative effects associated with emotionally detached relationships, counselors must simultaneously avoid becoming emotionally attached. To negotiate such a relationship requires people who understand themselves, who know their strengths and limitations, and who are self-sufficient enough to help others to become self-sufficient. The goal of developing and maintaining these skills and traits is a lifelong process that takes varied routes including supervision, consultation, advanced training, and personal counseling in individual or group settings.

Managing the Counselor's Issues

Being an effective counselor is both a personal and a professional challenge. While many other professions make use of tools and offer varied methods of protecting practitioners from the noxious influences that emanate from the subject of their work, the counselor's tool is himself or herself, and the counselor is expected to confront and experience the client's continuum of reactions. Kottler (1986, p. ix) illustrates the range of affects that counseling clients have on counselors when he writes, "The process of psychotherapy flows in two directions, obviously influencing the client, but also affecting the personal life of the clinician. This impact can be for better or worse, making the helping professions among the most spiritually fulfilling as well as the most emotionally draining human endeavors." His book, *On Being A Therapist*, offers counselors a unique opportunity to explore what it means to be a counselor from a professional as well as a personal perspective. His examination of the rigors of counseling provides counselors with an honest portrayal of how they are personally affected by their interaction with clients. Recommendations, for example, about ways to reduce counselor burnout, methods for making counseling a creative experience, and therapy alternatives for counselors make the book an excellent self-help text.

Much of the success of counseling relies upon the counselor's ability to translate theory into effective clinical practice, to establish and maintain a productive counseling relationship, and to manage personal issues in such a way that they do not counterproductively infiltrate or distort the counseling process. Given these demands and responsibilities, the need to expose clinical judgments to the scrutiny of others, to discuss reactions to clients, and to obtain suggestions and recommendations on how to best handle situations exists whenever counselors work with clients. Counselors, regardless of their level of experience, are always susceptible to countertransference reactions, errors in judgment, overestimating or underestimating levels of client pathology, mismanagement of the counseling relationship, and other pitfalls. To combat these counterproductive influences, counselors pursue varied forms of supervision and consultation as well as personal counseling in individual or group settings.

Our definition of consultation is limited—when we refer to consultation we mean the process of improving the quality of a counselor's delivery of services through regular meetings with one (individual consultation) or more experienced clinicians (group peer consultation). Thus, distinctions between supervision and consultation exist in only a couple of areas. First and most importantly, *supervision* is a required activity usually associated with course or licensing requirements. The supervisor bears legal and professional responsibility for the supervisee's clients. *Consultation* is an elective process where consultants are not legally or professionally responsible for the consultee's clients. Second, because supervision is required in the early stages of the counselor's professional development, the topics that are covered in supervision may be more elementary and more focused on skills training than those raised in consultation.

Bernard and Goodyear (1992) offer a useful classification system for different approaches to supervision that can also be extended to consultation. These authors use two major categories: psychotherapy-based supervision and conceptual models of supervision (see Bernard & Goodyear, p. 12). Psychotherapy-based approaches use the particular type of psychotherapy to form the model for supervision. Psychodynamic supervision, an example of a psychotherapy-based approach, is probably the original model for all forms of supervision. It now shares a position within the category of psychotherapy-based supervision with other approaches, each one modeled after each of the major counseling theories (e.g., Gestalt, person-centered, behavioral, etc.). There are good reasons for counselors to be supervised by or to consult with other professionals who share the same theoretical orientation.

On the other hand, conceptual models of supervision that are not linked to particular theories can also be quite helpful. Developmental supervision is one such approach. It "describes counselor growth as a series of sequential, hierarchical stages, each requiring different supervision interventions" (Borders, 1986, p. 9). Whether counselors want to pursue a deeper understanding of their work with clients through expanding their knowledge of and skills within a particular approach to counseling, or whether they select an approach that focuses more on the developmental stages that all counselors must progress through, is probably more a matter of personal preference than a well-founded scientific decision. Advantages and limitations can be found in each. (See Bernard & Goodyear, 1992, chapter 2 for a more complete discussion of the advantages and disadvantages found in various models of supervision.)

Regardless of which model of supervision a counselor selects and whether the counselor is completing the first practicum in a graduate counseling program or entering the twentieth year of clinical work, he or she will need to make productive use of supervision and consultation settings by being prepared to:

1. provide accurate and complete descriptions of counseling relationships
2. respond to supervisor or consultant questions openly and completely
3. carefully consider and evaluate suggestions and recommendations
4. implement changes
5. explore countertransference influences
6. pursue personal counseling and other forms of treatment when needed

These six activities can only be accomplished in an interpersonal environment that contains adequate levels of trust and respect—choosing a supervisor or consultant or deciding which peer consultation group to attend is a very serious decision. Contact with experienced and knowledgeable counselors who can provide honest reactions and useful suggestions is essential in both individual and group settings. In general, individual supervision or consultation is more useful in the early part of a counselor's career. Group consultation is a better choice for experienced counselors because it offers them a setting where they can discuss their own cases and where they can serve as consultants to others.

While there are valid ethical and legal reasons for counselors to obtain supervision or consultation, the most important reason to do so is because counselors cannot safely rely solely on their own perceptions, observations, and conclusions about a process in which they are so completely involved. Objectivity is increased through the involvement of other professionals. Counselors should plan to make use of supervision and consultation throughout the course of their professional lives.

Summary

Counseling is a personally and professionally challenging task. Counselors face a wide range of issues that come into play in the course of the counseling relationship. Different issues are associated with one or more of the three subcomponents of the counseling relationship—a working alliance, transference (countertransference) configuration, and a real relationship. Countertransference issues were covered first because of their wide-scale impact on the other components of the counseling relationship. Countertransference was shown to be a valuable force in the counseling process so long as the counselor was able to work through rather than act out his or her reactions to the client. Appropriate ways to manage feelings of hostility/frustration, boredom, and emotional pain/ suffering are vitally necessary if counselors are to be effective in their work with clients because these feelings surface in varying degrees in all counseling relationships.

Issues that counselors face with respect to the working alliance include manipulation, errors in clinical judgment, and problems with termination. The need to replace manipulation with confrontation was emphasized. The process of manipulation ignores the client's needs in favor of the counselor's. Confrontation, on the other hand, focuses exclusively on the client by helping the client become aware of conflicting thoughts and feelings. The fact that errors in clinical judgment occur was stressed and corrective measures that honor the need for the client to be aware of such errors were discussed. Issues of termination focused on essentially three types. The first is actually the ideal condition where both counselor and client agree that the goals have been achieved and that it is time to stop. Premature terminations at the counselor's or the client's request were shown to be potentially harmful, and strategies for reducing adverse effects were discussed. The process of termination was shown to be a critical aspect of counseling since the termination of a counseling relationship offers the client an opportunity to learn adaptive and useful ways to end other relationships in his or her life.

The real relationship between counselor and client has a substantial effect on the counseling process, yet it is the one that is least researched. The real relationship calls for a level of emotional intimacy that must be very carefully managed. Clients generally experience intimacy as a by-product of their discussions about their lives and the counselors' empathic responses. The counseling relationship was identified as having "one-way intimacy" for this reason. A healthy, well-bounded, real relationship was contrasted with emotionally attached and emotionally detached relationships. The devastating effects of attached or detached relationships were discussed. These relationships were shown to violate all of the basic assumptions of effective counseling, to be at odds with ethical and professional standards of care, and to be hazardous.

The chapter concludes with a discussion of what counselors can do to manage the issues that affect them in a manner that is both clinically and personally useful. Some form of supervision or consultation was shown to be necessary for counselors throughout the course of their professional lives. Peer consultation can be especially valuable for experienced counselors because it provides opportunities for the counselor both to serve as a consultant to other members of the group and to receive consultation from members of the group.

Counseling can be a very isolating profession. Counselors usually meet with clients, one after another, for relatively brief periods of time. Counseling relationships cannot and should not substitute for the interpersonal relationships that people require to lead healthy and fulfilling lives. Making time to meet with other professionals, taking time to meet personal needs through family and other personal relationships, and pursuing a range of interests helps counselors to remain healthy and able to work effectively with others.

⚜

Reflection Questions

1. A client makes a regular habit of entering the counseling office and asking if the counselor could help him make a decision. The counselor feels frustrated and somewhat angry each time the client asks.

   a. How would the counselor become aware of the incipient countertransference?

   b. What would this counselor say if she "acted out" the countertransference?

   c. What would be a good way to "work through" the countertransference?

2. No matter how "therapeutic" counselors try to be, few enjoy being the target of hostility. A client says to you, "How do you think

you can help me? I have children older than you, and I noticed that your nails are bitten and you're overweight, which means you're not handling things so well yourself."

   a. What is your immediate reaction to this response?

   b. What do you feel like saying?

   c. What do you feel like doing?

   d. What *do* you say?

   e. What *do* you do?

3. What is the one quality you want clients to see in you? How could the client's awareness of that quality and its importance to you be used to manipulate your behavior?

4. What is the one mistake you could make as a counselor that would be the most difficult to admit?

5. What signals would you expect to see that would suggest that emotional attachment to a client was becoming a possibility?

13

CRISIS INTERVENTION

In preceding chapters we illustrated the importance of offering counseling in an orderly sequence of stages. We buttressed this goal by describing many of the circumstances that can potentially disrupt counseling efforts (e.g., hazards brought about by mishandled countertransference reactions) and offered ways to overcome these pitfalls. While the goal is always to provide a carefully sequenced service to clients, this is not always possible. People are subject to many external, unpredictable events as well as surprising insights about themselves that can rapidly overwhelm defenses and outstrip their ability to cope. What happens when people encounter crises of one type or another and what counselors should do to help them form the focus of this chapter.

A basic rule of thumb in counseling dictates that counseling efforts cannot proceed in the face of a crisis, and the symptoms associated with the crisis must not be ignored. When people are in crisis their symptoms demand immediate and skilled attention. Such people are unable to channel sufficient energy to accomplish the broader counseling goals. Counselors must therefore adjust their focus from counseling to crisis intervention—the crisis must be managed first.

Crisis intervention is a form of short-term counseling that is the treatment of choice when the person seeking help is experiencing a state of acute psychological disequilibrium. Counselors may be called upon to handle crises when their own clients experience either internal or external traumatic events or they may encounter people who are first obtaining services because of a crisis. Some counselors even specialize in crisis intervention by serving on crisis intervention teams that provide services to one or more people who have been traumatized by some catastrophic event. School violence, natural disasters, and workplace violence are all examples of the type of trauma that can bring numbers of people to counselors for immediate services. Overall, counselors are being called upon increasingly to help people in crisis situations. Whether this is because life in modern times: (1) produces more crises, (2) produces more intense crisis situations, or because people are (3) less prepared to deal with crisis situations or (4) more aware of the help available to them, all counselors, at one time or another, will be called upon to help clients in crisis.

Traumas and Crises

A *crisis* is a state of cognitive disorganization and affective turmoil that is caused by perceiving a precipitating event as so threatening that it leaves someone incapable of functioning effectively. Kanel's "trilogy definition" of crisis identifies three component parts: "(1) A precipitating event occurs; (2) the perception of this event leads to subjective distress; and (3) usual coping methods fail, leading the person experiencing the event to function psychologically, emotionally, or behaviorally at a lower level than before the precipitating event occurred" (1999, p. 1).

Most people in the midst of crisis use similar ways of communicating their cognitive disorganization. They may say, "I'm so confused I don't know which way to turn" or "I think I'm going to lose my mind." They also express their affective turmoil in similar ways: "I'm absolutely terrified" or "I'm so distraught I can hardly see straight." While such symptoms can last for an indefinite period of time, crises typically are of short duration, lasting one day to a few weeks.

While the terms *trauma* and *crisis* are often used interchangeably, an important distinction exists when this language is applied to counseling efforts. A *trauma* or precipitating event is a powerful assault on the psychological well-being of a person and causes intense psychological pain (anxiety). A trauma may or may not precipitate a crisis. Whether it does or not depends on the severity of the trauma and the person's: (1) pretrauma psychological vulnerability or ego strength, (2) perception of the trauma, (3) ability to manage the painful emotions and reactions that the trauma produces, and (4) ability to obtain environmental (social and spiritual) support.

Basically a trauma is an objective event while a crisis is the individual's subjective reaction to that event. The difference between a trauma and a crisis is most clearly evident when the different reactions of different people to essentially the same trauma are explored—for example, the death of a child. A parent may:

1. grow in appreciation of the remaining children, feel closer to his or her spouse, and experience an increase in religious fervor
2. be so overcome with grief that he or she commits suicide
3. slip into an acute depression for several weeks
4. abuse alcohol or drugs
5. vow never to have another child
6. immediately try to have another child
7. initiate divorce proceedings
8. insist on moving immediately to another home
9. be relieved and grateful

When a trauma produces a crisis, intervention is necessary and often effective. While counseling cannot undo a trauma, it can help the person perceive and experience the trauma differently and in turn handle the psychological pain it produces more effectively. Crisis intervention strategies seek to correct the psychological processes that fuel the crisis before they can do more serious psychological damage. Ideally, crisis intervention leads the person to a path that will both resolve the crisis and strengthen the individual to the point where future traumas will be much less likely to result in crises. Accordingly, preventive mental health focuses on the variables that cause traumas to become crises, in order to be able to properly identify them and help people to effectively manage them.

Benefits of Crisis

The word *crisis* usually evokes fear and anxiety responses in most people and tends to have solely negative connotations. However, a crisis can have very beneficial results. A crisis can be therapeutic when it brings both the beauty and ugliness in a person's life into sharper focus. A crisis at work may help a woman appreciate her family in new ways. The death of a child may help parents gain a deeper and more meaningful appreciation of their marital relationship. An existential crisis may lead a man or woman to rearrange values and priorities so that life develops a fuller meaning.

A crisis can also introduce people to subconscious destructive elements in their lives that had previously been repressed and denied. For example, the explosion of serious marital problems may awaken the partners to the many ways they have been damaging themselves and sabotaging their relationship. Such realizations afford both partners opportunities to recognize and evaluate the downward trend of the marriage and motivate both to initiate steps to correct the difficulties.

Crises can be therapeutic especially when individuals are helped to successfully manage the overwhelming thoughts and feelings. Learning effective cognitive and affective skills psychologically strengthens them and produces greater levels of confidence. People who successfully work through crisis situations may even reframe the trauma and their response to it as "the best thing that ever happened." They learned more about themselves and about life in general than they would had the crisis never confronted them. A clear understanding of the fact that crises have the potential to produce both hazards and benefits has existed throughout history. According to Aguilera and Messick (1978):

> The Chinese characters that represent the word "crisis" mean both danger and opportunity. Crisis is a *danger* because it threatens to overwhelm the individual or his [sic] family, and it may result in suicide or a psychotic break. It is also an *opportunity* because during times of crisis individuals are more receptive to therapeutic influences. Prompt and skillful intervention may not only prevent the development of a serious long-term disability but may also allow new coping patterns to emerge that can help the individual function at a higher level of equilibrium than before the crisis. (p. 1)

Types of Traumas

While traumas can be categorized in various ways, we offer four specific types of traumas defined by the source of the traumatic event: situational, developmental, intrapsychic, and existential origins. Moderate to severe forms can be found in each of these four categories.

Situational traumas are precipitating events external to the individual. The death of a loved one, divorce, rape, loss of a job, serious financial reverses, discovery of a serious illness in oneself or a loved one, unwanted pregnancy, the discovery that a spouse has been unfaithful, the breakup of a close relationship or engagement, public embarrassment (such as being arrested or caught in a scandal), failure in business or school, and family stresses are all examples. Certain traumas can also affect large numbers of people. Natural disasters (e.g., fires, earthquakes, hurricanes, and floods) as well as workplace and school violence are examples of such situational traumas.

Developmental traumas arise as a function of maturation or progressing through life stages. These include traumas of childhood (birth of an unwanted sibling, peer rejection), adolescence (police, drug, or alcohol problems; sexual behaviors that cause shame and guilt; peer pressures to behave in ways that cause value conflict; dating pressures and stresses; academic or disciplinary problems at school), adulthood (stresses in dating, engagement, marriage, or parenthood; conflicts within the family and with in-laws and neighbors; dealing with the stresses of children leaving home; forced reduction of career expectations; waning attractiveness and sexual energy), and late life (retirement, failing health, loss of friends through death, loneliness, rejection by adult children, the specter of death). For a more complete review of common developmental conflicts that have the potential to develop into crises, see Erickson (1963). His eight-stage developmental model illustrates that the potential for developmental crises exists throughout one's lifetime and that counselors need to rely upon contributions from developmental psychology when working with clients in crisis. Many clients experience a sense of relief when they understand that the source of their discomfort is related to conflicts arising from developmental changes. Midlife crises, for example, are commonly understood as a recognizable crisis time for many. This is not to imply that all the events mentioned automatically cause a crisis. They *can* cause crises for certain people in specific situations.

Intrapsychic traumas are internal psychological events that create great anxiety because conflictual thoughts and feelings emerge. They can include the gradual or sudden recognition of homosexual feelings, the realization that one hates a person one "should" love (a parent, child, spouse, or friend), the gradual or sudden awareness of profound identity confusion, the realization that one must leave a job or marriage to salvage one's sanity, the increasing intensity of thoughts regarding suicide or homicide, and the arising of serious questions and doubts about one's religion, spiritual life, or belief in God.

Typically these types of intrapsychic thoughts and feelings are preconscious for some time and suddenly emerge into consciousness when the person's defenses become overburdened with related or unrelated stresses. At this point the person may have a crisis reaction or continue to carry the burden of the anxiety-producing realization for some time before it expands into a crisis reaction.

Existential traumas stem from the gradual or sudden recognition of a void, emptiness, or lack of meaning in one's life. Work, hobbies, and social and love relationships that once were compelling now seem vacuous and absurd. In a crisis reaction, the person feels a sense of emptiness that can create great levels of anxiety and panic. (See Bugental, 1978 and Jourard, 1968 for additional information on existential conflicts.)

How Crisis Intervention Differs from Other Types of Counseling

Kanel illustrated the most important difference between crisis counseling and other forms of therapy when she wrote, "Whereas other forms of counseling may focus on self-esteem building or personality modifications or even extinguishing maladaptive behaviors, in crisis intervention, the focus is on increasing the client's functioning" (1999, p. 1–2). In general, crisis intervention differs from other kinds of counseling, including short-term, noncrisis counseling, in four important practical ways.

Time

Crisis intervention is time limited, normally lasting from one to six sessions; short-term counseling of a noncrisis nature normally lasts from one to twenty sessions, and traditional counseling has no limited duration.

Focus

In crisis intervention, attention is focused tightly on the individual's problematic crisis responses to a particular trauma. In other types of counseling, a much wider range of issues is attended to, such as the person's history, unconscious processes, interpretation, interpersonal conflicts, career stresses, communication problems, transference, countertransference, sexual and identity confusion, personality constrictions, and value conflicts.

Active Participation

Crisis intervention demands more active participation on the part of the counselor than other kinds of counseling. Crisis counselors often direct, make suggestions, give advice, actively and directly seek the support of family and friends, and introduce the person to other referral sources. In some cases, counselors work directly with legal counsel for the person or with police agencies that are involved in the situation, and recommend environmental changes, such as taking a leave of absence from a job, temporarily moving out of a stressful family situation, or being hospitalized.

Goal

The goal of crisis intervention is to return the person to the level of precrisis adjustment. Of course, precrisis adjustment should not be confused with pretrauma adjustment. The following example illustrates the difference between precrisis and pretrauma adjustment. If a woman is experiencing a crisis reaction to the death of her husband, she may still be very upset by the loss of her husband at the end of a successful crisis intervention, but she is no longer in a crisis state. It would be inappropriate and unrealistic to expect crisis intervention to return this woman to the state of equilibrium she experienced prior to her husband's death.

Responses and Skills

Common Crisis Reactions

Although each person reacts to crisis differently, there are five common reactions.

Depression.   People may react to crisis with a sense of profound sadness, grief, or hopelessness. Their attitude is "What's the use? Nothing makes any difference now anyway." The sadness is often accompanied by sobbing or obvious attempts to refrain from weeping; by a substantial lack of energy, which is manifested in sitting and staring behavior; by a marked preoccupation with the precipitating event and a reluctance to discuss different but relevant issues; by apathy, sleeplessness, loss of appetite, and a seeming inability to care for oneself; by veiled hints and sometimes explicit statements that reflect the feeling that life is no longer worth living.

Anxiety. People may feel overwhelmed by a sense of fear, dread, and apprehension. They report feeling that their tension is going to cause them to burst or disintegrate. They have an overabundance of unchanneled energy, which causes them to behave in an agitated manner: constant motion, which is seen in frequent sitting, then standing, then pacing; feverish attempts to reduce anxiety by smoking, drinking, eating, praying, phoning, taking medications, and talking to "anyone who can help."

Common physical symptoms that usually accompany anxiety reactions include profuse sweating, headaches, palpitations, chest pain, tremors, hyperventilation, dizziness, and shortness of breath. Highly anxious people may relive the trauma in thought, fantasy, dreams, nightmares, and speech. Ordinary problems become magnified, assume extra importance, and seem insurmountable. Daily chores that were previously accomplished effortlessly become major obstacles that require great expenditures of energy and extensive planning.

Shock. People may be so stunned by the traumatic event that they feel numb and dazed. They partially dissociate themselves from the event, which leaves them with the feeling, "This isn't really happening to me." The psychological distance they have placed between themselves and the event is reflected in their almost zombielike appearance. Their eyes look glazed; their speech has a faraway sound; they have trouble hearing and concentrating; they walk in a rather stiff, unsteady way. They seem helpless and are often quite suggestible.

Violence. Some people react to stress caused by the precipitating event with physical attacks on others or against themselves. They may attack, or threaten to attack, the person whom they perceive as the cause of the crisis (for example, an unfaithful spouse). They believe that the only way they can vent their fury and recapture their self-esteem is to hurt or destroy the person whom they perceive as having injured them.

People who historically have turned their hurt and anger inward would be more inclined to react with violence toward themselves. This violence could manifest itself in potentially self-destructive behavior, such as jumping in a car and driving at high rates of speed along winding roads or drinking or taking drugs until one lapses into unconsciousness. The self-directed violence may also manifest itself in direct ways by suicidal gestures, genuine attempts, or actual suicide.

Pseudoadaptive reactions. This is the most subtle of all the crisis reactions. These individuals appear to be handling the trauma and the resultant stress well. The counselor's clue to pseudoadaptive reactions is that the person seems to be handling it *too well*. Their attitude toward the traumatic event is very philosophical or theological. Generally, their commentaries on the trauma are replete with platitudes that sound more rehearsed ("taped") than accurately felt. Some common "tapes" include: "Everything in life happens for a reason; so I'm sure there is some good reason for this"; "God works in our lives in strange ways; I'm sure God's doing this so I will grow"; "This is my chance to show people what I am really made of."

The pseudoadaptive reaction is a very brittle defense buttressed by repression, denial, and reaction formation. These people rarely seek help on their own but present themselves to a counselor with statements such as, "I'm handling this situation well, but my spouse (friend, doctor, minister) suggested that it might be good to talk with you. So here I am." When the repressed feelings of fear, hurt, anger, or guilt incubate and spread, they are likely to inundate the brittle defense of the pseudoadaptive response and cause a major upheaval.

The pseudoadaptive reaction can be differentiated from a genuinely adaptive reaction in the following ways:

1. The pseudoadaptive reaction is a source of concern and not of relief to the people who know the person best.

2. In the pseudoadaptive response, the person does not reflect a healthy integration and resolution between the painful feelings and the positive and redeeming aspects of the crisis. The person ignores and intellectualizes the painful elements while concentrating on or exaggerating the salutary aspects of the crisis.

3. The person strongly resists any suggestions by the counselor that there may be some painful and unresolved feelings to which the person is not attending. When the counselor probes this area, he or she is likely to be accused of trying to create a problem where no problem exists.

Although there is no clear-cut demarcation between a pseudoadaptive and a genuinely adaptive reaction to trauma, the counselor can be alert to the possibility that a person's seeming equanimity may be covering a wealth of conflict.

Dealing with Crisis Reactions

When dealing with crisis reactions, it is helpful for the counselor and the client to be aware of the following factors.

Dealing with reality. At the time of the crisis reaction, the person is unable to deal adequately with reality. Depressed people are so sad that they can see only the negative aspects of their lives and have little energy to move forward psychologically. Anxious people are so frightened that they seem unable to concentrate on the reality of the situation or to make helpful decisions. People who are in shock are sufficiently removed from the reality of the trauma that they are unable to take constructive steps to resolve it. Violent people are so intent on destruction that reality gets lost in their frenzy. Pseudoadaptive people are adapting so well to their hastily constructed defense system that they don't see any problem.

Counselors can help these people feel safe enough and hopeful enough to understand that there are more reality-oriented and constructive ways to deal with the trauma and resultant crisis.

Beneficial effects. Although none of the previously mentioned reactions are healthy, not all of them are necessarily maladaptive. Some are emergency reactions that temporarily help the person maintain an equilibrium until resources can be gained to deal with the trauma more constructively. For example, the self-pity in depression may have some healing effect, especially in the absence of genuine compassion from significant others. Also, the general "shutting down" in depression can protect the person from further hurt while the psyche is recovering.

The dissociation inherent in shock can allow people to acclimate themselves gradually to the full impact of the trauma as they develop psychological, social, and spiritual resources along the way. In the same manner, the intellectualization that forms the backbone of the pseudoadaptive response can act as a buffer between the harsh reality of the trauma and the sudden and unmitigated painful feelings that were evoked. This gives the person time to assimilate emotionally what has been perceived intellectually.

Although undoubtedly some could argue that even the reactions of anxiety and violence have some temporarily beneficial purpose, these reactions are considered to be the least helpful. In any case, counselors should be careful not to rush in and remove psychological supports that, while not adaptive, are still shielding the individual from the majority of the psychological distress, until the person is strong enough to manage the crisis with more adaptive responses.

Attempts to help. All these reactions to crisis make it difficult for most significant others in the person's life to respond helpfully. Typically, family and loved ones try to comfort these people but soon become frustrated, even antagonistic. This is especially true when the person in crisis reacts with depression, anxiety, or violence. After repeated and well-intentioned attempts to "pull these people out of it," family members often feel like telling them, "Stop feeling so sorry for yourself. My husband died, and I didn't fall apart" or "I'm so sick and tired of you; I don't care what happens to you." Such reactions can also be caused by the fact that family members may also be affected by the same trauma their loved one is experiencing and their weakened state makes it much more difficult for them to be realistic, supportive, and understanding. The overall result is that the person in crisis feels more alone, alienated, and hopeless.

Creating further anxiety. Counselors in crisis intervention often have a dual role: (1) to help the person through the original trauma, and (2) to help the person through the crisis that the trauma created. It is not helpful to lump what are often two psychodynamically different problems into one because one or both problems will not be resolved if this is done. Indeed, many crisis reactions create their own set of anxieties, separate from the original trauma. For example, a woman who has to deal with the death of a baby also has to deal with the personal problem of her depression and the interpersonal problem between herself and her husband caused by the depression. The person who reacts with violence to the discovery that a spouse has been unfaithful also has to deal with a new problem—that is, the intense anxiety caused by deciding toward whom to direct the violence, what form the violence will take, and what the consequences of the violence will be. If this person acts out the violent feelings, the crisis this creates may be more dramatic than the one currently being experienced.

Delayed reactions. While many crisis reactions follow immediately after the precipitating event, sometimes there can be a delayed reaction weeks or months after the initial trauma. A person may present himself or herself in a crisis state several months after the death of a loved one, the dissolution of a marriage, or the discovery of a serious illness. These people describe their symptoms as "coming out of the blue," and they appear to be genuinely perplexed and surprised. Their reactions are sometimes more intense than if they had experienced them at the time of the crisis because the painful feelings have had time to ferment and because there appears to be no obvious reason for the symptoms, making them all the more anxiety provoking.

Delayed reactions often occur when the original crisis was responded to with pseudoadaptive responses and the suppressed, painful feelings have finally eroded the defenses. Though the painful feelings have emerged, the traumatic quality of the original precipitating event may still be hidden. For example, the person may tell the counselor, "Oh, I forgot to tell you at our last visit, but six months ago I had a heart transplant, and the doctor told me I could die at any time." After the counselor recoups from this "incidental" piece of information, he or she explores this area with the person but is assured it is of no real consequence because the person has "made his peace with friends, family, and God."

Counselor Skills in Crisis Intervention

Although it would be inaccurate to state that crisis intervention requires different qualities in a counselor than do other types of counseling, some qualities assume a higher priority than others. The following are particularly important for counselors who do, or plan to do, crisis intervention.

Realistic perspective. Counselors must preserve a realistic perspective of their role in crisis intervention. This means that it is helpful for counselors to recognize both their strengths and their limitations when working with people in crisis. Hopefully, their strengths include being able to help the person in ways that the person's family and friends cannot. On the other hand, there are some realistic limitations that counselors will need to acknowledge.

First, precrisis personality and social problems contribute heavily to the individual's response to the current crisis. Faulty thinking, a poorly developed system of pyschological defenses, the social isolation that results from conflict laden relationships, and a history of poorly managed reactions to anxiety complicate the counselor's attempts to intervene. Hence, such personality weakness must be realistically considered and accommodated.

The second limiting factor is that traumas are objectively painful events, notwithstanding the fact that the person's subjective perspective increases the pain of the experience. Whatever the trauma, two elements are common. Traumas have the potential to take away from the person something needed to function well—namely, a source of security, love, or self-esteem—and they can add to the person something that significantly interferes with the person's functioning—namely, an overloading of stress. Thus the crisis counselor cannot return to the person the psychological resource that the trauma took away; the counselor can only help by reducing the overload of stress and by providing other resources to soften the pain.

The third limitation is that the counselor generally has little or no control over the reactions of family and friends to the person in crisis. These reactions may run the gamut from healthy support, to unhealthy support, antagonism, even outright rejection.

The counselor must enter this welter of psychological injury, painful feelings, psychological history, and family reactions with a clear and realistic understanding of each of these critical issues. The situation is somewhat analogous to the firefighter who is the first to arrive at the scene of a burning building that has people trapped inside. It is his or her duty to fight the fire as effectively as possible and to try to rescue the people. But the firefighter must also recognize the limitations inherent in the situation and calibrate expectations and behavior accordingly. In short, counselors need to correctly define their role and area of responsibility first and then work within it.

Holistic orientation. Crisis intervention demands a holistic approach. In crisis intervention, counselors must pursue and accept all the help they need. It is often necessary to refer the person to a physician for psychiatric evaluation and possibly medication. Ministers, priests, rabbis, and other clergy can be especially helpful when the person communicates a need for spiritual comfort. Sometimes it is appropriate to refer the person to a counselor of the opposite sex of the one initially contacted. For example, a woman who has been raped may feel more comfortable with a female counselor, or a man whose wife has just left him may feel more at ease with a male counselor.

In many situations, referral to other agencies is appropriate, either as a final referral or as ancillary to the work of the primary counselor. A woman who is in a crisis because she has been raped may be referred to a rape crisis center; a man who is drinking heavily as a means of handling a crisis may be referred to a detoxification center or a substance abuse counselor as a first step in the intervention process. Counselors must be familiar with the range of professional and paraprofessional resources in the community.

Flexibility.   Crisis intervention also requires flexibility. While setting limits and adhering to them is crucial to all types of counseling, limits usually have to be a bit more flexible in crisis intervention. Phone calls may be more appropriate; canceling or changing appointments may have more basis in reality; seeing the person in locations other than the counselor's office may, at times, be necessary; extending the length of sessions or increasing the agreed-upon number may also be appropriate. Intervening in family interactions may be more appropriate than it ordinarily would be. Making direct suggestions may be more helpful than is usually the case.

Crisis intervention ordinarily is not the time for counselors to behave and react as they would in more typical counseling situations. Usually it is not the time for confrontation; for lengthy, nondirective volleys; for delving into the developmental precursors of the crisis reaction; for interpreting behaviors or dreams; or for worrying much about transference and countertransference. A crisis atmosphere is much like that in any emergency situation. People do and say things that they may not ordinarily do or say in normal practice. They do what must be done to keep the person alive; it may not always follow the textbook. Counselors who have a fixed and firmly entrenched way of doing things are likely to be less effective in a crisis intervention situation.

Balance between empathy and strength.   Counselors who do crisis intervention need a great deal of empathy, a great deal of strength, and the ability to achieve a proper balance between the two. Some people are easy to feel empathy toward—for example, the parents whose child has just died or the young person who has just been told she has a terminal illness. Empathy may be much more difficult to feel toward other people—the man who is in a crisis because he has just been arrested for molesting children, including his own, and is now in an acute depression, or the woman who is in a state of shock because she violently assaulted her husband when he called her some vile names.

While counselors may feel the impulse to initially react to some people's crises with, "Well, they deserve to suffer for what they did," "They asked for it, and they got it," or "They're just *creating* a crisis to get attention," such impulses need to be acknowledged and carefully managed. Counselors are likely to experience such sentiments at one time or another because of social conditioning and personal experiences. Being aware of the possibility of such reactions places the counselor in a better position to control them and prevent them from unduly interfering with his or her attempts to help the person.

Counselors do encounter people in crisis who do not evoke much empathy, either because of their personality or the nature of their problem. If the counselor's negative sentiments are strong and lasting, it would be better to transfer the person to another counselor for the crisis intervention. The ability to develop empathy for people who evoke strong negative reactions is one of the great challenges that all counselors face, and to meet this challenge with a positive attitude is the mark of a good counselor.

Empathy without strength to balance it can slide into sympathy and malleability, which interfere with effective therapy. Strength means that counselors can maintain a healthy sense of separateness from the person and a willingness to stand by their decisions unless there is some compelling reason not to. A danger in crisis intervention is that the counselor may become so empathetic and immersed in the pain and pathos of the situation that he or she has no more objectivity or common sense than the person's family and friends. While counselors can empathize with the pain the client is experiencing, they must also remember that their main role is not solely to empathize but to help the person develop a more accurate perception of the situation and develop the skills and support needed to handle it effectively.

The Intervention Process

As is true with any type of counseling, crisis intervention follows a process. This does not mean that there is only one prescribed way of doing crisis intervention, any more than there is only one way to practice counseling. It simply means that it is necessary to follow basic guidelines, principles, and steps that will tie the process into a meaningful whole. Without this, crisis intervention would be comprised of scattered behaviors that are based more on intuition, good intentions, and panic than on sound counseling principles.

Kanel's (1999) ABC model for crisis intervention offers counselors a concise three-pronged approach to helping clients manage crisis situations. The three phases include: (A) developing and maintaining contact, (B) identifying the problem and the therapeutic interaction, and (C) coping.

The model helps counselors focus on the major elements of a crisis and identifies strategies and methods that improve the client's ability to cope. Reference is made to many of the elements of this model in the following sections, and her text should be considered required reading for anyone involved in crisis intervention.

Deciding to Do Crisis Intervention

The first consideration in the crisis intervention process is for the counselor to decide if he or she wants to get involved in a crisis intervention situation. Counselors usually consider several factors when deciding.

The first is formed from the qualifications and motivation of the counselor. Not all helpers are qualified to do crisis intervention. Some counselors are excellent in long-term treatment situations but have personalities that simply do not allow them to function well in crisis situations. When this is the case, it is better to transfer the person in crisis to an appropriate counselor or agency.

A counselor who feels qualified to do crisis intervention may, for any number of reasons, be unmotivated to do so or at least may be unmotivated at a particular time. There is nothing that dictates that counselors must agree to see everyone who seeks their help, though they must take steps to insure that the person is properly transferred to an appropriate agency or crisis intervention professional.

The second factor is the amount of time required. Crisis intervention may take a great deal of a counselor's time. While the crisis intervention literature suggests most crisis intervention work takes four to six sessions, the person in crisis does not know this. In acute crisis situations, especially when the trauma is great or there is an underlying disturbance, a counselor may be required to spend 15 hours or more in a month's time on one situation. With this in mind, counselors must balance the amount of time required with other professional and personal responsibilities. Counselors who find more demands on their time than they had initially expected can find *themselves* in their own semicrisis that creates resentment and diminishes their effectiveness as counselors.

The third factor is the nature of the crisis. Crisis intervention is often a more emotionally loaded situation than other types of counseling and hence may evoke strong feelings in the counselor. Will a counselor who has lost a child or spouse be the best helper for someone in a similar situation? Will a counselor who has been raped or had a loved one raped be the best person to help a rape victim or a rapist? Will a counselor who is experiencing painful marital stress or divorce be the best one to help a person in a similar situation? Although there are no obvious answers to these questions, counselors can legitimately ask themselves, "Do I really want to go through this again?" and "Will I be the most objective and healthily detached counselor for this person?"

The most important step in the crisis intervention process is for the counselor knowingly to consent to give his or her utmost energy and skill to the process. When the consent is uninformed or ambivalent, the rest of the process will lean precariously on a shaky foundation.

Factors Affecting a Positive Prognosis

The second consideration in the crisis intervention process is the question of what kinds of people in crisis get more out of crisis intervention. As is true with all counseling, some people are able to use crisis intervention better than others. The following are some factors that can be considered. While these factors are important, it should be remembered that a large portion of the success in crisis intervention can be attributed to the crisis intervention itself.

Duration of the crisis reaction. The majority of people in crisis seek help between 10 and 14 days after the precipitating trauma (Aguilera & Messick, 1978, p. 65). This is considered a relatively short time for the existence of a crisis reaction, and all other variables remaining the same, the prognosis for resolving the crisis is good. However, some people exist within the broader parameters of a crisis reaction for six months or a year before eventually deciding to seek professional help. A reasonable assumption in this situation is that the crisis reaction may have done some rather serious damage to the person and that the person's maladaptive coping mechanisms have become entrenched by sheer repetition, even though they were basically ineffective. To expect that these people will be significantly helped in 4 to 6 or even 20 sessions may be unrealistic.

Severity of the trauma and resultant symptoms. In general, there seems to be some relationship between the nature of the trauma and the resultant symptoms. Ordinarily, reactions are less severe when the trauma is being expelled from school than when it involves the loss of a job, when the trauma concerns marital stress than when it involves divorce, when the trauma is the breakup of a dating relationship than when it involves the loss of a loved one, and when the trauma is discovering one's child is a homosexual than being told that one has less than a year to live.

However, because the severity of the crisis reaction is contingent not only on the nature of the trauma but also on several other factors, a one-to-one relationship between a trauma and the resultant crisis reaction does not exist. It is possible that one person may have a minor crisis reaction to the death of a loved one while another may have a serious crisis reaction to the breakup of a dating relationship.

Consequently, when considering prognosis in crisis intervention, counselors must consider *both* the nature of the trauma *and* the severity of the symptoms. It seems reasonable to assume in most cases that mild traumas that have mild crisis reactions will be resolved more quickly and effectively than serious traumas that precipitate severe crisis reactions, with other combinations falling between these two points on a scale of prognosis.

Pretrauma personality. All other factors remaining the same, the weaker the pretrauma personality, the more counseling time and effort will be required to effect a successful resolution to the crisis reaction. Some people who are experiencing a crisis may have had normal, reasonably healthy personalities prior to the trauma. The trauma hit them in a particularly vulnerable area and created a crisis reaction, despite the presence of many psychological and environmental resources. With these people, the prognosis may be good.

However, as previously noted, many people who experience a crisis reaction to trauma had less than strong and healthy personalities before the trauma. Crisis intervention with these people will be more complicated and may not be as successful.

Although crisis intervention is not the place for a long and detailed psychological history, an abbreviated one taken at an opportune time can give the counselor some clues as to the strength of the pretrauma personality. This information can help the counselor obtain a clearer picture and establish realistic goals. While there are no foolproof ways of assessing the pretrauma strength of the person in crisis, some criteria can be helpful.

First, if a person has a history of crisis reactions or has behaved in maladaptive ways over a period of time, there would be some evidence pointing to personality problems that were present before the trauma.

Second, if the person's crisis reaction appears to be obviously disproportionate to the trauma, this could be another indication of a disturbed personality. For example, if a person is considering suicide because he failed to get into graduate school or is acutely depressed over not being selected for a fraternity, a counselor would be wise to conclude that psychological problems exist beyond those associated with the presenting crisis reaction.

Another criterion is the duration of the crisis reaction. If a person is still acutely depressed six months after the death of a loved one or is experiencing acute anxiety symptoms six months after an automobile accident, one could reasonably expect there is more to the picture than a crisis reaction.

A fourth criterion is how the person uses the crisis reaction. People with relatively healthy personalities do not *use* crisis reactions at all. They experience them and want to get rid of them as quickly as possible. People with personality problems may tend to use a crisis reaction for secondary gains. They may use the crisis reaction to elicit attention and sympathy past the point where it would be helpful or appropriate, to punish people whom they perceive as having caused the trauma or as having perpetrated injustices on them in the past, to escape facing some arduous or threatening responsibility at work or in marriage, or as a self-damaging tool that can further their veiled but ongoing efforts at ultimate self-destruction.

How the person uses the crisis can be seen in reactions to others during the crisis and the tenacity with which the person holds onto the symptoms. It also can be seen in the person's motivation or lack of motivation to follow through on the counselor's suggestions and the willingness to accept the environmental supports offered. If a person does have a pretrauma personality that is disturbed, this does not mean he or she is unsuitable for crisis intervention. It means that the counselor should be aware of these preexisting conditions and adjust counseling efforts, treatment strategies, prognoses, and recommendations accordingly.

Quantity and quality of environmental supports. In general, good environmental supports add significantly to a positive prognosis for crisis intervention. Environmental supports include family, friends, work, avocations, and religion. Some people in crisis receive a great deal of healthy support from family and friends who are willing to extend compassion, time, and material support in time of crisis. Other people may receive a great deal of unhealthy support. Parents, friends, or loved ones may try too hard to help, smothering the person and adding to the stress. One or more significant others may view the crisis period as an opportune time to take over the person's life or snatch him or her back into a dependency relationship. Still others are rejected by significant others because of the nature of the trauma. For example, parents may disown an unmarried daughter who becomes pregnant, or a husband may reject a wife who has been raped. Each of these responses from the environment increases stress in a person who is already overwhelmed.

Some people have satisfying jobs and understanding bosses, which help absorb some of the stress; others have jobs they abhor and bosses who refuse to give them time off from work during the crisis period. Some people have avocations, such as hobbies, sports, and volunteer work, that serve to reduce stress and distract them from a constant reliving of the trauma. They also may have a strong religious belief and a spiritual director who provides helpful ways of perceiving and handling the trauma. Other people in crisis have no avocations and/or no religious beliefs; hence, they must shoulder the brunt of the trauma more fully.

In weighing the positive and less positive aspects of the aforementioned variables, counselors will ultimately decide whether to agree to work with a person in a crisis intervention framework or whether another framework or counselor would be more helpful.

Sequence of Crisis Intervention

The third consideration in the process of crisis intervention is the sequence of steps that counselors can follow in helping people resolve crises. Each counselor, client, and crisis is different; therefore, no universally effective sequence can be postulated. However, by having a sequence of steps in mind, counselors can have a framework that they can modify according to their needs and the particular situation. The following is a four-step sequence that reflects one way of therapeutically intervening in a crisis situation. These steps are based on Beitman's (1987) four stages of counseling: engagement, pattern search, change, and termination. The content of the stages have been modified to accommodate a crisis intervention approach. Many of the skills discussed in earlier chapters of this text are equally useful in crisis intervention. The major difference is that the focus is narrowed to deal more directly with the presenting crisis, the client's perception of the traumatic event, the identification of intrapsychic and social and environmental supports, and the implementation of a course of action designed to help the client function and cope more effectively.

Step 1: Crisis engagement, reframing, and cognitive restructuring. During crisis engagement, the counselor needs first to establish a therapeutic alliance. The main difference here is that the alliance needs to form more quickly and in some ways more intensely, since very difficult emotions and reactions need to be shared very early in the intervention process. Empathy, support, and understanding form the basis of the counselor's early responses to the client. Once the relationship forms counselors need to quickly obtain some specific information about the client's affective, cognitive, and physical responses to the trauma. If the alliance is sufficiently strong the client should be able to reveal: the nature of the trauma, the kind and intensity of the crisis reaction, what the trauma and crisis reaction mean to the person, and what the person has been doing to resolve the crisis.

The client should be assessed for suicide risk, substance abuse history, prior trauma, physical symptoms, and medication history. This information will be used to assess the need for immediate referral to other mental health or medical professionals. Thoughts of suicide, sleep deprivation, and immobilizing anxiety are symptoms that demand immediate attention. In severe cases information may need to be obtained from significant others, especially when the client shows signs of a forming thought disorder or other serious psychiatric incapacity.

Unlike other forms of counseling, counselors during the crisis engagement phase are also expected to begin to reframe or cognitively restructure the client's perception of the trauma. Since much of what fuels the crisis can be found in the client's perception of the trauma, the counselor must, from the very outset, begin to help change those perceptions that are unrealistic and damaging. Crisis counselors often employ supportive statements that help the client understand that what has happened cannot be changed, though the client can control what he or she thinks about the events and what he or she will ultimately do in the face of the trauma.

It is important to recognize that it is not only the person who is being assessed and evaluated, but the counselor as well. At the end of the crisis engagement, there will be an explicit or implicit counseling agreement either to work together or not.

Step 2: Crisis pattern search. Once an alliance has been formed the counselor needs to obtain some historical information so that the counselor can obtain some sense of the client's personal, social, and environmental strengths and vulnerabilities. At this stage counselors will need to learn how the person has resolved crises in the past, what defenses the client is presently employing, what the client expects to obtain from the intervention, and why the person agreed to come for help.

Many times clients are so emotionally overwrought that it is necessary for them to express a wide range of feelings immediately. Counselors must walk the narrow line between stifling the feelings and allowing the feelings to control the session so that important information cannot be gathered.

It is better if the client volunteers the necessary information without being asked question after question. If the client does not volunteer, the counselor may need to ask a series of information-gathering questions, even though this practice would not ordinarily be used in other types of counseling.

After a counselor has reached an adequate understanding of the situation, it is important to invite ideas from the client as to how the client sees the counselor being of help. It is better to do this than compulsively to follow the next step in a prescribed outline. This does not mean the client in crisis always knows what is best for him or her. It simply means that people *can* know what is best for them, and it can be economical in terms of time and energy to ask before the counselor launches on a program of what he or she thinks will be helpful.

The main error to circumvent is the "This is what you need now" syndrome. The following are some verbal translations of this attitude:

1. "What you need now is to stop worrying about what you can't change." Perhaps. But most clients cannot follow such advice. A woman may lament, "My husband just died, and he was the only person in the world who loved me." Her worries about never finding what she had in her husband are real and intensely painful. At this point she needs compassion and time to ventilate these feelings.

2. "What you need now is to vent some painful feelings." Maybe. But it is possible that the client has vented feelings for a week and has gotten to a point of diminishing returns. He is simply regurgitating the same toxins day after day and is reinfecting himself. What he really needs now is to get at the source of the toxins and excise it.

3. "What you need now is to call upon your religious beliefs." Perhaps. But maybe the client is furious at God, whom she perceives

as having taken her child or husband away. She views God as punishing her for past sins and as being a very cruel and vengeful being. To encourage her to appeal to her religious beliefs as a source of comfort is to further stoke up her hatred of God and the fear and guilt that the hatred produces. Instead of reducing stress, appealing to her religious beliefs now could serve to increase it.

Contrary to what some of the literature states, experience indicates it is *people* who influence the sequence of reactions to the trauma and not the trauma that influences the reactions of the people. Naturally, if a counselor "leads" a client through certain prescribed steps of grieving, for example, the client will go through these steps. But when people are left to grieve according to their personalities, they often grieve differently from one another. When counselors fail to understand this, they may tend to force people through a resolution sequence that does not consider the client's unique personality and situation.

When a client is asked how the counselor might help, it is unlikely that the client will respond with a clear set of directions. But the behavioral reaction to the invitation will often provide the answer. One client may need to ventilate deep feelings of fear, anger, shame, guilt, grief, hurt, and despair. Another client may need to be educated by the counselor as to what is happening to him and how other people fare who have experienced similar traumas. A third client may need some practical advice. A fourth may need to ask the counselor what the counselor thinks of her after she "spilled her guts." A fifth client may be more concerned about someone else involved in the trauma than about himself and may need to discuss this situation.

Once the client is able to communicate directly or indirectly his or her needs, the counselor can judge whether it would be helpful to meet them at this point. People in crisis are often astute as to what will most reduce stress for them. Sometimes, however, they are so confused and frightened that it is necessary for counselors to use their best judgment as to what issues need immediate attention. At other times, people will ask counselors to meet their needs in ways that would be inappropriate or unhelpful. For example, a client may tell a counselor: "I'd sure appreciate it if you could call the district attorney's office and see if you can talk them out of filing charges against me" or "Maybe if you called my husband and told him what his leaving has done to me, he may come back and we can give our marriage one more try."

Once the counselor has a reasonably clear idea what steps will most quickly and effectively begin to reduce the crisis reaction, he or she begins the work necessary to free the client to move on to the next step in the sequence.

Environmental support is also explored in the crisis pattern search phase of the intervention. The purpose is to identify sources of help for the client outside of counseling. The client's environment can be helpful in two ways. It can afford the client some understanding, compassion, and practical support, such as food, lodging, and money. It also can remove or diminish stress, at least temporarily, while the client recovers. For example, an employer may give the client some time off work; in-laws may take care of the children for a while; a student may be excused from school or assignments for a period of time; creditors may allow extra time to pay bills. Counselors can help engender environmental supports by encouraging the client in crisis to use the available supports even though pride may be an obstacle. The counselor may invite family or friends to join some counseling sessions in order to reduce their anxiety about the crisis and to give them some ideas as to how they can be more helpful. The client may be encouraged to seek temporary changes in a work or school situation. The counselor may document the situation so that the client will be temporarily released from certain responsibilities. When people are in the midst of a crisis, common daily stresses associated with work and family responsibilities can become unbearable. Pressure to continue to shoulder these responsibilities can impede progress toward the successful resolution of the crisis.

Step 3: Crisis change. Step 3 includes planning for action, acting, and evaluating the action. By this step, the client should have progressed through whatever cognitive restructuring and emotional release was necessary to reduce the more acute aspects of the crisis reaction. The client is thinking more clearly and feeling more appropriately. The planning phase of the action step deals with the question, "What can you do outside of this room that will help reduce your anxiety and provide a little light at the end of the tunnel?" The next question is, "Exactly how are you going to accomplish this?"

More often than not, the answer to the first question will be "I don't know. If I knew, I wouldn't be here!" At this point, the counselor can patiently ask the client to list some options, regardless of how outlandish or impossible they sound. Sometimes the client is able to suggest some very plausible and helpful ideas. If, after a reasonable amount of time, the client genuinely cannot offer any options, the counselor may suggest some for consideration.

Counselors can be mindful of two points at this stage. One is that the proposed actions are not meant to resolve the crisis. A more realistic expectation is that each remedial activity will provide *some* symptomatic relief, and enough activities will provide *sufficient* relief so that, while the person continues to experience upset, he or she is no longer in a crisis state. This is in answer to the frequently heard response from the person in crisis to a suggestion from a counselor: "What good will *that* do—that won't solve anything."

A second point is that when two people earnestly struggle together to form some plan of action, it can be therapeutic in itself, even if no concrete plans are made during that particular session. Sometimes people leave such a session with the comment "Well, I still don't know what to do, but somehow I feel a little better."

Once some options for action are explored, the next phase is to try them out. What the actions are depends upon the nature of the trauma and the crisis. The trauma of failing in medical school will dictate different actions than that of an unwanted pregnancy, loss of a loved one, discovering that one's child is an addict, or being raped. If the proposed actions work to reduce stress, more options are explored in order to reduce symptoms further. If the actions do not bring about the desired result, new options are considered and acted upon.

Each action is evaluated. For the actions that worked, it is important to discover why they worked for future reference. It is equally important to find out why other options failed. Did the plan fail because it was a bad idea, or was it a good idea but poorly carried out? Successful actions are repeated and added to; unsuccessful ones are scuttled and replaced with effective ones.

It is important to realize that actions that work for one person may be unhelpful or even destructive to another. It is perilous to assume that what worked for the last rape victim will work for the next one. For example, it may be helpful for one person to share the crisis with parents, but for another this would be destructive. It may be helpful for one person to take a week off from work and disappear into the mountains, but this may be the worst thing someone else could do. It may be relatively easy for one woman to report to the police that she has been raped and very stressful for another.

Step 4: Crisis termination.   Step 4 is meant to tie up any loose ends and to be educative. It is both past and future oriented. The counselor and the person summarize what was learned during the previous sessions. The person, who is now in a state closer to equilibrium, is encouraged to reflect on how he or she turned a trauma into a crisis. Usually there are one or two things that the person did that exacerbated the trauma into a crisis. The person may have viewed the trauma in an overly catastrophic way, waited too long to take some action to prevent the crisis reaction from developing, pretended to have feelings that really did not exist, pretended not to have feelings that did exist, failed to use environmental supports wisely, underestimated his or her capacity to handle emergency situations, used defense mechanisms rather than adaptive behavior to handle the stress, or allowed himself or herself to get overly upset to garner some secondary gains.

This psychological reconnoitering is done with a positive spirit: "Let's see what we learned from this crisis that will help you next time a difficult situation arises." This invitation bridges the past and the future. The future dimension deals with the question, "What will you do differently next time if a trauma arises?" The discussion that these questions engender can give people the feeling that they learned something valuable about themselves, people, and life in general from the crisis intervention.

It is also at this time that the counselor may suggest further help in the form of short-term counseling of a noncrisis type or long-term counseling. It is helpful for counselors to approach this area with prudence. It may be that the person does not need any further professional help at this time, or the person may need further help, but this is not the time to approach the subject because the person is still quite tender psychologically and the suggestion would add further stress to the delicate postcrisis equilibrium. If this is the case, the counselor can set a definite time for a follow-up visit in the near future, at which time the recommendation can be made.

It may be that this is the exact time to recommend further help because the person needs it and the pain of the crisis is still fresh enough that the person would be willing to embark on any program that would help prevent a future occurrence. In any case, the termination should include an open invitation to return for "psychological refueling" any time the person feels the need.

Pitfalls

As counselors progress through these four steps, they will meet several potential pitfalls that are best avoided. The following are eight of the more common ones.

1. "Taking over" for the person in crisis who does not need this level of direction. It is not helpful for counselors to assume control of and responsibility for the welfare of all people in crisis. Many people in crisis are capable of making appropriate decisions, and if they are not, it may be better to encourage the person to enlist the aid of those family members or friends who are in a position to offer appropriate levels of support and sound guidance.

2. Giving false assurance. A common social response to those in crisis is to assure them that things aren't as bad as they seem and that the future is bright. However, false assurance is not a therapeutic response. False assurance simply communicates to the person in crisis that the counselor does not clearly understand the situation. A realistic appraisal of the trauma is ultimately more helpful.

3. Focusing on the cause of crisis rather than on the resolution. It may be tempting for counselors to focus on questions such as, "How did you get yourself into this mess anyway?" instead of "How are we going to get you some relief?" Analogously, while it is important to ascertain the cause of a fire, one must extinguish the fire first and only then seek its origin. It is only in the final step of the crisis intervention process that it is appropriate to examine the factors contributing to the crisis.

4. Assuming the psychological meaning of the trauma. The same trauma can have many meanings to different people. A counselor may assume that a man is experiencing acute anxiety because he loved his deceased wife so deeply. In reality, however, his crisis reaction may be caused by his guilt for *not* feeling sad.

A woman who is dropped from medical school in her final year reacts with acute depression, and the counselor interprets this as meaning she is crestfallen that she will not be a physician. In fact, the woman never wanted to be a physician. All she wanted to do was make her physician father proud of her, and now she feels she has failed. Some very erroneous paths can be followed when counselors assume the meaning of a trauma to be different from what it actually is.

5. "Catching" the panic of the person in crisis. Anxiety can be very contagious, and even experienced counselors are not immune to it. A counselor may be handling a crisis situation well until the person mentions doing something drastic (running away, suicide, homicide, going crazy), and then the counselor panics and makes imprudent decisions. Panic can be prevented by working closely with a colleague in very difficult cases, by being mindful that counselors are not responsible for what happens to the person but only for doing the best they can in the situation, and by using environmental supports, such as getting other agencies involved, advising the family of the potential dangers, and hospitalization.

6. Underestimating or overestimating the situation. Underestimating means communicating the attitude, "I realize you are terribly upset, but I work with these situations all the time, and it's no big deal." This conveys to the person in crisis that the counselor is cavalier about the biggest problem the person has probably ever encountered. Overestimating the crisis is to become as intense and worried as the person in crisis, which conveys the message, "You *are* in serious trouble." This adds even more stress to a seemingly intolerable situation.

7. Failing to ask for help when it is needed. Some crisis situations are extremely complicated and intense. But some counselors feel that they will "lose face" if they call in one or more colleagues for consultation. Just as it takes more than one surgeon to do complicated surgery, it may take more than one counselor to handle a crisis situation.

8. Assuming that the principles that are valid in one type of crisis are equally valid when applied to all types of crises. While there are some general principles that underlie all crisis intervention, many crises also have a specific set of counseling principles. Read-

ers who are interested in references that deal with specific types of crisis—such as grief, rape, suicide, and family and maturational crises—should review Aguilera and Messick (1978), Belkin (1980a), Dixon (1979), and Kanel (1999).

.⚜.
Summary

It is important to put crisis intervention into a proper perspective. The success of crisis intervention depends on the nature of the trauma, the severity of the crisis reaction, the pretrauma personality of the person, the level of available environmental/social support, and the skills of the counselor. In some ways, it is a very difficult type of counseling to do because the stakes are usually high and the time is short. On the other hand, because the person in crisis is often suggestible and motivated to try anything, a minimal amount of intervention can bring about a maximum amount of relief.

A crisis is never inherently beneficial, and mental health professionals must do all they can to educate people regarding how to avoid turning traumas into crises. However, good can come of a crisis in ways that may not have occurred in any other way in a particular individual. Leitner and Stecher illustrate this crucial point by writing that:

> When forces of life push our daily existence to some edge whereupon we find ourselves in the midst of crisis, then we have a chance to emerge as changed beings. Growth implies change and change may imply growth. Emerging from a crisis can be a movement toward a new being-state, one that we may not have been capable of before the crisis. . . . Crises call for risking. People in crisis, under intense pressure, become introspective—they can look at themselves more deeply and honestly than in times of tranquillity. (Quoted in Belkin, 1980a, p. 331)

.⚜.
Reflection Questions

1. What do you think is the most common mistake counselors make in doing crisis intervention?

2. What types of crises would you feel more comfortable dealing with, and what types would you feel less comfortable dealing with? Why?

3. What strengths do you possess that would make you particularly effective in crisis intervention? What qualities do you need to strengthen in order to feel confident doing crisis intervention?

4. What thoughts and feelings would arise within you if a person you had seen for the first of several scheduled crisis intervention sessions refused your help and the help of anyone else immediately following the first meeting? What would you do?

5. Under what specific circumstances would you feel it helpful to consult a colleague in a crisis intervention situation?

Appendix A

ACA CODE OF ETHICS AND STANDARDS OF PRACTICE

Preamble

The American Counseling Association is an educational, scientific, and professional organization whose members are dedicated to the enhancement of human development throughout the life-span. Association members recognize diversity in our society and embrace a cross- cultural approach in support of the worth, dignity, potential, and uniqueness of each individual.

The specification of a code of ethics enables the association to clarify to current and future members, and to those served by members, the nature of the ethical responsibilities held in common by its members. As the code of ethics of the association, this document establishes principles that define the ethical behavior of association members. All members of the American Counseling Association are required to adhere to the Code of Ethics and the Standards of Practice. The Code of Ethics will serve as the basis for processing ethical complaints initiated against members of the association.

ACA Code of Ethics

Section A: The Counseling Relationship
Section B: Confidentiality
Section C: Professional Responsibility

Section D: Relationships With Other Professionals
Section E: Evaluation, Assessment, and Interpretation
Section F: Teaching, Training, and Supervision
Section G: Research and Publication
Section H: Resolving Ethical Issues

Section A: The Counseling Relationship

A.1. Client Welfare
a. Primary Responsibility. The primary responsibility of counselors is to respect the dignity and to promote the welfare of clients.
b. Positive Growth and Development. Counselors encourage client growth
   and development in ways that foster the clients' interest and welfare;
   counselors avoid fostering dependent counseling relationships.
c. Counseling Plans. Counselors and their clients work jointly in devising
   integrated, individual counseling plans that offer reasonable promise of
   success and are consistent with abilities and circumstances of clients.
   Counselors and clients regularly review counseling plans to ensure their
   continued viability and effectiveness, respecting clients' freedom of
   choice. (See A.3.b.)
d. Family Involvement. Counselors recognize that families are usually important in clients' lives and strive to enlist family understanding and involvement as a positive resource, when appropriate.
e. Career and Employment Needs. Counselors work with their clients in
   considering employment in jobs and circumstances that are consistent
   with the clients' overall abilities, vocational limitations, physical restrictions, general temperament, interest and aptitude patterns, social skills,
   education, general qualifications, and other relevant characteristics and
   needs. Counselors neither place nor participate in placing clients in positions that will result in damaging the interest and the welfare of clients,
   employers, or the public.

A.2. Respecting Diversity
a. Nondiscrimination. Counselors do not condone or engage in discrimination based on age, color, culture, disability, ethnic group, gender, race, religion, sexual orientation, marital status, or socioeconomic status. (See
   C.5.a., C.5.b., and D.1.i.)
b. Respecting Differences. Counselors will actively attempt to understand
   the diverse cultural backgrounds of the clients with whom they work.
   This includes, but is not limited to, learning how the counselor's own cul-
   tural/ethnic/racial identity impacts her or his values and beliefs about the
   counseling process. (See E.8. and F.2.i.)

A.3. Client Rights
a. Disclosure to Clients. When counseling is initiated, and throughout the
   counseling process as necessary, counselors inform clients of the purposes, goals, techniques, procedures, limitations, potential risks, and benefits of services to be performed, and other pertinent information.
   Counselors take steps to ensure that clients understand the implications
   of diagnosis, the intended use of tests and reports, fees, and billing ar-

rangements. Clients have the right to expect confidentiality and to be provided with an explanation of its limitations, including supervision and/or treatment team professionals; to obtain clear information about their case records; to participate in the ongoing counseling plans; and to refuse any recommended services and be advised of the consequences of such refusal. (See E.5.a. and G.2.)

b. Freedom of Choice. Counselors offer clients the freedom to choose whether to enter into a counseling relationship and to determine which professional(s) will provide counseling. Restrictions that limit choices of clients are fully explained. (See A.1.c.)

c. Inability to Give Consent. When counseling minors or persons unable to give voluntary informed consent, counselors act in these clients' best interests. (See B.3.)

A.4. Clients Served by Others

If a client is receiving services from another mental health professional, counselors, with client consent, inform the professional persons already involved and develop clear agreements to avoid confusion and conflict for the client. (See C.6.c.)

A.5. Personal Needs and Values

a. Personal Needs. In the counseling relationship, counselors are aware of the intimacy and responsibilities inherent in the counseling relationship, maintain respect for clients, and avoid actions that seek to meet their personal needs at the expense of clients.

b. Personal Values. Counselors are aware of their own values, attitudes, beliefs, and behaviors and how these apply in a diverse society, and avoid imposing their values on clients. (See C.5.a.)

A.6. Dual Relationships

a. Avoid When Possible. Counselors are aware of their influential positions with respect to clients, and they avoid exploiting the trust and dependency of clients. Counselors make every effort to avoid dual relationships with clients that could impair professional judgment or increase the risk of harm to clients. (Examples of such relationships include, but are not limited to, familial, social, financial, business, or close personal relationships with clients.) When a dual relationship cannot be avoided, counselors take appropriate professional precautions such as informed consent, consultation, supervision, and documentation to ensure that judgment is not impaired and no exploitation occurs. (See F.1.b.)

b. Superior/Subordinate Relationships. Counselors do not accept as clients superiors or subordinates with whom they have administrative, supervisory, or evaluative relationships.

A.7. Sexual Intimacies With Clients

a. Current Clients. Counselors do not have any type of sexual intimacies with clients and do not counsel persons with whom they have had a sexual relationship.

b. Former Clients. Counselors do not engage in sexual intimacies with former clients within a minimum of 2 years after terminating the counseling relationship. Counselors who engage in such relationship after 2 years following termination have the responsibility to examine and document thoroughly that such relations did not have an exploitative nature, based on factors such as duration of counseling, amount of time since counseling, termination circumstances, client's personal history and mental status, adverse impact on the client, and actions by the counselor suggesting a plan to initiate a sexual relationship with the client after termination.

A.8. Multiple Clients

When counselors agree to provide counseling services to two or more persons who have a relationship (such as husband and wife, or parents and children), counselors clarify at the outset which person or persons are clients and the nature of the relationships they will have with each involved person. If it becomes apparent that counselors may be called upon to perform potentially conflicting roles, they clarify, adjust, or withdraw from roles appropriately. (See B.2. and B.4.d.)

A.9. Group Work

a. Screening. Counselors screen prospective group counseling/therapy participants. To the extent possible, counselors select members whose needs and goals are compatible with goals of the group, who will not impede the group process, and whose well-being will not be jeopardized by the group experience.

b. Protecting Clients. In a group setting, counselors take reasonable precautions to protect clients from physical or psychological trauma.

A.10. Fees and Bartering (See D.3.a. and D.3.b.)

a. Advance Understanding. Counselors clearly explain to clients, prior to entering the counseling relationship, all financial arrangements related to professional services including the use of collection agencies or legal measures for nonpayment. (A.11.c.)

b. Establishing Fees. In establishing fees for professional counseling services, counselors consider the financial status of clients and locality. In the event that the established fee structure is inappropriate for a client, assistance is provided in attempting to find comparable services of acceptable cost. (See A.10.d., D.3.a., and D.3.b.)

c. Bartering Discouraged. Counselors ordinarily refrain from accepting goods or services from clients in return for counseling services because such arrangements create inherent potential for conflicts, exploitation, and distortion of the professional relationship. Counselors may participate in bartering only if the relationship is not exploitative, if the client requests it, if a clear written contract is established, and if such arrangements are an accepted practice among professionals in the community. (See A.6.a.)

d. Pro Bono Service. Counselors contribute to society by devoting a portion of their professional activity to services for which there is little or no financial return (pro bono).

A.11. Termination and Referral

a. Abandonment Prohibited. Counselors do not abandon or neglect clients in counseling. Counselors assist in making appropriate arrangements for the continuation of treatment, when necessary, during interruptions such as vacations, and following termination.

b. Inability to Assist Clients. If counselors determine an inability to be of professional assistance to clients, they avoid entering or immediately terminate a counseling relationship. Counselors are knowledgeable about referral resources and suggest appropriate alternatives. If clients decline the suggested referral, counselors should discontinue the relationship.

c. Appropriate Termination. Counselors terminate a counseling relationship, securing client agreement when possible, when it is reasonably clear that the client is no longer benefiting, when services are no longer required, when counseling no longer serves the client's needs or interests, when clients do not pay fees charged, or when agency or institution limits do not allow provision of further counseling services. (See A.10.b. and C.2.g.)

A.12. Computer Technology

a. Use of Computers. When computer applications are used in counseling services, counselors ensure that (1) the client is intellectually, emotionally, and physically capable of using the computer application; (2) the computer application is appropriate for the needs of the client; (3) the client understands the purpose and operation of the computer applications; and (4) a follow-up of client use of a computer application is provided to correct possible misconceptions, discover inappropriate use, and assess subsequent needs.

b. Explanation of Limitations. Counselors ensure that clients are provided information as a part of the counseling relationship that adequately explains the limitations of computer technology.

c. Access to Computer Applications. Counselors provide for equal access to computer applications in counseling services. (See A.2.a.)

Section B: Confidentiality

B.1. Right to Privacy

a. Respect for Privacy. Counselors respect their clients right to privacy and avoid illegal and unwarranted disclosures of confidential information. (See A.3.a. and B.6.a.)

b. Client Waiver. The right to privacy may be waived by the client or his or her legally recognized representative.

c. Exceptions. The general requirement that counselors keep information confidential does not apply when disclosure is required to prevent clear and imminent danger to the client or others or when legal requirements demand that confidential information be revealed. Counselors consult with other professionals when in doubt as to the validity of an exception.

d. Contagious, Fatal Diseases. A counselor who receives information confirming that a client has a disease commonly known to be both communicable and fatal is justified in disclosing information to an identifiable third party, who by his or her relationship with the client is at a high risk of contracting the disease. Prior to making a disclosure the counselor should ascertain that the client has not already informed the third party about his or her disease and that the client is not intending to inform the third party in the immediate future. (See B.1.c and B.1.f.)

e. Court-Ordered Disclosure. When court ordered to release confidential information without a client's permission, counselors request to the court that the disclosure not be required due to potential harm to the client or counseling relationship. (See B.1.c.)

f. Minimal Disclosure. When circumstances require the disclosure of confidential information, only essential information is revealed. To the extent possible, clients are informed before confidential information is disclosed.

g. Explanation of Limitations. When counseling is initiated and throughout the counseling process as necessary, counselors inform clients of the limitations of confidentiality and identify foreseeable situations in which confidentiality must be breached. (See G.2.a.)

h. Subordinates. Counselors make every effort to ensure that privacy and confidentiality of clients are maintained by subordinates including employees, supervisees, clerical assistants, and volunteers. (See B.1.a.)

i. Treatment Teams. If client treatment will involve a continued review by a treatment team, the client will be informed of the team's existence and composition.

B.2. Groups and Families

a. Group Work. In group work, counselors clearly define confidentiality and the parameters for the specific group being entered, explain its importance, and discuss the difficulties related to confidentiality involved in group work. The fact that confidentiality cannot be guaranteed is clearly communicated to group members.

b. Family Counseling. In family counseling, information about one family member cannot be disclosed to another member without permission. Counselors protect the privacy rights of each family member. (See A.8., B.3., and B.4.d.)

B.3. Minor or Incompetent Clients

When counseling clients who are minors or individuals who are unable to give voluntary, informed consent, parents or guardians may be included in the counseling process as appropriate. Counselors act in the best interests of clients and take measures to safeguard confidentiality. (See A.3.c.)

B.4. Records

a. Requirement of Records. Counselors maintain records necessary for rendering professional services to their clients and as required by laws, regulations, or agency or institution procedures.

b. Confidentiality of Records. Counselors are responsible for securing the safety and confidentiality of any counseling records they create, maintain, transfer, or destroy whether the records are written, taped, computerized, or stored in any other medium. (See B.1.a.)

c. Permission to Record or Observe. Counselors obtain permission from clients prior to electronically recording or observing sessions. (See A.3.a.)

d. Client Access. Counselors recognize that counseling records are kept for the benefit of clients, and therefore provide access to records and copies of records when requested by competent clients, unless the records contain information that may be misleading and detrimental to the client. In situations involving multiple clients, access to records is limited to those parts of records that do not include confidential information related to another client. (See A.8., B.1.a., and B.2.b.)

e. Disclosure or Transfer. Counselors obtain written permission from clients to disclose or transfer records to legitimate third parties unless exceptions to confidentiality exist as listed in Section B.1. Steps are taken to ensure that receivers of counseling records are sensitive to their confidential nature.

B.5. Research and Training

a. Data Disguise Required. Use of data derived from counseling relationships for purposes of training, research, or publication is confined to content that is disguised to ensure the anonymity of the individuals involved. (See B.1.g. and G.3.d.)

b. Agreement for Identification. Identification of a client in a presentation or publication is permissible only when the client has reviewed the material and has agreed to its presentation or publication. (See G.3.d.)

B.6. Consultation

a. Respect for Privacy. Information obtained in a consulting relationship is discussed for professional purposes only with persons clearly concerned with the case. Written and oral reports present data germane to the purposes of the consultation, and every effort is made to protect client identity and avoid undue invasion of privacy.

b. Cooperating Agencies. Before sharing information, counselors make efforts to ensure that there are defined policies in other agencies serving the counselor's clients that effectively protect the confidentiality of information.

Section C: Professional Responsibility

C.1. Standards Knowledge
Counselors have a responsibility to read, understand, and follow the Code of Ethics and the Standards of Practice.

C.2. Professional Competence

a. Boundaries of Competence. Counselors practice only within the boundaries of their competence, based on their education, training, supervised experience, state and national professional credentials, and appropriate professional experience. Counselors will demonstrate a commitment to gain knowledge, personal awareness, sensitivity, and skills pertinent to working with a diverse client population.

b. New Specialty Areas of Practice. Counselors practice in specialty areas new to them only after appropriate education, training, and supervised experience. While developing skills in new specialty areas, counselors take steps to ensure the competence of their work and to protect others from possible harm.

c. Qualified for Employment. Counselors accept employment only for positions for which they are qualified by education, training, supervised experience, state and national professional credentials, and appropriate professional experience. Counselors hire for professional counseling positions only individuals who are qualified and competent.

d. Monitor Effectiveness. Counselors continually monitor their effectiveness as professionals and take steps to improve when necessary. Counselors in private practice take reasonable steps to seek out peer supervision to evaluate their efficacy as counselors.

e. Ethical Issues Consultation. Counselors take reasonable steps to consult with other counselors or related professionals when they have questions regarding their ethical obligations or professional practice. (See H.1.)

f. Continuing Education. Counselors recognize the need for continuing education to maintain a reasonable level of awareness of current scientific and professional information in their fields of activity. They take steps to maintain competence in the skills they use, are open to new procedures, and keep current with the diverse and/or special populations with whom they work.

g. Impairment. Counselors refrain from offering or accepting professional services when their physical, mental, or emotional problems are likely to harm a client or others. They are alert to the signs of impairment, seek assistance for problems, and, if necessary, limit, suspend, or terminate their professional responsibilities. (See A.11.c.)

C.3. Advertising and Soliciting Clients

a. Accurate Advertising. There are no restrictions on advertising by counselors except those that can be specifically justified to protect the public from deceptive practices. Counselors advertise or represent their services to the public by identifying their credentials in an accurate manner that is not false, misleading, deceptive, or fraudulent. Counselors may only advertise the highest degree earned which is in counseling or a closely related field from a college or university that was accredited when the degree was awarded by one of the regional accrediting bodies recognized by the Council on Postsecondary Accreditation.

b. Testimonials. Counselors who use testimonials do not solicit them from clients or other persons who, because of their particular circumstances, may be vulnerable to undue influence.

c. Statements by Others. Counselors make reasonable efforts to ensure that statements made by others about them or the profession of counseling are accurate.

d. Recruiting Through Employment. Counselors do not use their places of employment or institutional affiliation to recruit or gain clients, supervisees, or consultees for their private practices. (See C.5.e.)

e. Products and Training Advertisements. Counselors who develop products related to their profession or conduct workshops or training events ensure that the advertisements concerning these products or events are accurate and disclose adequate information for consumers to make informed choices.

f. Promoting to Those Served. Counselors do not use counseling, teaching, training, or supervisory relationships to promote their products or training events in a manner that is deceptive or would exert undue influence on individuals who may be vulnerable. Counselors may adopt textbooks they have authored for instruction purposes.

g. Professional Association Involvement. Counselors actively participate in local, state, and national associations that foster the development and improvement of counseling.

C.4. Credentials

a. Credentials Claimed. Counselors claim or imply only professional credentials possessed and are responsible for correcting any known misrepresentations of their credentials by others. Professional credentials include graduate degrees in counseling or closely related mental health fields, accreditation of graduate programs, national voluntary certifications, government-issued certifications or licenses, ACA professional membership, or any other credential that might indicate to the public specialized knowledge or expertise in counseling.

b. ACA Professional Membership. ACA professional members may announce to the public their membership status. Regular members may not announce their ACA membership in a manner that might imply they are credentialed counselors.

c. Credential Guidelines. Counselors follow the guidelines for use of credentials that have been established by the entities that issue the credentials.

d. Misrepresentation of Credentials. Counselors do not attribute more to their credentials than the credentials represent, and do not imply that other counselors are not qualified because they do not possess certain credentials.

e. Doctoral Degrees From Other Fields. Counselors who hold a master's degree in counseling or a closely related mental health field, but hold a doctoral degree from other than counseling or a closely related field, do not use the title "Dr." in their practices and do not announce to the public in relation to their practice or status as a counselor that they hold a doctorate.

C.5. Public Responsibility

a. Nondiscrimination. Counselors do not discriminate against clients, students, or supervisees in a manner that has a negative impact based on their age, color, culture, disability, ethnic group, gender, race, religion, sexual orientation, or socioeconomic status, or for any other reason. (See A.2.a.)

b. Sexual Harassment. Counselors do not engage in sexual harassment. Sexual harassment is defined as sexual solicitation, physical advances, or verbal or nonverbal conduct that is sexual in nature, that occurs in connection with professional activities or roles, and that either (1) is unwelcome, is offensive, or creates a hostile workplace environment, and counselors know or are told this; or (2) is sufficiently severe or intense to be perceived as harassment to a reasonable person in the context. Sexual harassment can consist of a single intense or severe act or multiple persistent or pervasive acts.

c. Reports to Third Parties. Counselors are accurate, honest, and unbiased in reporting their professional activities and judgments to appropriate third parties including courts, health insurance companies, those who are the recipients of evaluation reports, and others. (See B.1.g.)

d. Media Presentations. When counselors provide advice or co means of public lectures, demonstrations, radio or television programs, prerecorded tapes, printed articles, mailed material, or other media, they take reasonable precautions to ensure that (1) appropriate professional counseling literature and practice; (2) the statements are otherwise consistent with the Code of Ethics and the Standards of Practice; and (3) the recipients of the information are not encouraged to infer that a professional counseling relationship has been established. (See C.6.b.)

e. Unjustified Gains. Counselors do not use their professional positions to seek or receive unjustified personal gains, sexual favors, unfair advantage, or unearned goods or services. (See C.3.d.)

C.6. Responsibility to Other Professionals

a. Different Approaches. Counselors are respectful of approaches to professional counseling that differ from their own. Counselors know and take into account the traditions and practices of other professional groups with which they work.

b. Personal Public Statements. When making personal statements in a public context, counselors clarify that they are speaking from their personal perspectives and that they are not speaking on behalf of all counselors or the profession. (See C.5.d.)

c. Clients Served by Others.When counselors learn that their clients are in a professional relationship with another mental health professional, they request release from clients to inform the other professionals and strive to establish positive and collaborative professional relationships. (See A.4.)

Section D: Relationships With Other Professionals

D.1. Relationships With Employers and Employees

a. Role Definition. Counselors define and describe for their employers and employees the parameters and levels of their professional roles.

b. Agreements. Counselors establish working agreements with supervisors, colleagues, and subordinates regarding counseling or clinical relationships, confidentiality, adherence to professional standards, distinction between public and private material, maintenance and dissemination of recorded information, work load, and accountability. Working agreements in each instance are specified and made known to those concerned.

c. Negative Conditions. Counselors alert their employers to conditions that may be potentially disruptive or damaging to the counselor's professional responsibilities or that may limit their effectiveness.

d. Evaluation. Counselors submit regularly to professional review and evaluation by their supervisor or the appropriate representative of the employer.

e. In-Service. Counselors are responsible for in-service development of self and staff.

f. Goals.Counselors inform their staff of goals and programs.

g. Practices. Counselors provide personnel and agency practices that respect and enhance the rights and welfare of each employee and recipient of agency services. Counselors strive to maintain the highest levels of professional services.

h. Personnel Selection and Assignment. Counselors select competent staff and assign responsibilities compatible with their skills and experiences.

i. Discrimination. Counselors, as either employers or employees, do not engage in or condone practices that are inhumane, illegal, or unjustifiable (such as considerations based on age, color, culture, disability, ethnic group, gender, race, religion, sexual orientation, or socioeconomic status) in hiring, promotion, or training. (See A.2.a. and C.5.b.)

j. Professional Conduct. Counselors have a responsibility both to clients and to the agency or institution within which services are performed to maintain high standards of professional conduct.

k. Exploitative Relationships. Counselors do not engage in exploitative relationships with individuals over whom they have supervisory, evaluative, or instructional control or authority.

l. Employer Policies. The acceptance of employment in an agency or institution implies that counselors are in agreement with its general policies and principles. Counselors strive to reach agreement with employers as to acceptable standards of conduct that allow for changes in institutional policy conducive to the growth and development of clients.

D.2. Consultation (See B.6.)

a. Consultation as an Option. Counselors may choose to consult with any other professionally competent persons about their clients. In choosing consultants, counselors avoid placing the consultant in a conflict of interest situation that would preclude the consultant being a proper party to the counselor's efforts to help the client. Should counselors be engaged in a work setting that compromises this consultation standard, they consult with other professionals whenever possible to consider justifiable alternatives.

b. Consultant Competency. Counselors are reasonably certain that they have or the organization represented has the necessary competencies and resources for giving the kind of consulting services needed and that appropriate referral resources are available.

c. Understanding With Clients. When providing consultation, counselors attempt to develop with their clients a clear understanding of problem definition, goals for change, and predicted consequences of interventions selected.

d. Consultant Goals. The consulting relationship is one in which client adaptability and growth toward self-direction are consistently encouraged and cultivated. (See A.1.b.)

D.3. Fees for Referral

a. Accepting Fees From Agency Clients. Counselors refuse a private fee or other remuneration for rendering services to persons who are entitled to such services through the counselor's employing agency or institution. The policies of a particular agency may make explicit provisions for agency clients to receive counseling services from members of its staff in private practice. In such instances, the clients must be informed of other options open to them should they seek private counseling services. (See A.10.a., A.11.b., and C.3.d.)

b. Referral Fees. Counselors do not accept a referral fee from other professionals.

D.4. Subcontractor Arrangements

When counselors work as subcontractors for counseling services for a third party, they have a duty to inform clients of the limitations of confidentiality that the organization may place on counselors in providing counseling services to clients. The limits of such confidentiality ordinarily are discussed as part of the intake session. (See B.1.e. and B.1.f.)

Section E: Evaluation, Assessment, and Interpretation

E.1. General

a. Appraisal Techniques. The primary purpose of educational and psychological assessment is to provide measures that are objective and interpretable in either comparative or absolute terms. Counselors recognize the need to interpret the statements in this section as applying to the whole range of appraisal techniques, including test and nontest data.

b. Client Welfare. Counselors promote the welfare and best interests of the client in the development, publication, and utilization of educational and psychological assessment techniques. They do not misuse assessment results and interpretations and take reasonable steps to prevent others from misusing the information these techniques provide. They respect the client's right to know the results, the interpretations made, and the bases for their conclusions and recommendations.

E.2. Competence to Use and Interpret Tests

a. Limits of Competence. Counselors recognize the limits of their competence and perform only those testing and assessment services for which they have been trained. They are familiar with reliability, validity, related standardization, error of measurement, and proper application of any technique utilized. Counselors using computer-based test interpretations are trained in the construct being measured and the specific instrument being used prior to using this type of computer application. Counselors take reasonable measures to ensure the proper use of psychological assessment techniques by persons under their supervision.

b. Appropriate Use. Counselors are responsible for the appropriate application, scoring, interpretation, and use of assessment instruments, whether they score and interpret such tests themselves or use computerized or other services.

c. Decisions Based on Results. Counselors responsible for decisions involving individuals or policies that are based on assessment results have a thorough understanding of educational and psychological measurement, including validation criteria, test research, and guidelines for test development and use.

d. Accurate Information. Counselors provide accurate information and avoid false claims or misconceptions when making statements about assessment instruments or techniques. Special efforts are made to avoid unwarranted connotations of such terms as IQ and grade equivalent scores. (See C.5.c.)

E.3. Informed Consent

a. Explanation to Clients. Prior to assessment, counselors explain the nature and purposes of assessment and the specific use of results in language the client (or other legally authorized person on behalf of the client) can understand, unless an explicit exception to this right has been agreed upon in advance. Regardless of whether scoring and interpretation are completed by counselors, by assistants, or by computer or other outside services, counselors take reasonable steps to ensure that appropriate explanations are given to the client.

b. Recipients of Results. The examinee's welfare, explicit understanding, and prior agreement determine the recipients of test results. Counselors include accurate and appropriate interpretations with any release of individual or group test results. (See B.1.a. and C.5.c.)

E.4. Release of Information to Competent Professionals

a. Misuse of Results. Counselors do not misuse assessment results, including test results, and interpretations, and take reasonable steps to prevent the misuse of such by others. (See C.5.c.)

b. Release of Raw Data. Counselors ordinarily release data (e.g., protocols, counseling or interview notes, or questionnaires) in which the client is identified only with the consent of the client or the client's legal representative. Such data are usually released only to persons recognized by counselors as competent to interpret the data. (See B.1.a.)

E.5. Proper Diagnosis of Mental Disorders

a. Proper Diagnosis. Counselors take special care to provide proper diagnosis of mental disorders. Assessment techniques (including personal interview) used to determine client care (e.g., locus of treatment, type of treatment, or recommended follow-up) are carefully selected and appropriately used. (See A.3.a. and C.5.c.)

b. Cultural Sensitivity. Counselors recognize that culture affects the manner in which clients' problems are defined. Clients' socioeconomic and cultural experience is considered when diagnosing mental disorders.

E.6. Test Selection

a. Appropriateness of Instruments. Counselors carefully consider the validity, reliability, psychometric limitations, and appropriateness of instruments when selecting tests for use in a given situation or with a particular client.

b. Culturally Diverse Populations. Counselors are cautious when selecting tests for culturally diverse populations to avoid inappropriateness of testing that may be outside of socialized behavioral or cognitive patterns.

E.7. Conditions of Test Administration

a. Administration Conditions. Counselors administer tests under the same conditions that were established in their standardization. When tests are not administered under standard conditions or when unusual behavior or irregularities occur during the testing session, those conditions are noted in interpretation, and the results may be designated as invalid or of questionable validity.

b. Computer Administration. Counselors are responsible for ensuring that administration programs function properly to provide clients with accurate results when a computer or other electronic methods are used for test administration. (See A.12.b.)

c. Unsupervised Test Taking. Counselors do not permit unsupervised or inadequately supervised use of tests or assessments unless the tests or assessments are designed, intended, and validated for self-administration and/or scoring.

d. Disclosure of Favorable Conditions. Prior to test administration, conditions that produce most favorable test results are made known to the examinee.

E.8. Diversity in Testing

Counselors are cautious in using assessment techniques, making evaluations, and interpreting the performance of populations not represented in the norm group on which an instrument was standardized. They recognize the effects of age, color, culture, disability, ethnic group, gender, race, religion, sexual orientation, and socioeconomic status on test administration and interpretation and place test results in proper perspective with other relevant factors. (See A.2.a.)

E.9. Test Scoring and Interpretation

a. Reporting Reservations. In reporting assessment results, counselors indicate any reservations that exist regarding validity or reliability because of the circumstances of the assessment or the inappropriateness of the norms for the person tested.

b. Research Instruments. Counselors exercise caution when interpreting the results of research instruments possessing insufficient technical data to support respondent results. The specific purposes for the use of such instruments are stated explicitly to the examinee.

c. Testing Services. Counselors who provide test scoring and test interpretation services to support the assessment process confirm the validity of such interpretations. They accurately describe the purpose, norms, validity, reliability, and applications of the procedures and any special qualifications applicable to their use. The public offering of an automated test interpretations service is considered a professional-to-professional consultation. The formal responsibility of the consultant is to the consultee, but the ultimate and overriding responsibility is to the client.

E.10. Test Security

Counselors maintain the integrity and security of tests and other assessment techniques consistent with legal and contractual obligations. Counselors do not appropriate, reproduce, or modify published tests or parts thereof without acknowledgment and permission from the publisher.

E.11. Obsolete Tests and Outdated Test Results

Counselors do not use data or test results that are obsolete or outdated for the current purpose. Counselors make every effort to prevent the misuse of obsolete measures and test data by others.

E.12. Test Construction

Counselors use established scientific procedures, relevant standards, and current professional knowledge for test design in the development, publication, and utilization of educational and psychological assessment techniques.

Section F: Teaching, Training, and Supervision

F.1. Counselor Educators and Trainers

a. Educators as Teachers and Practitioners. Counselors who are responsible for developing, implementing, and supervising educational programs are skilled as teachers and practitioners. They are knowledgeable regarding the ethical, legal, and regulatory aspects of the profession, are skilled in applying that knowledge, and make students and supervisees aware of their responsibilities. Counselors conduct counselor education and training programs in an ethical manner and serve as role models for professional behavior. Counselor educators should make an effort to infuse material related to human diversity into all courses and/or workshops that are designed to promote the development of professional counselors.

b. Relationship Boundaries With Students and Supervisees. Counselors clearly define and maintain ethical, professional, and social relationship boundaries with their students and supervisees. They are aware of the differential in power that exists and the student's or supervisee's possible incomprehension of that power differential. Counselors explain to students and supervisees the potential for the relationship to become exploitive.

c. Sexual Relationships. Counselors do not engage in sexual relationships with students or supervisees and do not subject them to sexual harassment. (See A.6. and C.5.b)

d. Contributions to Research. Counselors give credit to students or supervisees for their contributions to research and scholarly projects. Credit is given through coauthorship, acknowledgment, footnote statement, or other appropriate means, in accordance with such contributions. (See G.4.b. and G.4.c.)

e. Close Relatives. Counselors do not accept close relatives as students or supervisees.

f. Supervision Preparation. Counselors who offer clinical supervision services are adequately prepared in supervision methods and techniques. Counselors who are doctoral students serving as practicum or internship supervisors to master's level students are adequately prepared and supervised by the training program.

g. Responsibility for Services to Clients. Counselors who supervise the counseling services of others take reasonable measures to ensure that counseling services provided to clients are professional.

h. Endorsement. Counselors do not endorse students or supervisees for certification, licensure, employment, or completion of an academic or training program if they believe students or supervisees are not qualified for the endorsement. Counselors take reasonable steps to assist students or supervisees who are not qualified for endorsement to become qualified.

F.2. Counselor Education and Training Programs

a. Orientation. Prior to admission, counselors orient prospective students to the counselor education or training program's expectations, including but not limited to the following: (1) the type and level of skill acquisition required for successful completion of the training, (2) subject matter to be covered, (3) basis for evaluation, (4) training components that encourage self-growth or self-disclosure as part of the training process, (5) the type of supervision settings and requirements of the sites for required clinical field experiences, (6) student and supervisee evaluation and dismissal policies and procedures, and (7) up-to-date employment prospects for graduates.

b. Integration of Study and Practice. Counselors establish counselor education and training programs that integrate academic study and supervised practice.

c. Evaluation. Counselors clearly state to students and supervisees, in advance of training, the levels of competency expected, appraisal methods, and timing of evaluations for both didactic and experiential components. Counselors provide students and supervisees with periodic performance appraisal and evaluation feedback throughout the training program.

d. Teaching Ethics. Counselors make students and supervisees aware of the ethical responsibilities and standards of the profession and the students' and supervisees' ethical responsibilities to the profession. (See C.1. and F.3.e.)

e. Peer Relationships. When students or supervisees are assigned to lead counseling groups or provide clinical supervision for their peers, counselors take steps to ensure that students and supervisees placed in these roles do not have personal or adverse relationships with peers and that they understand they have the same ethical obligations as counselor educators, trainers, and supervisors. Counselors make every effort to ensure that the rights of peers are not compromised when students or supervisees are assigned to lead counseling groups or provide clinical supervision.

f. Varied Theoretical Positions. Counselors present varied theoretical positions so that students and supervisees may make comparisons and have opportunities to develop their own positions. Counselors provide information concerning the scientific bases of professional practice. (See C.6.a.)

g. Field Placements. Counselors develop clear policies within their training program regarding field placement and other clinical experiences. Counselors provide clearly stated roles and responsibilities for the student or supervisee, the site supervisor, and the program supervisor. They confirm that site supervisors are qualified to provide supervision and are informed of their professional and ethical responsibilities in this role.

h. Dual Relationships as Supervisors. Counselors avoid dual relationships such as performing the role of site supervisor and training program supervisor in the student's or supervisee's training program. Counselors do not accept any form of professional services, fees, commissions, reimbursement, or remuneration from a site for student or supervisee placement.

i. Diversity in Programs. Counselors are responsive to their institution's and program's recruitment and retention needs for training program administrators, faculty, and students with diverse backgrounds and special needs. (See A.2.a.)

F.3. Students and Supervisees

a. Limitations. Counselors, through ongoing evaluation and appraisal, are aware of the academic and personal limitations of students and supervisees that might impede performance. Counselors assist students and supervisees in securing remedial assistance when needed, and dismiss from the training program supervisees who are unable to provide competent service due to academic or personal limitations. Counselors seek professional consultation and document their decision to dismiss or refer students or supervisees for assistance. Counselors ensure that students and supervisees have recourse to address decisions made to require them to seek assistance or to dismiss them.

b. Self-Growth Experiences. Counselors use professional judgment when designing training experiences conducted by the counselors themselves that require student and supervisee self-growth or self-disclosure. Safeguards are provided so that students and supervisees are aware of the ramifications their self-disclosure may have on counselors whose primary role as teacher, trainer, or supervisor requires acting on ethical obligations to the profession. Evaluative components of experiential training experiences explicitly delineate predetermined academic standards that are separate and do not depend on the student's level of self-disclosure. (See A.6.)

c. Counseling for Students and Supervisees. If students or supervisees request counseling, supervisors or counselor educators provide them with acceptable referrals. Supervisors or counselor educators do not serve as counselor to students or supervisees over whom they hold administrative, teaching, or evaluative roles unless this is a brief role associated with a training experience. (See A.6.b.)

d. Clients of Students and Supervisees. Counselors make every effort to ensure that the clients at field placements are aware of the services rendered and the qualifications of the students and supervisees rendering those services. Clients receive professional disclosure information and are informed of the limits of confidentiality. Client permission is obtained in order for the students and supervisees to use any information concerning the counseling relationship in the training process. (See B.1.e.)

e. Standards for Students and Supervisees. Students and supervisees preparing to become counselors adhere to the Code of Ethics and the Standards of Practice. Students and supervisees have the same obligations to clients as those required of counselors. (See H.1.)

Section G: Research and Publication

G.1. Research Responsibilities

a. Use of Human Subjects. Counselors plan, design, conduct, and report research in a manner consistent with pertinent ethical principles, federal and state laws, host institutional regulations, and scientific standards governing research with human subjects. Counselors design and conduct research that reflects cultural sensitivity appropriateness.

b. Deviation From Standard Practices. Counselors seek consultation and observe stringent safeguards to protect the rights of research participants when a research problem suggests a deviation from standard acceptable practices. (See B.6.)

c. Precautions to Avoid Injury. Counselors who conduct research with human subjects are responsible for the subjects' welfare throughout the experiment and take reasonable precautions to avoid causing injurious psychological, physical, or social effects to their subjects.

d. Principal Researcher Responsibility. The ultimate responsibility for ethical research practice lies with the principal researcher. All others involved in the research activities share ethical obligations and full responsibility for their own actions.

e. Minimal Interference. Counselors take reasonable precautions to avoid causing disruptions in subjects' lives due to participation in research.

f. Diversity. Counselors are sensitive to diversity and research issues with special populations. They seek consultation when appropriate. (See A.2.a. and B.6.)

G.2. Informed Consent

a. Topics Disclosed. In obtaining informed consent for research, counselors use language that is understandable to research participants and that (1) accurately explains the purpose and procedures to be followed; (2) identifies any procedures that are experimental or relatively untried; (3) describes the attendant discomforts and risks; (4) describes the benefits or changes in individuals or organizations that might be reasonably expected; (5) discloses appropriate alternative procedures that would be advantageous for subjects; (6) offers to answer any inquiries concerning the procedures; (7) describes any limitations on confidentiality; and (8) instructs that subjects are free to withdraw their consent and to discontinue participation in the project at any time. (See B.1.f.)

b. Deception. Counselors do not conduct research involving deception unless alternative procedures are not feasible and the prospective value of the research justifies the deception. When the methodological requirements of a study necessitate concealment or deception, the investigator is required to explain clearly the reasons for this action as soon as possible.

c. Voluntary Participation. Participation in research is typically voluntary and without any penalty for refusal to participate. Involuntary participation is appropriate only when it can be demonstrated that participation will have no harmful effects on subjects and is essential to the investigation.

d. Confidentiality of Information. Information obtained about research participants during the course of an investigation is confidential. When the possibility exists that others may obtain access to such information, ethical research practice requires that the possibility, together with the plans for protecting confidentiality, be explained to participants as a part of the procedure for obtaining informed consent. (See B.1.e.)

e. Persons Incapable of Giving Informed Consent. When a person is incapable of giving informed consent, counselors provide an appropriate explanation, obtain agreement for participation, and obtain appropriate consent from a legally authorized person.

f. Commitments to Participants. Counselors take reasonable measures to honor all commitments to research participants.

g. Explanations After Data Collection. After data are collected, counselors provide participants with full clarification of the nature of the study to remove any misconceptions. Where scientific or human values justify delaying or withholding information, counselors take reasonable measures to avoid causing harm.

h. Agreements to Cooperate. Counselors who agree to cooperate with another individual in research or publication incur an obligation to cooperate as promised in terms of punctuality of performance and with regard to the completeness and accuracy of the information required.

i. Informed Consent for Sponsors. In the pursuit of research, counselors give sponsors, institutions, and publication channels the same respect and opportunity for giving informed consent that they accord to individual research participants. Counselors are aware of their obligation to future research workers and ensure that host institutions are given feedback information and proper acknowledgment.

G.3. Reporting Results

a. Information Affecting Outcome. When reporting research results, counselors explicitly mention all variables and conditions known to the investigator that may have affected the outcome of a study or the interpretation of data.

b. Accurate Results. Counselors plan, conduct, and report research accurately and in a manner that minimizes the possibility that results will be misleading. They provide thorough discussions of the limitations of their data and alternative hypotheses. Counselors do not engage in fraudulent research, distort data, misrepresent data, or deliberately bias their results.

c. Obligation to Report Unfavorable Results. Counselors communicate to other counselors the results of any research judged to be of professional value. Results that reflect unfavorably on institutions, programs, services, prevailing opinions, or vested interests are not withheld.

d. Identity of Subjects. Counselors who supply data, aid in the research of another person, report research results, or make original data available take due care to disguise the identity of respective subjects in the absence of specific authorization from the subjects to do otherwise. (See B.1.g. and B.5.a.)

e. Replication Studies. Counselors are obligated to make available sufficient original research data to qualified professionals who may wish to replicate the study.

G.4. Publication

a. Recognition of Others. When conducting and reporting research, counselors are familiar with and give recognition to previous work on the topic, observe copyright laws, and give full credit to those to whom credit is due. (See F.1.d. and G.4.c.

b. Contributors. Counselors give credit through joint authorship, acknowledgment, footnote statements, or other appropriate means to those who have contributed significantly to research or concept development in accordance with such contributions. The principal contributor is listed first and minor technical or professional contributions are acknowledged in notes or introductory statements.

c. Student Research. For an article that is substantially based on a student's dissertation or thesis, the student is listed as the principal author. (See F.1.d. and G.4.a.)

d. Duplicate Submission. Counselors submit manuscripts for consideration to only one journal at a time. Manuscripts that are published in whole or in substantial part in another journal or published work are not submitted for publication without acknowledgment and permission from the previous publication.

e. Professional Review. Counselors who review material submitted for publication, research, or other scholarly purposes respect the confidentiality and proprietary rights of those who submitted it.

Section H: Resolving Ethical Issues

H.1. Knowledge of Standards
Counselors are familiar with the Code of Ethics and the Standards of Practice and other applicable ethics codes from other professional organizations of which they are member, or from certification and licensure bodies. Lack of knowledge or misunderstanding of an ethical responsibility is not a defense against a charge of unethical conduct. (See F.3.e.)

H.2. Suspected Violations
a. Ethical Behavior Expected. Counselors expect professional associates to adhere to the Code of Ethics. When counselors possess reasonable cause

that raises doubts as to whether a counselor is acting in an ethical manner, they take appropriate action. (See H.2.d. and H.2.e.)

b. Consultation. When uncertain as to whether a particular situation or course of action may be in violation of the Code of Ethics, counselors consult with other counselors who are knowledgeable about ethics, with colleagues, or with appropriate authorities.

c. Organization Conflicts. If the demands of an organization with which counselors are affiliated pose a conflict with the Code of Ethics, counselors specify the nature of such conflicts and express to their supervisors or other responsible officials their commitment to the Code of Ethics. When possible, counselors work toward change within the organization to allow full adherence to the Code of Ethics.

d. Informal Resolution. When counselors have reasonable cause to believe that another counselor is violating an ethical standard, they attempt to first resolve the issue informally with the other counselor if feasible, providing that such action does not violate confidentiality rights that may be involved.

e. Reporting Suspected Violations. When an informal resolution is not appropriate or feasible, counselors, upon reasonable cause, take action such as reporting the suspected ethical violation to state or national ethics committees, unless this action conflicts with confidentiality rights that cannot be resolved.

f. Unwarranted Complaints. Counselors do not initiate, participate in, or encourage the filing of ethics complaints that are unwarranted or intend to harm a counselor rather than to protect clients or the public.

H.3. Cooperation With Ethics Committees

Counselors assist in the process of enforcing the Code of Ethics. Counselors cooperate with investigations, proceedings, and requirements of the ACA Ethics Committee or ethics committees of other duly constituted associations or boards having jurisdiction over those charged with a violation. Counselors are familiar with the ACA Policies and Procedures and use it as a reference in assisting the enforcement of the Code of Ethics.

ACA Standards of Practice

All members of the American Counseling Association (ACA) are required to adhere to the Standards of Practice and the Code of Ethics. The Standards of Practice represent minimal behavioral statements of the Code of Ethics. Members should refer to the applicable section of the Code of Ethics for further interpretation and amplification of the applicable Standard of Practice.

Section A: The Counseling Relationship
Section B: Confidentiality
Section C: Professional Responsibility
Section D: Relationship With Other Professionals
Section E: Evaluation, Assessment and Interpretation
Section F: Teaching, Training, and Supervision
Section G: Research and Publication
Section H: Resolving Ethical Issues

Section A: The Counseling Relationship

Standard of Practice One (SP-1): Nondiscrimination. Counselors respect diversity and must not discriminate against clients because of age, color, culture, disability, ethnic group, gender, race, religion, sexual orientation, marital status, or socioeconomic status. (See A.2.a.)

Standard of Practice Two (SP-2): Disclosure to Clients. Counselors must adequately inform clients, preferably in writing, regarding the counseling process and counseling relationship at or before the time it begins and throughout the relationship. (See A.3.a.)

Standard of Practice Three (SP-3): Dual Relationships. Counselors must make every effort to avoid dual relationships with clients that could impair their professional judgment or increase the risk of harm to clients. When a dual relationship cannot be avoided, counselors must take appropriate steps to ensure that judgment is not impaired and that no exploitation occurs. (See A.6.a. and A.6.b.)

Standard of Practice Four (SP-4): Sexual Intimacies With Clients. Counselors must not engage in any type of sexual intimacies with current clients and must not engage in sexual intimacies with former clients within a minimum of 2 years after terminating the counseling relationship. Counselors who engage in such relationship after 2 years following termination have the responsibility to examine and document thoroughly that such relations did not have an exploitative nature.

Standard of Practice Five (SP-5): Protecting Clients During Group Work. Counselors must take steps to protect clients from physical or psychological trauma resulting from interactions during group work. (See A.9.b.)

Standard of Practice Six (SP-6): Advance Understanding of Fees. Counselors must explain to clients, prior to their entering the counseling relationship, financial arrangements related to professional services. (See A.10. a.-d. and A.11.c.)

Standard of Practice Seven (SP-7): Termination. Counselors must assist in making appropriate arrangements for the continuation of treatment of clients, when necessary, following termination of counseling relationships. (See A.11.a.)

Standard of Practice Eight (SP-8): Inability to Assist Clients. Counselors must avoid entering or immediately terminate a counseling relationship if it is determined that they are unable to be of professional assistance to a client. The counselor may assist in making an appropriate referral for the client. (See A.11.b.)

Section B: Confidentiality

Standard of Practice Nine (SP-9): Confidentiality Requirement. Counselors must keep information related to counseling services confidential unless disclosure is in the best interest of clients, is required for the welfare of others, or is required by law. When disclosure is required, only information that is essential is revealed and the client is informed of such disclosure. (See B.1. a.+f.)

Standard of Practice Ten (SP-10): Confidentiality Requirements for Subordinates. Counselors must take measures to ensure that privacy and confidentiality of clients are maintained by subordinates. (See B.1.h.)

Standard of Practice Eleven (SP-11): Confidentiality in Group Work. Counselors must clearly communicate to group members that confidentiality cannot be guaranteed in group work. (See B.2.a.)

Standard of Practice Twelve (SP-12): Confidentiality in Family Counseling. Counselors must not disclose information about one family member in counseling to another family member without prior consent. (See B.2.b.)

Standard of Practice Thirteen (SP-13): Confidentiality of Records. Counselors must maintain appropriate confidentiality in creating, storing, accessing, transferring, and disposing of counseling records. (See B.4.b.)

Standard of Practice Fourteen (SP-14): Permission to Record or Observe. Counselors must obtain prior consent from clients in order to record electronically or observe sessions. (See B.4.c.)

Standard of Practice Fifteen (SP-15): Disclosure or Transfer of Records. Counselors must obtain client consent to disclose or transfer records to third parties, unless exceptions listed in SP-9 exist. (See B.4.e.)

Standard of Practice Sixteen (SP-16): Data Disguise Required. Counselors must disguise the identity of the client when using data for training, research, or publication. (See B.5.a.)

Section C: Professional Responsibility

Standard of Practice Seventeen (SP-17): Boundaries of Competence. Counselors must practice only within the boundaries of their competence. (See C.2.a.)

Standard of Practice Eighteen (SP-18): Continuing Education. Counselors must engage in continuing education to maintain their professional competence. (See C.2.f.)

Standard of Practice Nineteen (SP-19): Impairment of Professionals. Counselors must refrain from offering professional services when their personal problems or conflicts may cause harm to a client or others. (See C.2.g.)

Standard of Practice Twenty (SP-20): Accurate Advertising. Counselors must accurately represent their credentials and services when advertising. (See C.3.a.)

Standard of Practice Twenty-One (SP-21): Recruiting Through Employment. Counselors must not use their place of employment or institutional affiliation to recruit clients for their private practices. (See C.3.d.)

Standard of Practice Twenty-Two (SP-22): Credentials Claimed. Counselors must claim or imply only professional credentials possessed and must correct any known misrepresentations of their credentials by others. (See C.4.a.)

Standard of Practice Twenty-Three (SP-23): Sexual Harassment. Counselors must not engage in sexual harassment. (See C.5.b.)

Standard of Practice Twenty-Four (SP-24): Unjustified Gains. Counselors must not use their professional positions to seek or receive unjustified personal gains, sexual favors, unfair advantage, or unearned goods or services. (See C.5.e.)

Standard of Practice Twenty-Five (SP-25): Clients Served by Others. With the consent of the client, counselors must inform other mental health professionals serving the same client that a counseling relationship between the counselor and client exists. (See C.6.c.)

Standard of Practice Twenty-Six (SP-26): Negative Employment Conditions. Counselors must alert their employers to institutional policy or conditions that may be potentially disruptive or damaging to the counselor's professional responsibilities, or that may limit their effectiveness or deny clients' rights. (See D.1.c.)

Standard of Practice Twenty-Seven (SP-27): Personnel Selection and Assignment. Counselors must select competent staff and must assign responsibilities compatible with staff skills and experiences. (See D.1.h.)

Standard of Practice Twenty-Eight (SP-28): Exploitative Relationships With Subordinates. Counselors must not engage in exploitative relationships with individuals over whom they have supervisory, evaluative, or instructional control or authority. (See D.1.k.)

Section D: Relationship With Other Professionals

Standard of Practice Twenty-Nine (SP-29): Accepting Fees From Agency Clients. Counselors must not accept fees or other remuneration for consultation with persons entitled to such services through the counselor's employing agency or institution. (See D.3.a.)

Standard of Practice Thirty (SP-30): Referral Fees. Counselors must not accept referral fees. (See D.3.b.)

Section E: Evaluation, Assessment, and Interpretation

Standard of Practice Thirty-One (SP-31): Limits of Competence. Counselors must perform only testing and assessment services for which they are competent. Counselors must not allow the use of psychological assessment techniques by unqualified persons under their supervision. (See E.2.a.)

Standard of Practice Thirty-Two (SP-32): Appropriate Use of Assessment Instruments. Counselors must use assessment instruments in the manner for which they were intended. (See E.2.b.)

Standard of Practice Thirty-Three (SP-33): Assessment Explanations to Clients. Counselors must provide explanations to clients prior to assessment about the nature and purposes of assessment and the specific uses of results. (See E.3.a.)

Standard of Practice Thirty-Four (SP-34): Recipients of Test Results. Counselors must ensure that accurate and appropriate interpretations accompany any release of testing and assessment information. (See E.3.b.)

Standard of Practice Thirty-Five (SP-35): Obsolete Tests and Outdated Test Results. Counselors must not base their assessment or intervention decisions or recommendations on data or test results that are obsolete or outdated for the current purpose. (See E.11.)

Section F: Teaching, Training, and Supervision

Standard of Practice Thirty-Six (SP-36): Sexual Relationships With Students or Supervisees. Counselors must not engage in sexual relationships with their students and supervisees. (See F.1.c.)

Standard of Practice Thirty-Seven (SP-37): Credit for Contributions to Research. Counselors must give credit to students or supervisees for their contributions to research and scholarly projects. (See F.1.d.)

Standard of Practice Thirty-Eight (SP-38): Supervision Preparation. Counselors who offer clinical supervision services must be trained and prepared in supervision methods and techniques. (See F.1.f.)

Standard of Practice Thirty-Nine (SP-39): Evaluation Information. Counselors must clearly state to students and supervisees in advance of training the levels of competency expected, appraisal methods, and timing of evaluations. Counselors must provide students and supervisees with periodic performance appraisal and evaluation feedback throughout the training program. (See F.2.c.)

Standard of Practice Forty (SP-40): Peer Relationships in Training. Counselors must make every effort to ensure that the rights of peers are not violated when students and supervisees are assigned to lead counseling groups or provide clinical supervision. (See F.2.e.)

Standard of Practice Forty-One (SP-41): Limitations of Students and Supervisees. Counselors must assist students and supervisees in securing remedial assistance, when needed, and must dismiss from the training program students and supervisees who are unable to provide competent service due to academic or personal limitations. (See F.3.a.)

Standard of Practice Forty-Two (SP-42): Self-Growth Experiences. Counselors who conduct experiences for students or supervisees that include self-growth or self-disclosure must inform participants of counselors' ethical obligations to the profession and must not grade participants based on their nonacademic performance. (See F.3.b.)

Standard of Practice Forty-Three (SP-43): Standards for Students and Supervisees. Students and supervisees preparing to become counselors must adhere to the Code of Ethics and the Standards of Practice of counselors. (See F.3.e.)

Section G: Research and Publication

Standard of Practice Forty-Four (SP-44): Precautions to Avoid Injury in Research. Counselors must avoid causing physical, social, or psychological harm or injury to subjects in research. (See G.1.c.)

Standard of Practice Forty-Five (SP-45): Confidentiality of Research Information. Counselors must keep confidential information obtained about research participants. (See G.2.d.)

Standard of Practice Forty-Six (SP-46): Information Affecting Research Outcome. Counselors must report all variables and conditions known to the investigator that may have affected research data or outcomes. (See G.3.a.)

Standard of Practice Forty-Seven (SP-47): Accurate Research Results. Counselors must not distort or misrepresent research data, nor fabricate or intentionally bias research results. (See G.3.b.)

Standard of Practice Forty-Eight (SP-48): Publication Contributors. Counselors must give appropriate credit to those who have contributed to research. (See G.4.a. and G.4.b.)

Section H: Resolving Ethical Issues

Standard of Practice Forty-Nine (SP-49): Ethical Behavior Expected. Counselors must take appropriate action when they possess reasonable cause that raises doubts as to whether counselors or other mental health professionals are acting in an ethical manner. (See H.2.a.)

Standard of Practice Fifty (SP-50): Unwarranted Complaints. Counselors must not initiate, participate in, or encourage the filing of ethics complaints that are unwarranted or intended to harm a mental health professional rather than to protect clients or the public. (See H.2.f.)

Standard of Practice Fifty-One (SP-51): Cooperation With Ethics Committees. Counselors must cooperate with investigations, proceedings, and requirements of the ACA Ethics Committee or ethics committees of other duly constituted associations or boards having jurisdiction over those charged with a violation. (See H.3.)

Appendix B

APA Ethical Principles of Psychologists and Code of Conduct

Introduction

The American Psychological Association's (APA's) Ethical Principles of Psychologists and Code of Conduct (hereinafter referred to as the Ethics Code) consists of an Introduction, a Preamble, six General Principles (A–F), and specific Ethical Standards. The Introduction discusses the intent, organization, procedural considerations, and scope of application of the Ethics Code. The Preamble and General Principles are aspirational goals to guide psychologists toward the highest ideals of psychology. Although the Preamble and General Principles are not themselves enforceable rules, they should be considered by psychologists in arriving at an ethical course of action and may be considered by ethics bodies in interpreting the Ethical Standards. The Ethical Standards set forth enforceable rules for conduct as psychologists. Most of the Ethical Standards are written broadly, in order to apply to psychologists in varied roles, although the application of an Ethical Standard may vary depending on the context. The Ethical Standards are not exhaustive. The fact that a given conduct is not specifically addressed by the Ethics Code does not mean that it is necessarily either ethical or unethical.

Membership in the APA commits members to adhere to the APA Ethics Code and to the rules and procedures used to implement it. Psychologists and students, whether or not they are APA members, should be aware that the Ethics Code may be applied to them by state psychology boards, courts, or other public bodies.

This Ethics Code applies only to psychologists' work-related activities, that is, activities that are part of the psychologists' scientific and professional functions or that are psychological in nature. It includes the clinical or counseling practice of psychology, research, teaching, supervision of trainees, development of assessment instruments, conducting assessments, educational counseling, organizational consulting, social intervention, administration, and other activities as well. These work-related activities can be distinguished from the purely private conduct of a psychologist, which ordinarily is not within the purview of the Ethics Code.

The Ethics Code is intended to provide standards of professional conduct that can be applied by the APA and by other bodies that choose to adopt them. Whether or not a psychologist has violated the Ethics Code does not by itself determine whether he or she is legally liable in a court action, whether a contract is enforceable, or whether other legal consequences occur. These results are based on legal rather than ethical rules. However, compliance with or violation of the Ethics Code may be admissible as evidence in some legal proceedings, depending on the circumstances.

In the process of making decisions regarding their professional behavior, psychologists must consider this Ethics Code, in addition to applicable laws and psychology board regulations. If the Ethics Code establishes a higher standard of conduct than is required by law, psychologists must meet the higher ethical standard. If the Ethics Code standard appears to conflict with the requirements of law, then psychologists make known their commitment to the Ethics Code and take steps to resolve the conflict in a responsible manner. If neither law nor the Ethics Code resolves an issue, psychologists should consider other professional materials and the dictates of their own conscience, as well as seek consultation with others within the field when this is practical.

The procedures for filing, investigating, and resolving complaints of unethical conduct are described in the current Rules and Procedures of the APA Ethics Committee. The actions that APA may take for violations of the Ethics Code include actions such as reprimand, censure, termination of APA membership, and referral of the matter to other bodies. Complainants who seek remedies such as monetary damages in alleging ethical violations by a psychologist must resort to private negotiation, administrative bodies, or the courts. Actions that violate the Ethics Code may lead to the imposition of sanctions on a psychologist by bodies other than APA, including state psychological associations, other professional groups, psychology boards, other state or federal agencies, and payors for health services. In addition to actions for violation of the Ethics Code, the APA Bylaws provide that APA may take action against a member after his or her conviction of a felony, expulsion or suspension from an affiliated state psychological association, or suspension or loss of licensure.

Preamble

Psychologists work to develop a valid and reliable body of scientific knowledge based on research. They may apply that knowledge to human behavior in a variety of contexts. In doing so, they perform many roles, such as researcher, educator, diagnostician, therapist, supervisor, consultant, administrator, social interventionist, and expert witness. Their goal is to broaden knowledge of behavior and, where appropriate, to apply it pragmatically to improve the condition of both the individual and society. Psychologists respect the central importance of freedom of inquiry and expression in research, teaching, and publication. They also strive to help the public in developing informed judgments and choices concerning human behavior. This Ethics Code provides a common set of values upon which psychologists build their professional and scientific work.

This Code is intended to provide both the general principles and the decision rules to cover most situations encountered by psychologists. It has as its primary goal the welfare and protection of the individuals and groups with whom psychologists work. It is the individual responsibility of each psychologist to aspire to the highest possible standards of conduct. Psychologists respect and protect human and civil rights, and do not knowingly participate in or condone unfair discriminatory practices.

The development of a dynamic set of ethical standards for a psychologist's work-related conduct requires a personal commitment to a lifelong effort to act ethically; to encourage ethical behavior by students, supervisees, employees, and colleagues, as appropriate; and to consult with others, as needed, concerning ethical problems. Each psychologist supplements, but does not violate, the Ethics Code's values and rules on the basis of guidance drawn from personal values, culture, and experience.

General Principles

Principle A: Competence

Psychologists strive to maintain high standards of competence in their work. They recognize the boundaries of their particular competencies and the limitations of their expertise. They provide only those services and use only those techniques for which they are qualified by education, training, or experience. Psychologists are cognizant of the fact that the competencies required in serving, teaching, and/or studying groups of people vary with the distinctive characteristics of those groups. In those areas in which recognized professional standards do not yet exist, psychologists exercise careful judgment and take appropriate precautions to protect the welfare of those with whom they work. They maintain knowledge of relevant scientific and professional information related to the services they render, and they recognize the need for ongoing education. Psychologists make appropriate use of scientific, professional, technical, and administrative resources.

Principle B: Integrity

Psychologists seek to promote integrity in the science, teaching, and practice of psychology. In these activities psychologists are honest, fair, and respectful of others. In describing or reporting their qualifications, services, products, fees, research, or teaching, they do not make statements that are false, misleading, or deceptive. Psychologists strive to be aware of their own belief systems, values, needs, and limitations and the effect of these on their work. To the extent feasible, they attempt to clarify for relevant parties the roles they are performing and to function appropriately in accordance with those roles. Psychologists avoid improper and potentially harmful dual relationships.

Principle C: Professional and Scientific Responsibility

Psychologists uphold professional standards of conduct, clarify their professional roles and obligations, accept appropriate responsibility for their behavior, and adapt their methods to the needs of different populations. Psychologists consult with, refer to, or cooperate with other professionals and institutions to the extent needed to serve the best interests of their patients, clients, or other recipients of their services. Psychologists' moral standards and conduct are personal matters to the same degree as is true for any other person, except as psychologists' conduct may compromise their professional responsibilities or reduce the public's trust in psychology and psychologists. Psychologists are concerned about the ethical compliance of their colleagues' scientific and professional conduct. When appropriate, they consult with colleagues in order to prevent or avoid unethical conduct.

Principle D: Respect for People's Rights and Dignity

Psychologists accord appropriate respect to the fundamental rights, dignity, and worth of all people. They respect the rights of individuals to privacy, confidentiality, self-determination, and autonomy, mindful that legal and other obligations may lead to inconsistency and conflict with the exercise of these rights. Psychologists are aware of cultural, individual, and role differences, including those due to age, gender, race, ethnicity, national origin, religion, sexual orientation, disability, language, and socioeconomic status. Psychologists try to eliminate the effect on their work of biases based on those factors, and they do not knowingly participate in or condone unfair discriminatory practices.

Principle E: Concern for Others' Welfare

Psychologists seek to contribute to the welfare of those with whom they interact professionally. In their professional actions, psychologists weigh the welfare and rights of their patients or clients, students, supervisees, human research participants, and other affected persons, and the welfare of animal subjects of research. When conflicts occur among psychologists' obligations or concerns, they attempt to resolve these conflicts and to perform their roles in a responsible fashion that avoids or minimizes harm. Psychologists are sensitive to real and ascribed differences in power between themselves and others, and they do not exploit or mislead other people during or after professional relationships.

Principle F: Social Responsibility

Psychologists are aware of their professional and scientific responsibilities to the community and the society in which they work and live. They apply and make public their knowledge of psychology in order to contribute to human welfare. Psychologists are concerned about and work to mitigate the causes of human suffering. When undertaking research, they strive to advance human welfare and the science of psychology. Psychologists try to avoid misuse of their work. Psychologists comply with the law and encourage the development of law and social policy that serve the interests of their patients and clients and the public. They are encouraged to contribute a portion of their professional time for little or no personal advantage.

Ethical Standards

1. General Standards

These General Standards are potentially applicable to the professional and scientific activities of all psychologists.

1.01 Applicability of the Ethics Code.

The activity of a psychologist subject to the Ethics Code may be reviewed under these Ethical Standards only if the activity is part of his or her work-related functions or the activity is psychological in nature. Personal activities having no connection to or effect on psychological roles are not subject to the Ethics Code.

1.02 Relationship of Ethics and Law.

If psychologists' ethical responsibilities conflict with law, psychologists make known their commitment to the Ethics Code and take steps to resolve the conflict in a responsible manner.

1.03 Professional and Scientific Relationship.

Psychologists provide diagnostic, therapeutic, teaching, research, supervisory, consultative, or other psychological services only in the context of a defined professional or scientific relationship or role. (See also Standards 2.01, Evaluation, Diagnosis, and Interventions in Professional Context, and 7.02, Forensic Assessments.)

1.04 Boundaries of Competence.

(a) Psychologists provide services, teach, and conduct research only within the boundaries of their competence, based on their education, training, supervised experience, or appropriate professional experience.

(b) Psychologists provide services, teach, or conduct research in new areas or involving new techniques only after first undertaking appropriate study, training, supervision, and/or consultation from persons who are competent in those areas or techniques.

(c) In those emerging areas in which generally recognized standards for preparatory training do not yet exist, psychologists nevertheless take reasonable steps to ensure the competence of their work and to protect patients, clients, students, research participants, and others from harm.

1.05 Maintaining Expertise.

Psychologists who engage in assessment, therapy, teaching, research, organizational consulting, or other professional activities maintain a reasonable level of awareness of current scientific and professional information in their fields of activity, and undertake ongoing efforts to maintain competence in the skills they use.

1.06 Basis for Scientific and Professional Judgments.

Psychologists rely on scientifically and professionally derived knowledge when making scientific or professional judgments or when engaging in scholarly or professional endeavors.

1.07 Describing the Nature and Results of Psychological Services.

(a) When psychologists provide assessment, evaluation, treatment, counseling, supervision, teaching, consultation, research, or other psychological services to an individual, a group, or an organization, they provide, using language that is reasonably understandable to the recipient of those services, appropriate information beforehand about the nature of such services and appropriate information later about results and conclusions. (See also Standard 2.09, Explaining Assessment Results.)

(b) If psychologists will be precluded by law or by organizational roles from providing such information to particular individuals or groups, they so inform those individuals or groups at the outset of the service.

1.08 Human Differences.

Where differences of age, gender, race, ethnicity, national origin, religion, sexual orientation, disability, language, or socioeconomic status significantly affect psychologists' work concerning particular individuals or groups, psychologists obtain the training, experience, consultation, or supervision necessary to ensure the competence of their services, or they make appropriate referrals.

1.09 Respecting Others.

In their work-related activities, psychologists respect the rights of others to hold values, attitudes, and opinions that differ from their own.

1.10 Nondiscrimination.

In their work-related activities, psychologists do not engage in unfair discrimination based on age, gender, race, ethnicity, national origin, religion, sexual orientation, disability, socio-economic status, or any basis proscribed by law.

1.11 Sexual Harassment.

(a) Psychologists do not engage in sexual harassment. Sexual harassment is sexual solicitation, physical advances, or verbal or nonverbal conduct that is sexual in nature, that occurs in connection with the psychologist's activities or roles as a psychologist, and that either: (1) is unwelcome, is offensive, or creates a hostile workplace environment, and the psychologist knows or is told this; or (2) is sufficiently severe or intense to be abusive to a reasonable person in the context. Sexual harassment can consist of a single intense or severe act or of multiple persistent or pervasive acts.

(b) Psychologists accord sexual-harassment complainants and respondents dignity and respect. Psychologists do not participate in denying a person academic admittance or advancement, employment, tenure, or promotion, based solely upon their having made, or their being the subject of, sexual harassment charges. This does not preclude taking action based upon the outcome of such proceedings or consideration of other appropriate information.

1.12 Other Harassment.

Psychologists do not knowingly engage in behavior that is harassing or demeaning to persons with whom they interact in their work based on factors such as those persons' age, gender, race, ethnicity, national origin, religion, sexual orientation, disability, language, or socioeconomic status.

1.13 Personal Problems and Conflicts.

(a) Psychologists recognize that their personal problems and conflicts may interfere with their effectiveness. Accordingly, they refrain from undertaking an activity when they know or should know that their personal problems are likely to lead to harm to a patient, client, colleague, student, research participant, or other person to whom they may owe a professional or scientific obligation.

(b) In addition, psychologists have an obligation to be alert to signs of, and to obtain assistance for, their personal problems at an early stage, in order to prevent significantly impaired performance.

(c) When psychologists become aware of personal problems that may interfere with their performing work-related duties adequately, they take appropriate measures, such as obtaining professional consultation or assistance, and determine whether they should limit, suspend, or terminate their work-related duties.

1.14 Avoiding Harm.

Psychologists take reasonable steps to avoid harming their patients or clients, research participants, students, and others with whom they work, and to minimize harm where it is foreseeable and unavoidable.

1.15 Misuse of Psychologists' Influence.

Because psychologists' scientific and professional judgments and actions may affect the lives of others, they are alert to and guard against personal, financial, social, organizational, or political factors that might lead to misuse of their influence.

1.16 Misuse of Psychologists' Work.

(a) Psychologists do not participate in activities in which it appears likely that their skills or data will be misused by others, unless corrective mechanisms are available. (See also Standard 7.04, Truthfulness and Candor.)

(b) If psychologists learn of misuse or misrepresentation of their work, they take reasonable steps to correct or minimize the misuse or misrepresentation.

1.17 Multiple Relationships.

(a) In many communities and situations, it may not be feasible or reasonable for psychologists to avoid social or other nonprofessional contacts with persons such as patients, clients, students, supervisees, or research participants. Psychologists must always be sensitive to the potential harmful effects of other contacts on their work and on those persons with whom they deal. A psychologist refrains from entering into or promising another personal, scientific, professional, financial, or other relationship with such persons if it appears likely that such a relationship reasonably might impair the psychologist's objectivity or otherwise interfere with the psychologist's effectively performing his or her functions as a psychologist, or might harm or exploit the other party.

(b) Likewise, whenever feasible, a psychologist refrains from taking on professional or scientific obligations when pre-existing relationships would create a risk of such harm.

(c) If a psychologist finds that, due to unforeseen factors, a potentially harmful multiple relationship has arisen, the psychologist attempts to resolve it with due regard for the best interests of the affected person and maximal compliance with the Ethics Code.

1.18 Barter (With Patients or Clients).

Psychologists ordinarily refrain from accepting goods, services, or other nonmonetary remuneration from patients or clients in return for psychological services because such arrangements create inherent potential for conflicts, exploitation, and distortion of the professional relationship. A psychologist may participate in bartering only if (1) it is not clinically contraindicated, and (2) the relationship is not exploitative. (See also Standards 1.17, Multiple Relationships, and 1.25, Fees and Financial Arrangements.)

1.19 Exploitative Relationships.

(a) Psychologists do not exploit persons over whom they have supervisory, evaluative, or other authority such as students, supervisees, employees, research participants, and clients or patients. (See also Standards 4.05–4.07 regarding sexual involvement with clients or patients.)

(b) Psychologists do not engage in sexual relationships with students or supervisees in training over whom the psychologist has evaluative or direct authority, because such relationships are so likely to impair judgment or be exploitative.

1.20 Consultations and Referrals.

(a) Psychologists arrange for appropriate consultations and referrals based principally on the best interests of their patients or clients, with appropriate consent, and subject to other relevant considerations, including applicable law and contractual obligations. (See also Standards 5.01, Discussing the Limits of Confidentiality, and 5.06, Consultations.)

(b) When indicated and professionally appropriate, psychologists cooperate with other professionals in order to serve their patients or clients effectively and appropriately.

(c) Psychologists' referral practices are consistent with law.

1.21 Third-Party Requests for Services.

(a) When a psychologist agrees to provide services to a person or entity at the request of a third party, the psychologist clarifies to the extent feasible, at the outset of the service, the nature of the relationship with each party. This clarification includes the role of the psychologist (such as therapist, organizational consultant, diagnostician, or expert witness), the probable uses of the services provided or the information obtained, and the fact that there may be limits to confidentiality.

(b) If there is a foreseeable risk of the psychologist's being called upon to perform conflicting roles because of the involvement of a third party, the psychologist clarifies the nature and direction of his or her responsibilities, keeps all parties appropriately informed as matters develop, and resolves the situation in accordance with this Ethics Code.

1.22 Delegation to and Supervision of Subordinates.

(a) Psychologists delegate to their employees, supervisees, and research assistants only those responsibilities that such persons can reasonably be expected to perform competently, on the basis of their education, training, or experience, either independently or with the level of supervision being provided.

(b) Psychologists provide proper training and supervision to their employees or supervisees and take reasonable steps to see that such persons perform services responsibly, competently, and ethically.

(c) If institutional policies, procedures, or practices prevent fulfillment of this obligation, psychologists attempt to modify their role or to correct the situation to the extent feasible.

1.23 Documentation of Professional and Scientific Work.

(a) Psychologists appropriately document their professional and scientific work in order to facilitate provision of services later by them or by other professionals, to ensure accountability, and to meet other requirements of institutions or the law.

(b) When psychologists have reason to believe that records of their professional services will be used in legal proceedings involving recipients of or participants in their work, they have a responsibility to create and maintain documentation in the kind of detail and quality that would be consistent with reasonable scrutiny in an adjudicative forum. (See also Standard 7.01, Professionalism, under Forensic Activities.)

1.24 Records and Data.

Psychologists create, maintain, disseminate, store, retain, and dispose of records and data relating to their research, practice, and other work in accordance with law and in a manner that permits compliance with the requirements of this Ethics Code. (See also Standard 5.04, Maintenance of Records.)

1.25 Fees and Financial Arrangements.

(a) As early as is feasible in a professional or scientific relationship, the psychologist and the patient, client, or other appropriate recipient of psychological services reach an agreement specifying the compensation and the billing arrangements.

(b) Psychologists do not exploit recipients of services or payors with respect to fees.

(c) Psychologists' fee practices are consistent with law.

(d) Psychologists do not misrepresent their fees.

(e) If limitations to services can be anticipated because of limitations in financing, this is discussed with the patient, client, or other appropriate recipient of services as early as is feasible. (See also Standard 4.08, Interruption of Services.)

(f) If the patient, client, or other recipient of services does not pay for services as agreed, and if the psychologist wishes to use collection agencies or legal measures to collect the fees, the psychologist first informs the person that such measures will be taken and provides that person an opportunity to make prompt payment. (See also Standard 5.11, Withholding Records for Nonpayment.)

1.26 Accuracy in Reports to Payors and Funding Sources.

In their reports to payors for services or sources of research funding, psychologists accurately state the nature of the research or service provided, the fees or charges, and where applicable, the identity of the provider, the findings, and the diagnosis. (See also Standard 5.05, Disclosures.)

1.27 Referrals and Fees.

When a psychologist pays, receives payment from, or divides fees with another professional other than in an employer–employee relationship, the payment to each is based on the services (clinical, consultative, administrative, or other) provided and is not based on the referral itself.

2. Evaluation, Assessment, or Intervention

2.01 Evaluation, Diagnosis, and Interventions in Professional Context.

(a) Psychologists perform evaluations, diagnostic services, or interventions only within the context of a defined professional relationship. (See also Standards 1.03, Professional and Scientific Relationship.)

(b) Psychologists' assessments, recommendations, reports, and psychological diagnostic or evaluative statements are based on information and techniques (including personal interviews of the individual when appropriate) sufficient to provide appropriate substantiation for their findings. (See also Standard 7.02, Forensic Assessments.)

2.02 Competence and Appropriate Use of Assessments and Interventions.

(a) Psychologists who develop, administer, score, interpret, or use psychological assessment techniques, interviews, tests, or instruments do so in a manner and for purposes that are appropriate in light of the research on or evidence of the usefulness and proper application of the techniques.

(b) Psychologists refrain from misuse of assessment techniques, interventions, results, and interpretations and take reasonable steps to prevent others from misusing the information these techniques provide. This includes refraining from releasing raw test results or raw data to persons, other than to patients or clients as appropriate, who are not qualified to use such information. (See also Standards 1.02, Relationship of Ethics and Law, and 1.04, Boundaries of Competence.)

2.03 Test Construction.

Psychologists who develop and conduct research with tests and other assessment techniques use scientific procedures and current professional knowledge for test design, standardization, validation, reduction or elimination of bias, and recommendations for use.

2.04 Use of Assessment in General and With Special Populations.

(a) Psychologists who perform interventions or administer, score, interpret, or use assessment techniques are familiar with the reliability, validation, and related standardization or outcome studies of, and proper applications and uses of, the techniques they use.

(b) Psychologists recognize limits to the certainty with which diagnoses, judgments, or predictions can be made about individuals.

(c) Psychologists attempt to identify situations in which particular interventions or assessment techniques or norms may not be applicable or may require adjustment in administration or interpretation because of factors such as individuals' gender, age, race, ethnicity, national origin, religion, sexual orientation, disability, language, or socioeconomic status.

2.05 Interpreting Assessment Results.

When interpreting assessment results, including automated interpretations, psychologists take into account the various test factors and characteristics of the person being assessed that might affect psychologists' judgments or reduce the accuracy of their interpretations. They indicate any significant reservations they have about the accuracy or limitations of their interpretations.

2.06 Unqualified Persons.

Psychologists do not promote the use of psychological assessment techniques by unqualified persons. (See also Standard 1.22, Delegation to and Supervision of Subordinates.)

2.07 Obsolete Tests and Outdated Test Results.

(a) Psychologists do not base their assessment or intervention decisions or recommendations on data or test results that are outdated for the current purpose.

(b) Similarly, psychologists do not base such decisions or recommendations on tests and measures that are obsolete and not useful for the current purpose.

2.08 Test Scoring and Interpretation Services.

(a) Psychologists who offer assessment or scoring procedures to other professionals accurately describe the purpose, norms, validity, reliability, and applications of the procedures and any special qualifications applicable to their use.

(b) Psychologists select scoring and interpretation services (including automated services) on the basis of evidence of the validity of the program and procedures as well as on other appropriate considerations.

(c) Psychologists retain appropriate responsibility for the appropriate application, interpretation, and use of assessment instruments, whether they score and interpret such tests themselves or use automated or other services.

2.09 Explaining Assessment Results.

Unless the nature of the relationship is clearly explained to the person being assessed in advance and precludes provision of an explanation of results (such as in some organizational consulting, pre-employment or security screenings, and forensic evaluations), psychologists ensure that an explanation of the results is provided using language that is reasonably understandable to the person assessed or to another legally authorized person on behalf of the client. Regardless of whether the scoring and interpretation are done by the psychologist, by assistants, or by automated or other outside services, psychologists take reasonable steps to ensure that appropriate explanations of results are given.

2.10 Maintaining Test Security.

Psychologists make reasonable efforts to maintain the integrity and security of tests and other assessment techniques consistent with law, contractual obligations, and in a manner that permits compliance with the requirements of this Ethics Code. (See also Standard 1.02, Relationship of Ethics and Law.)

3. Advertising and Other Public Statements

3.01 Definition of Public Statements.

Psychologists comply with this Ethics Code in public statements relating to their professional services, products, or publications or to the field of psychology. Public statements include but are not limited to paid or unpaid advertising, brochures, printed matter, directory listings, personal resumes or curriculum vitae, interviews or comments for use in media, statements in legal proceedings, lectures and public oral presentations, and published materials.

3.02 Statements by Others.

(a) Psychologists who engage others to create or place public statements that promote their professional practice, products, or activities retain professional responsibility for such statements.

(b) In addition, psychologists make reasonable efforts to prevent others whom they do not control (such as employers, publishers, sponsors, organizational clients, and representatives of the print or broadcast media) from making deceptive statements concerning psychologists' practice or professional or scientific activities.

(c) If psychologists learn of deceptive statements about their work made by others, psychologists make reasonable efforts to correct such statements.

(d) Psychologists do not compensate employees of press, radio, television, or other communication media in return for publicity in a news item.

(e) A paid advertisement relating to the psychologist's activities must be identified as such, unless it is already apparent from the context.

3.03 Avoidance of False or Deceptive Statements.

(a) Psychologists do not make public statements that are false, deceptive, misleading, or fraudulent, either because of what they state, convey, or suggest or because of what they omit, concerning their research, practice, or other work activities or those of persons or organizations with which they are affiliated. As examples (and not in limitation) of this standard, psychologists do not make false or deceptive statements concerning (1) their training, experience, or competence; (2) their academic degrees; (3) their credentials; (4) their institutional or association affiliations; (5) their services; (6) the scientific or clinical basis for, or results or degree of success of, their services; (7) their fees; or (8) their publications or research findings. (See also Standards 6.15, Deception in Research, and 6.18, Providing Participants With Information About the Study.)

(b) Psychologists claim as credentials for their psychological work, only degrees that (1) were earned from a regionally accredited educational institution or (2) were the basis for psychology licensure by the state in which they practice.

3.04 Media Presentations.

When psychologists provide advice or comment by means of public lectures, demonstrations, radio or television programs, prerecorded tapes, printed articles, mailed material, or other media, they take reasonable precautions to ensure that (1) the statements are based on appropriate psychological literature and practice, (2) the statements are otherwise consistent with this Ethics Code, and (3) the recipients of the information are not encouraged to infer that a relationship has been established with them personally.

3.05 Testimonials.

Psychologists do not solicit testimonials from current psychotherapy clients or patients or other persons who because of their particular circumstances are vulnerable to undue influence.

3.06 In-Person Solicitation.

Psychologists do not engage, directly or through agents, in uninvited in-person solicitation of business from actual or potential psychotherapy patients or clients or other persons who because of their particular circumstances are vulnerable to undue influence. However, this does not preclude attempting to implement appropriate collateral contacts with significant others for the purpose of benefiting an already engaged therapy patient.

4. Therapy

4.01 Structuring the Relationship.

(a) Psychologists discuss with clients or patients as early as is feasible in the therapeutic relationship appropriate issues, such as the nature and anticipated course of therapy, fees, and confidentiality. (See also Standards 1.25, Fees and Financial Arrangements, and 5.01, Discussing the Limits of Confidentiality.)

(b) When the psychologist's work with clients or patients will be supervised, the above discussion includes that fact, and the name of the supervisor, when the supervisor has legal responsibility for the case.

(c) When the therapist is a student intern, the client or patient is informed of that fact.

(d) Psychologists make reasonable efforts to answer patients' questions and to avoid apparent misunderstandings about therapy. Whenever possible, psychologists provide oral and/or written information, using language that is reasonably understandable to the patient or client.

4.02 Informed Consent to Therapy.

(a) Psychologists obtain appropriate informed consent to therapy or related procedures, using language that is reasonably understandable to participants. The content of informed consent will vary depending on many circumstances; however, informed consent generally implies that the person (1) has the capacity to consent, (2) has been informed of significant information concerning the procedure, (3) has freely and without undue influence expressed consent, and (4) consent has been appropriately documented.

(b) When persons are legally incapable of giving informed consent, psychologists obtain informed permission from a legally authorized person, if such substitute consent is permitted by law.

(c) In addition, psychologists (1) inform those persons who are legally incapable of giving informed consent about the proposed interventions in a manner commensurate with the persons' psychological capacities, (2) seek their assent to those interventions, and (3) consider such persons' preferences and best interests.

4.03 Couple and Family Relationships.

(a) When a psychologist agrees to provide services to several persons who have a relationship (such as husband and wife or parents and children), the psychologist attempts to clarify at the outset (1) which of the individuals are patients or clients and (2) the relationship the psychologist will have with each person. This clarification includes the role of the psychologist and the probable uses of the services provided or the information obtained. (See also Standard 5.01, Discussing the Limits of Confidentiality.)

(b) As soon as it becomes apparent that the psychologist may be called on to perform potentially conflicting roles (such as marital counselor to husband and wife, and then witness for one party in a divorce proceeding), the psychologist attempts to clarify and adjust, or withdraw from, roles appropriately. (See also Standard 7.03, Clarification of Role, under Forensic Activities.)

4.04 Providing Mental Health Services to Those Served by Others.
In deciding whether to offer or provide services to those already receiving mental health services elsewhere, psychologists carefully consider the treatment issues and the potential patient's or client's welfare. The psychologist discusses these issues with the patient or client, or another legally authorized person on behalf of the client, in order to minimize the risk of confusion and conflict, consults with the other service providers when appropriate, and proceeds with caution and sensitivity to the therapeutic issues.

4.05 Sexual Intimacies With Current Patients or Clients.
Psychologists do not engage in sexual intimacies with current patients or clients.

4.06 Therapy With Former Sexual Partners.
Psychologists do not accept as therapy patients or clients persons with whom they have engaged in sexual intimacies.

4.07 Sexual Intimacies With Former Therapy Patients.
(a) Psychologists do not engage in sexual intimacies with a former therapy patient or client for at least two years after cessation or termination of professional services.
(b) Because sexual intimacies with a former therapy patient or client are so frequently harmful to the patient or client, and because such intimacies undermine public confidence in the psychology profession and thereby deter the public's use of needed services, psychologists do not engage in sexual intimacies with former therapy patients and clients even after a two-year interval except in the most unusual circumstances. The psychologist who engages in such activity after the two years following cessation or termination of treatment bears the burden of demonstrating that there has been no exploitation, in light of all relevant factors, including (1) the amount of time that has passed since therapy terminated, (2) the nature and duration of the therapy, (3) the circumstances of termination, (4) the patient's or client's personal history, (5) the patient's or client's current mental status, (6) the likelihood of adverse impact on the patient or client and others, and (7) any statements or actions made by the therapist during the course of therapy suggesting or inviting the possibility of a post-termination sexual or romantic relationship with the patient or client. (See also Standard 1.17, Multiple Relationships.)

4.08 Interruption of Services.
(a) Psychologists make reasonable efforts to plan for facilitating care in the event that psychological services are interrupted by factors such as the psychologist's illness, death, unavailability, or relocation or by the client's relocation or financial limitations. (See also Standard 5.09, Preserving Records and Data.)
(b) When entering into employment or contractual relationships, psychologists provide for orderly and appropriate resolution of responsibility for patient or client care in the event that the employment or contractual relationship ends, with paramount consideration given to the welfare of the patient or client.

4.09 Terminating the Professional Relationship.
(a) Psychologists do not abandon patients or clients. (See also Standard 1.25e, under Fees and Financial Arrangements.)

(b) Psychologists terminate a professional relationship when it becomes reasonably clear that the patient or client no longer needs the service, is not benefiting, or is being harmed by continued service.

(c) Prior to termination for whatever reason, except where precluded by the patient's or client's conduct, the psychologist discusses the patient's or client's views and needs, provides appropriate pretermination counseling, suggests alternative service providers as appropriate, and takes other reasonable steps to facilitate transfer of responsibility to another provider if the patient or client needs one immediately.

5. Privacy and Confidentiality

These Standards are potentially applicable to the professional and scientific activities of all psychologists.

5.01 Discussing the Limits of Confidentiality.

(a) Psychologists discuss with persons and organizations with whom they establish a scientific or professional relationship (including, to the extent feasible, minors and their legal representatives) (1) the relevant limitations on confidentiality, including limitations where applicable in group, marital, and family therapy or in organizational consulting, and (2) the foreseeable uses of the information generated through their services.

(b) Unless it is not feasible or is contraindicated, the discussion of confidentiality occurs at the outset of the relationship and thereafter as new circumstances may warrant.

(c) Permission for electronic recording of interviews is secured from clients and patients.

5.02 Maintaining Confidentiality.

Psychologists have a primary obligation and take reasonable precautions to respect the confidentiality rights of those with whom they work or consult, recognizing that confidentiality may be established by law, institutional rules, or professional or scientific relationships. (See also Standard 6.26, Professional Reviewers.)

5.03 Minimizing Intrusions on Privacy.

(a) In order to minimize intrusions on privacy, psychologists include in written and oral reports, consultations, and the like, only information germane to the purpose for which the communication is made.

(b) Psychologists discuss confidential information obtained in clinical or consulting relationships, or evaluative data concerning patients, individual or organizational clients, students, research participants, supervisees, and employees, only for appropriate scientific or professional purposes and only with persons clearly concerned with such matters.

5.04 Maintenance of Records.

Psychologists maintain appropriate confidentiality in creating, storing, accessing, transferring, and disposing of records under their control, whether these are written, automated, or in any other medium. Psychologists maintain and dispose of records in accordance with law and in a manner that permits compliance with the requirements of this Ethics Code.

5.05 Disclosures.

(a) Psychologists disclose confidential information without the consent of the individual only as mandated by law, or where permitted by law for a valid purpose, such as (1) to provide needed professional services to the patient or the individual or organizational client, (2) to obtain appropriate professional consultations, (3) to protect the patient or client or others from harm, or (4) to obtain payment for services, in which instance disclosure is limited to the minimum that is necessary to achieve the purpose.

(b) Psychologists also may disclose confidential information with the appropriate consent of the patient or the individual or organizational client (or of another legally authorized person on behalf of the patient or client), unless prohibited by law.

5.06 Consultations.

When consulting with colleagues, (1) psychologists do not share confidential information that reasonably could lead to the identification of a patient, client, research participant, or other person or organization with whom they have a confidential relationship unless they have obtained the prior consent of the person or organization or the disclosure cannot be avoided, and (2) they share information only to the extent necessary to achieve the purposes of the consultation. (See also Standard 5.02, Maintaining Confidentiality.)

5.07 Confidential Information in Databases.

(a) If confidential information concerning recipients of psychological services is to be entered into databases or systems of records available to persons whose access has not been consented to by the recipient, then psychologists use coding or other techniques to avoid the inclusion of personal identifiers.

(b) If a research protocol approved by an institutional review board or similar body requires the inclusion of personal identifiers, such identifiers are deleted before the information is made accessible to persons other than those of whom the subject was advised.

(c) If such deletion is not feasible, then before psychologists transfer such data to others or review such data collected by others, they take reasonable steps to determine that appropriate consent of personally identifiable individuals has been obtained.

5.08 Use of Confidential Information for Didactic or Other Purposes.

(a) Psychologists do not disclose in their writings, lectures, or other public media, confidential, personally identifiable information concerning their patients, individual or organizational clients, students, research participants, or other recipients of their services that they obtained during the course of their work, unless the person or organization has consented in writing or unless there is other ethical or legal authorization for doing so.

(b) Ordinarily, in such scientific and professional presentations, psychologists disguise confidential information concerning such persons or organizations so that they are not individually identifiable to others and so that discussions do not cause harm to subjects who might identify themselves.

5.09 Preserving Records and Data.

A psychologist makes plans in advance so that confidentiality of records and data is protected in the event of the psychologist's death, incapacity, or withdrawal from the position or practice.

5.10 Ownership of Records and Data.

Recognizing that ownership of records and data is governed by legal principles, psychologists take reasonable and lawful steps so that records and data remain available to the extent needed to serve the best interests of patients, individual or organizational clients, research participants, or appropriate others.

5.11 Withholding Records for Nonpayment.

Psychologists may not withhold records under their control that are requested and imminently needed for a patient's or client's treatment solely because payment has not been received, except as otherwise provided by law.

6. Teaching, Training Supervision, Research, and Publishing

6.01 Design of Education and Training Programs.

Psychologists who are responsible for education and training programs seek to ensure that the programs are competently designed, provide the proper experiences, and meet the requirements for licensure, certification, or other goals for which claims are made by the program.

6.02 Descriptions of Education and Training Programs.

(a) Psychologists responsible for education and training programs seek to ensure that there is a current and accurate description of the program content, training goals and objectives, and requirements that must be met for satisfactory completion of the program. This information must be made readily available to all interested parties.

(b) Psychologists seek to ensure that statements concerning their course outlines are accurate and not misleading, particularly regarding the subject matter to be covered, bases for evaluating progress, and the nature of course experiences. (See also Standard 3.03, Avoidance of False or Deceptive Statements.)

(c) To the degree to which they exercise control, psychologists responsible for announcements, catalogs, brochures, or advertisements describing workshops, seminars, or other non-degree-granting educational programs ensure that they accurately describe the audience for which the program is intended, the educational objectives, the presenters, and the fees involved.

6.03 Accuracy and Objectivity in Teaching.

(a) When engaged in teaching or training, psychologists present psychological information accurately and with a reasonable degree of objectivity.

(b) When engaged in teaching or training, psychologists recognize the power they hold over students or supervisees and therefore make reasonable efforts to avoid engaging in conduct that is personally demeaning to students or supervisees. (See also Standards 1.09, Respecting Others, and 1.12, Other Harassment.)

6.04 Limitation on Teaching.

Psychologists do not teach the use of techniques or procedures that require specialized training, licensure, or expertise, including but not limited to hypnosis, biofeedback, and projective techniques, to individuals who lack the prerequisite training, legal scope of practice, or expertise.

6.05 Assessing Student and Supervisee Performance.
(a) In academic and supervisory relationships, psychologists establish an appropriate process for providing feedback to students and supervisees.
(b) Psychologists evaluate students and supervisees on the basis of their actual performance on relevant and established program requirements.

6.06 Planning Research.
(a) Psychologists design, conduct, and report research in accordance with recognized standards of scientific competence and ethical research.
(b) Psychologists plan their research so as to minimize the possibility that results will be misleading.
(c) In planning research, psychologists consider its ethical acceptability under the Ethics Code. If an ethical issue is unclear, psychologists seek to resolve the issue through consultation with institutional review boards, animal care and use committees, peer consultations, or other proper mechanisms.
(d) Psychologists take reasonable steps to implement appropriate protections for the rights and welfare of human participants, other persons affected by the research, and the welfare of animal subjects.

6.07 Responsibility.
(a) Psychologists conduct research competently and with due concern for the dignity and welfare of the participants.
(b) Psychologists are responsible for the ethical conduct of research conducted by them or by others under their supervision or control.
(c) Researchers and assistants are permitted to perform only those tasks for which they are appropriately trained and prepared.
(d) As part of the process of development and implementation of research projects, psychologists consult those with expertise concerning any special population under investigation or most likely to be affected.

6.08 Compliance With Law and Standards.
Psychologists plan and conduct research in a manner consistent with federal and state law and regulations, as well as professional standards governing the conduct of research, and particularly those standards governing research with human participants and animal subjects.

6.09 Institutional Approval.
Psychologists obtain from host institutions or organizations appropriate approval prior to conducting research, and they provide accurate information about their research proposals. They conduct the research in accordance with the approved research protocol.

6.10 Research Responsibilities.
Prior to conducting research (except research involving only anonymous surveys, naturalistic observations, or similar research), psychologists enter into an agreement with participants that clarifies the nature of the research and the responsibilities of each party.

6.11 Informed Consent to Research.
(a) Psychologists use language that is reasonably understandable to research participants in obtaining their appropriate informed consent (except as provided in Standard 6.12, Dispensing with Informed Consent). Such informed consent is appropriately documented.

(b) Using language that is reasonably understandable to participants, psychologists inform participants of the nature of the research; they inform participants that they are free to participate or to decline to participate or to withdraw from the research; they explain the foreseeable consequences of declining or withdrawing; they inform participants of significant factors that may be expected to influence their willingness to participate (such as risks, discomfort, adverse effects, or limitations on confidentiality, except as provided in Standard 6.15, Deception in Research); and they explain other aspects about which the prospective participants inquire.

(c) When psychologists conduct research with individuals such as students or subordinates, psychologists take special care to protect the prospective participants from adverse consequences of declining or withdrawing from participation.

(d) When research participation is a course requirement or opportunity for extra credit, the prospective participant is given the choice of equitable alternative activities.

(e) For persons who are legally incapable of giving informed consent, psychologists nevertheless (1) provide an appropriate explanation, (2) obtain the participant's assent, and (3) obtain appropriate permission from a legally authorized person, if such substitute consent is permitted by law.

6.12 Dispensing With Informed Consent.

Before determining that planned research (such as research involving only anonymous questionnaires, naturalistic observations, or certain kinds of archival research) does not require the informed consent of research participants, psychologists consider applicable regulations and institutional review board requirements, and they consult with colleagues as appropriate.

6.13 Informed Consent in Research Filming or Recording.

Psychologists obtain informed consent from research participants prior to filming or recording them in any form, unless the research involves simply naturalistic observations in public places and it is not anticipated that the recording will be used in a manner that could cause personal identification or harm.

6.14 Offering Inducements for Research Participants.

(a) In offering professional services as an inducement to obtain research participants, psychologists make clear the nature of the services, as well as the risks, obligations, and limitations. (See also Standard 1.18, Barter [With Patients or Clients].)

(b) Psychologists do not offer excessive or inappropriate financial or other inducements to obtain research participants, particularly when it might tend to coerce participation.

6.15 Deception in Research.

(a) Psychologists do not conduct a study involving deception unless they have determined that the use of deceptive techniques is justified by the study's prospective scientific, educational, or applied value and that equally effective alternative procedures that do not use deception are not feasible.

(b) Psychologists never deceive research participants about significant aspects that would affect their willingness to participate, such as physical risks, discomfort, or unpleasant emotional experiences.

(c) Any other deception that is an integral feature of the design and conduct of an experiment must be explained to participants as early as is feasible, preferably at the conclusion of their participation, but no later than at the conclusion of the research. (See also Standard 6.18, Providing Participants With Information About the Study.)

6.16 Sharing and Utilizing Data.

Psychologists inform research participants of their anticipated sharing or further use of personally identifiable research data and of the possibility of unanticipated future uses.

6.17 Minimizing Invasiveness.

In conducting research, psychologists interfere with the participants or milieu from which data are collected only in a manner that is warranted by an appropriate research design and that is consistent with psychologists' roles as scientific investigators.

6.18 Providing Participants With Information About the Study.

(a) Psychologists provide a prompt opportunity for participants to obtain appropriate information about the nature, results, and conclusions of the research, and psychologists attempt to correct any misconceptions that participants may have.

(b) If scientific or humane values justify delaying or withholding this information, psychologists take reasonable measures to reduce the risk of harm.

6.19 Honoring Commitments.

Psychologists take reasonable measures to honor all commitments they have made to research participants.

6.20 Care and Use of Animals in Research.

(a) Psychologists who conduct research involving animals treat them humanely.

(b) Psychologists acquire, care for, use, and dispose of animals in compliance with current federal, state, and local laws and regulations, and with professional standards.

(c) Psychologists trained in research methods and experienced in the care of laboratory animals supervise all procedures involving animals and are responsible for ensuring appropriate consideration of their comfort, health, and humane treatment.

(d) Psychologists ensure that all individuals using animals under their supervision have received instruction in research methods and in the care, maintenance, and handling of the species being used, to the extent appropriate to their role.

(e) Responsibilities and activities of individuals assisting in a research project are consistent with their respective competencies.

(f) Psychologists make reasonable efforts to minimize the discomfort, infection, illness, and pain of animal subjects.

(g) A procedure subjecting animals to pain, stress, or privation is used only when an alternative procedure is unavailable and the goal is justified by its prospective scientific, educational, or applied value.

(h) Surgical procedures are performed under appropriate anesthesia; techniques to avoid infection and minimize pain are followed during and after surgery.

(i) When it is appropriate that the animal's life be terminated, it is done rapidly, with an effort to minimize pain, and in accordance with accepted procedures.

6.21 Reporting of Results.

(a) Psychologists do not fabricate data or falsify results in their publications.

(b) If psychologists discover significant errors in their published data, they take reasonable steps to correct such errors in a correction, retraction, erratum, or other appropriate publication means.

6.22 Plagiarism.

Psychologists do not present substantial portions or elements of another's work or data as their own, even if the other work or data source is cited occasionally.

6.23 Publication Credit.

(a) Psychologists take responsibility and credit, including authorship credit, only for work they have actually performed or to which they have contributed.

(b) Principal authorship and other publication credits accurately reflect the relative scientific or professional contributions of the individuals involved, regardless of their relative status. Mere possession of an institutional position, such as Department Chair, does not justify authorship credit. Minor contributions to the research or to the writing for publications are appropriately acknowledged, such as in footnotes or in an introductory statement.

(c) A student is usually listed as principal author on any multiple-authored article that is substantially based on the student's dissertation or thesis.

6.24 Duplicate Publication of Data.

Psychologists do not publish, as original data, data that have been previously published. This does not preclude republishing data when they are accompanied by proper acknowledgment.

6.25 Sharing Data.

After research results are published, psychologists do not withhold the data on which their conclusions are based from other competent professionals who seek to verify the substantive claims through reanalysis and who intend to use such data only for that purpose, provided that the confidentiality of the participants can be protected and unless legal rights concerning proprietary data preclude their release.

6.26 Professional Reviewers.

Psychologists who review material submitted for publication, grant, or other research proposal review respect the confidentiality of and the proprietary rights in such information of those who submitted it.

7. Forensic Activities

7.01 Professionalism.

Psychologists who perform forensic functions, such as assessments, interviews, consultations, reports, or expert testimony, must comply with all other provisions of this Ethics Code to the extent that they apply to such activities. In addition, psychologists base their forensic work on appropriate knowledge of and competence in the areas underlying such work, including specialized knowledge concerning special populations. (See also Standards 1.06, Basis for Scientific and Professional Judgments; 1.08, Human Differences; 1.15, Misuse of Psychologists' Influence; and 1.23, Documentation of Professional and Scientific Work.)

7.02 Forensic Assessments.

(a) Psychologists' forensic assessments, recommendations, and reports are based on information and techniques (including personal interviews of the individual, when appropriate) sufficient to provide appropriate substantiation for their findings. (See also Standards 1.03, Professional and Scientific Relationship; 1.23, Documentation of Professional and Scientific Work; 2.01, Evaluation, Diagnosis, and Interventions in Professional Context; and 2.05, Interpreting Assessment Results.)

(b) Except as noted in (c), below, psychologists provide written or oral forensic reports or testimony of the psychological characteristics of an individual only after they have conducted an examination of the individual adequate to support their statements or conclusions.

(c) When, despite reasonable efforts, such an examination is not feasible, psychologists clarify the impact of their limited information on the reliability and validity of their reports and testimony, and they appropriately limit the nature and extent of their conclusions or recommendations.

7.03 Clarification of Role.

In most circumstances, psychologists avoid performing multiple and potentially conflicting roles in forensic matters. When psychologists may be called on to serve in more than one role in a legal proceeding—for example, as consultant or expert for one party or for the court and as a fact witness— they clarify role expectations and the extent of confidentiality in advance to the extent feasible, and thereafter as changes occur, in order to avoid compromising their professional judgment and objectivity and in order to avoid misleading others regarding their role.

7.04 Truthfulness and Candor.

(a) In forensic testimony and reports, psychologists testify truthfully, honestly, and candidly and, consistent with applicable legal procedures, describe fairly the bases for their testimony and conclusions.

(b) Whenever necessary to avoid misleading, psychologists acknowledge the limits of their data or conclusions.

7.05 Prior Relationships.

A prior professional relationship with a party does not preclude psychologists from testifying as fact witnesses or from testifying to their services to the extent permitted by applicable law. Psychologists appropriately take into account ways in which the prior relationship might affect their professional objectivity or opinions and disclose the potential conflict to the relevant parties.

7.06 Compliance With Law and Rules.

In performing forensic roles, psychologists are reasonably familiar with the rules governing their roles. Psychologists are aware of the occasionally competing demands placed upon them by these principles and the requirements of the court system, and attempt to resolve these conflicts by making known their commitment to this Ethics Code and taking steps to resolve the conflict in a responsible manner. (See also Standard 1.02, Relationship of Ethics and Law.)

8. Resolving Ethical Issues

8.01 Familiarity With Ethics Code.
Psychologists have an obligation to be familiar with this Ethics Code, other applicable ethics codes, and their application to psychologists' work. Lack of awareness or misunderstanding of an ethical standard is not itself a defense to a charge of unethical conduct.

8.02 Confronting Ethical Issues.
When a psychologist is uncertain whether a particular situation or course of action would violate this Ethics Code, the psychologist ordinarily consults with other psychologists knowledgeable about ethical issues, with state or national psychology ethics committees, or with other appropriate authorities in order to choose a proper response.

8.03 Conflicts Between Ethics and Organizational Demands.
If the demands of an organization with which psychologists are affiliated conflict with this Ethics Code, psychologists clarify the nature of the conflict, make known their commitment to the Ethics Code, and to the extent feasible, seek to resolve the conflict in a way that permits the fullest adherence to the Ethics Code.

8.04 Informal Resolution of Ethical Violations.
When psychologists believe that there may have been an ethical violation by another psychologist, they attempt to resolve the issue by bringing it to the attention of that individual if an informal resolution appears appropriate and the intervention does not violate any confidentiality rights that may be involved.

8.05 Reporting Ethical Violations.
If an apparent ethical violation is not appropriate for informal resolution under Standard 8.04 or is not resolved properly in that fashion, psychologists take further action appropriate to the situation, unless such action conflicts with confidentiality rights in ways that cannot be resolved. Such action might include referral to state or national committees on professional ethics or to state licensing boards.

8.06 Cooperating With Ethics Committees.
Psychologists cooperate in ethics investigations, proceedings, and resulting requirements of the APA or any affiliated state psychological association to which they belong. In doing so, they make reasonable efforts to resolve any issues as to confidentiality. Failure to cooperate is itself an ethics violation.

8.07 Improper Complaints.
Psychologists do not file or encourage the filing of ethics complaints that are frivolous and are intended to harm the respondent rather than to protect the public.

History and Effective Date

This version of the APA Ethics Code was adopted by the American Psychological Association's Council of Representatives during its meeting, August 13 and

16, 1992, and is effective beginning December 1, 1992. Inquiries concerning the substance or interpretation of the APA Ethics Code should be addressed to the Director, Office of Ethics, American Psychological Association, 750 First Street, NE, Washington, DC 20002-4242.

This Code will be used to adjudicate complaints brought concerning alleged conduct occurring after the effective date. Complaints regarding conduct occurring prior to the effective date will be adjudicated on the basis of the version of the Code that was in effect at the time the conduct occurred, except that no provisions repealed in June 1989, will be enforced even if an earlier version contains the provision. The Ethics Code will undergo continuing review and study for future revisions; comments on the Code may be sent to the above address.

Appendix C

TYPES OF
PSYCHOTROPIC MEDICATION

Table C. Types of psychotropic medication.

Antidepressant Names				Selective Action on Neurotransmitters[2]	
Generic	Brand	Sedation	ACH[1]	NE	5-HT
imipramine	Tofranil	+ +	+ +	+ +	+ + +
desipramine	Norpramin	+	+	+ + + + +	0
amitriptyline	Elavil	+ + + +	+ + + +	+	+ + + +
nortriptyline	Aventyl, Pamelor	+ +	+ +	+ + +	+ +
protriptyline	Vivactil	+ +	+ +	+ + + +	+
trimipramine	Surmontil[3]	+ + + +	+ + +	+ +	+ +
doxepin	Sinequan, Adapin[3]	+ + + +	+ +	+ + +	+ +
maprotiline	Ludiomil	+ +	+ +	+ + + + +	0
amoxapine	Asendin	+ +	+	+ + + +	+
trazodone	Desyrel	+ +	0	0	+ + + + +
fluoxetine	Prozac	+	0	0	+ + + + +
bupropion-S.R.	Wellbutrin-S.R.[4]	+	0	+ +	0
sertraline	Zoloft	+	0	0	+ + + + +
paroxetine	Paxil	+	+	0	+ + + + +
venlafaxine	Effexor	+	0	+ +	+ + +
nefazodone	Serzone	+ +	0	+	+ + + +
fluvoxamine	Luvox	+	+	0	+ + + + +
mirtazapine	Remeron	+ +	+ +	+ + +	+ + +
MAO Inhibitors					
phenelzine	Nardil[5]	+	0	+ + +	+ + +
tranylcypromine	Parnate[5]	+	0	+ + +	+ + +

Anti-Obsessional

Generic	Brand	Sedation	ACH Effects
Names			
clomipramine	Anafranil	++++	++++
fluoxetine	Prozac[6]	+	0
sertraline	Zoloft[6]	+	0
paroxetine	Paxil[6]	+	+
fluvoxamine	Luvox	+	+

Anti-Anxiety

Generic	Brand	Generic	Brand
Names		Names	
Benzodiazepines		*Other Anti-Anxiety Agents*	
diazepam	Valium	buspirone	BuSpar
chlordiazepoxide	Librium	hydroxyzine	Atarax, Vistrail
prazepam	Centrax	propranolol	Inderal
clorazepate	Tranxene	atenolol	Tenormin
clonazepam	Klonopin	clonidine	Catapres
lorazepam	Ativan	*Anti-Panic Medications*	
alprazolam	Xanax	High-potency benzodiazepines	
oxazepam	Serax	(e.g. alprazolam, clonazepam)	
		Antidepressants (e.g. SSRI's)	
		MAO inhibitors	

Psycho-Stimulants

Generic	Brand	Generic	Brand
Names		Names	
		Mood Stabilizers	
methylphenidate	Ritalin	lithium carbonate	Eskalith, Lithonate
dextroamphetamine	Dexedrine	carbamazepine	Tegretol
pemoline	Cylert	valproic acid	Depakote, Depakene

Hypnotics[7]

Generic	Brand
Names	
flurazepam	Dalmane
temazepam	Restoril
triazolam	Halcion
estazolam	ProSom
quazepam	Doral
zolpidem	Ambiem
diphenhydramine	Benadryl

Antipsychotic Names				
Generic	Brand	Sedation	EPS[8]	ACH Effects[9]
Low Potency				
chlorpromazine	Thorazine	++++	++	++++
thioridazine	Mellaril	++++	+	+++++
clozapine	Clozaril	++++	0	+++++
mesoridazine	Serentil	++++	+	+++++
High Potency				
Molindone	Moban	+	+++	+++
perphenazine	Trilafon	++	++++	++
loxapine	Loxitane	+	+++	++
trifluoperazine	Stelazine	+	++++	++
fluphenazine	Prolixin[10]	+	+++++	++
thiothixene	Navane	+	++++	++
haloperidol	Haldol[10]	+	+++++	+
pimozide	Orap	+	+++++	+
risperidone	Risperdal	+	+	+
olanzapine	Zyprexa	+	+/0	+
sertindole	Serlect	+	+/0	+

Common Side Effects Associated with Psychotropic Medications

Anticholinergic effects (block acetylcholine): dry mouth; constipation; urinary retention; blurred vision; memory impairment; confusional states.

Extrapyramidal effects (dopamine blockade in basal ganglia): Parkinson-like effects—rigidity, shuffling gait, tremor, flat affect, lethargy; dystonias—spasms in neck and other muscle groups; akathisia—intense, uncomfortable sense of inner restlessness; tardive dyskinesia—often a persistent movement disorder (lip smacking, writhing movements, jerky movements).

Autonomic effects: especially orthostatic hypotension, which can cause dizziness and imbalance in the elderly; especially can result in falls and fractures.

Sedation: drowsiness and impaired concentration and reaction time.

[1]ACH: Anticholinergic side effects.
[2]NE: Norepinephrine; 5-HT: Serotonin.
[3]Uncertain, but likely effects.
[4]Atypical antidepressant. Uncertain effects but likely to be a dopamine agonist, and indirect increase in norepinephrine.
[5]MAO inhibitors operate via a different mechanism of action than other antidepressants, and increase NE, 5-HT and dopamine.
[6]Often higher doses are required to control obsessive compulsive symptoms than the doses generally used to treat depression.
[7]To treat initial insomnia
[8]Acute: Parkinson's, dystonias, akathisia. Does not reflect risk for tardive dyskinesia. All neuroleptics may cause tardive dyskinesia, except clozapine.
[9]Anticholinergic side effects.
[10]Available in time-released IM format.

This is meant as a general reference only, and should not serve as a guideline for prescribing of medications. (Brand names are registered trademarks.)

Adapted from *Quick Reference to Psychotropic Medication*. Reprinted with permission of John Preston and P. A. Distributors.

REFERENCES AND RECOMMENDED READINGS

Adler, G., & Myerson, P. G. (Eds.). (1973). *Confrontation in psychotherapy.* New York: Science House.

Aguilera, D., & Messick, J. (1978). *Crisis intervention* (3rd ed.). St. Louis: Mosby.

American Counseling Association (ACA). (1995). *Code of ethics and standards of practice.* Alexandria, VA: Author.

American Psychiatric Association. (1994). *Diagnostic and statistical manual of mental disorders* (4th ed.). [*DSM-IV*]. Washington, DC: Author.

American Psychological Association (APA). (1992). *Ethical principles of psychologists and code of conduct.* Washington, DC: Author

Arnold, M. B. (1960). *Emotion and personality* (2 vols.). New York: Columbia University Press.

Arnold, M. B. (Ed.). (1970). *Feelings and emotions.* New York: Academic Press.

Barnard, C. P. (1994). Resiliency: A shift in our perception? *The American Journal of Family Therapy, 2(22),* 135–144.

Beardsley, R. S., Gardocki, G. J., Larsen, D. B., & Hidalgo, J. (1988). Prescribing of psychotropic medication by primary care physicians and psychiatrists. *Archives of General Psychiatry, 45,* 1117–1119.

Beck, A. T. (1967). *Depression: Causes and treatment.* Philadelphia: University of Pennsylvania Press.

Beck, A. T. (1976). *Cognitive therapy and the emotional disorders.* New York: International Universities Press.

Beier, E. G. (1966). *The silent language of psychotherapy.* Chicago: Aldine.

Beitman, B. D. (1987). *The structure of individual psychotherapy.* New York: The Guilford Press.

Belkin, G. S. (1980a). *An introduction to counseling.* Dubuque, IA: Brown.

Belkin, G. S. (1980b). *Contemporary psychotherapies.* Chicago: Rand McNally.

Bennet, B., Bryant, B., VanderBos, F., & Greenwood, A. (1990). *Professional liability and risk management.* Washington, DC: American Psychological Association.

Bergin, A. E. (1971). The evaluation of therapeutic outcomes. In A. E. Bergin & S. K. Garfield (Eds.), *Handbook of psychotherapy and behavior change.* New York: Wiley.

Bergin, A. E. (1975, November). Psychotherapy can be dangerous. *Psychology Today,* pp. 96–104.

Bernard, J. M., & Goodyear, R. K. (1992). *Fundamentals of clinical supervision.* Boston: Allyn and Bacon.

Bernstein, B. E., & Hartsell, T. L. (1998). *The portable lawyer for mental health professionals: An A-Z guide for protecting your clients, your practice, and yourself.* New York: Wiley.

Birdwhistell, R. L. (1970). *Kinesics and context.* Philadelphia: University of Pennsylvania Press.

Bischoff, M. M., & Tracey, T. J. G. (1995). Client resistance as predicted by therapist behavior: A study of sequential dependence. *Journal of Counseling Psychology, 42,* 487–497.

Blatt, S. J., & Erlich, H. S. (1982). Levels of resistance in the psychotherapeutic process. In P. L. Wachtel (Ed.), *Resistance: Psychodynamic and behavioral approaches* (pp. 69–91). New York: Plenum Press.

Blocher, D. H. (1987). *The professional counselor.* New York: Macmillan Publishing.

Borders, L. D. (1986). Facilitating supervisee growth: Implications of developmental models of counseling supervision. *Michigan Journal of Counseling and Development, 17(2),* 7–12.

Borders, L. D., & Leddick, G. R. (1987). *Handbook of counseling supervision.* Alexandria, VA: Association for Counselor Education and Supervision, a Division of the American Association for Counseling and Development.

Boy, A. V., & Pine, G. J. (1982). *Client-centered counseling: A renewal.* Boston: Allyn & Bacon.

Boy, A. V., & Pine, G. J. (1983). Counseling: Fundamentals of theoretical renewal. *Counseling & Values,* 248–255.

Brammer, L. M. (1979). *The helping relationship: Process and skills* (2nd ed.). Englewood Cliffs, NJ: Prentice-Hall.

Brammer, L. M., & MacDonald, G. (1999). *The helping relationship: Process and skills* (7th ed.). Boston: Allyn and Bacon.

Bugental, J. F. T. (1978). *Psychotherapy and process: The fundamentals of an existential-humanistic approach.* Menlo Park, CA: Addison-Wesley.

Burck, H. D., & Peterson, G. W. (1975). Needed! More evaluation, not research. *Personnel and Guidance Journal, 53(8),* 563–569.

Burns, D. D. (1999). *Feeling good: The new mood therapy.* New York: Harper Collins.

Burton, A. (1968). *Modern humanistic psychotherapy.* San Francisco: Jossey-Bass.

Candland, D. K., Fell, J. P., Keen, E., Leshner, A. I., Tarpy, R. M., & Plutchik, R. (1977). *Emotion.* Monterey, CA: Brooks/Cole.

Capuzzi, D., & Gross, D. R. (Eds.). (1995). *Counseling & psychotherapy: Theories and interventions.* New Jersey: Merrill.

Carkhuff, R. R., & Anthony, W. A. (1979). *The skills of helping.* Amherst, MA: Human Resource Development Press.

Coleman, J. C., Butcher, J. N., & Carson, R. C. (1980). *Abnormal psychology and modern life* (6th ed.). Palo Alto, CA: Scott, Foresman.

Combs, A. W., & Snygg, D. (1959). *Individual behavior* (2nd ed.). New York: Harper.

Copeland, M. E. (1992). *The depression workbook*. Oakland, CA: New Harbinger.

Corey, G. (1977). *Theory and practice of counseling and psychotherapy*. Monterey, CA: Brooks/Cole.

Corey, G., Corey, M. S., & Callanan, P. (1998). *Issues and ethics in the helping professions*. Pacific Grove, CA: Brooks/Cole.

Cormier, W. H., & Cormier, L. S. (1991). *Interviewing strategies for helpers* (3rd ed.). Pacific Grove, CA: Brooks/Cole.

Corsini, R. J. (Ed.). (1979). *Current psychotherapies* (2nd ed.). Itasca, IL: Peacock.

Cowan, M. A. (1995). *Sociocultural context of ministry*. New Orleans, LA: Institute for Ministry, Loyola University.

Cross, T. L., Bazron, B. J., Dennis, K. W., & Isaacs, M. R. (1989). *Towards a culturally competent system of care*. Washington, DC: Georgetown University Child Development Center.

Diller, J. V. (1999). *Cultural diversity: A primer for the human services*. Belmont, CA: Wadsworth.

Dixon, S. L. (1979). *Working with people in crisis*. St. Louis: Mosby.

Dowd, E. T. (1976). The gotterdammerung syndrome: Implications for counseling. *Counseling & Values, 20(3)*, 139–142.

Downing, C. (1988). *The goddess: Mythological images of the feminine*. New York: Cross Road Publishing.

Doyle, R. E. (1998). *Essential skills and strategies in the helping process* (2nd ed.). Pacific Grove, CA: Brooks/Cole.

Egan, G. (1982). *The skilled helper* (2nd ed.). Monterey, CA: Brooks/Cole.

Egan, G. (1994). *The skilled helper: A problem-management approach to helping* (5th ed.). Pacific Grove, CA: Brooks/Cole.

Egan, G. (1998). *The skilled helper* (6th ed.). Monterey, CA: Brooks/Cole.

Ellis, A. (1973). *Humanistic psychotherapy*. New York: Julian Press.

Ellis, A. (1977). Personality hypotheses of RET (rational-emotive therapy) and other modes of cognitive-behavior therapy. *The Counseling Psychologist, 7(1)*, 2–42.

Ellis, A. (1979). Rational-emotive therapy. In R. J. Corsini (Ed.), *Current psychotherapies* (2nd ed., pp. 185–229). Itasca, IL: Peacock.

Ellis, A. (1984). Forward. In W. Dryden, *Rational-emotive therapy: Fundamentals and innovations* (pp. i–xv). London: Croom Helm.

Ellis, A. (1989). Rational-emotive therapy. In R. J. Corsini & D. Wedding (Eds.), *Current psychotherapies* (4th ed., pp. 197–240). Itasca, IL: Peacock.

Erickson, E. H. (1963). The A-B-C method of crisis management. *Mental Hygiene, 52*, 87–89.

Everstein, L., Everstein, D. S., Heymann, G., True, R. H., Frey, D. H., Johnson, H. G., & Seiden, R. H. (1980). Privacy and confidentiality in psychotherapy. *American Psychologist, 35(9)*, 828–840.

Eysenck, H. J. (1966). *The effects of psychotherapy*. New York: International Sciences Press.

Fauman, M. A. (1994). *Study guide to DSM-IV*. Washington, DC: American Psychiatric Press, Inc.

Fierman, L. B. (1965). Myths in the practice of psychotherapy. *Archives of General Psychiatry, 12*, 408–414.

Frank, J. D. (1971). Therapeutic factors in psychotherapy. *American Journal of Psychotherapy, 25*, 350–361.

Frank, J. D. (1973). *Persuasion and healing* (Rev. ed.). Baltimore: Johns Hopkins University Press.

Frankl, V. E. (1992). *Man's search for meaning: An introduction to logotherapy* (4th ed.). Boston: Beacon Press.

Freud, A. (1966). (Original work published 1936). *The ego and the mechanisms of defense*. New York: International Universities Press, Inc.

Freud, S. (1953). The psychopathology of everyday life. In J. Strachey (Ed.), *The standard edition of the complete psychological works of Sigmund Freud* (Vol. 6). London: Hogarth.

Fromme, A. (1972). *The ability to love*. Hollywood, CA: Wilshire.

Garfield, S. L. (1980). *Psychotherapy: An eclectic approach*. New York: Wiley.

Gelso, C. J., & Carter, J. A. (1985). The relationship in counseling and psychotherapy: Components, consequence, and theoretical antecedents. *The Counseling Psychologist, 8*, 7–36.

Gelso, C. J., & Carter, J. A. (1994). Components of the psychotherapy relationship: Their interaction and unfolding during treatment. *Journal of Counseling Psychology, 41*, 296–306.

Gill, M. M. (1982). *Analysis of transference* (Vol. 1). Madison, CT: International Universities Press.

Ginter, E. J. (1988). Stagnation in eclecticism: The need to recommit to a journey. *Journal of Mental Health Counseling, 10*, 3–8.

Glasser, W. (1965). *Reality therapy*. New York: Harper & Row.

Goldberg, C. (1977). *Therapeutic partnership: Ethical concerns in psychotherapy*. New York: Springer.

Goldman, L. (1976). A revolution in counseling research. *Journal of Counseling Psychology, 23(6)*, 543–552.

Goodman, A. (1991). Organic unit theory: The mind-body problem revisited. *American Journal of Psychiatry, 148*, 553–563.

Gorkin, M. (1987). *The uses of countertransference*. Northvale, NJ: Jason Aronson.

Greenson, R. R. (1967). *The technique and practice of psychotherapy* (Vol. 1). New York: International Universities Press.

Greist, J. H., Jefferson, J. W., & Marks, I. M. (1986). *Anxiety and its treatment*. Washington, DC: American Psychiatric Press.

Gurman, A. S., & Razin, A. M. (Eds.) (1977). *Effective psychotherapy*. New York: Pergamon.

Hahn, M. E. (1953). Conceptual trends in counseling. *Personnel and Guidance Journal, 31*, 232.

Hammer, M. (1972). *The theory and practice of psychotherapy with specific disorders*. Springfield, IL: Charles C Thomas.

Hanna, F. J., & Shank, G. (1995). The specter of metaphysics in counseling research and practice: The qualitative challenge. *Journal of Counseling and Development, 74*, 53–59

Hare-Mustin, R. T., Marecek, M., Kaplan, A. G., & Liss-Levinson, N. (1979). Rights of clients, responsibilities of therapists. *American Psychologist, 34(1)*, 3–16.

Hayes, J. A., McCracken, J. E., McClanahan, M. K., Hill, C. E., Harp, J. S., & Carozzini, P. (1998). Therapists' perspectives on countertransference: Qualitative data in search of a theory. *Journal of Counseling Psychology, 45*, 468–482.

Herlihy, B., & Corey, G. (1997). *Boundary issues in counseling: Multiple roles and responsibilities*. Alexandria, VA: American Counseling Association.

Herman, K. C. (1997). Embracing human science in counseling research. *Counselor Education and Supervision, 36,* 270–283.

Higgins, R. L., Snyder, C. R., & Berglas, S. B. (1990). *Self-handicapping: The paradox that isn't.* New York: Plenum Press.

Ivey, M. (1994). *Intentional interviewing and counseling* (3rd ed.). Pacific Grove, CA: Brooks/Cole.

Izard, C. E. (1977). *Human emotions.* New York: Plenum.

Jourard, S. M. (1968). *Personal adjustment: An approach through the study of healthy personality* (2nd ed.). New York: The Macmillan Company.

Jourard, S. M., & Landsman, T. (1980). *Healthy personality* (4th ed.). New York: Macmillan.

Kalodner, C. R. (1995). Cognitive-behavioral theory. In D. Capuzzi & D. R. Gross (Eds.), *Counseling and psychotherapy: Theories and interventions.* Englewood Cliffs, NJ: Merrill.

Kanel, K. (1999). *A guide to crisis intervention.* Pacific Grove, CA: Brooks/Cole.

Kelly, G. A. (1970). A brief introduction to personal construct theory. In D. Bannister (Ed.), *Perspectives in personal construct theory.* New York: Academic Press.

Kitchener, K. S. (1984). Intuition, critical evaluation, and ethical principles: The foundation for ethical decisions in counseling psychology. *Counseling Psychologist, 12,* 43–55.

Knapp, M. L. (1978). *Nonverbal communication in human interaction* (2nd ed.). New York: Holt, Rinehart & Winston.

Kottler, J. A. (1986). *On being a therapist.* San Francisco: Jossey-Bass.

Kottler, J. A., & Brown, R. W. (1992). *Introduction to therapeutic counseling* (2nd ed.). Pacific Grove, CA: Brooks/Cole.

Lambert, M. J., & Cattani-Thompson, K. (1996). Current findings regarding the effectiveness of counseling: Implications for practice. *Journal of Counseling & Development, 74,* 601–608.

Lauver, P., & Harvey, D. R. (1997). *The practical counselor: Elements of effective helping.* Pacific Grove, CA: Brooks/Cole.

Lazarus, A. A., & Beutler, L. E. (1993). On technical eclecticism. *Journal of Counseling and Development, 71,* 381–385.

Leeman, C. P., & Mulvey, C. H. (1973). Brief psychotherapy of the dependent personality: Specific techniques. *Psychonometrics, 25,* 36–42.

Levy, L. H. (1962). *Psychological interpretation.* New York: Holt, Rinehart & Winston.

Livneh, H., & Wright, P. E. (1995). Rational-emotive theory. In D. Capuzzi & D. R. Gross (Eds.), *Counseling and psychotherapy: Theories and interventions.* Englewood Cliffs, NJ: Merrill.

Loesch, L. C., & Vacc, N. A. (Eds.). (1996). *Research in counseling and therapy.* Eric Clearing House on Counseling and Student Services, Greensboro, NC, Office of Educational Research and Improvement Contact # RR93002004.

Luborsky, L., Chandler, M., Auerbach, A. H., Cohen, J., & Bachrach, H. M. (1971). Factors influencing the outcome of psychotherapy. *Psychological Bulletin, 75,* 145–185.

Mahalik, J. R. (1994). Development of the client resistance scale. *Journal of Counseling Psychology, 41,* 58–68.

Mahoney, M. J. (1991). *Human change processes: The scientific foundations of psychotherapy.* New York: Basic Books.

Mann, J. (1973). *Time-limited psychotherapy.* Cambridge, MA: Harvard University Press.

Martin, B. (1977). *Abnormal psychology: Clinical and scientific perspectives*. New York: Holt, Rinehart & Winston.

Maslow, A. H. (1968). *Toward a psychology of being*. Princeton, NJ: Van Nostrand Reinhold.

May, R. (1967a). *The art of counseling*. Nashville: Abingdon Press.

May, R. (1967b). *Psychology and the human dilemma*. Princeton, NJ: Van Nostrand.

Mayer, J. D., Salovey, P., Gomberg-Kaufman, S., & Blainey, K. (1991). A broader conception of mood experience. *Journal of Personality and Social Psychology, 60,* 100–111.

Mayer, J. D., & Salovey, P. (1997). What is emotional intelligence? In P. Salovey & D. J. Saluter (Eds.) *Emotional development and emotional intelligence: Educational implications* (pp. 3–34). New York: Basic Books.

McGonicle, D. (1988). Making self-talk positive. *American Journal of Nursing, 88,* 725–726.

Murphy, B. C., & Dillon, C. (1998). *Interviewing in action: Process and practice*. Pacific-Grove, CA: Brooks/Cole.

Nugent, F. A. (1994). *An introduction to the profession of counseling*. New York: Merrill Publishing.

Osipow, S. H., Walsh, W. B., & Tosi, D. J. (1980). *A survey of counseling methods*. Homewood, IL: Dorsey.

Ottens, A. J., Shank, G. D., & Long, R. J. (1995). The role of abductive logic in understanding and using advanced empathy. *Counselor Education and Supervision, 34,* 199–211.

Pacht, A. R. (1984). Reflections on perfection. *American Psychologist, 39,* 386–390.

Page, J. D. (1975). *Psychopathology: The science of understanding deviance*. Chicago: Aldine.

Perez, J. F. (1979). *Family counseling: Theory and practice*. New York: Van Nostrand.

Perls, F. S. (1969). *Gestalt therapy verbatim*. Lafayette, CA: Real People Press.

Physician's desk reference (53rd ed.). (1999). Montvale, NJ: Medical Economics Company.

Pietrofesa, J. J., Hoffman, A., Splete, H. H., & Pinto, D. V. (1978). *Counseling: Theory, research and practice*. Chicago: Rand McNally.

Pietrofesa, J. J., Leonard, G. E., & Van Hoose, W. (1978). *The authentic counselor* (2nd ed.). Chicago: Rand McNally.

Plutchik, R. (1962). *The emotions: Facts, theories, and a new model*. New York: Random House.

Preston, J. D., O'Neal, J. H., & Talaga, M. C. (1997). *Handbook of clinical psychopharmacology for therapists*. Oakland, CA: New Harbinger Publications.

Raimy, V. (1975). *Misunderstandings of the self*. San Francisco: Jossey-Bass.

Ramey, L. (1998). The use of Gestalt interventions in the treatment of the resistant alcohol-dependent client. *Journal of Mental Health Counseling, 20,* 202–215.

Reid, W. H., & Wise, M. G. (1995). *DSM-IV training guide*. New York: Brunner/Mazel.

Rogers, C. R. (1951). *Client-centered therapy*. Boston: Houghton Mifflin.

Rogers, C. R. (1957). The necessary and sufficient conditions of therapeutic personality change. *Journal of Consulting Psychology, 21,* 95–103.

Rogers, C. R. (1961). *On becoming a person*. Boston: Houghton Mifflin.

Ruesch, J. (1973). *Therapeutic communication*. New York: Norton.

Saarni, C. (1997). Emotional competence and self-regulation in childhood. In P. Salovey & D. J. Saluter (Eds.), *Emotional development and emotional intelligence: Educational implications* (pp. 35–66). New York: Basic Books.

Salovey, P., & Mayer, J. D. (1990, Spring). On emotional intelligence. *Dialogue, 9–10.*

Salovey, P., & Mayer, J. D. (1994). Some final thoughts about personality and intelligence. In R. J. Sternberg & P. Ruzgis (Eds.), *Personality and intelligence* (pp. 303–318). New York: Cambridge University Press.

Salovey, P., & Sluyter, D. J. (Eds.) (1997). *Emotional development and emotional intelligence: Educational implications.* New York: Basic Books.

Sanford, J. A. (1987). *The kingdom within: The inner meaning of Jesus' sayings* (Rev. ed.). New York: Harper Collins.

Shaffi, M., & Shaffi, S. L. (1982). *Pathways of human development: Normal growth and emotional disorders in infancy, childhood, and adolescence.* New York: Thiema-Stratton.

Singer, E. (1965). *Key concepts in psychotherapy.* New York: Random House.

Singer, B. A. & Luborsky, L. (1977). Countertransference: The status of clinical versus quantitative research. In A. S. Gurman & A. M. Radzin (Eds.), *Effective psychotherapy: A handbook of research* (pp. 433–451). New York: Pergamon Press.

Small, L. (1972). The uncommon importance of diagnosis. *Professional Psychology, 3(2),* 111–119.

Smith, D., & Fitzpatrick, M. (1995). Patient therapist boundary issues. An integrative review of theory and research. *Professional Psychology: Research and Practice, 25(1),* 499–506.

Sonne, J. L. (1994). Multiple relationships: Does the new ethics code answer the right questions? *Professional Psychology: Research and Practice, 25,* 336–343.

Source encyclopedia of world problems and human potential, Union of International Associations, retrieved 3/15/2001, from http://db.uia.org/scripts/sweb.dll/uiaf? SC=9177 & XP=U1 & DD=HU & DR=H0217 & AB=3 & RT=0 & PG=1 &.

Stott, R. L. (1981). *A summary of laws relating to the practice of psychology as a health profession in California and a discussion of relevant legal concepts and procedures* (3rd ed.). Orange, CA: California State Psychological Association.

Strongman, K. T. (1974). *Decent exposure: Living with your emotions.* New York: St. Martin's.

Strupp, H. H. (1971). Psychotherapy: Research and practice: An overview. In A. E. Bergin & S. K. Garfield (Eds.), *Handbook of psychotherapy and behavior change.* New York: Wiley.

Sullivan, H. S. (1953). *The interpersonal theory of psychiatry.* New York: Norton.

Tauber, E. S. (1954). Exploring the therapeutic use of countertransference data. *Psychiatry, 17,* 332–336.

Teyber, E. (1997). *Interpersonal process in psychotherapy: A relational approach* (3rd ed.). Pacific Grove, CA: Brooks/Cole.

Tolbert, E. L. (1972). *Introduction to counseling* (2nd ed.). New York: McGraw-Hill.

Vaihinger, H. (1924). *The philosophy of "as if."* New York: Harcourt Brace Jovanovich.

Vaillant, G. E. (1977). *Adaptation to life.* Cambridge, MA: Harvard University Press.

Vaillant, L. M. (1997). *Changing character: Short-term anxiety-regulating psychotherapy for restructuring defenses, affects, and attachment.* New York: Basic Books.

Vaimy, V. (1975). *Misunderstandings of the self.* San Francisco: Jossey-Bass.

Vinicor, F., & Cooper, J. (1979, December). Early recognition of endocrine disorders. *Hospital Medicine,* pp. 38–47.

Wachtel, P. L. (Ed.). (1982). *Resistance: Psychodynamic and behavioral approaches.* New York: Plenum.

Wallace, W. A. (1986). *Theories of counseling and psychotherapy: A basic issues approach.* Boston: Allyn and Bacon.

Warga, R. G. (1974). *Personal awareness: A psychology of adjustment.* Englewood Cliffs, NJ: Prentice-Hall.

Watts, R. E. (1993). Developing a personal theory of counseling: A brief guide for students. *TCA-Journal, 21,* 103–104.

Weiner, I. B. (1975). *Principles of psychotherapy.* New York: Wiley.

Welfel, R. R. (1998). *Ethics in counseling and psychotherapy: Standards, research and emerging issues.* Pacific Grove, CA: Brooks/Cole.

Williamson, E.G. (1965). *Vocational counseling.* New York: McGraw-Hill.

Wolberg, L. R. (1977). *The techniques of psychotherapy* (3rd ed., Part 1). New York: Grune & Stratton.

Young, J. Z. (1987). *Philosophy and the brain.* Oxford: Oxford University Press.

INDEX